A Companion to Europe si

CW01461155

WILEY BLACKWELL COMPANIONS TO HISTORY

This series provides sophisticated and authoritative overviews of the scholarship that has shaped our current understanding of the past. Defined by theme, period and/or region, each volume comprises between twenty-five and forty concise essays written by individual scholars within their area of specialization. The aim of each contribution is to synthesize the current state of scholarship from a variety of historical perspectives and to provide a statement on where the field is heading. The essays are written in a clear, provocative, and lively manner, designed for an international audience of scholars, students, and general readers.

For further information on these and other titles in the series please visit our website at

www.wiley.com

A COMPANION TO EUROPE SINCE 1945

Edited by

Klaus Larres

WILEY Blackwell

This paperback edition first published 2014
© 2014 John Wiley & Sons Ltd

Edition history: Blackwell Publishing Ltd (hardback, 2009)

Registered Office
John Wiley & Sons Ltd, The Atrium, Southern Gate, Chichester, West Sussex, PO19 8SQ, UK

Editorial Offices
350 Main Street, Malden, MA 02148-5020, USA
9600 Garsington Road, Oxford, OX4 2DQ, UK
The Atrium, Southern Gate, Chichester, West Sussex, PO19 8SQ, UK

For details of our global editorial offices, for customer services, and for information about how to apply for permission to reuse the copyright material in this book please see our website at www.wiley.com/wiley-blackwell.

The right of Klaus Larres to be identified as the author of the editorial material in this work has been asserted in accordance with the UK Copyright, Designs and Patents Act 1988.

All rights reserved. No part of this publication may be reproduced, stored in a retrieval system, or transmitted, in any form or by any means, electronic, mechanical, photocopying, recording or otherwise, except as permitted by the UK Copyright, Designs and Patents Act 1988, without the prior permission of the publisher.

Wiley also publishes its books in a variety of electronic formats. Some content that appears in print may not be available in electronic books.

Designations used by companies to distinguish their products are often claimed as trademarks. All brand names and product names used in this book are trade names, service marks, trademarks or registered trademarks of their respective owners. The publisher is not associated with any product or vendor mentioned in this book.

Limit of Liability/Disclaimer of Warranty: While the publisher and editor have used their best efforts in preparing this book, they make no representations or warranties with respect to the accuracy or completeness of the contents of this book and specifically disclaim any implied warranties of merchantability or fitness for a particular purpose. It is sold on the understanding that the publisher is not engaged in rendering professional services and neither the publisher nor the author shall be liable for damages arising herefrom. If professional advice or other expert assistance is required, the services of a competent professional should be sought.

Library of Congress Cataloging-in-Publication Data

A companion to Europe since 1945 / edited by Klaus Larres.
    p. cm. – (Blackwell companions to European history)
  Includes bibliographical references and index.
  ISBN 978-1-4051-0612-2 (hardcover : alk. paper) – ISBN 978-1-118-72998-4 (paperback: alk. paper)
  1. Europe–History–1945– 2. Cold War. I. Larres, Klaus.
  D1051.C65 2009
  940.55–dc22

                    2008037346

A catalogue record for this book is available from the British Library.

Cover image: 'People in Desolation' by Maxim Kantor. © Maxim Kantor/Galerie Nannen, Emden, Germany/The Bridgeman Art Library.
Cover design by Richard Boxall Design Associates.

Set in 10 on 12 Galliard by Toppan Best-set Premedia Limited
Printed in Malaysia by Ho Printing (M) Sdn Bhd

1 2014

In memory of

My brother Norbert Larres (1962–2005)

and my mother Änni Larres (1927–2007)

Contents

Contributors

Ingolfur Blühdorn is reader in politics and political sociology at the University of Bath, England.

David R. Devereux is associate professor in history at Canisius College, Buffalo, NY, USA.

Ralph Dietl is senior lecturer in European Studies at Queen's University, Belfast, Northern Ireland.

Desmond Dinan is Jean Monnet professor Public Policy at George Mason University, Arlington, VA, USA.

Laura den Dulk is assistant professor in sociology at the University of Utrecht, the Netherlands.

Roger Eatwell is professor in comparative European politics and Dean of Humanities and Social Sciences, University of Bath, England.

Alfred E. Eckes is Ohio Eminent Research professor in contemporary history, at Ohio University, Athens, OH, USA, and former commissioner and chairman of the US International Trade Commission.

Christopher Flockton is emeritus university professor of European Economic Studies University of Surrey, England.

Carine Germond is a research fellow of the German Historical Institute in Paris.

Mark Gilbert is associate professor of contemporary international history at the University of Trento, Italy.

Robert Hutchings is diplomat-in-residence at the Woodrow Wilson School of Public and International Affairs, Princeton University, NJ, USA. He is the former chair of the US National Intelligence Council and former special adviser to the Secretary of State with the rank of ambassador.

Ian Jackson is a lecturer in politics and international relations at De Montfort University, Leicester, England.

Dianne Kirby is senior lecturer in history and international affairs at University of Ulster, Northern Ireland.

Mark Kramer is director of the Cold War studies program at Harvard University and senior fellow at Harvard's Gavis Center for Russian and Eurasian Studies.

Klaus Larres is professor in history and international affairs at the University of Ulster in Northern Ireland and the former holder of the Herry A. Kissinger chair in foreign policy and international relations at the Library of Congress in Washington, DC.

Stephen (Steen) Mangen is senior lecturer in European social policy at the London School of Economics and Political Science, England.

Panikos Panayi is professor of European history at De Montfort University, Leicester, England.

John Pinder is emeritus professor in politics at the College of Bruges, Belgium, and Chairman, Federal Trust, London.

Claire Sutherland is lecturer in politics at the University of Manchester in England.

Paul Wilkinson is emeritus professor of international relations, and chairman of the advisory board, Centre for the Study of Terrorism and Political Violence, University of St. Andrews, Scotland.

Ruth Wittlinger is senior lecturer in politics at the University of Durham, England.

Acknowledgments

I am most grateful to the individual authors for their willingness to contribute to this volume. As the completion of this volume was considerably delayed, first due to a year of research in Washington, DC, and then because of two family tragedies which struck rather unexpectedly in short succession, I am most grateful for the understanding and patience of all of the contributors. I am also very grateful for the support and untiring help I received from Wiley-Blackwell. In particular my sincere gratitude goes to Tessa Harvey, Gillian Kane, and Virginia Graham, and also Carole Drummond from The Running Head, without whose support and infinite patience this book would not have seen the light of day.

Map labels:
ICELAND
NORWAY
SWEDEN
FINLAND
GREAT BRITAIN
DENMARK
IRELAND
THE NETHER-LANDS
SOVIET UNION
Atlantic Ocean
BELGIUM
GER. FED. REP. (1955)
GER. DEM. REP.
POLAND
CZECHOSLOVAKIA
FRANCE
SWITZ.
AUSTRIA
HUNGARY
ROMANIA
ITALY
YUGOSLAVIA
BULGARIA
Black Sea
PORTUGAL
SPAIN (1982)
ALBANIA
GREECE (1952)
TURKEY (1952)
Mediterranean Sea

Legend:
☐ Neutral country
▨ Warsaw Pact organization
▧ Communist country, not member of Warsaw Pact
■ North Atlantic Treaty Organization, plus Canada and the United States. France withdrew from integrated Military Command in 1966

Map 1 Europe during the Cold War, 1945/46–1990/91, (Source: William R. Keylor, *A World of Nations*, Oxford University Press, Oxford, 2003 p. 42).

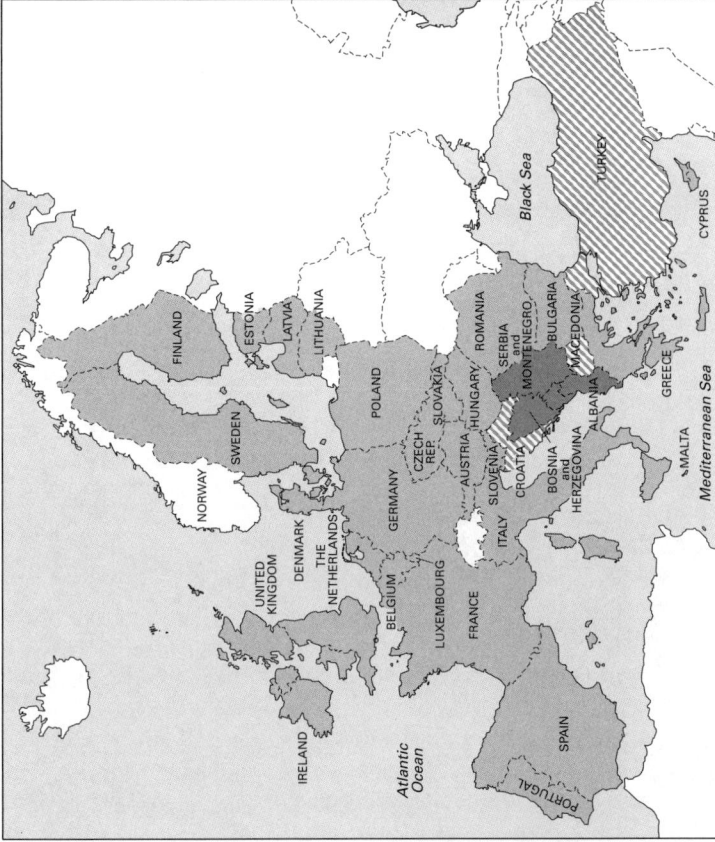

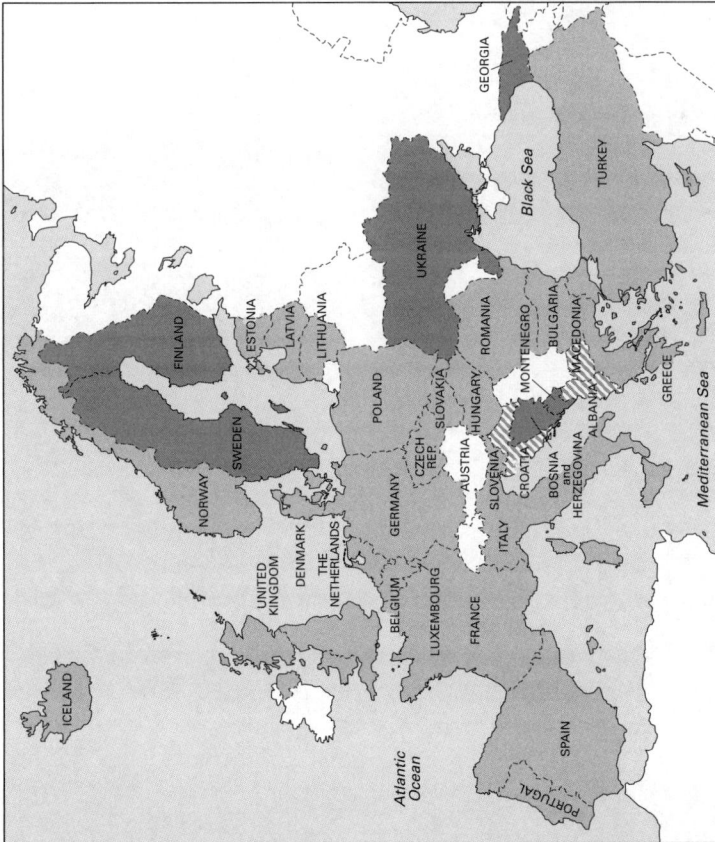

Map 2 Post-Cold War Europe

NATO members

Candidates for NATO membership

Potential candidates for NATO membership

European Union members

Candidates for European Union membership

Potential candidates for European Union membership

Introduction

KLAUS LARRES

When World War II in Europe ended in early May 1945 the crushing defeat of the European continent became obvious. The entire continent lay in ruins, many of its people were homeless, severely wounded (both physically and mentally) or never returned from war service at all. The war provoked by Hitler's Germany had not only brought misery and death to many millions of people, it also ensured that the once proud nations of the European continent would for years be preoccupied with physical survival, reconstruction, and political and social reconciliation.

Even the victorious British found that they had hugely overstretched their resources and would soon not only face austerity and economic deprivation at home but also witness the collapse of their global influence, economic prowess, and the ever faster disappearance of their empire. In a very short period of time even fewer overseas possessions would remain in the hands of the French, Italians, Portuguese, Dutch, and Belgians. The entire eastern part of the European continent would be swallowed up by the Soviet Union within three years. Once fully sovereign countries such as Poland, Czechoslovakia, Hungary, the Baltic states, Bulgaria, Romania were forcibly integrated into Moscow's hugely expanded communist sphere of influence, which soon developed into a new sort of dictatorial and ideologically underpinned empire.

The only country which benefited from World War II, both economically and with regard to its global standing and immense military power, which included possession of the atomic secret, was the United States of America. Contrary to the expectations of many and contrary to America's decision to withdraw from Europe after World War I, the US made a deliberate effort to learn from history. Not withdrawal but further participation in the affairs of Europe appeared to be the recipe for preventing yet another world war originating on the European continent. Economic reconstruction, democratic re-education in for example Germany, Austria, and Italy, and the creation of a Franco-German rapprochement as part of an overarching process of European integration were deemed vital.

The Truman and subsequent Eisenhower administrations embarked upon an "empire by invitation," as Geir Lundestad has called it, and used Marshall Plan aid

A Companion to Europe since 1945, First Edition. Edited by Klaus Larres.
© 2014 John Wiley & Sons, Ltd. Published 2014 by John Wiley & Sons, Ltd.

in the economic field and the North Atlantic Treaty Organization in the security and political areas to impose its will and ideas about the future shape of western Europe on the helpless European governments. Particular attention was paid to Germany, the divided nation, with the divided former capital Berlin at the frontline of the Cold War, to Franco–German relations and the economic revival of Europe to prevent the continent from once again becoming seduced by the promises of radical ideologies. The impetus to overcome the ingrained animosities of the past with the help of a process of European integration mostly came from British, French, and Italian thinkers who had first introduced such schemes in the 1920s and resuscitated and developed them during the most despairing times of World War II.

Within a mere decade most of the continent's most pressing economic, social, and political problems had been overcome. Both outside help and the enormous energy, imagination, and sheer will for survival of the peoples of western Europe had transformed the continent from a helpless colossus to a democratic, fairly prosperous and well-functioning half-continent. Europe had again become a force to be reckoned with in the world, in particular in economic terms. European integration – though initially only advocated by the Schuman Plan "Six" for a limited number of economic sectors – had played a vital role in overcoming the economic deprivation and the political dislocation which had characterized the initial postwar years.

To a considerable extent this also applied to the years after the end of the Cold War in 1990/1991 and the resulting reunification of the European continent. The Maastricht Treaty, in particular, but also the Nice, Amsterdam, and Lisbon treaties as well as perhaps the Lisbon Reform Treaty of 2008 had a decisive influence on shaping the difficult transition from the Cold War era to the post-Cold War years and indeed to the post-9/11 era. Within Europe the creation of a single European market, the transformation of the European Community into the European Union (EU), the introduction of a common currency a decade later, the insistence on a normative process of democratization and not least the resulting waves of enlargement which led to the incorporation of the former communist states into the EU have dramatically changed the character of the European continent. Despite many difficulties and at times unnecessary complexities and stifling bureaucracies, Europe has certainly become a more coherent and more united continent which projects its influence, even power, increasingly beyond the confines of the European continent.

The enlargement of the EU and the integration of the former eastern European communist states preoccupied the EU to a substantial extent during the first decade and a half after the end of the Cold War. In the aftermath of the events of September 11, 2001 and the highly controversial US–British invasion of Iraq in March 2003 (which put an unprecedented strain on transatlantic and intra-European relations), it was above all international terrorism which engaged the EU. The EU countries were forced to respond to that threat and to the American-led "war against terror" with increasing domestic vigilance, that led to ever greater governmental meddling in the private lives of their citizens. They also felt it imperative to become much more involved than hitherto in peacekeeping and indeed peacemaking activities far beyond the borders of Europe. The EU also took the lead in facing up to the climate and energy crises that plague global affairs in the post-Cold War years; Brussels attempted to develop a strategic policy of international sustainability.

The failure of the "war on terror" in both Iraq and Afghanistan and the uneasy stalemate of Washington's relations with important countries such as China, Russia, and Iran resulted in a deep political and – under the influence of the global "credit crunch" and other recessionary economic factors – financial crisis in the USA. Consequently there was increasing pressure on the EU to become a more active international player. The partial replacement of the dollar as the global reserve currency by the euro was not just of symbolic importance.

Towards the end of the first decade of the twenty-first century the EU appears to be on the threshold of becoming a global power and a crucially important international mediator. However, it is still an open question if the EU will accept this challenge and continue with the development of a streamlined institutional set-up, including the creation of an effective common foreign, security, and defense policy. Perhaps the EU will lose courage again and shrink away from the global responsibilities of the future; instead it may once again focus on intra-European squabbles, navel-gazing and confine itself to largely dealing with common market and trade questions. Only the developments in the second decade of the twenty-first century can tell.

A Companion to Europe since 1945 has a two-fold objective. The many authors who have contributed to this volume look back and analyze the developments which took place on the European continent during the Cold War. They also consider present-day Europe, the Europe which has taken shape since the end of the Cold War in 1990/1991, and analyze current developments from a plethora of angles.

The book is divided into four major parts. Part I considers the transition from war to cold war. In the first chapter Mark Gilbert analyzes the political and military developments, in particular, the origins of the Cold War in Europe. In the following chapter John Pinder considers the roots of the ideas for European integration and how these ideas spread and developed into a proposal for the establishment of a federalist and united European state.

The seven chapters of Part II analyze developments in Europe during the Cold War. Ian Jackson considers the western European perspective while Mark Kramer views the developments from the Soviet and eastern European angle. In chapter three Ian Jackson compares the different economic developments and experiences in western and eastern Europe between 1945 and 1990. David Devereux considers the process of decolonization, that affected in particular Britain and France but also some other European countries, and looks at the impact huge-scale migration from the former colonies had on the home countries. Desmond Dinan then follows the development and execution of the European idea from the Schuman Plan of 1950 through to the establishment of the single market in the early 1990s. Klaus Larres looks at the role the United States played in shaping the process of European integration. The American insistence on their continued hegemony in transatlantic relations which in particular the Nixon and Reagan administrations pursued gave a decisive impetus to the European efforts in the 1970s and above all in the 1980s to create more coherent and effective federal European institutions. Subsequently Dianne Kirby analyzes the role of religion and the main churches in shaping the Cold War world, a theme which has been recognized only recently as a crucial factor of influence. Last but not least Carine Germond considers the impact of the sudden and entirely unexpected end of the Cold War on the newly reunified European continent.

Parts III and IV of this book deal with the developments from 1990 to the present, the former with the political and economic developments and the latter with social and cultural developments since 1990.

Part III begins with a chapter by Robert Hutchings who analyzes the state of transatlantic relations since 1990 and considers whether or not the transatlantic alliance will survive in the post-Cold War world. Alfred E. Eckes investigates the impact the strong European economic performance has had on the forces of globalization. Subsequently Christopher Flockton analyzes in detail the economic developments within the EU since the Maastricht Treaty of 1991. Roger Eatwell then compares the political parties and the respective party systems in a large number of European countries. Ralph Dietl looks at the origins and current developments of the European Security and Defence Policy (ESDP) and Paul Wilkinson considers the impact of domestic and international terrorism in the major European countries since 1945.

Part IV, the final section of this book, considers social and cultural developments in Europe since the end of the Cold War. Ruth Wittlinger questions in her chapter whether or not something approximating a European identity has been able to develop during the past five decades and in particular since 1990. Claire Sutherland looks at the development and rising popularity of post-Cold War nationalism not only in the liberated countries of eastern Europe but also in the countries of the western part of the continent. Ingolfur Blühdorn analyzes the development of new social and political movements, such as the Green Party, in present-day Europe and the impact this has had on European civil society. Panikos Panayi analyzes the politics of the EU and the various European countries towards migrants who wish to settle in the EU. Laura den Dulk considers the changing roles and norms in gender relations and family structures in both western and eastern Europe. Finally, Steen Mangen analyzes the crisis of the present-day welfare state affecting almost all European countries and traces its developments.

On the whole the book offers the reader an attempt at evaluating some of the most important aspects which have influenced the political, economic, and social and cultural nature and character of the European continent. All of the chapters have been written by experts on the themes discussed and they introduce the reader to the most crucial aspects of the topics under discussion and guide him/her through the rich literature and lively scholarly debates. Taken together, the 22 chapters enable the reader to obtain a comprehensive picture of some of the crucial developments that have shaped Europe in the aftermath of both World War II and the Cold War.

Klaus Larres
Belfast, November 2008

PART I

Europe in Transition: From War to Cold War

CHAPTER ONE

From War to Cold War

MARK GILBERT

By late summer 1944, the Red Army had crossed the Soviet Union's borders into Poland and Romania and would shortly invade and occupy Bulgaria. A million American and British troops had invaded France in June 1944 and, with the assistance of General Charles de Gaulle's Free French forces, would liberate Paris at the end of August. Athens was occupied by the British in October 1944 and Italy had been liberated as far north as Florence. Despite the tenacious resistance of the German forces, who fought on all three fronts with a determination born of desperation, it was clear that Nazi Germany was doomed. Her casualties in the east were totalled in the millions; in the West and the Mediterranean theaters of war she was unable to match the allies' massive superiority in tanks, aeroplanes, and artillery.

In Poland, Greece, Italy, Yugoslavia, and France, the German forces were fighting savage wars of repression against the peoples of the occupied territories. As Russian armies neared Warsaw, the Polish Home Army raised a heroic insurrection against the Nazi occupiers in August 1944. The Red Army remained passive, however, for two months as SS troops crushed the uprising and killed over 200,000 Polish civilians. Terrible episodes of repression took place elsewhere in Europe. To give just one example, in September 1944, 1,836 civilians, including many children, were murdered at Marzabotto, near Bologna, as a brigade commanded by SS officer Walter Rader concluded its "march of death" through Emilia-Romagna and Tuscany. By late 1944 and early 1945 the grim machinery of the Final Solution was being wound down. Europe would soon discover the full extent of the human damage done by the Nazis' ideological madness (although it had been known since the end of 1942 that the Jews were being systematically slaughtered). Almost six million Jews had been killed by the *Einsatzgruppen* or in the extermination camps located in eastern Poland. Hundreds of thousands of other "undesirables" – the Roma, the mentally and physically handicapped, homosexuals – had also been murdered.

Faced with evil on this scale, the Allies responded by waging the war with a terrible brutality of their own. Dresden, Hamburg, and the cities of the Ruhr were bombed to destruction in British and American "obliteration raids" in 1944 and early 1945: hundreds of thousands of tons of bombs were dropped on by now defenseless

A Companion to Europe since 1945, First Edition. Edited by Klaus Larres.
© 2014 John Wiley & Sons, Ltd. Published 2014 by John Wiley & Sons, Ltd.

Germany in the first quarter of 1945. The advancing Soviet forces treated the enemy with the same ruthlessness that the Nazis themselves had applied in Russia. Captured German soldiers were either shot out of hand or sent eastwards to windswept labor camps far behind the lines. Few ever returned.

The central question facing the Allies in the postwar world was whether they would be able to cooperate together to undo the damage of the war and to revive a morally and physically devastated continent. In the summer of 1944, there was still optimism on this score. The President of the United States, Franklin Delano Roosevelt, believed he had established a good working relationship with Stalin. British premier Winston Churchill was more suspicious of the Soviet leader's intentions, but certainly believed that Stalin was a leader with whom deals could be made. Over the next three years, this optimism was shattered by events. The continent was divided in two, with the lands east of the Elbe being dominated by Soviet-backed regimes that gradually eliminated all domestic political opposition. The allies that had been united in fighting against Hitlerite Germany found it impossible to agree on a peace settlement. As a result, Germany was partitioned economically and politically as early as 1947, although the formal political separation of East and West Germany only came in the summer of 1949.

The task of this chapter is to reconstruct how and why this process of division occurred. Its argument is that unfolding events confirmed ideological stereotypes, on both sides, and transformed the normal friction of great-power coexistence into a clash of civilizations and values. In an age where, to paraphrase Stalin's notorious remark to the Yugoslav intellectual Milovan Djilas, every victorious power inevitably imposed its own social system, neither side could make the calculated territorial arrangements that had characterized traditional European diplomacy without fearing that a loss had been made.[1] Poland or Hungary could not be "awarded" to the Soviet Union without democrats believing that a vital principle was at stake; Germany could not be rebuilt by the Allies without provoking Russian fears that a capitalist plot was being hatched. Neither side was satisfied with mere territory; both believed that their ideals had to prevail as well.

The High Tide of Cooperation: October 1944–June 1945

Great Britain and the United States went as far as was consistent with ordinary decency to satisfy Stalin's territorial ambitions and security fears between the autumn of 1944 and the late spring of 1945. Over Poland, in particular, the Western allies, especially the US, followed a highly conciliatory policy towards Stalin, allowing the Soviet leader to dictate the precise boundaries of the new Polish state and to construct a provisional government that was only dubiously in accordance with the USSR's commitment at the Yalta conference in February 1945 to widen the democratic composition of the Soviet-backed government. Churchill and Roosevelt arguably had little choice – although they had committed themselves in the Atlantic Charter in August 1941 to making no territorial changes that did not accord with the wishes of affected populations. The Red Army dominated the country and the two Western allies needed Stalin's cooperation: the US because, still unsure whether the atomic bomb would work, it thought it would need Russian military help against Japan and Russian participation in the new international organization, the United Nations, in which Roosevelt placed so many of his hopes for the postwar world; Britain because Churchill's reactionary policy of backing conservative, preferably monarchist, governments in Greece and Italy would run into difficulties if the Soviet Union gave covert support to the powerful and well-armed communist parties of those countries.

This process of engagement with the ambitions of Stalin began October 9, 1944, when Churchill and his foreign secretary Anthony Eden met the Soviet leader in Moscow. During this meeting, Churchill presented the Soviet leader with a "naughty document" that proposed to share out influence in the Balkans according to the following percentages: in Romania, the USSR would have 90% influence; in Bulgaria 75% (which was amended by the foreign ministers, Molotov and Eden, to 80% in the following days). Hungary and Yugoslavia would be shared 50:50, while Britain would have 90% influence in Greece.[2] Stalin scrawled a large tick on the document, but for all its notoriety, it should not be thought that the "percentages' agreement" was decisive for the political future of the Balkans as a whole. Josip Broz Tito, the communist leader in Yugoslavia, would demonstrate over the next three years that he was his own man, not Stalin's; Britain had no illusions about its ability to influence politics in Bulgaria. On the other hand, in both Greece and Romania, the percentages agreement had a clear and immediate effect on events.

In Greece, Stalin did not so much as raise his voice in December 1944–January 1945 when the British army suppressed a rebellion by the communist-controlled National Liberation Front (EAM) and forced its military wing, the National People's Liberation Army (ELAS) to disarm. Bowing to reality, Britain renounced its long-standing support for King George II of the Hellenes, whose association with the prewar Metaxas dictatorship weakened him as a force, but Churchill still remained determined to exclude the left. Churchill, who flew to Athens on Boxing Day 1944, persuaded the King to accept Archbishop Damaskinos of Athens as Regent and backed a new government that was initially led by a veteran soldier with a colorful past as a coup leader, Nikolaos Plastiris. There was persistent political violence in Greece between January 1945 and elections in March 1946, when the parties of the left, making a serious lapse of judgment, boycotted the polls and threw away perhaps the last hope of avoiding civil war.[3]

In Romania, the provisional government of an anti-Nazi general, Nicolae Radescu, was subverted by the communist-controlled National Democratic Front (NDF), composed of the Communist Party, the Social Democrat Party, the Union of Patriots and the "Ploughman's Front," which was to all intents and purposes the rural wing of the Communist Party. Radescu fought hard to keep his position, but on February 27, 1945 Soviet troops compelled King Michael – to whom Stalin had awarded the Order of Victory, the Soviet Union's highest honor, for his part in overthrowing the pro-Hitler dictator, Ion Antonescu, in August 1944 – to accept a NDF government. A few days later, the USSR further imposed Petru Groza, the leader of the "Ploughman's Front," as premier. In August 1944, when Antonescu fell, there had not been a thousand communists in the country.[4] Events in Romania, which coincided with the Crimea conference between the leaders of the "Big Three," disturbed both Churchill and Roosevelt, but as the British premier wrote, "in order to have the freedom to save Greece, Eden and I at Moscow in October recognized that Russia should have a largely preponderant voice in Roumania and Bulgaria . . . Stalin adhered very strictly to this understanding during the thirty days fighting against the communists and ELAS in the city of Athens."[5] Britain and the United States nevertheless did not recognize the legitimacy of the Groza government until February 1946.

Both Churchill and Roosevelt seemingly hoped against hope that Stalin, despite his high-handedness in Romania, would allow at least a façade of democracy in the countries falling into the Soviet orbit. At the Crimea conference at Yalta (February 4–11, 1945), the three leaders negotiated a "Declaration on Liberated Europe" that committed them to assist the "peoples liberated from the domination of Nazi Germany and the peoples of the former Axis satellite states of Europe to solve by democratic means their pressing political and economic problems." The declaration added that the three allies would help "form interim governmental authorities broadly representative of all democratic elements in the population" and facilitate the holding of "free elections." It is sometimes suggested that the Declaration was an ambiguous call for postwar democracy, but this interpretation is hard to justify. Stalin plainly put his name to a document whose specific content he had every intention of flouting. Churchill and Roosevelt, despite their having by now very few illusions about the likelihood of democratic evolution within the Soviet system itself, nevertheless sincerely clung to the belief that Stalin might permit political pluralism in neighboring states so long as Soviet security was guaranteed.

The test case was Poland. Great Britain had entered the war to defend Poland; Polish soldiers, sailors, and airmen had fought heroically with the allied forces; the resistance of the Polish Home Army to the Nazis had been brave almost beyond belief; Poland had suffered proportionately more than any other country from the ravages of the Nazis.[6] How could such a people not be allowed to choose its own destiny after the conflict? It was also true that the USSR, mindful of the bloody aggressive war against Russia fought by Poland in 1919–1920, and of Poland's strategic position as a cushion between Russia and Germany, was determined to ensure that any postwar Polish government was a friendly one.

The problem was that since, during the war, Poland had suffered almost as much from the Soviet Union as it had from the Nazis, finding Poles willing to cooperate with Stalin was almost impossible. The Soviet Union had colluded with the Nazis in August 1939 to partition Poland and had treated the Polish populations of the territories it had occupied with the same appalling brutality that had been visited upon the peoples of the Baltic states. Over two million Poles and Balts, especially from the professional classes, had been arrested and transported to Siberia in order to rip up the social fabric of the newly occupied territories and make them more amenable to communist rule. Hundreds of thousands never returned. The culmination of this process had been the secretive mass murder in 1940 of approximately 15,000 captured Polish army officers, thousands of whose bodies were discovered by the Germans in April 1943 at Katyn wood near Smolensk. The Soviet Union claimed that the Germans themselves had killed the officers (and persisted in this claim until *glasnost* in the 1980s), but no Pole in any position of responsibility could accept this.[7] The Polish government in exile in London refused to believe the Soviet denials and asked the International Red Cross to conduct an impartial investigation. This led the USSR to brand the London government as "fascist collaborators" and to establish a rival government, the so-called "Polish Committee of National Liberation," of its own. When Soviet troops entered Poland in July 1944, Stalin recognized the Committee (whom Churchill described as "the greatest villains imaginable") as the legitimate Polish government. It was, in fact, the only Polish government that could have accepted, or even contemplated, the Soviet Union's pretensions to Polish territory.[8]

At Yalta, the two Western allies, anxious to keep Stalin's good will, conceded both of Stalin's main demands on the Polish question. First, they confirmed that Poland's eastern frontier would be, with some slight modifications in Poland's favor, a line drawn in 1920 by Lord Curzon, the then British foreign secretary. Poland was to be compensated in the west with German territory at the envisaged peace conference. The Curzon line restored to the Soviet Union most of the gains obtained by the Nazi–Soviet pact. At the Teheran conference in November 1943, when the war had not yet been won and when Russia had been doing most of the fighting, Churchill and Roosevelt had informally promised Stalin, with the aid of three matches symbolizing the borders of Poland, the USSR, and Germany, the territories in question. They knew there was no possibility of reneging on their bargain at Yalta. The Red Army was *in situ*. Second, they recognized that the Committee of National Liberation, rather than the legal government in London, should provide the nucleus of the provisional government in Poland. The conference communiqué did assert, however, that the Committee should be "reorganized on a broader democratic basis with the inclusion of democratic leaders from Poland itself and from Poles abroad." Representatives of the Home Army and of the London government in exile would, in short, be grafted onto the existing puppet regime. Stalin acknowledged, too, that "free and unfettered" elections would be held in Poland in which "all democratic and anti-Nazi parties shall have the right to take part."

Stalin did not keep his word. The Russian delegate on the Commission charged with reorganizing the Polish government, foreign minister Molotov, tried to block the inclusion of Stanisław Mikołajczyk, the Peasant Party leader, and of other representative Polish politicians. The free movement of British and American missions was being obstructed by Russian officials in all the countries that had fallen under Soviet domination. By mid-March, Churchill was willing to state, in a letter to Roosevelt, that "we are in the presence of a great failure and utter breakdown of what was settled at Yalta."[9] Stalin, by contrast, was seemingly convinced that the arch-anti-Bolshevist Churchill was reneging on Yalta and trying to foist a hostile government upon him. The Americans, conscious that "the Soviet Union then had in the United States a deposit of good will, as great, if not greater than that of any other country," tried to bridge the divide.[10] At the end of May, Harry S. Truman, who had replaced Roosevelt as President when the latter died on April 12, 1945, sent Harry Hopkins, "who embodied Roosevelt's legacy of diplomacy," as his special emissary to Moscow to find a solution to the Polish crisis.[11] Stalin out-argued Hopkins and persuaded him to accept that the Polish government be supplemented merely by Mikołajczyk and four other non-communist members.

The British, who had not been consulted about Hopkins's mission, went along with his breakthrough in the talks, even though there was a striking contrast between Stalin's behavior in Poland and their own behavior in Italy, where almost contemporaneously they presided over the formation of a provisional government led by a resistance hero, Ferruccio Parri, that contained several pro-Moscow Communist Party or Socialist Party officials in key positions. Equally important, Mikołajczyk himself agreed to return to Poland, despite the opposition of most of the London Poles. His view was that it was necessary "to create a provisional government which would attempt to prepare democratic elections as the first step towards re-establishing Poland as a free and sovereign state."[12] Sometimes criticized for being indecisive, Mikołajczyk was in fact a singularly brave man. His decision to accept membership of a government that was dominated by the communists should be interpreted as the last act of good faith in the Soviets' promises to allow "free and unfettered" elections in his war-battered country.

Mikołajczyk's good faith would prove, like Roosevelt's and Churchill's before him, to be woefully misplaced. His Peasant Party rapidly became the most authentically popular party in the country, with 600,000 members in January 1946, despite the fact that its activities were subjected to often brutal intimidation by the communist-controlled police. Elections were postponed in Poland until January 1947, when they were conducted in an atmosphere of "escalating terror." The Peasant Party's candidates were arbitrarily excluded from the ballot in large swathes of the country, and many of its candidates were arrested or beaten during the campaign. Ballot-stuffing was *de rigueur* throughout the country. Officially, the so-called "Democratic Bloc" composed of the communists and the socialists won 80% of the poll and the Peasant Party just over 10%, but these figures bore no relationship to the facts. Mikołajczyk was forced to flee Poland in October 1947.[13]

Similar intimidation of non-communist forces in Romania (where the Moscow-backed National Democratic Front obtained a two-thirds majority in elections held in November 1946) and Bulgaria (where preliminary elections held in November 1945 were blatantly rigged and where the government of the independent-minded agrarian leader Nikola Petkov was subjected to heavy-handed pressure from the Soviet Union) formed the backdrop to the wartime allies' attempts to negotiate a postwar settlement with the defeated nations. Such intolerance of dissent and such cavalier disregard for both the letter and spirit of the Declaration on Liberated Europe bred a corrosive atmosphere of distrust. Genuinely free elections in Hungary in November 1945, where the local communists, intent on not scaring the Anglo-Saxons, initially took a progressive line of cooperating with other forces to establish liberal institutions, showed all too clearly the real electoral strength of communism east of the Elbe: only 17% voted communist, while nearly 60% voted for the Peasant Party.[14] In a free poll, similar figures would unquestionably have been registered throughout central and southeastern Europe. Only in Czechoslovakia, where the communists managed to get 38% of the vote in free elections in May 1946, did communism have real popular support.

Dealing with the Enemy: July 1945–January 1947

The war in Europe ended on May 7, 1945, a week after Hitler had taken his own life in the deranged atmosphere of his Berlin bunker.[15] Hitler left behind him a devastated city – almost a million died in its defense – that was prey to the victorious Soviet armies. The fall of Berlin (and Vienna, which the Red Army captured on April 13, and Budapest, which had fallen in mid-February) was marked by an orgy of looting and rape unmatched in modern history – perhaps all history. A couple of days before Hitler killed himself, his Italian erstwhile sidekick Mussolini had been shot by partisans and his body strung up by the heels in Milan's Piazza Loreto, together with the corpses of his mistress and several of the Fascist regime's senior leaders, or "hier-archs." The bodies were vilely treated by the crowds.[16] British troops had captured Belsen on April 15, 1945 and the photographs they took of skeletal inmates dying of typhoid were published throughout the world, hammering the final nail into the macabre coffin of the Nazi regime's reputation.

How were the defeated nations, above all Germany, to be treated? Back in the 1930s, it had been believed that the disastrous outcome of the harsh peace treaties of 1919–1920 would rob Europeans of any desire for a punitive peace in any future war. In the summer of 1945, a handful of warm-hearted British intellectuals aside, nobody contemplated anything but a "Super Versailles" for Germany, or indeed for Hungary and Italy (Romania, Finland, and Bulgaria, Germany's other allies, were more hopeful), although the Italians protested that they should be regarded as victims of Fascism, not its perpetrators. The only question was how Carthaginian the peace should be.

All were agreed that the Nazi elite should be publicly tried and punished for the "crimes against humanity" that they had committed. Starting on November 20, 1945, 24 of the regime's former leaders, including Hermann Göring, Rudolf Hess, Joachim von Ribbentrop and Julius Streicher, were placed on trial at Nuremberg before a court consisting of a panel of judges drawn from the four victorious allies. The court sat until October 1, 1946. Twelve death sentences were pronounced, although only ten were carried out since Martin Bormann was tried *in absentia* and Göring managed to kill himself the night before his execution. Three leading Nazis (Hans Fritzsche, the head of the news division at the ministry of propaganda, Franz von Papen, the conservative chancellor who preceded Hitler, and Hjalmar Schacht, a financier and economist) were actually acquitted; one who was executed, General Alfred Jodl, was posthumously rehabilitated by a German court. In addition to this major trial of war criminals, the Nuremberg court and associated military tribunals handled approximately 2,000 other cases between 1945 and 1949.

The German people were to be punished: to be regarded as complicit in the crimes of the regime. The Red Army's looting and use of rape – which was officially sanctioned – has already been mentioned. British and American troops were initially refused permission to fraternize with German citizens. Above all, Germans living outside the national borders – in Bohemia, Transylvania, the Baltic states and Poland – were now uprooted and driven westwards to join the millions who had already fled from the Red Army or had been evacuated by the Nazi government in the dying days of the "Third Reich." The mostly German territories east of the Neisse river were handed over to Poland by Stalin (a fait accompli that was authorized, pending the decisions of the final peace treaty at the Potsdam conference) in July 1945. Over the next months, literally millions of people were forced out of their homes and compelled, battered cardboard suitcases in hand, to begin a new life hundreds of miles away from their homes and jobs. As an eloquent British historian has com-mented, such forced transfers "represented an uprooting of peoples unlike anything seen in Europe since the Dark Ages."[17]

Germany ran the risk of complete national "dismemberment," to use the word that the Yalta communiqué prefigured as a potential solution for the political future of Germany. Germany was divided into four occupation "zones" at Yalta, with Britain taking responsibility for the Rhineland; the US for Bavaria and the South; the French for the Saarland; and the Russians for the East. Berlin was similarly divided and so was Austria. There were plenty of people in the Soviet and French governments who thought that the division of Germany into four or more states should become a permanent feature of the political map of Europe: de Gaulle's view was that "certain western regions of the Reich" should be "permanently removed" from German sovereignty.[18]

The US, too, initially favored tough treatment. In the summer of 1944, the US Treasury Secretary Henry Morgenthau Jr. had hypothesized that the Ruhr valley "should not only be stripped of all presently existing industries, but so weakened and so controlled that it cannot in the foreseeable future become an industrial area."[19] Morgenthau thought Germany should lose territory to France and Poland and that the rest of the country should be divided into a "North German State" and a "South German State" based on Bavaria, with the Ruhr being under international administration. Roosevelt broadly sympathized with Morgenthau's ideas for the economic emasculation of Germany and at Yalta indicated that he preferred a harsh peace. The Soviet Union asked for substantial reparations at Yalta ($20,000 million, with half at least going to the USSR), and Roosevelt sided with the Soviet request, which was put in the communiqué only against British opposition. By July 1945, after "the Russians had already spread over Germany and its satellites like the locusts of biblical Egypt, grabbing an enormous war booty haphazardly and without consulting their allies," the Americans had become more cautious.[20] But there was more initial awareness, in the country of John Maynard Keynes, of the centrality of the German economy for the prosperity of Europe as a whole and of the "economic consequences of the peace."

The question of what to do with the political and economic organization of Germany was the principal topic of the conference between the "Big Three" held at Potsdam near Berlin between July 17 and August 2, 1945. By the end of the conference, Stalin was the only one of the three nations' leaders who had been in post at Yalta. Truman had replaced Roosevelt, and Churchill, the great war leader, was evicted from office at the end of July by a Labour landslide in the general election. Churchill's place as prime minister was taken by the prim, schoolmasterly figure of Clement Attlee, but his role as Britain's voice in foreign affairs went to the massive, boisterous, shrewd, and vindictive Ernest Bevin, a proletarian who would soon prove that he would not be hectored by the representatives of the workers' paradise.

The Potsdam conference established a Council of Foreign Ministers, composed of the foreign ministers of Britain, the US, the USSR, France, and China, charged with drawing up treaties of peace with Italy, Romania, Bulgaria, Hungary, and Finland, and preparing a peace settlement to be presented to Germany at such time that it had a government "adequate for the purpose." Until this time, Germany would be administered by a "Control Council" of the military commanders in charge of the four zones. The Control Council was to dismantle and eliminate Germany's war-making potential, "convince the German people that they have suffered a total military defeat and that they cannot escape responsibility for what they have brought upon themselves," and "prepare the ground" for democracy in Germany and for the reintegration of a democratic Germany into international society. Germany was not to be broken up into separate states, but the federal principle was to be encouraged and local government "on democratic principles" was to be restored as soon as possible.

Germany, in short, was to be for the foreseeable future a mandated territory shared by the four allies. She was also to be treated as an economic unit and common policies were to be established by the Control Council to establish a functioning economy. Somewhat contradicting this ambition, however, it was also decided at Potsdam that each country would take reparations from its own zone, while the USSR would meet Poland's reparations claims from its own share. The Western allies would further transfer from their zones 15% of capital stock "unnecessary for the German peace economy" to the Soviets in exchange for food and raw materials of equal value from the Soviet zone. A further 10% was to be transferred to the USSR without any kind of return payment at all.

The Potsdam conference, though it issued an agreed communiqué and a clear plan of action, was marked by some sharp exchanges in its early stages between Stalin and Churchill, who, using a phrase that would become famous, accused the Soviet leader of having drawn an "iron curtain" (some accounts say "iron fence") across the continent and of failing to implement the Yalta accords. Britain and the US refused to recognize the governments constructed in Romania, Hungary, and Bulgaria and protested against Tito's elimination of rivals in Yugoslavia; as a counter-measure, Stalin blocked Italian access to the United Nations and pointed to the situation in Spain, where the US and Britain, fearing the spread of communist influence, were loath to undertake any action that might destabilize the Franco regime.[21] He might just as well have reproached the West for the colonial policy of France, who massacred thousands of Arab civilians after riots in Algiers and Oran in May 1945, and who shelled Damascus in the same month, but in fact French premier Charles de Gaulle was more severely reprimanded for his actions by Washington and London than by Stalin since de Gaulle was following a slavishly pro-Soviet line on the question of democracy in central Europe. Stalin did not take France seriously as a potential ally, however, and refused to allow de Gaulle a place at Potsdam, even though France had become a permanent member of the Security Council of the United Nations at the San Francisco conference in April 1945.[22]

The Council of Foreign Ministers met four times between September 1945 and July 1946. And from July 29, 1946 to October 15, 1946 the CFM was engaged in the Paris Peace Conference that decided the five treaties of peace with Italy, Hungary, Romania, Bulgaria, and Finland. From the first, at London in September 1945, the conferences were characterized by repeated clashes between V.M. Molotov and Ernest Bevin, whose language was blunt to the point of rudeness, but whose unwillingness to be browbeaten was probably the only rational response to the relentless Soviet negotiating style. The US were represented by James F. Byrnes, who like Bevin was a tougher negotiator than his wartime predecessors.

The peace treaties were an important moment in international diplomacy and were proof that all cooperation between East and West had not yet broken down – though the tensions aroused during the meetings of the Council no doubt contributed to making a breakdown inevitable. Formally signed in Paris on February 10, 1947, the treaties compelled Finland to make minor territorial concessions to the USSR; rewarded Groza's Romania, which had arguably been Hitler's most assiduous ally, with the return of Transylvania, although Bessarabia and northern Bukovina were lost to the USSR; and reduced Hungary to its 1920 frontiers. Bulgaria was compelled to return Western Thrace to Greece, but retained territory it had gained from Romania during the war.

The most important treaty was with Italy, which had held free and unfettered elections on June 2, 1946 in which the centrist Christian Democrats (DC) had emerged as the largest party, with 35% of the vote, but in which the two pro-Moscow parties, the socialists (PSI) and communists (PCI), had together taken 40%. Italy regarded itself as both a democratic success story and as a co-belligerent in the war that had proved its antifascist character by its sacrifices after 1943. Italy had, after all, been a battlefield for two years. Italy's leaders, of all parties, were shocked by the severity of the terms being demanded of her. Premier Alcide de Gasperi, when he responded to the terms agreed by Italy's victims on August 9, 1946, began his speech by saying that he realized that "everything, except for your personal courtesy, is against me." In a reasoned but perhaps too indignant speech, De Gasperi made a case for Italy that contained "too little anti-fascism and perhaps too much national-ism."[23] It was anyway to no avail. Italy lost the Dodecanese islands to Greece, most of the province of Trieste to Yugoslavia, and all her colonies. Trieste itself became an international territory. Italy had to pay considerable reparations to Albania, Ethiopia, Greece, the USSR, and, above all, Yugoslavia. These provisions were greeted with outrage. On the day the treaty was signed, flags were lowered to half-mast, a symbolic ten-minute silence was held, the Constituent Assembly stopped work on the new constitution for half an hour, and the DC newspaper *Il Popolo*'s headline was "the people of Rome are united in dignified protest while at Paris Italy is being mutilated."[24]

Over Germany, East–West tensions were intense and the intention, expressed at Potsdam, to treat Germany as a whole swiftly became a dead letter. In 1946, the Western allies followed a policy of economic rebuilding. The Soviet Union did not keep its promises to send raw materials and foodstuffs to western Germany; in May 1946, American commander Lucius D. Clay responded by stopping the flow of repa-rations from the western zones. Britain and the US merged their zones to form "Bizonia" in July 1946 and speaking in Stuttgart on September 6, 1946, secretary Byrnes warned that the US would not favour any controls that would subject the Ruhr and the Rhineland to the political domination of outside powers. In the same month, Britain introduced bread rationing at home to help feed hungry Germans. The Western allies' motives were clear and significant. Clay and his British counter-parts believed that unless the level of nutrition was raised in the Western zones, which meant producing goods for export in order to pay for food imports, Germany would be at risk of going communist.[25] This fear arguably underestimated the depth of the opposition of the German masses to communism. Christian Democracy was quick to take root in the western zones of Germany, while the leader of the German socialists (SPD), Kurt Schumacher, a Marxist by conviction and training, was opposed to any attempt to bring Germany within the Soviet sphere of influence and resisted attempts by the philo-Soviet wing of his party to allow the fusion of the SPD with the communists (KPD) in the Soviet zone. In local elections in the Soviet zone in January 1946, the KPD was heavily defeated by the SPD. In late April 1946 Otto Grotewohl, eastern German SPD leader, was instrumental in merging the SPD in the Soviet zone with the Communist Party into the new *Sozialistische Einheitspartei Deutschlands* ("Socialist Unity Party": SED). Backed by the Russians, this party swiftly occupied power and marginalized the democratic opposition. In the west, by contrast, free and unfettered local elections were held as in the US zone early as the spring of 1946.

A year on from Potsdam, in short, Germany was already becoming a divided country. Only a major effort at collaboration could have prevented Germany being divided in two and neither side was willing to make the compromises necessary to do it. The former allies met at foreign ministers' level to discuss the future of Germany and Austria in Moscow between March 10 and April 24, 1947, but the talks ended in failure. Britain and the United States were not disposed to accept a Soviet proposal for a centralized German government, preferring a federal solution, and rejected a further Soviet proposal for a voice in the control of the industrial production of the Ruhr. The Soviet Union reinstated its demand for a fixed sum of $10,000 million in reparations, despite the Potsdam agreement; the two Western democracies argued instead that it was more important to raise Germany's productive potential and build an integrated economy with freedom of movement throughout the country. Bevin, at least, thought that the USSR, having stripped its own zone of its assets, now wanted to "rehabilitate" it at the expense of British and American taxpayers.[26] Over Austria, the two sides were just as far apart. Even an American proposal to sign a four-power treaty to keep Germany disarmed for 25 years was opposed by Molotov – ironically, in view of the turn events would take in the 1950s.

Constructing New Enemies: September 1945–March 1947

The Moscow meeting of the Council of Foreign Ministers was conditioned by President Harry S. Truman's famous speech to Congress on March 12, 1947 in which he announced what would become known as the "Truman Doctrine," the conviction that it was the task of the United States "to support free peoples who are resisting attempted subjugation by armed minorities or outside pressures." Truman was asking Congress for cash to support the governments of Greece and Turkey (which Britain could no longer afford to do). Civil war had flared in Greece following the election of a right-wing government in March 1946, and Washington believed – wrongly, in fact – that the Soviet Union was supplying the EAM, the National Liberation Front, via Yugoslavia. Tito was in fact acting on his own account, showing the personal independence that would shortly lead him to break with Moscow. The US was, however, extra-sensitive to Soviet involvement in this region. In August 1946, during the "war scare of 1946," Truman had been prepared to meet aggression against Turkey with "force of arms." Informed of Truman's determination by British spy Donald Maclean, Stalin backed off, as he had in the earlier March 1946 crisis in Iran.[27]

Truman's speech highlighted just how far relations between the two "superpowers" – to use a term that was just beginning to have currency – had deteriorated since Roosevelt's presidency. The US had become convinced both that the Soviet Union represented a menace to democracy comparable to the Nazis and that it was the moral duty of the US to meet this "implacable challenge" by showing political leadership.[28]

Several factors had combined in 1946 to make this conviction latent in the thoughts of American policy-makers. The first can only be described as a psychological retreat from the consequences of the decisions taken as the war drew to a close. In March 1946, at Fulton, Missouri, Winston Churchill, no longer British premier but still obviously an authoritative figure, had put the new mood into words in a remarkable speech from which, usually, only a single phrase is remembered:

From Stettin in the Baltic to Trieste in the Adriatic an iron curtain has descended across the Continent. Behind that line lie all the capitals of the ancient states of central and eastern Europe. Warsaw, Berlin, Prague, Vienna, Budapest, Belgrade, Bucharest and Sofia, all these famous cities and the populations around them lie in what I must call the Soviet sphere, and all are subject in one form or another, not only to Soviet influence but to a very high and, in some cases, increasing measure of control from Moscow. Athens alone – Greece with its immortal glories – is free to decide its future at an election under British, American and French observation. The Russian-dominated Polish government has been encouraged to make enormous and wrongful inroads upon Germany, and mass expulsions of millions of Germans on a scale grievous and undreamed-of are now taking place. The Communist parties, which were very small in all these Eastern States of Europe, have been raised to pre-eminence and power far beyond their numbers and are seeking everywhere to obtain totalitarian control. Police governments are prevailing in nearly every case, and so far, except in Czechoslovakia, there is no true democracy.[29]

Churchill had been personally complicit in the creation of this situation, as, even more egregiously, had the American administrations of both Roosevelt and Truman, and his speech, which was delivered with the president sitting in the audience, was surely a way of expiating his guilt for what he now believed to be a serious lapse of judgment (significantly, the speech makes an explicit justification for the favorable treatment given to the USSR at Yalta). Churchill, Roosevelt, and the foreign policy establishment of the Western allies had been hopeful that a lasting peaceful settlement, and perhaps even a measure of democracy, might be won by conciliatory methods, but they had been proved wrong. Their instinct was to reverse the policy – not least because the possession of the atomic bomb strengthened their position. On January 5, 1946, Truman had expostulated to his secretary of state, Byrnes, "At Potsdam we were faced with an accomplished fact and were by circumstances almost forced to agree to Russian occupation of eastern Poland and that part of Germany east of the Oder river by Poland. It was a high-handed outrage . . . I'm tired of babying the Soviets."[30]

George F. Kennan's famous "Long Telegram," sent from Moscow on February 22, 1946 and rapidly diffused at all levels of the American government, essentially provided a conceptual justification for this change of mood. Kennan argued that world communism, with its base in the USSR, was "a political force committed fanatically to the belief that with the US there can be no permanent modus vivendi . . . [T]his political force has complete power of disposition over the energies of one of world's greatest peoples . . . [and] . . . an elaborate and far flung apparatus for exertion of its influence in other countries, an apparatus of amazing flexibility and versatility managed by people whose experience and skill in underground methods are presumably without parallel in history."[31] Democracy was at risk, in short, not just east of the "iron curtain" but nearer to home.

There was therefore a growing conviction that the West was facing a remorseless, well-equipped foe dedicated to the destruction of democratic values. But this was linked to a parallel conviction, based on the experience of the first year of economic reconstruction, that the US could not stay aloof from Europe. Without the US's material support, the democracies of western Europe would struggle to rebuild their economies and might fall prey to communist propaganda. In the first year after the war, it had been expected that the British ally would take the lead in western Europe. But it became apparent in 1946 that Britain was no longer strong enough to manage alone. The magnitude of the task was simply beyond the strength of her war-torn, indebted economy. The US somewhat reluctantly gave socialist Britain a loan of $3,750 million in December 1945, thus averting, in John Maynard Keynes's phrase, a "financial Dunkirk," but throughout 1946 Britain's reserves leached away as it tried to finance reconstruction, a nascent welfare state and huge military commitments round the globe. In August 1947 the Labour government was compelled to end the convertibility of sterling for dollars despite the convertibility of sterling having been one of the conditions of the American loan.[32]

Britain was in the same fix as its neighbors on the continent. Everybody in western Europe was desperate for dollars to finance the imports necessary for reconstruction. In 1946, Britain had a trade deficit of $764 million with the US; France's deficit was nearly as high at $650 million. Smaller countries, such as the Netherlands ($187 million) were running deficits of comparable size relative to GNP. In 1947, the deficits were even larger. Western Europe had a collective trade deficit with the US of nearly $4,750 million in 1947.[33] Europe needed American raw materials such as coal, wheat, and other foodstuffs because local producers could not yet churn out enough of these products. But above all, western Europe needed capital goods. According to Milward, "the deterioration of western Europe's balance of trade with the United States was largely caused by the very high and increasing level of imports of machinery, steel and transport equipment."[34] Paying for such goods was difficult, however. It required a lot of Scotch whisky, or French perfume, to pay for ships, tractors, and aeroplanes. Europe was only kept afloat financially by ad hoc US loans and, from 1948 onwards, Marshall Plan aid. Between July 1945 and December 1946, the US loaned western Europe nearly $3,500 million; in 1947, she loaned another $4,000 million. The US government, in effect, was buying American industry's own products.

Such largesse, in the tense political climate of 1946–1947, obviously came at a price, although whether the Americans specifically named that price, or merely allowed it to be inferred, remains an open question. In May 1947, the French and Italian communist parties were excluded from government. In France, this event came about after a harsh winter had led to increases in the prices for basic necessities. Factory workers throughout the country struck for wage increases. The French Communist Party (PCF) took the view that it was their duty to lead the workers' protests and refused to support the government in a parliamentary vote of confidence on May 1. Premier Paul Ramadier, deeply aware of how dependent France was on American loans ($1,000 million in 1946 alone), seized his chance to get rid of his communist ministers. France subsequently "moved towards open acceptance of the 'western strategy' and, in 1948, agreed to co-sponsor the establishment of a west German state."[35]

In Italy, tensions had been high since the election of the Constituent Assembly in June 1946. The Treasury minister in De Gasperi's government, Epicarmo Corbino, and the governor of the Bank of Italy, the political economist Luigi Einaudi, followed a strict deflationary policy after June 1946, hoping to raise Italy's competitiveness and boost exports. This policy, however rational from the economic point of view, caused severe social unrest, which the PCI took advantage of, campaigning for state direction of the economy and for higher wages. De Gasperi unquestionably used this unrest to stir up the fear in Washington that another important European country was about to fall to the Reds. In January 1947, he visited the US and carried out a "carefully choreographed public relations campaign" designed to maximize pressure from the Italo-American community for US aid to their former homeland.[36]

De Gasperi returned home with the promise of a $100 million loan. In May 1947, determined to drive the PCI out of government, De Gasperi resigned. The US promised him increased aid if he formed a government without the extreme left, which he did ten days later, although he had to rely on the neo-fascists for a parliamentary majority. Although it seems unlikely that the Truman administration imposed the exclusion of the communists from government as a price for US loans, it is quite clear that Italian leaders realized that they could manipulate the American dread of communism to gain their political ends.[37] This is not to dispute that the PCI, with its two million members, huge stocks of hidden arms and strong revolutionary wing, was a potential menace. There is little doubt that without the strong will and political moderation of the PCI's leader, Palmiro Togliatti, Italy could have followed the path of Greece in 1946–1947. De Gasperi and Togliatti, who continued to collaborate even after May 1947 to draw up the delicate and intricate amalgam of compromises that is Italy's constitution, were the founding fathers of modern Italian democracy.

Events in Greece, France, and Italy in the spring of 1947, along with the failure of the foreign ministers' talks over the future of Germany, marked the end of the transitional period between the defeat of the Nazis and the onset of what the American journalist Walter Lippmann was soon to call, in a series of articles deeply critical of the Truman administration, the "Cold War." The US convinced itself – though contemporary statistics do not entirely bear this conclusion out – that Europe was starving and on the verge of revolution and needed a systematic program of economic aid.[38] This conclusion led directly to Secretary of State George Marshall's famous Harvard speech on June 5, 1947 promising to aid the reconstruction of Europe, but it is a mistake to see Marshall's move purely as an act of charity. It was, rather, the "most dedicated effort yet to reduce communist influence in Europe" and was offered to the countries of central Europe only on condition that they reoriented their economies away from the USSR and towards integration with the West.[39]

The USSR interpreted these events ideologically in its turn. Reflecting an analysis that had been in circulation at the highest levels in Moscow since at least September 1946, when the Soviet Ambassador in Washington, Nikolai Novikov, had sent a lengthy telegram to foreign minister Molotov claiming that the US's postwar ambition was "war against the Soviet Union, which in the eyes of the American imperialists is the main obstacle in the path of the United States,"[40] Stalin circled the communist wagons rather than allow the states under Soviet control to participate in the Plan. As John Lewis Gaddis has argued, "Stalin fell into the trap that the Marshall Plan laid for him, which was to get *him* to build the wall that would divide Europe."[41] In September 1947, at a meeting of Europe's major communist parties in Poland, Stalin's henchman Andrei Zhdanov berated the French and Italian parties for their passivity and attachment to parliamentary methods and dictated the need for communist solidarity in the face of American expansionism and imperialist plots. A new organization, the Cominform, would be set up to counter the Americans' propaganda towards the European masses.[42] The split in the wartime Grand Alliance was moot.

New enemies had been created in both Moscow and Washington to replace the monsters of the Third Reich.

Notes

I have not provided notes for quotations taken from the official communiqués of the Yalta and Potsdam conferences, or the Truman declaration. These are all available online at http://avalon.law.yale.edu/subject_inenus/wwii.asp.

1   Djilas, *Conversations with Stalin*, 114.
2   Churchill, *The Second World War*, vol. 6, 198; Jenkins, *Churchill*, 757–763.
3   Clogg, *A Concise History of Greece*, 136–141.
4   Schöpflin, *Politics in Eastern Europe*, 65.
5   Kimball, *Churchill and Roosevelt: The Complete Correspondence*, vol. 3, 547.
6   Davies, *Heart of* Europe, says, 55, that Poland lost 18% of her population during the war. The nearest rivals were the USSR (11. 2%) and Yugoslavia (11.1%). The US lost 0.2%.
7   Charlton, *The Eagle and the Small Birds*, 15–30; Zaslavsky, *Pulizia di classe*, 61–83.
8   Quoted Jenkins, *Churchill*, 762.
9   Kimball, *Churchill and Roosevelt*, 565.
10 Byrnes, *Speaking Frankly*, 71.
11 Senarclens, *From Yalta to the Iron Curtain*, 39.
12 Hanson, "Stanisław Mikołajczyk: November 1944–June 1945," 62.
13 Rothschild and Wingfield, *Return to Diversity*, 81–83.
14 Gati, "Hegemony and Repression in the Eastern Alliance," 179.
15 Byrnes, in *Speaking Frankly*, 68, says that Stalin believed Hitler had escaped to Spain or Argentina!
16 Bosworth, *Mussolini*, 411.
17 Bell, *Twentieth-Century Europe*, 142.
18 Quoted Lacouture, *De Gaulle: The Ruler 1945–1970*, 63.
19 "Morgenthau Plan," included in Morgenthau, *Germany is Our Problem*, 4.
20 Senarclens, *From Yalta to the Iron Curtain*, 57.
21 Moradiellos, "The Potsdam Conference and the Spanish Problem," 73–90.
22 Lacouture, *De Gaulle: The Ruler 1945–1970*, 62, 95.
23 Lorenzini, op. cit., 75.
24 Lorenzini, *L'Italia e il trattato di pace*, 107.
25 Trachtenberg, *A Constructed Peace*, 52.
26 Bullock, *Ernest Bevin: Foreign Secretary*, 388.
27 Mark, "The War Scare of 1946 and Its Consequences."
28 Kennan, "The Sources of Soviet Conduct," 106.
29 Churchill, "The Sinews of Peace," at http://www.winstonchurchill.org
30 Truman, *Year of Decisions*, 492.
31 George F. Kennan, "Long Telegram," at http://www.trumanlibrary.org
32 For Britain's financial problems, see Skidelsky, *John Maynard Keynes*, 375–458.
33 Milward, *Reconstruction of Western Europe 1945–1951*, 26–27.
34 Milward, op. cit., 36.
35 Creswell and Trachtenberg, "France and the German Question," 14.
36 William I. Hitchcock, *The Struggle for Europe*, 87.
37 Harper, *America and the Reconstruction of Italy, 1945–1948*, 137–158.
38 As early as 1948 the Food and Agriculture Organization (FAO) of the United Nations concluded in a report on nutrition in western Europe that Denmark, Sweden, Greece, and Switzerland had restored their prewar levels of food consumption, although in the

case of Greece this was at a low figure of 2,300 calories per day. Norway, the Netherlands, Britain, Belgium, and Finland were all over 2,500 calories per day – an adequate though not luxurious level of nutrition. France, Italy, and Austria remained below prewar averages, at just over 2,000 calories per day. The danger zone was Germany, where people still had less than 2,000 calories per day, 1,000 calories per day less than before the war. Figures cited in Hubert d'Hérouville, *L'Economie Européenne*, 56.

39 Cox and Kennedy-Pipe, "The Tragedy of American Diplomacy," 109–110.
40 Novikov Telegram, Cold War International History Project, http://cwihplib.si.edu
41 Gaddis, *The United States and the Origins of the Cold War*, 32.
42 See Anna Di Biagio, "The Marshall Plan and the Founding of the Cominform" for a detailed account.

Bibliography

Beevor, Anthony, *Berlin: The Downfall 1945* (London: Penguin, 2007).

Bell, P.M.H., *Twentieth-Century Europe* (London: Hodder Arnold, 2006).

Bosworth, R.J.B., *Mussolini* (London: Arnold, 2002).

Bullock, Alan, *Ernest Bevin: Foreign Secretary* (Oxford: Oxford University Press, 1983).

Byrnes, James F., *Speaking Frankly* (New York: Harper & Row, 1947).

Charlton, Michael, *The Eagle and the Small Birds: Crisis in the Soviet Empire: From Yalta to Solidarity* (Chicago: Chicago University Press, 1984).

Churchill, Winston Spencer, *The Second World War*, vol. 6 (London: Cassell, 1954).

Clogg, Richard, *A Concise History of Greece* (Cambridge: Cambridge University Press, 1995).

Cox, Robert and Caroline Kennedy-Pipe, "The Tragedy of American Diplomacy? Rethinking the Marshall Plan," *Journal of Cold War Studies* 7, no. 1, Winter 2005, 97–134.

Creswell, Michael and M. Trachtenberg, "France and the German Question, 1945–1955," *Journal of Cold War Studies* 5, no. 3, Summer 2003, 5–28.

Davies, Norman, *Heart of Europe: The Past in Poland's Present* (Oxford: Oxford University Press, 2001).

Davies, Norman, *Europe at War 1939–1945: No Simple Victory* (London: Pan Books, 2007).

Di Biagio, Anna, "The Marshall Plan and the Founding of the Cominform, June–September 1947," in Francesca Gori and Silvio Pons (eds), *The Soviet Union and Europe in the Cold War, 1943–1953* (London: Macmillan, 1996).

Djilas, Milovan, *Conversations with Stalin* (New York: Harcourt, Brace, Jovanovich, 1962).

Gaddis, John Lewis, *The United States and the Origins of the Cold War* (New York: Columbia University Press, 2000).

Gaddis, John Lewis, *The Cold War* (London: Allen Lane, 2006).

Gati, Charles, "Hegemony and Repression in the Eastern Alliance," in Melvyn P. Leffler and David S. Painter (eds.), *Origins of the Cold War* (London: Routledge, 1994).

Hanson, Joanna, "Stanisław Mikołajczyk: November 1944–June 1945," *European History Quarterly* 21, no. 1, 1991, 39–73.

Harper, John Lamberton, *America and the Reconstruction of Italy, 1945–1948* (Cambridge: Cambridge University Press, 2002).

Hérouville, Hubert d', *L'Economie Européenne* (Paris: Presses Universitaires de France, 1949).

Hitchcock, William I., *The Struggle for Europe: The Turbulent History of a Divided Continent* (London: Profile, 2003).

Jenkins, Roy, *Churchill* (London: Macmillan, 2001).

Judt, Tony, *Postwar* (New York: Penguin, 2005).

Kennan, George F., "The Sources of Soviet Conduct," in Kennan, *American Diplomacy 1900–1950* (New York and Toronto: New American Library, 1951).

Kennedy-Pipe, Caroline, *Russia and the World 1917–1991* (London: Arnold, 1998).

Kennedy-Pipe, Caroline, *The Origins of the Cold War* (London: Palgrave, 2007).

Kimball, Warren F., *Churchill and Roosevelt: The Complete Correspondence*, vol. 2 (Princeton, NJ: Princeton University Press, 1984).

Lacouture, Jean, *De Gaulle: The Ruler 1945–1970* (London: Collins Harvill, 1991).

Leffler, Melvyn and David Painter (eds.), *The Origins of the Cold War* (London: Routledge, 2005).

Lorenzini, Sara, *L'Italia e il trattato di pace del 1947* (Bologna: Il Mulino, 2007).

Mark, Eduard, "The War Scare of 1946 and Its Consequences," *Diplomatic History* 21, no. 3 (Summer 1997), 383–415.

Mastny, Vojtech, *Russia's Road to the Cold War* (New York: Columbia University Press, 1979).

Milward, Alan S., *The Reconstruction of Western Europe 1945–1951* (London: Routledge, 1984).

Moradiellos, Enrique, "The Potsdam Conference and the Spanish Problem," *Contemporary European History* 10, no. 1, 73–90.

Morgenthau, Henry, *Germany is Our Problem* (New York: Harper & Brothers, 1945).

Naimark, Norman, *The Russians in Germany: A History of the Soviet Zone of Occupation 1945–1949* (Cambridge, MA: Harvard University Press, 1995).

Rothschild, Joseph and Nancy M. Wingfield, *Return to Diversity: A Political History of East Central Europe since World War II* (Oxford: Oxford University Press, 2000).

Schöpflin, George, *Politics in Eastern Europe 1945–1992* (Oxford: Blackwell, 1996).

Senarclens, Pierre de, *From Yalta to the Iron Curtain: The Great Powers and the Origin of the Cold War* (Oxford: Berg, 1995).

Skidelsky, Robert, *John Maynard Keynes: Fighting for Britain 1937–1946* (London: Macmillan, 2001).

Thomas, Hugh, *Armed Truce: The Beginnings of the Cold War 1945–1946* (London: Sceptre, 1986).

Trachtenberg, Marc, *A Constructed Peace: The Making of the European Settlement 1945–1963* (Princeton, NJ: Princeton University Press, 1999).

Truman, Harry S., *Year of Decisions* (London: Hodder and Stoughton, 1955).

Tusa, John, *The Nuremberg Trial* (London: Atheneum, 1984).

Zaslavsky, Victor, *Pulizia di classe: il massacro di Katyn* (Bologna: Il Mulino, 2007).

Further Reading

The literature on the end of World War II in Europe is vast and growing daily. Two important recent additions to the literature that provide a vivid picture of the sheer horror of the war, and of moral complexities created by five years of total war, are Norman Davies, *Europe at War 1939–1945: No Simple Victory* (London: Pan Books, 2007) and Anthony Beevor, *Berlin: The Downfall 1945* (London: Penguin, 2007). The trial of the leading Nazis has been the subject of many works of popular history, but one which stands out for rigor and seriousness is John Tusa, *The Nuremberg Trial* (London: Atheneum, 1984).

Life in the Soviet occupation zone of Germany is brilliantly depicted by Norman Naimark, *The Russians in Germany: A History of the Soviet Zone of Occupation 1945–1949* (Cambridge, MA: Harvard University Press, 1995); how the communists came to power throughout east-central Europe is the subject of Joseph Rothschild and Nancy M. Wingfield, *Return to Diversity: A Political History of East Central Europe since World War II* (Oxford: Oxford University Press, 2000), pp. 75–123.

Classic accounts of the origins of the Cold War in Europe include Hugh Thomas's highly readable *Armed Truce: The Beginnings of the Cold War 1945–1946* (London: Sceptre, 1986) and John Lewis Gaddis, *The United States and the Origins of the Cold War* (New York: Columbia University Press, 2000). Pierre de Senarclens, *From Yalta to the Iron Curtain: The Great Powers and the Origin of the Cold War* (Oxford: Berg, 1995) is a well-paced book that wears its political sympathies on its sleeve. Soviet policy is skillfully summarized in two chapters of Caroline Kennedy-Pipe's *Russia and the World 1917–1991* (London: Arnold, 1998) and in Vojtech Mastny, *Russia's Road to the Cold War* (New York: Columbia University Press, 1979). Kennedy-Pipe's *The Origins of the Cold War* (London: Palgrave, 2007) is the most up-to-date treatment of the subject. An important collection of essays by acknowledged experts is Melvyn Leffler and David Painter (eds.), *The Origins of the Cold War* (London: Routledge, 2005).

The economic reconstruction of Europe is magisterially depicted in Alan S. Milward, *The Reconstruction of Western Europe* (London: Routledge, 1984). The first five chapters of Tony Judt's *Postwar* (New York: Penguin, 2005) are a superb synthesis of political, cultural, and economic history.

CHAPTER TWO

Federalism and the Beginnings of European Union

JOHN PINDER

Federalism became an *idée-force* in Europe following the devastating experience of the two World Wars in the first half of the twentieth century. But its influence on the creation of the European Communities in the 1950s had roots in earlier developments of the idea.

Roots in the Years 1918–1940

Already in 1918 Luigi Einaudi, a distinguished professor of economics in Turin who was to become the first president of the Italian Republic in 1948, wrote two articles explaining that a League of Nations, based on the absolute sovereignty of states, would not prevent another war; so federation, in which states share sovereignty to deal with common problems, was required to keep the peace and deal with the fact of economic interdependence. Then a book by the industrialist Giovanni Agnelli and Professor Attilio Cabiati expounded a similar argument, for a European federation. They cited predominantly British sources, including leading scholars such as Acton, Bryce, Mill, Seeley, and Sidgwick, whose writings on federalism had been inspired by the example of the United States Constitution. But this early emergence of European federalism was cut short by Mussolini's seizure of power in 1922.[1]

In the same year Richard Coudenhove-Kalergi's book *Paneuropa*, advocating the uniting of Europe as the only alternative to its decline, had enormous success and influenced the French foreign minister Aristide Briand's proposal in 1930 for a European "federal union" which, however, like Coudenhove's own ideas, failed to grasp the nettle of national sovereignty. The Pan-Europe movement continued to enjoy support, though many lost confidence in Coudenhove when he tried to recruit Mussolini to his cause.[2]

In Paris a brilliant group of intellectuals, including Alexandre Marc and Denis de Rougement, developed a theory of "integral federalism," rejecting both Soviet Marxism and liberal democracy, and proposing federal structures in the economy, society, and polity in response to a "crisis of civilisation."[3] Having generalized their

A Companion to Europe since 1945, First Edition. Edited by Klaus Larres.
© 2014 John Wiley & Sons, Ltd. Published 2014 by John Wiley & Sons, Ltd.

critique of the French political system in the 1930s into a rejection of parliamentary democracy as such, however, they lacked influence over the beginnings of European Union in the 1950s.

Ironically, in contrast with the relative influence of France and Britain on the foundation of the Communities in the 1950s, it was the British who in the 1930s made the outstanding contribution to federalist thinking in Europe. Stemming from the same tradition of federalism as had influenced Einaudi, Agnelli, and Cabiati, they produced a growing volume of high-quality literature in the period up to 1940. In 1935 Lord Lothian made the general case for federation most eloquently in his short book *Pacifism is not Enough*. This was followed in 1937 by Lionel Robbins's *National Planning and International Order*, explaining that the international economy required, like a national economy, an effective framework of law and policy, hence federal judicial, legislative, and executive institutions; and in 1939 he demonstrated in *The Economic Causes of War* that absolute sovereignty, not as marxists contended capitalism, was to blame and concluded the book, a few days after World War II had begun, with a passionate appeal to establish a European federation after the war had been won.[4]

The Federal Union organization had already been launched to campaign for federation as the antidote to war. It rapidly gained the support of notables such as Lord Lothian, Sir William Beveridge, Ernest Bevin, and the Archbishop of York who observed that "the whole scheme of Federal Union has made a staggeringly effective appeal to the British mind." By April 1940 it had ten thousand members and editorial support from the *The Times*, the *Manchester Guardian*, and the *New Statesman*. Many of the members had been influenced by the message of Clarence Streit's *Union Now*, advocating a federal union of the democracies including the United States. But as the approach of war confirmed American isolationism, a European federation such as Robbins envisaged became the main objective. The Federal Union Research Institute was established, under Beveridge's leadership, to work on its constitutional and economic aspects. In addition to Beveridge and Robbins, the participants included such luminaries as James Meade, Friedrich von Hayek and Ivor Jennings, the foremost constitutional jurist of his generation.[5]

On June 17, 1940 Winston Churchill, attempting to forestall French surrender to Hitler's conquering army, made his offer of Union between Britain and France, with federal elements in its institutions. It was Jean Monnet, then in London as chairman of the joint Franco-British coordinating committee for war supplies, who had pressed the idea on the British government.[6] Churchill was to recall his surprise at the enthusiasm of the cabinet. But given the prevalence of support for the federal idea, including public commitment by the cabinet's two leading Labour members as well as its leading Liberal, that was not so surprising.[7] Paul Reynaud, the French prime minister, was also enthusiastic. But he was immediately replaced by Marshal Pétain and France capitulated on the following day. Britain became fully absorbed in the struggle for survival, then for victory; and after the war it was to be France, not Britain, that took the lead in moves towards a federal Europe. Meanwhile Monnet was in Washington, continuing to play an important part in the procurement of war supplies, thus gaining practical experience of the federal system and forging strong relations with people such as Dean Acheson, George Ball, and John McCloy, whose support as leading

Americans was to be crucial in the launching of the European Community after the war.[8]

Federalism and the Resistance, 1939–1945

By 1939 Altiero Spinelli, a former communist, had for 12 years been a political prisoner of Italy's fascist regime, first in jail and after that confined on the island of Ventotene, where Ernesto Rossi, a brilliant economics professor and former student of Einaudi, was likewise confined. They read, in a collection of Einaudi's writings, his federalist articles of 1918 and, communication with him being permitted, Rossi asked Einaudi for some literature on the subject. Einaudi sent some of the British federalists' writings, including the two books by Lionel Robbins, with an astounding result. Spinelli was to recall that the British federalist thinking, which gave him a "key to understanding the chaos into which Europe was plunging and for devising alternatives," had remained impressed on his memory "like a revelation."[9] It gave him the cause to which he devoted the rest of his life. The first result was the Ventotene manifesto, which he wrote with Rossi and which became an iconic statement for postwar federalist movements, above all in Italy.[10] An essay that Spinelli then wrote before being freed from Ventotene in 1943 demonstrated a clear understanding of what was to become known as a "hamiltonian" federation for Europe, with democratic government and the rule of law at both federal and state level, the division of powers between them constitutionally guaranteed, and enough federal powers to serve the common economic and security interests.[11] So while the thinking of British federalists who had sought to apply the basic principles of the American founding fathers to the problems of contemporary Europe was to be neglected in Britain, it was transmitted to the mainstream of Continental federalism through Spinelli, who was to play a major part in federalist developments both in Italy and at European level.

Directly after his liberation, Spinelli convened a meeting in Milan at which the Movimento Federalista Europeo was founded.[12] Believing that there must be like-minded people in resistance movements elsewhere, Spinelli and Rossi then went to Switzerland to locate their representatives. By March 1944 they had arranged a series of meetings in Geneva, including French, German, and Dutch participants, at which a declaration was adopted proposing a European federation, which was sent to all accessible resistance movements.[13]

There was no answer from Germany, understandably given the circumstances. But despite the dangers of any activity that the Gestapo might regard as subversive, the Kreisau Circle, led by Helmuth von Moltke, had envisaged a democratic federal Germany in a federal European state, with powers relating to foreign affairs, armed forces, and the economy; and other groups favored federal outcomes, though there is not much evidence of detailed proposals.[14] Von Moltke was executed early in 1945; and Hans and Sophie Scholl, with other students of the White Rose group, were likewise executed after distributing leaflets denouncing state absolutism and proposing, among other things, a federal political organization for Europe.[15]

Communication was generally difficult, so clear responses to the Geneva declaration came only from the Netherlands and France. Although the principal Dutch resistance journals had favored a European "federal community," and a penetrating analysis of the question of European federation had been circulated, the Dutch response to the declaration was cautious, preferring joint action on "a common task" as a move towards a federation.[16]

The encouraging reaction came from France. Henri Frenay, later a minister in the first postwar government and subsequently chairman of the European Union of Federalists, in 1941 had founded Combat, which became one of the strongest French resistance groups. Albert Camus was editor of its journal. Frenay had already proposed "a federation of equal states in Europe, with Germany cured of its megalomania."[17] Soon after receiving the communication from Geneva, the leaders of resistance groups in southern France met, created the Comité Français pour la Fédération Européenne (CFFE), and issued a similar declaration.[18]

At Spinelli's instigation a conference was organized in Paris in March 1945, not long after the liberation, with French, British, German, Italian, and Spanish participants, in order to follow up what had been begun in Geneva. The participants, in addition to Spinelli and Camus, included André Philip, who in London during the war had been responsible for the relations of General de Gaulle's Free French with the resistance movements; was soon to be a minister in de Gaulle's government; and did much to promote federalist influence in the following years.[19] The conference issued another declaration like that of Geneva, providing further demonstration of support for the federal idea in Continental Europe, which was to be manifested in the growth of federalist organizations and their increasingly prominent activities.

Federalists and the Council of Europe, 1945–1950

In France in July 1945, 73% thought that Europe "should form a federation," against 17% who did not.[20] But leading members of the CFFE such as Camus, not seeing the basis for a realistic federalist strategy, withdrew from its activities.[21] In Italy Spinelli, after his dynamic and promising start, observed in June 1945 that, with almost all the Continent occupied by the Americans, the British, and the Soviet Union, there was no chance of exercising initiative, for in the Soviet bloc there was no democracy and hence no prospect of federalism, while the Americans and British opposed activities that might upset relations with Stalin. So for the time being he suspended his activity in the federalist movement.[22] It was left to the British and Swiss movements to take the initiative at European level.

The Swiss Europa Union organized a conference at Hertenstein in September 1946, with federalist groups from 13 countries, which issued a declaration calling for the transfer of part of economic, political, and military sovereignty to a European federation and for a European organization of federalist movements. In October, Federal Union organized a conference in Luxembourg, with representatives from organizations in twelve countries, whose main proposal was the creation of two umbrella organizations, one for European and one for world federalists. The outcome of these two initiatives was a congress at Montreux in August 1947 to establish the European Union of Federalists, followed by one to establish a world federalist movement.[23]

Denis de Rougement opened the EUF congress with an inspiring speech on integral federalist lines, reflected in the concluding resolution which saw federalism as "a dynamic principle which transforms all human activities." The resolution also emphasized the need to create a European federation, seen as an incremental process.[24] Spinelli pointed out that the Marshall Plan, a product of democratic and liberal America, now gave west Europeans the chance to federate; and he foresaw that if they failed to do so the US, lacking an equal partner, would be liable to shift from the liberal to the imperial alternative. So federation was the condition for ensuring that there would be not only a properly democratic Europe but also a liberal rather than imperial America.[25]

Meanwhile Churchill, in a speech at Zurich University in September 1946, had put new life into the idea of a united Europe, affirming that "we must build a kind of United States of Europe," to make "Europe as free and happy as Switzerland is today." The project would have to be supported by America and Britain, but "the first step must be a partnership between France and Germany . . . France and Germany must take the lead together"; and "we must begin now."[26] He may have been vague about the structure of a United States of Europe and he certainly envisaged that Britain would not be a part of it, but his insistence on Franco-German partnership as a condition of progress towards European Union was prophetic and his words had an electric effect on many people who wanted to unite Europe.

This was followed in May 1948 by a spectacular Congress at The Hague, presided over by Churchill and organized by Duncan Sandys, who as well as being a very able politician was Churchill's son-in-law. Among the eight hundred participants were many former and future political leaders, including Konrad Adenauer, Alcide De Gasperi, François Mitterrand, Paul Reynaud and Paul-Henri Spaak. The participants were divided between the federalists, led by Reynaud, and intergovernmentalists, led by Sandys, presaging the split between the Continental group of states prepared to take steps towards European Union and those, led by Britain, that were to prefer cooperation among governments.[27]

Not all the British agreed with Sandys. R.W.G. Mackay, a leading federalist since 1940, who was now a Labour MP and who led a delegation of British federalists to the Congress, had a few weeks earlier secured the signatures of two hundred MPs for a motion calling for a long-term policy to create a European federation, designed by a constituent assembly to be convoked as soon as possible. Prime minister Attlee, replying to the debate, said that "ultimately we must come to federation of Europe" – but not yet.[28]

The British government was less conciliatory. The Congress had called for a European parliament to prepare plans for a European Union; and three months later, the French government pressed for such a parliament to form "the nucleus of a federal organization of Europe."[29] The British government responded by proposing a permanent council of ministers, taking decisions by unanimity. When Robert Schuman, the French foreign minister, had intimated that France would if necessary go ahead without Britain, the reaction of Ernest Bevin, by now foreign secretary and suspicious of the idea of European federation, was "We've got to give them something. I think we'll give them this talking-shop in Strasbourg."[30] So the Council of Europe was set up with a Consultative Assembly of member states' parliamentarians alongside a Committee of Ministers to take the decisions.

When the Assembly first met in August 1949 Mackay, with André Philip and Senator Pierre de Félice, took the initiative in calling for "a European Political Authority with limited functions but real powers." Their resolution, supported by Reynaud, was passed by near unanimity, before being rejected by the Committee of Ministers.[31] This reflected the strength of federalist support among parliamentarians, particularly those from France, Germany, and Italy.

Italy's federalist movement had been gaining political influence since Spinelli returned to the Movimento Federalista Europeo (MFE) as secretary general in June 1948, when it already had twelve thousand members and substantial support among parliamentarians and political parties but lacked an effective political strategy.[32] Not long after the opening session of the Consultative Assembly of the Council of Europe, the MFE Congress called for its transformation into "a Constituent Assembly, in order to draw up a Federal Pact of the United States of Europe";[33] and by May 1949 Spinelli had persuaded the EUF to urge the Assembly to draft a Federal Pact.[34] A campaign for the Federal Pact ensued, with impressive impact in France, Germany, and Italy. Several thousand French mayors signed a petition in support.[35] In Germany, where a powerful federalist organization was being developed, the *Bundestag* passed a resolution approving the project.[36] In Italy some half a million signatures were collected for a petition which was approved by the parliament and finally signed by prime minister De Gasperi and foreign minister Sforza in the presence of President Einaudi.[37] De Gasperi's signature was particularly significant, for when Spinelli had approached him earlier with the petition, he had requested that the word federal be removed and, when Spinelli refused, had "coldly" concluded their meeting.[38] De Gasperi's support was crucial to the federalist policy of the Italian government and mainstream political parties from then on. Indeed, the campaign helped to evoke the generally federalist stance of both Italy and Germany which was to be a major influence in favor of steps towards European Union during the following half-century.

Frustrated by the British-led vetoes in the Committee of Ministers on action proposed by the Consultative Assembly, in August 1950 André Philip moved, on behalf of French delegates in the Assembly, that willing states should sign a Federal Pact instituting a democratically elected European parliament and a government responsible to it.[39] In November the EUF organized a major conference at Strasbourg to promote the idea; and Spinelli recounted, as an object lesson, the example of the Annapolis and Philadelphia Conventions.[40] The primary sources for Italian federalists have, indeed, remained until this day not only the Federal Union literature to answer the question "why make Europe?," but also the American experience as the basis for their focus on the constitutional convention as the answer to the question "how make Europe?."[41]

The split between British intergovernmentalism and Continental federalism had also occurred in the European Movement, though here it was the federalists who gained control of the organization. Sandys had been chairman of its International Executive Committee since the Movement's foundation in October 1948. But in January 1950 the federalists, by then predominant in the Committee, secured the passage of a resolution for opening the way towards a federation among those willing.[42] This led to Sandys's resignation and replacement in November by

Paul-Henri Spaak, the Belgian statesman who was currently President of the Consultative Assembly. Spaak, who had been in London in Belgium's government in exile during the war, had hoped for British leadership in the uniting of Europe but, frustrated like André Philip by Britain's obstruction, was to resign his presidency in December 1951, saying that "to rely on Britain is to give up the very idea of building Europe." He added, in his memoirs, that he decided to support Monnet's view: "Create a united Europe and Britain will join. It is by succeeding that you will convince her."[43] Spaak was indeed to play a leading part in the steps towards European Union that were to follow Monnet's initiative in creating the first European Community.

Monnet, Schuman, Adenauer, and the ECSC, 1950–1952

The campaign for the Federal Pact had demonstrated Continental support for European Union and British rejection of moves towards it but had not succeeded in circumventing that obstacle. Monnet devised a way to do so, through a specific step towards Union that would be accepted by the French, German, Italian, and Benelux (Belgian, the Netherlands, Luxembourg) governments, with crucial American support from which Monnet was able to derive full benefit through the relationships he had forged in wartime Washington. He initiated his proposal, which resulted in the establishment of the European Coal and Steel Community, by drafting, with his principal advisers, in particular Etienne Hirsch and Pierre Uri, the Declaration made by Robert Schuman, the French foreign minister, on May 9, 1950, which called it "a first step in the federation of Europe."

Monnet was to recall that, for him, the proposal in 1940 for Anglo-French union "had no federalist overtones" and that the normal course of his life had not conditioned him "to look at international problems in terms of national sovereignty."[44] But the following years in Washington had familiarized him with the workings of a federal system and evidently also with *The Federalist* of Hamilton, Jay, and Madison, for when he arrived in Algiers in 1943 and joined the French Committee of National Liberation, he gave the Committee's secretary general a copy, saying "Read it from end to end. It is good throughout"; and he wrote, in a note for the Committee, that European states must, after the war, "form a federation or economic entity that will make a single economic unit."[45] Hirsch, who was one of Monnet's closest collaborators from that time onwards, later expressed the view that Monnet never really was a federalist.[46] But it may well be that Hirsch, who was himself deeply committed to Monnet's approach to the building of a federal system, was applying the term to those who had a clearer notion than Monnet of the meaning of a federal constitution.[47] Spinelli, who had several opportunities to discuss federal institutions with Monnet in relation both to the ECSC and to the project for a European Political Community, judged that Monnet "certainly" wanted to arrive at a federation, even if he had "no idea how to make a constitution" and thought that "a few scraps of improvised ideas were enough."[48] Monnet's own idea in 1950 was focused on the creation of a European executive of federal type, but he was ready to incorporate complementary federal elements proposed by others, sufficient to set in train a series of steps that have led far towards a completed federal system.

The idea of a European organization for heavy industries had long been germinating in Monnet's mind. Spaak was to recall him explaining, in 1941 in Washington, "the rough outlines of what later became known as the Schuman Plan."[49] By 1950, with the control of German steel production by the International Ruhr Authority evidently due for reform, ideas for replacing it were in the air. Adenauer, Reynaud, and Philip were among those who had floated them.[50] The French foreign ministry had been preparing plans for international agreements with the orthodox formula of "a common ministerial organization" and "ministerial committees with regular meetings."[51] But Monnet's idea was to establish an organization that would put a definitive end to wars between the French and the Germans, for which he envisaged two conditions to be essential: complete equality between France and Germany; and institutions that would become a basis for permanent peace and, as he was later to put it, "civilize international relations," i.e. replace power relationships by the rule of law.[52] The coal and steel industries were the perfect terrain for such institutions, as they were still the industrial basis for armed force: governed in common, they would no longer offer the means for war between Germany and France; and the French government urgently needed a plan to replace the Ruhr Authority as the Americans and British were insisting that, as a basis for the revival of the German economy, the control of German steel production must be relaxed – to intense French alarm on both economic and strategic grounds.

Monnet, with Hirsch and Uri, rapidly produced the proposal that became the Schuman Declaration. Hirsch, after working with him for many years, then becoming the first President of the European Atomic Energy Community, was later to be president of federalist movements; and it was probably he who introduced the federal concept into the Schuman Declaration.[53] Pierre Uri was an outstandingly creative economist who provided a coherent intellectual framework for Monnet's ideas including, among other things, the idea of the common market.[54]

The first draft of the Declaration already expressed Monnet's essential political objective: "to make a breach in the ramparts of national sovereignty which will be narrow enough to secure consent but deep enough to open the way towards the unity that is essential to peace."[55] The word "narrow" reflected Monnet's determination to propose a step that governments would accept, while "deep" reflected the strength of the means for dealing with the problem: in Monnet's view, a European executive independent of the member states' governments. His experience of dealing with governments had taught him that a requirement to secure agreement between them on each decision would lead to little or nothing being decided in good time and hence to the project's failure. Thus the essence of the Declaration was, for Monnet, summarized in its final sentence: "By the pooling of basic production and the establishment of a new High Authority whose decisions will be binding on France, Germany, and the countries that join them, this proposal will lay the first concrete foundations of the European Federation which is indispensable to peace."[56] The High Authority's significance for Monnet was indicated when, in a speech after becoming its first president in 1952, he referred to it as "Europe's first government."[57] This was the crucial federal element around which the other federal elements in the project were to coalesce.

Robert Schuman, despite the words he used in the Declaration, was not an avowed federalist, though he had expressed the hope, when signing the treaty establishing the Council of Europe, that it would lay the foundations of a "vast and durable supranational union."[58] But he belonged to the frontier region between France and Germany and was profoundly conscious of the need for an effective way of ensuring peace, and hence ready to take responsibility for what became known as the Schuman Plan. Chancellor Konrad Adenauer accepted the plan with no hesitation whatever. As a Rhinelander, he too came from near the frontier. His first political speech, in 1919, had advocated European unity; already in March 1946 he had expressed the hope for a United States of Europe "in the not too distant future"; and as Chancellor, he was determned to put a definitive end to the potential for Franco-German conflict and underlined the importance of the article in the Federal Republic's Basic Law that provided for the transfer of sovereignty to inter-state institutions in order to secure peace.[59] He evidently saw a federal system as compatible with his aim of restoring Germany to international respectability, with Franco-German partnership a fundamental necessity. So he warmly welcomed the Monnet–Schuman proposal and later moves towards European Union in the 1950s.

The negotiations, chaired by Monnet, which opened in June 1950 and concluded in April 1951 with the ECSC Treaty, brought other federalist influences to bear on shaping the Community's institutions, in particular Walter Hallstein and Carl Friedrich Ophüls. Hallstein, who led the German delegation, was a distinguished law professor who went into these and subsequent negotiations in the 1950s with carefully thought-out proposals based on "German, US and Swiss federalism"; was to become the first President of the Commission of the European Economic Community; and was later to provide a theoretical basis for the stepwise approach to federation.[60] Ophüls led a group of official jurists who were to champion the cause of federalism as a basis for stability and security in Europe's inter-state system.[61]

Without a broader federalist perspective, Monnet's insistence on the federal-type executive would not have fulfilled his aim of replacing power relationships by the rule of law. Judicial and parliamentary institutions were also needed. The Germans brought to the negotiations a proposal for a two-chamber institution, comprising a directly elected parliament and a council of ministers, to control the High Authority.[62] Hirsch, moreover, to whom André Philip suggested that "an element of democratic structure" should be added, had passed the suggestion on to Monnet; and the memorandum which Monnet, as leader of the French delegation, presented at the opening of the negotations proposed that the High Authority be answerable to a parliamentary body.[63] The result was the Community's "Common Assembly," with the power to dismiss the High Authority, whose members were to be directly elected by the citizens when the governments should unanimously agree, which finally led to the first direct elections to the European Parliament in 1979, but meanwhile were appointed by the member states' parliaments. The Council of Ministers, which was both to become the equivalent of a chamber of the states, akin to the German Bundesrat, and to exercise intergovernmental tutelage over the Community's executive (then the High Authority and later the European Commission), was introduced at the behest of the Benelux governments, who hoped it would enable the smaller states to defend their interests.

The memorandum also proposed, somewhat vaguely, "an arbiter":[64] This was transformed during the negotiations into the Court of Justice, responsible for ensuring that in matters of Community competence "the law is observed"; and these words have remained in the Treaties to this day, enabling the Court to make the rule of Community, now Union, law a reality. So Hallstein was able, in an address at Georgetown University in April 1951, to explain the essential constitutional functions of the Court; and he went on to describe the High Authority as a potential federal executive, the Council as corresponding to a Bundesrat and the Common Assembly as an embryonic European Parliament, with the Community as a whole comprising a dynamic first step which "in its constitution-type structures already intentionally anticipates the structure of the future complete federation."[65]

Monnet, in his inaugural address as President of the High Authority in August 1952, more modestly enumerated the federal elements in the Community: the High Authority independent of governments and responsible to a European Assembly; the Assembly, likewise independent of the member states, with power to dismiss the Commission and with the prospect of direct elections; the Court of Justice, independent of the states' courts; and direct relations with legal persons in the states, including the power to tax enterprises.[66] The precise knowledge of federalism came from Spinelli. Monnet, impressed by the clarity of his thinking, had invited him to draft the speech; and Monnet then suggested that he stay to write a series of speeches, on the pattern of *The Federalist*. But Spinelli was determined to pursue his own federalist path, returning to the Community in a political capacity;[67] and this he did when he became a Commissioner in 1970, then a leading member of the European Parliament.

Already in the the spring of that year, Monnet had written a very short note in which he listed the further stages that he evidently envisaged for the process of integration: "single market, single currency, Federation."[68] That was an indication of the path which he, for his part, intended to pursue.

Spinelli, Spaak and the European Political Community, 1952–1954

Five days after the Schuman Plan negotiations began in June 1950, North Korea invaded South Korea. The US, burdened with this new commitment, insisted on a German contribution to western Europe's defense. With German occupation of France so raw in French memories, Monnet feared that French political reactions could derail the Community project. The idea of a European army to preempt German national rearmament was being discussed; Churchill himself had proposed it at the Council of Europe Assembly in August, though later explaining that he meant it for the Continentals "and not for us."[69] Monnet may well have thought that the idea was "at best premature," but he judged that the only way to safeguard the ECSC project would be to propose a European Defence Community on similar lines.[70] So he devised a detailed proposal to present to prime minister René Pleven, who set in train an intergovernmental conference (IGC) to draft an EDC in parallel with that for the ECSC. Monnet's memoirs record that the matter "touched on the core of national sovereignty" and "now, the federation of Europe would have to become an immediate objective."[71] But he did not then realize that institutions such as those envisaged for the ECSC would be an inadequate framework for a European army. Nor did most of those who started the EDC negotiations in February 1951.

Spinelli, however, was quick to identify the contradiction implicit in an army without a state and to grasp the relevance for the federalists' constitutional project. In April the European Union of Federalists organized a conference in Lugano, which approved detailed proposals for a constituent assembly that had been drafted by a committee of jurists chaired by the Belgian Senator Fernand Dehousse.[72] In June General Eisenhower, following a conversation with Monnet, made a speech in London favoring a European federation to deal with the problem.[73] Early in July Spinelli visited Monnet, who agreed that a European constitution was required and considered that the Community's Common Assembly should draft it.[74] Later that month the IGC issued an interim report containing a draft treaty; and Spinelli reacted with a memorandum criticizing its inadequacy and proposing that a constituent assembly design the necessary federal powers and institutions, including a directly elected European parliament with a political executive responsible to it.[75] Spinelli had discussions with Ivan Matteo Lombardo, the head of the Italian delegation to the IGC and a long-standing member of the federalist movement, following which the Italian government sent a memorandum to the other delegations underlining the need to transfer sovereignty to constitutionally defined institutions; and at a meeting of the six foreign ministers in December, De Gasperi, who like Adenauer was both foreign minister and head of government, insisted that the Common Assembly be required to propose the powers and structure of a democratically elected assembly which would replace it and to which the EDC's executive would be responsible. This was accepted and incorporated in Article 38 of the EDC Treaty, signed in May 1952.[76]

Spaak, in his speech on resigning from the presidency of the Council of Europe's Assembly in frustration at British obduracy, had said that although he had "never belonged to the federalists," he had voted "in the same spirit and with the same will" as they did.[77] Spinelli, sensing the prospect of an important ally, visited him in January 1952, and, before the end of February, Spaak had agreed to launch a major campaign for the constitution. This led to an Action Committee for the European Constituent, chaired by Spaak and with membership including Spinelli, Frenay, and Philip, as well as a Study Committee for the European Constitution, also chaired by Spaak, with Dehousse as secretary general and with Spinelli, de Félice and Frenay and seven others, mostly federalists and distinguished lawyers, as members, together with two eminent Harvard academics, Professors Robert R. Bowie and Carl J. Friedrich, as advisers.[78] Spinelli found Spaak to be "a pure political animal," with imagination and courage, but "with a fantastic ignorance of all federal problems," though with a nose for the path to follow so long as there was a good chance of immediate results; and Monnet, he found, was in agreement that Spaak was "on our side, but won't press the battle to the conclusion."[79] Meanwhile, however, Spaak was indeed with the federalists, and contributed his outstanding gifts as chairman and orator to their cause.

The Study Committee worked intensively, on the basis of Spinelli's drafts of resolutions aiming at a federal constitution; and Friedrich had particular praise for Spaak, Spinelli, and Dehousse for the results, which were presented to the Assembly responsible for drafting the European Political Community Treaty, at its first session in September 1952.[80] On Monnet's initiative, France had proposed that the treaty be drafted by the ECSC Assembly (whose membership was slightly enlarged into an "Ad Hoc Assembly" for the purpose).[81] Spaak was elected its president, Dehousse was appointed rapporteur of the committee on institutions, and Ludovico Benvenuti, an active Italian federalist, rapporteur of the committee on powers and competences.

Though federalists had key positions in the Assembly and Spinelli was active behind the scenes, the draft treaty that emerged in March 1953 was only partly federal, with, for example, unanimous approval by a Council of Ministers required for various important decisions.[82] Spinelli nevertheless thought it contained enough federal structures to permit a struggle against the nation states to be victorious – "within fifty years."[83] Spaak struck a more optimistic note, presenting it to the foreign ministers with George Washington's opening words when presenting the US Constitution to the then US Congress in 1787. But it had become apparent in the meetings of ministers, who had shadowed the Assembly's proceedings, that France intended to block anything beyond a minimalist outcome.[84]

This was confirmed in the IGC on the Draft Treaty, where the main point at issue was Johan Beyen's proposal that the EPC should be concerned, alongside the EDC and the ECSC, with the creation of a general common market. Beyen was a former banker and currently Dutch foreign minister, whose relationship with federalism was similar to Schuman's. He avoided using the word but favored a European executive "answerable not to the national governments but before a supranational parliament":[85] a democratically responsible federal executive wielding a substantial federal power. He wanted to create a common market as a sound basis for Europe's economy and argued, moreover, that political integration concerned mainly with military affairs would be inadequate. So he had secured inclusion of the common market in the terms of reference for the Assembly, which had accordingly included it in the Draft Treaty.[86]

Provision for the common market was supported by all participants in the IGC save France, which was resolutely opposed and continued to maintain a generally minimalist stance.[87] So the IGC remained deadlocked until, following elections which had given Gaullists, antagonistic to the Community, a powerful position in both parliament and government, the EDC Treaty fell in August 1954 and the EPC fell with it. What looked like a disaster for federalism was, however, turned round by the success of the Treaties of Rome.

Monnet, Spaak, Beyen, Hallstein, and the Treaties of Rome, 1954–1958

Early in September 1954, Spaak visited Monnet to discuss what should be done to relaunch the integration process after the collapse of the EDC. They agreed that it should be something "in the economic field" and that Monnet would prepare proposals and Spaak take the diplomatic initiative. Thus Spaak, having done what he could for Spinelli's constitutional project, turned to Monnet's more incremental approach. Monnet's ideas were to extend the ECSC to include transport and energy as a whole, and to create a new Community for civil nuclear power; and an elected European parliament figured in the earlier drafts. He also decided to resign from the High Authority so as to be free to press for the necessary further delegations of sovereignty; and to enhance his effectiveness in this, he established the Action Committee for the United States of Europe, whose members were the member states' parties and trade unions, represented by their leaders, and which acted as a very high-level pressure group for Monnet's proposals.[88]

In April 1955 Spaak, by then Belgian foreign minister, wrote to the other foreign ministers about Monnet's proposals for further sectoral integration, but the response was not encouraging. On the same day, however, Beyen wrote to Spaak renewing his advocacy of a common market and stressing the need for supranationality to enable it to work properly and to ensure a strong enough framework to contain Germany effectively.[89] Monnet, in view of the prevalent French aversion to the idea, was resistant. But Germany was likewise averse to the atomic energy proposal and favored the common market for its institutional potential, with Hallstein in particular continuing to insist that a federal constitution was the ultimate aim.[90] Monnet was persuaded that Germany would not accept EURATOM without the common market, so that a viable project had to comprise both together; but he continued to emphasize EURATOM, as the only way to kindle French interest in the relaunching of integration.[91] So it was a "Benelux memorandum," drafted by Beyen and Spaak, which proposed the combined project that was the basis for the "Messina conference" in June.

The prospects for French engagement had improved since elections in January 1955 had almost annihilated the Gaullist parliamentary presence, and Guy Mollet, who was for a while at least to treat Monnet as his "mentor" for European policy, had become prime minister.[92] But with France favoring EURATOM and opposing the common market that was central for the other five, a positive outcome to the conference was far from assured. The German delegation was led by Hallstein. But it was Spaak who had been developing close relations with Antoine Pinay, the French foreign minister, and who finally persuaded him to accept further "exploratory talks" on the combined project. Pinay also agreed to the principle of appointing a "political figure" to lead them – who was crucially, in the event, Spaak himself.[93]

Spaak chaired the resulting "Spaak Committee" with outstanding ability. In April 1956 it produced its report, brilliantly constructed by Uri.[94] Ophüls as head of the German delegation in the Committee and Benvenuti of the Italian delegation ensured federalist backing, to add to that of the Belgians and the Dutch; Félix Gaillard, who headed the French delegation, was a "pragmatic Europeanist." So they approved the "Spaak Report."[95] But while French backing for EURATOM remained firm, there was still scant support for a common market. Robert Marjolin, the top official in the French delegation to the ensuing negotiations, who was to write that he "leant, almost instinctively, towards the idea of European federation," encountered resistance throughout the government machine.[96] But the political climate changed radically in November 1956, when the failure of the Anglo-French Suez expedition against American opposition convinced the French political class that they must accept these steps towards a united Europe. Mollet was able to sign the Treaties of Rome, establishing the European Economic Community and EURATOM, in March 1957. Monnet then turned his Action Committee's pressure from its focus on EURATOM to the two Rome Treaties together;[97] and after some final concessions to France, they were ratified in time to enter into force in January 1958. Hallstein then became the first President of the Commission and did much to consolidate the foundations for the Community's future development.

Conclusion

Four men in particular had outstanding influence on the beginnings of European Union in the 1950s: Monnet, Hallstein, Spaak, and Spinelli.

Monnet, as the instigator of the treaties establishing the European Communities, was later to call the ECSC, as the first of them, the foundation that "made possible all the rest."[98] Despite his incomplete knowledge of federalism, he put in place federal bases on which a Union with many further federal elements has been developed.

Hallstein, with his deep knowledge of federalism, consistently applied the incremental approach towards federation from the Schuman Plan negotiations to his time as the first President of the Commission, then articulated its theory and practice in his scholarly book on the subject.[99] He did much to ensure that federalism would remain a constant element in German policy.

Spaak's federalist period lasted five years, when he played a key part in creating the EPC Treaty, then made his crucial contribution to the establishment of the European Economic Community (EEC) and EURATOM. He at the same time eliminated remaining intergovernmentalist tendencies among the Belgians.[100]

Spinelli transmitted federalist thought to postwar movements, ensured that federalism was entrenched in Italy's European policy and inspired the campaigns for a European constitution. After the EPC Treaty was set aside, he campaigned again for a constituent assembly, but had to wait until the 1980s before he could, as a directly elected Member of the European Parliament, lead the drafting and secure the approval by the citizens' elected representatives of a treaty-constitution for the European Union, which has presaged its further federal development into the European Union of today.[101]

Not least of their achievements has been their enduring influence on their own countries' European policies: in Belgium, Germany, and Italy in the form of a commitment to federal institutions; in France in a tradition of initiatives to endow the Community, now the Union, with federal competences. This has sustained the process that they launched in the 1950s, together with others such as Schuman, Adenauer, and De Gasperi, who, aware of the federal implications, took political responsibility for the first steps, and Beyen, who gave the impulse to the creation of the common market and hence of the EEC; and thus they initiated the development of what has become the European Union with its pronounced federal features. The neglect of the federalism which they, in their various ways, instilled into the process has been a critical weakness of the neo-functionalist and neo-realist theories that have attempted to explain it as well as of citizens' understanding of the Union that has emerged; and it has inhibited the British in particular from playing the constructive part in the Union's development which their earlier contribution to federalist thinking might have led one to expect.

Notes

1   Agnelli and Cabiati, *Federazione Europea*; Pinder, "Federalism in Britain and Italy," 201–203.
2   Lukaszewski, "Richard Coudenhove-Kalergi," 81–108.
3   Loughlin, "French Personalist and Federalist Movements," 188–200.
4   Pinder, "Federal Union, 1939–1941", 203–205; Robbins, *The Economic Causes of War*, 109.
5   Mayne and Pinder, *Federal Union*, 1–49, citation on 26; Pinder, "Federal Union 1939–1941," 26–155.
6   Monnet, *Memoirs*, 28–29.
7   Churchill, *Second World War*, 180–181; Mayne and Pinder, op. cit., 27–29.
8   Duchêne, *Jean Monnet*, 83–97.
9   Spinelli, *Come ho tentato di diventare saggio*, 307–308; Pinder, *Altiero Spinelli and British Federalists*, 3–4.
10 Spinelli and Rossi, *Il Manifesto di Ventotene*; in English in Pinder, ibid., 73–85.
11 Ibid, 87–119.
12 Lipgens, *Documents*, vol. 1, 514–519.
13 Lipgens, *Documents*, vol. 1, 661–683.
14 Lipgens, *Documents*, vol. 1, 381–395, 402, 405–409, 442–444.
15 Lipgens, *Documents*, vol. 1, 413–415.
16 Lipgens, *Documents*, vol. 1, 559, 593–601, 686–689.
17 Lipgens, *Documents*, vol. 1, 284–285.
18 Lipgens, *Documents*, vol. 1, 347–350.
19 Lipgens, *A History of European Integration*, 125–130.
20 Lipgens, *Documents*, vol. 4, 585.
21 Lipgens, *Documents*, vol. 3, 37.
22 Lipgens, *Documents*, vol. 3, 145–148.
23 Lipgens, *A History of European Integration*, 303–316.
24 Lipgens, *Documents*, vol. 4, 23–41, citation on 35.
25 Lipgens, *Documents*, vol. 3, 172–175.
26 Lipgens, *Documents*, vol. 3, 662–666.
27 Lipgens, *Documents*, vol. 4, 319–324, 332–353; Mayne and Pinder, op. cit., 99–100.
28 Lipgens, *Documents*, vol. 3, 703–706; Mayne and Pinder, op. cit., 100, 120.
29 Lipgens, *Documents*, vol. 3, 9.
30 Charlton, *Price of Victory*, 77.
31 Mayne and Pinder, op. cit., 103.
32 Lipgens, *Documents*, vol. 3, 235; Pistone "Italian Parties and Pressure Groups," 135–141.
33 Lipgens, *Documents*, vol. 3, 236.
34 Lipgens, *Documents*, vol. 4, 80–91.
35 Gouzy, *Les Pionniers*, 65–66.
36 Lipgens, *Documents*, vol. 3, 441–457, 555–556.

37 Gouzy, op. cit., 65–66; Spinelli, *Diario*, 64.

38 Spinelli, *Appunti*, 80.

39 Lipgens, *Documents*, vol. 3, 119–123.

40 Levi and Pistone, *Trent'anni*, 130–132.

41 See Pinder, "Mario Albertini," 157.

42 Lipgens, *Documents*, vol. 4, 323, 424–425.

43 Spaak, *Continuing Battle*, 224–225.

44 Monnet, *Memoirs*, 34.

45 Joxe, "Contribution," 252–253; Monnet, *Memoirs*, 222.

46 Duchêne, op. cit., 367.

47 Hirsch later became President of the Mouvement Fédéraliste Européen (see *Ainsi va la vie*, 268–269), where the discourse was of the constitutional approach to federalism.

48 Spinelli, *Diario*, 142–143.

49 Spaak, op. cit., 213.

50 Monnet, *Memoirs*, 282; Dieter Dettke, in Jansen and Mahncke, *Persönlichkeiten*, 242.

51 Milward, *Reconstruction of Western Europe*, 396.

52 Duchêne, op. cit., 400–401.

53 See n.47 above, and Mayne and Pinder, op. cit., 187; Monnet, *Memoirs*, 295; Duchêne, op. cit., 367.

54 Monnet, *Memoirs*, 297–298.

55 Monnet, *Memoirs*, 296.

56 Monnet, *Memoirs*, 298.

57 Duchêne, op. cit., 235.

58 Brugmans, *Prophètes et fondateurs*, 342–343.

59 Werner Weidenfeld, in Jansen and Mahncke, op. cit., 301, 302, 313, 315.

60 Frank Bärenbrinker, in Loth et al., *Walter Hallstein*, 114; Hallstein, *Europe in the Making*.

61 Hanns Küsters, in Loth et al., op. cit., 85.

62 "Einleitung," in Loth et al., op. cit., 18.

63 Hirsch, op. cit., 107; Monnet, *Memoirs*, 321.

64 Monnet, *Memoirs*, 321.

65 Lipgens, *45 Jahre*, 304–306.

66 Monnet, *Etats-Unis d'Europe*, 55–60.

67 Spinelli, *Diario*, 140–145.

68 Rieben et al., *A l'Ecoute de Jean Monnet*, 97–98.

69 Mayne and Pinder, op. cit., 106; Charlton, op. cit., 137.

70 Duchêne, op. cit., 229.

71 Monnet, *Memoirs*, 342–348, citation from 343.

72 Lipgens, *45 Jahre*, 299–303.

73 Monnet, *Memoirs*, 358–360.

74 Spinelli, *Diario*, 84.

75 Majocchi and Rossolillo, *Parlamento europeo*, 47–49, 193–216.

76 Griffiths, *Europe's First Constitution*, 65–66; Majocchi and Rossolillo, *Parlamento europeo*, 179, 181–183, 188–199; Spinelli, *Diario*, 100.

77 Schöndube and Ruppert, *Eine Idee*, 167.

78 Spinelli, *Diario*, 125–133; Friedrich, "Introduction," xxv–xlii.

79 Spinelli, *Diario*, 135, 140.

80 Friedrich, "Introduction," xxvii, xxix; Spinelli, *Diario*, 146, 149, 161.

81 Duchêne, op. cit., 234; Spinelli, *Diario*, 137–138.

82 Friedrich, "Introduction," xxxii-xxxiii; Griffiths, op. cit., 71–94, 189–226.

83   Spinelli, *Diario*, 171.
84   Griffiths, op. cit., 92–93, 96.
85   Duchêne, op. cit., 273.
86   Griffiths, op. cit., 69, 100, 214.
87   Ibid., 118–148.
88   Duchêne, op. cit., 263ff.
89   Duchêne, op. cit., 271–274.
90   Duchêne, op. cit., 275–276; Küsters, in Jansen and Mahncke, op. cit., 85–86.
91   Duchêne, op. cit., 292.
92   Duchêne, op. cit., 275–276, 287.
93   Duchêne, op. cit., 281–282.
94   Spaak, op. cit., 231.
95   Lipgens, *Documents*, vol. 3, 98.
96   Marjolin, *Travail d'une vie*, 274–303, citation from 312.
97   Duchêne, op. cit., 306.
98   Monnet, *Memoirs*, 383.
99   Hallstein, *Europe in the Making*.
100   Duchêne, op. cit., 285.
101   See Pinder, "Altiero Spinelli's Federal Odyssey," 581–587.

Bibliography

Agnelli, Giovanni and Attilio Cabiati, *Federazione Europea o Liga delle Nazioni?* (Turin: Fratelli Bocca, Editori, 1918).

Brugmans, Henri, *Prophètes et fondateurs de l'Europe* (Bruges: College of Europe, 1974).

Charlton, Michael, *The Price of Victory* (London: BBC, 1983).

Churchill, Winston Spencer, *The Second World War*, vol. 2 (London: Cassell, 1948).

Coudenhove-Kalergi, Count Richard, *Paneuropa* (Vienna, 1923), published in English as *Paneurope* (New York, 1926).

Duchêne, François, *Jean Monnet: The First Statesman of Interdependence* (New York and London: W.W. Norton, 1994).

Friedrich, Carl J., "Introduction," in Robert R. Bowie and Carl J. Friedrich (eds.), *Studies in Federalism* (Boston and Toronto: Little, Brown, 1954).

Friedrich, Carl J., "Federal Constitutional Theory and Emergent Proposals," in A.W. Macmahon (ed.), *Federalism: Mature and Emergent* (New York: Doubleday, 1955).

Gouzy, Jean-Pierre, *Les Pionniers de l'Europe communautaire* (Lausanne: Centre de Recherches Européennes, 1968).

Griffiths, Richard, *Europe's First Constitution: The European Political Community, 1952–1954* (London: Federal Trust, 2000).

Hallstein, Walter, *Der unvollendete Bundesstaat, Europäische Erfahrungen und Erkenntnisse* (Düsseldorf: Econ Verlag, 1969), published in English as *Europe in the Making* (London: Allen and Unwin, 1972).

Hirsch, Etienne, *Ainsi va la vie* (Lausanne: Fondation Jean Monnet pour l'Europe, 1988).

Jansen, Thomas and Dieter Mahncke (eds.), *Persönlichkeiten der Europäischen Integration: Vierzehn biographische Essays* (Bonn: Europa Union Verlag, 1981).

Joxe, Louis, "Contribution," in Henri Rieben, *Des Guerres européennes à l'Union de l'Europe* (Lausanne: Fondation Jean Monnet pour l'Europe, 1987).

Levi, L. and S. Pistone (eds.), *Trent'anni di vita del Movimento Federalista Europeo* (Milan: Franco Angeli Editore, 1973).

Lipgens, Walter, *A History of European Integration 1945–1947: The Formation of the European Unity Movement* (Oxford: Clarendon Press, 1982).

Lipgens, Walter (ed.), *Documents on the History of European Integration*, vol. 1: *Continental Plans for European Union 1939–1945* (Berlin and New York: Walter de Gruyter, 1985).

Lipgens, Walter (ed.), *Documents on the History of European Integration*, vol. 2: *Plans for European Union in Great Britain and in Exile 1939–1945* (Berlin and New York: Walter de Gruyter, 1986).

Lipgens, Walter, *45 Jahre Ringen um die Europäische Verfassung: Dokumente 1939–1984: Von den Schriften der Widerstandsbewegung bis zum Vertragsentwurf des Europäischen Parlaments* (Bonn: Europa Union Verlag, 1986).

Lipgens, Walter and Wilfried Loth (eds.), *Documents on the History of European Integration*, vol. 3: *The Struggle for European Union by Political Parties and Pressure Groups in Western European Countries 1945–1950* (Berlin and New York: Walter de Gruyter, 1988).

Lipgens, Walter and Wilfried Loth (eds.), *Documents on the History of European Integration*, vol. 4: *Transnational Organizations of Political Parties and Pressure Groups in the Struggle for European Union, 1945–1950* (Berlin and New York: Walter de Gruyter, 1991).

Loth, Wilfried, William Wallace, and Wolfgang Wessels (eds.), *Walter Hallstein: Der vergessene Europäer?* (Bonn: Europa Union Verlag, 1995).

Lothian, Philip Kerr, 11th Marquess of, *Pacifism Is Not Enough – Nor Patriotism Either* (Oxford: Clarendon Press, 1935).

Loughlin, John, "French Personalist and Federalist Movements in the Interwar Period," in Peter M.R. Stirk (ed.), *European Unity in Context: The Interwar Period* (London and New York: Pinter, 1989).

Lukaszewski, Jerzy, "Richard Coudenhove-Kalergi," in Lukaszewski, *Jalons de l'Europe* (Lausanne: Fondation Jean Monnet pour l'Europe, 1985).

Majocchi, Luigi Vittorio and Francesco Rossolillo, *Il Parlamento europeo* (Naples: Guida editori, 1979).

Marjolin, Robert, *Travail d'une vie: Mémoires 1911–1986* (Paris: Robert Laffont, 1986).

Mayne, Richard, *The Recovery of Europe: From Devastation to Unity* (London: Weidenfeld and Nicolson, 1970).

Mayne, Richard and John Pinder, with John Roberts, *Federal Union: The Pioneers – A History of Federal Union* (Basingstoke: Macmillan, 1990).

Milward, Alan, *The Reconstruction of Western Europe* (London: Methuen, 1984).

Monnet, Jean, *Les Etats-Unis d'Europe ont commencé: Discours et allocutions 1952–1954* (Paris: Laffont, 1955).

Monnet, Jean, *Memoirs* (London: Collins, 1978).

Pinder, John, "Federal Union 1939–1941," in Walter Lipgens (ed.), *Documents on the History of European Integration*, vol. 2: *Plans for European Union in Great Britain and in Exile 1939–1945* (Berlin and New York: Walter de Gruyter, 1986).

Pinder, John, "Federalism in Britain and Italy: Radicals and the English Liberal Tradition," in Peter M.R. Stirk (ed.), *European Unity in Context: The Interwar Period* (London and New York: Pinter, 1989).

Pinder, John (ed.), *Altiero Spinelli and the British Federalists: Writings by Beveridge, Robbins and Spinelli 1937–1943* (London: Federal Trust, 1998).

Pinder, John, *The Building of the European Union*, 3rd edition (Oxford: Oxford University Press, 1998).

Pinder, John, "Mario Albertini in the History of Federalist Thought," *The Federalist*, Year 44, no. 3, 2002, 157–170.

Pinder, John, "Altiero Spinelli's European Federal Odyssey," *International Spectator* 42, no. 4, December 2007, 571–588.

Pistone, Sergio, "Italian Political Parties and Pressure Groups in the Discourse on European Union," in Walter Lipgens and Wilfried Loth (eds.), *Documents on the History of European Integration*, vol. 3: *The Struggle for European Union by Political Parties and Pressure Groups in Western European Countries 1945–1950* (Berlin and New York: Walter de Gruyter, 1988).

Rieben, Henri, Claire Camperio, and Françoise Nicoud (eds.), *A l'Ecoute de Jean Monnet* (Lausanne: Fondation Jean Monnet pour l'Europe and Centre de recherches européennes, 2004).

Robbins, Lionel, *National Planning and International Order* (London: Macmillan, 1937).

Robbins, Lionel, *The Economic Causes of War* (London: Jonathan Cape, 1939).

Schöndube, Claus and Christel Ruppert, *Eine Idee setzt sich durch: Der Weg zum vereinigten Europa* (Hangelar bei Bonn: Verlag Heinrich Warnecke, 1964).

Schuman, Robert, "Statement Made by M. Robert Schuman on May 9, 1950." Full text at http://europa.eu/abc/symbols/9-may/decl.en.htm.

Spaak, Paul-Henri, *The Continuing Battle: Memoirs of a European* (London: Weidenfeld and Nicolson, 1971).

Spinelli, Altiero, *Come ho tentato di diventare saggio: Io, Ulisse* (Bologna: iI Mulino, 1984).

Spinelli, Altiero, *Appunti per una biographia*, compiled by Edmondo Paolini (Bologna: Il Mulino, 1988).

Spinelli, Altiero, *Diario europeo 1948/1969*, edited by Edmondo Paolini (Bologna: Il Mulino, 1989).

Spinelli, Altiero and Ernesto Rossi, *Il Manifesto di Ventotene* (Milan: Oscar Mondadori, 2006).

Streit, Clarence, Union Now: A Proposal for a Federal Union of the Democracies of the North Atlantic (London and New York: Jonathan Cape and Harper, 1939).

Further Reading

The literature in English has largely neglected this subject, which has to be extracted from a variety of sources. But there is a monumental exception regarding the build-up to the 1950s: Lipgens's four volumes of *Documents on European Integration* during 1940–1950, comprising excerpts of documents with explanatory introductions to each document and section. For "integration" read "federalism" for those volumes as well as for his valuable *History of European Integration, 1945–1947*.

For background up to 1945, there are the first three entries under Pinder in the list of sources above; Loughlin on "French Personalist and Federalist Movements in the Interwar Period"; and Mayne and Pinder on *Federal Union*, continuing through the postwar period. Gouzy's *Les Pionniers de l'Europe commmunautaire* records what European federalist movements did from the 1940s through the 1950s.

Duchêne's *Jean Monnet* is an indispensable account of the central figure in the foundation of the Communities; and Monnet's *Memoirs*, inevitably subjective, though factually reliable, covers similar ground. There is little in English on Hallstein, but his own book was published as *Europe in the Making* and there are several German sources, some of which can be found in the notes above.

The EPC Treaty gave rise to impressive contemporary books by American scholars: Robert R. Bowie and Carl J. Friedrich (eds.), *Studies in Federalism* (Boston: Little, Brown, 1954), and A. W. Macmahon (ed.), *Federalism: Mature and Emergent* (New York: Doubleday, 1955). Griffiths's *Europe's First Constitution* analyzes the background to the EPC Treaty and its reception by governments. Most of the literature on Spinelli's influence from 1943 through the 1950s is in Italian, with his *Diario europeo 1949* being a particularly illuminating, if notably subjective, source. Pinder's article on "Altiero Spinelli's European Federal Odyssey" includes a section on his thought and action in the 1950s.

An illuminating history of the period and of the creation of the Communities is to be found in Mayne's *The Recovery of Europe*. The development of federal elements in the powers and institutions up to the 1990s is included in Pinder, *The Building of the European Union*, and summarized in its chapter ten.

PART II

Europe and The Cold War World

CHAPTER THREE

The Cold War: The Western European Perspective

IAN JACKSON

Until the opening of western European government archives in the 1970s and 1980s, the Cold War was largely viewed by historians as a bipolar conflict between the United States and the Soviet Union. The thousands of declassified documents that scholars have drawn upon in reconstructing the key turning points of the Cold War in the past two decades have cast significant light on the role of western Europe in the shaping of the post-World War II international order. The research of the "new" Cold War history, in particular, has painted a more sophisticated and complex portrait of power politics within the US-led Western alliance. Studies of bilateral and multilateral relationships between the United States and its European allies have demonstrated the moderating influence of the western European governments over Washington's policy in the formative decades of the Cold War. From the available evidence it now appears, for example, that Britain and France not only took the lead in inviting a reluctant United States into the affairs of western Europe, but also sought to manage and orchestrate the American response to Soviet expansionism in the east. With research well underway on the events of the Cold War in the 1950s, the 1960s and the 1970s, scholars have continued to stress the influential role played by western European governments in East–West relations. A number of recent studies have shown that Britain, France, and West Germany advocated détente with the Soviet Union long before such a policy was embraced by Presidents Johnson and Nixon. While historians will not be able to write with full authority about the events leading up to the end of the Cold War in the late 1980s until a substantial number of government documents have been released on both sides of the Atlantic, several recent works based on political memoirs and secondary sources have emphasized the important role of western Europe in encouraging the change in Soviet policy that paved the way to German reunification in 1990.

The intention of this chapter is to provide not only a relatively brief overview of the Cold War from the western European standpoint, but also to offer a synthesis of the most recent historical research on the early decades of the East–West conflict. First, the chapter reviews the origins of the Cold War with special focus

A Companion to Europe since 1945, First Edition. Edited by Klaus Larres.
© 2014 John Wiley & Sons, Ltd. Published 2014 by John Wiley & Sons, Ltd.

on the influence of Britain and France in the forging of the Western alliance. It also highlights the tension that existed between the West and the Soviet Union over Germany, which culminated in the establishment of two separate states in 1949. Second, the western European challenge to American leadership of the Atlantic alliance is the subject of the proceeding section of this chapter. During the 1960s the western Europeans began to question Washington's Cold War policies. The French president, Charles de Gaulle, was an especially vocal critic of the United States' management of the Western alliance, its decision to intervene in Vietnam, and the privileged status of the dollar in the international monetary order. The chapter concludes with a retrospective assessment of the Cold War after 1969. The western European desire for détente with the Soviet Union and eastern Europe in the 1970s and the underlying friction with Washington over alliance policy will be analyzed. Finally, the response of the western Europeans to the renewal of tensions between the United States and the Soviet Union in the early 1980s and the subsequent demise of the Cold War system at the end of the decade are explored.

The Origins of the Cold War, 1945–1955

Despite forging a victorious alliance against Nazi Germany, the "Big Three" powers of the United States, the Soviet Union and Britain had contrasting visions about the structure of the post-World War II peace settlement. In the spirit of the Atlantic Charter they had signed in August 1941, the American president, Franklin D. Roosevelt, and the British prime minister, Winston Churchill, sought to build a new world order based on the principles of democracy, collective security, and commercial liberalism. Roosevelt, however, did not attempt to impose this new world order on the Soviet Union. Recognizing that Josef Stalin would be anxious to consolidate Soviet power in eastern Europe, the president proposed the creation of a collective security framework. Roosevelt's "Four Policemen" concept envisaged a world of four main spheres of influence controlled by the United States, Britain, the Soviet Union, and China. This great power condominium was enshrined in the United Nations (UN) Charter, which was agreed by the three powers and France in San Francisco in June 1945. Like Woodrow Wilson, Roosevelt believed that world peace could only be achieved through the establishment of a permanent international security organization. Unlike Wilson's League of Nations, however, Roosevelt's UN would be managed by the United States and the other great powers.[1] While Stalin participated in the formation of the UN and accepted a seat on the organization's Security Council, he was extremely suspicious of Western motivations with regard to the postwar international order. Recent research has demonstrated that the Soviet dictator did not have any grandiose plans for a global communist revolution, but he was determined to prevent the capitalist encirclement of the USSR and preserve Moscow's domination over eastern Europe.[2]

Although the "Big Three" differed over their perceptions of world order, Roosevelt, Churchill, and Stalin were prepared to cooperate on the question of Germany. The three leaders were unanimous in the conviction that the history of the interwar period should not repeat itself and that Germany must never again be in a position to compete for the hegemony of Europe. As the war was ending, they gathered for a summit in Yalta to discuss the future of Germany, the borders of Poland and spheres of influence in Europe. On the German problem, the three statesmen agreed that the country should be divided into four zones, occupied and administered by the United States, Britain, the Soviet Union, and France repectively. Roosevelt and Churchill acquiesced in Stalin's plan to preserve the Polish borders and create a network of governments "friendly" to the Soviet Union in eastern Europe.[3] Five months later a second conference was convened at Potsdam. Once again, the three countries failed to reach consensus on a satisfactory peace treaty for Germany. It was agreed that the four military zones would not presage the eventual division of Germany and the country was to be treated as a single economic unit. The conference was adjourned in August 1945 with only vague understandings about the issues of German reparations and a peace treaty.[4]

The Potsdam accords on Germany were subsequently disavowed by the Western powers and the Soviet Union in 1946–1947. In the East, Stalin increased his stranglehold over eastern Europe through military intervention and a series of coups leading to the incorporation of Poland, Romania, and Bulgaria into the Soviet sphere in 1946. Hungary and Czechoslovakia became satellites of Moscow in 1947 and 1948 respectively and Stalin looked to extend his empire into the Near East.[5] The new American president, Harry S. Truman, initially persisted with Roosevelt's policy of cooperation and accommodation with the Soviet Union, but grew increasingly wary of Stalin's brutal and ruthless expansionism in eastern Europe. In March 1946 an American attaché in the Moscow embassy, George F. Kennan, forwarded his influential "Long Telegram" to Washington outlining the dangers of unchecked Soviet expansionism. Now out of government, Winston Churchill traveled to Fulton in Missouri to deliver a grave warning to the American public about the prospect of an "iron curtain" descending across the continent of Europe. While taking cognizance of Kennan's and Churchill's geopolitical views, the Truman administration proceeded cautiously. Initially, neither Truman nor his secretary of state, James F. Byrnes, wanted Washington to become involved in the power politics of Europe. The UK foreign secretary, Ernest Bevin, however, pressed Byrnes to merge the British and American zones in the summer of 1946 thus paving the way for the establishment of a provisional government in West Germany.[6] Britain's financial weakness and her withdrawal from the Near East in February 1947 precipitated Truman's famous doctrine pledging assistance to peoples seeking to preserve their liberty from the tyranny of communism. Truman did not offer military support to Greece and Turkey, but $400 million in financial assistance was provided by the US government to protect the region from Soviet expansionism.[7]

In January 1947 George C. Marshall replaced Byrnes as secretary of state. On assuming office, the veteran American general was concerned about two interlinked European problems: the future of Germany and western European economic weakness and vulnerability. During the early months of 1947 Marshall was still hopeful that an agreement could be reached with the Soviet Union over the future of Germany based on the Potsdam accords. Yet, his 46 sessions with the Soviet foreign minister, Molotov, in Moscow during March and April proved unproductive. Marshall's solution to the second problem was to propose an ambitious plan of financial assistance to rebuild the continent, with the German industrial heartland in the center of a rejuvenated European economic system.[8] While Stalin was invited to participate in the Marshall Plan, in the words of David Reynolds, Moscow was "adroitly excluded" by Bevin and the French foreign minister, Georges Bidault, from playing any meaningful role in the discussions concerning the American initiative.[9] As a result, Stalin ensured that Moscow's satellites, most significantly the eastern German zone, would not be involved in the scheme. When the Marshall Plan was finally approved by Congress in April 1948, approximately $13 billion was provided to the countries of western Europe. What was more, the Marshall Plan was instrumental in completing the economic division of Germany and, thus, Europe.

In strategic terms, the Marshall Plan had dual objectives. First, the Truman administration hoped that financial assistance would help to bolster the western European nations, fill the power vacuum that had developed in central Europe and create a "third force" to check potential Soviet aggression in Eurasia. In encouraging the western European governments to pool their resources and collaborate under the multilateral auspices of the Organization for European Economic Cooperation (OEEC), Washington signalled its intention not to build a sphere of influence in the region. During 1947–1948, American officials were wedded to the concept of the European "third force" and appeared to be extremely reluctant to send troops to western Europe, despite their circumspection with regard to Stalin's geopolitical objectives in Eurasia.[10] Second, the Marshall Plan aimed to dissuade public opinion in western European nations from the election of communist political parties to high office. In fact, only countries with democratic governments committed to capitalist domestic economic systems were eligible for financial assistance from Washington under the European Recovery Program (ERP). From a political standpoint, therefore, Marshall Aid was designed to weaken the influence of European communist parties sympathetic to Moscow and deter the type of Soviet-inspired military and political coups that were occurring in eastern Europe.[11]

As well as dividing the continent economically, Stalin's decision not to participate in the ERP exacerbated East–West tensions over Germany. Virtually no progress was made at the foreign ministers' meeting in London between Molotov and his Western counterparts in December 1947. No longer hamstrung in a coalition government with the French Communist Party, Bidault dramatically shifted the orientation of Paris's foreign policy towards the acceptance of a West German state. The French zone was subsumed into the British and American zones to form a distinct economic unit in western Germany.[12] The London program, which was finalized in the spring of 1948, endorsed the creation of a non-sovereign West German state under allied occupation, with the prospect of democratic elections for the establishment of a provisional government.[13] Stalin reacted to these developments by closing off supply routes to West Berlin (like Germany, the city of Berlin had been divided between the wartime allies in 1945) in an attempt to pull the whole city into the Soviet orbit. Although the blockade of Berlin was to last for 11 months, a war was not triggered between the Soviet Union and the West. Truman and Attlee responded to the crisis by supplying West Berlin through airlifts. The blockade, nonetheless, ushered in a period of confrontation between East and West that not only divided Europe indefinitely, but also heightened the risk of war between Moscow and its former wartime allies.

The military coup in Czechoslovakia in February 1948, encouraged by Stalin, was viewed with trepidation by the Attlee government. Bevin, with French support, was instrumental in forming the western European Union (WEU) on March 17. Under the Brussels Pact, Britain, France, Belgium, the Netherlands, and Luxembourg forged a military alliance with a view to defending western Europe from Soviet aggression. Bevin, however, had grander plans for the alliance. He believed that if Britain could demonstrate its commitment to the common defense of western Europe, the United States could be coaxed into guaranteeing the security of the continent against the threat of a Soviet military invasion. Historians of the origins of the Cold War have now widely accepted that it was the astute diplomacy of the British foreign secretary that opened the door to the signature of the North Atlantic Treaty (NAT) in Washington in April 1949.[14]

By establishing and joining the North Atlantic Treaty Organization (NATO), the Truman administration abandoned the concept of the "third force" in western Europe and accepted the role of military guardian of western Europe.[15] By breaking its time-honored tradition of avoiding entanglements outside the Western Hemisphere, Washington sent a strong message to Moscow that its national security interests were now inextricably bound with the fate of the European balance of power. Following the creation of the Federal Republic of Germany (FRG) by the Western allies in September 1949, Stalin transformed the Soviet-controlled eastern zone into the German Democratic Republic (GDR). The formal division of Germany in 1949, then, was symbolic in that it split Europe into two spheres: an American-led bloc in the West and a Soviet-led bloc in the east.

Despite having managed to secure a written guarantee from Washington in the form of NATO, the western Europeans still feared that Stalin would be able to take advantage of the vulnerability of the continent and launch an invasion against the region. While a military alliance organization, NATO did not yet have a finalized command structure and the United States was only beginning to station troops in western Europe. Ironically, developments in Southeast Asia were to provide the catalyst that transformed NATO from being a tacit American commitment to the defense of western Europe into a fully-fledged international security organization. When the communist-controlled North Korea invaded its pro-Western southern counterpart in June 1950, alarm bells sounded not only in Washington, but also in western Europe.[16] For one, Konrad Adenauer, the West German chancellor, worried that the United States would abandon its commitment to western Europe in order to contain communism in the Far East and thus leave the continent unguarded against Soviet expansionism.[17]

In an effort to assuage western European fears, Dean Acheson, the US secretary of state, met with Ernest Bevin and Robert Schuman, the French foreign minister, in September 1950. During the talks held in New York City, Acheson pledged to send further troop divisions to western Europe and nominated the distinguished World War II general, Dwight D. Eisenhower, as the supreme commander of the combined armed forces of NATO. While this went a long way to appease Bevin and Schumann, secretary of state Acheson insisted on a quid pro quo. In return for American troops, he insisted that West Germany be rearmed.[18]

This demand sent shock waves across both London and Paris. But French strategic thinking had changed markedly since the mid-1940s. The government of René Pleven was alarmed by the prospect of a fully armed West German state from the standpoint of French security, but accepted the realities of the situation: if France opposed German rearmament, the United States might rethink its pledge to the defense of western Europe. As the scholarship of Georges-Henri Soutou, Marc Trachtenberg, and William I. Hitchcock has recently shown through extensive research in French government archives, Paris was prepared to overcome its innate suspicions of German *revanchism* and sanction the militarization of the FRG within a supranational framework.

The resulting Pleven Plan, in essence, was similar to the economic rapprochement with West Germany sought by Schumann in his initiative to establish a supranational coal and steel community: German troops would be incorporated into a European army. The centerpiece of Pleven's plan was the concept of the European Defence Community (EDC), which was approved by the participating governments of the European Coal and Steel Community (ECSC) in a treaty signed on May 1952. Yet, French public opinion increasingly turned against the idea of ceding sovereignty to a supranational defense community. On August 30, 1954 the National Assembly decided to postpone the decision on the EDC indefinitely and thus in fact voted against the EDC initiative.[19]

Just 20 months in office, the Eisenhower administration, which had supported the EDC initiative, was deeply angered by the decision of the French parliament to block France's participation in the community and, in effect, scupper any chance of rearming West Germany within a European supranational community. John Foster Dulles, the US secretary of state, warned the European allies that failure to settle the contentious issue of German rearmament satisfactorily would lead to an American reappraisal of its military commitment to western Europe. Kevin Ruane has convincingly argued that Dulles was probably calling the bluff of the western Europeans.

Nonetheless, the Churchill government, which had refused to participate in the EDC proposal, was forced to salvage the situation. Actually, it was the diplomatic skill of both Anthony Eden, the British foreign secretary, and Adenauer that won the day. Eden proposed that West Germany sign the Brussels Pact (under whose new terms supervised West German rearmament was to take place), and then also become a member of NATO under the American military umbrella. Not only did this satisfy the demands of the Americans, but, moreover, French fears of a powerful West Germany and uncontrolled German rearmament were allayed by London's commitment to the security of Europe. Moreover, Britain was assured that Washington would honor its military pact to defend the region from Soviet aggression.[20] It was not until May 1955, however, that the FRG finally became a member of NATO and at the same time also obtained its full sovereignty (except with regard to matters concerning German reunification) as a state within the community of nations. Obtaining sovereignty was the price Adenauer had insisted upon in order to give his agreement to West German rearmament and inclusion into the Western alliance.

Perhaps the most significant event in the history of the Cold War during the first decade of the conflict was the death of Stalin in March 1953. In his final year, the Soviet dictator hinted at reviving diplomatic efforts to solve the German problem.

In March and April 1952, despite the fact that independent states had been formed in East and West Germany, Moscow proposed reunification of the country. In an attempt to make the prospect enticing to the Western allies, Stalin appeared to be amenable to the creation of a unified Germany, fully rearmed and administered by a freely elected government. The Western governments spurned Stalin's overtures, preferring to maintain the status quo and the pivotal role that the FRG was now playing in the tentative steps towards the economic and political integration of western Europe. In his last act of diplomacy prior to retirement, Winston Churchill launched a campaign to bring about a détente with the Soviet Union. This was primarily aimed at restoring Britain's status as an influential power in the international system, but Churchill failed to convince President Eisenhower of the need to effect a peaceful settlement of the Cold War through summitry with the Soviets.[21] Following a change in Soviet policy towards "peaceful coexistence" with the West after Stalin's death, the USSR, the United States, Britain, and France met in Geneva for talks about the German question in the summer of 1955. The "spirit" of Yalta did not prevail on this occasion. Despite empty rhetoric on both sides about German unity and liberty, the Cold War division of Europe that was finally completed with Moscow's decision to sign the Warsaw Pact with its eastern European satellites in response to West German membership of NATO became a reality.

The Troubled Partnership: Europe between the Superpowers, 1955–1969

By 1955 the battle lines in Europe had been drawn. As the Cold War entered its second decade, the newly constituted balance of power between the US-led Western alliance and Soviet-dominated Warsaw Pact defined a period of tension short of war. The threat of nuclear war prevented an outbreak of conflict between the Eastern and Western blocs, but both sides were determined to demonstrate their resolve, especially with regard to the German question. During 1955–1957 in a drive to pool resources, increase productivity, and pave the way for political integration, the continental European states, including West Germany, formed the European Economic Community (EEC).

Meanwhile, having decided to opt out of the EEC negotiations, Britain witnessed the further decline of its global influence when the Eisenhower administration refused to support its ill-timed invasion of Egypt in 1956. The Suez Crisis damaged Anglo-American relations and led British policy-makers to question the firmness of Washington's commitment to the "special relationship." In Moscow Nikita Khrushchev finally consolidated his control over the Kremlin in October 1957. Although he had denounced Stalin's policies, Khrushchev had ordered Soviet troops into Hungary to crush a rising in Budapest in November 1956. The launching of the Sputnik space satellite and the acquisition of the Intercontinental Ballistic Missile (ICBM) system, moreover, imbued the Soviet leadership with renewed confidence to challenge the United States in potential "hot spots" in Europe and other regions in the international system.

In late November 1958 Khrushchev presented the Western occupying powers with an ultimatum over Berlin: if the United States, Britain, and France did not withdraw from the divided city within six months, Moscow would sign a separate peace treaty with the GDR. Khrushchev's ultimatum produced friction among the allies over the best possible response to the Kremlin's threat to West Berlin.[22] Both the United States and Britain reacted cautiously to the Soviet initiative. The British prime minister, Harold Macmillan, favored negotiations with Moscow and was determined to avoid war with the Soviets over Berlin at all costs. Eager to continue Churchill's campaign for détente between East and West, Macmillan flew to Moscow for talks with Khrushchev in February 1959. By contrast, France and West Germany, to differing degrees, chafed at any thought of conciliation with the Soviet Union on the issue of Berlin. The French president, Charles de Gaulle, felt that Khrushchev was attempting to call the Western allies' bluff over Berlin and did not believe that Moscow was prepared to go to war over the status of the city. He nevertheless sought to preserve the status quo and offered his full support to Adenauer in the defense of West Berlin.

The West German chancellor was most disturbed by Macmillan's attitude to the crisis, which he viewed as a form of appeasement of the Soviet Union. As events transpired, Khrushchev did not force the issue over Berlin, and Eisenhower and Macmillan tried in vain to resolve the problem of Western occupation rights in the city at a summit held in Paris in June 1960.[23] It was not until the building of the Berlin Wall on August 11, 1961 that the Berlin question was resolved between the Soviet Union and the Western allies. Khrushchev's decision to erect a barrier to prevent refugees from flowing into the FRG from the GDR cemented the division of the city and preserved the status quo in Berlin so readily desired by the Western powers in 1958.

The confrontation between the United States and the Soviet Union was in evidence not only in Europe, but also in other parts of the world.[24] Most significantly, the clash between Khrushchev and President John F. Kennedy over Berlin in June 1961 resulted in a confrontation between Moscow and Washington over Cuba in October 1962. Sensing that Kennedy was inexperienced and weak, the Soviet leader had placed nuclear weapons in Cuba, some 90 miles from the American seaboard. Khrushchev, however, miscalculated. Kennedy, it seemed, was prepared to risk nuclear war with the Soviet Union over Cuba. Forced to withdraw the missiles from Cuba, the Soviet leader's reputation in the Kremlin was damaged irrevocably. Kennedy was hailed as winning an important victory in the Cold War against the Soviet Union. Clearly, the clash between the superpowers over Cuba highlighted the futility of conflict in an age of thermonuclear power. The aftermath of the Cuban Missile Crisis culminated in a general relaxation of tensions between Washington and Moscow, as talks concerning arms control yielded the Comprehensive Test Ban Treaty in August 1963.[25] The Western allies had unanimously pledged their solidarity with Kennedy on the Cuban crisis, but began to seriously doubt the future of Washington's security commitment to Europe. De Gaulle, in particular, reasoned that the Cuban Missile Crisis demonstrated that the United States would take action at any price to protect its national interests. The French president was skeptical that those national interests included the future security of western Europe.[26]

One of the most striking developments of the 1960s was de Gaulle's challenge to the American leadership of the Western alliance.[27] Even before the general assumed power in 1958, France was undoubtedly the most independent of

Washington's European allies. Paris was the leading voice in the EEC and viewed European integration as a means of limiting American influence on the continent. The rapid economic expansion and the political stability that the new Fifth Republic had produced enabled de Gaulle to project a more ambitious French diplomacy. By 1960 Paris had acquired the capacity to develop a nuclear weapons program, and with the decision to withdraw from the Algerian conflict in 1962 the French president began to implement his vision of an autonomous western Europe between the superpowers.[28]

What policies did de Gaulle implement in pursuit of his grand design for Europe? In November 1958 the general approached Eisenhower and Macmillan with a view to creating a tripartite directorate to centralize policy-making within NATO. Only by sharing power with the United States and the United Kingdom in the organization, according to de Gaulle, could France and continental Europe have an influential voice in the Western alliance. Having been rebuffed by Eisenhower and Macmillan over his idea for a tripartite directorate in NATO, the French president increasingly began to disengage from the organization during the 1960s. Unimpressed by Eisenhower and Kennedy's handling of the Berlin crisis, de Gaulle turned his attention towards buttressing France's national defense. In developing an independent nuclear deterrent he hoped to provide a shield for the continental powers against the threat of Soviet aggression in the east. He also believed that a French nuclear program would somewhat help to break western Europe's dependence on the US military guarantee.[29] As he asserted France's autonomy from Washington and London, de Gaulle gravitated towards an entente with Adenauer. Like the French president, Adenauer was suspicious of American intentions in western Europe. Far from satisfied with the Anglo-American response to the Berlin crisis, the German chancellor was receptive to the idea of a Franco-German alliance. On January 14, 1963 the two statesmen signed a treaty of friendship in Paris (the so-called Elysée Treaty), which formalized the new Paris–Bonn axis. More significantly, in reaffirming his ties to Adenauer, de Gaulle further alienated the Anglo-Saxon powers with his so-called "double *non.*" With characteristic forthrightness, the French president rejected London's bid for membership of the EEC and declared that Paris would not be participating in the American-led multilateral force (MLF) exercise, which aimed to create a single nuclear deterrent for western Europe.[30]

Adenauer's retirement from the West German political stage in October 1963 deprived de Gaulle of an indispensable ally in his crusade against American hegemony. The new German chancellor, Ludwig Erhard, was anxious to build bridges with Washington after the relative coolness that had characterized the Adenauer–Kennedy relationship. From the outset, Erhard wanted to forge a special relationship with Lyndon Johnson, who had acceded to the presidency after Kennedy's assassination in November 1963. Unlike his predecessor, Erhard was a proponent of both the MLF concept and a strong Atlantic alliance under American leadership.

Despite the changes in the orientation of West German foreign policy, de Gaulle stepped up his campaign against Washington's involvement in European political affairs. The general expressed his opposition to the Johnson administration's increasing embroilment in the Vietnam War and called for the neutralization of Southeast Asia in the Cold War conflict. He also criticized US foreign economic policy. Pointing to the privileged position of the dollar in the Bretton Woods system, de Gaulle stood firm against American foreign direct investment and efforts to remove European barriers to trade in agricultural products during the Kennedy Round of the General Agreement on Tariffs and Trade (GATT). The president's most dramatic act in defiance of Washington was his decision to pull France out of the combined military command of NATO on March 7, 1966.[31] This diplomatic maneuver stunned the Western alliance. While Paris did not withdraw from NATO, it ended its military participation within the organization. Foreign troops had to leave French soil by mid-1968 and the headquarters of NATO were relocated to Brussels.

De Gaulle's initiative came at a most inopportune time in the history of NATO. Britain had declined as a global power. The weakness of sterling led to devaluation of the pound in November 1967. Given its financial woes, London was no longer able to meet its overseas military obligations, and British troops east of Suez were called home as the Wilson government grappled with the ailing British economy. What was more, relations between Washington and Bonn soured over the military offset crisis. Throughout the 1960s West Germany had agreed to meet the foreign exchange costs of US troops stationed in the FRG in order to help the United States with its ballooning balance-of-payments deficit, which threatened to weaken the dollar and destabilize the international financial system. In September 1966, Erhard told Johnson that West Germany was no longer in a position to carry out the offset arrangement. Although the United States, Britain, and West Germany succeed in restoring confidence in NATO through the tripartite negotiations of 1966–1967, Johnson faced intense pressure from the US Senate to substantially reduce the American troop commitment in western Europe.[32] Thus, by the end of the 1960s NATO's *raison d'être* was being called into question.

In June 1966 de Gaulle visited Moscow for talks about the East–West confrontation and the German problem. As part of his strategy of European independence, the French president sought to end the stranglehold of the two superpowers over the continent. He thought that Europe could wrest itself from the Cold War bipolar structure and establish autonomy from East–West domination. A Europe from the Atlantic to the Urals, he believed, would only be possible if a lasting détente could be achieved with the Soviet Union. In contrast with Washington, de Gaulle was convinced that German unification could become a reality only when the Cold War ended. The Americans held the opinion that German reunification was the first step before détente with the Soviet Union and Warsaw Pact. By pursuing détente with Moscow, de Gaulle envisaged a pan-European settlement of the Cold War, involving the two superpowers but led by France and the continental powers. A reunified Germany would be the epicenter of the East–West settlement, which would witness the demise of the superpower blocs and the emergence of Europe as an independent force in world politics.[33] De Gaulle did not live to see his dream become a reality, but his diplomacy, much like Churchill's peace campaign of the early 1950s, was certainly instrumental in the move towards détente by the two superpowers at the beginning of the 1970s.

From Détente to the End of the Cold War, 1969–1991

De Gaulle was not the only Western leader to engage in détente with the Soviet Union in the late 1960s. Pausing momentarily from his absorption with the Vietnam War, President Johnson conducted talks with the Soviet premier, Alexei Kosygin, in 1967 with regard to arms control and nuclear non-proliferation. The Johnson–Kosygin talks eventually bore fruit and in the summer of 1968 the Nuclear Non-Proliferation Treaty (NPT) was signed.[34] During this time, Washington and Moscow began to prepare the ground for extensive discussions on reducing their respective nuclear arsenals. Both de Gaulle and Johnson, however, departed office in 1969. The West German foreign minister, Willy Brandt, whose Social Democratic Party had formed a coalition with the Christian Democrats under the leadership of Chancellor Kurt Kiesinger, engineered a shift in Bonn's policy towards the GDR in 1967. Under the Hallstein Doctrine of 1957, the FRG had refused to acknowledge the existence of East Germany. In the late 1960s Brandt developed political and economic contacts with both the GDR and some of the other Warsaw Pact countries.

European efforts to pursue détente separately from Washington created friction in the Atlantic alliance in the early 1970s. After becoming chancellor in 1969, Brandt inaugurated a new policy towards the GDR, which aimed to improve relations between the two Germanies. Brandt's *Ospolitik* worried President Richard Nixon and his national security advisor, Henry Kissinger. Kissinger, in particular, was concerned that Brandt would reach an accommodation with Moscow, split the Western alliance, and undermine Washington's policies of linkage and triangular diplomacy.[35] Despite American misgivings about Brandt's initiative, the West German chancellor convinced his allies to sign an agreement with Moscow in September 1971 that confirmed the division of Berlin. Brandt also signed non-aggression pacts with the Soviet Union and Poland and followed these diplomatic successes with the Basic Treaty between East and West Germany in December 1972. The Basic Treaty recognized the existence of the FRG and GDR as two distinct political entities, but did not rule out German reunification as a future prospect. In compliance with the agreement, the two countries would build economic contacts and begin the gradual process of political and diplomatic cooperation.[36]

Another Western leader who sought autonomy from Washington was Edward Heath, the Conservative British prime minister. In an unusual break with past tradition, Heath did not desire an intimate relationship with the United States and preferred a more Eurocentric focus in his foreign policy. Kissinger pretended to be more amused than disturbed by this radical shift in British policy and in his memoirs depicted Heath as a "benign" version of de Gaulle.[37]

Progress on the German question led to two years of discussions between the Eastern and Western bloc countries on a political settlement for Europe. Signed by 35 nations, the Helsinki accords of 1975 marked only the second occasion in three decades that the Western allies and the Soviet Union met collectively to discuss European security.[38] The Helsinki accords were essentially the result of a compromise between Moscow and the Western powers. The West, in the words of Frank Ninkovich, would acquiesce in the Soviet desire "to normalize and legitimize the post-World War II status quo in Europe."[39] In return, the Soviet Union would respect universal human rights in eastern Europe. The Helsinki agreement, neverthe-less, was not binding on any of the signatories. As support for détente crumbled in the United States and Kissinger's linkage policies failed to secure satisfactory conces-sions from Moscow, relations between East and West, despite the Helsinki accords, deteriorated.[40] Forced to adopt a stronger stand against Moscow, President Ford jettisoned détente in favor of a more confrontational approach towards the Soviet Union.

Jimmy Carter won the 1976 presidential election in the United States. Charged with revamping post-Vietnam US foreign policy, Carter emphasized human rights rather than *realpolitik* in his diplomacy towards the Soviet Union. The new presi-dent's insistence that the Kremlin comply with the Helsinki accords infuriated Leonid Brezhnev and Carter never achieved the high level of personal contact with the Soviet leadership that both Nixon and Ford had enjoyed. Carter and Brezhnev did manage to strike an agreement on arms control and initialled the SALT II Treaty in the summer of 1979.[41] Neither France nor West Germany could fathom the objectives of President Carter's European policy. While committed to the pursuit of détente with the Soviet Union, Paris and Bonn did not have much faith in Carter and fretted about the future of the US military guarantee in western Europe.[42] A further attempt to build on the achievements of the Helsinki accords under the guise of the Conference on Security and Cooperation in Europe (CSCE) in 1977–1978 did not garner much in the way of progress. By the late 1970s both NATO and the Warsaw Pact were following ambivalent policies: as they held talks with the other side on the question of arms control they were simultaneously bolstering their military capabilities. The Soviet invasion of Afghanistan in December 1979 stimulated divergent responses from Washington and its NATO allies. While Carter abruptly ended détente with Moscow and braced the United States for renewed conflict with the Soviet Union, the Europeans viewed Brezhnev's act as a defense measure and not a direct threat to the status quo in Europe.

Paradoxically, it was the renewal of US–Soviet tensions during 1979–1985 that presaged the end of the Cold War. In January 1981 Ronald Reagan became US president with the intention of standing firm against communism not only in eastern Europe, but also in Central America, the Middle East and Africa. Ideologically hostile to communism, Reagan was morally repulsed by what he viewed as the repressive nature of the Soviet political and economic systems. Given the failure of détente to extract adequate concessions from Moscow in eastern Europe and with regard to arms control, Reagan launched a massive program of military spending in 1981–1983. However, his bellicose anti-Soviet rhetoric belied a deep fear of a nuclear holocaust. Reagan's Strategic Defense Initiative (SDI) of March 1983, although dubbed "star wars" by scornful critics, was designed to protect the United States from the threat of anti-ballistic missiles. Despite his unwavering abhorrence of the Soviet Union, arms control negotiations with Moscow were never far from Reagan's mind.[43] The western European governments were for the most part startled by Reagan's remilitarization of the Cold War.[44] Reagan found a natural ally in his anti-communist crusade in the Conservative British prime minister, Margaret Thatcher.[45] When the Christian Democrats finally returned to power in West Germany in 1982, the new chancellor, Helmut Kohl became a solid supporter of Washington. Even

François Mitterrand, the socialist French president, shared some of Reagan's views on the Soviet Union.

By the early 1980s the Soviet Union was enfeebled both in terms of its economy and its political leadership. The strain of attempting to keep pace in the new arms race stimulated by Reagan sent the centrally planned Soviet economy into steep decline. After Brezhnev's death in 1982, the political reins passed in quick succession to two ageing Communist Party stalwarts, Yuri Andropov and Konstantin Chernenko, neither of whom was long enough in power to arrest the demise of the Soviet Union as a superpower. In 1985, however, Chernenko's death brought the young and dynamic Mikhail Gorbachev to office. Reform-minded and conscious of the parlous state of the Soviet economy, Gorbachev introduced a series of new measures. His *perestroika* and *glasnost* reforms aimed not only to put the domestic economy on a more secure footing, but also to partially "open" Soviet society. Moreover, the Soviet premier was convinced that the Soviet Union could only remain an influential actor in the international system through engagement with the West.[46] As part of his reform package, Gorbachev was prepared to uphold human rights and respect the right to self-determination in eastern Europe. He also wanted to build a more conciliatory relationship with western Europe. He visited the major western European capitals and spoke about the future possibility of a unified continent, echoing de Gaulle's vision of a Europe from the "Atlantic to the Urals."[47]

Arms control was high on the agenda for both Reagan and Gorbachev when they met for their first summit in Geneva in November 1985. The two leaders were united in their determination to take significant steps towards the reduction of nuclear weapons. They met again at a summit in Reykjavik in Iceland in October, but aside from mutually acknowledging that intermediate range missiles should be abolished, made no progress towards agreeing an arms control treaty. Ostensibly, the major bone of contention at Reykjavik was Washington's future possession of the SDI system. It appeared that Reagan was willing to share the SDI with Gorbachev, but the latter misconstrued the American president's intentions with regard to the creation of the anti-ballistic missiles system. In March 1987, however, Gorbachev announced that notwithstanding the SDI issue he was prepared to negotiate an Intermediate Nuclear Forces (INF) treaty with Reagan. An agreement was reached in September, and at a special signing ceremony in Washington the first major bridge towards ending the nuclear arms race and the Cold War was crossed when Reagan and Gorbachev initialled the INF treaty. The INF committed the United States and the Soviet Union to destroying their intermediate-range nuclear missiles.[48]

Within two years of the historic Reagan–Gorbachev accords on nuclear arms control, the Soviet empire in eastern Europe began to crumble. In line with his policy of political and social openness in the Soviet Union, Gorbachev recognized the right of the eastern European countries to self-determination. His decision to remove Soviet troops from Afghanistan in 1988 marked a radical departure from the Brezhnev Doctrine, which sanctioned the use of force to prevent member countries from seceding from the Warsaw Pact. Over the course of 1989, the year of the "velvet revolutions," Moscow legitimized the Solidarity movement in Poland and allowed Hungary and Czechoslovakia to once again become sovereign nations. The former Soviet republics of Latvia, Lithuania, and Estonia, moreover, declared their independence from Moscow. Dramatically, Gorbachev did not intervene on behalf of the East German government to prevent the tearing down of the Berlin Wall in October, which was the catalyst for German reunification. In February 1990, the Kohl government entered into negotiations with Gorbachev, Reagan's successor as the US president, George Bush and its East German counterpart.[49] In a matter of months a monetary union between the FRG and the GDR was planned, and on October 31 a treaty of unification was finalized and signed, effectively ending the Cold War division between East and West Germany.

The reunification of Germany posed potential challenges to both the western European governments and the Soviet Union.[50] Neither prime minister Thatcher in London nor President Mitterrand in Paris was fully comfortable with the inevitability of a powerful Germany at the center of Europe.[51] Gorbachev, moreover, was fearful that a united Germany linked to NATO would encroach on Moscow's sphere of influence in the east and threaten Soviet security. He, at any rate, consented to East Germany leaving the Warsaw Pact and joining NATO. Just as Germany was being unified and Europe transformed, the Soviet Union started to implode. The revolution in eastern Europe had inspired the Soviet republics to declare their independence from Moscow. Despite Gorbachev's heavy-handed attempts to deny the Baltic states their sovereignty from the Soviet Union, the tide had turned against the Kremlin and the architect of economic reform and political openness. In May 1990 Russia, under the leadership of the politically shrewd Boris Yeltsin, became an independent state, thereby diluting Gorbachev's power and influence in the Soviet capital. Although he survived a coup by hard-liners in August 1991, Gorbachev failed to stall the march of the post-communist era in Russian history.[52] Upon the Soviet president's resignation on December 25 the Commonwealth of Independent States (CIS) was established and the former Soviet republics rejected communism for market reforms and the ambition to adopt democratic forms of government.

Conclusion

What was the significance of western Europe's role in the Cold War? In the first instance, the continent of Europe, like Southeast Asia and the Middle East, was an important strategic theater in the conflict between the two superpowers. The Cold War began after the breakdown of the cooperation between the Soviet Union and its Western allies that had characterized World War II. The Potsdam conference sowed the seeds for the division of Europe into two competing blocs with divergent political and economic ideologies. By 1949, the western European states had forged a military alliance with the United States, and Moscow had consolidated its dominant position over the countries of eastern Europe. During the near half-century of the Cold War, Germany was a central battleground in the confrontation between East and West. Only with the reunification of Germany in 1990 was the Cold War finally declared over.

Cold War historiography has assigned a pivotal role to western Europe in the bipolar conflict between the United States and the Soviet Union. In fact, the continent was more than merely a strategic "hot spot" in which the superpowers confronted each other. The leading states of western Europe, in particular Britain, France, and the FRG, were instrumental in assisting the United States in the struggle to contain communism both in Europe and around the world. While firm allies of Washington, these countries often disagreed with American strategic objectives and, on occasion, successfully modified the Cold War policies of the United States. Despite the loss of its empire and relative economic weakness after World War II, Britain was Washington's most stalwart ally, ably supporting successive presidential administrations in waging the Cold War during the 1940s and 1950s. British officials were influential in convincing the United States to make a long-standing commitment to the defense of Europe and highlighting to American policy-makers the potential "threat" that Moscow posed the region. France and the FRG, at various times during the Cold War, carried the torch for détente in Europe between East and West. Seeking to restore France to great power status in the 1960s, President Charles de Gaulle's envisaged a western Europe independent of the United States and acting as a third force between the superpowers. Chancellor Willy Brandt, also challenged the status quo by abandoning the Hallstein Doctrine and opening dialogue and encouraging contacts between the FRG and GDR. Despite the abandonment of détente by the United States after the Helsinki conference of 1975, western Europe, for the most part, remained committed to the peaceful settlement of the Cold War. After the uncertainty of the period of renewed tensions between Washington and Moscow during 1979–1985, the western European governments welcomed the Reagan–Gorbachev arms control negotiations of the late 1980s. They encouraged Gorbachev's internal reforms and welcomed the Soviet leader to their capitals for discussions about the future of European security. Gorbachev's political engagement with the former adversaries of Moscow and his decision to permit the reunification of Germany ultimately contributed to the end of the Cold War.

Notes

1 Ninkovich, *The Wilsonian Century*, 137–142.
2 Young, *Cold War Europe, 1945–1991: A Political History 2nd edition*, 12–14.
3 Zubok and Pleshakov, *Inside the Kremlin's Cold War*, 36–40.
4 Trachtenberg, *A Constructed Peace*, 55–65.
5 Kennedy-Pipe, *Stalin's Cold War*, 120–138.
6 American historians of the Cold war have tended to focus on the confrontation of the two superpowers at the expense of the western European powers. The Europeans, especially Britain, had begun to distrust Soviet intentions towards Germany and eastern Europe several years before the Truman administration launched its containment doctrine. In fact, the evidence suggests that it is plausible to speak of an "Anglo-Soviet Cold War" in 1945–1946. See Miscamble, *From Roosevelt to Truman: Potsdam, Hiroshima, and the Cold War*, 277–278. For an alternative view, which argues that American involvement in western Europe was motivated by fear of Soviet expansionism in Eurasia and Washington's desire to extend its global influence after World War II, see Leffler, *For The Soul of Mankind: The United States, the Soviet Union and the Cold War*, 78–79.
7 Reynolds, "Great Britain," 80–83.

8   For details see Hogan, *The Marshall Plan: America, Britain and the Reconstruction of Western Europe, 1947–52*

9   Reynolds, *Britannia Overruled*, 175.

10 Gaddis, *The Long Peace*, 56–67.

11 Gaddis, *We Now Know*, 37–39.

12 Eisenberg, *Drawing the Line*, 402–404.

13 Soutou, "France," 102–105.

14 For an extended discussion on the degree to which the Europeans "determined" US foreign policy towards the continent in the early years of the Cold War see Lundestad, *The United States and Western Europe since 1945*, 55–59.

15 Ikenberry, "Rethinking the Origins of American Hegemony," 391–395; Schwabe, "The Origins of the United States' Engagement in Europe, 1946–52," 176–180.

16 Leffler, *A Preponderance of Power*, 383–390.

17 The United States also placed great faith in Adenauer remaining in power. Washington believed that only Adenauer could ensure the integration of the FRG into the Western alliance. See Beisner, *Dean Acheson: A Life in the Cold War* 258–263; Gaddis, *The Cold War*, 135.

18 See, for example, Dockrill, *Britain's Policy for West German Rearmament, 1950–55*, 21–44; Mawby, *Containing Germany*, 41–52.

19 Soutou, "France," 112–117; Hitchcock, *France Restored*, 152–185; Trachtenberg, *A Constructed Peace*, 103–125.

20 Runane, *The Rise and Fall of the European Defence Community*, 183–197.

21 Two influential studies are Young, *Winston Churchill's Last Campaign: Britain and the Cold War, 1951–55* and Larres, *Churchill's Cold War: The Politics of Personal Diplomacy*.

22 Taubman, *Khrushchev: The Man and his Era*, 406–412.

23 Trachtenberg, *A Constructed Peace*, 263–282.

24 Ashton, *Kennedy, Macmillan and the Cold War*, 48–63.

25 Freedman, *Kennedy's Wars: Berlin, Cuba, Laos, and Vietnam*, 218–237.

26 An illuminating recent account based on French and American primary sources can be found in Mahan, *Kennedy, de Gaulle and Western Europe*, 137–140.

27 Recent scholarship has explored de Gaulle's challenge to American leadership in extensive detail. See Layne, *The Peace of Illusions*, 100–101; Leffler, *For The Soul of Mankind*, 179–180.

28 Bozo, *Two Strategies for Europe*, xi–xiii.

29 Mahan, op. cit., 58–66.

30 Soutou, *L'alliance incertaine*, 241–259; Giaque, *Grand Designs and Visions of Unity*, 197–224.

31 Vaïsse, *La Grandeur: Politique étrangère du Général de Gaulle, 1958–1969*, 363–412.

32 For two excellent recent accounts see Zimmermann, *Money and Security*, 202–221; Gavin, *Gold, Dollars*, and *Power*, 148–164.

33 Bozo, op. cit., 176–178.

34 For a recent convincing analysis of the Johnson administration's policies towards western Europe and the Soviet Union see Schwartz, *Lyndon Johnson and Europe*, 227–234.

35 Kissinger, *The White House Years*, 409–410.

36 Hanrieder, *Germany, America, Europe: Forty Years of German Foreign Policy*, 195–209.

37 Kissinger, *The White House Years*, 965.

38 Ryan, *The United States and Europe in the Twentieth Century*, 91–94.

39 Ninkovich, *The Wilsonian Century*, 239.

40 Garthoff, *Détente and Confrontation*, 526–555.

41 Dumbrell, *American Foreign Policy: Carter to Clinton*, 17–21, 40–45.
42 LaFeber, *America, Russia*, and *the Cold War, 1945–92*, 299.
43 Cannon, *President Reagan: The Role of a Lifetime*, 759–760.
44 Garthoff, *The Great Transition*, 542–545, 553.
45 Ovendale, *Anglo-American Relations in the Twentieth Century*, 144–146.
46 Paterson, *On Every Front*, 223–225.
47 Cohen, *America in the Age of Soviet Power*, 231–234.
48 Garthoff, *The Great Transition*, 300–337.
49 Stent, *Russia and Germany Reborn*, 114–148.
50 The diplomacy behind German reunification and the role of NATO after the Cold War is discussed in Zelikow and Rice, *Germany Unified and Europe Transformed*, 169–170.
51 Greenwood, *Britain and the Cold War, 1945–1991*, 187.
52 McCauley, *Russia, America and the Cold War, 1949–1991*, 77–86.

Bibliography

Ashton, Nigel, *Kennedy, Macmillan and the Cold War* (Basingstoke: Palgrave Macmillan, 2002).

Beisner, Robert L., *Dean Acheson: A Life in the Cold War* (New York: Oxford University Press, 2006).

Bozo, Frédéric, *Two Strategies for Europe: De Gaulle, the United States and the Atlantic Alliance* (New York: Rowman and Littlefield, 2001).

Cannon, Lou, *President Reagan: The Role of a Lifetime* (New York: Publicaffairs, 2000).

Cohen, Warren I., *America in the Age of Soviet Power* (Cambridge: Cambridge University Press, 1993).

Dockrill, Saki, *Britain's Policy for West German Rearmament, 1950–55* (Cambridge: Cambridge University Press, 1991).

Dumbrell, John, *American Foreign Policy: Carter to Clinton* (Basingstoke: Macmillan, 1997).

Eisenberg, Carolyn Woods, *Drawing the Line: The American Decision to Divide Germany, 1944–1949* (Cambridge: Cambridge University Press, 1996).

Freedman, Lawrence, *Kennedy's Wars: Berlin, Cuba, Laos and Vietnam* (New York: Oxford University Press, 2000).

Gaddis, John Lewis, *The Long Peace: Inquiries into the History of the Cold War* (Oxford: Oxford University Press), 1987.

Gaddis, John Lewis, *We Now Know: Rethinking Cold War History* (Oxford: Oxford University Press, 1997).

Gaddis, John Lewis, *The Cold War* (London: Allen Lane, 2005).

Garthoff, Raymond L., *Détente and Confrontation: American–Soviet Relations from Nixon to Reagan* (Washington, DC: Brookings, 1994).

Garthoff, Raymond L., *The Great Transition: American–Soviet Relations and the End of the Cold War* (Washington, DC: Brookings, 1994).

Gavin, Francis J., *Gold, Dollars and Power: The Politics of International Monetary Relations, 1958–1971* (Chapel Hill, NC: University of North Carolina Press, 2004).

Giaque, Jeffrey Glen, *Grand Designs and Visions of Unity: The Atlantic Powers and the Reorganization of Western Europe, 1955–1963* (Chapel Hill, NC: University of North Carolina Press, 2002).

Greenwood, Sean, *Britain and the Cold War, 1945–1991* (Basingstoke: Macmillan, 2000).

Hanrieder, Wolfram F., *Germany, America, Europe: Forty Years of German Foreign Policy* (New Haven, CT: Yale University Press, 1989).

Hitchcock, William I., *France Restored: Cold War Diplomacy and the Quest for Leadership in Europe, 1944–54* (Chapel Hill, NC: University of North Carolina Press, 1998).

Hogan, Michael J., *The Marshall Plan: America, Britain and the Reconstruction of Western Europe, 1954–52* (Cambridge: Cambridge University Press, 1987).

Ikenberry, G. John, "Rethinking the Origins of American Hegemony," *Political Science Quarterly* 104, no. 3 (1989).

Kennedy-Pipe, Caroline, *Stalin's Cold War: Soviet Strategies in Europe 1943–56* (Manchester: Manchester University Press, 1995).

Kissinger, Henry, *The White House Years* (Boston: Little, Brown, 1979).

LaFeber, Walter, *America, Russia and the Cold War, 1945–92* (New York: McGraw-Hill, 1993).

Larres, Klaus, *Churchill's Cold War: The Politics of Personal Diplomacy* (New Haven, CT: Yale University Press, 2002).

Layne, Christopher, *The Peace of Illusions: American Grand Strategy from the 1940s to the Present* (Ithaca, NY: Cornell University Press, 2006).

Leffler, Melvyn P., *A Preponderance of Power: The Truman Administration, National Security and the Cold War, 1945–53* (Stanford, CA: Stanford University Press, 1992).

Leffler, Melvyn P., *For the Soul of Mankind: The United States, the Soviet Union and the Cold War* (New York: Hill and Wang, 2007).

Lundestad, Geir, *The United States and Western Europe since 1945: From "Empire" by Invitation to Transatlantic Drift* (New York: Oxford University Press, 2003).

McCauley, Martin, *Russia, America and the Cold War, 1949–1991* (London: Longman, 1998).

Mahan, Erin, *Kennedy, de Gaulle and Western Europe* (Basingstoke: Palgrave Macmillan, 2002).

Mawby, Spencer, *Containing Germany: Britain and the Arming of the Federal Republic* (Basingstoke: Macmillan, 1999).

Miscamble, Wilson D.C.S.C., *From Roosevelt to Truman: Potsdam, Hiroshima, and the Cold War* (Cambridge: Cambridge University Press, 2007).

Ninkovich, Frank, *The Wilsonian Century: US Foreign Policy since 1900* (Chicago, IL: University of Chicago Press, 1999).

Ovendale, Ritichie, *Anglo-American Relations in the Twentieth Century* (Basingstoke: Macmillan, 1998).

Paterson, Thomas G., *On Every Front: The Making and Unmaking of the Cold War* (New York: Norton, 1993).

Reynolds, David, *Britannia Overruled* (London: Longman, 1991).

Reynolds, David, "Great Britain," in Reynolds (ed.), *The Origins of the Cold War in Europe: International Perspectives* (New Haven, CT: Yale University Press, 1994).

Runane, Kevin, *The Rise and Fall of the European Defence Community: Anglo-American Relations and the Crisis of European Defence, 1950–54* (Basingstoke: Macmillan, 2000).

Ryan, David, *The United States and Europe in the Twentieth Century* (London: Pearson Education, 2003).

Schwabe, Klaus, "The Origins of the United States' Engagement in Europe, 1946–52," in Francis H. Heller and John R. Gillingham (eds.), *NATO: The Founding of the Atlantic Alliance and the Integration of Europe* (New York: St. Martin's Press, 1992).

Schwartz, Thomas Allan, *Lyndon Johnson and Europe* (Cambridge, MA: Harvard University Press, 2003).

Soutou, Georges-Henri, "France," in David Reynolds (ed.), *The Origins of the Cold War in Europe: International Perspectives* (New Haven, CT: Yale University Press, 1994).

Soutou, Georges-Henri, *L'Alliance incertaine: Les Rapports poltico-stratégiques franco-allemands, 1954–1996* (Paris: Fayard, 1996).

Stent, Angela E., *Russia and Germany Reborn: Unification, the Soviet Collapse and the New Europe* (Princeton, NJ: Princeton University Press, 1999).

Taubman, William, *Khrushchev: The Man and His Era* (New York: The Free Press, 2003).

Trachtenberg, Marc, *A Constructed Peace: The Making of the European Settlement, 1945–63* (Princeton, NJ: Princeton University Press, 1999).

Vaïsse, Maurice, *La Grandeur: Politique étrangère du Général de Gaulle, 1958–1969* (Paris: Fayard, 1998).

Young, John W., *Cold War Europe, 1945–1991: A Political History*, 2nd edition (London: Arnold, 1996).

Young, John W., *Winston Churchill's Last Campaign: Britain and the Cold War, 1951–55* (Oxford: Clarendon Press, 1996).

Zelikow, Philip and Condoleezza Rice, *Germany Unified and Europe Transformed: A Study in Statecraft* (Cambridge, MA: Harvard University Press, 1995).

Zimmermann, Hubert, *Money and Security: Troops, Monetary Policy and West Germany's Relations with the United States and Britain, 1950–71* (Cambridge: Cambridge University Press, 2002).

Zubok, Vladislav and Constantine Pleshakov, *Inside the Kremlin's Cold War: From Stalin to Khrushchev* (Cambridge, MA: Harvard University Press, 1996).

Further Reading

The literature on the Cold War is voluminous. A good starting point for readers new to the subject is John Lewis Gaddis, *The Cold War* (London: Allen Lane, 2005). Gaddis's *We Now Know: Rethinking Cold War History* (New York: Oxford University Press, 1997) analyze the central debates in Cold War historiography with a particular focus on the German question. A solid narrative overview of the western European dimension of the Cold War can be found in John W. Young, *Cold War Europe, 1945–1991: A Political History*, 2nd edition (London: Arnold, 1996). David Reynolds (ed.), *The Origins of the Cold War in Europe: International Perspectives* (New Haven, CT: Yale University Press, 1994), a stimulating collection of essays on the historiography of the Cold War experience of the leading European protagonists in the conflict, is required reading for an advanced study of post-1945 international relations.

Geir Lundestad, *The United States and Western Europe since 1945* (New York: Oxford University Press, 2005), a study of the transatlantic alliance since World War II, is a well-written and thought-provoking analysis of the powerful influence the western European states exercised on American cold war strategy. For a concise and accessible interpretation of the state of US–European relations during the Cold War see David Ryan, *The United States and Europe in the Twentieth Century* (London: Pearson, 2003). Ryan's book contains a number of useful documents outlining significant European policy positions towards the United States and the Soviet Union.

An extensive discussion of the division of Germany and tensions between western and eastern Europe in the formative decades of the Cold War can be found in Marc Trachtenberg, *A Constructed Peace: The Making of the European Settlement, 1945–63* (Princeton, NJ: Princeton University Press, 1999). On France in the de Gaulle era, Frédéric Bozo, *Two Strategies for Europe: De Gaulle, the United States and the Atlantic Alliance* (New York: Rowman and Littlefield, 2001) is highly recommended.

The story of the diplomacy behind the reunification of Germany and the end of the Cold War is told in fascinating detail in Philip Zelikow and Condoleezza Rice, *Germany Unified and Europe Transformed: A Study in Statecraft* (Cambridge, MA: Harvard University Press, 1995). This should be read in conjunction with Raymond L. Garthoff, *The Great Transition: American–Soviet Relations and the End of the Cold War* (Washington, DC: Brookings, 1994) and Melvyn P. Leffler's magisterial *For The Soul of Mankind: The United States, the Soviet Union and the Cold War* (New York: Hill and Wang, 2007).

CHAPTER FOUR

The Soviet Bloc and the Cold War in Europe

MARK KRAMER

This chapter provides an assessment of the Soviet–east European bloc from 1945, when the Soviet Union emerged as the dominant power in eastern Europe, until 1991, when the last vestiges of Soviet hegemony in the region were dissolved.[1] The formation of the bloc was one of the chief precipitants of the Cold War, and the demise of the bloc brought an end to the Cold War. The chapter is divided into six parts. The first part lays out an analytical framework for the rest of the chapter. The second part provides a brief historical overview of Soviet–east European relations from 1945 to 1985. The third part discusses the military, political, and economic factors that contributed to Soviet hegemony in eastern Europe. The fourth part highlights the limits of Soviet power in eastern Europe during the post-World War II period. The fifth part recounts the fundamental changes in Soviet–east European relations after 1985. The final part determines what broad analytical conclusions can be drawn from the four-and-a-half decades of Soviet–east European relations.

Spheres of Influence and Asymmetrical Power Relationships

For analytical purposes, it is useful to compare the postwar Soviet–east European relationship with other highly unequal interstate relationships that have existed in various parts of the world. One way of approaching this task might be through the use of "dependency theory," a neo-Marxist perspective developed in the 1970s as an outgrowth of earlier theories of economic imperialism.[2] The original proponents of dependency theory were interested solely in studying relationships between developed capitalist states and underdeveloped countries (e.g., US–Latin American relations), rather than devising a comparative framework that would also encompass relations among communist states. Subsequently, a few scholars specializing in the study of communist systems applied the main tenets of dependency theory to Soviet–east European relations.[3] Their efforts were useful in underscoring the many shortcomings of dependency theory, but their work shed relatively little light on the dynamics of Soviet policy in eastern Europe.

A Companion to Europe since 1945, First Edition. Edited by Klaus Larres.
© 2014 John Wiley & Sons, Ltd. Published 2014 by John Wiley & Sons, Ltd.

A more fruitful approach to the study of Soviet–east European relations (and of other highly asymmetrical relationships) has emerged from analyses done in the late 1970s and 1980s on "spheres of influence" and interactions between "preponderant and subordinate states" – concepts that are related to but distinct from long-standing notions of "empire."[4] These concepts have facilitated cross-regional comparisons of unequal power relationships over broad periods of history. It is now possible, for example, to compare post-1945 Soviet–east European relations with post-1933 US–Central American relations, with the pre-1990 relationship between South Africa and its neighbors, or with the post-1991 relationship between Russia and the countries of central Asia and the Caucasus. The differences among these cases may be at least as great as the similarities, but that is precisely what a comparative framework is designed to show.

As used in this chapter, a sphere of influence can be defined as a region of the world in which a preponderant external actor (State A) is able to compel the local states to conform with State A's own preferences. Other outside powers may also have some leverage over the countries in State A's sphere of influence, but that leverage is relatively circumscribed and is greatly eclipsed by the power that State A exerts. By this definition, eastern Europe was clearly a sphere of influence for the Soviet Union after World War II. Although Western countries had some effect on the behavior of the east European states, the dominant external influence in the region came from the Soviet Union. The Soviet sphere of influence was never formally recognized as such by Western governments, but the *de facto* existence of the sphere was widely understood. The Soviet sphere of influence in eastern Europe was simultaneously a military buffer against West Germany and other members of the North Atlantic Treaty Organization (NATO) and an ideological extension of Soviet-style communist rule. In that sense, the east European sphere was quite different from the US sphere of influence in Central America, which was never a full-fledged buffer zone for the United States and was not regarded as an ideological extension of American democracy.

A further specification is needed to distinguish among the possible ways that the preponderant state can exploit its political, economic, and military leverage to gain influence or control over the group of weaker states. Despite the peculiar nature of the Soviet bloc (especially in the ideological sphere), the post-1945 Soviet–east European relationship fits well into a broad typology that Hedley Bull devised of relationships between a preponderant state and a group of subordinate states. His typology included the three alternatives of "dominance," "hegemony," and "primacy," which are best conceived of as points on a continuum, ranging from the most coercive to the least coercive.[5] Only the first two alternatives can truly be regarded as "spheres of influence." In a relationship of *dominance*, the preponderant state exercises tight, pervasive control over the subordinate states, paying little heed to modern norms of international law. In a relationship of *hegemony*, the preponderant state exercises looser control and usually abides by most norms of international law, but it still seeks – if necessary, through the use of armed force – to ensure that the internal and external orientation of the subordinate states is in accord with its own preferences. In a relationship of *primacy*, the preponderant state makes no recourse to the threat or use of force in its dealings with the weaker states, and instead relies solely on standard means of diplomatic and economic influence.

At any given time, a highly unequal relationship in the modern state system, including all sphere-of-influence relationships, will approximate one of these three ideal-types. No such relationship, however, is static over the long term. Even the Soviet Union's sphere of influence in eastern Europe, as discussed below, was more dynamic and variable than often assumed. What began as outright Soviet "dominance" over eastern Europe during the era of Josef Stalin evolved after the mid-1950s into a "hegemonic" and more complex relationship.

Even so, the changes in Soviet–east European relations over time, important though they may have been, were never far-reaching enough to prevent the whole structure from collapsing in 1989–1990. If at some point long before 1989 the transition from "dominance" to "hegemony" had been carried further to leave the Soviet Union with something closer to "primacy," the Soviet–east European relationship might have proven more durable. No such transition was ever forthcoming. The basic structure of the relationship that was imposed on the east European countries just after World War II – a structure requiring them to maintain Marxist-Leninist systems at home and to pursue "socialist internationalist" policies abroad – was left essentially intact even after pressures for drastic change had set in. Those pressures occasionally burst into the open, forcing the Soviet Union to defend and restore its sphere of influence, though at ever greater cost and with ever greater difficulty. In the late 1980s, when the Soviet Union itself finally became intent on abolishing the old order, the pressures that had been building for so long in eastern Europe came rapidly to the surface, leaving the whole Soviet bloc in tatters and ending the Cold War.

Historical Overview, 1945–1985

In the closing months of World War II, Soviet troops occupied most of eastern Europe. Over the next few years, the establishment of communism in eastern Europe proceeded at varying rates. In Yugoslavia and Albania, the indigenous communist parties led by Josip Broz Tito and Enver Hoxha had obtained sufficient political leverage and military strength through their role in the anti-Nazi resistance to eliminate their opponents (with ruthless violence) and assume outright power as the war drew to a close. In the Soviet zone of Germany, the Soviet occupation forces enabled the Socialist Unity Party of Germany (SED) to gain preeminence well before the German Democratic Republic (GDR) was formally created in 1949. Similarly, in Bulgaria and Romania, communist-dominated governments were imposed under Soviet pressure in early 1945. Elsewhere in the region, events followed a more gradual pattern. Not until the spring of 1948 were "People's Democracies" in place all over east-central Europe.[6] Moreover, in June 1948, only a few months after the Soviet sphere of influence was finally consolidated, a significant breach in it occurred. A bitter rift with Yugoslavia nearly provoked Soviet military intervention, but in the end Stalin refrained from using military force. From then on, Yugoslavia was able to pursue a more or less independent course.

Despite the "loss" of Yugoslavia, Soviet influence in eastern Europe came under no further threat during Stalin's time. From 1947 through the early 1950s, the east European states embarked on crash industrialization and collectivization programs, causing vast social upheaval yet also leading to rapid short-term economic growth.

No conflict between "viability" and "cohesion" yet existed, for Stalin was able to rely on the presence of Soviet troops, a tightly woven network of security forces, the wholesale penetration of the east European governments by Soviet agents, the use of mass purges and political terror, and the unifying threat of renewed German militarism to ensure that regimes loyal to Moscow remained in power.[7] By the early 1950s, Stalin had established a degree of control over eastern Europe to which his successors could only aspire.

Following Stalin's death in March 1953, a shift began in Soviet–east European relations, as the new Soviet leaders encouraged the east European governments to loosen economic controls, adopt "New Courses" of development, and downgrade the role of the secret police.[8] The severe economic pressures that had built up on workers and farmers during the relentless drive for industrialization and collectivization were gradually eased, and many victims of the Stalinist purges were rehabilitated, often posthumously. As a result, the socioeconomic turmoil that had earlier been contained now began to surface, rendering all but impossible a full-fledged return to the pervasive control of the Stalinist years. Thus, from 1953 until the late 1980s the fundamental problem for the Soviet Union in eastern Europe was how to preserve its sphere of influence while adapting to the changed social and political conditions that made such a sphere far more difficult to maintain.

In the first few months after Stalin's death, the situation in eastern Europe was greatly exacerbated by the initial stages of the succession struggle in the Soviet Union and the analogous struggles in several of the east European countries. The pronouncements and recommendations about reform that emanated from the Soviet Union in the spring of 1953 were erratic and haphazard, enabling several of the hard-line east European leaders to retrench and avoid any real movement away from Stalinism. Only after the outbreak of a violent uprising in Plzeň and unrest in other Czechoslovak cities in early June 1953, stemming from the Czechoslovak government's adoption of a harsh "currency reform," did the urgent need for greater economic and political liberalization become apparent. This need was demonstrated even more vividly two weeks later by a mass uprising in East Germany against communist rule. Coming at a time of profound uncertainty and leadership instability in both Moscow and East Berlin, the uprising in the GDR threatened the very existence of the SED regime and, by extension, vital Soviet interests in Germany. Although the Soviet Army put down the rebellion rather easily and with relatively little bloodshed – roughly two dozen demonstrators were killed, several hundred wounded, and many thousands arrested – the military intervention was crucial both in forestalling an escalation of the violence and in reasserting Soviet control.[9]

Despite the resolution of the June 1953 crisis, the use of Soviet military power in East Germany did not impart greater consistency to Soviet policy or eliminate the prospect of further turmoil in eastern Europe. Most Soviet leaders were preoccupied with domestic affairs, and they failed to appreciate the implications of the changes taking place in the Eastern bloc. They hoped that the events in Czechoslovakia and East Germany were an aberration, rather than a portent of more explosive unrest to come. Not until the events of October and November 1956 in Poland and Hungary did a modicum of direction finally return to Soviet policy. The peaceful outcome of the Soviet Union's standoff with Poland demonstrated that some Soviet flexibility would continue and that a return to Stalinism was not in the offing. At the same time, the Soviet Union's armed intervention in Hungary in early November 1956 made clear to all the Warsaw Pact countries the bounds of Soviet restraint and the limits of what could be changed in eastern Europe.[10] Far more than the uprisings of 1953 in Czechoslovakia and East Germany, the Hungarian revolution posed a fundamental threat to Soviet hegemony in the region. By reestablishing military control over Hungary and by exposing – more dramatically than in 1953 – the emptiness of the "roll-back" and "liberation" rhetoric in the West, the Soviet invasion stemmed any further loss of Soviet power in eastern Europe.

By the time the next major challenge to the Soviet sphere of influence emerged, in 1968, Soviet–east European relations had undergone several notable changes. Certain developments had facilitated greater Soviet control over eastern Europe and better cohesion among the Warsaw Pact states. On balance, though, most developments since 1956 had pointed not towards an increase of Soviet control but towards a loosening of that control. In part, this trend reflected the growing heterogeneity of the east European societies and the continued impact of the "thaw" introduced under Nikita Khrushchev in the 1950s, but it was also due to the schism in world communism that resulted from the increasingly bitter Sino-Soviet conflict. Less than a year after the Sino-Soviet split became public knowledge in 1960, Albania sparked a crisis with the Soviet Union by openly aligning itself with China – a precedent that caused deep concern in Moscow. To compound matters, Romania in the early 1960s began to embrace foreign and domestic policies that were at times sharply at odds with the Soviet Union's own policies. Although Romania had never been a crucial member of the Warsaw Pact, Nicolae Ceauşescu's growing recalcitrance on military affairs and foreign policy posed obvious complications for the cohesion of the alliance.

Developments outside the bloc also contributed to the loosening of Soviet control in eastern Europe. The perceived threat of German aggression, which for so long had unified the Warsaw Pact governments, had gradually diminished. In the mid-1960s, West Germany had launched its *Ostpolitik* campaign to increase economic and political contacts in eastern Europe (especially the GDR), a campaign whose potentially disruptive impact on the Soviet bloc was well recognized in Moscow. Soviet policy in eastern Europe also was increasingly constrained by the incipient US–Soviet détente, with its promise of strategic nuclear arms accords and increased East–West economic ties. This new relationship gave Soviet leaders an incentive to proceed cautiously in eastern Europe before taking actions that could undermine the détente.

Against this backdrop, the events of 1968 unfolded in Czechoslovakia. Sweeping internal reforms during the "Prague Spring" brought a comprehensive revival of political, economic, and cultural life in Czechoslovakia, but it also provoked anxiety in Moscow about the potential ramifications.[11] Both the internal and the external repercussions of the liberalization in Czechoslovakia were regarded by Soviet leaders as a fundamental threat to their sphere of influence in eastern Europe. The Prague Spring raised doubts about the cohesion of the Warsaw Pact, and those doubts were bound to multiply if the developments in Czechoslovakia proved "contagious." Soviet efforts to compel the Czechoslovak leader, Alexander Dubček, to change course were of little efficacy, as all manner of troop movements, thinly veiled threats, and political and economic coercion failed to bring an end to the Prague Spring. If anything, the Czechoslovak reformers seemed to benefit domestically the stronger the pressure from the Warsaw Pact became.

On August 17, 1968, after a three-day session focusing on the crisis, the CPSU (Communist Party of the Soviet Union) Politburo unanimously approved an invasion of Czechoslovakia to bring an end to the Prague Spring.[12] The following day, the CPSU general secretary, Leonid Brezhnev, informed his East German, Polish, Bulgarian, and Hungarian counterparts of the decision at a hastily convened meeting in Moscow. Unlike in 1956, when Soviet troops intervened in Hungary unilaterally, Brezhnev was determined to give the invasion in 1968 a multilateral appearance. As a result, some 80,000 soldiers from Poland, East Germany, Bulgaria, and Hungary ended up taking part. In reality, though, Operation "Danube" (the codename of the invasion) could hardly be regarded as a "joint" undertaking. Soviet paratroopers and special operations forces spearheaded the invasion, and a total of more than 400,000 Soviet troops eventually moved into Czechoslovakia, roughly five times the number of east European forces. Moreover, the invasion was under strict Soviet command at all times, rather than being left under Warsaw Pact command as originally planned.

The invasion of Czechoslovakia explicitly introduced what became known in the West as the "Brezhnev Doctrine" into Soviet–east European relations. In effect, the Doctrine linked the fate of each socialist country with the fate of all others, stipulated that every socialist country must abide by the norms of Marxism-Leninism as interpreted in Moscow, and rejected "abstract sovereignty" in favor of the "laws of class struggle." The Brezhnev Doctrine thus laid out even stricter "rules of the game" than in the past for the "socialist commonwealth":

> Without question, the peoples of the socialist countries and the Communist parties have and must have freedom to determine their country's path of development. Any decision they make, however, must not be inimical either to socialism in their own country or to the fundamental interests of other socialist countries . . . A socialist state that is in a system of other states composing the socialist commonwealth cannot be free of the common interests of that commonwealth. The sovereignty of individual socialist countries cannot be set against the interests of world socialism and the world revolutionary movement . . . The weakening of any of the links in the world system of socialism directly affects all the socialist countries, and they cannot look indifferently upon this.[13]

The enunciation of the Brezhnev Doctrine codified Soviet attitudes towards eastern Europe as they had developed over the previous two decades. The doctrine owed as much to Stalin and Khrushchev as to Brezhnev, inasmuch as the policies of these earlier leaders were merely reaffirmed in the Brezhnev era. Nonetheless, the promulgation of the Doctrine was significant both in restoring a firmer tone to Soviet–east European relations and in defining the limits of permissible deviations from the Soviet model of communism.

For twelve years after the 1968 crisis, the Soviet bloc seemed relatively stable, despite crises in Poland in 1970–1971 and 1976. In mid-1980, however, the façade of stability came to an abrupt end when a severe and prolonged crisis erupted in

Poland. The crisis started out modestly enough as a wave of protests against higher meat prices announced in July 1980; but it intensified with remarkable celerity and soon posed graver complications for Soviet policy than any event had since the late 1940s.[14] The formation of *Solidarność* (Solidarity), an independent and popularly based trade union that soon rivaled the Polish United Workers' Party for political power and that represented the interests of the very same working class in whose name the party had always purported to rule, posed a fundamental challenge to Poland's communist system. From the outset, as the magnitude of that challenge became apparent, officials in Moscow reacted with unremitting hostility towards Solidarity and other unofficial groups. Soviet leaders were equally dismayed by the growing political influence of Poland's Catholic church, which they regarded as "one of the most dangerous forces in Polish society" and a fount of "anti-socialist" and "hostile" elements.[15]

Because of Poland's location in the heart of Europe, its communications and logistical links with the Group of Soviet Forces in Germany, its contributions to the "first strategic echelon" of the Warsaw Pact, and its numerous storage sites for Soviet tactical nuclear warheads, the prospect of having a non-communist government come to power in Warsaw or of a drastic change in Polish foreign policy was a cause for alarm in Moscow. Soviet foreign minister Andrei Gromyko spoke for all his colleagues when he declared at a CPSU Politburo meeting in October 1980 that "we simply *cannot* lose Poland" under any circumstances.[16] Although Khrushchev had been willing in 1956 to reach a *modus vivendi* with the Polish leader Władysław Gomułka, the situation in 1980–1981 was totally different. Gomułka, despite his initial defiance of Moscow's strictures, was a devoted communist, and Khrushchev could be confident that socialism in Poland and the Polish–Soviet "fraternal relationship" would continue and even thrive under Gomułka's leadership. Brezhnev and his colleagues had no such assurances about Poland in 1980 and 1981.

By stirring Soviet anxieties about the potential loss of a key member of the Warsaw Pact and about the spread of political instability throughout eastern Europe, the Polish crisis demonstrated, as the events of 1953, 1956, and 1968 had previously, the degree of "acceptable" change in the Soviet bloc. The crisis in Poland was more prolonged than those earlier upheavals, but the leeway for genuine change was, if anything, narrower than before. Plans for the imposition of martial law began almost from the very first day of the crisis.[17] Although the plans were drafted by the Polish General Staff, the whole process was supervised and moved along by the Soviet Union. The constant pressure exerted by Soviet political leaders and military commanders on Polish officials thwarted any hope that Stanisław Kania, the Communist Party first secretary until October 1981, might have had of reaching a genuine compromise with Solidarity and the Catholic church. From the Soviet Politburo's perspective, any such compromise would have been, at best, a useless diversion or, at worst, a form of outright capitulation to "hostile" forces. The only thing Soviet leaders truly wanted during the crisis was to get the Polish authorities to implement "decisive measures" as soon as possible against the "anti-socialist and counterrevolutionary opposition."

The Soviet Union's pursuit of an "internal solution" to the Polish crisis was by no means a departure from its responses to previous crises in eastern Europe. In

Hungary and Poland in 1956 and Czechoslovakia in 1968, the Soviet Union applied pressure short of direct military intervention and sought to work out an "internal solution" that would preclude the need for an invasion. In each case, Soviet officials viewed military action as a last-ditch option, to be used only after all other measures had failed. In Poland in 1956 an internal solution that left Gomułka in power did prove feasible, whereas in Hungary and later in Czechoslovakia all attempts to reassert Soviet control "from within" proved futile, leading in the end to direct Soviet military intervention. During the 1980–1981 Polish crisis, one of the first steps taken by the CPSU Politburo was to mobilize Soviet tank and infantry forces "in case military assistance is provided to Poland."[18] Soviet military officers drew up plans for a full-scale invasion, but these plans were to be implemented only if the Polish authorities failed to restore order on their own. Preparations for the imposition of martial law began in 1980 even before the Soviet High Command started laying the groundwork for an invasion, and the "internal" option was deemed throughout to be vastly preferable to direct "fraternal assistance" from outside. Only in a worst-case scenario, in which the martial law operation collapsed and full-scale civil war erupted in Poland, would the Soviet Union have gone with the "external" option.

If "Operation X" (the codename of the martial law operation) had indeed collapsed amid widespread violence in December 1981 and the Soviet Politburo had been forced to decide whether to send in troops, the consequences of such a choice would have been immense. The extreme difficulty of carrying out an invasion of Poland and of coping with its aftermath would have been so great that it would have changed the course of Soviet policy in eastern Europe for many years to come. As it was, the success of Wojciech Jaruzelski's "internal solution" precluded any test of Moscow's restraint and restored conformity to the Soviet bloc at relatively low cost. The surprisingly smooth imposition of martial law (*stan wojenny*) in Poland also helped to prevent any further disruption in Soviet–east European relations during Brezhnev's final year and the next two-and-a-half years under Yuri Andropov and Konstantin Chernenko.

The lack of any major political turmoil in eastern Europe from 1982 to 1985 seems especially surprising at first glance, for this was a period of great uncertainty not only because of the post-Brezhnev succession in Moscow but also because of the impending successions in most of the other Warsaw Pact countries. The last time the Soviet Union had experienced a prolonged leadership transition, from 1953 to 1956, numerous crises arose in the Eastern bloc: in Czechoslovakia and East Germany in June 1953, in Poznań in June 1956, and in Poland and Hungary in October–November 1956. Moreover, during the 1953–1956 period, all the east European countries underwent changes at the top of their communist parties, just as the Soviet Union did. By contrast, no such upheavals or leadership changes occurred in 1982–1985. This unusual placidity cannot be attributed to any single factor, but the martial law crackdown of December 1981 and the Soviet invasions of 1956 and 1968 are probably a large part of the explanation. After Stalin's death in March 1953, the limits of what could be changed in eastern Europe were still unknown, but by the early 1980s the Soviet Union had evinced its willingness and ability to use extreme measures, when necessary, to prevent or reverse "deviations from socialism." Thus, by the time Mikhail Gorbachev became CPSU general secretary in March 1985, the internal political complexion of eastern Europe seemed destined to remain within the narrow bounds of orthodox communism as interpreted in Moscow.

The Dynamics of Soviet Hegemony in Eastern Europe

Soviet hegemony in eastern Europe after 1945 had three key dimensions: military, political, and economic. The different forms of Soviet power tended to reinforce one another insofar as the Soviet Union's military and economic influence in the region strengthened its political control. Warsaw Pact maneuvers, for example, often achieved political ends, and economic pressure helped to bring wayward states into line.

This section discusses the different aspects of Soviet power in eastern Europe, focusing on only one side of the Soviet–east European power relationship. The other side of the relationship – that is, the east European states' leverage vis-à-vis the Soviet Union – was by no means unimportant, but the chief concern in this section is with the dynamics of Soviet hegemony in the region. The extent to which the east European states were able to constrain, inhibit, and influence Soviet power is discussed in the section after this.

Military aspects

The most conspicuous element of Soviet power in eastern Europe was the deployment of formidable military strength. Hundreds of thousands of Soviet troops were stationed in Poland (1945–1993), Romania (1945–1958), Czechoslovakia (1968–1991), Hungary (1945–1991), and the former East Germany (1945–1994), and hundreds of thousands more were based in the western military districts of the Soviet Union. Large quantities of Soviet weapons, including tanks, armored combat vehicles, artillery, fighter aircraft, bombers, and nuclear and conventional missiles, were deployed on east European soil. The Soviet Union maintained exclusive control over Warsaw Pact nuclear weapons, communications networks, joint air defense systems, and logistical supply lines. In addition, the extensive links between Soviet and east European Communist Party and military leaders, the influence of the Soviet and allied state security organs, and the dependence of the east European armed forces on the Soviet Union for weapons and spare parts enabled Soviet commanders to wield a good deal of formal and informal control over the non-Soviet Warsaw Pact military units.[19] Soviet control was especially pervasive over the East German *Nationale Volksarmee* (NVA), which even in peacetime was wholly subordinated to the Soviet-dominated Joint Command of the Warsaw Pact. In wartime, the NVA and all the other Warsaw Pact armies (other than the Romanian) would have been placed under the direct control of the Soviet High Command, in accordance with an array of secret bilateral agreements concluded in the late 1970s and early 1980s.[20]

Nor was Soviet military power in eastern Europe maintained merely for appearance' sake. In the first 15 years after Stalin's death, Soviet troops intervened on three occasions – in East Germany in 1953, Hungary in 1956, and Czechoslovakia in 1968

– to counter perceived threats to Soviet interests in the region. The Soviet Union's demonstrated willingness to use force in these instances was at least as important as the presence of Soviet troops on east European territory in precluding violent challenges to the local communist regimes. By the same token, when specific challenges did arise in eastern Europe, the record of previous Soviet interventions lent greater credibility to Moscow's warnings and threats, and thus helped forestall the need for direct intervention. During a political crisis, conspicuous Soviet and Warsaw Pact troop maneuvers were often enough to bring overwhelming pressure to bear on both the government and the population.

Soviet military power in eastern Europe was reinforced by the military strategy of the Warsaw Pact, which in effect preserved a Soviet capability to intervene in other member states. The Pact's strategy was essentially identical to Soviet strategy for Europe in its emphasis on a blitzkrieg-style assault by combined Soviet and east European forces against western Europe.[21] To support this strategy, the military establishments in eastern Europe (other than Romania) geared most of their training, tactics, and military planning towards offensive operations and devoted little time to defensive arrangements that might have been adopted to resist Soviet intervention in their own countries. Even the unique system of National Territorial Defence (*Obrona terytorium kraju*) in Poland, though defensive in nature, was designed entirely to protect against nuclear air attacks from the West. By compelling the east European states to concentrate exclusively on perceived threats from the West and not on more plausible threats from the East, the Warsaw Pact's strategy prevented those states from developing an adequate defensive capacity against "fraternal" invasions.

In other ways as well, the Warsaw Pact bolstered Soviet military control over eastern Europe. The formation of the pact in May 1955, the day after the Austrian State Treaty was signed, served to legitimize the continued deployment of Soviet troops in Hungary and Romania. The ostensible justification for the presence of those troops was eliminated by the signing of the Austrian State Treaty, but the establishment of this new multilateral alliance provided a fresh rationale for keeping them. The status-of-forces agreements concluded with Poland (1956), Hungary (1957), East Germany (1957), and Czechoslovakia (1968) gave the Soviet Union a further safeguard for the "temporary" presence of its forces in the region while passing off a large share of the stationing costs to the host countries. The Warsaw Pact also became a leading organ for the defense of "socialist internationalism" and "socialist gains" – that is, for joint military intervention against refractory allies, as was done in Czechoslovakia in August 1968. To that end, the pact's joint military exercises that began in October 1961, in addition to serving as a form of coercive diplomacy during intra-bloc and East–West crises, were valuable in providing coordinated training and preparations for the Warsaw Pact armies in case direct intervention against another East-bloc country proved necessary.

The Soviet Union's *global* military power also played a vital role in maintaining hegemony over eastern Europe. The threat of Soviet nuclear or conventional retaliation helped to deter the United States and its Western allies from coming to the defense of east European countries when the Soviet Union intervened. Similarly, the NATO governments recognized that even if they responded with military force to Soviet incursions into eastern Europe, they would have little chance of success, given the USSR's local force preponderance and logistical advantages. Past Soviet interventions in eastern Europe thus helped to consolidate Moscow's claim to a sphere of influence in the region – a sphere that was further buttressed by the emergence of strategic nuclear parity between the superpowers in the 1960s and early 1970s. US secretary of state Dean Rusk acknowledged as much in 1964 when he declared that "our capacity to influence events and trends within the communist world is very limited. But it is our policy to do what we can . . ."[22]

Political/ideological aspects

Compared to most other highly unequal interstate relationships, the Soviet relationship with eastern Europe was marked by a far greater number of intrusive political controls. Some of these controls were overt and widely discussed; others were surreptitious and never mentioned in open sources. One of the standard ways in which Soviet officials gained broad influence was by cultivating close personal and political ties with east European Communist Party leaders, both in their initial selection and during their subsequent careers. During the Stalin era, Soviet control over east European leaders was pervasive and conspicuous. The situation changed after Stalin's death, with the dissolution of the Communist Information Bureau in April 1956 and the gradual removal of the most blatant forms of Soviet interference in east European domestic affairs in the 1950s and early 1960s. Nevertheless, Moscow still retained at least some say over most leadership changes in the Eastern bloc. The long-time Communist Party leader in Hungary, János Kádár, was installed after a Soviet invasion of his country. Many other east European Communist leaders – Gustáv Husák and Miloš Jakeš in Czechoslovakia; Edward Gierek, Stanisław Kania, and Wojciech Jaruzelski in Poland; and Erich Honecker in East Germany – came to power under Soviet auspices after their predecessors had incurred Moscow's displeasure. Similarly, Todor Zhivkov's emergence as a compromise leader in Bulgaria in 1954 was effected through direct Soviet support. The pivotal role that the Soviet Union played in the selection of these and other east European leaders usually enabled Soviet authorities to exert far-reaching influence on the policies of the new leaders. The close relationships fostered by high-level Soviet officials with their east European counterparts also helped to ensure that party leaders in eastern Europe would not attempt, at a later stage, to assert too great a degree of autonomy.

Besides exerting influence over leadership selection, the Soviet Union sought to strengthen its ties and to coordinate policies with East-bloc officials through regular bilateral and multilateral meetings. Because bilateral meetings were more effective in allowing Moscow to communicate and enforce its views, Soviet leaders traditionally preferred this sort of consultation with their allies. That was especially the case under Stalin and Khrushchev, and it continued during the Brezhnev era, when bilateral summits were held annually at summer resorts in the Crimea. Top-level bilateral meetings also occurred regularly under Brezhnev's successors. Further bilateral contacts took place via the Soviet liaison officers and embassy representatives stationed in each of the bloc countries, as well as through meetings held by officials from the CPSU Secretariat and the CPSU Central Committee department responsible for intra-bloc relations with their east European counterparts. Starting in the early 1970s, Soviet leaders also showed greater interest in multilateral forums, such as the Council for Mutual Economic Assistance (CMEA), the Warsaw Pact's joint political and military committees, and various cultural and scientific exchanges under the CPSU's close supervision. New multilateral organs were formed within the Warsaw Pact, including the Council of Defence Ministers in 1969 and the Council of Foreign Ministers in 1976. These and other multilateral bodies proved to be a useful instrument for coordinating policies and for strengthening the "organic" links between the Soviet and east European military, economic, and scientific bureaucracies.[23] Those links, in turn, facilitated greater Soviet control over the region's Communist Party leaders.

As a further means of retaining political and ideological sway in eastern Europe, the Soviet Union was able to rely on the monitoring and clandestine activities of the Soviet state security and intelligence services. When the communist regimes were first established in eastern Europe, Soviet officials were instrumental in creating local secret police forces analogous to those operating in the USSR itself. For many years, and particularly during the Stalin era, the east European internal security organs were mere appendages of the Soviet state security apparatus. The situation was aptly described by one of Stalin's top aides (and eventual successor), Nikita Khrushchev, in his memoirs:

> The security organs [in eastern Europe] worked under the direct supervision of "advisers" who had been sent from the Soviet state security apparatus, rather than under the supervision of the East European governments themselves . . . Our "advisers" were in all the [East European] countries, and their role [under Stalin] was very shameful.[24]

Later on, the east European secret police forces were not quite as pervasively controlled by the Soviet Union as they had been in Stalin's time, but they remained the most steadfastly pro-Moscow element in the east European states, consistently placing Soviet interests ahead of their own national interests. Furthermore, even in the 1970s and 1980s the Soviet security forces, in particular the Committee for State Security (KGB) still kept a tight rein on the East-bloc intelligence agencies and still used those agencies to promote Soviet political and military objectives. What is more, the KGB's activities extended well beyond its dealings with the allied secret police and foreign intelligence forces to include the recruitment and installation of Soviet agents in key positions throughout the political and military command structures of the east European countries.[25] In other ways as well, such as providing information to Soviet political leaders about social and economic trends in the east European countries, the Soviet state security and intelligence services played a crucial role in the maintenance of the Soviet sphere of influence in eastern Europe.

These various methods of political control were reinforced by the commonality of interests that usually existed between Soviet and east European political elites. Their common interests stemmed from more than the fact that the east European leaders were ultimately beholden to the CPSU Politburo and the Soviet armed forces for their security and continued tenure. Even if the east European regimes had had less of a stake in maintaining good relations with the USSR, most of the leaders in the region would have been willing to adhere to Soviet methods of "socialist development." By doing so they could bolster their own political positions and solidify the dominant role of their communist parties. In this sense, the measures that were desired by Soviet leaders for the countries of eastern Europe – the maintenance of supreme authority by the Communist Party, the retention of a highly centralized party structure and official Marxist-Leninist ideology, and state control over the press and all publishing outlets – were also likely to be the measures preferred by the leaders of those countries themselves. Given this natural overlapping of interests between Soviet and east European elites, the efficacy of Soviet political power in the region was greatly enhanced.

Economic aspects

The Soviet Union also wielded far-reaching economic power vis-à-vis the East European states, of which five – Poland, Czechoslovakia, Hungary, Bulgaria, and Romania – were founding members of the CMEA in January 1949. (Albania was admitted a month later, and the newly created GDR was admitted the following year.) In the 1940s and 1950s, Soviet economic power in the region was augmented by the transfer of German industrial plants to Soviet territory, by the extraction of war reparations from East Germany, Hungary, Romania, and Bulgaria, by the establishment of Soviet-dominated joint enterprises, and by trading arrangements slanted in favor of the Soviet Union. The net outflow of resources from eastern Europe to the Soviet Union was approximately $15 billion to $20 billion in the first decade after World War II, an amount roughly equal to the total aid provided by the United States to western Europe under the Marshall Plan.[26] Moreover, during Stalin's time, Soviet leaders directly controlled the economic policies of the bloc governments as they steered the east European countries – all of which except Czechoslovakia had been predominantly agrarian during the prewar era – along the path of crash industrialization.

In later years, Soviet economic power stemmed from the sheer size of the Soviet economy compared to the east European economies, as well as from the Soviet Union's abundant natural resources and certain structural features of CMEA. The Soviet gross national product (GNP) was three to four times the size of the combined GNPs of all the other members of CMEA, and the Soviet Union possessed vast supplies of oil, natural gas, and raw materials, producing 97.7% of CMEA's crude oil, 90.4% of its natural gas, 97.4% of its iron ore, 72.7% of its steel, 98.2% of its manganese, and similar percentages of other resources in any given year.[27] The east European states, by contrast, were largely devoid of natural resources and were unable to purchase oil and other commodities in sufficient quantity on the world market because of their dearth of hard currency. What is more, from the mid-1970s on, the east European states found the relative prices for trade with the Soviet Union to be far more advantageous than the prices for comparable trade with non-CMEA countries. Hence, for economic as well as political reasons, the Soviet Union remained the dominant supplier and market for all the east European countries (except Romania after the early to mid-1960s). In the first half of the 1980s, roughly 40–50% of total east European foreign trade (including that of Romania) was conducted with the Soviet Union.

The extent of Soviet economic preponderance was even greater than this percentage may imply, for it does not take into account the nature of the bilateral trade relationship between the Soviet Union and each of its east European partners. In return for exports of oil, natural gas, and raw materials, which could easily have been sold for greater returns in the West, the Soviet Union imported machinery, electronic equipment, and consumer and agricultural products from eastern Europe, most of which were of inferior quality by Western (though not Soviet) standards and therefore would have been unmarketable outside the Soviet bloc or at least would have had to be sold at highly disadvantageous prices.[28] This "radial" trading pattern, with the USSR at the center, reinforced east European economic dependence on the Soviet Union in two respects.

First, the potentially autarkic Soviet economy, unlike the east European economies, depended relatively little on foreign trade, including trade with eastern Europe. Trading activities represented only 6–8% of the Soviet GNP compared to 45–50% of the east European GNPs, and most of the products the Soviet Union imported, especially those from eastern Europe, could have been replaced rather easily. In contrast, the energy supplies and other raw materials purchased by the east European countries from the USSR, especially those imported by the GDR, Hungary, Poland, and Bulgaria, were so vital to their economic development that a cutoff of the supplies would have resulted in economic chaos almost immediately.

Second, the capacity of the Soviet economy to absorb goods that would have been unacceptable on the world market allowed the east European countries to continue production of low-quality items without due regard for international competitiveness. This situation ultimately retarded economic progress in the east European states and forced even greater reliance on the Soviet market. The importance of the Soviet market, in turn, encouraged east European planners to concentrate on products whose sole customer was the Soviet Union, thus further distorting sectoral development in the east European economies and further attenuating the range of market options outside the Soviet Union. In all these ways, the Soviet Union avoided becoming economically vulnerable in its trade with other CMEA members, whereas the east European states found, by contrast, that "all aspects of [their] trade with the USSR – the level, the composition, the terms, and the balance and how it [was] financed – [were] critical for [their] economic development."[29]

The Soviet Union's economic power vis-à-vis eastern Europe was further strengthened by CMEA's non-convertible currency system. The individual east European currencies were "commodity non-convertible," meaning that currency from one east European country could not be converted for commodities in another country unless detailed arrangements based on national five-year plans were worked out in advance by the respective foreign trade ministries. To simplify these transactions, the CMEA countries used an accounting unit known as the "transferable ruble," which, despite its name, was not transferable at all even within the bloc, much less outside CMEA. Although limited multilateral clearing facilities for intra-CMEA trade did exist (at least after the early 1970s), in very few cases could one country's trade surpluses with another CMEA member actually be transferred to help balance trade deficits with a third. Instead, almost all trade within the bloc had to be conducted bilaterally, a pattern that, because of the USSR's dominant economic position, slanted intra-CMEA trade even further towards the Soviet Union.

The CMEA currencies were also "externally" non-convertible – that is, financially non-convertible outside the bloc. Hence, the east European states could not ordinarily obtain hard currency on foreign exchange markets and had to make do with what they could receive from exports, Western loans, and the limited reserves of CMEA's two banks.[30] Added to this were the protectionist pressures, inefficiency, and constraints on innovation generated by the centralized foreign-trading system in each east European country. These financial and systemic pressures inhibited the east European governments from conducting a greater portion of their trade with non-CMEA countries, leaving them with no real alternative but to conduct most of their trade bilaterally with other CMEA members, particularly the Soviet Union. The maintenance of a separate financial bloc among CMEA countries thereby reinforced Soviet economic preponderance.

In turn, the USSR was able to use its economic leverage to promote "socialist integration" within CMEA. In accord with Soviet preferences, "socialist integration" was pursued through greater intra-bloc coordination of centralized planning and control, especially in areas of advanced science and technology. Although this policy ensured that economic integration would not cause undue reliance on market mechanisms, the inefficiencies of centralized planning deprived most integrationist programs of even minimal flexibility, an obstacle compounded by the objections of some east European countries (most notably Romania) to plans for a precise "division of labor" among CMEA countries. Consequently, most attempts to develop formal mechanisms of economic integration, particularly supranational institutions, never came to fruition. Only a very modest degree of integration actually took place. Still, Soviet leaders were able to use informal pressure to help make up for the dearth of formal supranational institutions. Moreover, some of CMEA's multilateral and bilateral joint ventures, including joint energy production and refining, were successful. The CMEA countries also managed to form two multilateral banks – the International Bank for Economic Cooperation in 1964 and the International Investment Bank in 1971 – and to establish a Comprehensive Program of Integration in 1971 and a Comprehensive Program on Science and Technology in December 1985. These programs encouraged more coherent long-range planning and capital ventures within CMEA and a certain degree of specialization, and they also facilitated the implementation of reforms that, though market-oriented, were largely compatible with the exigencies of centralized planning.[31] In the end, however, intra-CMEA integration produced few tangible benefits for the Soviet Union.

The Limits of Soviet Power in Eastern Europe

In the first forty years after World War II, the Soviet Union at times fell short in its ability to control political trends in eastern Europe. This was due, in part, to the limited utility of Soviet military power. The USSR's armed presence in eastern Europe was formidable indeed, but not so formidable as to deter and overcome all threats to Soviet hegemony. Soviet military forces did not forestall challenges in Yugoslavia in 1948, East Germany in 1953, Poland and Hungary in 1956, Albania in 1961, Romania in the mid-1960s, and other countries on other occasions. Nor did they prevent certain of these challenges – in Yugoslavia and Albania and to a lesser extent in Romania – from succeeding. In addition, there were further constraints on the most obvious manifestation of Soviet military power, namely, the use of armed force. Invasions and the direct use of military force occurred only in the east European countries that were of critical geostrategic importance to the Soviet Union (i.e. the northern tier states and Hungary). Moreover, the prospect of incurring heavy casualties and of being compelled to undertake a bloody occupation of a "fraternal" east European country helped to induce Soviet leaders to forgo the direct use of force when it seemed likely that invading troops would encounter large-scale resistance among the indigenous armed forces and population. Such was the case, for example, with Yugoslavia, Romania, and Poland. Although this consideration did not figure as prominently when the decision was made in December 1979 to invade Afghanistan, the embroilment of Soviet troops in Afghanistan underscored the dangers of military intervention. During the Soviet Politburo's deliberations about Poland in 1980–1981, several of the highest leaders kept emphasizing that the Soviet Union must not become bogged down in a "second Afghanistan."[32]

Furthermore, even in cases when the Soviet Union did resort to the use of force, there were limits on what military power could accomplish in and of itself. This was especially apparent in Czechoslovakia after the August 1968 invasion, and it would have been equally true of Poland if Soviet troops had intervened massively in 1981. The use and the threat of armed force, though crucial for precluding unfavorable developments and safeguarding perceived Soviet interests in eastern Europe, were insufficient to assure long-term control in the region. To be sure, military power – whether in the form of Soviet troop deployments, the deterrent effect of past invasions, coercive pressure brought on by troop maneuvers, "internal solutions" such as occurred in Poland in 1981, or direct military intervention – was the underpinning of Soviet influence in eastern Europe during the whole period from 1945 to 1985. But the extent of Moscow's success in preserving a sphere of influence could not be determined by its military strength alone.

Much as there were limits on the efficacy of Soviet military power, so too were there limits on Soviet political leverage. Despite the extensive network of formal and informal controls wielded by Soviet leaders, and despite the commonality of interests that often existed between Soviet and east European elites, several east European countries attempted to deviate sharply from Soviet policy and even to seek outright autonomy. Such was the case in Yugoslavia and Albania (and to a lesser extent Romania), where Tito and Hoxha (and Ceauşescu) took the precautionary step of eliminating the pro-Moscow factions in their communist parties while staking out positions independent of the Soviet Union. A similar situation might have arisen in Czechoslovakia had Soviet tanks not moved in shortly before the Extraordinary 14th Congress of the Czechoslovak Communist Party was due to convene. Equally important, Soviet political controls were not able to forestall occasional revolts "from below," especially those originating from economic turmoil, as in East Germany in 1953, Hungary in 1956, and even more dramatically in Poland in 1980–1981.

Soviet political leverage in eastern Europe was also limited – in a more subtle but no less important way – by domestic political constraints within the Soviet Union itself. The legacy of Stalin's tight grip on the east European countries in the 1940s and early 1950s meant that any appreciable loosening of Soviet control over the region would encounter staunch opposition in the CPSU Politburo, as Khrushchev discovered in 1956–1957. Later on, when Brezhnev made a commitment to preserve the "socialist commonwealth" at all costs, the stakes of maintaining or losing that commitment were bound to grow over time. Hence, Soviet leaders became increasingly unwilling to take steps that could endanger the short-term cohesion of the socialist commonwealth. Proposals that might have engendered a looser but, in the long run, more viable Soviet–east European relationship – akin to the Soviet Union's relationship with Finland after World War II – were almost certainly rejected at an early stage, if they were broached at all. This constraint, in turn, circumscribed the flexibility of almost every aspect of Soviet policy in the region.

Perhaps the greatest limits on Soviet power in eastern Europe were on the economic side. On most of the occasions when the Soviet Union attempted to use its regional economic preponderance for coercive purposes – against Yugoslavia in 1948, Albania in 1961, and Romania in 1964–1965 – the sanctions and pressure achieved little and in many respects were counterproductive.[33] Yugoslavia and Romania escaped any lasting economic damage when they turned to the West for trade and assistance, and Albania ended up relying on the People's Republic of China to make up for the loss of Soviet aid (though the Albanian economy was more seriously hurt by the sanctions than either the Yugoslav or the Romanian economy). Thus, in each of these cases, the main effect of Soviet economic coercion was to widen the split between the east European state and the Soviet Union. In other cases where the *potential* for economic coercion would have been much greater, the actual *use* of coercion would have made no sense. During the crisis in 1980–1981, for example, a cutoff of Soviet oil shipments to Poland would have quickly brought the Polish economy to a halt. Such a step, however, would have served no purpose other than to create even greater turmoil. Hence, Soviet oil and natural gas exports and economic aid to Poland flowed without interruption during the entire crisis and, indeed, substantially increased. In private, Soviet officials complained bitterly about the economic burden that these extra shipments were imposing on the USSR, but they realized they had little choice.[34] The actual leverage that the Soviet Union could bring to bear in this case, as in numerous others, was much less than the country's economic potential alone would have suggested.

The limits of Moscow's economic power were also apparent in the perennial inability of the Soviet Union to alleviate the economic woes of the east European countries. From the mid-1950s on, Soviet officials were well aware that economic grievances in eastern Europe could easily translate into political discontent. Yet Moscow's efforts to promote better economic conditions in the region repeatedly faltered, at times because of a lack of concerted attention to the problem but more often because of limits on the Soviet Union's own economic vitality. The highly centralized economic system set up by Stalin was of some use in promoting "extensive" growth in the 1930s–1950s, but the system's pervasive inefficiencies, distorted incentives, and other shortcomings stymied efforts in the 1960s and 1970s to shift to an "intensive" growth strategy based on greater productivity and rapid technological progress.[35] Fundamental reform seemed the only way to rectify these deficiencies, but neither Brezhnev nor his two immediate successors were willing to venture far down this path, in part because of worries that sweeping economic reform might eventually require major political concessions as well. As a result, the Soviet Union in the early to mid-1980s was confronted by deepening stagnation at home and was still unable to assume more than a negligible role in the world economy. Vis-á-vis eastern Europe, Soviet economic power was of far greater importance, but even there the range of options was constrained by the Soviet economy's inherent weaknesses.

The Transformation of Soviet Policy in Eastern Europe, 1985–1991

After Mikhail Gorbachev came to power in March 1985, the Soviet–east European relationship initially changed very little. By the spring of 1988, however, Soviet policy towards eastern Europe started to loosen, adumbrating a fundamental shift in Gorbachev's approach. As the pace of *perestroika* and *glasnost* accelerated in the Soviet Union, the "winds of change" gradually filtered throughout the Eastern bloc, bringing long-submerged grievances and social discontent to the surface. Under growing popular pressure, the regimes in Hungary and Poland embarked in 1988–1989 on much more ambitious paths of reform than even Gorbachev himself had yet adopted. As ferment in those two countries and elsewhere in the region continued to increase, the tone of Gorbachev's public comments about eastern Europe grew bolder. By early 1989 it had become clear that the USSR was willing to permit far-reaching internal changes in eastern Europe that previously would have been ruled out and forcibly suppressed under the Brezhnev Doctrine.

Significant though the first wave of reforms in Hungary and Poland had been, the full magnitude of the forces unleashed by Gorbachev's policy in eastern Europe became apparent only during the last few months of 1989. Events that would have been unthinkable even a year or two earlier suddenly happened: peaceful revolutions from below in East Germany and Czechoslovakia, the dismantling of the Berlin Wall, popular ferment, and the downfall of Todor Zhivkov in Bulgaria, and violent upheaval and the execution of Nicolae and Elena Ceauşescu in Romania. As one orthodox communist regime after another collapsed, the Soviet Union expressed approval and lent strong support to the reformist governments that emerged. Soviet leaders also joined their east European counterparts in condemning previous instances of Soviet military interference in eastern Europe, particularly the 1968 invasion of Czechoslovakia.[36] Unlike in the past, when the Soviet Union had done all it could to stifle and deter political liberalization in eastern Europe, there was no doubt by the end of 1989 that the east European countries would have full leeway to pursue drastic economic, political, and social reforms, including the option of abandoning communism altogether.

In every respect, Gorbachev's approach to Soviet–east European relations from mid-1988 on was radically different from that of his predecessors. Previous Soviet leaders had sought to maintain communism in eastern Europe, if necessary through the use of armed force. Gorbachev, by contrast, wanted to avoid military intervention in eastern Europe at all costs. Hence, his paramount objective was to defuse the pressures in the region that might eventually have led to violent, anti-Soviet uprisings. This objective, in turn, required him to go much further than he initially anticipated. In effect, the Soviet Union ended up *promoting* internal crises in eastern Europe while there was still some chance of benefiting from them, rather than risk being confronted later on by widespread violence that would leave Gorbachev with little alternative other than to send in troops. The hope was that by supporting sweeping but peaceful change in the region over the near term, the USSR would never again have to contend with large-scale outbreaks of anti-Soviet violence, as Khrushchev had to do in 1956. This basic strategy, of encouraging and managing intra-Pact crises in order to prevent much more severe crises in the future, achieved its immediate aim, but in the process it both necessitated and ensured the complete demise of east European communism.[37]

By effectively doing away with the communist bloc, Gorbachev vastly improved the climate for East–West relations (including East–West trade) and eliminated the burden that eastern Europe had long imposed on Soviet economic and military resources. He also removed a major impediment to his domestic reform program. Whereas previous Soviet leaders had invoked the concepts of "socialist international-ism" and a "socialist commonwealth" to confer legitimacy on the traditional Marxist–Leninist model, Gorbachev and his aides could point to the developments in eastern Europe as evidence of the model's bankruptcy. The turmoil that Gorbachev allowed and even encouraged in the east-bloc countries thereby negated a key external prop on which his opponents in the CPSU might have relied for a rearguard attack. In all these respects, the dissolution of Soviet hegemony over eastern Europe was highly beneficial for Gorbachev's larger program.

On the other hand, Gorbachev's policy, for all its positive aspects, was fraught with serious costs. By late 1990, the Soviet Union was unable to salvage what little remained of its leverage in eastern Europe. Even before the Warsaw Pact was formally abolished at the beginning of July 1991, the limited effectiveness of the alliance had disappeared. All the internal political changes in eastern Europe that the Warsaw Pact was supposed to prevent ended up occurring in 1989–1990, most notably in the GDR. The elaborate command-and-control infrastructure that Soviet leaders worked so long to develop for the pact disintegrated, and pressures rapidly mounted for the withdrawal of all Soviet troops and weapons from the region. All Soviet forces were gone from Hungary and Czechoslovakia by mid-1991 and from Poland by September 1993. The final pullout of troops from eastern Germany in September 1994 brought to an end the presence of the former Soviet Army in eastern Europe, thus completing the demise of the Warsaw Pact.

The fate of CMEA was no better. Although most of the east European states after 1989 still relied heavily on the Soviet Union for trade and energy supplies, the in-exorable trend in the region was towards much greater economic interaction with the West, especially western Europe. The new east European governments regarded CMEA as a cumbersome, antiquated organization that should be abolished, and they drafted formal proposals to that effect. Soviet leaders, too, soon acknowledged that the organization had never come close to living up to its stated aims and that its functions had been overtaken by events. Even if drastic reforms could have been implemented in CMEA (which they were not), the organization was doomed by the upheavals of 1989–1990. Hence, like the Warsaw Pact, it was formally disbanded in mid-1991.

In all these ways, events moved so far and so fast in eastern Europe, and the Soviet Union's influence in the region declined so precipitously, that the fate of the whole continent eluded Gorbachev's control. The very notion of a "socialist common-wealth" lost its meaning once the Soviet Union not only permitted, but actually facilitated, the collapse of communist rule in eastern Europe. Despite the benefits Gorbachev gained from the disintegration of the bloc, his political fortunes at home suffered once the lingering remnants of the socialist commonwealth were formally dissolved. Domestic recriminations and controversy over the "loss" of eastern Europe contributed to the resurgence of harder-line forces in Moscow from the late summer of 1990 through the spring of 1991.[38] Not until after the aborted coup attempt in Moscow in August 1991, and the dissolution of the Soviet Union as a whole four months later, was it clear that Soviet hegemony in eastern Europe was gone for good. Any hopes that orthodox communist elements in Moscow might have had of someday resurrecting the "socialist bloc" and Soviet military hegemony were shattered once the Soviet state itself followed the Warsaw Pact and CMEA into oblivion.

Conclusion

Until the late 1980s the Soviet Union's determination to preserve a communist sphere of influence in eastern Europe was not in doubt. Despite important changes in Soviet policy and the growing complexity of the east European societies, the main Soviet objective in the region – the maintenance of a political-ideological bloc and a military buffer zone – remained unchanged. The gradual transition from "dominance" to "hegemony" after Stalin's death was never followed by a transition to "primacy" or anything close to it. Until Gorbachev came to power, the "rules of the game" within the communist bloc, as codified by Soviet military interventions in East Germany in 1953, Hungary in 1956, and Czechoslovakia in 1968, as well as by the threats against Poland in 1980–1981, still prohibited meaningful "deviations" from the basic principles of Marxism-Leninism. Under the Brezhnev Doctrine, any threat to the security of an east European com-munist regime, whether internal or external, was regarded as a threat to Soviet secu-rity as well. The Soviet Union's failure to relax its hegemony over eastern Europe and move towards a relationship of genuine primacy is what ultimately ensured the collapse of Soviet power in the region. The maintenance of a hegemonic relationship depended on the Soviet Union's willingness to resort, in extreme cases, to military force. Once the military option was no longer deemed viable in either Moscow or the east European countries, the whole edifice crumbled and there was nothing to take its place.

This is not to imply, however, that the collapse of the Soviet sphere of influence in the region was inevitable. Everything seems inevitable in retrospect, but the reality is always more complex. If Gorbachev had been determined to uphold communist rule in eastern Europe, as all his predecessors were, he undoubtedly could have succeeded. The Soviet Union in the late 1980s still had more than enough military strength to enforce the Brezhnev Doctrine, provided that officials in

Moscow had been willing to shed a good deal of blood if necessary. Gorbachev's acceptance and even encouragement of the peaceful disintegration of the communist bloc thus stemmed from a conscious choice on his part, a choice bound up with his domestic priorities and his desire to do away with the legacies of the Stalin era that had blighted the Soviet economy and Soviet technological prowess. Any Soviet leader who was truly intent on overcoming Stalinism at home had to be willing to implement drastic changes in policy vis-à-vis eastern Europe. Far-reaching liberalization and greater openness within the Soviet Union were incompatible with, and eventually would have been undermined by, a policy requiring military intervention on behalf of orthodox communist regimes in eastern Europe. The fundamental reorientation of Soviet domestic goals under Gorbachev therefore necessitated the relinquishment of Soviet hegemony over eastern Europe, and that in turn swiftly led to the outright collapse of Soviet power in the region, bringing an end to the Cold War.

Notes

1   As used in this chapter, the term "eastern Europe" refers primarily to the six countries other than the Soviet Union that were members of the Warsaw Pact until 1991: Bulgaria, Czechoslovakia, East Germany, Hungary, Poland, and Romania. A few references will also be made to Albania and Yugoslavia.

2   For an overview and critiques of dependency theory, see Rosen and Kurth, *Theories of Economic Imperialism*.

3   See, in particular, Zimmerman, "Dependency Theory and the Soviet–east European Hierarchical Regional System," 604–623; Clark and Bahry, "Dependent Development: A Socialist Variant," 271–293; Gochman and Ray, "Structural Disparities in Latin America and Eastern Europe, 1950–1970," 231–254; and Ray, "Dependence, Political Compliance, and Economic Performance," 111–136.

4   See, for example, Bull, *The Anarchical Society*, 213–225; Keal, *Unspoken Rules and Superpower Dominance*; Kaufman, *The Superpowers and their Spheres of Influence*; and Triska, *Dominant Powers and Subordinate States*. For recent samples of the vast literature on empire, see Doyle, *Empires*; Snyder, *Myths of Empire*; Kupchan, *The Vulnerability of Empire*; Lundestad, *The Fall of Great Powers* (Oxford: Oxford University Press, 1994); Kennedy, *The Rise and Fall of the Great Powers*; Gilpin, *War and Change in World Politics*; Lieven, *Empire: The Russian Empire and Its Rivals*; Demandt, *Das Ende der Weltreiche*; Muldoon, *Empire and Order*; Duverger et al., *Le Concept d'empire*; Eisenstadt, *The Political Systems of Empires*; Beissinger, "The Persisting Ambiguity of Empire," 149–184; and Beissinger, "Demise of the Empire State," 97–124. Beissinger rightly emphasizes that subjective perceptions underlie what we mean by "empire" and thereby make it a malleable concept over time – a concept dependent on prevailing attitudes.

5   This way of categorizing unequal power relationships is similar, though not identical, to the discussion in Bull, *The Anarchical Society*, 213–219.

6   For an overview, see Naimark and Gibianskii, *The Establishment of Communist Regimes in Eastern Europe*.

7   The notion of a trade-off between "viability" and "cohesion" is well presented in Brown, *Relations between the Soviet Union and Its East European Allies*.

8   On the early post-Stalin era in the Soviet bloc, see the relevant essays in Larres and Osgood, *The Cold War after Stalin's Death: A Missed Opportunity for Peace?*

9 Kramer, "The Early Post-Stalin Succession Struggle and Upheavals in East-Central Europe: Internal–External Linkages in Soviet Policymaking (Part 1)," 3–55.

10 These events are covered in detail in Kramer, *Crisis, Compromise, and Coercion in the Communist Bloc, 1956*. See also Kramer, "The Soviet Union and the 1956 Crises in Hungary and Poland," 163–215.

11 For a valuable overview of the Prague Spring, see Skilling, *Czechoslovakia's Interrupted Revolution*.

12 "K voprosu o polozhenii v Chekhoslovakii: Vypiska iz protokola no. 95 zasedaniya Politbyuro TsK ot 17 avgusta 1968 g.," no. P95/1 (Top Secret), August 17, 1968, in Arkhiv Prezidenta Rossiiskoi Federatsii (APRF), Fond (F.) 3, Opis' (Op.) 496, Delo (D.) 2, Prot. no. 38.

13 Kovalev, "Suverenitet i internatsional'nye obyazannosti sotsialisticheskikh stran," *Pravda* (Moscow), September 26, 1968, 4.

14 For an overview of the Solidarity era in Poland, see Paczkowski, *Drogo do "mniejszego zła": Strategia i taktika obozu władzy, lipiec 1980-stycień 1982*.

15 "Vneshnyaya politika PNR na nyneshnem etape (Politpis'mo)," July 9, 1981, Cable no. 595 (Top Secret) from Aristov, Soviet ambassador in Poland, in Rossiiskii Gosudarstvennyi Arkhiv Noveishei Istorii (RGANI), F. 5, O84, D. 596, Listy (Ll.) 21–34.

16 "Zasedanie Politbyuro TsK KPSS 29 oktyabrya 1980 goda: Materialy k druzhestvennomu rabochemu vizitu v SSSR pol'skikh rukovoditelei," October 29, 1980 (Top Secret), in RGANI, F. 89, O42, D. 31, L. 3.

17 See Kramer, *Soviet Deliberations during the Polish Crisis*, 41–45, 53–58. See also the interview with Colonel Ryszard Kukliński in "Wojna z narodem widziana od środka," *Kultura* (Paris), no. 4/475 (April 1987), 6–7, 17–19. Kukliński, as the top aide to General Wojciech Jaruzelski in 1980–1981, was one of five officers on the Polish General Staff responsible for devising the plans for martial law. He also was a spy for the US Central Intelligence Agency. He had to flee to the West in November 1981.

18 "TsK KPSS," no. 682-op (Top Secret/Special Dossier), August 28, 1980, from Mikhail Suslov, Andrei Gromyko, Yuri Andropov, Dmitrii Ustinov, and Konstantin Chernenko, in APRF, F. 83-op, O20, D. 5, L. 1.

19 Kramer, "Civil–Military Relations in the Warsaw Pact," 45–68.

20 "Grundsätze über die Vereinten Streitkräfte der Teilhenmerstaaten des Warschauer Vertrages und ihre Führungsorgane (für den Krieg)," GVS-Nr. A 468 858 (Top Secret), March 18, 1980, in Bundesarchiv-Militärarchiv in Freiburg, Archiv Zugangsnummer 32584.

21 See, for example, "Doświadczenia i wnioski z ćwiczenia 'Mazowsze,'" Military Exercise Report (Top Secret – Special Designation), compiled by the Polish General Staff, June 1963, in Archiwum Akt Nowych, Archiwum Komitetu Centralnego PZPR, Sygnatura 5008.

22 "Why We Treat Communist Countries Differently," *Department of State Bulletin*, 51 (April 1964), 13.

23 See, for example, Bluth, *The Two Germanies and Military Security in Europe*.

24 Khrushchev, *Vospominaniya – Vremya, lyudi, vlast'*, vol. 3, 10.

25 Andrew and Mitrokhin, *The Sword and the Shield*, esp. 262–275.

26 For estimates on the resource outflow, see Marer, "The Political Economy of Soviet Relations with Eastern Europe," 231–260.

27 US Central Intelligence Agency, *Handbook of Economic Statistics, 1987*, CPAS-870002 (September 1987), 103–104.

28 Smith, *The Planned Economies of Eastern Europe*, 155–157.

29 Bornstein, "Soviet–East European Economic Relations," 105–106.

30   Holzman, "CMEA Hard Currency Deficits and Rouble Convertibility," 73–91.
31   Stone, "CMEA's International Investment Bank and the Crisis of Developed Socialism,"
     47–70.
32   See Kramer, *Soviet Deliberations during the Polish Crisis*, 151, 162.
33   Freedman, *Economic Warfare in the Communist Bloc*.
34   Kramer, *Soviet Deliberations during the Polish Crisis*, 45, 78, 111–114, 127–128, 161–
     170. This same point was made in "Polozhenie v PORP posle IX S"ezda," Report no.
     857 (Top Secret), November 4, 1981, from Mal'tsev to Konstantin Rusakov, in RGANI,
     F. 5, O84, D. 596, Ll. 35–53, esp. 53.
35   Kornai, *The Socialist System*.
36   "Zayavlenie rukovoditelei Bolgarii, Vengrii, GDR, Pol'shi, i Sovetskogo Soyuza" and
     "Zayavlenie Sovetskogo pravitel'stva," *Izvestiya* (Moscow), December 5, 1989, 2.
37   Kramer, "The Collapse of East European Communism and the Repercussions within the
     Soviet Union (Part 1)," 178–256.
38   Kramer, "The Collapse of East European Communism and the Repercussions within the
     Soviet Union (Part 3)," 3–97.

Bibliography

Aleksandrov-Agentov, A.M., *Ot Kollontai do Gorbacheva: Vospominaniya diplomata, sovetnika
     A.A. Gromyko, pomoshchnika L.I. Brezhneva, Yu. V. Andropova, K.U. Chernenko i M.S.
     Gorbacheva* (Moscow: Mezhdunarodnye otnosheniya, 1993).
Andrew, Christopher M. and Vasili Mitrokhin, *The Sword and the Shield: The Mitrokhin Archive
     and the Secret History of the KGB* (New York: Basic Books, 1999).
Beissinger, Mark R., "Demise of the Empire State: Identity, Legitimacy, and the Deconstruction
     of Soviet Politics," in Crawford Young (ed.), *The Rising Tide of Cultural Pluralism: The
     Nation-State at Bay?* (Madison: University of Wisconsin Press, 1993).
Beissinger, Mark R., "The Persisting Ambiguity of Empire," *Post-Soviet Affairs* 11, no. 2,
     April–June 1995, 149–184.
Bluth, Christoph, *The Two Germanies and Military Security in Europe* (New York: Palgrave
     Macmillan, 2002).
Bornstein, Morris, "Soviet–East European Economic Relations," in Morris Bornstein, Zvi
     Gitelman, and William Zimmerman (eds.), *East–West Relations and the Future of Eastern
     Europe: Politics and Economics* (Boston: Allen & Unwin, 1981).
Brown, James F., *Relations between the Soviet Union and Its East European Allies: A Survey*,
     Report R–1742-PR (Santa Monica, CA: RAND Corporation, 1975).
Brzezinski, Zbigniew K., *The Soviet Bloc: Unity and Conflict*, revised and expanded edition
     (Cambridge, MA: Harvard University Press, 1967).
Bull, Hedley, *The Anarchical Society: A Study of Order in World Politics* (New York: Columbia
     University Press, 1977).
Clark, Cal and Donna Bahry, "Dependent Development: A Socialist Variant," *International
     Studies Quarterly* 27, no. 3, September 1983, 271–293.
Demandt, Alexander (ed.), *Das Ende der Weltreiche: vom Persen bis zur Sowjetunion* (Munich:
     C.H. Beck, 1997).
Domański, Paweł (ed.), *Tajne dokumenty Biura Politycznego, Grudzień 1970* (London: Aneks,
     1991).
"Doświadczenia i wnioski z ćwiczenia 'Mazowsze,'" Military Exercise Report (Top Secret –
     Special Designation), compiled by the Polish General Staff, June 1963, in Archiwum Akt
     Nowych, Archiwum Komitetu Centralnego PZPR, Sygnatura 5008.
Doyle, Michael W., *Empires* (Ithaca, NY: Cornell University Press, 1986).

Dubček, Alexander, *Hope Dies Last: The Autobiography of Alexander Dubček*, trans. by Jiří Hochman (New York: HarperCollins, 1993).

Duverger, Maurice et al. (eds.), *Le Concept d'empire* (Paris: Presses universitaires de France, 1980).

Eisenstadt, Shmuel, *The Political Systems of Empires* (New York: Free Press of Glencoe, 1963; republished by Transaction Books in 1993 with a new introduction by Eisenstadt).

Eisler, Jerzy (ed.), *Grudzień 1970 w dokumentach MSW* (Warsaw: Instytut Studiów Politycznych, 2000).

Eisler, Jerzy (ed.), *Co nam zostało z tych lat: Opozycja polityczna 1976–1980 z dzisiejszej perspektywy* (Warsaw: Instytut Pamięci Narodowej, 2003).

Freedman, Robert Owen, *Economic Warfare in the Communist Bloc: A Study of Soviet Economic Pressure against Yugoslavia, Albania, and Communist China* (New York: Praeger Publishers, 1970).

Gilpin, Robert, *War and Change in World Politics* (New York: Cambridge University Press, 1981).

Gochman, Charles S. and James Lee Ray, "Structural Disparities in Latin America and Eastern Europe, 1950–1970," *Journal of Peace Research* 16, no. 3, 1979, 231–254.

"Grundsätze über die Vereinten Streitkräfte der Teilnehmerstaaten des Warschauer Vertrages und ihre Führungsorgane (für den Krieg)," GVS-Nr. A 468 858 (Top Secret), March 18, 1980, in Bundesarchiv-Militärarchiv in Freiburg, Archiv Zugangsnummer 32584.

Hájek, Jiří, *Dix Ans après: Prague 1968–1978* (Paris: Éditions du Seuil, 1978).

Holzman, Franklyn D., "CMEA Hard Currency Deficits and Rouble Convertibility," in Nita G.M. Watts (ed.), *Economic Relations between East and West* (London: Macmillan, 1979).

Holzman, Franklyn D., *The Economics of Soviet Bloc Trade and Finance* (Boulder, CO: Westview Press, 1988).

Huszár, Tibor, *1968: Prága, Budapest, Moszkva. Kádár János és a csehszlovákiai intervenció* (Budapest: Szabad Tér, 1998).

Hutchings, Robert L., *Soviet–East European Relations: Consolidation and Conflict, 1968–1980* (Madison: University of Wisconsin Press, 1983).

Islamov, T.M. et al. (eds.), *Sovetskii Soyuz i vengerskii krizis 1956 goda: Dokumenty* (Moscow: ROSSPEN, 1998).

"K voprosu o polozhenii v Chekhoslovakii: Vypiska iz protokola no. 95 zasedaniya Politbyuro TsK ot 17 avgusta 1968 g.," no. P95/1 (Top Secret), August 17, 1968, in Arkhiv Prezidenta Rossiiskoi Federatsii (APRF), Fond (F.) 3, Opis' (Op.) 496, Delo (D.) 2, Prot. no. 38.

Kamiński, Łukasz, *Przed i po 13 grudnia: Państwa bloku wschodniego wobec kryzysu w PRL, 1980–1982* (Warsaw: Instytut Pamié8ci Narodowej, 2006–2007).

Kaufman, Edy, *The Superpowers and Their Spheres of Influence: The United States and the Soviet Union in Eastern Europe and Latin America* (London: Croom Helm, 1976).

Keal, Paul, *Unspoken Rules and Superpower Dominance* (New York: St. Martin's Press, 1983).

Kennedy, Paul M. *The Rise and Fall of the Great Powers: Economic Change and Military Conflict from 1500 to 2000* (New York: Random House, 1987).

Khrushchev, N.S., *Vospominaniya – Vremya, lyudi, vlast'*, 4 vols. (Moscow: Moskovskie novosti, 1999).

Kornai, János, *The Socialist System: The Political Economy of Communism* (Princeton, NJ: Princeton University Press, 1992).

Kovalev, S., "Suverenitet i internatsional'nye obyazannosti sotsialisticheskikh stran," *Pravda* (Moscow), September 26, 1968, 4.

Kowalski, Lech, *Generał ze skaza: Biografia wojskowa gen. armii Wojciecha Jaruzelskiego* (Warsaw: Oficyna Wydawnicza, 2001).

Kramer, Mark, "Civil–Military Relations in the Warsaw Pact: The East European Component," *International Affairs* 61, no. 4, Winter 1984–1985, 45–68.

Kramer, Mark, "The Czechoslovak Crisis and the Brezhnev Doctrine," in Carole Fink, Philipp Gassert, and Detlef Junker (eds.), *1968: The World Transformed* (New York: Cambridge University Press, 1998).

Kramer, Mark, "The Soviet Union and the 1956 Crises in Hungary and Poland: Reassessments and New Findings," *Journal of Contemporary History* 33, no. 2, April 1998, 163–215.

Kramer, Mark, "The Early Post-Stalin Succession Struggle and Upheavals in East-Central Europe: Internal–External Linkages in Soviet Policymaking (Part 1)," *Journal of Cold War Studies* 1, no. 1, Winter 1999, 3–57.

Kramer, Mark, "The Early Post-Stalin Succession Struggle and Upheavals in East-Central Europe: Internal–External Linkages in Soviet Policymaking (Part 2)," *Journal of Cold War Studies* 1, no. 2, Spring 1999, 3–39.

Kramer, Mark, "The Early Post-Stalin Succession Struggle and Upheavals in East-Central Europe: Internal–External Linkages in Soviet Policymaking (Part 3)," *Journal of Cold War Studies* 1, no. 3, Fall 1999, 3–67.

Kramer, Mark, *Soviet Deliberations during the Polish Crisis, 1980–1981* (Washington, DC: Cold War International History Project, 1999).

Kramer, Mark, "The Collapse of East European Communism and the Repercussions within the Soviet Union (Part 1)," *Journal of Cold War Studies* 5, no. 4, Fall 2003, 178–256.

Kramer, Mark, "The Collapse of East European Communism and the Repercussions within the Soviet Union (Part 2)," *Journal of Cold War Studies* 6, no. 4, Fall 2004, 3–64.

Kramer, Mark, "The Collapse of East European Communism and the Repercussions within the Soviet Union (Part 3)," *Journal of Cold War Studies* 7, no. 1, Winter 2005, 3–97.

Kramer, Mark, *Crisis, Compromise, and Coercion in the Communist Bloc, 1956: The Soviet Union and Upheavals in Hungary and Poland* (Cambridge, MA: Harvard University Press, 2009).

Kula, Henryk, *Dwa oblicza grudnia "70: Oficjalne-rzeczywiste* (Gdańsk: Wydawnictwo DJ, 2000).

Kula, Henryk, *Grudzień 1970: "Oficjalny" i rzeczywisty* (Gdańsk: Wydawnictwa L & L, 2006).

Kupchan, Charles A., *The Vulnerability of Empire* (Ithaca, NY: Cornell University Press, 1994).

Larres, Klaus and Kenneth A. Osgood (eds.), *The Cold War after Stalin's Death: A Missed Opportunity for Peace?* (Lanham, MD: Rowman & Littlefield, 2006).

Lieven, Dominic, *Empire: The Russian Empire and Its Rivals* (New Haven, CT: Yale University Press, 2000).

Lundestad, Geir (ed.), *The Fall of Great Powers* (Oxford: Oxford University Press, 1994).

McAdam, Doug, Sidney Tarrow, and Charles Tilly, *Dynamics of Contention* (New York: Cambridge University Press, 2001).

Marer, Paul, "The Political Economy of Soviet Relations with Eastern Europe," in Steven J. Rosen and James R. Kurth (eds.), *Theories of Economic Imperialism* (Lexington, MA: Lexington Books, 1978).

Mastny, Vojtech and Malcolm Byrne (eds.), *A Cardboard Castle? An Inside History of the Warsaw Pact, 1955–1991* (Budapest: Central European University Press, 2005).

Mlynář, Zdeněk, *Nachtfrost: Erfahrungen auf dem Weg vom realen zum menschlichen Sozialismus* (Cologne: Europäische Verlagsanstalt, 1978).

Muldoon, James, *Empire and Order: The Concept of Empire, 800–1800* (New York: St. Martin's Press, 1999).

Murrell, Peter, *The Nature of Socialist Economies: Lessons from Eastern European Foreign Trade* (Princeton, NJ: Princeton University Press, 1990).

Naimark, Norman and Leonid Gibianskii (eds.), *The Establishment of Communist Regimes in Eastern Europe* (Boulder, CO: Westview Press, 1997).

Nalepa, Edward Jan, *Wojsko Polskie w Grudniu 1970* (Warsaw: Bellona, 1990).

Nalepa, Edward (ed.), *Wojsko Polskie w wydarzeniach grudniowych 1970 roku: Materiały z sympozjum 17 grudnia 1970 r.* (Warsaw: Wojskowy Instytut Historyczny, 1991).

Paczkowski, Andrzej, *Drogo do "mniejszego zła": Strategia i taktika obozu władzy, lipiec 1980-stycień 1982* (Kraków: Wydawnictwo Literackie, 2002).

Perović, Jeronim, "The Tito–Stalin Split: A Reassessment in Light of New Evidence," *Journal of Cold War Studies* 9, no. 2, Spring 2007, 32–63.

"Polozhenie v PORP posle IX S″ezda," Report no. 857 (Top Secret), November 4, 1981, from V.F. Mal'tsev to Konstantin Rusakov, in RGANI, F. 5, O84, D. 596, Ll. 35–53.

Poznanski, Kazimierz Z., "Pricing Practices in the CMEA Trade Regime: A Reappraisal," *Europe–Asia Studies* 45, no. 5, 1993, 923–930.

Ray, James Lee, "Dependence, Political Compliance, and Economic Performance: Latin America and Eastern Europe," in Charles W. Kegley Jr. and Pat McGowan (eds.), *The Political Economy of Foreign Policy Behavior* (Beverly Hills, CA: Sage Publications, 1981).

Rosen, Steven J. and James R. Kurth (eds.), *Theories of Economic Imperialism* (Lexington, MA: Lexington Books, 1978).

Skilling, H. Gordon, *Czechoslovakia's Interrupted Revolution* (Princeton, NJ: Princeton University Press, 1976).

Smith, Alan H., *The Planned Economies of Eastern Europe* (London: Croom Helm, 1983).

Snyder, Jack, *Myths of Empire: Domestic Politics and International Ambition* (Ithaca, NY: Cornell University Press, 1991).

Stone, David R., "CMEA's International Investment Bank and the Crisis of Developed Socialism," *Journal of Cold War Studies* 10, no. 3, Summer 2008, 47–70.

Triska, Jan F. (ed.), *Dominant Powers and Subordinate States: The United States in Latin America and the Soviet Union in Eastern Europe* (Durham, NC: Duke University Press, 1986).

"TsK KPSS," no. 682-op (Top Secret/Special Dossier), August 28, 1980, from Mikhail Suslov, Andrei Gromyko, Yuri Andropov, Dmitrii Ustinov, and Konstantin Chernenko, in APRF, F. 83-op, O20, D. 5, L. 1.

US Central Intelligence Agency, *Handbook of Economic Statistics, 1987*, CPAS-870002 (September 1987).

"Vneshnyaya politika PNR na nyneshnem etape (Politpis'mo)," July 9, 1981, Cable no. 595 (Top Secret) from B.I. Aristov, Soviet ambassador in Poland, in Rossiiskii Gosudarstvennyi Arkhiv Noveishei Istorii (RGANI), F. 5, O84, D. 596, Listy (Ll.) 21–34.

Volokitina, T.V. et al. (eds.), *Vostochnaya Evropa v dokumentakh rossiiskikh arkhivov, 1944–1953*, 2 vols., vol. 1: *1944–1948 gg.* and vol. 2: *1949–1953 gg.* (Novosibirsk: Sibir'skii khronograf, 1997 and 1999).

Volokitina, T.V. et al. (eds.), *Sovetskii faktor v Vostochnoi Evrope, 1944–1953: Dokumenty*, 2 vols., vol. 1: *1944–1948* and vol. 2: *1949–1953* (Moscow: ROSSPEN, 1999 and 2002).

"Why We Treat Communist Countries Differently," *Department of State Bulletin*, 51 (April 1964), 13.

Williams, Kieran, *The Prague Spring and Its Aftermath: Czechoslovak Politics, 1968–1970* (New York: Cambridge University Press, 1997).

"Wojna z narodem widziana od środka," interview with Colonel Ryszard Kukliński, in *Kultura* (Paris), no. 4/475, April 1987, 5–57.

"Zasedanie Politbyuro TsK KPSS 29 oktyabrya 1980 goda: Materialy k druzhestvennomu rabochemu vizitu v SSSR pol'skikh rukovoditelei," October 29, 1980 (Top Secret), in RGANI, F. 89, O42, D. 31, Ll. 1–6.

"Zayavlenie rukovoditelei Bolgarii, Vengrii, GDR, Pol'shi, i Sovetskogo Soyuza" and
    "Zayavlenie Sovetskogo pravitel'stva," *Izvestiya* (Moscow), December 5, 1989, 2.
Zimmerman, William, "Dependency Theory and the Soviet–East European Hierarchical
    Regional System: Initial Tests," *Slavic Review* 37, no. 4, December 1978, 604–623.

Further Reading

For a standard work covering the formation and evolution of the Soviet bloc from the 1940s
through the early 1960s, see Zbigniew K. Brzezinski, *The Soviet Bloc: Unity and Conflict*,
revised and expanded edition (Cambridge, MA: Harvard University Press, 1967). A more
recent set of essays on the formation and early years of the Soviet bloc, drawing on newly
available archival sources, is Norman M. Naimark and Leonid Gibianskii (eds.), *The Establishment
of Communist Regimes in Eastern Europe* (Boulder, CO: Westview Press, 1997). For a concise
survey of the Soviet–Yugoslav split, drawing on newly available documents and analyses, see
Jeronim Perović, "The Tito–Stalin Split: A Reassessment in Light of New Evidence," *Journal
of Cold War Studies* 9, no. 2, Spring 2007, 32–63. Valuable essays on the Soviet bloc in the
larger East–West context during the first few years after Stalin's death can be found in Klaus
Larres and Kenneth A. Osgood (eds.), *The Cold War after Stalin's Death: A Missed Opportunity
for Peace?* (Lanham, MD: Rowman & Littlefield, 2006). A lucid survey of Soviet–east European
relations in the period from the aftermath of the invasion of Czechoslovakia to the rise of
Solidarity in Poland is Robert L. Hutchings, *Soviet–East European Relations: Consolidation
and Conflict, 1968–1980* (Madison: University of Wisconsin Press, 1983).

Among many useful works on Soviet–east European economic relations are Alan H. Smith,
The Planned Economies of Eastern Europe (London: Croom Helm, 1983); Peter Murrell, *The
Nature of Socialist Economies: Lessons from Eastern European Foreign Trade* (Princeton, NJ:
Princeton University Press, 1990); Franklyn D. Holzman, *The Economics of Soviet Bloc Trade
and Finance* (Boulder, CO: Westview Press, 1988); and Kazimierz Z. Poznanski, "Pricing
Practices in the CMEA Trade Regime: A Reappraisal," *Europe–Asia Studies* 45, no. 5, 1993,
923–930.

On the periodic crises within the Soviet bloc, see Mark Kramer, "The Early Post-Stalin
Succession Struggle and Upheavals in East-Central Europe: Internal–External Linkages in
Soviet Policymaking" (parts 1, 2, and 3), *Journal of Cold War Studies* 1, no. 1, Winter 1999,
3–54; 1, no. 2, Summer 1999, 3–38; and 1, no. 3, Fall 1999, 3–65; Mark Kramer, *Crisis,
Compromise, and Coercion in the Communist Bloc, 1956: The Soviet Union and the Upheavals
in Hungary and Poland* (Cambridge, MA: Harvard University Press, 2008); Mark Kramer,
"The Czechoslovak Crisis and the Brezhnev Doctrine," in Carole Fink, Philipp Gassert, and
Detlef Junker (eds.), *1968: The World Transformed* (New York: Cambridge University Press,
1998), 111–175 (and my forthcoming book, *The Soviet–Czechoslovak Crisis and the Brezhnev
Doctrine, 1968: The Prague Spring and the August Invasion*); Mark Kramer, *Soviet Deliberations
during the Polish Crisis, 1980–1981* (Washington, DC: Cold War International History Project,
1999); and the collection of articles and translated documents in the *Cold War International
History Project Bulletin*, issue no. 11 (Winter 1998), 5–133. On the collapse of communism
in eastern Europe and the impact it had on the Soviet Union, see Mark Kramer, "The Collapse
of East European communism and the Repercussions within the Soviet Union" (parts 1, 2,
and 3), *Journal of Cold War Studies* 5, no. 4, Fall 2003, 178–256; 6, no. 4, Fall 2004, 3–64;
and 7, no. 1, Winter 2005, 3–97.

Of the many document collections that have appeared on the early period of Soviet–east
European relations, two are particularly worth mentioning, both published as large two-volume
sets: T.V. Volokitina et al. (eds.), *Vostochnaya Evropa v dokumentakh rossiiskikh arkhivov,
1944–1953*, 2 vols., vol. 1: *1944–1948 gg.* and vol. 2: *1949–1953 gg.* (Novosibirsk: Sibir'skii
khronograf, 1997 and 1999); and T.V. Volokitina et al. (eds.), *Sovetskii faktor v Vostochnoi*

Evrope, 1944–1953: Dokumenty, 2 vols., vol. 1: *1944–1948* and vol. 2: *1949–1953* (Moscow: ROSSPEN, 1999 and 2002). For a valuable collection of documents on the Soviet Union and the Hungarian revolution, see T.M. Islamov et al. (eds.), *Sovetskii Soyuz i vengerskii krizis 1956 goda: Dokumenty* (Moscow: ROSSPEN, 1998). For declassified documents on the Polish crisis of 1980–1981, see the two-volume collection edited by Łukasz Kamiński, *Przed i po 13 grudnia: Państwa bloku wschodniego wobec kryzysu w PRL, 1980–1982* (Warsaw: Instytut Pamięci Narodowej, 2006–2007). For a collection of translated East-bloc documents on the Warsaw Pact from the beginning of the alliance to the end, see Vojtech Mastny and Malcolm Byrne (eds.), *A Cardboard Castle? An Inside History of the Warsaw Pact, 1955–1991* (Budapest: Central European University Press, 2005).

CHAPTER FIVE

Economic Developments in Western and Eastern Europe since 1945

IAN JACKSON

While western and eastern Europe pursued profoundly different approaches to organizing their economies after 1945, the two regions shared some similar experiences in terms of their economic fortunes in the second half of the twentieth century. Despite the slump of the 1930s, the western Europeans remained committed to capitalism and the market economy. The eastern European nations, however, traveled in a radically different economic direction. Before World War II the Soviet Union had achieved relatively high levels of growth through central planning, and, with Moscow's determination to build a strategic sphere of influence as a means of preventing encirclement by the capitalist nations, communism was imposed on several central and eastern European countries during the 1940s. Whereas western European capitalism was characterized by the interplay of the private and public sectors of the economy, Soviet-style central planning rejected the private market in favor of state direction and ownership of the economic means of production.

Nevertheless, both western and eastern Europe enjoyed a substantial period of economic growth from the early 1950s to the mid-1970s. As this chapter will demonstrate, economic growth was achieved in the two regions by radically divergent objectives and means. During the 1970s, moreover, western and eastern Europe endured an arduous phase of economic decline and adjustment. The western Europeans shifted the focus of their economic policies from government intervention to deregulation and the free market. As central planning failed to deliver the high economic growth levels of the 1950s and 1960s, the eastern European governments attempted to reform communism by reducing state involvement in economic life. By the late 1980s, reform only succeeded in highlighting the deficiencies of the command economy approach. In less than a decade eastern Europe and the former Soviet republics dispensed with communism and embraced democracy and the market economy. It is a supreme irony that in May 2004 a number of these former communist states would join the European Union (EU). Among the ten countries that became EU members in 2004, the largest number of countries ever admitted at one time, were the eastern European countries Hungary, Poland, the Czech Republic,

A Companion to Europe since 1945, First Edition. Edited by Klaus Larres.
© 2014 John Wiley & Sons, Ltd. Published 2014 by John Wiley & Sons, Ltd.

Slovakia, Slovenia, and the three Baltic countries Estonia, Latvia, and Lithuania. In January 2007 the former Soviet satellite states Romania and Bulgaria became members of the European Union.

Western Europe: Reconstruction and Economic Boom, 1945–1973

The global economic malaise of the interwar period together with the devastation wrought by World War II profoundly influenced western European economic thinking and policy-making in the second half of the twentieth century. After 1945, governments turned increasingly to the concept of the "mixed economy" in the quest for growth, stability, and prosperity. The concept of the mixed economy essentially called for direct government intervention in the financial affairs of the state through fiscal management, i.e. taxation and public spending, state-owned enterprise in tandem with the private sector, and the creation of a welfare state.

Why did the western European governments seek a larger role for the state in the economy in the three decades following the war? According to Yergin and Stanisław, there were three motivating factors. First, the parlous state of the economies of the European nations after the conflict necessitated immediate government action to organize and direct recovery programs to tackle the problems of food shortages, physical destruction, which had brought industry and agriculture to a standstill, the obsolescence of machinery and shortage of capital equipment. Second, governments had learnt the harsh lessons of the global recession of the 1930s. Anxious to avoid future slumps and mass unemployment, European leaders and civil servants believed that the state should be actively involved in organizing, directing, and regulating economic life. Finally, in the immediate aftermath of the war, capitalism appeared to many to be a largely discredited economic system. The Soviet Union had financed a successful war effort against Nazi Germany through central planning and communist parties in western Europe seized the opportunity to proclaim a viable alternative to the market economy in their political manifestos.[1]

Another major influence on European economic policy-making in the middle of the twentieth century was the economist John Maynard Keynes. In many ways, Keynes was the intellectual godfather behind the concept of the mixed economy model that was implemented by the western European governments after World War II. Having combined an illustrious career as an academic economist with extensive government service, Keynes was a vocal critic of the market approach that was in vogue in the 1920s and 1930s. In his masterwork *General Theory of Employment, Interest and Money* published in 1936, Keynes presented his grand scheme for an approach to economic management based on active government intervention and regulation. Shifting the focus from monetary to fiscal policy, he eloquently argued that the most important object of governments should be full employment. Since full employment could not be achieved by relying on market forces and the simple balance between supply and demand as suggested by classical economists, Keynes concluded that public investment and expenditure on public works could not only create employment opportunities, but also increase the purchasing power of consumers and thus increase productivity and prosperity. Governments could finance budget deficits through borrowing and draw on a range of fiscal tools to macro-manage the economy. For example, during a recession an increase in public expenditure could expedite economic recovery or taxation could be reduced to stimulate economic activity.[2] What made Keynes's ideas appealing to many western European leaders in the 1940s was that through his theories about fiscal management he was offering an alternative to both the market economy model and socialist central planning. By suggesting that government become the central actor in the economy, Keynes was not abandoning capitalism, but merely reforming it.[3]

With the cessation of hostilities in 1945, all of the European governments were faced with the arduous task of reconstructing their economies, rebuilding their infrastructure, and feeding their destitute populations. Perhaps the biggest problems confronting each of the western European states were the loss of production, the shortage of raw materials and foodstuffs, and the paralysis of industry, commerce, and agriculture.[4] Financial troubles also abounded. Many of the European governments were plagued by financial crises that had been produced by huge budget deficits, swollen money supplies, and a scarcity of foreign currency supplies caused by the war effort. In fact, the acute shortage of dollars in western Europe created an imbalance in the world economy, which elicited a generous offer of financial assistance from the United States in the form of the Marshall Plan.[5] The role of the Marshall Plan in the economic recovery of western Europe has long been a contentious issue in the literature on post-World War II international relations.

The American historian Michael J. Hogan contends that Marshall Aid was crucial to both the economic and political stability of the continent in the late 1940s. For Hogan the Marshall Plan helped not only to revitalize production and encourage cooperation between the European states, but also to deter the rise to power of communist parties sympathetic to the Soviet Union. American financial assistance, he also asserts, was important from a strategic point of view: the Marshall Plan was instrumental in bolstering the region against the threat of a potential Soviet invasion and takeover of the continent.[6] Conversely, the British economic historian Alan S. Milward has sought to demonstrate through a quantitative analysis of the western European economies in the 1940s that the Marshall Plan had little effect on the industrial and commercial revival of the region. Rather, Milward believes that the economic recovery of western Europe had actually commenced before the first shipments of aid reached the continent. He concedes that American financial assistance did provide European states with valuable capital goods, which were essential for much-needed public investment, but points out that US exports to western Europe during the Marshall Plan period fell and the rise of communism in countries such as Italy and France was thwarted by domestic politics rather than the psychological impact of external financial assistance.[7] Contemporary scholarship has tended to support the findings of Milward's thesis, but it is important to note that the Marshall Plan certainly expedited the economic recovery of the western European nations by providing governments with the finance to pursue expansionary policies and counterpart funds which complemented domestic sources of capital.[8]

If Keynesian thinking and foreign assistance were two of the pillars on which the edifice of western Europe's economic boom of the 1950s and 1960s was built, interventionist government economic policies provided the third pillar. Public-sector spending in the industrial world mushroomed from 27% of GDP in 1950 to 43% in 1973. The social safety net provided by welfarism, furthermore, compressed unemployment levels to just 3% during 1950–1973.[9] While the leading governments in western Europe shared similar objectives in domestic economic management, there were subtle differences in terms of the approaches of individual countries.[10] The big three economies of West Germany, France, and Britain, for example, were each more or less committed to the twin goals of economic growth and stability during the formative decades after the war.

The West German approach involved a strong focus on price stability and balance-of-payments equilibrium at the expense of full employment and growth. The country nevertheless, enjoyed extraordinary levels of growth Marshall Plan in the first half of the 1950s, of almost 10% and thereafter an annual GDP increase of 4% until 1973. As a result of West Germany's commitment to price stability, inflation remained low throughout the 1950s and 1960s, and the FRG ran regular balance-of-payments surpluses, which fortified the Deutschmark in the foreign exchange markets.[11] The West German economy, moreover, became the economic powerhouse of the European Economic Community (EEC) from the inception of the common market in January 1958.

Successive French governments tended to target growth as the central aim in macroeconomic policy during the 1950s. France's exceptionally high GDP growth rate of 6.8% between 1945 and 1975 was due to both heavy public investment and flexibility within the labor force as successive governments sought to move the economy away from its traditional concerns with agriculture and mining towards manufacturing industry. Under the Rueff–Pinay reforms of 1958, the de Gaulle government opened the French economy to external competition and set in motion an export-drive approach to domestic economic growth.[12]

The British approach contrasted sharply with those of West Germany and France. Far from an exclusive preoccupation with either monetary stability or economic growth, British governments tried simultaneously to balance full employment against price stability, growth, external equilibrium, and social equality. While undoubtedly this constituted the most Keynesian approach to fiscal management, British policy goals placed severe strains on the economy. Lagging behind its continental neighbors with GDP annual growth of just 3% during the 1950s, the United Kingdom's political commitment to full employment and the welfare state resulted in so-called "stop–go" cycles.[13] Essentially, during a period of economic growth governments could not restrain demand, culminating in monetary instability as inflation rose, the balance-of-payments deficit grew and sterling, as an international monetary reserve currency, was buffeted in the international money markets. In the 1960s economic weakness not only undermined growth and internal monetary stability, but also forced the Wilson government to devalue sterling, end the prestigious position of the pound sterling as an international currency, and curtail Britain's global defense commitments east of Suez.[14]

Recent research has indicated that the economic boom experienced by western Europe and the rest of the industrialized world during the first two postwar decades was due to the rapid expansion of trade under the Bretton Woods regime. The Bretton Woods international trade and monetary arrangements married global economic openness with national autonomy for governments to pursue welfarism and demand management insulated from the harsh socioeconomic implications of debilitating adjustments required to correct balance-of-payments deficits. As Jeffrey A. Frieden has pointed out, world trade doubled in volume every ten years between 1945 and 1970. This was a faster rate of growth than even the "Golden Liberal Age" of 1880–1914 when the world economy was virtually free of barriers to trade and investment under the Gold Standard. In the case of western Europe, exports ballooned from US$19 billion in 1950 to US$244 billion in 1973.[15]

The success of European manufacturers in world markets was, in part, owing to the existence of the General Agreement on Tariffs and Trade (GATT), a rule-based liberal trade regime, which was instrumental in reducing tariffs on non-agricultural goods to below 9% by the 1990s. The establishment of the EEC, moreover, intensified trade among the western European nations, provided protection from foreign competition outside the continent and allowed member governments to fund domestic welfare states and regional economic development. In the words of Frieden, "European economic integration fused classical liberalism and social democracy, with great success."[16]

Eastern Europe: Challenging the West, 1945–1975

By 1949 seven eastern European countries had organized their economies along the principles of central planning. The Soviet Union had been the first country to adopt the command economic model in the 1920s. With their incorporation into the Soviet sphere of influence after World War II, Bulgaria, Poland, Hungary, Czechoslovakia, and Romania employed the central planning approach in economic policy. While autonomous from the Soviet Union, Yugoslavia also favored a variation on the command economy model, and Josef Stalin, the Soviet leader, ensured that the economy of the newly created German Democratic Republic (GDR) was based on the tenets of socialist planning and state ownership of the means of production. In the first three postwar decades, eastern Europe enjoyed economic growth levels comparable with those of the Western capitalist states. Derek H. Aldcroft and Steven Morewood estimate that the Soviet Union and eastern Europe were responsible for 30% of total world industrial output by 1970.[17] Yet, economic growth came at a high price. While the command economy model enabled the eastern Europe states to industrialize rapidly, growth and stability proved unsustainable owing to the inflexibility of the system. Indeed, by the 1970s the eastern European socialist economies were suffering critical food shortages, technology was becoming obsolete, and the policy of central planning had failed to adapt to the changing conditions of the world economy.

The command economic model was comprised of three distinct features. First, whereas, in the mixed economy model, industry was partially nationalized, in the communist economic system the state directed, managed, and owned the means of production. The state chose the industries in which it wanted to invest and to which it wanted to allocate resources and labor. In the absence of private industry, a free market, and competition, state-owned corporations that possessed

monopolies within their specific sectors conducted all commerce. Central bureaucracies controlled by the Communist Party operated other aspects of economic
activity such as banking and finance, trade, and transport. Second, the eastern
European economies that followed the Soviet model were centrally planned.
In essence, a vast state bureaucracy regulated economic life. The bureaucracy
was divided into different ministries, with each department responsible for
a specific aspect of the economy. The central bureaucracy's main functions were to
select and set growth targets for particular industries; oversee the progress and development of each industrial sector; and apportion adequate capital resources and labor
to fulfill the aims of the plan. Finally, the Soviet-style command economy was
geared specifically towards obtaining faster levels of growth than the Western
capitalist nations.[18]

After all, the communist governments perceived themselves to be in an ideological
struggle with capitalism. This was due, in part, to the Cold War that raged between
the Western and Soviet blocs during the second half of the twentieth century. To be
sure, the Soviet economy had been designed by Stalin and his successors not only
for the purposes of rapid industrialization, but also for advanced military production.
Thus, given their preoccupation with surpassing the capitalist nations in terms of
economic growth and development, the Soviet bloc countries concentrated their
efforts on heavy goods industries. Central plans de-emphasized agriculture, consumer
goods and services in favor of industrial sectors such as machinery, iron, steel, chemicals, and electronics.

Additionally, some of the eastern European countries created a regional economic
regime designed to intensify trade contact and pool resources between governments.
In January 1949 the Soviet Union together with Czechoslovakia, Poland, Hungary,
and Bulgaria formed the Council for Mutual Economic Assistance (CMEA). By 1950
the founding members were joined by Albania, Poland, and the GDR. Scholars have
debated whether the CMEA was created primarily as an economic vehicle for consolidating Soviet control over eastern Europe or reflected a genuine attempt by the
communist governments to establish an organization to facilitate trade between their
nations.[19] As the process of central planning made trade problematic between the
eastern European countries, the CMEA was to provide an integrated framework to
overcome the obstacles to commercial contact inherent in domestic protectionism
and currency inconvertibility. During 1958–1961 the central organs of the CMEA
began to emerge: the membership adopted the "transferable rouble" to overcome
the problem of inconvertibility, a goods pricing system was introduced and the governments agreed to adopt an "international socialist division of labour." Under the
international socialist division of labor, some of the members would concentrate their
economies on agricultural production, while others would specialize in industrialization. It was hoped that the combined efforts of the CMEA nations would yield
maximum growth in the agricultural and industrial sectors and raise living standards
throughout the region.[20]

If the economies of the eastern European countries are assessed in terms of growth
during 1945–1975, then the command economy experiment can be judged a success.
After an initially slow period of recovery after World War II, the communist nations
recorded industrial output levels of 10% over a 20-year period from 1950 to 1970.

Moreover, the major shift from agrarian concerns to industrialization across the region modernized the economies of the eastern European countries and closed the gap with the advanced capitalist economies of their neighbors in the west of the continent. Under the centrally planned economic system, full employment was achieved and a noticeable transformation occurred in the number of workers moving from jobs in agriculture to industry. Another major success was the expansion of heavy industry in eastern Europe. The process of central planning ensured that investment and resources were concentrated in the key industries of machinery, chemicals, coal, iron, and steel.[21]

Yet, despite high economic growth levels, the command economy model did not produce financial stability or adequate standards of living in eastern Europe. It could be argued that the biggest shortcoming of central planning was that it neglected consumption. Eastern European living standards remained much lower than those in western Europe throughout the remaining decades of the twentieth century. More significantly, food shortages caused periodic crises of confidence in the efficacy of central planning, as the state funnelled vast amounts of resources into heavy industry to the detriment of agricultural production. By the standards of the Western capitalist countries, goods produced in the communist countries were often poorly manufactured and of inferior quality.

Central planning also failed because of its inflexibility. Until the reforms of the 1970s, state bureaucrats adhered rigidly to the planning process, motivated solely by the realization of targets. As a result, there was little investment in new technologies and little regard for the efficient utilization of resources across all sectors of the economy. In this regard, the Soviet Union paid the heaviest price for its commitment to the military–industrial complex and its economic and strategic rivalry with the West. Nuclear parity with the United States, which can be viewed as a remarkable achievement of the Soviet command economy and its central planning procedures, brought the Soviet Union to the fringes of economic and financial meltdown by the early 1980s and was arguably a crucial contribotry factor in the fall of communism as a viable economic system in the immediate aftermath of the Cold War.[22] The reforms implemented in the 1970s and 1980s actually weakened rather than strengthened the Soviet economy and highlighted the fatal flaws of central planning.

Western Europe: Stagflation and Stability, 1973–2000

By the early 1960s most of western Europe experienced economic growth and prosperity. The economies of the western European countries registered annual GDP growth rates of 5% on average. Industrial production had tripled in France, Italy, and West Germany since the 1940s; agricultural production across the continent also reached new postwar high levels; and the formation of the EEC had stimulated economic cooperation and trade between the member countries.[23] Yet by the mid-1970s the economic boom had run its course. What were the reasons for this sudden reversal in western Europe's economic fortunes? The economic malaise of the 1970s can be explained by a number of external and internal factors. The chief external factor was the oil crisis of 1973, which triggered a recession in the economies of the industrial nations. Internally, inflation was the scourge that undermined the performance of the European mixed economies and called into question the efficacy of Keynesian demand–management.[24] In their struggle to respond to the dual problems of low growth and high inflation, or "stagflation," governments jettisoned fiscal for monetary policy approaches in the late 1970s and early 1980s.

The decision by the Middle Eastern oil producers to increase the price of fuel in 1973 sent economic shock waves throughout the industrial world. Much of the postwar economic boom had been due to the growth of what were termed the "energy-intensive sectors" of the Western economies. The new scarcity of oil as a result of astronomical energy prices increased industrial production costs and squeezed profit margins. As production costs rose and profits fell, other parts of the domestic economy became caught in the vicious circle: tax revenues declined, unemployment climbed, and inflation spiralled. What was more, as the terms of trade swung in favor of the Organization of Petroleum Exporting Countries (OPEC), the balance-of-payments surpluses that many European countries had enjoyed in the 1960s were replaced by debilitating deficits.

While the energy crises contributed to the economic slowdown of western Europe in the 1970s, the major economies of the continent were affected to varying degrees. Worst hit by the oil shock were Britain, France, and Italy. Each of these countries had to implement austere deflationary programs to reduce their burgeoning balance-of-payments deficits and stabilize their exchange rate positions.[25] In fact, in 1976 Britain was forced to seek financial assistance from the International Monetary Fund (IMF) to bail out the Labour government and rescue the pound sterling in the international currency markets. West Germany was least affected by the energy crisis. Like the United States and Japan, the FRG's relatively stable monetary position enabled it to counterbalance the oil deficits with a surge in exports in the middle of the decade.

The oil crisis, however, was not the main cause of the economic downturn that bedeviled western Europe in the 1970s. The seeds of the economic malaise were sown by the very Keynesian fiscal policies that had paved the way for the two decades of sustained growth that followed World War II. As we observed, the mixed economy model placed heavy emphasis on government intervention to maintain high levels of employment, social security spending and market regulation. Keynesian fiscal management, nevertheless, could not reconcile full employment with low inflation. This was the conundrum that most of the leading western European countries, with the exception of West Germany which enjoyed low inflation levels, were required to grapple with throughout the 1950s and 1960s. For Britain and France, in particular, inflation gave rise to persistent economic instability in the latter part of the twentieth century. The limitations of the Keynesian approach proved that it was not possible to pursue full employment and run budget deficits conterminously without experiencing high levels of inflation. Low levels of growth, moreover, were attributable to the fact that western Europe began to lose its industrial competitiveness and technological superiority to the newly industrializing nations, specifically in the automobile, steel, and capital goods sectors.[26]

During the course of the 1970s a highly influential school of economists championing free enterprise and limited government emerged on the political scene. Strongly influenced by the writings of Friedrich von Hayek, an Austrian economist based in London, the Monetarist School argued that the only way inflation could be suppressed and economic growth restored was if governments recognized the primacy of monetary over fiscal policy. Monetarists such as the Nobel laureate Milton Friedman profoundly influenced the United States and the United Kingdom governments in the 1980s. Even the continental European countries began to embrace monetarist ideas in an effort to overcome their inflationary epidemics.

Friedman and the Monetarists believed that governments had placed too much faith in pump-priming fiscal tools and that, instead, economic stability could be achieved if political leaders and civil servants attended to the growth of the domestic money supply. By regulating the supply of money in the economy through interest rate manipulation, governments could keep inflation in check and ensure steady growth. The Monetarists were convinced that less government was better. They called for lower taxes and reduced spending on social services and public works, and opposed state intervention in the economy. By keeping the public and private sectors of the economy separate, industry and enterprise would be allowed to flourish, generating employment and prosperity. The Monetarists also advocated free trade and floating exchange rates. Currency exchange rates, they argued, should be determined by market conditions and not by governments or international organizations. Similarly, with regard to free trade they stressed the importance of removing barriers to external commerce and creating a competitive world economic environment.[27]

The 1980s was a decade of economic recovery for western Europe after the slump that had characterized the 1970s. Borrowing liberally from the ideas of the Monetarist School, the leading European governments placed financial stability at the center of their economic agendas. They took action on a number of fronts to control inflation. In particular, they instituted measures to improve the state of public finances, including reducing public expenditure and international borrowing, two of the cornerstones of the Keynesian mixed economy approach. western European interest rates also began to rise in the early 1980s both in response to inflation and the strength of the dollar.

While western Europe succeeded for the most part in stemming the inflationary tide, the continent was subject to levels of unemployment not witnessed since the 1920s. High unemployment in western Europe was largely caused by the OPEC oil shock and the subsequent recession from the beginning of the 1970s, inflexible labor markets, and the weakening of industrial bargaining, especially in Britain.[28] During the postwar boom, the western European economies enjoyed full employment. By contrast, during the decade of the economic slump, levels of unemployment across the continent accelerated from 2.5% in 1973 to over 10% in the mid-1980s.[29]

On the positive side, the European integration project was given new impetus with the accession of Greece in 1981 and Spain and Portugal in 1986 as members of the EEC. Under the Single European Act (SEA) of 1987, the 12 member states agreed to create a single market by 1992. The single European market (SEM) was designed to remove all barriers to trade, investment, and competition within the European Community (EC). It was to become the largest trading area in the world, boasting a potential market of 344 million consumers in the early 1990s. The SEM was to be the prelude to monetary unification and eventual political integration.[30]

In economic terms, the 1990s are synonymous with the great American boom. From 1994 to 2000 the US economy grew at an annual rate of almost 4% of GDP. No comparable economic expansion occurred in the big three economies of the European Union. The average EU growth rate for the decade was in the region of 2.1%. Although some countries such as the United Kingdom and Ireland recorded growth in excess of the western European average, Germany and France continued to struggle with sluggish economic performances. For Germany, the two chief obstacles to growth were the persistence of unsatisfactory levels of unemployment and the ongoing costs of reunification that had been achieved in October 1990. The French economy was also hampered by high unemployment, with the annual rate touching 12% before dipping slightly at the end of the decade. France did manage to record an impressive growth rate of 3% in the late 1990s, with inflation falling to just 1% per year.[31] In new millennium, the major challenges facing the EU generally are the fortunes of the new currency, the euro, the future threat to the provision of social security posed by the continent's ageing population, and the financial uncertainty posed by a global credit crisis, which began with the collapse of the sub-prime mortgage market in the United States in the autumn of 2007.

Eastern Europe: Crisis and Reform, 1975–2000

Much like the Western capitalist countries, the eastern European communist states experienced a downturn in their economic fortunes in the 1970s. But unlike their counterparts in the West, the economic crisis that afflicted in the Soviet bloc countries was precipitated not by energy shortages, but the cracks that were beginning to appear in the command economy approach. The CMEA failed to live up to its members' expectations. Multilateral trade appeared to be virtually impossible given the absence of market mechanisms and the incompatibility of the diverse planning apparatuses of the CMEA membership. In response, eastern European countries had increasingly looked West to their capitalist counterparts for trade agreements to supply consumer goods and industrial products in the late 1960s.[32]

The 1970s began in a positive vein for the Soviet Union and its eastern European satellites. The United States appeared keen to improve relations with the communist countries, commence arms controls talks with Moscow, and expand commercial contacts with eastern Europe. Partially liberalized trade and commercial contact with the West was to have both a positive and negative effect on eastern Europe. On the positive side, the communist governments could import much-needed technology and consumer goods for their ailing economies. Yet trade liberalization was to have an adverse impact on the financial stability of the centrally planned eastern European economies. The attempt to bridge the technology gap with the West through imports drove the balance-of-payments positions of countries such as Poland into deficit. With little or no demand for Soviet or eastern European manufactured goods in the West, exports in the communist countries struggled to keep apace with imports. The problem was compounded by the region's heavy dependence on borrowing from

Western banks. As a result, high indebtedness coupled with enormous trade imbalances stunted economic growth in eastern Europe during the late 1970s and early 1980s.[33]

The eastern European economies were hindered by a series of internal setbacks. During the 1970s and 1980s, agricultural production declined rapidly across the region. Environmental factors were blamed for much of the hardship and food shortages created by the agrarian crisis. But it had become apparent that severe winters and crop failures were not the only reasons for inadequate agricultural production. State farms, in particular, were becoming increasingly inefficient and unable to deliver the levels of production required by the central bureaucracies to feed the population. The renewed arms race of the early 1980s brought the economy of the Soviet Union to the brink of bankruptcy. As military expenditure touched 15% of total GNP, the manufacturing, industrial, and agricultural sectors of the economy were starved of investment and the Soviet Union was encumbered by shortages of basic consumer goods and services.

Soviet foreign policy was another huge strain on the economy. The invasion of Afghanistan proved to be an expensive misadventure, which committed Moscow to billions of roubles in annual occupation costs over a nine-year period. The effectiveness of the central planning model, moreover, was called into question. Although the command economy approach had delivered quite impressive results for the first two decades after World War II, its rigidity and incapacity to incorporate new technologies and practices into the production process led to diminished growth and inefficiency.

There had been some attempts to reform the communist economic system in the 1960s and 1970s. Several eastern European countries had tried to increase worker productivity and growth by improving living standards and allowing the directors of factories and manufacturing plants more autonomy with regard to managing their enterprises.[34] It was not until the mid-1980s, however, that sweeping changes to the operation of the command economy were proposed and implemented. Following in the footsteps of one of his predecessors, Yuri Andropov, Mikhail Gorbachev was determined to resuscitate the Soviet economy on coming to power in 1985. While he did not want to discard the communist principles that had defined the Soviet Union since the beginning of the twentieth century, Gorbachev believed that structural reform of both the political and economic life of the country was urgently needed. To achieve his ambitious aims he expounded a dual policy approach of *glasnost*, or "openness," and *perestroika*, or "economic reform."

Glasnost involved gradually liberalizing Soviet society. In effect, Gorbachev relaxed the strict ban of free speech and the restriction on religious worship, and sought to make the Communist Party more accountable to the people. He envisaged a more transparent political system that would root out corruption and separate the role and functions of the Communist Party and the state.[35] The policy of *perestroika* was an outgrowth of *glasnost*, in that the Soviet economy would also be subject to limited liberalization. Even though Gorbachev did not wish to jettison the socialist ethos inherent in the centrally planned economy, he believed that some sectors of economic activity could operate more effectively in private hands. In order to allow for private ownership andthe profit incentive, Gorbachev passed a law in 1988 which permitted the establishment of cooperatives. These were enterprises usually in the consumer goods and service sectors of the economy, which were owned by groups of individuals and traded for private profits. The Soviet leader's most significant break with the command economy model was his decision to dramatically reduce the role of the Communist Party in economic activity. Control of the state economic apparatus was retained by central ministries but was overseen by Gorbachev after his election as president of the Soviet Union by the Congress of People's Deputies.[36]

Undoubtedly, Gorbachev's reforms transformed the political and economic systems of the Soviet Union. The decision to partially liberalize Soviet society and the command economy proved the catalyst that led the eastern European countries to relinquish communism in favor of democracy and capitalism. Over the course of Gorbachev's tenure as leader, the Soviet economy ground to a halt. It was evident that his efforts to restructure the command economy were not having the desired effect. In fact, *glasnost* and *perestroika* may have expedited the demise of the Soviet Union, as the policies unearthed the fatal flaws of the system. The centrally planned economy could not coexist with, let alone function in, an open society with a private market. Gorbachev's reforms provided no solutions to the growing food shortages, the lack of consumer goods, and the ballooning budget deficits that were a product of the Soviet Union's commitment to military spending and defense. Military expenditure did fall in the late 1980s because of the arms controls talks and agreements between the Soviet Union and the United States, but by this stage the economy was in a state of virtual collapse. Low growth rates produced stagflation and popular unrest as the Soviet people, inspired by developments in eastern Europe, took to the streets to protest against their meager standard of living.[37] Even Gorbachev's well-documented and well-meaning crusade to tackle the problem of alcoholism backfired. New laws restricting the consumption of alcohol and taxes on the beverage deprived the state of what would have been valuable revenues during a period of high inflation and negative economic growth.

Encouraged by the liberal policies of Gorbachev, especially his decision to dispense with the Brezhnev Doctrine and pull Soviet troops out of Afghanistan in 1988, the eastern European countries started to loosen the shackles that had bound them to Moscow for the past four decades. Together with political and social transformation, which resulted in the ousting of communist leaders, the holding of democratic elections, and the formation of open societies, the eastern European countries desired rapid reform in the economic sphere. During 1989–1992 the six eastern European communist countries and the newly independent states that had comprised the former Soviet Union completed the transition from centrally planned to market economies.

As Robert Solomon notes, the process had three phases. First, the eastern European countries had to institute strict macroeconomic measures that entailed the abolition of price controls and subsidies and a monetary policy geared towards deflation. Second, new institutions were established to create the financial infrastructure required for a market economy. In a short period of time, laws concerned with property rights, a central and private banking system, a tax system, and free enterprise culture were hastily assembled. Finally, once the conditions governing supply and demand had begun to function smoothly, the eastern European countries embarked on the privatization of industry, as firms were sold to investors. The barriers to international trade were also removed, as private firms sought to sell their goods and services in external as well as internal markets.[38]

How have the eastern European countries fared since the market revolution of the early 1990s? It is instructive to examine the examples of the Czech Republic and Poland, two new entrants into the EU in 2004, and the economic adjustment troubles of Russia. The Czech Republic and Poland were two of the economic success stories of the so-called velvet revolutions of 1989. As a newly created sovereign state in 1992, the Czech Republic became a model newly emerging market economy in less than a decade. The relatively smooth path to capitalism was due to several major reforms, which swept away the last vestiges of the Soviet-style command economy that had caused social unrest and economic stagnation in the 1970s and 1980s. By and large the Czech Republic adhered to the above-mentioned three-phase transition model identified by Solomon. Price controls were removed, currency convertibility was introduced, and tight monetary policy was observed in order to stabilize public finances and suppress inflation. Massive privatization of publicly owned industries provided important revenue for the state, and the latent Czech enterprise culture that had lain dormant during almost half a century of communism quickly replaced the void left by the central planned economy.[39]

For Poland the situation was similar, if more dramatic. The new Polish government applied a type of "shock therapy" to hasten the transition to capitalism. Despite some initial public apprehension regarding the new economic system, an enterprise culture was fostered and macroeconomic policies aimed at stabilizing Poland's financial position were put in place.[40]

Russia, by contrast, experienced a rocky transition to market capitalism. The high inflation caused by the Gorbachev reforms spilled into the 1990s, leaving Russia's external accounts in a hazardous state. In March 1994 a loan of US$1.5 billion from the IMF was secured with the assistance of the United States, but little could be done to reverse the shaky position of the Russian economy. Some commentators even called for a Marshall Plan for the country.[41] Unlike privatization in the Czech Republic and Poland, privatization in Russia was tinged with corruption, nepotism, and favoritism. Capital flight ensued as investors moved their money out of the country after the international financial crisis of 1997–1998 during which the rouble was devalued. By the turn of the millennium the Russian economy was so feeble that not only the country's capitalist system but also its precarious democratic political system was threatened.[42]

Russia nevertheless rebounded from the economic meltdown of the late 1990s to become one of the world's leading oil producers and an "energy superpower" of the twenty-first century.[43] The country's energy reserves, at the time of writing, comprise of 20% of the world's supply of natural gas and 7% of global oil output.[44] Through the state-run energy company *Gazpron*, Russia has become one of the world's major oil and gas producers and suppliers. As well as yielding Russia an abundance of currency reserves, oil has proved to be a potent political weapon in the hands of the Kremlin. In 2006 and 2007, Moscow curtailed gas exports to Ukraine and cut off oil supplies to Belarus. While Russia eventually agreed to recommence energy supplies to both countries, the EU expressed concern at President Vladimir Putin's willingness to use oil as a tool of economic statecraft. As global energy reserves have begun to dwindle, the EU has become dependent on Russia for its oil and gas needs, currently importing 30% of its oil and 44% of its natural gas supplies from Russia. Clearly, European leaders fear that the EU members could be held to ransom by Moscow over energy supplies if there is deterioration in diplomatic relations. There is no consensus within the EU on how to address the issue of Russia's "hard soft power." The European governments, for the most part, have aimed to balance the maintenance of existing supplies through political engagement with Moscow against attempting to locate new energy markets to reduce reliance on Russian oil and gas. [45]

Conclusion

After 1945, western and eastern Europe pursued divergent economic models and approaches on the paths to growth and prosperity. Anxious to avoid the policy mistakes of the Great Depression which engulfed the world economy in the 1930s, the western European governments implemented what the economic historian Barry Eichengreen has termed "coordinated capitalism." Coordinated capitalism involved direct government action in economic affairs in the form of fiscal management, state-owned and private enterprise, and welfarism. Strongly influenced by Keynesian economic theory, western European governments prioritized full employment together with public investment and expenditure. With the recovery of the western European economies after World War II, the region enjoyed an uninterrupted period of economic growth lasting into the late 1960s. The rapid recovery of western Europe was due not only to effective domestic demand management, but also the international financial and trade arrangements negotiated at Bretton Woods in 1944. The continent benefited from the boom in global trade from 1945 to 1970 facilitated by significant reductions in tariffs under the GATT. Moreover, the creation of the EEC in 1958 intensified regional trade between the continental neighbors while providing manufacturers with insulation from foreign competition in the form of a common external tariff. The global economic slowdown of the 1970s had a profound impact on the western European economy as a whole. While inflation spiralled, economic growth dwindled. Despite the shift from Keynesianism to monetarism, western European economic growth remained slack in the 1980s and 1990s. By the turn of the millennium, the region's economic performance paled in comparison with the double-digit growth levels of the Asian newly industrializing countries.

For the first two postwar decades, the eastern European economy also experienced high levels of growth. Employing the command economic model, the eastern European socialist governments eschewed private industry in favor of state control of the means of production. Economic affairs were regulated by a vast state bureaucracy which set growth targets for specified industries and monitored the progress and development of each industrial sector. By the 1970s, however, the shortcomings of the command economic model had become apparent. The eastern European countries were unable to sustain the high levels of growth they had experienced in the 1950s and 1960s. Facing shortages in critical technology components, they sought an expansion of East–West trade and began to borrow heavily from Western banks. In the 1980s, Gorbachev's internal economic reforms and attempt to integrate the Soviet Union into the world economy only appeared to hasten the demise of the command system, pushing the country to the verge of financial collapse. As the eastern European countries seceded from the Soviet empire, they began to democratize and build market economies. Within two decades a number of the former satellite states had joined the EU as fully fledged democracies with burgeoning economic growth rates. For Russia, the 1990s were to prove a decade of economic toil as it grappled with the vagaries of market capitalism. Yet, under Putin's presidency the country re-emerged as a powerful force in Eurasia and a significant actor in world politics thanks to its vast energy resources.

Notes

1 Yergin and Stanisław, *The Commanding Heights*, 21–22.
2 Skidelsky, *John Maynard Keynes: The Economist as Saviour, 1920–1937*, 537–571.
3 Yergin and Stanisław, *The Commanding Heights*, 39–42.
4 Wegs and Ladrech, *Europe since 1945: A Concise History*, 4th edition, 65–69.
5 Aldcroft, *The European Economy, 1914–2000*, 4th edition, 104–111.
6 Hogan, *The Marshall Plan*, 26–28, 430–443.
7 Milward, *The Reconstruction of Western Europe*, 92–113, 465–471.
8 See, for example, Newton, *The Global Economy*, pp 36–40.
9 Frieden, *Global Capitalism*, 299.
10 Urwin, *A Political History of Western Europe since 1945*, 4th edition, 125–130.
11 Hallett, "West Germany," 87–94.
12 Lynch, "France," 55–69.
13 Cairncross, "The United Kingdom," 30–39.
14 Dell, *The Chancellors*, 315–346.
15 Frieden, *Global Capitalism*, 288–289.
16 Frieden, op. cit, 287.
17 Aldcroft and Moorewood, *Economic Change in Eastern Europe*, 125.
18 Hanson, "The Soviet Union," 205–211.
19 van Brabant, *Socialist Economic Integration*, 19–20; van Brabant, *Economic Integration in Eastern Europe*, 18.
20 Bideleux and Jeffries, *A History of Eastern Europe*, 543–544.
21 Aldcroft, *The European Economy*, 167.
22 Aldcroft and Moorewood, *Economic Change in Eastern Europe*, 156–169.
23 Hitchcock, *The Struggle for Europe*, 131–133.
24 Aldcroft, *The European Economy*, 197–204.
25 For details see Aldcroft, *The European Economy*, 195–196; Yergin, *The Prize*, 613–617.
26 Wegs and Ladrech, *Europe since 1945*, 287–288.
27 Friedman's ideas are succinctly summarized in Friedman, *Capitalism and Freedom*.
28 Lawson, *The View from No. 11*, 76–100, 287–299; Middleton, *The British Economy since 1945*, 93–96.
29 Eichengreen, *The European Economy since 1945*, 263.
30 Armstrong and Bulmer, *The Governance of the Single European Market*, 13–22.
31 Solomon, *The Transformation of the World Economy*, 2nd edition, 56–61.
32 Kornai, *The Socialist System*, 356–357.

33 Aldcroft, *The European Economy*, 251–257.
34 Swain and Swain, *Eastern Europe since 1945*, 118–145.
35 McCauley, *Gorbachev*, 63–66.
36 Sakwa, *Gorbachev and his Reforms*, 268–295.
37 McCauley, *The Soviet Union, 1917–1991*, 2nd edition, 364–366.
38 Solomon, *Transformation of the World Economy*, 99–100.
39 Crampton, *Eastern Europe in the Twentieth Century and Beyond*, 2nd edition, 441–442.
40 Fowkes, *The Post-Communist Era*, 111–116.
41 Cox, *US Foreign Policy after the Cold War*, 58–61.
42 Gustafson, *Capitalism Russian-Style*, 137–149, 219–234.
43 Gvosdev, "The Bear's Croquet Ground," 54.
44 Simpson, "Russia Wields the Energy Weapon".
45 Stent, "Berlin's Russia Challenge," 46–47.

Bibliography

Aldcroft, Derek, *The European Economy, 1914–2000*, 4th edition (London: Routledge, 2001).

Aldcroft, Derek and Steven Moorewood, *Economic Change in Eastern Europe since 1918* (London: Edward Elgar, 1995).

Armstrong, Kenneth and Simon Bulmer, *The Governance of the Single European Market* (Manchester: Manchester University Press, 1998).

Bideleux, Robert and Ian Jeffries, *A History of Eastern Europe: Crisis and Change* (London: Routledge, 1998).

Cairncross, Alec, "The United Kingdom," in Andrew Graham with Anthony Seldon (eds.), *Government and Economies in the Postwar World: Economic Policies and Comparative Performance, 1945–85* (London: Routledge, 1990).

Cox, Michael, *US Foreign Policy after the Cold War: Superpower without a Mission?* (London: Pinter, 1995).

Crampton, R.J., *Eastern Europe in the Twentieth Century and Beyond*, 2nd edition (London: Routledge, 1997).

Dell, Edmund, *The Chancellors: A History of the Chancellors of the Exchequer since 1945* (London: HarperCollins, 1996).

Eichengreen, Barry, *The European Economy since 1945: Coordinated Capitalism and Beyond* (Princeton, NJ: Princeton University Press, 2006).

Fowkes, Ben, *The Post-Communist Era* (Basingstoke: Macmillan, 1999).

Frieden, Jeffrey A., *Global Capitalism: Its Rise and Fall in the Twentieth Century* (New York: W.W. Norton, 2006).

Friedman, Milton, *Capitalism and Freedom* (Chicago: Chicago University Press, 1962).

Gustafson, Thane, *Capitalism Russian-Style* (Cambridge: Cambridge University Press, 1999).

Gvosdev, Nikolas K., "The Bear's Croquet Ground," *National Interest* no. 94, March/April 2008, 54–55.

Hallett, Graham, "West Germany," in Andrew Graham with Anthony Seldon (eds.), *Government and Economies in the Postwar World: Economic Policies and Comparative Performance, 1945–85* (London: Routledge, 1990).

Hanson, Philip, "The Soviet Union" in Andrew Graham with Anthony Seldon (eds.), *Government and Economies in the Postwar World: Economic policies and comparative performance, 1945–85* (London: Routledge, 1990), 205–211.

Hitchcock, William I., *The Struggle for Europe: The History of the Continent since 1945* (London: Profile Books, 2003).

Hogan, Michael J., *The Marshall Plan: America, Britain and the Reconstruction of Western Europe, 1947–1952* (Cambridge: Cambridge University Press, 1987).

Kornai, János, *The Socialist System: The Political Economy of Socialism* (Oxford: Oxford University Press, 1992).

Lawson, Nigel, *The View from No. 11: Memoirs of a Tory Radical* (London: Bantam, 1992).

Lynch, Frances B., "France," in Andrew Graham with Anthony Seldon (eds.), *Government and Economies in the Postwar World: Economic Policies and Comparative Performance, 1945–85* (London: Routledge, 1990).

McCauley, Martin, *The Soviet Union, 1917–1991*, 2nd edition (London: Longman, 1993).

McCauley, Martin, *Gorbachev* (London: Longman, 1998).

Middleton, Roger, *The British Economy since 1945* (Basingstoke: Macmillan, 2000).

Milward, Alan S., *The Reconstruction of Western Europe, 1945–1951* (London: Methuen, 1984).

Newton, Scott, *The Global Economy, 1945–2000: The Limits of Ideology* (London: Arnold, 2004).

Sakwa, Richard, *Gorbachev and His Reforms, 1985–1990* (London: Philip Allan, 1990).

Simpson, Emma, "Russia Wields the Energy Weapon," February 2, 2006, BBC News, http://www.news.bbc.co.uk/go/pr/fr/-/1/hi/world/europe/4708256.stm (accessed April 9, 2008).

Skidelsky, Robert, *John Maynard Keynes: The Economist as Saviour, 1920–1937* (London: Macmillan, 1992).

Solomon, Robert, *The Transformation of the World Economy*, 2nd edition (Basingstoke: Macmillan, 1999).

Stent, Angela, "Berlin's Russia Challenge," *National Interest*, no. 88, March/April 2007, 46–51.

Swain, Geoffrey and Nigel Swain, *Eastern Europe since 1945* (Basingstoke: Palgrave Macmillan, 1998).

Urwin, Derek W., *A Political History of Western Europe since 1945*, 4th edition (London: Longman, 1997).

van Brabant, Josef M., *Socialist Economic Integration* (Cambridge: Cambridge University Press, 1980), 19–20.

van Brabant, Josef M., *Economic Integration in Eastern Europe* (London: Harvester Wheatsheaf, 1989), 18.

Wegs, J. Robert and Robert Ladrech, *Europe since 1945: A Concise History*, 4th edition (New York: St. Martin's Press, 1996).

Yergin, Daniel, *The Prize: The Epic Quest for Oil, Money and Power* (New York: The Free Press, 1991).

Yergin, Daniel and Joseph Stanisław, *The Commanding Heights: The Battle between Government and the Marketplace that Is Remaking the Modern World* (New York: Simon and Schuster, 1998).

Further Reading

Readers interested in exploring the themes of this chapter in more detail should begin with Barry Eichengreen's *The European Economy since 1945: Coordinated Capitalism and Beyond* (Princeton, NJ: Princeton University Press, 2006). Eichengreen, a leading economic historian of Europe, provides a lucid and stimulating account of the main economic developments in both western and eastern Europe that is useful to both economists and non-specialists.

For the global background to economic developments in Europe and the impact of ideas on policy, see Daniel Yergin and Joseph Stanisław, *The Commanding Heights: The Battle between Government and the Marketplace that Is Remaking the Modern World* (New York: Simon and Schuster, 1998) and Jeffrey A. Frieden, *Global Capitalism: Its Rise and Fall in the Twentieth Century* (New York: W.W. Norton, 2006). Another accessible general survey is Derek H. Aldcroft, *The European Economy, 1914–2000*, 4th edition (London: Routledge, 2001).

For more specific information on the eastern European economic experience, see Derek Aldcroft and Steven Moorewood, *Economic Change in Eastern Europe since 1918* (London: Edward Elgar, 1995).

Chapter Six

The End of Empires: Decolonization and Its Repercussions

David R. Devereux

The withdrawal of European powers from their colonial possessions outside of the continent represents one of the most critical changes in the geopolitical balance in the world in the post-1945 period. Not only did this process transform the place European nations held in the world in general, it also unleashed political and social forces that continue to transform the European continent in the twenty-first century. Although the age of empire is now over, its impact on both the "colonizing" nations and those that were "colonized" was deep and profound. Europe today is still in the process of accepting the legacies of empire, be it in terms of reduced world power, diminished influence overseas, but perhaps most importantly, in the communities of recent immigrants from the old empires that transform the whole idea of what being "European" means.[1] After years of obscurity, the study of imperialism and decolonization has enjoyed a resurgence owing to renewed interest in the interactions between colony and the metropolis and also the legacy of empire found in much of the developing world and indeed in Europe. This resurgence has also influenced a wide range of disciplines, from literature to politics and sociology, as well as history.[2]

The European Empires in 1945

Six western European nations could be considered "imperial" powers: the United Kingdom, France, the Netherlands, Belgium, Portugal, and Spain. A seventh European nation, Russia, could also be considered an "imperial" power by virtue of its domination of the Soviet Union, a group of theoretically equal republics representing a vast and diverse region of Europe and Asia. Although not normally classed with the other six in discussions of imperialism and decolonization (in part because of the contiguous nature of the country and because of its ideological aversion to imperialism), the Soviet Union would prove to be the last of the great imperial systems to disappear, in the early 1990s.

Of the six western European empires, those of Britain and France were the only ones that were truly global in scope, and conferred upon the two nations the status

A Companion to Europe since 1945, First Edition. Edited by Klaus Larres.
© 2014 John Wiley & Sons, Ltd. Published 2014 by John Wiley & Sons, Ltd.

of great powers, thus ensuring them a primary role in the shaping of the postwar world. Both, but especially Britain, played a fundamental part in the decision-making that led to the United Nations, the postwar settlements of territories, and the creation of new multilateral bodies such as the International Monetary Fund and the World Bank. Both were also granted permanent seats on the United Nations Security Council, perhaps the last remnant of the old concept of Great Powers. Without their empires, neither could claim equality with the United States and the Soviet Union, and both continued to assume a global role for their militaries.

The other four European empires were concentrated in specific areas: that of the Netherlands was in the East Indies (modern Indonesia), with a few small islands in the West Indies and a mainland territory in South America; that of Belgium was in the Congo and in the small adjoining territories of Ruanda-Urundi; and Portugal and Spain also had African territories (and Portugal also held a few small possessions in Asia). Although the Netherlands and Belgium regarded their empires as important parts of the national realm, none of the lesser European powers equated their imperial possessions with great-power status.

Britain's empire was arguably at its greatest extent ever in 1945. Although the "white settlement" colonies of Canada, Australia, New Zealand and South Africa had achieved full statehood, Britain continued to regard itself as "first among equals" within the British Commonwealth, that curious successor to empire that would continue to provide a faint echo of Britain's imperial past up to the present day. However, most of the remaining parts of the British empire continued under British rule in 1945: in the West Indies, Africa, the Middle and Far East and especially India, Britain could still claim to hold sway over the largest collection of territories under one sovereignty in world history. British forces also controlled many other territories that had been part of the defeated Italian and Japanese empires, and also occupied French territories in the Middle and Far East. The maintenance of a significant empire was considered essential to Britain's postwar reconstruction and to its role as a great power along with the United States and the Soviet Union. The shape the postwar empire would take, however, was an important question that confronted the Labour government elected in July 1945. W.R. Louis and Ronald Robinson, among others, have argued that the problem must be seen in terms of the important relationship to the United States and to Britain's financial condition in 1945; thus what confronted the new Attlee government was an integral connection between empire, transatlantic relations and financial stability.[3]

Second in size only to the British, the French empire was also global, consisting of territories in the West Indies and mainland South America, large parts of Africa, Madagascar, Indochina, and islands in the Indian Ocean and the Pacific. As with Britain, the retention of an overseas empire was considered by French leaders to be an integral part of France's reconstruction and its position as a great power. The defeat of France by Germany in 1940, and its subsequent role as a collaborationist regime under the discredited Vichy government, placed the French empire in a much more precarious state than that of Britain in 1945. Not only did the Free French interim government have to restore constitutional rule to France, it had to assert its authority in the colonies and restore French control of Syria, Lebanon, and French Indochina, all of which had fallen out of French control in the course of World War II.[4]

The Netherlands and Belgium also hoped to use their colonial possessions to assist in postwar reconstruction, but as with the case of France, the occupation of both countries by Germany from 1940 to 1945 made restoration of colonial authority a potential problem. This was particularly true in the Netherlands East Indies, which like French Indochina, had been occupied by Japan.[5]

In summary, none of the European countries with colonial empires anticipated the process of decolonization that would follow over the next three decades. All were confident that the prewar order could be restored and that the homeland and overseas possessions would continue to benefit mutually from this arrangement. Although they were prepared to accept the possibility of reform, none anticipated the rising tide of nationalism and demands for independence that would bring the colonial era to an end.[6]

Changes in Direction

Although the end of empire was not desired or even vaguely anticipated by any of the colonial powers, all made significant efforts to restore colonial rule in a modified way. In the case of Britain, the wartime government passed two Colonial Development and Welfare Acts, in 1940 and 1945, that anticipated spending significant money to encourage economic development in underfunded tropical colonies, particularly in Africa and Malaya. The Labour Party's electoral victory in July 1945 also brought a change, in that although Labour supported the idea of enlightened development of the empire (particularly favored by the Fabian Society's colonial bureau), it intended to fulfill promises of self-government to India and Burma. Stephen Howe has written extensively of this in *Anticolonialism in British Politics: The Left and the End of Empire 1918–64*.

Although the Labour Party presided over the tumultuous first stage of decolonization (in India and Palestine) in 1945–1948, this did not mean a wholesale dissolution of the empire; prime minister Clement Attlee in fact hoped to free "deficit areas" like India and Palestine that had long posed political difficulties for the British government. Through the use of careful funding and economic development, the Colonial Office would step to the fore in the 1940s and 1950s to create what it hoped would be a new era of imperial collaboration in sub-Saharan Africa and Malaya, where economic and political development (so the theory went) could operate hand in hand. This optimistic approach remained for about a dozen years after 1945, before growing nationalist pressure and a series of crises in the Middle East (Egypt, Iran, and Suez) and numerous military commitments in such diverse places as Cyprus, Kenya, and Malaya, led the Macmillan government to begin the wholesale withdrawal from empire and a concurrent turn towards Europe. Nevertheless, the demands of domestic programs and the construction of the welfare state competed constantly for funds. With Britain desperately in debt to the US and to the Commonwealth, John Maynard Keynes commented "we cannot police half the world at our own expense when we have already gone into pawn to the other half."[7]

The classic era of British decolonization could be said to span roughly the decade from the independence of Ghana (1957) to the final grant of independence to the West Indian possessions in the early 1970s (Rhodesia/Zimbabwe provided a unique case and did not achieve independence until 1980; there were also a few remaining vestiges of empire like the Falkland Islands, Hong Kong, and Gibraltar that would continue to influence British policy long after the era of empire was gone.)[8]

The gradualist approach of the British (in which economic and political "development" was emphasized) would be derailed by events; as has been argued by W.R. Louis, "the British lurched from one crisis to the next, sometimes turning adversity to advantage."[9] The extensive historiography of British decolonization reveals a good deal of official misgivings about any withdrawal, and in many cases it was Britain's dire economic state after 1945 that influenced the timing of events. In February 1947, for example, in the midst of the worst winter in 50 years and with rationing and serious fuel shortages to contend with, the Attlee government took three momentous decisions that suggested to the world that the British empire was in the throes of collapse: Indian independence would be granted by June 1948; Britain would end financial and military support to Greece and Turkey; and the Palestine Mandate would be referred to the United Nations.[10]

All three issues had profound repercussions: Indian independence was actually brought forward to August 1947, and the partition of India into what would become three nations (India, Pakistan, and Bangladesh) would cost a million lives and create a border conflict in Kashmir that remains unresolved.[11] The British Notes to the US on the termination of funding for Greece and Turkey led directly to the Truman Doctrine of March 1947, arguably the first sign of an evolving American Cold War policy. Finally, the referral of the Palestine problem to the United Nations relieved Britain of a costly and seemingly insoluble commitment, but the resultant Arab–Israeli dispute would damage British relations with other Middle East states and led ultimately to the fiasco at Suez in 1956.

Louis and Robinson in "The Imperialism of Decolonization" argue that the decisions made in the late 1940s cannot be understood in isolation but only in the context of Britain's dire financial situation after World War II and of the developing Cold War. Indeed, despite a history of antagonism towards the British empire and its continuation, "as the Cold War intensified from 1947–1951, competition between the two superpowers came to the rescue of the Empire. Faced with the Czech Crisis and the Berlin Blockade (1948), the United States hastened to strengthen Britain and France in defence of Western Europe . . . after 1947 the Americans subsidized the imperial system generously in one way or another as a measure of national defence."[12]

The French reoccupied their empire in 1945 with two ominous signs: the brutal suppression of Arab nationalists in Algiers in May, and the declaration of Vietnamese independence by Ho Chi Minh in August. In the latter case, the French did not actually return until the spring of 1946, and found themselves up against a well-entrenched and intractable foe. The French empire in Asia came to an end in the humiliating defeat at Dien Bien Phu in the spring of 1954 and the recognition of the independence of Cambodia, Laos, and Vietnam. Vietnam, partitioned "temporarily" between north and south, would of course go on to frustrate the Cold War aims of a much greater power than France. Otherwise, the French "metropolitan" view of empire achieved its manifestation in the Fourth Republic of 1946, in which the

Overseas Departments (Algeria, Caribbean islands, St. Pierre and Miquelon, and Réunion), were combined with the Overseas Territories in Africa and the Pacific to form a new French Union.[13]

Unlike the British, who had always considered the empire (apart from Ireland) separate from the home island, the French saw their colonies as "*France Outremer*" and part of a seamless whole with France itself (the overseas departments actually sent representatives to the French National Assembly in Paris). Charles de Gaulle's idea for a French Union, first proposed at Brazzaville in 1944 to rally the support of France's African colonies, would in theory tie the colonies closer to France while granting limited local autonomy. All inhabitants of the French Union were made French citizens with equal civil rights, thus abolishing the old prewar distinction between "citizen" and "subject" in the French empire. Unlike the British empire, where as we will see the nationalist leaders grew out of the local political landscape and went on to demand independence, the potential nationalist leaders of the French colonies (with the exception of Ho Chi Minh) were drawn off to Paris to be part of the new French Union. This would have profound consequences for the nature and direction of French decolonization.[14]

The Dutch government, restored to power after the German defeat in 1945, hoped to regain control of its valuable East Indian possessions with the defeat of Japan. However, as the French also found in Vietnam, the sudden Japanese surrender in August 1945 meant that no forces were available to accept the surrender and hence arrange for a rapid restoration of colonial rule. The Viet Minh, which declared Vietnamese independence, had fought the Japanese and then turned on the French. In the Dutch East Indies, nominal independence had been granted by the Japanese to a group led by Achmed Sukarno, who proclaimed the independence of Indonesia upon the defeat of Japan. Although the British (who, as in Vietnam, provided the first allied troops to disarm the Japanese) and the Americans preferred some kind of recognition of the new nationalist government, the Dutch insisted on resuming their colonial rule, although with some nod to local autonomy.

After a year of hostilities, the Dutch recognized an independent state in Java and Sumatra, but hoped to federate the rest of Indonesia with the Dutch state in a kind of "Commonwealth" arrangement. This satisfied neither side. After continued fighting, the United Nations became more involved, and, under growing US pressure to concentrate their resources in the reconstruction of Europe, the Dutch finally relinquished control in August 1949. They would continue to govern Western New Guinea (Irian Jaya) until 1963 as a face-saving measure in what had in effect been a forced withdrawal by a long-standing colonial power.[15]

Unlike the Dutch, for whom German and Japanese occupation fatally weakened their grip on empire, the Belgians resumed their rule of the Congo with little difficulty. Although the homeland itself was occupied, the Belgian Congo was not and remained under its colonial administration throughout the war. Indeed, its raw materials such as copper, manganese, and uranium, were placed at the disposal of the allies by the Belgian government in exile. Thus, in 1945, the Belgian Congo resumed its place as one of the most prosperous and apparently stable of the European possessions in Africa, with political development a low priority.[16]

The Politics of Partition: Britain, India, and the Middle East

Although the new British Labour government led by Clement Attlee continued to believe in the maintenance of British power both military and imperial, the independence of India within the Commonwealth had long been a goal of party leaders. Its achievement, however, proved to be of monumental difficulty in the first two postwar years, and because of its significance for Britain itself and for the eventual long-term progress of decolonization, is worth analyzing at some length. The Labour government's pursuit of a solution to the problem of Indian nationalism did not merely reflect its ideological sympathies. It reflected the hard realities of US anti-imperialism and opposition to the full restoration of the Raj, as well as Britain's own financial difficulties in 1945–1946, which were alleviated in part by a large US loan. In addition, Lord Wavell, the British viceroy in India since 1943, was not confident that the military could maintain security as anti-British and Hindu-Muslim communal violence grew in 1945–1946. With Britain's security and oil interests in the Middle East located in predominantly Muslim countries (Egypt, Iraq, and Iran), the extrication of Britain from India and Palestine without becoming caught in ruinous communal violence was perhaps the highest priority for the British Cabinet.[17]

The decision to grant independence to India by June 1948, taken in the difficult weeks of February 1947, coincided with the appointment of Lord Louis Mountbatten as the last viceroy and he was given a wider mandate than his predecessor to negotiate the transfer of power. Perhaps the biggest task confronting him was negotiating with the leaders of the Congress Party (particularly Jawaharlal Nehru) who favored a united India, and of the Muslim League (particularly Muhammad Ali Jinnah) who favored the partition of India to allow the creation of a Muslim state to be called Pakistan. The inability to achieve the British goal of a united India with sufficient powers allotted to the Muslim areas resulted in acceptance of the need for a strong India with its Muslim provinces detached in some way to form the new nation of Pakistan. By advancing the date of final British withdrawal to August 15, 1947, Mountbatten was able to finalize plans for the partition of the subcontinent with the approval of both the Labour government and the opposition Conservative Party, while also achieving acceptance of Dominion status within the Commonwealth by both Nehru and Jinnah. Although the speed of the transfer and the ensuing violence caused by the drawing of boundaries has led to much historical re-evaluation of Mountbatten, he succeeded in his primary goal, which was to extract Britain peacefully and to maintain the goodwill of the two successor states.[18]

Although celebrated at the time as a triumph of British policy in maintaining the good will of India and Pakistan and retaining both within the Commonwealth, Mountbatten's decision to accelerate the pace of partition and British withdrawal has been increasingly criticized by historians for the slapdash manner of the departure. Partition itself may perhaps have been unavoidable, but the precipitous departure of British authority before subsequent security could be provided for has been widely blamed for the death of at least a million Hindu and Muslim refugees and the displacement of at least ten million people. The tendency of post-partition accounts (and of his official biographer Philip Ziegler) to credit Mountbatten for his brilliant work has been replaced by a significant rethinking, in part due to the further break-down of Pakistan in 1971 and its ongoing problems to the present day. The intrac-table dispute between India and Pakistan over Kashmir can also be traced directly to decisions made in haste in the aftermath of partition. Stanley Wolpert in his book *Shameful Flight*, places the blame squarely upon Mountbatten, the British govern-ment, and the leading Indian nationalist leaders.[19]

Along with India, Palestine was the most intractable problem faced by the Labour government in its plans for a renewal of the empire. Under strong US pressure to admit 100,000 Jewish refugees from Europe, but unwilling to inflame the Middle East further by granting wholesale access, the British made a number of efforts to reconcile Jewish, Arab, and American interests. Facing rising violence, the govern-ment resorted to referring the Palestine question to the United Nations in February 1947, and in September the date of May 15, 1948 was set for a final termination of the mandate. In November, the United Nations Special Committee on Palestine (UNSCOP) recommended the partition of Palestine into Jewish and Arab states, thus setting the region on the path of war that began immediately upon the termination of the British mandate.[20]

The near-simultaneous withdrawals from India and Palestine (and soon after, Greece) lead to events that continue to have consequences to this day, but, from the British perspective, the country was rid of problems that could only worsen and require more British troops and money. The Palestine withdrawal was part of a broader scheme to place British relations with the Arab states, particularly Egypt, on a better footing. However, the inability of the British to negotiate a satisfactory defense arrangement in the Middle East, and the expulsion of British staff from the oilfields of Abadan, Iran, in 1951, made a continued informal British presence in the region less tenable. Arab nationalism, symbolized best by the accession to power of Gamal Nasser in Egypt in 1952, inflamed the Arab world against both continued imperialism and the state of Israel, which was (and still is) considered a creature of Western "domination" of the region.

Against the background of the Cold War, British and US security interests in the Middle East were tested in the Suez Crisis in 1956, when Nasser nationalized the Canal which, with India lost, best symbolized continued British influence outside Europe. An Anglo-French invasion, in collusion with an Israeli attack across the Sinai desert, proceeded without consultation with the United States, and, facing US and Soviet anger, the invasion forces had to be withdrawn, thereby handing Nasser an important political victory. Not only did Britain's remaining influence in the Middle East rapidly decline thereafter, Suez came to represent the "nail in the coffin" of the British imperial experience, and tends to be perceived that way even today. Whether Suez was truly a watershed, however, remains unclear from the documentary record.[21] The Suez episode has been particularly important in British historiography, as it has come to symbolize the moment of Britain's demise as a great power.[22]

The first phase of British decolonization just discussed also witnessed several other successes and failures. The British departure from India in 1947 was followed by the successful transition of Ceylon to independence within the Commonwealth, and that of Burma outside, a loss keenly felt by Attlee. Malaya and Singapore were considered of vital importance to the British economy because of their rubber and tin resources.

A Chinese communist insurgency (a legacy of anti-Japanese activity in World War II) threatened to undermine British attempts to place Malaya on a new constitutional footing, and considerable military resources were committed to the defeat of the guerillas, culminating in a federal solution that led successfully to the independence of Malaya in 1957 (soon joined by Sarawak and Sabah to create Malaysia, but losing Singapore in 1965).[23]

The End of Empire: France, Belgium, and Portugal

Nationalist movements in Asia, and the British withdrawal from India, forced the hands of the remaining European empires in Asia, those of France and the Netherlands. The inability of both countries to re-establish their authority without military force led to lengthy conflicts that were resolved only when the two powers, under pressure at home and with the need to participate in European security and integration, withdrew from their Asian possessions (the Netherlands in 1949; France in 1954). However, the humiliating French defeat at Dien Bien Phu in 1954 coincided with the breakdown in order in Algeria, a territory physically closer to France itself and inhabited by nearly 1 million *colons* (French settlers), who enjoyed full rights of French citizenship and voted in national elections. The growing importance of Arab nationalism, symbolized by Egypt's Nasser, led to the formation of the Algerian National Liberation Front (FLN), in November 1954. French attempts to suppress the FLN led to an increasingly vicious war in which the French military, supported by the politically influential *colons*, attempted to root out the rebellion.

Atrocities on both sides led to widespread condemnation of the war. The fragmented nature of the Fourth Republic political system ensured that the war became a stalemate and by 1958 brought the wartime hero, Charles de Gaulle, to power with the understanding that he would terminate the Algerian war on acceptable terms. In addition to founding France's Fifth Republic (which granted the president enhanced powers), de Gaulle sought to extract France from Algeria against the vicious opposition of conservative French public opinion, and the French military, which strongly backed the *colons*. At considerable personal and political risk, de Gaulle convened several conferences at Evian with FLN representatives in 1961–1962, and successfully negotiated Algerian independence in July 1962. Referenda in both France and Algeria passed overwhelmingly. Despite careful provision for the French *colons*, they chose overwhelmingly to leave Algeria and settled in the south of France, where they and their descendants tend to support the anti-immigrant policies of France's political right.[24]

De Gaulle's efforts to resolve the crippling crisis in Algeria had profound implications for the remaining French territories in Africa. Faced with mounting Algerian nationalist resistance, and watching the neighboring British territories move to self-government and independence, French African leaders, particularly in Guinea, clamored for greater autonomy. In 1956, in order to accede to these pressures without dissolving the French Union, the Fourth Republic passed the *loi cadre* (outline law), which retained the federal structure but granted greater representative government at the local level. The French Union was renamed the French Community in 1958, and the territories in Africa were give the option of continued membership (and French support) or outright independence. At the time only Guinea chose independence and was precipitately cut loose by France.

However, the French Community proved to be short-lived: with the war in Algeria moving to a climax and with major British colonies like Nigeria achieving independence, de Gaulle chose to grant independence to French West Africa and French Equatorial Africa in 1960. Unlike the former British colonies, which generally chose continued membership in the Commonwealth but otherwise became fully independent, the new states that emerged from French Africa continued to rely extensively on France for their currency (the French franc remained the standard), security and economic well-being. Many of the new leaders, like Leopold Senghor of Senegal, had spent much time in Paris and were considered reliable allies of France. Therefore, the degree to which France truly decolonized in this era is debatable.[25]

With the largest parts of the former French empire gone by 1962, only residual parts remained in the Pacific, the Indian Ocean, and the West Indies. Those that had substantial French populations (such as Martinique, Guadeloupe, St. Pierre and Miquelon, and Réunion) were deemed Overseas Departments of France and thus elected members to the legislature in Paris. Others, such as French Guiana and New Caledonia, were considered Overseas Territories and became internally autonomous, but did not have political representation in Paris. This quasi-colonial situation remains intact to this day.

Belgium's gigantic colony in the Congo was considered "the most peaceful and tranquil of colonies" by a Belgian journalist in 1955, thanks to the territory's vast mineral wealth. However, the Belgian government made no provision for political development and preferred to keep the population at a low level of education. As a result, the Congo had no indigenous nationalist movement such as could be found in the British colonies, nor even an educated collaborating class like that in the French territories. When it achieved independence in 1960 it had only 16 university graduates. Only minor political reforms were instituted by Belgium when the strong wind of independence began to blow in from other parts of Africa. Patrice Lumumba emerged as a nationalist leader of some skill who returned from an All-African Conference in Accra with demands for independence. Riots broke out in the Congo's cities, and faced with mounting international pressure and financial costs, the Belgian government decided to grant independence on a shortened timetable; it was granted on June 30, 1960 with only the most minimal level of preparation. The result, predictably, was chaos, and as the new country slid into civil war, the United Nations had to mount a major operation that took place in the shadow of the Cold War. In 1962, Belgium also withdrew from the small neighboring territories of Rwanda and Burundi, where ethnic politics continues to inflame tensions to this day.[26]

Portugal was the oldest European colonial presence in Africa and Asia, yet proved the most tenacious. While Britain and France moved towards autonomy and independence for their colonies in the 1950s and 1960s, Portugal sought closer union between its overseas possessions and the metropolis. Portugal's empire consisted of four territories in Africa (Angola, Mozambique, Guinea-Bissau, and the islands of

São Tomé and Principe), and remnants of trading settlements in India (Goa), China (Macao), and the East Indies (East Timor). In 1951, the Salazar government declared the colonies "Overseas Provinces" and encouraged settlement from Portugal. So, at a time when the process of decolonization was going forward in neighboring territories, Portugal was actively seeking closer ties. This combination of a growing European settler population, particularly in Angola, and the increasing importance of African nationalism in general, led to growing discontent and outright rebellion.

By the mid-1960s, Portugal found itself in the middle of full-scale war which brought not only international criticism (although the United States supported the anti-communist Portuguese government), but increasing financial and military exhaustion. A military coup in April 1974 brought an end to the right-wing dictatorship in Portugal, ushering in a transition to democracy. An immediate side effect was the rapid withdrawal from the colonies in Africa and East Timor (Goa was forcibly seized by India in 1961). This left only Macao as a Portuguese overseas possession, and it was returned to China in 1999.[27]

The Climax of British Decolonization

By 1957, Britain had withdrawn from India, parts of the Middle East, and the Sudan, and was preparing to grant independence to Malaya. But large areas of the empire remained intact, particularly in Africa, the Caribbean, and various island groups throughout the world. British leaders remained committed to a global role and were aloof from the growing movement to European integration. It took only a few years for this attitude to shift substantially. This was partly due to the humiliation of the Suez Crisis of November 1956, during which Britain found itself at odds with its most important ally, the United States. The crisis also illustrated the rising power of nationalism in the Arab world and beyond, and forced the British to diminish rapidly their military commitments in Jordan and Iraq. We have also seen how Arab nationalism would overwhelm the French in Algeria.

The advent of Harold Macmillan as British prime minister in early 1957 initiated a decisive period in Britain's abandonment of an imperial role. Unlike his Conservative predecessors Winston Churchill and Anthony Eden, Macmillan was a pragmatist who recognized that the empire was not sacrosanct and that Britain's place between a close American alliance and a European community had to be reconciled. He also saw that the rising tide of nationalism was already forcing Britain to commit resources in such far-flung places as Cyprus, Kenya, and Malaya. Certain territories in Africa, notably the Gold Coast and the federation of Nigeria, were well on their way to internal self-government when Macmillan took office; indeed the Gold Coast became independent as Ghana in March 1957. As a model for the rest of Africa, it was quickly followed by Nigeria in 1960, and Sierra Leone and Gambia soon after. East Africa was on a parallel path of evolutionary development; although the concerns of the white settler minority delayed Kenyan independence till 1963, that territory along with Tanganyika and Uganda had been among the early candidates for independence.[28]

While presiding over the first and critical stages of the dissolution of the British empire in Africa, Macmillan's government continued to see British power in global terms and insisted on preserving key bases on several continents. Traditional naval facilities in the West Indies and South Africa were declining in importance, but the British developed significant naval and air bases in Malta, Cyprus, Aden, Kenya, and Singapore during the 1960s, even as those territories achieved independence. Schemes for federating colonies as a prelude to independence, most notably in Malaysia and Nigeria, were deemed successes, whereas central Africa (1953–1963) and the West Indies (1958–1962) proved untenable for various reasons, and the constituent parts were rushed to independence in the early to mid-1960s, a period which was the crest of British decolonization.

Macmillan delivered his famous "Wind of Change" speech in 1960, used several times during a tour of Africa. His speech was seen at the time as aligning Britain with the growing force of African nationalism, but also as a warning to Apartheid-era South Africa that Britain would not support white minority rule. It can also now perhaps be seen as a sign that Britain did not intend to remain in Africa much longer, as proved to be the case. Equally significant was the Macmillan government's decision to apply for admission to the European Economic Community in 1962; although the outcome was unsuccessful, the unmistakable message was that Britain saw its future tied to Europe, not to the diminishing empire or its successor body, the Commonwealth.[29]

Although the key period of British decolonization was over by 1965, numerous residual responsibilities remained and continued to influence British policy overseas. The decision of Southern Rhodesia to maintain white-minority rule and illegally declare independence in 1965 was a difficult problem for the Labour government under Harold Wilson (1964–1970), as was the failed effort to keep a base in Aden surrounded by a federation of South Arabian emirates.[30] Britain withdrew defeated from Aden in 1967, the same year that the decision was made for financial reasons to terminate Britain's military role east of Suez. Over the next five years, base facilities in Singapore, the Indian Ocean, and the Persian Gulf were wound down. Rhodesia (as the white-minority regime called itself) was blockaded by Britain, but received sustenance from white-ruled South Africa. Only the growing revolt of the African majority in Rhodesia made possible the transition to the majority-ruled state of Zimbabwe negotiated in 1980, making it the last British territory in Africa to achieve independence.[31]

Although, like France, Britain has minor overseas territories to this day, they no longer symbolize any kind of global ambition; the British military remains the most flexible in the world after the United States, but this is unrelated to the legacy of empire. In 1982, that flexibility was put to the test by Argentina's seizure of the Falkland Islands, which were successfully recovered by an expeditionary force that briefly revived the British public's interest in projecting military power into a distant (and until then obscure) part of the old empire. The last major British territory abroad was Hong Kong, which returned to Chinese rule in June 1997 after China agreed to keep the territory's free market system intact for 50 years.[32]

According to John Darwin, the study of British and indeed other European processes of decolonization must fuse three different approaches to the problem: the domestic politics of "decline," the relative shifts in European power at the international and Cold War level, and the local circumstances in each colonial territory.

Indeed, in their *British Imperialism* (1993), P.J. Cain and A.G. Hopkins argue that the economic imperatives of the British situation determined the need to abandon empire and that indeed the financial and currency situations cannot be separated from a broader understanding of imperial decline.[33]

The European empires are gone, and apart from minor remnants that are still under British, French or Dutch sovereignty by choice, they play little role in the broader national life of their countries. The British even have special passports for their territories that do not allow residents to move automatically to Britain; ironically, European Union citizens do have that right.

Legacies of Empire

In a rather ironic twist, the European nations that possessed colonial empires have since 1945 become much more diverse and cosmopolitan, often through immigration from the old empires. The need for postwar reconstruction in Europe and the existence of a common citizenship made it relatively easy for people from the overseas colonies to emigrate to the metropolis in search of work. This phenomenon of course preceded 1945; Britain and France had communities of Indians and Africans dating to the nineteenth century, but they grew rapidly from the 1940s onwards and continued after the age of decolonization ended.

The first great wave of immigration to postwar Britain came from the Caribbean, famously beginning aboard the *Empire Windrush* in 1948. Soon after, large-scale immigration began from the Indian subcontinent, which continued into the 1970s, particularly as a result of crises in Bangladesh. Smaller numbers of immigrants came from Africa (not least Uganda), Cyprus, and Malaysia, among others. Despite immigration controls imposed in the 1960s because of the concerns of many conservative Britons, British cities in particular became the home of large communities of immigrants from the Commonwealth, which swelled because of family unification. In certain areas, these "minority" communities became the majority.[34] In the 1991 census, there were 1.5 million people of South Asian origin in Britain, about 2.7% of the total.[35] The evolution of Britain into a multiracial society has had a profound effect on what it means to be "British," but also particularly English or Scottish. Racial discrimination on many levels grew in proportion to the size of immigrant communities, but as the multicultural nature of modern Britain become more the norm for new generations, inter-community marriage has grown and the level of public tolerance has grown with it.[36]

Official Britain still has ties on many levels with the former empire, through the Commonwealth (based in London) and through ordinary trade and diplomatic channels. The former British colonies in the West Indies, for example, have enjoyed preferential access to the European Union for their sugar products, largely because of British support. Informal ties such as the use of the English language and contacts made through students in Britain continue to give the country a special role in many parts of the developing world. Direct intervention is rare, but occurred in the former colony of Sierra Leone in 2002 to stop a bitter civil war.

As with Britain, France, the Netherlands and Belgium have communities of immigrants from their former colonies in the West and East Indies, Southeast Asia, and

Africa. Many came as students or to seek jobs in a better-paying environment. France has a particularly large population of immigrants from Morocco, Algeria, and Tunisia, its former possessions in North Africa. The close proximity to France and Spain has made moving to Europe very popular; once within the European Union it is very easy to move around. The largely Muslim Arab communities in France (numbering about 5 million people) have experienced economic and social discrimination and a tendency towards ghettoization, but as can be found in Britain, successive generations become more assimilated to the French mainstream. However, all the countries discussed have parties of the right that wish to discourage immigration for fear of diluting the "original" culture.[37]

France has maintained a more active role than Britain in its former empire. As well as treating the imperial remnants as part of the French state at the institutional level (something the British never did), the French have ensured their sense of cultural connection with the French-speaking world through *La Francophonie*, a body of countries that have large populations of francophones or were at one time part of the French empire. It has come to have a role similar to the Commonwealth for Britain. France has also intervened frequently in Africa to support friendly regimes, including the central African Republic, Chad, and Côte d'Ivoire. France also used its territories in the Pacific to test nuclear weapons during the Cold War.

With the passage of time, the absorption of large immigrant populations from the former empires has contributed to economic and social growth because they initially provided a cheap labor source and eventually began moving into the ordinary working and middle classes. Political power came through organizations devoted to the interests of each group and eventually through certain individuals achieving elected office at the local and national level. In all cases, the threat these groups posed to "traditional" ethnic, religious, and linguistic assumptions has forced the former colonial powers to adapt to the numerous new populations within them and to transform their sense of themselves. Although education continues to be in the national language of each country, the presence of sizeable minorities of people with languages and religions different from the mainstream has created issues about whether assimilation should or should not occur, and what degree of tolerance should be expected from the state. Finally, the existence of open borders and labor markets within the European Union has permitted these immigrant communities to expand far beyond their original place of settlement; therefore countries like Ireland, Denmark, and Germany have also experienced the phenomenon of new immigrant communities.

More recently, the growth of substantial Muslim communities in many western European countries has exacerbated social tensions. Particularly since the 9/11 bombings in the United States, the July 7, 2005 bombings in London, and attacks in Madrid and elsewhere, there has been growing concern that these communities are not sufficiently integrated into metropolitan society and are indeed possible breeding grounds for extreme Islamist behavior. This has led to open hostility in both directions, particularly in France which saw outbreaks of violence in suburban Paris in 2006. In Britain the perpetrators of the London bombings and subsequent plots to cause damage have been linked not to foreign terrorists but to young men born in Britain within long-standing Muslim communities. This has raised substantial questions about what can be done to confront the problem and whether assimilation is desirable or not. Similar debates are heard in France, Germany, and Spain, to name but three examples.[38]

The End of the Soviet Union

As suggested at the beginning of this chapter, the Soviet Union was an empire but of a different type than those of western Europe. As a revolutionary state, the Soviet Union restored the old Russian empire in the 1920s in a different guise; the territories were made Soviet socialist republics within a Soviet Union, and thus were technically equal to each other and to the bulk of the country, Russia. In practice, the Communist Party of the Soviet Union (CPSU) held a monopoly on power in all areas, and party members of Russian origin tended to dominate. Tightly controlled from Moscow, the Soviet Union allowed minimal autonomy in the republics and was in practice an authoritarian regime that showed little tolerance for regional or local customs. Local party leaders had to become effectively "Russified" to rise up the chain of command, and centralized economic planning for the benefit of Russia had a profound impact on the economies of the Soviet republics. Local religious and political institutions, particularly in Islamic central Asia, were repressed, and immigration from Russia ensured sizeable populations that would (it was hoped) maintain Russian political dominance.[39]

The policy of *glasnost* instituted by Soviet president Mikhail Gorbachev in the late 1980s, and his unwillingness to intervene in satellite states in eastern Europe, unleashed long-repressed feelings of nationalism throughout the Eastern bloc. Beginning in Poland in 1989 and quickly spreading, the growing political whirlwind swept away discredited communist governments, and spread into the Soviet Union itself. The formerly independent Baltic states (Estonia, Latvia, Lithuania) were the first to challenge Soviet power directly by declaring independence early in 1990. Georgia, briefly independent in 1918–1920, also fell into internal turmoil. The rise of Boris Yeltsin as president of the Russian republic in 1991 symbolized a growing Russian identity separate from the larger Soviet state, whose underlying rationale was not nationalism but communist ideology. As that rationale crumbled, the more potent forces of nationalism took over, and in central Asia, Islam reasserted itself as a rallying force. By December, efforts by Gorbachev to assemble a new "union of sovereign states" collapsed when the important republics of Ukraine, Belarus, and Russia itself seceded. Gorbachev's resignation on December 25, 1991 brought an end to the Soviet Union, and its constituent republics were now recognized as independent states.[40]

The rapidity of the Soviet collapse meant that the leadership of the new republics was often the same people, but without the Communist Party label. In theory, all were trying to transform into representative democracies with free market economies, but this has proved very difficult after decades, if not centuries, of authoritarian rule and centrally planned economies. Russia, the largest and most powerful remnant of the Soviet state, is still a "federation" of 21 republics and numerous small ethnically based units. In that sense, the empire of the Tsars still exists in a reduced way.[41]

Conclusion

The period of decolonization since 1945 has had dramatic impacts on world as well as European history. The study of the period has gone from predominantly an analysis of the political process leading to the end of empire and after, to a far more nuanced understanding of the many levels on which decolonization operated. In this chapter we have examined primarily the process by which each state found ways to withdraw from empire on its own terms, but the recent trend to return to imperial history has taken many new and different directions. The continued immigration from former colonies has opened up many new avenues for analysis, just as the integration of much of Europe into the European Union has called into question national identities. What role will these growing communities play in their respective states and indeed in Europe as a whole? What will the impact be of religious groups who embrace their faith far more than largely secular Europe? And of course what role should Europe play in the "developing" world, so much of which used to be part of the European colonial experience until quite recently.

Postcolonial theory has emerged from the work of Edward Said and also from cultural studies, including the work of such significant intellectual figures as Foucault, Barthes, and Derrida. While understanding the end of empire used to be confined primarily to the fields of political and economic history, it has now broadened dramatically to include literature, gender studies, queer theory, environmentalism, and beyond. While it is sometimes difficult to synthesize different disciplines and forms of analysis into a coherent whole, it does nevertheless point to an ongoing re-evaluation of the process of decolonization and its transformative effects on both the metropolis and its people and those territories that experienced colonialism. There is little doubt then that the extensive historiography on the end of empire will only continue to grow as interest in the era remains both relevant and intense.[42]

The end of empire has radically transformed the position European states hold in world affairs and has ushered in a new era of states still grappling with the challenges of independence. Although some have privileged access to the European Union, Europe for the most part has turned back to its own shores and concerns. Nevertheless, the experience of decolonization has brought with it demographic and social changes that would have been unimaginable to the leaders of 1945, who envisioned empires lasting centuries. While within few decades, these vanished few would question the impact the existence of a colonial past has had on much of the continent.

Notes

1 The traditional study of empire and its end has gone through a vast transformation. Instead of focusing exclusively on politics and government, recent scholarship on the end of empire has embraced cultural studies and postcolonial literary theory, which has resulted in a burst of new work on interpreting the experience of empire and its influence on the metropolitan nations. A sampling of recent literature would include Childs and Williams, *An Introduction to Post-colonial Theory* and Mongia, *Contemporary Post-colonial Theory: A Reader*. Much of the writing on these topics has been strongly influenced by

Edward Said's pathbreaking work *Orientalism,* which while devoted primarily to perceptions of the Middle East is significant in its use of the "other" in European perceptions of the wider world.

2   Much of the recent literature on imperialism and colonialism has explored hitherto little-examined subjects such as culture, gender, and sexuality, and these have strongly influenced postcolonial literary studies. Among the important works to consult are Chaudhuri and Strobel, *Western Women and Imperialism: Complicity and Resistance*; Hyam, *Empire and Sexuality: The British Experience*; Midgley, *Gender and Imperialism*; Prakash, *After Colonialism: Imperial Histories and Post-colonial Displacements*; and Said, *Culture and Imperialism.*

3   See Louis and Robinson, "The Imperialism of Decolonization," 451–42.

4   Ansprenger, *The Dissolution of the Colonial Empires,* 208–209.

5   Ansprenger, op. cit., 253.

6   There are relatively few books that cover the entirety of the colonial experience of each of the European powers, but three that attempt to be comprehensive are Holland, *European Decolonization 1918–1981: An Introductory Survey*; Ansprenger, *Dissolution of the Colonial Empires*; and Chamberlain, *Decolonization: The Fall of the European Empires.* Two recent books are Betts, *Decolonization* and Duara, *Decolonization: Perspectives from Now and Then.*

7   Quoted in Louis and Robinson, op. cit., 455.

8   Darwin, *Britain and Decolonisation,* 1–30.

9   Louis, "The Dissolution of the British Empire," 329.

10 Louis and Robinson, op. cit., 457.

11 Louis, "The Dissolution of the British Empire," 334–35.

12 Louis and Robinson, op. cit., 459–60.

13 Ansprenger, op. cit., 211–13.

14 See Betts, *France and Decolonisation 1900–1960* and Aldrich and Connell, *France's Overseas Frontier.*

15 Van Goor, *De Nederlandse Koloniën. Geschiedensis van de Nederlanse expansie 1600–1975*; Legge, *Sukarno.*

16 Stengers, "Precipitous Decolonization: The Case of the Belgian Congo," 319.

17 Darwin, *Britain and Decolonization,* 69–97. There is of course a huge historiography on the intricacies of the Palestine issue from every possible angle, but among the best studies are Cohen, *Palestine and the Great Powers 1945–48* and Louis, *The British Empire in the Middle East 1945–51,* which has an extensive section on Palestine. Much of the discussion on the issue in recent years has centered on the work of "new" Israeli historians such as Shlaim's *Collusion across the Jordan: King Abdullah, the Zionist Movement and the Partition of Palestine* and Morris, *The Birth of the Palestinian Refugee Problem, 1947–49*; both are very critical of the "triumphalist" view of the emergence of the State of Israel.

18 Holland, *European Decolonization,* 74–86.

19 Wolpert, *Shameful Flight: The Last Years of the British Empire in India,* 1–11.

20 Darwin, *Britain and Decolonization,* 110–125.

21 Louis, *The Dissolution of the British Empire,* 339–43.

22 Important works on the Suez Crisis and its significance for Britain and its relationship to the US and the empire include Kyle, *Suez*; Lucas, *Divided We Stand*; and Louis, *Suez: The Crisis and its Consequences.*

23 Louis, *The Dissolution of the British Empire,* 336–55.

24 See Clayton, *The Wars of French Decolonization.*

25 See Manning, *Francophone Sub-Saharan Africa 1880–1985.*

26 See Stengers, op. cit., and also Young, *Politics in the Congo.*

27   See Bender, *Angola under the Portuguese* and Clarence-Smith, *The Third Portuguese Empire*.
28   Darwin, *Britain and Decolonization*, 222–26.
29   Louis, *The Dissolution of the British Empire*, 343–35.
30   Shula Marks, "Southern Africa," 571.
31   See Louis, "The Dissolution of the British Empire in the Era of Vietnam."
32   Hastings and Jenkins, *The Battle for the Falklands*; Tsang, *A Modern History of Hong Kong*.
33   Darwin, "Decolonization and the End of Empire," 552.
34   Fryer, *Staying Power*; Holmes, *John Bull's Island*.
35   Marwick, *British Society since 1945*, 4th edition, 390–391.
36   See Alibhai-Brown, *Imagining the New Britain*.
37   Lucassen, *The Immigrant Threat*.
38   See Bawer, *While Europe Slept*; Vidino and Emerson, *Al Qaeda in Europe*.
39   See von Laue, *Why Lenin? Why Stalin?*
40   See White, *After Gorbachev* and Remnick, *Lenin's Tomb*.
41   See Dannreuther, *Creating New States in Central Asia*.
42   Winks, "Future of Imperial History," 658–69.

Bibliography

Aldrich, Robert and John Connell, *France's Overseas Frontier: Départements et territoires d'outre-mer* (Cambridge: Cambridge University Press, 2006).

Alibhai-Brown, Y., *Imagining the New Britain* (London: Routledge, 2001).

Ansprenger, Franz, *The Dissolution of the Colonial Empires* (London: Routledge, 1989).

Bawer, Bruce, *While Europe Slept: How Radical Islam Is Destroying the West from Within* (New York: Doubleday, 2006).

Bender, Gerald H., *Angola under the Portuguese: The Myth and the Reality* (New York: Africa World Press, 2004).

Betts, Raymond, *France and Decolonization 1900–1960* (London: Palgrave Macmillan, 1991).

Betts, Raymond, *Decolonization* (New York: Routledge, 2004).

Cain, P.J. and A.G. Hopkins, *British Imperialism: Crisis and Deconstruction 1914–1990* (London: Longman, 1993).

Chamberlain, M.E., *Decolonization: The Fall of the European Empires* (Oxford: Basil Blackwell, 1985).

Chaudhuri, Nupur and Margaret Strobel, *Western Women and Imperialism: Complicity and Resistance* (Bloomington: Indiana University Press, 1992).

Childs, Peter and R.J. Patrick Williams, *An Introduction to Post-colonial Theory* (New York: Prentice Hall, 1997).

Clarence-Smith, G. *The Third Portuguese Empire, 1825–1975: A Study in Economic Imperialism* (Manchester: Manchester University Press, 1985).

Clayton, Anthony, *The Wars of French Decolonization* (London: Longman, 1994).

Cohen, Michael, *Palestine and the Great Powers 1945–48* (Princeton, NJ: Princeton University Press, 1982).

Dannreuther, Roland, *Creating New States in Central Asia* (New York: Routledge, 1994).

Darwin, John, *Britain and Decolonization: The Retreat from Empire in the Post-war World* (London: Macmillan, 1988).

Darwin, John, "Decolonisation and the End of Empire," in Robin Winks (ed.), *Oxford History of the British Empire*, vol. 5: *Historiography* (Oxford: Oxford University Press, 1999).

Duara, Prasenjit, *Decolonization: Perspectives from Now and Then* (New York: Routledge, 2003).

Fryer, Peter, *Staying Power: The History of Black People in Britain* (London: Pluto, 1984).

Hastings, Max and Simon Jenkins, *The Battle for the Falklands* (New York: Norton, 1984).

Holland, R.F., *European Decolonization 1918–1981: An Introductory Survey* (London: Macmillan, 1985).

Holmes, Colin, *John Bull's Island: Immigration and British Society 1871–1971* (London: Sheridan House, 1988).

Hyam, Ronald, *Empire and Sexuality: The British Experience* (Manchester: Manchester University Press, 1990).

Legge, J.D. *Sukarno* (New York: Butterworth Heinemann, 2003).

Louis, W.R., *The British Empire in the Middle East 1945–51* (Oxford: Clarendon Press, 1984).

Louis, W.R. "The Dissolution of the British Empire," in J. Brown and W.R. Louis (eds.), *The Oxford History of the British Empire: The Twentieth Century* (Oxford: Oxford University Press, 1999).

Louis, W.R. (ed.), *The Oxford History of the British Empire*, 5 vols. (Oxford: Oxford University Press, 1999).

Louis, W.R., "The Dissolution of the British Empire in the Era of Vietnam," *American Historical Review*, vol. 107, no. 1, 2002, pp. 1–25.

Louis, W.R. and Ronald Robinson, "The Imperialism of Decolonization," in W. R. Louis (ed.), *Ends of British Imperialism: The Scramble for Empire, Suez and Decolonization* (London: Tauris, 2006).

Lucassen, Leo, *The Immigrant Threat: The Integration of Old and New Migrants in Western Europe since 1850* (Champaign-Urbana: University of Illinois Press, 2005).

Manning, Patrick, *Francophone Sub-Saharan Africa, 1880–1995* (Cambridge: Cambridge University Press, 1999).

Marks, Shula, "Southern Africa," in J. Brown and W.R. Louis (eds.), *The Oxford History of the British Empire: The Twentieth Century* (Oxford: Oxford University Press, 1999).

Marshall, D. Bruce, *The French Colonial Myth and Constitution-Making in the Fourth Republic* (New Haven, CT: Yale University Press, 1973).

Marwick, Arthur, *British Society since 1945*, 4th edition (Harmondsworth: Penguin, 2003).

Midgley, Clare (ed.), *Gender and Imperialism* (Manchester: Manchester University Press, 1998).

Mirsky, G.I., *On Ruins of Empire: Ethnicity and Nationalism in the Former Soviet Union* (Westport, CT: Greenwood Press, 1997).

Mongia, Padmini (ed.), *Contemporary Post-colonial Theory: A Reader* (New York: Hodder Arnold, 1998).

Morris, Benny, *The Birth of the Palestinian Refugee Problem 1947–49* (Cambridge: Cambridge University Press, 1988).

Prakash, Gyan (ed.), *After Colonialism: Imperial Histories and Postcolonial Displacements* (Princeton, NJ: Princeton University Press, 1995).

Remnick, David, *Lenin's Tomb: The Last Days of the Soviet Empire* (New York: Vintage, 1994).

Said, Edward W., *Orientalism* (New York: Vintage, 1979).

Said, Edward W., *Culture and Imperialism* (New York: Knopf, 1993).

Shlaim, Avi, *Collusion across the Jordan: King Abdullah, the Zionist Movement and the Partition of Palestine* (Oxford: Clarendon Press, 1988).

Sorum, Paul C., *Intellectuals and Decolonization in France* (Chapel Hill, NC: UNC Press, 1977).

Stengers, Jean, "Precipitous Decolonization: The Case of the Belgian Congo," in P. Gifford and W.R. Louis (eds.), *The Transfer of Power in Africa: Decolonization 1940–1960* (New Haven, CT: Yale University Press, 1982).

Suny, R.G., *The Soviet Experiment: Russia, the USSR and the Successor States* (1997). . . . ??

Tsang, Steve, *A Modern History of Hong Kong* (New York: Tauris, 2007).

Van Goor, J. *De Nederlanse Kolonën. Geschiedenis van de Nederlanse expansie 1600–1975* (The Hague: SDU Uitgerverij, 1994).

Vidino, Lorenzo and Steven Emerson, *Al Qaeda in Europe: The New Battleground of International Jihad* (New York: Prometheus, 2005).

Von Laue, Theodore, *Why Lenin? Why Stalin? Why Gorbachev? The Rise and Fall of the Soviet System*, 3rd edition (New York: Longman, 1997).

White, Stephen, *After Gorbachev* (Cambridge: Cambridge University Press, 1993).

Winks, Robin, "Future of Imperial History," in Winks (ed.), *Oxford History of the British Empire*, vol. 5: *Historiography* (Oxford: Oxford University Press, 1999).

Wolpert, Stanley, *Shameful Flight: The Last Years of the British Empire in India* (Oxford: Oxford University Press, 2006).

Young, Crawford, *Politics in the Congo: Decolonization and Independence* (Princeton, NJ: Princeton University Press, 1965).

Further Reading

The literature on the end of empire is vast and growing; after several decades of comparative neglect, the subject has returned to the forefront of academic research. While this can only be a brief survey, several works stand out. Without question, the most up to date and comprehensive survey of the British empire is the *Oxford History of the British Empire* (5 vols., Oxford, Oxford University Press, 1999), edited by W.R. Louis. This covers the entire historical span of the empire, but volumes 4 and 5 (*The Twentieth Century* and *Historiography*) contain significant discussion of the post-1945 period. These have been followed by several supplementary volumes focusing on particular cases. Other important recent books on the end of the British empire include John Darwin, *Britain and Decolonization: The Retreat from Empire to the Postwar World* (London: Macmillan, 1988) and P.J. Cain and A.G. Hopkins, *British Imperialism: Crisis and Deconstruction 1914–1990* (London: Longman, 1993). An excellent ongoing series is the British Documents on the End of Empire Project (BDEEP), which has thus far produced four volumes each on the Labour government of 1945–1951 and the Conservative government of 1957–1963.

More general works published in English that consider the whole phenomenon of the European withdrawal are less numerous, but among the most useful are Robert Holland, *European Decolonization 1918–81: An Introductory Survey* (London: Macmillan, 1985) and Franz Ansprenger, *The Dissolution of the Colonial Empires* (London: Routledge, 1989). A short introduction to the topic is M.E. Chamberlain, *Decolonization: The Fall of the European Empires* (Oxford: Blackwell, 1985).

There are surprisingly few books about the French empire published in English, but two older works of importance are D. Bruce Marshall, *The French Colonial Myth and Constitution-Making in the Fourth Republic* (New Haven, CT: Yale University Press, 1973) and Paul C. Sorum, *Intellectuals and Decolonization in France* (Chapel Hill, NC: UNC Press, 1977). For Marxist approach to the last Portuguese empire see Gervase Clarence-Smith, *The Third*

Portuguese Empire 1825–1975: A Study in Economic Imperialism (Manchester: Manchester University Press, 1985).

Finally, there is a growing scholarship assessing the end of the Soviet Union and the birth of new nations, including G.I. Mirsky, *On Ruins of Empire: Ethnicity and Nationalism in the Former Soviet Union* (Westport, CT: Greenwood Press, 1997) and R.G. Suny, *The Soviet Experiment: Russia, the USSR and the Successor States* (1997).

CHAPTER SEVEN

European Integration: From the Common Market to the Single Market

DESMOND DINAN

Western European countries launched a process of highly institutionalized economic integration in the aftermath of World War II. This began with the European Coal and Steel Community (1952), in which the six founding member states (France, West Germany, Italy, Belgium, the Netherlands and Luxembourg) agreed to share responsibility for regulatory policy-making in their crucial coal and steel sectors. Although seemingly narrow and highly technical, the new Community was of immense political importance. It epitomized both Franco-German rapprochement and the member states' willingness to pool cherished national sovereignty in order to resolve otherwise intractable problems. The legacy of close cooperation and shared sovereignty animated the inauguration in 1958 of the European Economic Community (EEC), the next major building block of today's European Union (EU). With its core objective of a common market in which goods, services, capital, and people would move freely across national borders, the EEC was a hugely ambitious undertaking.

The course of European economic integration was anything but smooth over the following two decades. Only in the late 1980s, with the launch of a new legislative program, did national governments make a concerted effort to go beyond the customs union (established in 1968) and achieve the original goal of a common market, now called the single market. In the meantime, the EEC had constructed a common agricultural policy and enlarged to 12 member states (Denmark, Ireland and the UK joined in 1973; Greece in 1981; Portugal and Spain in 1986). In the Single European Act of 1987, member states agreed to complete the single market by 1992, to take other policy initiatives, and to alter the EEC's institutional arrangements with a view to improving efficiency and legitimacy.

The prevailing view among historians of European integration is that economic interests principally motivated member states to share sovereignty and establish supranational institutions. Only when separate national policies and traditional international cooperation proved inadequate did national governments opt for deeper integration. Strategic objectives, notably embedding West Germany into western Europe under the umbrella of the Atlantic alliance, were important considerations,

A Companion to Europe since 1945, First Edition. Edited by Klaus Larres.
© 2014 John Wiley & Sons, Ltd. Published 2014 by John Wiley & Sons, Ltd.

but economic interests predominated. Dreams of European unity or visions of a federal Europe had little tangible effect.

This chapter provides an overview of the course of European integration from the launch of the EEC in the late 1950s to the single market program 30 years later. First, it discusses the commitment to a customs union despite a British proposal to subsume the EEC into a wider free trade area. It then explores the causes and consequences of French president Charles de Gaulle's political challenges to the EEC, manifested in a veto of Britain's membership application and boycott of the Council of Ministers, the EEC's main decision-making institution. The next section covers the revival of European integration following de Gaulle's departure, encapsulated in the "Spirit of The Hague." The chapter then assesses the political and economic setbacks of the 1970s, ranging from the impact of British accession, to stagflation, to the pernicious effect of non-tariff barriers to trade. The final section describes the fortuitous combination of political, economic, and personal circumstances that led to the launch of the single market program, a development that coincided with, and perhaps contributed to, the reform movement in central and eastern Europe.

Customs Union or Free Trade Area?

Britain, which preferred not to join a supranational organization and feared the impact on its exports of a continental customs union, tried to thwart the establishment of the EEC by proposing instead a European free trade area. The idea appealed to many influential Europeans who were ambivalent about or opposed to the EEC. For instance, Ludwig Erhard, Germany's economics minister, feared that the EEC would be too protectionist. An economic liberal, Erhard favored global trade liberalization under the auspices of the General Agreement on Tariffs and Trade. Some French politicians, uninterested in liberalization, feared being trapped in a "little Europe" of six member states with an economically powerful Germany.

When the Six ended their negotiations and concluded the Rome Treaties on March 25, 1957, the founding document of the EEC, Britain took a new tack and proposed that the EEC, as an entity, join with other European countries in a free trade area. Britain wanted above all to prevent the Six from taking the first step towards implementing the customs union, in January 1959. Having vested so much in the EEC, and having included provisions in the Rome Treaty for agricultural policy and assistance for overseas colonies, French business and political leaders rejected Britain's overtures. Erhard was still interested in them, but German chancellor Konrad Adenauer remained committed less to the Rome Treaty itself than to the treaty's significance as a manifestation of Franco-German rapprochement.

The survival of the fledgling EEC would depend on French president Charles de Gaulle, who came to power in early 1958 following the collapse of the Fourth Republic. De Gaulle was notorious for his opposition to supranationalism and defense of national sovereignty, positions that resonated in Britain. The British could be forgiven for assuming that de Gaulle (to paraphrase Churchill) would strangle the Community baby at birth and dissolve the EEC into a broader free trade area. Indeed de Gaulle disliked the EEC's political pretensions, but he appreciated its economic potential. In particular, the EEC could help to modernize French industry, one of de Gaulle's overriding goals. Moreover, the common agricultural policy (CAP), promised in the Rome Treaty but not yet negotiated, could help defray the increasing costs of French farm subsidies.

To Britain's dismay, de Gaulle embraced the EEC. He signalled this unequivocally by announcing in October 1958 that France would honor the timetable for implementing the customs union and in November 1958 that the EEC would not participate in negotiations for a wider free trade area. This enraged British prime minister Harold Macmillan, who threatened to retaliate politically within the North Atlantic Treaty Organization (NATO), which would hardly have upset de Gaulle. The United States eventually intervened to calm Macmillan down. Britain then proposed a rival free trade area for non-EEC member states, which resulted in the European Free Trade Association (EFTA) in 1960. Seeing the EEC as a fait accompli, and preferring to be inside its tariff walls, Britain soon abandoned EFTA and, in a remarkable about-face, applied to join the EEC in 1961.[1]

The Gaullist Challenge

De Gaulle may have appreciated the EEC economically, but he distrusted it politically. De Gaulle espoused close intergovernmental cooperation among European states. He despised the Cold War and the global supremacy of the United States and the Soviet Union. In order to transcend the Cold War, he wanted to build bridges to the countries of central and eastern Europe, while transforming NATO into an equal partnership between western Europe and the United States. In the early 1960s, he thought that the EEC might form an organizational basis for a "European Europe," independent of American political control. He launched the Fouchet Plan to graft an intergovernmental political superstructure onto the EEC, but was thwarted by the Atlanticist, and pro-British, Belgians and Dutch. Instead, in January 1963, de Gaulle signed the Elysée Treaty with Adenauer. Far from spearheading an intergovernmental association of European states, the treaty later became one of the institutional planks of deeper supranational integration.[2]

De Gaulle's misgivings about the EEC's political orientation were generally in accord with those of the British government. Where de Gaulle and the British diverged, of course, was in their attitude towards the United States. Whereas de Gaulle distrusted the United States, the British embraced Washington in a supposed special relationship. The extent of the Anglo-American relationship became clear in December 1962 when Macmillan and US president John Kennedy reached an agreement in Nassau to supply US missiles for Britain's putatively independent nuclear force. De Gaulle, then striving for a truly independent French nuclear force, saw this as damning evidence of British subservience to the United States. As Britain was then negotiating EEC membership, and de Gaulle hoped to use the EEC as the basis for a "European Europe," the Nassau agreement convinced de Gaulle that he should not let Britain into the EEC.

De Gaulle may have already made up his mind, for economic reasons, to keep the British out. Having committed himself in 1958 to implementing the customs union for industrial goods, he turned his attention to implementing the common agricultural policy, which, because of the size and structure of the French farming sector, he considered a vital national interest. Putting the CAP in place involved a series of intensive negotiations among the member states throughout the early 1960s. Although by now an applicant for EEC membership, Britain, with a small and open agricultural sector, strongly opposed the CAP. If admitted to the EEC at this stage, de Gaulle knew, the British would ally with economic liberals in Germany and other member states to prevent the CAP from ever being implemented. It was a risk that de Gaulle, sensitive to the welfare of French farmers, would not take. He therefore vetoed Britain's application in January 1963, and again in November 1967 after Britain applied a second time.[3]

De Gaulle's first veto provoked a minor crisis in the EEC. Yet the other member states were more irritated by the manner than the consequences of de Gaulle's action. Even fervently pro-British member states suspected that British membership might be premature in the early 1960s. A combination of political and economic motives led de Gaulle to provoke a far greater crisis in 1965. Deeply resentful of Commission president Walter Hallstein's Euro-federalist ambitions, and eager to prevent a treaty-mandated change to qualified majority voting on agricultural and commercial policy issues, de Gaulle withdrew French representation from the Council of Ministers in July 1965. By trying to bring forward from 1970 (the deadline stipulated in the treaty) to mid-1965 a mechanism whereby the CAP would be funded directly from the EEC's own budget, instead of by national contributions, and linking it to an increase in the political authority of the supranational Commission and European Parliament, Hallstein gave de Gaulle an excellent pretext to act. Having pulled France out of the Council to protest Hallstein's proposals and the failure of the member states to reach an interim agreement on CAP funding, de Gaulle announced that France would not resume its full participation in the EEC unless the others agreed not to introduce qualified majority voting for decisions concerning the CAP and commercial policy, key areas in which de Gaulle feared that France would be outvoted by its more liberal partners.

If de Gaulle's high-handedness over Britain's application annoyed the other member states, his antics in the empty chair crisis pushed them over the edge. By that time Erhard, not the Francophile Adenauer, was chancellor of Germany. Under his informal leadership, the other member states stood their ground and refused to renegotiate the treaty. The impasse ended after de Gaulle received a salutary message from the French electorate. Although he won the presidential election of December 1965, de Gaulle did not receive the overwhelming majority that he thought his due. His opponent, none other than future president François Mitterrand, played the EEC card and garnered a lot of support. French farmers, in whose interests de Gaulle supposedly acted, signalled their concern that his obstructionism might kill the EEC – the goose that laid their golden egg (the CAP).

Under the terms of the so-called Luxembourg Compromise of January 1966, the Council would indeed make decisions by qualified majority vote, but a country could prevent the presidency from calling for a vote by claiming that a "very important national interest" was at stake. As national interests are notoriously difficult to define, and "very important" is an imprecise criterion, in effect the Luxembourg Compromise gave recalcitrant member states a means of perpetuating the veto in Council decision-making, a practice that became prevalent in the recessionary 1970s. In the meantime, he got his revenge by blocking Hallstein's reappointment. He also bullied the Commission into a decade of relative inaction.[4]

Thus the Luxembourg Compromise was a pyrrhic victory for the other member states, whose leaders took quiet satisfaction in de Gaulle's domestic difficulties, when strikers almost overthrew the regime in May 1968. Although he survived the immediate crisis, de Gaulle resigned in April 1969, having turned a referendum on minor institutional reforms into a vote of confidence in his presidency. De Gaulle's departure seemed to remove a major obstacle on the road to European integration. With the customs union completed in 1968, 18 months ahead of schedule, the CAP almost entirely in place, the common commercial policy coming on-stream, the Court of Justice establishing an impressive body of Community law, and the Commission seemingly rebounding under new leadership, it looked as if the EEC was in the ascendant.[5]

The Spirit of The Hague

Georges Pompidou, de Gaulle's successor, called for a summit meeting of EEC leaders to revive European integration. Pompidou was a Gaullist, but not a dogmatic one. Like de Gaulle, he appreciated the EEC's economic importance for France while opposing supranationalism. On the key question of British accession, however, he differed from de Gaulle. Once the CAP was firmly in place, which it would be when the EEC had its "own resources" (monies that accrued to the EEC's coffers rather than to national exchequers), Pompidou had no objection to Britain entering the EEC. On the contrary, with Germany powerful economically and assertive politically, Pompidou wanted Britain inside the Community as a counterbalance to Germany. Geopolitical considerations became uppermost for Pompidou as the new German government, under Willy Brandt, pursued *Ostpolitik* (a policy of rapprochement with the communist countries to the east).

The summit took place in The Hague in December 1969 (the Netherlands was then in the Council presidency). One of the most evocative events ever in the history of the EEC, it gave rise to the "spirit of The Hague," a sense that European integration was bouncing back. The summit communiqué committed the EEC to three related goals: completion, deepening, and enlargement. Completion meant wrapping up the unfinished business of the Rome Treaty, namely negotiating a budgetary agreement whereby the EEC could receive its own resources (from industrial tariffs and agricultural import duties), from which it would fund the CAP. Given that Hallstein's proposal to expedite the introduction of own resources had triggered the empty chair crisis, this was a sensitive subject.

Deepening meant moving the EEC in new directions, specifically towards economic and monetary union (EMU) and foreign policy cooperation. Pompidou's and Brandt's interest in these issues was pragmatic, not ideological. Neither wanted deeper integration for the sake of "building Europe." Both were interested in practical solutions to real problems, although Brandt, unlike Pompidou, was amenable to sharing national sovereignty in order to enhance monetary policy and foreign policy cooperation. The pressing reason for EMU was the international financial turmoil of the late 1960s, which culminated in 1971 in the formal collapse of the Bretton Woods system. One of the main reasons for foreign policy cooperation was French suspicion of *Ostpolitik*. By devising a procedure to share information and limit unilateralism in the foreign policy realm, Pompidou hoped to be able to keep *Ostpolitik* in check.[6]

The meaning of enlargement was self-evident. Britain's exclusion from the EEC had become synonymous with de Gaulle. Now that de Gaulle was gone, British accession seemed inevitable. But the situation was not that simple. For one thing, Pompidou insisted that member states conclude a budgetary agreement ("completion") before allowing Britain to join. Only then would the CAP be impervious to British efforts to change it. For another thing, British accession negotiations were bound to be arduous. Apart from the CAP, which was not negotiable, Britain demanded special access to the EEC market for Commonwealth producers, who already enjoyed preferential treatment in Britain. For sentimental and political reasons, Britain wanted to protect New Zealand farmers (Britons with family members in New Zealand were an influential lobby). Finally, because Britain, with its different agricultural system, would benefit relatively little from the CAP, the government wanted to contribute relatively less to the EEC budget, or else receive financial transfers from Brussels in other policy areas.

The heady mix of policies and preferences ensured that "completion, deepening, enlargement" would not be easy or straightforward. Moreover, the favorable atmospherics at the summit obscured deep personal and political differences between Brandt and Pompidou, the EEC's most prominent leaders. Pompidou, a bourgeois conservative, disliked Brandt and distrusted Germany, especially because of *Ostpolitik*. Brandt, a working-class socialist, appreciated the political importance of placating France but felt no particular affinity for Pompidou. Like all spectral beings, the spirit of The Hague, which hovered over the EEC in the early 1970s, proved ephemeral.

Member states reached a budget agreement without much difficulty in April 1970. It provided for the transfer to Brussels of tariffs and other monies collected at points of entry into the EEC. On the expenditure side, the CAP would be the largest item covered by the autonomous EEC budget. As part of the arrangement, the European Parliament received considerable budgetary authority to compensate for the transfer of some budgetary powers from the national to the European level. It is difficult to imagine that de Gaulle would have accepted such a proviso.

Completion cleared the way for enlargement, or at least for the start of British accession negotiations. As expected, these proved difficult. The sticking points were Britain's contribution to the Budget, New Zealand butter (lamb, the other big New Zealand export, was not yet covered by the CAP), and Commonwealth preferences. Quickly grasping that the member states were not about to allow cheap Commonwealth products, largely agricultural, to flood the EEC, Britain soon abandoned that demand, much to the ire of Commonwealth countries and their supporters in Britain. New Zealand was an exception, so much so that the Six made an obvious link. In return for allowing New Zealand butter into the EEC, Britain would have to agree to contribute more to the budget that it initially offered. This was acceptable to Britain. Nevertheless the extent of Britain's budgetary contribution caused a festering sore in Britain's relationship with the EEC, which British prime minister Margaret Thatcher resolved to cure in the early 1980s. Yet it was a problem for which the British had themselves, or their New Zealand kinsmen, to blame. The British parliament ratified the accession agreement in 1972 (Britain did not hold a referendum on whether to join).[7]

Three other countries – Denmark, Ireland, and Norway – applied to join along with Britain, and held referenda on the question in 1972. All were tied economically to Britain's coattails. Of the three, Ireland had the most intense economic and the most fraught political relationship with Britain. If Britain joined the EEC, Ireland could not afford to stay out. Yet EEC membership gave Ireland great economic and political opportunities. Having recently abandoned autarky in favor of openness, Ireland would avail of preferential access to a large European market, not to mention the bounty of the CAP. Having been dominated by Britain for hundreds of years, Ireland might also become more self-assured and, paradoxically, more sovereign in the EEC. Little wonder that the Irish electorate voted overwhelmingly for membership.

Denmark and Norway were less enamored of the EEC. Like Britain, both feared a diminution of sovereignty as a result of membership and looked at accession largely as an economic issue. With Britain and Germany, its two main markets, in the EEC, Denmark could hardly stay out. Nevertheless a sizeable minority of Danes chose that option in the referendum. In Norway, a small majority, fearful of the political and economic costs, prevailed against membership. The issue proved extremely divisive, and became the dividing line in Norwegian politics for a generation to come.

By the end of 1972, completion and enlargement were clearly on track, but what about deepening? Superficially, at least, the third leg of the EEC's post-de Gaulle revival was well on track. In October 1970 Pierre Werner, the prime minister of Luxembourg, produced a report on EMU which the other national leaders subsequently endorsed. The plan called for a phased approach, culminating in the launch of a single monetary policy (and possibly a single currency) in 1980. Yet the plan was shallow and disguised bitter differences among member states. Some, like Belgium and France, wanted monetary union to precede economic convergence; others, like Germany and the Netherlands, wanted economic convergence to prepare the way for monetary union. It was no coincidence that Belgium and France were weak-currency countries, and Germany and the Netherlands strong-currency countries. Germany and the Netherlands, whose strong currencies rested on sound macro-economic policies, wanted a single European currency, whether virtual or real, to rest on sound EEC-wide macro-economic policies. In their view, Belgium and France wanted to gain from EMU without suffering the pain of fiscal rectitude.

There was another fundamental difference between France and the others on the question of EMU. Pompidou, an intergovernmentalist, did not want to share any more sovereignty. The others, although not necessarily committed to supranationalism, agreed that EMU could not work without pooling sovereignty in a European central bank. For the sake of political expediency, the Werner Report fudged the issue. Like a Holy Scripture, it was all things to all men. It is doubtful that the Werner Plan could have been implemented even had economic circumstances in the 1970s been propitious. As it happened, the oil crisis and ensuing recession blew the Werner Plan way off course.[8]

Member states disputed neither the desirability nor the feasibility of foreign policy cooperation, the other area in which they hoped to deepen European integration.

All agreed that such cooperation should be strictly intergovernmental and limited to an exchange of information and ideas. Foreign ministers easily endorsed a plan drawn up by Etienne Davignon, a Belgian diplomat, to hold regular meetings on "European Political Cooperation," in order to exchange information about international issues. Germany gladly used European Political Cooperation as a way to defuse French and others' concerns about *Ostpolitik*.

In December 1972, on the eve of enlargement, national leaders held a summit in Paris both to celebrate the spirit of The Hague and to discuss the future of the enlarged EEC. The summit communiqué included a commitment, much derided in retrospect, "to transform, before the end of the present decade . . . the whole complex of the relations of [the] member states into a European Union."[9] This should not be taken at face value. Pompidou, an arch-intergovermentalist, was not endorsing a supranational European Union of the kind that came into being in 1993. For him, and for many in the postwar decades, "European Union" did not have a precise meaning. Instead, it conveyed the ideal of peaceful, cooperative relations among the countries of western Europe (central and eastern Europe being cutoff by the Cold War). Thus the call for European Union in December 1972, with a target date of 1980, did not imply a master plan for a far-reaching federation. On the contrary, it was a declaration of faith in Europe's future, inspired by the terminally ill French president, who was concerned about his place in history.

Setbacks

Britain and Denmark took a long time to settle into the EEC (some would say that they have not yet settled into the EU). For Britain in particular, the first decade of EEC membership was a trial for it and for the original member states. Britain entered the EEC under the leadership of Edward Heath, the country's most pro-European prime minister until Tony Blair formed a government in 1997. No sooner was Britain in, however, than Labour Party leader Harold Wilson won the general election and formed a new government. Wilson was acutely aware that few Britons were enthusiastic about the EEC and that membership deeply divided his party. Having campaigned in the general election on a mildly anti-EEC platform, Wilson demanded a renegotiation of Britain's membership terms once he became prime minister, and promised to put the results to a referendum.

Britain's EEC partners were appalled. German chancellor Helmut Schmidt, a fellow social democrat, urged restraint. Schmidt explained to Valéry Giscard d'Estaing, the new president of France, that Wilson faced domestic political difficulties and that it was best, for the sake of Britain's continued membership, to resolve the situation to everyone's satisfaction. A patrician conservative, Giscard disliked Wilson personally and politically, but agreed to play along. The renegotiation of Britain's membership terms, which focused on financial issues, dominated the EEC in late 1974 and early 1975, ending at a summit in Dublin in March. Under the terms of the settlement, EEC leaders agreed to double the size of the European Regional Development Fund, most of which would go to Britain in lieu of large-scale agricultural subsidies, and accepted the principle of a "correcting mechanism" to provide a budget rebate.

Both measures were intended in large measure to help Wilson win the ensuing referendum and thereby keep Britain in the EEC. An extraordinary political event, this was the first nationwide referendum in Britain, a country that cherished the sanctity of parliamentary sovereignty (the idea that elected parliamentarians were solely responsible for legislative and other major decision-making). Thatcher, the new leader of the Conservative Party, strongly opposed the idea of holding a referendum. Once parliament approved the referendum, however, she campaigned wholeheartedly for Britain to stay in the EEC. That seems surprising in view of her later hostility to the EU. But in the mid-1970s, for Thatcher as for most Britons, the EEC meant simply a common market (indeed, Britons referred colloquially to the EEC as "the Common Market"). Despite their concerns about national sovereignty, Thatcher and most other Conservatives supported the EEC for economic reasons. With strong Conservative and split Labour support, the outcome of the referendum was hardly in doubt. Sixty-seven percent voted in favor of staying in the EEC (the turnout was 64%).[10]

That should have ended the matter. No sooner was Thatcher elected prime minister in 1979, however, than she returned to the fray. This time she asked not to renegotiate Britain's membership terms, but to put the principle of the "correcting mechanism" into practice by winning for Britain a huge, annual budget rebate. On a purely financial basis, Britain paid too much into the EEC and got too little in return. Thatcher had a reasonable case to make. But the way that she made it exasperated her EEC colleagues and dragged the issue out for five years, when it dominated countless ministerial meetings.

Demanding Britain's money back, Thatcher hectored and lectured her fellow national leaders. Mutual antipathy between Thatcher and Giscard (both conservatives, but one radical and the other moderate) exacerbated the problem. Only when Mitterrand became president of France was it possible to find a way out of the impasse. Mitterrand, who found Thatcher fascinating in a freakish way, and who wanted to end the British budgetary question in order to reinvigorate European integration, was instrumental in finding a mutually acceptable solution during his country's EEC presidency in early 1984. Under the terms of the settlement, Britain won a generous annual rebate and national leaders agreed to review the budget as a whole.

The British renegotiations of 1974–1975 and resolution of the British budgetary question ten years later bracketed a difficult and disappointing period in the history of European integration. Britain's experience in the EEC, not to mention the EEC's experience of British membership, was made much worse by the harsh economic climate that coincided with enlargement. The combined effects of international financial turmoil and the oil crisis of late 1973 and 1974 caused massive disruption. The golden age of high and persistent postwar growth came to an abrupt end. Rising unemployment, spiraling inflation, and plummeting growth swept western Europe, although some countries fared better than others. Here was a true test for the EEC. Would economic integration wither in the face of stagflation or would the Community provide its member states with the will and the means to pull through together?

Both at the time and in retrospect, the EEC seemed to be gripped by Eurosclerosis: a bloated bureaucracy, a CAP out of financial control, and a Council incapable of

making decisions. As they saw it, Giscard and Schmidt came to the rescue by inau-
gurating the European Council – regular meetings of national leaders to direct the
beleaguered Community. Not only that, but by launching the European Monetary
System in 1979, a far-sighted initiative for exchange rate stability, they pointed the
otherwise moribund EEC towards completion of the single market program and the
Holy Grail of monetary union.

The truth is less dramatic than that. European integration certainly stalled in the
late 1970s, but the situation was not entirely bleak. The biggest problem, hardly
perceptible to most Europeans, was the proliferation of non-tariff barriers to trade.
Since implementation of the customs union in 1968, there were no more tariff barriers among member states. But non-tariff barriers, ranging from different national
product standards to different testing requirements, were pervasive. Goods could not
travel freely throughout the EEC as long as those barriers existed. The Rome Treaty
included provision for the harmonization of national laws, through qualified majority
voting in the Council, in order to complete the internal market. As the recession
intensified, governments became less and less willing to make concessions in the
Council. Far from being to everyone's benefit, harmonization looked increasingly
like a zero-sum game. Moreover, the Luxembourg Compromise gave national governments an excuse to block decision-making in the Council by claiming that a very
important national interest was at stake (the interest often being pressure from
domestic lobbies). As a result, proposals for harmonization languished in Council
working groups, sometimes for years on end.[11]

Implementation of the single market, originally envisioned as a gradual but relentless process, quickly ground to a halt. Enlargement made matters worse because
Britain and Denmark, jealous of their national sovereignty, championed the national
veto. Little wonder that "political attitudes to harmonization in Denmark and the
United Kingdom . . . [varied] from the politically skeptical to the stridently hostile."[12]
Far from eradicating non-tariff barriers, member states introduced new ones in
response to straitened economic circumstances.

In other respects the EEC fared surprisingly well. Greece, Portugal, and Spain
emerged from dictatorial regimes in the mid-1970s and promptly applied for membership. At a time of rampant Eurosclerosis, it was comforting for the Community
to be courted by three potential new members. For emotional rather than practical
reasons, the EEC put Greece on a fast track for membership (prime minister
Constantine Karamanlis's evocation of ancient Athenian democracy swayed his
European counterparts). Following relatively short negotiations, Greece entered the
EEC in January 1981. Portugal and Spain, which presented more formidable economic challenges, went through a longer and more arduous accession process, joining
only in January 1986.

Regardless of prevailing economic circumstances, the road to Mediterranean
enlargement cast the EEC as a beacon of stability for newly democratic countries. A
major international initiative in the 1970s also reflected well on the EEC. That was
the negotiation of the Lomé Convention, a generous trade and aid agreement
between the EEC and 46 developing countries scattered throughout Africa, the
Caribbean, and Pacific (ACP), all former colonies of EC member states. Instead
of renegotiating an existing relationship (the Yaoundé Convention) with the ACP

countries, the EEC sought a new departure in keeping with global concerns about the growing North–South divide. Although later criticized for being post-colonial and exploitative, and viewed by the United States at the time as a threat to American trade interests, the first Lomé Convention won plaudits in development circles and boosted the EEC's profile and morale.

Institutionally, the launch of the European Council gave national leaders an opportunity to meet frequently to resolve contentious problems and keep the Community afloat during a generally turbulent time. By its nature – a gathering of national leaders in an informal decision-making capacity – the European Council was an intergovernmental body. That alarmed supporters of supranationalism, including small member states that feared big-member state dominance. Given Giscard's disinterest in the small member states and disdain for the Commission, their putative champion, such fears were understandable. To counterbalance the European Council, supranationalists advocated the introduction of direct elections to the European Parliament, something envisioned in the Rome Treaty but not within a particular time frame. A directly elected parliament, they presumed, would be a politically more powerful one. Giscard, an intergovernmentalist, was happy to improve the appearance of democracy at the European level by agreeing to direct elections, without necessarily increasing the Parliament's powers. Eventually, after intensive negotiations about the reallocation of seats in the Parliament for each member state, the first direct elections took place in June 1979.

An otherwise seemingly dismal decade ended on the high point of both direct elections and the launch of the European Monetary System (EMS). Following the demise of EMU in the mid-1970s, a new monetary policy initiative only a few years later looked foolhardy. But the proposed EMS was a relatively modest step. Far from envisioning monetary union, the EMS sought only to promote exchange rate stability at a time of wild fluctuations among member state currencies and between European currencies and the US dollar. Commission President Roy Jenkins launched the idea in 1977, but Schmidt, more irritated with US international financial management (or mismanagement) than enamored of the EEC, hijacked the proposal in early 1978. He ran it by Giscard, his close friend and fellow former finance minister. Thereafter the EMS became synonymous with Giscard and Schmidt and went down in history as a Franco-German initiative.[13]

With some input from the Commission, French and German officials worked out the details of the EMS, which EU leaders approved at the end of 1978. Partly out of pique but mostly for reasons of national sovereignty, the British declined to participate in the system's Exchange Rate Mechanism (ERM). The ERM used a parity grid based on the European currency unit (ECU), an artificial currency drawn from a basket of participating currencies, weighted according to their values. Currencies could fluctuate against each other within a band of plus or minus 2.25% of their value. National authorities would have to approve parity changes and take fiscal and monetary policy measures to stay within the band.

The success of the EMS, both economically and symbolically, became apparent in the early 1980s after a number of parity changes. Big fluctuations in exchange rates among participating currencies became a thing of the past, and the discipline of staying in the ERM helped with the fight against inflation. Yet its highly technical nature, as well as the continuing British budgetary question, obscured the success of the new monetary system. The EEC's apparent obsession with Britain's budget rebate also obscured other important developments. Perhaps the most consequential of these was a growing realization on the part of politicians, officials, and business people throughout the EEC that non-tariff barriers to trade had to be tackled and the single market finally implemented if Europe was ever to overcome the economic setbacks of the 1970s. Pragmatism (the need for harmonization) and ideology (the onset of neo-liberalism) combined to infuse new life into the EEC. The result was a dramatic acceleration of European integration in the late 1980s.

The Acceleration of Integration

Jacques Delors, who became Commission President in January 1985, is often credited with causing the dramatic improvement in the EEC's fortunes. Undoubtedly Delors envisioned a stronger, deeper EEC, with responsibility for many more policy areas and greater supranational powers. He wanted both EMU and political union, although he was not sure exactly what the latter meant. As a charismatic, skilled politician (but with little experience of elective office) from a large and influential member state (France), with close ties to the leader of the largest and most influential member state (Germany), Delors was ideally placed to personify the acceleration of European integration. Yet Delors was an enabler rather than an architect of the EEC's revival, which was already well on track by the time he moved to Brussels.

The Commission that Delors took over was finally emerging from a long, post-de Gaulle depression. Roy Jenkins, Commission President from 1977 to 1981, was an activist who tried to inject new life into the institution. A former British finance minister, he spent most of his time consumed by the British budgetary question, which he called the "Bloody British Question," and battling Giscard for the right to sit in the European Council and in meetings of the newly launched group of seven most industrialized countries (G7). Disillusioned, he returned to London to fight Thatcher on her own turf (he helped found the new Social Democratic Party).[14]

Gaston Thorn, a former prime minister of Luxembourg and Jenkins's successor, was a weak Commission President. Nevertheless the Commission began to stir to life during his tenure, thanks largely to the influence of Vice-President Etienne Davignon, author of the plan for foreign policy cooperation a decade earlier. As Commissioner for industrial affairs, Davignon reached out to European business, hoping to combine private sector pressure and Commission leadership in the service of greater market integration. European business people increasingly lamented the fragmentation of the European market. A group of leading industrialists, including the chief executive officers of Philips (the Dutch electronics firm), Volvo (the Swedish car manufacturer), and Olivetti (the Italian computer maker), banded together to form the European Round Table, a high-level lobby for completion of the single market.

Their rationale for market integration was simple. In the face of stiff competition from the United States and the Asian tigers, western European firms were unable to compete internationally. This was hardly a novelty. As long ago as 1968 J.J. Servan-Schreiber, a French pundit, had written *The American Challenge*, a book with a catchy title that advocated deeper European integration in order to ward off the threat from US multinationals. Europe's plight was far worse nearly 15 years later. Especially in the automobile and electronics sectors, European manufacturers felt besieged by cheaper, more reliable American and Asian imports. Their response was to call for a united European market in which they could maximize economies of scale, regain market share, and learn to compete globally.

The Commission and the European Round Table made strange bedfellows, not least because business people routinely dismissed Commissioners and their staff as ineffectual bureaucrats. Yet Davignon's no-nonsense approach impressed them. By launching a successful research program for collaboration between the Commission, industry, and universities in the high-technology sector, Davignon demonstrated that he could deliver the goods. The resurgent Commission, under Davignon's rather than Thorn's sway, and the European Round Table lobbied national leaders to revisit the internal market. In effect, that meant picking up the pace in the Council of harmonization of national rules and regulations on product manufacturing, testing, and certification.

National leaders were highly susceptible to such lobbying. Thatcher, elected in 1979 with a mandate for economic reform, urged European-wide deregulation and liberalization. By 1983, Britain was beginning to emerge from the initially disastrous impact of Thatcher's domestic economic policies. The bracing winds of neo-liberalism were about to blow over the continent, where left-of-center social democratic and right-of-center Christian democratic leaders grasped the need for fundamental change. Without endorsing Reaganite or Thatcherite ideology, presidents and prime ministers like Mitterrand in France, Helmut Kohl in Germany, and Felipe Gonzalez in Spain understood the need to abandon old nostrums and failed approaches. This was most obvious in France, where Mitterrand, elected in May 1981 on a doctrinaire socialist platform, made a dramatic U-turn in March 1983 and embraced market principles. Had he not done so, the franc would have been forced out of the ERM, with disastrous financial consequences.

Reflecting changing attitudes in the EEC, the communiqués of several summit meetings in the early 1980s included promises to complete the internal market. The directly elected European Parliament passed resolutions to the same effect. Led by Altiero Spinelli, the veteran Italian Euro-federalist and former Commissioner, a parliamentary committee produced the "Draft Treaty Establishing the European Union," which parliament as a whole approved in February 1984. Going far beyond a call for completion of the single market, the draft treaty contained a blueprint for a supranational EU, including EMU and closer foreign policy cooperation. Mitterrand, in the Council presidency in early 1984, endorsed the draft treaty and cast himself as the leader of a resurgent EEC. He bent over backwards to resolve the British budgetary question in order to clear the decks for new policy initiatives. At Mitterrand's urging, the other national leaders agreed at a summit in June 1984 to appoint a committee to consider whether and how the Rome Treaty might be revised.[15]

Thatcher viewed Mitterrand's behavior with some suspicion. She had no interest in EMU or other new initiatives, but simply wanted completion of the single market and, possibly, closer foreign policy cooperation – but on a strictly intergovernmental basis. Thatcher saw no need to revise the Rome Treaty in order to achieve what was, after all, one of the treaty's main objectives. She argued that an informal agreement among national leaders to dispense with the national veto would suffice to get the single market going again. Kohl, who came to power in 1982, was detached from the debate. Preoccupied with domestic political issues, he had not yet formed a close friendship with Mitterrand in the service of deeper European integration.

The committee duly met in late 1984 under the chairmanship of Jim Dooge, a former Irish foreign minister. In its report to EEC leaders in March 1984, the committee recommended the convening of an intergovernmental conference (a forum of national representatives) to revise the Rome Treaty, with a view to formally launching the single market program, strengthening the powers of the European Parliament, and incorporating areas such as environmental policy and foreign policy cooperation into the treaty. National leaders took note of the report but did not act on it yet, being caught up in a Greek demand for compensation because of the supposedly negative impact of Portuguese and Spanish accession. Nevertheless they took the time to authorize Delors to draw up a white paper, or policy document, on completing the single market.

The Milan summit of June 1985, at which national leaders considered both the Dooge Report and the Commission's white paper, was one of the most important in the history of European integration. Delors and Arthur Cockfield, a British Conservative and the internal market Commissioner, drew up the white paper in record time because many of the proposals in it had been lying around Council working groups for years, victims of the national veto. Cockfield's contribution was to organize the proposals into categories of barriers – physical, technical, and fiscal – and present a detailed action plan against which officials, politicians, and business people could measure progress towards the single market. National leaders endorsed the white paper and, over Thatcher's opposition, decided to hold an intergovernmental conference that autumn.

This was the genesis of the Single European Act (SEA).[16] Concluded at the Luxembourg summit in December 1985 and signed by foreign ministers in February 1986, the SEA committed member states to completing the single market, defined as an area in which goods, services, people, and capital could move freely, by the end of December 1992. In order to make it happen, national governments agreed to use qualified majority voting for the majority of harmonization measures in the Commission's white paper, the blueprint for the single market program.

The SEA contained other institutional and policy provisions. One of the most important of these was the cooperation procedure for legislative decision-making, whereby the European Parliament won the right to a second reading of Commission proposals. Although relatively modest, the cooperation procedure set a precedent for the more far-reaching co-decision procedure, introduced in the Maastricht Treaty of 1992 and strengthened in subsequent treaty reforms. The rationale for the cooperation procedure was not simply to strengthen supranationalism in the EEC, about which some governments were far from enthusiastic, but to close what was already being called the "democratic deficit" – the growing gap between the governed and the governing in the EEC – by boosting the decision-making role of the directly elected parliament.

The main policy innovation in the SEA was a commitment to increase spending on so-called cohesion (efforts to bring poorer countries and regions closer to the Community-wide economic norm). Here was an issue that pitted Thatcher against Delors and other EEC leaders. As a die-hard economic liberal, Thatcher saw no need for the EEC, or national governments for that matter, to help less-advantaged regions. Like a rising tide, she argued, a rising economy would lift all boats. The salvation of the poorer regions lay in the single market program, not in cohesion policy. The other national leaders, less enamored than Thatcher of the free market and firm believers in government intervention, upheld the principle of transfer payments from rich EEC regions, mostly in the northwest, to poor ones, mostly on the Celtic and Mediterranean periphery.

It was one thing for them to proclaim the merit of cohesion policy, but quite another to come up with adequate funding for it. A row soon erupted over Delors's proposal for EEC expenditure covering the period 1988–1992 to include generous allocations for the structural funds, the means by which cohesion policy would be implemented. The "Club Med" countries (Greece, Portugal, Spain, and Ireland, an honorary member) made principled arguments in favor of generous financial transfers, before threatening to block implementation of the single market program unless they got their way. Finally Delors prevailed on Kohl, the paymaster of the EEC, who by that time was keenly interested in European integration, to cover the extra costs. Agreement on the Delors budgetary package paved the way for completion of the single market.

With two new member states (Portugal and Spain), a generous cohesion policy, and a renewed drive to complete the single market, the EEC appeared in the late 1980s to have a new lease on life. Thatcher was the fly in the ointment. While strongly supporting the single market program, she bitterly opposed related efforts to deepen European integration. She focused her fury on Kohl and Mitterrand, now working in tandem to accelerate European integration, and especially Delors, whom she accused of pushing Euro-federalism. Thatcher and Delors outlined their contending views of Europe in a series of legendary speeches on the future of the EEC. Delors's famous declaration in July 1988 that, in ten years' time, "80 per cent of our economic legislation and perhaps even of our fiscal and social legislation will be of Community origin,"[17] infuriated Thatcher. Her response was a clarion call to Euroskeptics: "We have not successfully rolled back the frontiers of the state in Britain only to see them reimposed at the European level with a European superstate exercising a new dominance from Brussels."[18]

What Thatcher most feared was the growing momentum to build EMU on the back of the successful single market program. Against the advice of her finance minister, she acquiesced in a clause in the SEA mentioning EMU, which nonetheless stated that it could not happen without another intergovernmental conference. In June 1988, again against Thatcher's wishes, the European Council agreed to establish a committee, under Delors's chairmanship, to chart the road to EMU. At the same time, they approved the full liberalization of capital movements, a key element of the single market program and a necessary precondition for EMU. These decisions, and the cotemporaneous changes brewing in central and eastern Europe, led inexorably to EMU and, parenthetically, contributed to Thatcher's political downfall.[19]

Conclusion

The SEA, which came into effect in July 1987, provided the institutional machinery (in the form of qualified majority voting and a new legislative procedure) used to enact most single market measures. The Commission duly submitted legislative proposals, and the Council and Parliament began the lengthy process of turning them into law. The phrase "single market" became widely used instead of "internal market" or "common market," largely because of the prominence of the SEA. The single market program, known colloquially as the "1992 program," became synonymous with the revival of European integration, leading to the establishment of the EU. For the first and perhaps only time in its history, the European project evoked warm and friendly feelings among ordinary people, before anxieties about democratic accountability, national identity, and globalization overshadowed the course and conduct of European integration.

Notes

1 On Britain's free trade area, see Milward, *National Strategy*, 231–309; Ellison, *Threatening Europe*; Lynch, "De Gaulle's First Veto."
2 On de Gaulle's plans for Europe, see Bozo, *Two Strategies for Europe*; Giauque, *Grand Designs*.
3 On Britain's application and de Gaulle's first veto, see Milward, op. cit., 310–441.
4 On the empty chair crisis and its outcome, see Palayret, Wallace, and Winand, *Visions, Votes and Vetoes*.
5 On the EEC development in the 1960s, see Von der Groeben, *Formative Years*.
6 On the spirit of The Hague and Franco-German relations, see Simonian, *Privileged Partnership*.
7 On the Britain negotiations, see O'Neill, *Britain's Entry*.
8 On the Werner Plan and its fate, see Tsoukalis, *Politics and Economics of European Monetary Integration*.
9 European Commission, *Sixth Report*, 6–9.
10 On the British renegotiation and referendum, see Butler and Kitzinger, *The 1975 Referendum*.
11 On harmonization and market integration, see Egan, *Constructing a European Market*.
12 Dashwood, "Hastening Slowly," 291.
13 On the EMS, see Ludlow, *Making of the European Monetary System*.
14 See Jenkins, *Life at the Centre*, 470–471.
15 On Mitterrand's commitment to European integration, see Cole, *François Mitterrand*, 35–72.
16 On the origin and negotiation of the SEA, see Moravcsik, *Choice for Europe*, 314–378.
17 Delors, *Speech to the Parliament*, 140.
18 See Thatcher, *Downing Street Years*, 742.
19 On the road to EMU, see Dyson and Featherstone, *Road to Maastricht*.

Bibliography

Bozo, Frederic, *Two Strategies for Europe: De Gaulle, the United States, and the Atlantic Alliance* (Lanham, MD: Rowman & Littlefield, 2001).

Butler, David and Uew Kitzinger, *The 1975 Referendum* (London: Macmillan, 1976).

Cole, Alistair, *François Mitterrand: A Study in Political Leadership* (London: Routledge, 1994).

Dashwood, Alan, "Hastening Slowly: The Community's Path towards Harmonization," in Helen Wallace, William Wallace, and Carole Webb (eds.), *Policy-Making in the European Communities* (London: John Wiley & Sons, 1977).

Delors, Jacques, *Speech to the Parliament*, July 6, 1988, OJ-EP, 2–367.

Dinan, Desmond, *Europe Recast: A History of European Union* (Basingstoke: Palgrave Macmillan, 2004).

Dyson, Kenneth and Kevin Featherstone, *The Road to Maastricht: Negotiating Economic and Monetary Union* (Oxford: Oxford University Press, 1999).

Egan, Michelle, *Constructing a European Market: Standards, Regulation, and Governance* (Oxford: Oxford University Press, 2001).

Eichengreen, Barry, *The European Economy since 1945: Coordinated Capitalism and Beyond* (Princeton, NJ: Princeton University Press, 2007).

Ellison, James, *Threatening Europe: Britain and the Creation of the European Community, 1955–1958* (London: Macmillan, 2000).

European Commission, *Sixth Report on the General Activities of the European Communities* (Luxembourg: European Communities, 1973).

Giauque, Jeffrey Glen, *Grand Designs and Visions of Unity: The Atlantic Powers and the Reorganization of Western Europe, 1955–1963* (Chapel Hill: University of North Carolina Press, 2002).

Gilbert, Mark, *Surpassing Realism: The Politics of European Integration since 1945* (Lanham, MD: Rowman and Littlefield, 2003).

Gillingham, John, *European Integration, 1950–2002: Superstate or New Market Economy?* (Cambridge: Cambridge University Press, 2003).

Jenkins, Roy, *Life at the Center: Memoirs of a Radical Reformer* (New York: Random House, 1991).

Ludlow, Peter, *The Making of the European Monetary System* (London: Butterworths, 1982).

Lynch, Frances, "De Gaulle's First Veto: France, the Rueff Plan and the Free Trade Area," *Contemporary European History* 19, no. 1, March 2000, 111–136.

Milward, Alan, *The UK and the European Community*, vol. 1: *The Rise and Fall of a National Strategy, 1945–1963* (London: Whitehall History Publishing in association with Frank Cass, 2002).

Moravcsik, Andrew, *The Choice for Europe: Social Purpose and State Power from Messina to Maastricht* (Ithaca: Cornell University Press, 1998).

O'Neill, Con, *Britain's Entry into the European Community: Report by Sir Con O'Neill on the Negotiations, 1970–1972* (London: Whitehall History Publishing in association with Frank Cass, 2000).

Palayret, Jean Marie, Helen Wallace, and Pascaline Winand (eds.), *Visions, Votes and Vetoes: The Empty Chair Crisis and the Luxembourg Compromise Forty Years On* (Brussels: Peter Lang Publishing, 2006).

Servan-Schreiber, J.J., *The American Challenge* (New York: Atheneum, 1968).

Simonian, Haig, *Privileged Partnership: Franco-German Relations in the European Community, 1969–1984* (Oxford: Clarendon Press, 1985).

Thatcher, Margaret, *Downing Street Years* (New York: HarperCollins, 1993).

Tsoukalis, Loukas, *The Politics and Economics of European Monetary Integration* (London: Allen & Unwin, 1977).

Von der Groeben, Hans, *The European Community: The Formative Years* (Brussels: Commission of the European Communities, 1985)

Further Reading

Three good histories of the EU, which include detailed accounts of the period covered in this chapter, are Desmond Dinan, *Europe Recast: A History of European Union* (Basingstoke: Palgrave Macmillan, 2004); Mark Gilbert, *Surpassing Realism: The Politics of European Integration since 1945* (Lanham: Rowman and Littlefield, 2003); and John Gillingham, *European Integration, 1950–2002: Superstate or New Market Economy?* (Cambridge: Cambridge University Press, 2003). Barry Eichengreen, *The European Economy since 1945: Coordinated Capitalism and Beyond* (Princeton, NJ: Princeton University Press, 2007), provides a detailed analysis of economic developments in Europe in the postwar period.

CHAPTER EIGHT

The United States and European Integration, 1945–1990

Klaus Larres

During the entire Cold War all US administrations were in support of the ever closer integration of western Europe. The American enthusiasm for the creation of a united Europe was greatest in the decade after the Marshall Plan had been launched. A certain coolness towards the idea occurred in the years since 1958, after the EEC had come into being. Yet, it will be argued in this chapter that a decisive turning point was only reached in the early 1970s when economic and also increasing political competition from the EEC made Washington rethink its basic attitude towards the process of European integration in a more fundamental way.

One can thus discern two major stages of intensity with respect to the American enthusiasm for European integration between 1945 and 1990.[1] During the initial stage, encompassing the first two postwar decades until the end of the Johnson administration in 1968/69, all American governments were in strong support of the integration of the European continent within an Atlantic framework. Charles de Gaulle's challenge to American leadership of Europe throughout the 1960s did not fundamentally alter Washington's pro-integration policy.[2] The late 1960s/early 1970s, however, proved to be a decisive turning point as far as America's European strategy was concerned. In the course of the second stage, from the advent of the Nixon administration in early 1969 to the end of the Cold War in 1989/90, American support for the further integration of the European continent deteriorated considerably. After all, the world of the 1970s and 1980s was much more complex, interconnected, and economically more competitive than had been the case during the previous two decades which were largely characterized by the bipolarity of the early Cold War. By the early 1970s, not so much traditional foreign policy matters but rather a climate of severe trade competition and economic jealousy had begun to dominate America's relations with the European Economic Community (EEC). This crisis culminated during the second half of Jimmy Carter's presidency and the first years of Ronald Reagan's first term in office, when Helmut Schmidt was West German chancellor and Giscard d'Estaing and James Callaghan governed in Paris and London. Moreover, from the late 1970s the economic difficulties were complemented by serious European–American differences over security issues

A Companion to Europe since 1945, First Edition. Edited by Klaus Larres.
© 2014 John Wiley & Sons, Ltd. Published 2014 by John Wiley & Sons, Ltd.

and NATO's policy towards the Soviet Union. Trade and security matters became closely intertwined and this situation contributed to the bitterness of transatlantic conflicts.

With hindsight it is clear that the transatlantic crisis during the last two decades of the Cold War was strongly influenced by the gradual emancipation of western Europe from American tutelage; in particular the Europeans were questioning America's predominance in the economic sphere. Washington, however, was not prepared to accept this challenge to its pre-eminent position within the Western world. With its support for European reconstruction and integration after World War II the USA had never intended to nourish a genuinely independent "third force" on the European continent. The Europeans were always meant to remain secondary in importance and influence to the United States. This also applied to the Kennedy era in the early 1960s when the United States appeared to be much more prepared than hitherto to grant the Europeans a greater input into transatlantic relations and view them as genuinely independent actors on the world stage.[3]

Despite all early generosity and genuine idealistic enthusiasm for European unity, Washington always had its own advantages in mind when supporting European integration. Although it may be claimed with some justification that there was something unique about the way the American "empire" and American "hegemony" developed,[4] throughout the entire Cold War the United States resembled very much a traditional great power, at least as far as its willingness to remain the undisputed leader of the Atlantic system was concerned.[5] Equally, in the post-Cold War era, and in particular in the post-9/11 years, it was difficult to detect any willingness on the part of the United States to surrender its hegemonic position within the Atlantic alliance. Instead, and in particular in connection with the invasion of Iraq in March 2003, the underlying increasing rivalry in transatlantic relations which had taken root since the early 1970s came ever more to the forefront.[6]

It will be argued in this chapter that in the 1970s and 1980s transatlantic mistrust and Washington's ever greater preoccupation with its own economic competitiveness and global hegemonic standing pushed the leading EC governments into cooperating increasingly closely, for example, by means of the creation of the European Monetary System and the Single European Act. These developments were viewed with great distrust by the USA. What set the stone rolling was the Nixon administration's policy of attempting to uphold America's global position while at the same time neglecting both the economic-financial dimension of such a role and genuine political and military cooperation with its European allies. Both gradually encouraged the western Europeans to develop common economic, financial, and even political institutions.

While to a large extent President Carter benignly neglected European integration in the late 1970s, the Reagan administration's attempt to reimpose 1950s-style American unilateralism on the transatlantic alliance and ignore the European integration process led to a severe crisis in transatlantic relations and pushed the European countries even further together in the 1980s. Only in the course of the dramatic events of 1989/90 did President George H.W. Bush manage to realign the USA with the process of European integration and, at least for a short time, link Washington's policy once again with America's old pro-integrationist vision as formulated in the aftermath of World War II.

In the following, Washington's broad geopolitical strategy towards the process of European integration from the late 1940s until the early 1990s will be analyzed. The chapter juxtaposes the continuities of Washington's policy with the abrupt change in policy which took place in the early to mid-1970s and in 1989/90.

Europe and America during the Years of Reconstruction

Beginning with the 1947 Marshall Plan it was Washington's intention to stabilize and reconstruct the continent with the help of generous economic and financial aid. It would not be wrong to claim that a number of Euro-centric influential "wise men" in Washington developed a visionary strategy that was characterized by America's enthusiastic support for European reconstruction and unification.[7] The thinking of Jean Monnet, the French bureaucrat and political strategist who had extensive personal ties to many influential American policy-makers, had clearly fallen on fruitful ground in the United States.[8] American politicians thus developed the insight that only a united western Europe at peace with itself would be able to create a concerted front against the military and ideological threat from the Soviet Union. Moreover, only such a Europe would ensure the reconciliation of the Federal Republic of Germany with the countries of the Western world and thereby generate lasting Franco-German friendship while avoiding tendencies towards neutralism and defeatism.[9]

In this respect, the term "double containment," introduced into the literature by Wilfried Loth and Wolfram Hanrieder, has proven a helpful explanatory construct. American "double containment" was aimed at keeping the Soviet Union in check by means of military containment through NATO. At the same time this strategy had the aim to control the West Germans by safely integrating them into the Western alliance in military but, above all, political and economic terms while making it possible to fulfill Chancellor Konrad Adenauer's desire to be treated as a more or less equal and sovereign partner. This would enable the Federal Republic to develop new self-respect and confidence and thus turn it into a constructive partner within the Western alliance. It was hoped that the "double containment" of the Soviet Union and Germany would lead to the pacification of the European continent.[10]

Underlying America's postwar vision was, above all, the assumption that only a fully integrated, stable, and economically viable Europe would develop into a peaceful and democratic continent. Achieving prosperity in western Europe appeared to depend on the creation of a unified single market. The lessons from America's own past as well as the country's federalist structure were to serve as the model to achieve a single European market. This would prevent economic nationalism and lead to a truly free and multilateral transatlantic economic system. In due course this strategy would have the advantage of making unnecessary the continuation of American economic aid to western Europe. After all, it would close the dollar gap, permit the convertibility of European currencies, allow the Europeans to export to the USA, and, in addition, create a huge market for American exporters. On the whole, it was hoped by many in Washington that in due time European integration would enable the "self-healing" forces of the free market to take over. Active American governmental support and interference were always regarded as limited and temporary.[11] In the heady, enthusiastic days of the late 1940s and throughout the 1950s it appeared as if the eventual unification of the European continent would not only ensure permanent peace and well-being on the continent but also America's long-term economic prosperity.

Thus, Washington's reasons for supporting European integration were not altruistic but they nevertheless were of great benefit to the western Europeans.[12] Economic historian Alan Milward's thesis that the Marshall Plan was not essential for European economic revival is not supported by the majority of scholars and also ignores the important psychological impact American support had on western Europe. His argument that the Marshall Plan made the Europeans focus on their national recoveries rather than on cooperating with each other and that thus the receipt of Marshall Plan monies delayed genuine European economic integration is not widely accepted either.[13]

European integration must be regarded as the "deus ex machina" with which the Truman administration intended to solve the daunting economic but also military problems of the postwar world. Both President Truman and his successor Dwight D. Eisenhower expected that an economically healthy Europe would be able to build up strong military forces and abide by a policy of strength towards the Soviet Union. In particular President Eisenhower believed that a prosperous Europe would enable Washington to reduce the large number of American troops still based in Europe. With the exception of the 1970s, throughout the Cold War US troop levels in Europe were well above the 300,000 mark; the vast majority of these troops were based in West Germany (on average four times as many as were stationed in France or the UK).[14] This was an important dimension; after all Congress had to give its support to America's expensive western European and Cold War policies. Furthermore, it was expected that the creation and development of NATO and the successful implementation of the containment strategy would help the Europeans to foster a sense of security and stability.[15] This would prevent any internal challenges to the NATO framework, the security roof which Washington superimposed on Western political and economic integration.[16] It was expected that the system would work and become mutually reinforcing, as it would give considerable advantages to both the United States and western Europe.[17] In addition, Eisenhower hoped that the unity of western Europe "would solve the peace of the world" and "ultimately attract to it all the Soviet satellites."[18] Thus, it was expected that the unity of western Europe, to be achieved through the European integration process, would ultimately lead to the unification of the divided European continent and overcome the Cold War.

However, European integration did not function as well as had been expected in Washington. Instead of being all-embracing, initially it appeared to tend to concentrate on a limited number of countries and just a few economic sectors (e.g. the coal and steel industries). Moreover, it was clearly protectionist and discriminatory. There were ever increasing European endeavors to keep economic competition from the United States and the dollar area out of Europe.[19] Thus, genuine liberalization of trade and payments and the introduction of multilateralism and currency convertibility as desired by Washington did not occur. Instead, European regionalism prevailed and the creation of the European Payments Union (EPU) in July 1950 was not able to change this fundamentally.[20]

Yet, throughout the 1950s Washington continued to regard this as a temporary phenomenon which would not be able to prevent the gradual development of full multilateralism. Short-term American economic sacrifices were regarded as affordable and would later be counterbalanced by the immense economic advantages accruing from a huge unified market.[21] As long as the United States was economically and militarily predominant, Washington was prepared to postpone temporarily both the creation of a new export market for American goods and the full realization of its economic vision. Despite an increasingly worrying balance of trade deficit, policy-makers in the USA did not yet worry about American international economic competitiveness.[22] Instead, at the height of the Cold War, full European supranational unity and within this framework the integration of the Federal Republic with the West were viewed as vital to the national interest of the USA.[23]

The Transition to Economic Interdependence in the late 1950s

By the end of the 1950s the view that geopolitics was more important than mere economic and trade matters was increasingly challenged from within the American government. The speedy recovery of the European economies, above all epitomized by the West German "economic miracle," and the discovery of structural deficiencies in the American economic performance ensured that the Europeans and in particular the Six – the founding members of the fledgling EEC – came to be seen as serious competitors. Even during the negotiations that led to the Rome Treaties of 1957, which created both the EEC and the European Atomic Energy Community (EURATOM), a number of American policy-makers based in the economic and trade ministries voiced their fear that the US was giving its support to the establishment of a future rival. However, most policy-makers, in particular those in the State Department, were not convinced; they were almost exclusively focused on the geopolitical importance of creating a solid western European bloc to counter the threat posed by the Soviet Union, its satellites, and not least its powerful communist ideology.[24] Within a matter of years, however, the United States had to grow accustomed to the dawning of an age of interdependence between the European and American economies and to a more forthright assertion by Europe of its political independence. In fact, Federico Romero and Alan Milward have argued that from 1958, the year the EEC began working, America's attitude towards European integration became much more skeptical.[25] This appears to be doubtful. As will be outlined below, Washington's disappointment with the results of the process of European integration only manifested itself when America's economic problems mounted during the late 1960s and early 1970s. Geir Lundestad also believes that the "Milward–Romero interpretation seems considerably overstated."[26]

Still, in the 1960s economic aspects of transatlantic relations gained increasing importance, not least because the American payments deficit had greatly increased in 1958–1959. Thus, genuine currency convertibility and the termination of all protective European tariffs and trade discriminations began to be regarded as long overdue. American coolness to the British-inspired free trade area and then to the free trade association (EFTA) can be explained by the fact that both entailed trade discriminations against the USA without having any of the expected integrationist advantages of the EEC.[27] The West German–American squabbles about German off-set payments as a contribution to the cost of American troops and equipment based on West German soil which burdened German-American relations throughout the 1960s and 1970s also indicates the increasing importance of economic and financial matters to Washington.[28]

Part of the American reaction to the increasing economic competition from western Europe was the Dillon and Kennedy rounds in the General Agreement on Tariffs and Trade (GATT) which aimed at creating a more liberal world trading system by, above all, reducing EEC tariffs on American goods. The attempt to strengthen the role of the restructured and renamed Organization for Economic Coperation and Development (OECD) had a similar aim. Not surprisingly, John F. Kennedy's "grand design" contained the expectation that an ever more united and independent Europe would have a strong and lasting American connection.[29] Kennedy and his advisers continued to regard it as dangerous if Europe "struck off on its own" in order to play an independent role in international politics. Even as far as America's most loyal European ally, Britain, was concerned, Washington was not thinking of independence and genuine partnership but had something very different in mind. Former secretary of state Dean Acheson, a pro-European ad hoc adviser of Kennedy's, was convinced that London should be used "to act as our lieutenant (the fashionable word is partner)" to help unite the European continent under clear American leadership. Acheson and his colleagues, however, were not opposed to America creating the impression of European participation in decision-making, with the real power still residing in the US capital.[30] US historian Frank Costigliola concluded that on the whole "Kennedy paid even less attention to the allies' views than Eisenhower had."[31]

In the security sphere Washington also began to pay more attention to accommodating the Europeans and their attempts to achieve greater independence. Part of this strategy was the effort made during the Kennedy and Johnson administrations to introduce a sea-based Multilateral Force (MLF) to give the Europeans, in particular the West Germans and the French, the impression of participating in NATO's nuclear decision-making process while keeping them firmly under the US-controlled Western nuclear umbrella. It was hoped that any Franco-German nuclear collaboration and the development of a German atomic bomb could thus be avoided. The 1967 establishment of NATO's Nuclear Planning Group as well as the creation of the Eurogroup in 1968 were part of this policy. It was obvious that that for Washington European integration was always subordinate in importance to upholding the Atlantic framework and US hegemony within this framework.[32]

Washington had no desire to give up any real power. For example, it was not Europe but the US that insisted on terminating the "massive retaliation" doctrine in favor of the "flexible response" strategy in the late 1960s. The raising of the nuclear threshold by the new doctrine appeared to make war by conventional means in the middle of Europe much more likely again; a worrisome prospect for the West Germans and most other continental European politicians.[33] It was also characteristic that the last Cold War summit in which the Europeans (i.e. Britain and France) were invited to participate was the abortive Paris summit of

1960. Thereafter, summitry was conducted bilaterally between Washington and Moscow.[34]

In the course of the 1960s, Washington's political, military, as well as economic predominance within the transatlantic alliance was criticized more often than hitherto, but on the whole it was not yet seriously challenged. The only notable exception was de Gaulle's openly anti-American policy and the French withdrawal from the military section of NATO in 1966/67. Although the USA was deeply angered and quite perturbed by the general's deep-seated anti-American attitude, it was realized in Washington that not so much France but West Germany and its booming economy was the key to America's role in Europe. It was thus not so much France but the Bonn Republic which had to be kept in NATO. Without West Germany, NATO – including Washington's dominance within the Atlantic alliance and in Europe – was bound to unravel; without France the alliance system could survive, as it did.[35]

Fortunately for the United States, West Germany was much more dependent on American goodwill than France, which ever since the Suez Crisis of 1956 had decided to develop its own global power position as much as possible, France's leading role in the EEC being part of this scheme. Successful US economic and political pressure on both France and Britain to make them abort the invasion of Egypt in November 1956 had led to great anti-American resentment in Paris.[36] Owing to the division of Germany, Bonn's reunification ambitions, the Berlin problem, and the country's front-line status in the Cold War, with its need for military protection from the US, the Federal Republic could not afford to antagonize the US by for example seriously embarking on the idea of leaving NATO or developing nuclear weapons itself. Chancellor Konrad Adenauer and all of his Cold War successors were well aware of this fact.[37]

Thus, while the ageing de Gaulle posed a serious and quite unprecedented challenge to US hegemony, on the whole both the Kennedy and the subsequent Johnson administrations believed that the US could afford to wait patiently for the tiresome general's departure. It did not seem to be necessary to placate him too much by for example agreeing to the establishment of a Tripartite Directorate (US, Britain, and France) for the Western alliance as de Gaulle had desired when he had come to office in the late 1950s or to grant him a veto over the use of US nuclear weapons in Europe. Washington had no intention of giving up its predominance within the Western alliance to please France. Above all, it did not seem to make sense to exclude West Germany in favor of closer relations with France and Britain. Washington remained convinced that for both strategic and economic reasons the Federal Republic was western Europe's most important state and that Britain's loyalty in a crisis could be relied upon in any case. It was also feared that any real concessions to de Gaulle's somewhat illusory ambition to turn France once again into Europe's foremost power would only whet his appetite and make him ask for even more favors.[38]

Therefore, despite de Gaulle's challenge, US's hegemony in the Western alliance as well as Washington's still largely positive view of the constructive and mutually beneficial nature of European integration for both Europe and the United States itself remained largely unimpaired throughout the 1960s. There were an increasing number of politicians in the United States who questioned whether the process of

European integration would in fact eventually lead to economic, political, and military benefits for the United States but they were still in a minority. On the whole, most politicians in Washington still regarded the process towards a more integrated and thus economically and militarily stronger Europe under US leadership as vital to compete successfully in the Cold War with the Soviet Union. This would only change with the "era of negotiations" and the coming to power of the Nixon administration in January 1969.

The Turning Point in America's European Policy in the Early 1970s

Throughout the global recessions of the 1970s the world's leading economies found themselves increasingly exposed to the often contradictory necessities of "global interdependence, regional integration, and national self-assertion."[39] Washington resented the ever growing competition and exclusionary trade habits of the EC which seemed to challenge America's leadership position. Moreover, in the wake of Vietnam and Watergate, the United States underwent a deep identity crisis. This situation encouraged policymakers in Washington to indulge in "navel-gazing." They were only ready to concentrate on the larger themes of international politics and neglected the many complex regional European affairs. Above all, the financial burden of the Vietnam War, the lingering costs of financing the domestic "great society" programs of the 1960s, as well as the two oil crises of the 1970s which were accompanied by rising energy prices meant that America's economic and financial position was much less secure than in the previous decades. The United States had not only accumulated a considerable balance-of-payments deficit, but from 1971, for the first time for almost one hundred years, it also had a considerable trade deficit as well as inflationary problems, rising unemployment, and almost stagnant wages and the position of the dollar, the world's leading reserve currency, was weakening.[40] The reputation of many European currencies, in particular that of the West German mark, as a solid "safe haven" for investors meanwhile was becoming stronger.

President Richard Nixon accused the EC of unfair trade practices and demanded that the Europeans should lower their tariffs and allow more US goods to enter the common market. In particular, he made the EC's protectionist new common agricultural policy (CAP) responsible for the US's trade deficit. While this was not entirely wrong, in fact one of the main reasons for Washington's problems was the relative overvaluation of the dollar which helped European (particularly West German) and Japanese exports. Ever since the devaluation of most European currencies in 1949, the dollar had remained overvalued. Moreover, both the EC and EFTA had discriminated against all non-essential US goods by imposing quotas, exchange controls, and import licences.[41]

The lingering monetary crisis came to a head in the summer of 1971. In August Nixon decided on the sudden suspension of the dollar's convertibility into gold. This resulted in the free floating of international currencies and, above all, in an effective devaluation of the dollar. Simultaneously, the president imposed a 10% protective tariff on imported goods. In practice, these decisions terminated the 1944 Bretton

Woods system of fixed exchange rates.[42] Moreover, they were solely dictated by American domestic-economic requirements and disregarded any consequences for the country's allies. Secretary of the Treasury, John Connally, did not hesitate to admit that the American action had been taken "to screw the Europeans before they screw us."[43]

Thus, America's relative economic and financial decline in combination with global détente and the accompanying perception that the military threat from the Warsaw Pact was receding, decisively contributed to undermining the Nixon administration's commitment to the European continent.[44] In addition, Congress had grown increasingly skeptical about the benefits of America's involvement in Europe. During the 1970s, Senator Mike Mansfield introduced eight amendments for American troop reductions in Europe.[45] Within the administration, national security adviser Henry Kissinger, a keen student of nineteenth-century European power politics, continued to pursue America's relations with its western European allies on a purely bilateral nation-state basis within the Atlantic framework.[46] The administration had not much time for the fledgling common European institutions and took the European integration process not terribly seriously. Kissinger's well-known quip that he did not know which number to call if he wanted to call Europe appears to have been made during this time.[47] Still, Kissinger was realistic enough to recognize that it was unlikely that "Europe would unite in order to share *our* burdens or that it would be content with a subordinate role once it had the means to implement its own views." Kissinger also noted that once "Europe had grown economically strong and politically united, Atlantic Cupertino could not be an American enterprise in which consultations elaborated primarily American designs." He advised that a "common focus had to be achieved among sovereign equals; partnership had to be evoked rather than assumed."[48]

Like previous administrations the Nixon administration continued speaking out in favor of a united federal Europe with a big single market and fully integrated into the Atlantic system. In such a case it was assumed in Washington that Europe would be capable of sharing with the United States "the burdens and obligations of world leadership."[49] The Nixon administration therefore favored the envisaged first major expansion of the EC. In particular, it hoped that Britain's entry and the revival of the Anglo-American "special relationship" would lead to an improvement in transatlantic relations. However, the Nixon White House was no longer interested in actively supporting the creation of a supranational Europe with common federal political and economic decision-making bodies. Washington intended to leave the initiative with respect to any further steps towards a more united continent to the Europeans. Whether Nixon, as many authors maintain, and Kissinger were convinced that America was a declining power, which only had a limited degree of influence on the EC must be questioned.[50] Instead policy-makers in Washington had come to the conclusion that a federally organized supranational Europe might well turn against the United States; it certainly could be expected that such a Europe would become an even more serious trade and economic rival to the United States.[51]

Despite Kissinger's insights about the consequences of burden-sharing with the Europeans for American hegemony, which seemed to indicate a willingness to accept the realities of a more pluralistic and interdependent world, in practice the Nixon administration still expected a largely docile Europe. In particular, as far as East–West relations and the NATO alliance were concerned, Washington certainly wished to be in full control. *Ostpolitik*, West Germany's fairly independent variant of détente, was also only grudgingly accepted by the Nixon administration.[52] The Brandt government received only very belated praise from Kissinger for its initiatives. Although, the acceptance of the Cold War status quo and the *de facto* recognition of the GDR had been urged on West Germany since the Kennedy era, Kissinger initially believed that the Bonn government had embarked on a new Rapallo policy.[53] Eventually, however, Kissinger and Nixon, as well as their counterparts in London and Paris, realized that West Germany was finally accepting political realities. It was thus concluded with great relief that *Ostpolitik* "was more likely to lead to a permanent division of Germany than to healing its breach."[54] Naturally these sentiments were not revealed to the West German ally.

It had been the independence and confidence with which the West Germans had proceeded with *Ostpolitik* and had competed with Washington's own strategy of superpower détente which had been particularly disliked by the US administration. Within a general climate of American suspicion of growing European independence, this factor contributed considerably to the apprehension with which Chancellor Brandt's policy and West Germany's leading position in the EC had been regarded initially by the Nixon administration.[55]

By 1973 Kissinger realized that transatlantic relations were in urgent need of revision and repair and, to the utter surprise and then anger of the EC countries, he grandly announced the "Year of Europe."[56] It did not help that Kissinger's staff had only informed the Europeans in a most perfunctory way about Kissinger's intention; most European leaders felt that they had not been consulted.[57] But at the core of Kissinger's "Year of Europe" idea was the intention to breathe new constructive life into the transatlantic relationship. After all, the Nixon administration had been largely occupied with the Vietnam War and the development of détente with China and the Soviet Union during its first years in office. Thus, the "Year of Europe" was Kissinger's attempt to improve US–EC relations while safeguarding Washington's leadership role.[58]

In his speech on April 23, 1973 to an Associated Press luncheon in Washington, DC, Kissinger proposed a new Atlantic Charter and did not hesitate to emphasize that America had global responsibilities while the EC countries only had to deal with regional problems. Moreover, he insisted on a greater degree of military burden-sharing, as only Europe's economic contribution would guarantee the further functioning of America's security umbrella. Both points, but particularly the linkage between economic and security concerns, led to severe difficulties between Washington and the western Europeans. Kissinger however managed to persuade the Europeans to agree to a clause in the Atlantic Declaration, signed in June 1974, which stated that Washington should be consulted before the EC countries arrived at important decisions which impacted on transatlantic issues. Thus, American ideas of the nature of the transatlantic relationship had largely won the day.[59]

In practice, however, allied relations remained tense. Severe friction occurred during the Yom Kippur War of October 1973 when Washington full-heartedly backed Israel while many European countries hesitated to do so. At the time most EC countries were much more dependent on Middle Eastern oil than the USA, and many countries (like France, the UK, the FRG) had strong economic links with the Arab countries in the region.[60] Thus, the war and the energy question were closely connected with both security and economic prosperity.

The American-European differences with respect to the "Year of Europe" and the Yom Kippur War pushed the EC into developing more sophisticated processes of cooperation, not least in order to be able to resist pressure to fall in line with American wishes. The 1973 Declaration on European Identity was influential in gradually leading to a tentative common European foreign policy. It encouraged EC members to make a serious attempt to use the instrument of European Political Cooperation (EPC), created in 1970, to ensure that foreign policy positions would be coordinated among all EC countries.[61] Yet this only worked initially, and most authors view the 1970s largely as a "dark age" or a "stagnant decade" for European integration.[62]

The two oil crises and the accompanying economic recession (best characterized by the phrase "stagflation") as well as the expansion of the EC from six to nine countries with the addition of the UK, Ireland, and Denmark on January 1, 1973 caused a severe long-lasting crisis of adaptation within the Community.[63] On the whole, "the disarray of Europe" worked to the benefit of the USA. Washington was able to insist on the importance of the Atlantic framework and was thus able, as Alfred Grosser has argued, to regain "its position as the leading power among the partners who were unified only when under its direction."[64] However, under Nixon and Kissinger an important re-evaluation of US–EC relations had taken place. Washington had begun to look after its own economic and political interests much more than hitherto. It was not prepared anymore to accept unilateral economic disadvantages in the hope of obtaining vaguely defined benefits in the long run. The age of American patience and benevolence with regard to European integration and European economic competition had come to an abrupt end. While essentially this had long been foreshadowed since at least the late 1950s, at the time most European leaders were taken by surprise and many viewed it quite mistakenly as merely a temporary phenomenon which would be overcome in the near future.

The Limits of American Power

Despite Jimmy Carter's professed pro-European attitude and his intention to concentrate on re-establishing more cooperative and constructive trilateral relations among the US, western Europe, and Japan, his ever increasing domestic and international difficulties did not leave him much time to look after European integration issues.[65] Carter was, however, the first President who visited and thus symbolically acknowledged the importance of the EC Commission.[66] Still, due to the recession in the West, continuing American economic difficulties and growing EC self-confidence, the economic differences in transatlantic relations were not overcome. During the Carter presidency the existence of monetary disputes and rivalries among the allies was often revealed in the course of the various economic summits which had become established practice in the Western world since 1975. They constituted an active strategy to once again attempt to coordinate the Western world's economic and financial policies.[67]

In the past such initiatives had usually come from the USA; in the mid- to late 1970s, however, the EC became increasingly active in this respect. The EC countries, for example, attempted to put Western currency exchange rates on a new stable footing with the help of first the Smithsonian Agreement, then the so-called "currency snake," and eventually by creating the European Monetary System (EMS) in 1978, the forerunner of the European Monetary Union (EMU). The main aim of the EMS was the establishment of a zone of stable exchange rates floating in tandem against the dollar thus obtaining a certain protection in a volatile world of international trade dominated by the increasingly unstable dollar. This benefited, above all, the position of the Deutschmark – which became ever more important not only as the EC's leading currency but also increasingly as a global reserve currency.[68] In the long run this had a positive effect on the West German economy and the country's political influence within the EC, thus enhancing the rivalry between Bonn and Washington.

West German chancellor Schmidt, a trained economist who together with French president Giscard d'Estaing increasingly appeared to become the EC's economic spokesman, expected Washington to coordinate its expansionary economic strategies with the EC. However, Carter refused to do so.[69] Instead, continued American economic problems during Carter's term in office led to Washington's unpopular suggestion that in order to diminish the American trade deficit with the EC, the West German and American economies should form an economic "axis." Bonn was asked to act as a "locomotive" for Western economic growth by ending its restrictive monetary policy and embarking on an expansionist economic strategy instead. Schmidt, however, believed that this would be detrimental to his policy of stabilizing inflation and the value of the Deutschmark. He suggested to Carter that the dollar be stabilized by curtailing inflation and cutting America's surging payments deficit (for instance by increasing taxes on the USA's huge energy consumption, hardly a suggestion the embattled Carter could accept as it would have made him even more unpopular). With the support of his European partners, Schmidt argued that continuing American monetary and fiscal irresponsibility were responsible for the devaluation of the dollar and thus for undermining the competitiveness of European exports. This situation was destabilizing the entire Western economic system.[70]

Washington's willingness to resort increasingly to protectionist measures to defend the competitiveness of American goods was also much resented by the EC. The summit meeting in Venice in the summer of 1980 must be regarded as one of the low points of transatlantic and, in particular, West German–American relations. The conference led to an unprecedented personal clash between Schmidt and Carter. Carter speaks of an "unbelievable meeting" and "the most unpleasant personal exchange I ever had with a foreign leader."[71]

However, on the whole, in the course of its last two years in office the Carter administration adopted more restrained macroeconomic and trade policies with a greater emphasis on cooperation with the EC. Carter, for example, began to pay more attention to stabilizing the value of the dollar and he made important concessions during the Tokyo round of multilateral trade negotiations in April 1979. The president seemed to have realized that America's relative weakness and the EC's growing strength made transatlantic cooperation and mutual accommodation imperative. In effect, it appears that the Carter administration had become "educated to the new limits of American power."[72]

These limits also became apparent as far as security policy issues were concerned. Differences over arms control negotiations and rearmament issues including Carter's unilateral decisions first to develop and then to cancel the so-called neutron bomb as well as disputes over the divisibility of détente characterized the dire state of transatlantic relations during the Carter era. The EC countries sharply criticized the president's erratic leadership in the security arena.[73] Under severe pressure from the dramatic shift to the right in American domestic opinion during the 1970s, in 1978/79, even before the USSR's invasion of Afghanistan in December 1979, Carter underwent a transformation from apostle of détente to rigid cold warrior.[74] In Europe, however, and in particular in West Germany, there was much stronger interest in the continuation of détente under almost all circumstances than in America. Therefore, Carter's imposition of trade sanctions on the USSR (including stopping grain sales) and the American boycott of the Olympic Games in Moscow were regarded as exaggerated reactions to the Afghanistan invasion.[75] Carter was also strongly criticized for deliberately mixing economic and security policies. In effect, it seemed that Carter had resorted to Kissinger's hard-headed realist policy of "linkage" but with a much greater emphasis on the "stick" than on the "carrot."

Most EC countries viewed American politics under Carter as ambiguous and unpredictable, while the president regarded the EC as unhelpful, unsympathetic, and even ruthless as far as Washington's global predicaments were concerned. Despite Carter's approval, in principle, of American support for further progress towards a united European continent, the constant crisis atmosphere of his presidency had not given him the chance to play an active role in this respect. While transatlantic and particularly German–American relations suffered severely, European integration was largely benignly neglected by American policymakers during Carter's spell in office. In principle the Carter administration and the president himself supported the process of European integration but, owing to the immensely difficult economic and political environment in which Carter had to operate and in view of the tension in transatlantic relations, this resulted in very few American activities in support of a united Europe during Carter's term in the White House.

The Reimposition of American Hegemony

When Ronald Reagan became President in January 1981, he was intent on reimposing America's leadership on transatlantic relations. In the meantime, however, the EC had begun to occupy a much stronger economic position, accompanied by greater political confidence, than had been the case hitherto. Moreover, many Europeans were wondering whether, in the era of Cold War détente firm hegemonic leadership by the United States as in the past was still necessary. While superpower détente, had all but collapsed, détente in Europe seemed to be working just fine, at least when seen from the western European perspective.[76] Yet these considerations were largely ignored by Reagan; for the US administration these developments appeared never to have taken place. Thus, while during the Nixon administration transatlantic tension had largely resulted from economic and trade issues, under Reagan, even more so than under Carter, economics as well as security issues and severely differing perceptions regarding the East–West conflict affected the transatlantic alliance.[77]

Above all, Reagan was not interested in supporting the creation of a supranational Europe. In fact, his new policy of strength towards Moscow even precluded a reassessment of Washington's relations with its allies.[78] As far as Reagan's policy towards the Soviet Union was concerned, it is useful to differentiate between Reagan's first and second term in office; as in 1984/1985 the president began to embark upon a less hard-line approach towards the USSR.[79] Although this helped to improve Washington's relations with its allies to a considerable degree, Reagan still expected the Europeans to follow America's "hegemonic" lead without questioning any of its policies. Thus, with respect to transatlantic relations a deliberate policy of arrogant neglect rather than benign neglect as during the Carter years can be observed throughout Reagan's terms in office.[80]

Early in Reagan's presidency, for example, the administration talked casually of developing nuclear war fighting capabilities and the possibility of entering into tactical nuclear exchanges with the Soviet Union. Such exchanges would of course have taken place over European territory, destroying much of the continent in the process. The same apparent willingness to distance himself from European security concerns appeared to apply to the president's enthusiasm for the development of the Strategic Defense Initiative (SDI; star wars). If this project ever came to fruition, it would make the United States immune to nuclear attacks from the Soviet Union, while in all likelihood such protection would not be available to the Europeans.[81] Equally, Reagan's negotiations with Soviet leader Mikail Gorbachev in Reykjavik in October 1986 almost led to the elimination of all ballistic missiles in East and West and the tabling of plans for the eradication of all nuclear weapons in the foreseeable future. Although such a development would have dramatically affected the future of the European continent, the president never consulted the Europeans.[82] The same applied to Reagan's and Gorbachev's so-called "double-zero" agreement of 1987/88 which foresaw the removal of all medium-range missiles from Europe, and Reagan's 1988 proposal to modernize NATO's short-range nuclear Lance missiles in Europe. As the latter were mostly deployed in West Germany and could only reach German territory, the lack of consultation with Bonn deeply angered the Kohl government.[83]

The Reagan administration's disinterest in consulting the Europeans can also be observed with respect to economic issues. The EC's and in particular West Germany's and France's increasing trade with the GDR, the Soviet Union, the developing world as well as certain Arab nations was viewed with a combination of great suspicion and envy in Washington. Reagan attempted to restrain the competition of the EC countries and did not hesitate to explain the rationale of American trade policy with the help of Cold War security reasons which frequently resulted in the development of severe economic conflicts among the transatlantic allies.[84] Such crises emerged, for example, in connection with the envisaged European gas pipeline deal with Moscow,

Bonn's intentions to export a nuclear power plant to Brazil or to sell sophisticated Leopard tanks to Saudi Arabia.[85] Reagan's controversial trade sanctions on the Soviet Union in the wake of the declaration of martial law in Poland in December 1981 ensured that transatlantic relations deteriorated further. American policies with respect to Nicaragua, the Middle East, and "Irangate" brought about further strong European criticism, while in particular CAP had to bear the brunt of (partially quite justified) American attacks on European protectionism.[86]

However, as usual the EC was ready to compromise as far as security and political issues were concerned, fully realizing that reasonable transatlantic relations and a functioning NATO alliance were still the indispensable pillars of the Cold War world. Moreover, Reagan's close relationship with British prime minister Margaret Thatcher, who had little sympathy for further progress towards a united Europe, helped to undermine any common approach by the EC countries towards Washington. Thus, from November 1983, after the negotiations with Moscow within NATO's "dual track" framework had failed, most EC countries went along with the deployment of new intermediate-range missiles, despite very hostile peace movements in many countries, not least in West Germany where most of the new cruise missiles were to be deployed.[87] Indeed, the deployment of the missiles even reassured some European governments that the Reagan administration did not intend to "recouple" from the European continent. Eventually, the EC countries compromised over SDI and also agreed to the imposition of sanctions (though largely symbolic ones) on Moscow after the Polish crisis of late 1981.[88]

On important economic issues, however, the EC was much less disposed to compromise. Reagan's emphasis on the market appeared to be at odds with his willingness to use protectionist measures to defend the competitiveness of American goods and his authoritarian attempts to curtail western Europe's trade with eastern Europe by degree. Thus, with regard to the envisaged gas pipeline with Moscow, the EC countries were resolute in defying American attempts to undermine the deal by, for example, not allowing American companies and American technology to be employed in the construction of the pipeline. Reagan's attempts to impose what amounted to extra-territorial sanctions on European companies who were willing to participate led to an outcry. Eventually, Reagan had no option but to quietly give in with the help of a face-saving argument.[89]

Above all, "Reaganomics," the catchword for the president's emphasis on relying on the uninhibited forces of the free market to revive the American economy, was viewed with great skepticism in Europe (whether "Reaganomics" amounted to anything approximating a thoughtful economic strategy is questionable). Only Britain's Margaret Thatcher sympathized with the Reagan's administration's economic approach. The US administration seemed to rely on a policy which consisted of a mixture of laissez-faire, supply-side economics, tight money, and total governmental passivity (apart from support for the defense industries) that relied on the forces of the market to kick-start the economy.[90] This economic ideology led to renewed monetary difficulties between Washington and the EC. Reagan's tax cuts and simultaneous huge investments in the defense industry with the help of immense governmental borrowing created a large American budget deficit. As the value of the dollar increased while interest rates were kept artificially high to allow the government to obtain cheap loans from abroad, from 1984 an enormous American trade deficit was built up. This meant that European countries felt they also had to attempt to maintain high interest rates to avoid the flow of savings and investments from the EC to the US; yet such a high interest rate policy slowed down economic growth in the individual EC countries.[91]

Reagan's economic and financial policies showed yet again that the EC was helpless in the face of unilateral American policies and was forced to react to the decisions which had been taken in Washington. Thus, once again, "the precarious dependence of European economies on decisions taken by a fundamentally unsympathetic US administration pushed the EC countries towards closer cooperation."[92] The EC under Commission President Jacques Delors began developing plans for a single European market (SEM) to liberate itself from overwhelming American influence on western Europe's economic and financial fate. It intended to develop a fully free and integrated internal European market by 1992 and to design a common European currency system for shortly afterwards.[93]

Moreover, the French-led, though rather short-lived, revival of the Western European Union (WEU) in 1984 helped to contribute to the development of new ideas for creating a genuine common European foreign and defense policy as later articulated in the Maastricht Treaty of 1991.[94] After all, America's economic and financial predicament, made worse by a rapid decline of the dollar's value in the second half of the 1980s, seemed to indicate the possibility of American troop withdrawals from Europe for financial reasons. The negotiations between Gorbachev and Reagan and the winding down of the Cold War also appeared to make this a distinct possibility for political reasons. At the least, further conflicts regarding financial "burden sharing" within NATO could be expected.[95]

The Reagan administration viewed the European activities towards an economically and politically more integrated and independent Europe with great suspicion. Despite its own protectionist and discriminatory trade policies, it did not hesitate to speak of a "Fortress Europe" and was deeply disturbed by European protectionist measures, particularly in agricultural goods.[96] By the end of the Reagan years it appeared that not much was left of America's pro-European unity design as it had been developed in the late 1940s and early 1950s. The United States appeared not to be able to cope with an increasingly independent Europe emancipating itself from American guidance. Adapting America's once predominant and unchallenged economic and financial position to the interdependent realities of the 1970s and 1980s was proving very difficult.

According to Geir Lundestad in the 1950s the United States had only been prepared to impose its "Empire" on the Europeans because it had been invited by them to do so.[97] Thirty years later Washington did not find it easy to accept the notion that in certain respects the US was no longer regarded as a welcome guest, but rather as an uninvited distant relative who was becoming bothersome. While the Reagan administration instigated a fundamental and very successful review of its Cold War strategy after 1984/85, it did not attempt to do the same with regard to transatlantic relations. Neither the president nor his secretary of state George Shultz appeared to recognize the need for a "year of Europe." By 1989, when Reagan's vice president George H.W. Bush entered the White House in his own right, the Atlantic alliance was at breaking point.

The Maturing of Transatlantic Relations towards the End of the Cold War

Transatlantic relations considerably improved during George Bush's presidency; Bush's policy towards Europe did indeed "represent a real change of heart" as Geir Lundestad has written.[98] Unlike Reagan, Bush became less involved in the economic and military squabbles with America's allies. Instead he concentrated on the larger picture and realized the importance of reviewing European–American relations.[99] After some initial hesitation, in late 1989/early 1990 Bush quickly realized that further European integration, transatlantic interdependence as well as German unification were inevitable. Thus, the Bush administration embarked on a course of accepting realities and attempting to influence and shape events.[100] This was made easier by the fact that the USA achieved a trade surplus with the EC in early 1990. Moreover, it had been possible to work out transatlantic compromises as far as the many conflicts with respect to the single European market were concerned.[101] Bush also realized that the end of the Cold War and the fall of communism in central and eastern Europe would make the newly liberated countries ask for immense financial support from the Western world. As Washington was no longer in the financial position to offer a Marshall Plan, this time for the countries of eastern Europe, the Bush administration was happy to learn that the western Europeans might be induced to participate in such an enterprise. In November 1990 a new Transatlantic Declaration was signed to strengthen American–EC relations. The Bush administration wished to create "a more united European Community, with stronger, more formal links with the United States."[102]

By late 1990 it appeared that the United States had again succeeded in superimposing a somewhat modified and more interdependent Atlantic framework on the process of European integration. This would hardly have been possible if Washington had not begun to express support for the EC's increasingly successful endeavors to unite the continent in economic and monetary terms. Support was even expressed for the development of a common European foreign and security policy.

Above all, President Bush realized that the answer to the question of how to overcome the difficulties and uncertainties of the post-Cold War world might well be similar to the solution found in the late 1940s. In view of the uneasiness expressed by countries such as France, Poland, Britain, the Soviet Union, and others regarding the unification of Germany, once again the stabilization of the European continent seemed to require the subtle containment of Germany by means of the country's voluntary integration into an ever closer Europe and a firm Atlantic system. Once again the western Europeans including the Germans were happy to oblige. After all, according to Chancellor Helmut Kohl, German unification and further European integration were "two sides of the same coin."[103] Moreover, and much to the relief of the United States and the European members of the Atlantic alliance, the newly united German nation was happy to remain a member of NATO. This had been Bush's only major condition for extending American support for German unification.[104]

Conclusion

It was obvious, however, that European–American relations in the post-Cold War world would have to be based on a much more interdependent and equal basis than had ever been the case during the Cold War. Yet, despite his impressive role in bringing about German unification, managing the relationship with a dissolving Soviet Union and winning the Gulf War of 1991, Bush was voted out of office before his administration developed a new vision for the future of the transatlantic alliance in the post-Cold War world.

Bush's "new world order" which he had referred to several times in the years 1990–1991 remained a vacuous and nebulous project that was never filled with any real substance.[105] Former national security advisor Zbigniew Brzezinski wrote with some justification that "as a global leader" President George H.W. Bush "did not seize the opportunity to shape the future or leave behind a compelling sense of direction. The historical moment called for a great vision for the world at large . . . It called for a burst of global architectural innovation like the one that followed World War II, in keeping with the new opportunities for international cooperation . . . None was forthcoming, and not much was foreshadowed should Bush have won a second term."[106]

Bush certainly never articulated a vision for the future of American–European relations. Perhaps this contributed to the difficulties which plagued the transatlantic alliance in the 1990s, during the Clinton administration's two terms in office, and which led, in the context of 9/11, to the "war on terror" and the invasion of Iraq, and the explosion of an unprecedented crisis in transatlantic relations during George W. Bush's eight years in office. Some analysts began to dismiss transatlantic relations and the Atlantic alliance altogether as a thing of the past while others spoke of the "near-death" of that long-standing relationship. Even more optimistic experts were still deeply concerned about the "transatlantic drift."[107] Towards the end of the first decade of the twenty-first-century, relations may well have stabilized again under president Barack Obama, George W. Bush's successor in the White House, and close transatlantic cooperation and the continuation of the Atlantic alliance may well be taken for granted again. The United States continues to support the creation of a united Europe though the Europeans will have to achieve this themselves; there is little Washington can or wishes to do to bring this about.

Yet a genuine vision, an architecture, an overarching design for the future of transatlantic relations in their crucial political, military, and economic dimensions is still lacking. In a world which many still characterize, despite all evidence to the contrary, as a "clash of civilizations" between fundamentalist Islam and Western liberal democracy, the transatlantic alliance seems to be based on nothing much more substantial than the perceived existence of a common external enemy – al Qaeda and similar terrorist groups. Unlike in the Cold War, this time, however, the external threat is too nebulous, too multifaceted, too imprecise, and too fluid and changeable to give the enlarged alliance much coherence and stability.[108] Moreover, the perceived threat is very different from what it was during the Cold War. It is no longer nuclear annihilation of all civilization which is widely feared but the random attacks of international terrorism which, however, are most likely to result in "merely" local and regional attacks and disasters. The development of a common threat perception has thus been hampered and it is little wonder that the seriousness of the perceived threat is viewed very differently on both sides of the Atlantic.

Thus, in the twenty-first century the transatlantic alliance can no longer rely on being kept together by external threats as was the case during the Cold War. Instead there is no alternative but to keep the alliance together by common democratic values and, in an increasingly materialistic world, perhaps also by the maintenance of similar high standards of living across the alliance. The tasks for political leaders on both sides of the Atlantic would appear to consist of acting as guarantors of the economic well-being of the transatlantic peoples and ensuring the further development of democratic values. Above all, the crucial implantation and observation of these values in everyday life in both Europe and the United States of America must be regarded as vital.

Notes

1   While there is an abundance of literature on certain aspects of American–European relations particularly in the security field, there are only very few comprehensive accounts. Among the best are Lundestad, *"Empire" by Integration: The United States and European Integration, 1945–1997*; Lundestad, *The United States and Western Europe since 1945*; and the older one by Grosser, *The Western Alliance: European–American Relations since 1945*. But see also Burk and Stokes, *The United States and the European Alliance since 1945*; and Forsberg, *Divided West: European Security and the Transatlantic Relationship*. A first provisional draft of part of this article has appeared online in the electronic journal *Cercles* (ed. Capet), vol. 5 (2002).

2   See Mahan, *Kennedy, de Gaulle and Western Europe*; Pagedas, *Anglo-American Strategic Relations and the French Problem*; Bozo, *Two Strategies for Europe*; Paxton and Wahl, *De Gaulle and the United States*; also Simonian, *The Privileged Partnership*.

3   Brinkley and Griffith, *John F. Kennedy and Europe*.

4   See Lundestad, "Empire by Invitation? The United States and Western Europe, 1945–1952" Lundestad, *The American "Empire,"* 31ff.; Ikenberry, "Rethinking the Origins of American Hegemony."

5   See Mark Kramer's chapter in this book for a useful differentiation among "dominance," "hegemony," and "primacy." By this definition it appears that the US was only really dominant during the years of reconstruction and perhaps until the mid-1950s, while it clearly had a hegemonic position in transatlantic relations during the remainder of the Cold War. It is too early to tell whether or not current developments indicate a gradual shift from US hegemony to merely US primacy in transatlantic relations.

6   See for example Hoffmann with Bozo, *Gulliver Unbound: America's Imperial Temptation and the War in Iraq*; Cohen-Tanugi, *An Alliance at Risk*; Andrews, *The Atlantic Alliance under Stress*; Pond, *Friendly Fire*; Kashmeri, *America and Europe after 9/11 and Iraq*; Coker, *Empires in Conflict*; Shawcross, *Allies*.

7   See the articles in Heller and Gillingham, *The United States and the Integration of Europe*; Schwabe, "The United States and European Integration, 1947–1957," 115–35; Hogan, *The Marshall Plan*; and also more generally, Isaacson and Thomas, *The Wise Men*.

8   See Hackett, *Monnet and the Americans*, Harper, *American Visions of Europe* and Duchêne, *Jean Monnet*.

9   See *Foreign Relations of the United States (FRUS)* 1955–57, vol. IV, 399 (26 January 1956); also the various articles in Herbst et al., *Vom Marshall-Plan zur EWG*.

10 See the brief discussion in Schröder, "USA und westdeutscher Wiederaufstieg (1945–1952)," 106–107.

11 Romero, "US Attitudes towards Integration and Interdependence: The 1950s," 103–21; Killick, *The United States and European Reconstruction*, 65ff., 171ff.

12 It seems to be more appropriate to speak of "enlightened self-interest" rather than US altruism. See Killick, op. cit., 185.

13 Milward, *The Reconstruction of Western Europe*; Milward, *The European Rescue of the Nation State*. For an opposing view, see Hogan, *The Marshall Plan*.

14 See Kane, "Global US Troop Deployment, 1950–2003." For the precise troop levels divided by continent, countries, and years, see http://www.heritage.org/Research/NationalSecurity/troopMarch2005.xls. During the 1970s there were approximately 270,000 American soldiers based in western Europe.

15 For the strategy of containment, see still Gaddis, *Strategies of Containment: A Critical Appraisal of American National Security Policy during the Cold War*, revised and expanded edition.

16 For an overview, see Larres, "North Atlantic Treaty Organization"; Kaplan, *NATO Divided, NATO United*.

17 See *FRUS*, 1955–57, vol. IV, 349 (21 November 1955): While the US would be able "to sit back and relax somewhat," Eisenhower cited the "American historical patterns as an illustration" and expressed the belief that "each and every one" of the western Europeans "would profit by the union of them all and none would lose"; also Lundestad, *"Empire" by Integration*, 18, 71. See also Winand, *Eisenhower, Kennedy and the United States of Europe*.

18 See *FRUS* 1955–57, vol. IV, 349 (21/11/1955).

19 See for example *FRUS* 1958–60, vol. VII, Part 1, 61–64 (29 July 1958), 218–20 (16 December 1959).

20 See Romero, "Interdependence and Integration in American Eyes," 164–165.

21 See Romero, "US Attitudes towards Integration and Interdependence," 114–118; see also Romero, "Interdependence and Integration in American Eyes, 164–165.

22 Romero, "Interdependence and Integration in American Eyes, 164–165.

23 For recent accounts of German–American relations in the European context see above all Hanrieder, *Germany, America, Europe*; see also the articles in Larres and Oppelland, *Deutschland und die USA im 20. Jahrhundert*.

24 See Larres, "The United States and the Rome Treaties of 1957," 599–616.

25 See the discussion in Lundestad, *"Empire" by Integration*, 83ff., esp. 86–89; Romero, "US Attitudes towards Integration and Interdependence," 114–118; Romero, "Interdependence and integration in American Eyes, 164–165; Zeiler, *American Trade and Power in the 1960s*; Kunz, "Cold War Diplomacy: The Other Side of Containment," 80–114.

26 Lundestad, *"Empire" by Integration*, 88.

27 Lundestad, *"Empire" by Integration*, 89–90.

28 In particular, Congress had become increasingly suspicious of the EC. See Morgan, *The United States and West Germany, 1945–1973*, 200–204; Thiel, *Dollar-Dominanz*; Treverton, *The Dollar Drain and American Forces in Germany*. See also Hentschel, *Ludwig Erhard*.

29 See Grosser, op. cit., 200–201; Mahan, *Kennedy, de Gaulle and Western Europe*, 167–68; Cleva, *Henry Kissinger and the American Approach to Foreign Policy*, 165–166; Giuque, *Grand Designs and Visions of Unity*; Kraft, *The Grand Design: From Common Market to Atlantic Partnership*.

30 Quotes: Costigliola, "The Pursuit of Atlantic Community," 27, 29.

31 Costigliola, op. cit., 28.
32 See also Romero, "Interdependence and Integration," 159.
33 See Larres, "Sicherheit mit und vor Deutschland," 58–59; also Schake, "NATO-Strategie und deutsch-amerikanisches Verhältnis," 364ff.
34 The exception was the quadripartite Berlin negotiations in 1971, but this was a special case.
35 See for example Heuser, *NATO, Britain, France, and the FRG.*
36 On the important "Suez factor" in British and French politics, see Larres, "Britain and Europe from Churchill to Blair and Brown."
37 This immediately becomes apparent when reading Adenauer's memoirs.
38 See Schwartz, *Lyndon Johnson and Europe*; Gardner, "Lyndon Johnson and de Gaulle"; Pierre, "Conflicting Visions," 257ff., 279ff.; Costigliola, "The Pursuit of Atlantic Community," 33–35; Paxton and Wahl, *De Gaulle and the United States.*
39 Quoted in Hanrieder, "The German–American Connection in the 1970s and 1980s," 116. See also Dittgen, "Die Ära der Ost-West-Verhandlungen und der Wirtschafts- und Währungskrisen (1969–1981)," 188–190.
40 See Lawrence et al., "An Analysis of the 1977 US Trade Deficit"; Gavin, *Gold, Dollars and Power.*
41 See Killick, op. cit., 173; also Kirshner, *The Bretton–Woods–GATT system.*
42 See Gavin, op. cit., ch.s 7 and 8.
43 Quoted in Peterson, *Europe and America in the 1990s*, 41. See also James, *Rambouillet, 15 November 1975*, 131ff.
44 See Gavin, op. cit., 197ff. The best account of the Nixon administration and European integration is still Schaetzel, *The Unhinged Alliance*, 48ff., but also see the literature in note 58 below. For Nixon's détente policy see Garthoff, *Détente and Confrontation.*
45 Andrianopoulos, *Western Europe in Kissinger's Global Strategy*, 132ff.
46 Schaetzel, *The Unhinged Alliance*, 50; Andrianopoulos, op. cit., 66ff., 152ff.
47 In conversation with the author in early 2003 Kissinger said, however, that he could not remember ever having actually made this comment.
48 Kissinger, *Years of Upheaval*, 131–132, also 595.
49 Kissinger, op. cit., 143–148.
50 Lundestad, *"Empire" by Integration*, 101; Litwak, *Détente and the Nixon Doctrine*: Kissinger vigorously denied this assumption in conversation with the author in October 2002.
51 See Romero, "Interdependence and Integration," 176–181.
52 See Larres, "Germany and the West," 303–318.
53 See Kissinger, *White House Years*, 409–410, 529–530; also *Years of Upheaval*, 145.
54 Kissinger, *White House Years*, 411.
55 Brandt, *Erinnerungen*, 189–190, 192; Frank, *Entschlüsselte Botschaft*, 287; Hersh, *The Price of Power: Kissinger in the Nixon White House*, 416.
56 Brandt, op. cit., 192; also Kissinger, *Years of Upheaval*, 128ff., 151ff.
57 This was disputed by Kissinger as well as by most members of his staff whom I spoke to in the course of the autumn/spring 2002/03.
58 See, above all, Devuyst, *American Attitudes on European Political Integration*; Burr and Wampler, "With Friends Like These . . ." See also Williams, *The Permanent Alliance:*, 267–277.
59 See Kissinger, *Years of Upheaval*, 192–194; also Cromwell, *The United States and the European Pillar: The Strained Alliance*, 79ff.
60 Lavy, *Germany and Isreal: Moral Debt and National Interest*, 175ff.; for a popular account, see Rabinovich, *The Yom Kippur War.*

61   See Dinan, *Ever Closer Union?* 75–87.

62   Peterson, *Europe and America in the 1990s*, 42; Middlemas, quoted in Lundestad, *"Empire" by Integration*, 109.

63   See Urwin, *The Community of Europe: A History of European Integration since 1945*, 2nd edition, 157ff.

64   Grosser, op. cit., 281.

65   On Carter's domestic and foreign policy see Kaufman and Kaufman, *The Presidency of James Earl Carter*, 2nd edition; R.A. Strong, *Working in the World: Jimmy Carter and the Making of American Foreign Policy*; Dumbrell, *The Carter Presidency*; G. Smith, *Morality, Reason and Power*.

66   See Lundestad, *"Empire" by Integration*, 108–109.

67   See James, op. cit.

68   See Morgan, *The United States and West Germany*, 204–208; Hanrieder, *Germany, America, Europe*, 290ff.; also Hellmann, *Gold, the Dollar, and the European Currency Systems*; Ilgen, *Autonomy and Independence*.

69   See Schmidt, *Menschen und Mächte*, 188ff., 202ff, 222ff.; also Heep, *Helmut Schmidt und Amerika. Eine schwierige Partnerschaft*; Hanrieder, *Germany, America, Europe*, 282ff.; Haftendorn, *Sicherheit und Stabilität*, 35ff.; Keohane, "US Foreign Economic Policy toward Other Advanced Capitalist States," 91–122.

70   See Schmidt, op. cit., 192ff.; Dittgen, "Ära der Ost-West-Verhandlungen," 188–190. See also Biven, *Jimmy Carter's Economy*; Horowitz, *Jimmy Carter and the Energy Crisis*; Lieber, *The Oil Decade*.

71   Quoted in Carter, *Keeping Faith*, 536, 538. For the clashes between Carter and Schmidt, see Wiegrefe, *Das Zerwürfnis*.

72   Cohen, "An Explosion in the Kitchen?" 113.

73   See Wasserman, *The Neutron Bomb Controversy*; Dittgen, "Ära der Ost-West-Verhandlungen," 190–196; also Dittgen, *Deutsch-Amerikanische Sicherheitsbeziehungen in der Ära Helmut Schmidt*.

74   See Skidmore, *Reversing Course*; see also the literature in note 68 above.

75   See Schmidt, op. cit., 243ff.; also Czempiel, *Machtprobe: Die USA und die Sowjetunion in den achtziger Jahren*.

76   See van Oudenaren, *Détente in Europe*.

76   For a succinct analysis of Carter's policies see (despite the title) Kahler, "The United States and Western Europe," 276–289.

77   See Bell, *The Reagan Paradox*, esp. 121ff.; also Czempiel, op. cit.; Jochum, "Der Zerfall des sicherheitspolitischen Konsenses und die Verschärfung der Wirtschafts- und Währungskrisen (1981–89)," 204ff.; Talbott, *Deadly Gambits*.

78   For a good analysis see Lundestad, "The United States and Western Europe under Ronald Reagan," 47–62; also Goldstein, *Reagan's Leadership and the Atlantic Alliance*.

79   See Fischer, *The Reagan Reversal*.

80   See Knudsen, *Europe versus America*.

81   Drell, *The Reagan Strategic Defense Initiative*.

82   See Bell, *The Reagan Paradox*, 27ff.; Lundestad, "The United States and Western Europe," 48ff.; Kahler, "The United States and Western Europe," 290ff.; also Matlock, *Reagan and Gorbachev*.

83   See Genscher, *Erinnerungen*, 581ff.; Hanrieder, *Germany, America, Europe*, 364–366; Broer, *Die nuklearen Kurzstreckenraketen in Europa*; Wells, "Reagan, Euromissiles and Europe."

84   See Knapp, "Das Dilemma der europäischen NATO-Staaten zwischen ökonomischen Machtzuwachs und sicherheitspolitischer Abhängigkeit," 95–111.

85   Wilker, "Das Brasiliengeschäft – Ein, diplomatischer Betriebsunfall?'" 191–208.

86   See Lundestad, "The United States and Western Europe," 50ff.
87   For the protests, see Kohl, *Erinnerungen 1982–1990*, 194–197; Müller and Risse-Kappen, "Origins of Estrangement; see also Broer, op. cit.; Benien, *Der SDI-Entscheidungsprozeß in der Regierung Kohl/Genscher 1983–86*.
88   See also Layritz, *Der NATO-Doppelbeschluß*; Risse-Kappen, *Zero-option: INF, West Germany and Arms Control*.
89   Blinken, *Ally versus Ally*; Jentleson, *Pipeline Politics*; also Tsoukalis, "Euro–American Relations and Global Economic Interdependence," 12–14.
90   See Busch, "Ronald Reagan and Economic Policy"; Sloan, *The Reagan Effect: Economics and Presidential Leadership*; Kimzey, *Reaganomics*; Buchanan, *Reagonomics and After*.
91   See Cohen, op. cit., 113ff.; Kreile, "Aufschwung und Risiko"; also Sahu and Tracy, *The Economic Legacy of the Reagan Years*; Smith and Wertman, *US–West European Relations during the Reagan Years*.
92   Peterson, *Europe and America in the 1990s*, 45.
93   See Grant, *Inside the House that Jacques Built*.
94   See Urwin, op. cit., 180ff.; Stirk, *A History of European Integration since 1914*, 203ff.; also Rees, *The Western European Union at the Crossroads*; Deighton, *Western European Union, 1954–1997*.
95   See Beschloss and Talbott, *At the Highest Levels*; Oberdorfer, *The Turn: From Cold War to a New Era*; Hutchings, *American Diplomacy and the End of the Cold War*.
96   See Knapp "EG 1992 und die USA."
97   See Lundestad, "Empire by Invitation," 263–277.
98   Lundestad, *The United States and Western Europe*, 241.
99   Lundestad, *"Empire" by Integration*, 111–116; see also the interesting essays in Haftendorn and Tuschhoff, *America and Europe in an Era of Change*; a convincing account of the Bush administration's European policy can be found in Lundestad, *The United States and Western Europe*, 233ff. For a succinct overview of the Bush presidency, see Naftali, *George H.W. Bush*.
100 See Zelikow and Rice, *Germany Unified and Europe Transformed*; Merkl, *German Unification in the European Context*. See also the chapter by Robert Hutchings in this volume and his book *American Diplomacy and the End of the Cold War*.
101 See Rode, "Transatlantische Wirtschaftsbeziehungen zwischen Freihandel und Protektionismus," 70ff.; Randall,"Europe's Monetary Union and the United States."
102 Lundestad, *"Empire" by Integration*, 114.
103 Quoted in Schwabe, "The United States and European Integration," 115. See also Kahler and Link, *Europe and America*; and Larres, "Die USA, die europäische Einigung und die Politik Helmut Kohls."
104 See the literature in notes 95 and 100.
105 Hurst, *The Foreign Policy of the Bush Administration*.
106 Brzezinski, *Second Chance*, 82.
107 See the literature in note 6 above.
108 Biscop and Lembke, *EU Enlargement and the Transatlantic Alliance*.

Bibliography

Andrews, David M. (ed.), *The Atlantic Alliance under Stress: US–European Relations after Iraq* (Cambridge: Cambridge University Press, 2005).
Andrianopoulos, Argyris G., *Western Europe in Kissinger's Global Strategy* (Basingstoke: Macmillan, 1987).

Bell, Coral, *The Reagan Paradox: US Foreign Policy in the 1980s* (Aldershot: Edward Elgar, 1989).

Benien, Theodor, *Der SDI-Entscheidungsprozeß in der Regierung Kohl/Genscher 1983–86: Eine Fallstudie über Einflußfaktoren sicherheitspolitischer Entscheidungsfindung under den Bedingungen strategischer Abhängigkeit* (Munich: Tuduv, 1991).

Beschloss, M.R. and S. Talbott, *At the Highest Levels: The Inside Story of the End of the Cold War* (Boston: Little, Brown, 1993).

Biscop, Sven and Johan Lembke (eds.), *EU Enlargement and the Transatlantic Alliance: A Security Relationship in Flux* (Boulder, CO: Lynne Rienner Publishers, 2008).

Biven, W. Carl, *Jimmy Carter's Economy: Policy in an Age of Limits* (Chapel Hill: University of North Carolina Press, 2002).

Blinken, Antony J., *Ally versus Ally: America, Europe, and the Siberian Pipeline Crisis* (New York: Praeger, 1987).

Bozo, Frederic, *Two Strategies for Europe: De Gaulle, the US and the Atlantic Alliance* (Lanham, MD: Rowman & Littlefield, 2001).

Brandt, Willy, *Erinnerungen* (Frankfurt am Main: Ferenczy, 1989).

Brinkley, Douglas and Richard T. Griffith (eds.), *John F. Kennedy and Europe* (Baton Rouge: Louisiana State University Press, 1999).

Broer, M., *Die nuklearen Kurzstreckenraketen in Europa: Eine Analyse des Deutsch–Amerikanischen Streits über die Einbeziehung der SRINF in den INF-Vertrag und der SNF-Kontroverse* (Frankfurt/M.: Peter Lang, 1993).

Brzezinski, Zbigniew, *Second Chance: Three Presidents and the Crisis of American Superpower* (New York: Basic Books, 2007).

Buchanan, James M., *Reagonomics and After* (London: Institute of Economic Affairs, 1989).

Burk, Kathleen and Melvyn Stokes (eds.), *The United States and the European Alliance since 1945* (Oxford: Berg, 1999).

Burr, William and Robert A. Wampler, "With Friends like these . . . Kissinger, the Atlantic Alliance and the Abortive Year of Europe, 1973–74," paper presented at the international conference on NATO, the Warsaw Pact and the Rise of Détente, 1965–1972, Machiavelli Center for Cold War Studies, Dobbiaco, September 2002.

Busch, Andrew E., "Ronald Reagan and Economic Policy," in Paul Kengor (ed.), *The Reagan Presidency: Assessing the Man and His Legacy* (Lanham, MD: Rowman & Littlefield, 2005).

Carter, Jimmy, *Keeping Faith: Memoirs of a President* (London: Collins, 1982).

Cleva, Gregory D., *Henry Kissinger and the American Approach to Foreign Policy* (Lewisburg, PA: Bucknell University Press, 1989).

Cohen, Benjamin J., "An Explosion in the Kitchen? Economic Relations with Other Advanced States," in Kenneth A. Oye et al. (eds.), *Eagle Defiant: United States Foreign Policy in the 1980s* (Boston: Little, Brown, 1983).

Cohen-Tanugi, Laurent, *An Alliance at Risk: The United States and Europe since September 11* (Baltimore: Johns Hopkins University Press, 2003).

Coker, Christopher, *Empires in Conflict: The Growing Rift between Europe and the United States* (London: RUSI, 2003).

Costigliola, Frank, "The Pursuit of Atlantic Community: Nuclear Arms, Dollars, and Berlin," in Thomas G. Paterson (ed.), *Kennedy's Quest for Victory: American Foreign Policy, 1961–63* (New York: Oxford University Press, 1989).

Cromwell, William C., *The United States and the European Pillar: The Strained Alliance* (New York: St. Martin's Press, 1992).

Czempiel, E.O., *Machtprobe: Die USA und die Sowjetunion in den achtziger Jahren* (Munich: Beck, 1989).

Deighton, Anne (ed.), *Western European Union, 1954–1997: Defence, Security, Integration* (Reading: European Interdependence Research Unit, 1997).

DePorte, Anton W., *Europe between the Superpowers: The Enduring Balance*, 2nd edition (New Haven, CT: Yale University Press, 1986).

Devuyst, Youri, *American Attitudes on European Political Integration: The Nixon–Kissinger Legacy* (Brussels: Vrije Universiteit. Institute for European Studies, 2007), IES Working Paper 2.

Dinan, Desmond, *Ever Closer Union? An Introduction to the European Community*, 3rd edition (Basingstoke: Macmillan, 2005).

Dittgen, Herbert, *Deutsch-Amerikanische Sicherheitsbeziehungen in der Ära Helmut Schmidt: Vorgeschichte und Folgen des NATO-Doppelbeschlußes* (Munich: Fink, 1991).

Dittgen, Herbert, "Die Ära der Ost-West-Verhandlungen und der Wirtschafts- und Währungskrisen (1969–1981)," in Klaus Larres and Torsten Oppelland (eds.), *Deutschland und die USA im 20. Jahrhundert: Geschichte der politischen Beziehungen* (Darmstadt: WGB, 1997), 178–203.

Drell, Sidney D. et al., *The Reagan Strategic Defense Initiative: A Technical, Political, and Arms Control Assessment* (Cambridge, MA: Ballinger, 1984).

Duchene, François, *Jean Monnet: The First Statesman of Interdependence* (New York: Norton, 1994).

Dumbrell, John, *The Carter Presidency: A Re-evaluation* (Manchester: Manchester University Press, 1993).

Fischer, Beth A., *The Reagan Reversal: Foreign Policy and the End of the Cold War* (Columbia, MO: University of Missouri Press, 1997).

Forsberg, Tuomas and Graeme P. Herd, *Divided West: European Security and the Transatlantic Relationship* (Oxford: Blackwell, 2006).

Frank, Paul, *Entschlüsselte Botschaft: Ein Diplomat macht Inventur* (Stuttgart: DVA, 1981).

Gaddis, John Lewis, *Strategies of Containment: A Critical Appraisal of American National Security Policy during the Cold War*, revised and expanded edition (Oxford: Oxford University Press, 2005).

Gardner, Lloyd, "Lyndon Johnson and de Gaulle," in Robert O. Paxton and Nicholas Wahl (eds.), *De Gaulle and the United States: A Centennial Reappraisal* (Oxford: Berg, 1994).

Garthoff, Raymond, *Détente and Confrontation: American–Soviet Relations from Nixon to Reagan*, revised edition (Washington, DC: Brookings, 1994).

Gavin, F.J., *Gold, Dollars and Power: The Politics of International Monetary Relations, 1958–1971* (Chapel Hill: University of North Carolina Press, 2004).

Genscher, Hans-Dietrich, *Erinnerungen*, 2nd edition (Berlin: Siedler, 1995).

Giauque, Jeffrey G., *Grand Designs and Visions of Unity: The Atlantic Power and the Reorganization of Western Europe, 1955–1963* (Chapel Hill: University of North Carolina Press, 2002).

Goldstein, Walter (ed.), *Reagan's Leadership and the Atlantic Alliance: Views from Europe and America* (Washington, DC/London: Pergamon/Brassey, 1986).

Grant, Charles, *Inside the House that Jacques Built* (London: Brealey Publishing, 1994).

Grosser, Alfred, *The Western Alliance: European–American Relations since 1945* (New York: Seabury Press, 1980).

Hackett, Clifford, *Monnet and the Americans: The Father of a United Europe and his US Supporters* (Washington, DC: American Council for Jean Monnet Studies, 1995).

Haftendorn, Helga, *Sicherheit und Stabilität: Außenbeziehungen der Bundesrepublik zwischen Ölkrise und NATO-Doppelbeschluß* (Munich: dtv, 1986).

Haftendorn, Helga and C. Tuschhoff (eds.), *America and Europe in an Era of Change* (Boulder, CO: Westview, 1993).

Hanrieder, Wolfram, *Germany, America, Europe: Forty Years of German Foreign Policy* (New Haven, CT: Yale University Press, 1989).

Hanrieder, Wolfram, "The German–American Connection in the 1970s and 1980s: The Maturing of a Relationship," in Carl C. Hodge and Cathal J. Nolan (eds.), *Shepherd of Democracy? America and Germany in the Twentieth Century* (Westport, CT: Praeger, 1992).

Harper, John L., *American Visions of Europe: Franklin D. Roosevelt, George F. Kennan, and Dean G. Acheson* (Cambridge: Cambridge University Press, 1996).

Heep, Barbara D., *Helmut Schmidt und Amerika. Eine schwierige Partnerschaft* (Bonn: Bouvier, 1990).

Heller, Francis H. and John R. Gillingham (eds.), *The United States and the Integration of Europe: Legacies of the Postwar Era* (New York: St. Martin's Press, 1996).

Hellmann, Rainer, *Gold, the Dollar, and the European Currency Systems: The Seven Year Monetary War* (New York: Praeger, 1979).

Hentschel, Volker, *Ludwig Erhard: Ein Politikerleben* (Berlin: Ullstein, 1998).

Herbst, Ludolf et al. (eds.), *Vom Marshall-Plan zur EWG: Die Eingliederung der Bundesrepublik in die westliche Welt* (Munich: Oldenbourg, 1990).

Hersch, Seymour M., *The Price of Power: Kissinger in the Nixon White House* (New York: Summit, 1983).

Heuser, Beatrice, *NATO, Britain, France, and the FRG: Nuclear Strategies and Forces for Europe, 1949–2000* (Basingstoke: Macmillan, 1997).

Hoffmann, Stanley with Frederic Bozo, *Gulliver Unbound: America's Imperial Temptation and the War in Iraq* (Lanham, MD: Rowman & Littlefield, 2004).

Hogan, Michael J., *The Marshall Plan: America, Britain and the Reconstruction of Western Europe, 1947–1952* (Cambridge: Cambridge University Press, 1987).

Horowitz, Daniel (ed.), *Jimmy Carter and the Energy Crisis of the 1970s: The "Crisis of Confidence" Speech of July 15, 1979: A Brief History with Documents* (Boston: St. Martin's, 2005).

Hurst, Steven, *The Foreign Policy of the Bush Administration: In Search of a New World Order* (New York: Cassell, 1999).

Hutchings, Robert, *American Diplomacy and the End of the Cold War: An Insider's Account of US Policy in Europe, 1989–1992* (Washington, DC/Baltimore, MD: Woodrow Wilson Center Press/Johns Hopkins University Press, 1997).

Ikenberry, John G., "Rethinking the Origins of American Hegemony," *Political Science Quarterly* 104, 1989, 375–400.

Ilgen, T.L., *Autonomy and Independence: US–Western European Monetary and Trade Relations, 1958–84* (Totowa, NJ: Rowman & Allanheld, 1985).

Isaacson, Walter and E. Thomas, *The Wise Men: Six Friends and the World They Made* (London: Faber, 1986).

James, Harold, *Rambouillet, 15 November 1975: Die Globalisierung der Wirtschaft* (Munich: dtv, 1997).

Jentleson, Bruce W., *Pipeline Politics: The Complex Political Economy of East–West Energy Trade* (Ithaca, NY: Cornell University Press, 1986).

Jochum, Michael, "Der Zerfall des sicherheitspolitischen Konsenses und die Verschärfung der Wirtschafts- und Währungskrisen (1981–89)," in Klaus Larres and Torsten Oppelland (eds.), *Deutschland und die USA im 20. Jahrhundert: Geschichte der politischen Beziehungen* (Darmstadt: WGB, 1997).

Kahler, Miles, "The United States and Western Europe: The Diplomatic Consequences of Mr. Reagan," in Kenneth A. Oye et al. (eds.), *Eagle Defiant: United States Foreign Policy in the 1980s* (Boston: Little, Brown, 1983).

Kahler, M. and W. Link, *Europe and America: A Return to History* (New York: Council on Foreign Relations, 1996).

Kane, Tim, "Global US Troop Deployment, 1950–2003," October 27, 2004, http://www.heritage.org/research/nationalsecurity/cda04-11.cfm

Kaplan, Lawrence S., *NATO Divided, NATO United: The Evolution of an Alliance* (Westport, CT: Praeger, 2004).

Kashmeri, Sarwar A., *America and Europe after 9/11 and Iraq: The Great Divide* (Westport, CT: Praeger, 2007).

Kaufman, Burton I. and Scott Kaufman, *The Presidency of James Earl Carter*, 2nd revised edition (Lawrence, KS: University Press of Kansas, 2006).

Keohane, Robert O., "US Foreign Economic Policy toward Other Advanced Capitalist States," in Kenneth A Oye et al. (eds.), *Eagle Entangled: US Foreign Policy in a Complex World* (New York: Longman, 1979).

Killick, John, *The United States and European Reconstruction, 1945–1960* (Edinburgh: Keele University Press, 1997).

Kimzey, Bruce W., *Reaganomics* (St. Paul: West Publishing Company, 1983).

Kirshner, Orin (ed.), *The Bretton Woods–GATT System: Restrospect and Prospect after Fifty Years* (Armonk, NY: M.E. Sharpe, 1995).

Kissinger, Henry, *White House Years* (Boston: Little, Brown, 1979).

Kissinger, Henry, *Years of Upheaval* (Boston: Little, Brown, 1982).

Knapp, Manfred, "Das Dilemma der europäischen NATO-Staaten zwischen ökonomischen Machtzuwachs und sicherheitspolitischer Abhängigkeit," in Christian Hacke and Manfred Knapp (eds.), *Friedenssicherung und Rüstungskontrolle in Europa* (Cologne: Verlag Wissenschaft und Politik, 1989).

Knapp, Manfred, "EG 1992 und die USA: Transatlantische Beziehungen zwischen Wirtschaftskonkurrenz und Sicherheitspartnerschaft," in Manfred Knapp (ed.), *Transatlantische Beziehungen: Die USA und Europa zwischen gemeinsamen Interessen und Konflikt* (Stuttgart: Steiner, 1990).

Knudsen, Bard B., *Europe versus America: Foreign Policy in the 1980s* (Paris: Atlantic Institute for International Affairs, 1984).

Kohl, Helmut, *Erinnerungen 1982–1990* (Stuttgart: Droemer/Knaur, 2005).

Kraft, Joseph, *The Grand Design: From Common Market to Atlantic Partnership* (New York: Harper, 1962).

Kreile, M. "Aufschwung und Risiko: Die Wirtschafts- und Haushaltpolitik der Reagan-Administration;" in Hartmut Wasser (ed.), *Die Ära Reagan: Eine erste Bilanz* (Stuttgart, 1988).

Krige, John, *American Hegemony and the Postwar Reconstruction of Science in Europe* (Cambridge, MA: MIT Press, 2006).

Kunz, Diane B., "Cold War Diplomacy: The Other Side of Containment," in Kunz (ed.), *The Diplomacy of the Crucial Decade: American Foreign Policy during the 1960s* (New York: Columbia University Press, 1994).

Larres, Klaus, "Germany and the West: The 'Rapallo Factor' in German Foreign Policy from the 1950s to the 1990s," in K. Larres and P. Panayi (eds.), *The Federal Republic of Germany since 1949: Politics, Society and Economy before and after Unification* (London and New York: Longman, 1996).

Larres, Klaus, "North Atlantic Treaty Organization," in Alexander DeConde et al. (eds.), *Encyclopedia of American Foreign Relations: Studies of the Principal Movements and Ideas*, revised and expanded 2nd edition, 3 vols., vol. 2 (New York: Scribner's, 2002).

Larres, Klaus, "Die USA, die europäische Einigung und die Politik Helmut Kohls," *Historisch-Politische Mitteilungen* 14, 2007, 245–262.

Larres, Klaus, "Sicherheit mit und vor Deutschland. Der Einfluss der Bundesrepublik auf die USA und das westliche Bündnis in den 50er und 60er Jahren," in Frank Nägler (ed.), *Die Bundeswehr 1955 bis 2005. Rückblenden, Einsichten, Perspektiven* (Munich: Oldenbourg, 2007).

Larres, Klaus, "Britain and Europe from Churchill to Blair and Brown," in Jürgen Elvert and Jürgen Nielsen-Sikora (eds.), *Leitbild Europa? Europabilder und ihre Wirkungen in der Neuzeit* (Stuttgart: Steiner Verlag, 2008).

Larres, Klaus, "The United States and the Rome Treaties of 1957," in Michael Gehler (ed.), *The Rome Treaties after 50 Years* (Cologne: Böhlau Verlag, 2008).

Larres, Klaus and Torsten Oppelland (eds.), *Deutschland und die USA im 20. Jahrhundert: Geschichte der politischen Beziehungen* (Darmstadt: WGB, 1997).

Lavy, George J., *Germany and Israel: Moral Debt and National Interest* (London: Frank Cass, 1996).

Lawrence, Robert Z. et al., "An Analysis of the 1977 US Trade Deficit," *Brookings Papers on Economic Activity* 9, no. 1, 1978, 159–190.

Layritz, Stephan, *Der NATO-Doppelbeschluß: Westliche Sicherheitspolitik im Spannungsfeld von Innen-, Bündnis- und Außenpolitik* (Frankfurt am Main: Peter Lang, 1992).

Lieber, Robert J., *The Oil Decade: Conflict and Cooperation in the West* (New York: Praeger, 1983).

Litwak, Robert S., *Détente and the Nixon Doctrine: American Foreign Policy and the Pursuit of Stability, 1969–1976* (Cambridge: Cambridge University Press, 1984).

Lundestad, Geir, "Empire by Invitation? The United States and Western Europe, 1945–1952," *Journal of Peace Research* 23, no. 3, 1986, 263–277.

Lundestad, Geir, *The American "Empire" and other Studies of US Foreign Policy in a Comparative Perspective* (Oslo: Norwegian University Press, 1990).

Lundestad, Geir, "The United States and Western Europe under Ronald Reagan," in David E. Kyvig (ed.), *Reagan and the World* (New York: Praeger, 1990).

Lundestad, Geir, *"Empire" by Integration: The United States and European Integration, 1945–1997* (Oxford: Oxford University Press, 1998).

Lundestad, Geir, *The United States and Western Europe since 1945: From "Empire" by Invitation to Transatlantic Drift* (Oxford: Oxford University Press, 2003).

Mahan, Erin R., *Kennedy, de Gaulle and Western Europe* (Basingstoke: Palgrave Macmillan, 2002).

Matlock, Jack F. *Reagan and Gorbachev: How the Cold War Ended* (New York: Random House, 2004).

Merkl, P.H., *German Unification in the European Context* (University Park, PA: Pennsylvania State University Press, 1993).

Milward, Alan, *The Reconstruction of Western Europe, 1945–1951* (London: Methuen, 1984).

Milward, Alan, *The European Rescue of the Nation State* (London: Routledge, 1992).

Moore, R. Laurence and Maurizio Vaudagna (eds.), *The American Century in Europe* (Ithaca, NY: Cornell University Press, 2003).

Morgan, Rogan, *The United States and West Germany, 1945–1973: A Study in Alliance Politics* (London: Oxford University Press, 1974).

Müller, Harald and Thomas Risse-Kappen, "Origins of Estrangement: The Peace Movement and the Changed Image of America in West Germany," *International Security* 12, 1987, 52–88.

Naftali, Timothy, *George H.W. Bush* (New York: Macmillan, 2007).

Oberdorfer, Don, *The Turn: From Cold War to a New Era. The United States and the Soviet Union 1983–1990* (London: Jonathan Cape, 1992).

Oudenaren, John van, *Détente in Europe: The Soviet Union and the West since 1953* (Durham, NC: Duke University Press, 1991).

Pagedas, Constantine A., *Anglo-American Strategic Relations and the French Problem, 1960–63: A Troubled Partnership* (London: Frank Cass, 2000).

Paxton, Robert O. and Nicholas Wahl (eds.), *De Gaulle and the United States: A Centennial Reappraisal* (Oxford: Berg, 1994).

Pells, Richard, *Not Like Us: How Europeans Have Loved, Hated, and Transformed American Culture since World War II* (New York: Basic Books, 1997).

Peterson, John, *Europe and America in the 1990s: The Prospects for Partnership* (Aldershot: Edward Elgar, 1993).

Pierre, Andrew J., "Conflicting Visions: Defence, Nuclear Weapons, and Arms Control in the Franco-American Relationship during the de Gaulle Era," in Robert O. Paxton and Nicholas Wahl (eds.), *De Gaulle and the United States: A Centennial Reappraisal* (Oxford: Berg, 1994).

Pond, Elizabeth, *Friendly Fire: The Near-Death of the Transatlantic Alliance* (Washington, DC: Brookings Press, 2004).

Rabinovich, Abraham, *The Yom Kippur War: The Epic Encounter that Transformed the Middle East* (New York: Schocken Books, 2004).

Randall, Henning C., "Europe's Monetary Union and the United States," *Foreign Policy* 102, 1996, 83–104.

Rees, W.G., *The Western European Union at the Crossroads: Between Transatlantic Solidarity and European Integration* (Boulder, CO: Westview, 1998).

Reynolds, David (ed.), *The Origins of the Cold War in Europe: International Perspectives* (New Haven, CT: Yale University Press, 1994).

Risse-Kappen, Thomas, *Zero-Option: INF, West Germany and Arms Control* (Boulder, CO: Westview, 1988).

Rode, Reinhard, "Transatlantische Wirtschaftsbeziehungen zwischen Freihandel und Protektionismus," in Manfred Knapp (ed.), *Transatlantische Beziehungen: Die USA und Europa zwischen gemeinsamen Interessen und Konflikt* (Stuttgart: Steiner, 1990).

Romero, Frederico, "Interdependence and Integration in American Eyes: From the Marshall Plan to Currency Convertibility," in Alan Milward et al. (eds.), *The Frontier of National Sovereignty: History and Theory 1945–1992* (London: Routledge, 1993).

Romero, Frederico, "US Attitudes towards Integration and Interdependence: The 1950s," in Francis H. Heller and John R. Gillingham (eds.), *The United States and the Integration of Europe: Legacies of the Postwar Era* (New York: St. Martin's Press, 1996).

Ryan, David, *The United States and Europe in the Twentieth Century* (Harlow: Longman, 2003).

Sahu, Anandi P. and Ronald L. Tracy (eds.), *The Economic Legacy of the Reagan Years: Euphoria or Chaos?* (New York: Praeger, 1991).

Schaetzel, J. Robert, *The Unhinged Alliance: America and the European Community* (New York: Harper & Row, 1974).

Schake, Kori N., "NATO-Strategie und deutsch-amerikanisches Verhältnis," in Detlef Junker (ed.), *Die USA und Deutschland im Zeitalter des Kalten Krieges. Ein Handbuch*, Bd.1: 1945–1968 (Munich: DVA, 2001).

Schmidt, Helmut, *Menschen und Mächte* (Berlin: Siedler, 1987).

Schröder, Hans-Jürgen, "USA und westdeutscher Wiederaufstieg (1945–1952)," in Klaus Larres and Torsten Oppelland (eds.), *Deutschland und die USA im 20. Jahrhundert: Geschichte der politischen Beziehungen* (Darmstadt: WGB, 1997).

Schwabe, Klaus, "The United States and European Integration, 1947–1957," in Clemens Wurm (ed.), *Western Europe and Germany: The Beginnings of European Integration, 1945–1960* (Oxford: Berg, 1995).

Schwabe, Klaus, *Weltmacht und Weltordnung. Amerikanische Außenpoltik von 1989 bis zur Gegenwart. Eine Jahrhundertgeschichte* (Paderborn: Schöningh 2006).

Schwartz, Thomas A., *Lyndon Johnson and Europe: In the Shadow of Vietnam* (Cambridge, MA: Harvard University Press, 2003).

Shawcross, William, *Allies: The US, Britain, Europe and the War in Iraq* (London: Atlantic, 2003).

Simonian, Haig, *The Privileged Partnership: Franco-German Relations in the European Community, 1969–1984* (Oxford: Clarendon Press, 1985).

Skidmore, David, *Reversing Course: Carter's Foreign Policy, Domestic Politics, and the Failure of Reform* (Nashville, TN: Vanderbilt University Press, 1996).

Skogmar, Gunnar, *The United States and the Nuclear Dimension of European Integration* (Basingstoke: Palgrave Macmillan, 2004).

Sloan, John W., *The Reagan Effect: Economics and Presidential Leadership* (Lawrence, KS: University Press of Kansas, 1999).

Smith, Gaddis, *Morality, Reason and Power: American Diplomacy in the Carter Years* (New York: Hill and Wang, 1986).

Smith, Steven K. and Douglas A. Wertman (eds.), *US–West European relations during the Reagan Years: The Perspective of West European Publics* (London: Macmillan, 1991).

Stirk, P.M.R., *A History of European Integration since 1914* (London: Continuum, 2001).

Strong, Robert A., *Working in the World: Jimmy Carter and the Making of American Foreign Policy* (Baton Rouge: Louisiana State University Press, 2000).

Talbott, Strobe, *Deadly Gambits: The Reagan Administration and the Stalemate in Nuclear Arms Control* (London: Picador, 1984).

Thiel, Elke, *Dollar-Dominanz. Lastenteilung und amerikanische Truppenpräsenz in Europa* (Baden-Baden: Nomos, 1979).

Trachtenberg, Marc, *A Constructed Peace: The Making of the European Settlement, 1945–1963* (Princeton, NJ: Princeton University Press, 1999).

Treverton, Gregory F., *The Dollar Drain and American Forces in Germany: Managing the Political Economies of Alliance* (Athens, OH: Columbia University Press, 1978).

Tsoukalis, Loukas, "Euro-American Relations and Global Economic Interdependence," in Tsoukalis (ed.), *Europe, America and the World Economy* (Oxford: Blackwell, 1986).

Urwin, Derek W., *The Community of Europe: A History of European Integration since 1945*, 2nd edition (London: Longman, 1995).

Wasserman, Sherri L., *The Neutron Bomb Controversy: A Study in Alliance Politics* (New York: Praeger, 1983).

Wells, Samuel F. Jr, "Reagan, Euromissiles, and Europe," in Brownlee W. Elliot (ed.), *The Reagan Presidency: Pragmatic Conservatism and Its Legacies* (Lawrence, KS: University Press of Kansas, 2003).

Wiegrefe, Klaus, *Das Zerwürfnis: Helmut Schmidt, Jimmy Carter und die Krise der deutsch-amerikanischen Beziehungen* (Berlin: Propyläen, 2005).

Wilker, Lothar, "Das Brasiliengeschäft – ein 'diplomatischer Betriebsunfall?'," in Helga Haftendorn et al. (eds.), *Verwaltete Außenpolitik: sicherheits- und entspannungspolitische Entscheidungsprozesse in Bonn* (Cologne: Verlag Wissenschaft und Politik, 1978).

Williams, Geoffrey L., *The Permanent Alliance: The European–American Partnership, 1945–1984* (Leyden: A.W. Sijthoff, 1977).

Winand, Pascal, *Eisenhower, Kennedy and the United States of Europe* (London: Macmillan, 1993).

Zeiler, Thomas W., *American Trade and Power in the 1960s* (New York: Columbia University Press, 1992).

Zelikow, Philip and Condoleezza Rice, *Germany Unified and Europe Transformed: A Study in Statecraft* (Cambridge, MA: Harvard University Press, 1995).

Further Reading

While most of the essential reading on the theme of this chapter has been referred to in the notes, students will find it particularly beneficial to consult the books by Geir Lundestad. Accessible and very readable accounts are in particular *The United States and Western Europe since 1945: From "Empire" by Invitation to Transatlantic Drift* (2005) and *"Empire" by Integration: The United States and European integration, 1945–1997* (1998). Lundestad's original thesis that the United States established an "empire by invitation" in western Europe was published as a journal article. See "Empire by Invitation? The United States and Western Europe, 1945–1952," *Journal of Peace Research* 23, no. 3, 1986, 263–277.

Other good comprehensive accounts are Alfred Grosser, *The Western Alliance: European–American Relations since 1945* (1980); Klaus Schwabe, *Weltmacht und Weltordnung* (2006); Geoffrey L. Williams, *The Permanent Alliance* (1987); William C. Cromwell, *The United States and the European Pillar* (1992); the rather short book by David Ryan, *The United States and Europe in the Twentieth Century* (2003); and with an emphasis on transatlantic security issues Ronald E. Powaski, *The Entangling Alliance* (1994). Several edited volumes are also useful introductions to the study of transatlantic relations in the post-World War II era, such as Francis H. Heller and John R. Gillingham (eds.), *The United States and the Integration of Europe: Legacies of the Postwar Era* (1996), Kathleen Burk and Melvyn Stokes (eds.), *The United States and the European Alliance since 1945* (1999), and R. Laurence Moore and Maurizio Vaudagna (eds.), *The American Century in Europe* (2003).

Very few studies exist which deal directly with the main theme of this chapter, the policy of the United States towards the process of European integration and European unity. Geir Lundestad partially deals with it in his publications, as does the edited volume by Heller and Gillingham. An older but still useful book on the matter was written by Max Beloff, *The United States and the Unity of Europe* (1963).

Until the rise of the post-revisionist school within Cold War studies in the early to mid-1970s, European–American relations had been somewhat neglected in favor of studies on the bilateral Soviet–American rivalry. Good balanced post-revisionst accounts are Anton W. DePorte, *Europe between the Superpowers: The Enduring Balance*, 2nd edition (1986) and David Reynolds (ed.), *The Origins of the Cold War in Europe: International Perspectives* (1994).

Numerous good articles on American–European relations during the Cold War tend to be published in the journals *Diplomatic History*, the *Journal of Cold War Studies*, *Diplomacy and Statecraft* and not least the *Journal of Transatlantic Studies*.

Most works on European–American relations have dealt with the years of reconstruction from the Marshall Plan to the establishment of the EEC in 1958. Among a very large number of studies in particular the books by Alan Milward, Michael Hogan, and the provocative study by Marc Trachtenberg, *A Constructed Peace* (1999) are of interest here as well as the innovative recent book by John Krige, *American Hegemony and the Postwar Reconstruction of Science in Europe* (2006). The nuclear dimension of transatlantic relations is convincingly dealt with by Gunnar Skogmar, *The United States and the Nuclear Dimension of European Integration* (2004).

The most interesting studies on transatlantic relations in the political, economic, and security fields during the Kennedy/Johnson era, the Nixon/Ford/Kissinger years, and during the Carter and Reagan/Bush administrations are referred to in the notes of this chapter. For the best introduction to the cultural dimension of transatlantic relations, consult Richard Pells, *Not Like Us: How Europeans Have Loved, Hated, and Transformed American Culture since World War II* (1997).

CHAPTER NINE

The Churches and Christianity in Cold War Europe

DIANNE KIRBY

After the 1648 Treaty of Westphalia, which removed religion as a justification for war, the salience of religion for international affairs declined.[1] Nonetheless, the widespread separation of religion from the ensemble of political institutions that constitute the modern national state and geopolitical system did not mean that religion ceased to play a role in politics or in the constitution of the world order.[2] The potency of religious "soft power"[3] meant that religion was never discarded from state arsenals. The actions of Christian leaders and institutions during World War II highlighted its national and international value to the nation state, however secular. The war itself renewed the determination of the churches to secure political influence and a meaningful position in the postwar world, convinced that Christianity was the means to a more just and equitable society for all. While Roosevelt and Stalin seemingly thought religion a potential bridge between East and West, others identified Marxist atheism as the window of vulnerability through which to attack and curtail the Soviet experiment. Consequently, the postwar period and the emerging Cold War were endowed with a critical religious dimension. The "religious cold war" that followed, plus the Christian component of transatlantic relations, a shared religious heritage between Europe and the US, had profound implications for European Christianity and its churches.

The Catholic theologian John Henry Newman noted that the church is not "placed in a void, but in the crowded world," meaning that it must adapt to "persons and circumstances, and must be thrown into new shapes according to the form of society" in which it exists.[4] The Cold War divided Europe and subjected its societies to two competing models of modernization: the communist-socialist, represented by the Soviet Union, versus the liberal capitalist, represented by the US. A reliable source of emotion, ready-made symbols, and rituals, Christianity offered the potential to extend the appeal of the competing political and economic models throughout what had once been Christendom. The historical, cultural, and indeed national roots of continental Europe remained intimately linked to Christianity, the dominant religion for over 1,500 years. It had been supported by a social and legal framework that involved coercion, control, and an alliance with state authority. In the early Cold

A Companion to Europe since 1945, First Edition. Edited by Klaus Larres.
© 2014 John Wiley & Sons, Ltd. Published 2014 by John Wiley & Sons, Ltd.

War, Christianity became a means through which the US and its Western allies could de-legitimate Soviet influence and enhance the appeal of the transatlantic alliance for European peoples wary of American capitalism.[5] The West's Manichaean Cold War rhetoric presented US–Soviet rivalry as the defense of Western civilization and Christianity against the atheistic communism of a Soviet Union determined on the destruction of one and the eradication of the other. The appropriation of Christianity for Cold War purposes is an area in which new research is now being undertaken after many years of neglect.[6] This essay is a contribution that examines how some key "Christian" institutions responded to the challenges represented by Europe's "religious Cold War."[7]

At war's end the old European order verged on disintegration, convulsed by conflict and the radicalism it fostered. The Soviet Union and the US, one devastated and the other revitalized by the war, emerged as the world's major powers. As negotiations about the postwar arrangements in Europe broke down, each side moved to secure its sphere of influence. At the Potsdam conference, Secretary of State James Byrnes initially refused reparations, then made concessions in what historian Marc Trachtenberg has interpreted as a policy of "amicable divorce" by which the Americans demonstrated their willingness to tolerate a Soviet "security zone."[8] It was clear that Stalin also preferred a *modus vivendi*. The British, on the other hand, were concerned that an amicable understanding between the two anti-colonial, anti-imperialist powers might prove detrimental to British interests. Even while fighting against Germany in alliance with the Soviet Union, Britain had planned for possible future conflict with it and continued to regard it as the main hostile force in the world. Britain viewed American power as the safeguard against Soviet power. From the end of the war, the major objective of British foreign policy was what became the Atlantic Pact, when, for the first time, the US committed itself to the defense of western Europe.[9]

Knowing that the American public and policy-makers alike were wary of British intentions, especially towards the Soviet Union, the Foreign Office thought that "the process of inducing the United States to support a British resistance to Russian penetration in Europe will be a tricky one."[10] It would require the inclusion of values and principles. Religion had proven an effective component in British wartime efforts to persuade the American public to support their resistance to the Nazi onslaught and, after June 1941, the Anglo-Soviet alliance.[11] Religion subsequently became integral to postwar British endeavors to reverse attitudes towards their former Soviet ally and to educate publics either side of the Atlantic about its threat potential to world peace. Winston Churchill's 1946 Fulton speech, carefully coordinated between the British and American administrations, notably referred to the "growing challenge and peril to Christian civilisation."[12]

Through the Church of England's Council on Foreign Relations, the British Foreign Office had numerous links with Orthodox churches in eastern Europe. As the Cold War intensified, Foreign Office opinion was that Orthodoxy was more likely to collaborate with than challenge Soviet domination. In contrast, Roman Catholicism was regarded as "one of the most powerful anti-communist influences."[13] More than 50 million Catholics came into the Soviet sphere of influence with its postwar extension into eastern Europe. The institutional Catholic Church had been crushed in the Soviet Union in the 1930s. The war's end, however, brought Soviet overtures to the

Vatican offering a deal: "Potential enemies could be neutralised in return for concessions which would permit Catholics to exercise their faith without molestation."[14] Although favored by elements within the Catholic Church itself, as well as the US State Department at the time, Pope Pius XII and his principal advisers resolutely opposed an agreement. The Vatican's hard-line stance towards the new communist regimes was unwelcome to bishops, clergy, and laity who considered church interests could best be protected by cooperation. This was the case in Poland, Hungary, Czechoslovakia, Romania, and Bulgaria where the church was initially treated relatively well.[15]

The British Foreign Office was reluctant to be openly identified with the Vatican: "they are rather in disgrace all over Europe for trimming during the war." But it supported the Vatican's anti-Soviet stand by "inconspicuous means." During the Anglo-Soviet Cold War of 1945–1946, the Foreign Office's Russia Committee advised Heads of Missions abroad to be aware of "the potential importance of organised religion in combating the spread of Communism."[16] Moscow's suspicions that its enemies would use religion for subversive purposes were confirmed in mid-August 1950 when the Hungarian secret police uncovered the Hungarian Catholic Resistance Movement. Set up in 1947 by the British Intelligence Service, the Hungarian Catholic Resistance Movement was controlled by its Vienna Station. In addition to maintaining caches of arms, its initial operational role was to gather intelligence.[17]

The US supplanted the covert and cautious use made of religion by the British with a much more overt, indeed dramatic and confrontational approach. Beginning with the return of Roosevelt's wartime Vatican envoy Myron C. Taylor in 1946, Truman flaunted his alliance with Pius XII, a self-avowed Soviet enemy.[18] In 1949, Truman demonstrated his satisfaction with the election of the Archbishop of North and South America as Patriarch of Constantinople, achieved with a significant degree of Anglo-American collusion, by having him flown in his personal presidential plane to Istanbul to assume his new position.[19] He thus directly signalled to Moscow his overt support for the heads of the two major religions in the Soviet sphere of influence. Roman Catholicism and Eastern Orthodoxy were each closely connected to the national identity, history, and sentiment of key countries in the Soviet bloc.[20] The equation of religious unity with political unity and national identity was the motivational force behind autocephaly in the Orthodox world, considered a key element in the drive towards statehood.[21] While the influence of the Ecumenical Patriarch did not match that of the pope, the appointment of an American citizen to the primary position in the Orthodox world was calculated to impress an Orthodox community susceptible to political intrigue and full of poor churches seeking financial support. Above all, it was intended to thwart the alleged aspirations of the Moscow patriarchate to become the "Third Rome." It challenged potential Soviet influence in the Orthodox world through the Russian Orthodox Church with Western influence via the Ecumenical Patriarch. Even more worrying for the Soviets, it threatened a combination of Roman Catholicism and Orthodoxy against Soviet communism.[22]

With his Marxist-Leninist background, the calculated use of religion by the West confirmed Stalin's worst beliefs about organized religion and Western hostility. The attempt to rally the religious into a global anti-Soviet crusade played to Stalin's fears about the subversive potential of religion. World War II had demonstrated that significant numbers of Soviet citizens would turn against the regime in response to religious appeals. The Soviets knew that religion remained a focus for dissent and were deeply disturbed by the West's recruitment of religion in a way all too reminiscent of Hitler. The Soviet leadership could not revert to the sort of historical alliance that existed between the church and regimes from which the communist revolution was meant to be a radical departure. Communism had its own internal legitimation that would be called into question should it seem to be seeking "sacralization." An alliance with religion risked alienating communist adherents for whom religion remained a reactionary and anti-progressive force from which the masses had to be liberated. Rather than eradicate, however, Soviet efforts were directed towards controlling and domesticating religion within its sphere and rallying believers with socialist sympathies everywhere in its defense. Nonetheless, no matter how domesticated, religion retained the potential to at least compromise, if not challenge, communist power. The result was vacillating and contradictory policies towards religion throughout the Soviet era.

In contrast, shared religious values facilitated popular support for the US–European alliance. Post-revisionists stress that the "empire" created by the US in western Europe was made possible by the willingness of host governments to collaborate with America in pursuit of their own interests. Truman's rhetoric and overtures to Europe's Christian leaders revealed an assumption that in the struggle between the godless, atheistic Soviet Union and the God-fearing US and its allies, among whom the president included the faithful behind the Iron Curtain, the world's religious forces would be in the American camp. European statesmen were less certain, aware from their own histories that religious organizations were well able to ally themselves with dissident sectors of society to challenge established elites and could be rivals to, as well as supporters of, state power. They knew churchmen were able to transgress the boundaries between the sacred and profane to assert their own political, social, and economic influences and would not necessarily be passive recipients of state-imposed ideological conformity.

Nonetheless, recognizing the importance of ideological solidarity with the US, west European leaders responded by presenting the basic division between their democracies and the totalitarian states as a conflict between religion and communism. In doing so they formulated the basis for a theory of totalitarianism that raised the question of the structural similarities between National Socialism and Stalinism. It provided a useful taxonomy of repressive regimes, justifying the postwar switch from one enemy to another. In the process, the defense of Western civilization and Christianity became anti-communism's central rhetorical device, consolidating the two fundamental contentions on which Cold War policies rested: that communism was a supreme and unqualified evil and that its purpose was world domination. Consequently, in many ways the strongest key common denominator facilitating church–state cooperation in the early Cold War was absolutist anti-communism which, couched in extreme moralistic terms with strongly religious connotations, insisted that the Soviet Union was the incarnation and main source of evil. The result was the "godless Soviet bogey," perhaps the key construction responsible for the European nations, united since the Treaty of Versailles in their determination to halt

Soviet influence, putting aside their differences and supporting America's Cold War leadership.

The potency of religious themes, symbols, and metaphors facilitated a process by which anti-communism, with its deep religious roots, was accorded a doctrinal-like status that served as the cement that bonded the "Free World." Anti-communism also provided a powerful ideological basis of agreement between the governing conservative forces in the US and their Social and Christian Democratic counterparts in western Europe. The latter played a vital role in legitimizing the Cold War, in enrolling labor movements into the anti-communist crusade and in bringing to fruition a form of social reformism that did not threaten the established order.[23]

A decimated Soviet Union, preoccupied with its own future survival and wary of America's "empire of modernity" beginning in Europe, was naturally concerned by the prospect of an anti-communist Christian front as advocated by Truman and Pius XII. The possibility of uniting an otherwise divided eastern Christianity in an ecumenism of suffering or struggle was deeply worrying for a Soviet bloc made up of deeply religious peoples, including significant Catholic populations. Stalin's need to reduce anti-Soviet hostility within and without the communist bloc, as well as his desire to improve his regime's image abroad, militated against the crude anti-religious policies he had once implemented.[24] This deprived Western leaders of a key tool that had been crucial in consolidating an anti-communist consensus in the aftermath of the Russian Revolution. Instead, admiration for "Uncle Joe," the victorious Red Army and the communist role in resistance movements prevailed in western Europe.

Consequently, European leaders, already concerned that Stalin might not remain content with a security zone, also feared that many of their peoples might be attracted to the Soviet ideological and socioeconomic system. The Vatican was particularly aware that communism spoke to the poor, the oppressed, and the downtrodden, its own traditional constituency. It worried that the crucible of war might merge the Orthodox conception of a messianic Russia with the Marxist conception of a messianic proletariat, representing a fusion of ideas that appealed to a Europe in which a return to the prewar status quo was unthinkable.[25]

The difficulties of combining political and social loyalties with religious identity were exacerbated for churches in communist regimes owing to the atheism of Marxist-Leninist ideology. However, unable to eradicate religious faith and confronted with its power and persistence, a weakened Soviet Union saw advantages in accommodating and working with the churches. Stalin had hopes that religion might be one means of bridging the gulf that remained between him and his allies. While religion may have been a mobilizing device for transformational purposes that could eventually be transcended, Soviet generals and local communist leaders honored Greek Orthodox clergy in the Balkans and courted Roman Catholic clergy in Poland. Stalin, albeit by maladroit means, attempted reconciliation with the pope in the spring of 1944.[26] Hitler's invasion had impressed upon Stalin the value of closer church–state relations.[27]

In October 1917 the Bolsheviks had declared the new Soviet state to be non-religious, not anti-religious. The Bolshevik decree of 1918 "on freedom of conscience and religious societies" theoretically safeguarded "Free practice of religious customs." Religious believers were not denied admission to the party, as opposition to religion was subordinated to the class struggle. Some Christian churches flourished under the new regime, including Evangelical Christians who increased their adherents from about 100,000 to over a million in the first decade of Soviet rule.[28] However, under the regime that Stalin gradually introduced, the free conflict of ideas, especially on the subject of religion, became impossible. Although the March 1919 Communist Party program had warned against offending religious sentiments in order not to strengthen religious fanaticism, religious harassment and persecution marked the history of the post-revolutionary years. By 1940 the Russian Orthodox Church was on the verge of institutional elimination in Russia. The most church leaders could have hoped for was survival. By 1946, however, the church had the power to become involved in Soviet foreign policy objectives, largely derived from its wartime cooperation with the state.

The Soviet regime elected to use the patriarchal church and recognized its need to re-establish its power throughout Russia. The relationship was mutually beneficial, although far from a partnership of equals. The state supported the church out of both domestic and foreign policy considerations. The strengthening of the Russian Orthodox Church outside Russia was designed primarily to facilitate the assertion of political control over the liberated territories, challenge Catholic power and curtail indigenous nationalist movements. Allowed to play a missionary role, the Othodox Church became complicit in aiding the Soviet government's destruction of the Uniate Church, made possible owing to a convergence of interest reflected also in their joint attacks on the underground churches. Members of the underground churches avoided participation in Soviet society and the patriarchal Orthodox Church. The Moscow patriarchate and the Soviet state therefore had a joint interest in their eradication.

While the Soviets were able to manipulate the church's concern for self-preservation to help ensure the survival of their regime,[29] they also relied upon the patriotism that had revealed itself so compellingly following the Nazi invasion. Metropolitan Sergi, then patriarchal locum tenens, condemned the German invasion on day one, while Soviet leaders and media remained silent. In a fiery sermon, he warned the clergy to remain with the people and not be tempted by "the other side." In 1942 he spoke of "Holy Rus," "the sacred borders of our country," and "holy hatred towards the enemy." Beyond the identification with the Soviet state, the terms emphasize the bonds between church and nation.[30]

During the Cold War it was both the patriotic disposition of the church, as well as the coercive power of the Soviet leadership, that informed church–state relations. The identification of church and national interests, as well as the usurpation of religion by politics, was not unique to the Russian church and the Soviet Union. During the interwar period, Christian leaders had deprecated the identification of national interests with righteousness.[31] With its history marred by religious wars, the admixture of religion and politics was regarded with skepticism in Europe. However, Cold War rivalry included the competing universal claims through which each side created the space in which their respective states and churches could come together. The West's declaration that it was defending Western civilization and

Christianity from atheistic communism was matched by the East's promotion of the "peace movement," supposed to save the world from nuclear destruction. Europe's leaders knew that for many people, religion was more relevant and meaningful than democracy, a malleable and a contested concept to which each side laid claim.[32]

Churchmen, after the Depression and two global conflicts and conscious of their own culpability as well as systemic failures, saw the war's end as an opportunity for Christianity. The outbreak of another European war in 1939 fostered a widespread conviction that the fight must be not just to defeat the Axis enemy, but to win a new social and political order. Acknowledging the guilt of the churches in contributing to the historical processes that climaxed in global conflict, Christian leaders still considered faith the solution, advocating the new order be built on a renewed relationship between political and moral power. Christian leaders harbored aspirations that Europe's common Christian traditions combined with Christianity's supranationalism and universalism could provide the foundation for a new Christendom and beyond that a supranational world community, the brotherhood of man, that transcended national interests, political differences, and ideology.[33]

Lacking shared racial origins, ethnicity, or language, Christian thinkers have posited that Europe is a historical creation that emerged from European culture, from "Christendom." During World War II, Christian intellectuals such as Arnold Toynbee argued that the disappearance after World War I "of the sense of common Christendom" contributed to the inability to construct a viable international order. Convinced that religion was central to the historical development of world order, Toynbee stressed the necessity of a shared religious ethos as a basis for political order.[34] His ideas were reflected in a variety of Christian groups focused on the postwar world.[35] Believing Christianity was essential for world order, significant Christian leaders wanted to exercise a decisive influence on international policy and behavior.[36] Amid the chaos of war-torn Europe, despite significant collaboration and quietism, the churches were the only organized bodies that consistently and successfully resisted the National–Socialist *Weltanschauung*. In many cases the clergy and the bishops of the various churches became leaders, trusted by their people. Significantly, however, although church leaders engaged meaningfully in postwar planning, the victorious Allies, unwilling to relinquish any power, excluded them from peace negotiations. Even the Vatican, possessed of state status as well as being the center of the worldwide Catholic faith, was excluded.[37]

The Vatican was in many ways another European state looking to the US. Mutual global interest lay at the heart of their alliance. The Vatican hierarchy had been preparing for the *dopo-fascismo* (the post-Fascist era) for a long time, and had been seeking a relationship with the US from well before the war.[38] Cardinal Pacelli, the future Pius XII, visited America in 1936, warning that the greatest threat to the future was the Soviet Union and that a time would come when all the churches would need to combine in order to resist and defeat atheistic communism.[39] The first papal condemnation of the "unspeakable doctrine of Communism" came in 1846.[40] In May 1931 Pius XI delivered *Quadregesimo anno*. With the world suffering the deprivations of the Great Depression, the pope could do no other than acknowledge the failings of modern liberal capitalism, but his main indictments were reserved for communism and socialism. He exhorted Christians to "lay aside internal quarrels, link up harmoniously into a single battle-line, and strike with united forces towards the common aim."[41] Pius XII's exhortations were therefore in line with those of his predecessors.

Pius XII remains an extremely controversial historical figure, mainly over his wartime role, but his Cold War activities are also a source of scholarly contention. Frank Coppa argues that Pius XII led the way in the Cold War, followed by the US, becoming deeply implicated in the political realm as he mobilized Catholic forces to combat communism in his initiation of a global campaign against Bolsheviks in general and the Soviet Union in particular.[42] Peter C. Kent agrees with Coppa that the Roman Catholic Church in the twentieth century was among the first ranks of the Cold Warriors. Kent, however, challenges assumptions about the Vatican's initiation of the Cold War and Pius XII's central role in determining the course of international events in the 1940s.[43] Pius XII's aspirations for Europe certainly differed greatly from those of the US.[44] Pius XII was the locus of ideological opposition to the Soviet Union. Hence, US relations with the Vatican prove an effective yardstick for measuring the scale and degree of changes in American policy towards the Soviet Union, from the wartime alliance to a more rigid stance in the early part of 1946, to confrontation in 1947. Most important, Truman's approaches to the Vatican indicate how far from seeking to resolve, or at least ameliorate, postwar crises, the president chose to heighten the Cold War by aligning himself with the foremost advocate of a "crusade" against America's former ally.

Following the Truman Doctrine[45] and the Marshall Plan, in August 1947 the pope and the president conducted a highly publicized exchange of letters. President and pope pledged their resources to a lasting peace that could only be built on Christian principles.[46] Calling on all persons, regardless of divergent religious allegiances, to unite to preserve freedom, morality, and justice, Truman denounced "the chains of collectivist organization," encouraged religious freedom, and expressed his belief that the greatest need of the world was for a renewal of faith. The president acknowledged Pius XII as a central figure in the Western alliance. The pope endorsed US policy, for which he begged God's assistance, portraying the battle against communism as an extension of the conflict in which the church had been involved for the past two thousand years, that against evil. As well as a symbolic repudiation of accommodation and negotiation, the exchange was strategic. It provided moral justification for containment, blamed the Soviet Union for deteriorating international relations, and, like the Marshall Plan, encouraged dissent within the Soviet sphere.

With the Vatican and the US as arbiters of Italy's fate in the immediate postwar period, the left was resoundingly defeated by their combination of material and spiritual power. The left-leaning *New Statesmen and Nation* wryly observed of the Italian electorate:

> Invited by Togliatti and Nenni to dispense with material aid from the West and spiritual salvation from the Church – to forgo the good offices of both Mr Hoffman and St Peter – they have firmly declined to do without the 700 million dollars proffered under ERP, and have shown an unmistakable reluctance to risk hell fire by voting for the Popular Front.[47]

Nonetheless, substantive differences remained between Pius XII and his Western allies, revealed when Stalin publicly expelled Tito's Yugoslavia from the Cominform. To the pope, Tito was simply another communist bandit hostile to Catholicism. For the West, Tito represented an opportunity to "penetrate and disunite the Soviet bloc."[48] It became increasingly clear that the pope had compromised papal neutrality and exposed the Vatican to criticism from the Left for an alliance with anti-communist statesmen whose aims diverged significantly from his.[49]

In contrast to the course followed by the Vatican stood the World Council of Churches, which was determined to try and transcend the conflict dividing Europe and its churches. It endeavored to adhere to the traditional conviction that the church ought not to be "identified with any particular political or social system."[50] Headquartered in Geneva, WCC attitudes towards the Soviet Union reflected those of west European statesman generally rather than of Pius XII. While not unmoved by the Soviet threat, they perceived it less in ideological than geo-political and historical terms, as yet another episode in the age-old balance-of-power struggle. Moreover, WCC commitment was to the ecumenical ideal, the unity of all Christians regardless of doctrinal divisions or differences, and this, in theory, took no account of state affairs.[51] The WCC was intended to provide a voice for non-Roman Christendom. Importantly, it was a collective voice that did not command but which served the churches. WCC authority consisted "in the weight which it carries with the churches by its own wisdom."[52] It lacked a titular head that carried supreme authority, such as the pope, and was in fact forbidden to act in the name of its participating churches except so far as all or any of them had commissioned it to do so.

Visser 't Hooft, Secretary General from the inception of the WCC, recalled in his *Memoirs* that "some of the gravest tensions in the life of the council were caused by the political and ideological divisions of the cold war period."[53] Major financial support came from the US, and in the early stages of formation west European and American influence predominated. On the whole, WCC officers were naturally inclined to a Western perspective that blamed the Soviet Union for deteriorating East–West relations. Europe's churches were inherently conservative institutions, naturally anti-communist and suspicious of the Soviet Union. However, for the WCC to align with one side in the Cold War would destroy its very *raison d'être*, Christian unity, as became apparent following the church conference of heads and representatives of the Autocephalous Orthodox Churches held in Moscow from July 8 to 17, 1948. The Patriarchs of Moscow, Antioch, Jerusalem, Alexandria, and the Orthodox in the satellite countries, all subject to Soviet influence, decided against participation in the ecumenical movement owing to a "deeply rooted suspicion that the World Council was controlled by Western political influences."[54]

On the eve of its inaugural conference, the WCC was confronted with the same Cold War challenge that divided Europe's trade unions, students, and intellectuals.[55] Preparations for the WCC inaugural assembly, held in Amsterdam in August 1948, took place in the shadow of the Berlin blockade. Naturally, the international tension and the polarization of the world into two competing blocs had a profound impact, reflected in the debates. But the assembly's final report notably stated:

The greatest threat to peace today comes from the division of the world into mutually suspicious and antagonistic blocs. This threat is all the greater because national tensions are confused by the clash of economic and political systems. Christianity cannot be equated with any of these . . .

The final report advised that "The Christian Church should reject the ideologies of both communism and laissez-faire capitalism and should draw men from the false assumption that these extremes are the only alternatives." It recommended that men seek new creative solutions. As 't Hooft later pointed out: "The real significance of this declaration was that the World Council refused to identify itself with any political or social ideology and thus to let itself be used as an instrument in the cold war."[56] Although this stand helped maintain a form of relations with churches in the Soviet bloc, tension increased between the WCC and the Vatican.[57]

However, with increasing European anti-Americanism, generated by McCarthyism and the Korean War, and sensitive to left-wing charges that he was a warmonger, Pius XII himself began to incline towards neutralism. Stalin's death, the hydrogen bomb and the proliferation of nuclear weapons moved the pope towards coexistence. By the end of 1955 the pope was warning the West about its indiscriminate opposition to any form of coexistence. At the same time he indicated to the communist bloc his readiness to engage in dialogue. Positive responses from the Soviet Union led to a shift from the Vatican's alliance with the West towards nonalignment in order to reach an accommodation with the Soviet system. The seeds were sown for Christian–Marxist engagement in the 1960s, as well as John XXIII's *aggiornamento* and Paul VI's *Ostpolitik*.[58]

Changing Perspectives

From the late 1950s, striking changes in global affairs tore apart the post-World War II anti-communist consensus, rendering the depiction of the East–West confrontation as between good and evil less and less tenable. The concept was challenged by Khrushchev's domestic thaw, his appeal for "peaceful coexistence," plus the denunciation of Stalin's crimes along with the repudiation of his doctrine of the inevitability of war between capitalist and socialist countries. It was becoming increasingly clear that not only was the Soviet government far from being a rigid, unchangeable monolithic entity, the communist movement was itself fracturing. Some east European leaders were adopting notably independent positions, while Chinese communists attacked Soviet "revisionism." There were even military skirmishes between the two countries. As the world changed, so too did the composition of church hierarchies. Of particular significance was the growing influence within international church circles of non-white, developing-world participants.[59] They were outraged by the brutal responses of some European powers to the decolonization process and as aware as their white counterparts of the way in which morally questionable US policies undermined America's self-righteous claim to free-world leadership.[60]

Western policies and practices came under increasing scrutiny and criticism as churchmen from the developing world, and in some cases the Soviet bloc, became more involved and active in the high level church affairs that had once been dominated by European and American churchmen.[61] Disagreements and conflicts within the WCC were further exacerbated by the anti-war, anti-imperialist, socio-political concerns of its youth wings. Although the "desire of ecumenical leaders to be in the front line of the church's witness to the world and a partner in its renewal," was a defining trait of the WCC, member churches were alarmed by what seemed to them the "left radicalism" of its youth and student organizations.[62] A notable consequence of the intellectual and ideological turmoil that afflicted the ecumenical movement in the sixties and seventies was a series of financial crises that weakened and damaged the WCC.[63] The peace movement and the arms race were contested questions within the WCC and Europe's churches generally. The Cuban Missile Crisis and American involvement in Vietnam stimulated the peace movement throughout western Europe, drawing in significant churchmen, militating against its easy dismissal as "Soviet inspired." Supported by church leaders throughout the Soviet bloc, the peace movement had appealed directly to Western Christians through a prism of religious and moral arguments that advocated coexistence, repudiated the iron curtain and claimed ideological differences could reside peacefully in one world. Rejected by key Western churchmen, as well as secular statesmen, as a communist ploy intended to weaken the West, it still struck a visceral chord among Europeans, of all political and religious persuasions, who feared a third world war and the terrible potential of nuclear weapons.

Although by the end of his pontificate Pius XII sought to move from his alliance with the West towards nonalignment,[64] it was the election of John XXIII that proved the significant turning point for the Vatican's attitude towards the Soviet bloc and the Cold War. John XXIII saw communism as an outgrowth of modernity, and his response transformed what was meant to be a transitional papacy into a revolutionary one, quite distinct from its predecessors, by seeking better relations with the communist world. His 1961 encyclical, *Mater et magistra*, adapted Catholic social teaching to the changed conditions of the postwar world, proffering the hand of peace to "all men of goodwill." That the Cold War was a key factor in his thinking was illustrated by the 1963 encyclical, *Pacem in terris*, tellingly composed in the aftermath of the Cuban Missile Crisis that brought the world to the brink of nuclear warfare. The pope not only repudiated the concept of a just war in a nuclear world, he drew a notable distinction between unchristian Marxist philosophy and the positive practices to which it could give rise. His statement that the time had come for Catholics to cooperate in good causes with non-Christians began the "opening to the East" that led to the *Ostpolitik* that permitted the "opening to the left."[65]

After John XXIII's death in June 1963, Paul VI continued his policies. The radically changed stance of the Vatican was reflected in the 1965 "Pastoral Constitution," *Gaudium et spes*, which made an unprecedented acknowledgment of past failures. It also repudiated the church's political alignments under Pius XII, subsequently demonstrated by dialogue with the communist regimes, particularly the sustained campaign conducted by Mgr. Casaroli aimed at alleviating conditions for the churches in Czechoslovakia, Hungary, and Yugoslavia. Most importantly, *Gaudium et spes* established the church's independence from any political community or system, denouncing doctrines opposing reform "on the pretext of a false notion of freedom" and those that subordinated personal rights to the "collective organisation of production."[66]

With the papal "peace offensive" reflecting ongoing concern over the East–West confrontation, and *Popolorum progressio* (1967) emphasizing social justice between nations, conservative sentiment criticized the Vatican for moving to the left and being overly sympathetic towards Marxism.[67] Eurocommunists did not regard the denial of religion as necessary, and by the late sixties there were Christians and Marxists throughout Europe who believed that each could learn from the other.[68] Reflecting that the evolving relationship between communism and Christianity in western Europe was more than simply accommodation, the Italian Communist Party's 1979 program stated: "In the reality of the contemporary world, the Christian conscience can stimulate commitment to the struggle towards society's socialist transformation."[69] Although popular perceptions are that the Vatican secretly collaborated with the US in orchestrating the demise of communism in eastern Europe, the collapse of the Soviet bloc had more to do with internal rather than external pressures.[70] While John Paul II shared the American interest in supporting human rights in Poland, he and the Polish bishops opposed America's call for economic sanctions. Moreover, his 1987 encyclical, *Sollicitudo rei socialis*, accused both East and West of betraying "humanity's legitimate expectations."[71] The demise of communism was preceded by the decreasing ideological persuasiveness of socialism as it departed from its own claims and objectives and failed to deliver material benefits, ultimately destroying its own legitimacy. However, rather than the "truly rich inheritance" that the pope hoped the church could secure in the post-communist world, it was confronted with *kairos*, a time of challenge and danger.

Christian Democracy

The impact of the Cold War on organized Christianity in Europe was ultimately damaging and divisive, compromising aspirations to effective and independent socio-political influence. It was Christian Democratic parties that became the major beneficiaries of the Cold War-induced fear of Soviet communism. As anti-communism divided and weakened the socialist left and contributed to the resurgence of Christianity, it paved the way for confessional parties to become a dominant force in European politics. The interwar Catholic parties moved after the war not simply to consolidate their old confessional constituencies, but to reach out across the Catholic–Protestant divide, a gesture of which the church leadership seemed at the time incapable, to establish genuinely inter-confessional "Christian" parties.[72]

As political efforts to promote a Christian anti-communist front foundered and America Protestants speculated that the pope was manipulating US foreign policy to help build up a Catholic western Europe, Christian Democracy offered distinct advantages to western Europe's transatlantic ally. Its political principles matched those of America's own mainstream political parties: integration, compromise, accommodation, and pluralism, plus commitments to human rights and liberal democracy. They also held "that private property constitutes an inviolable right, that communism is an abhorrent movement, and that the state should be confined and carefully watched in terms of its interventionist zeal."[73] Above all, Christian Democrats opted for the Atlantic alliance and what seemed to be its essential corollary, a united western Europe.[74] By the 1950s they were established as parties of government, devoted to a Cold War political agenda of capitalist economics and defense of western Europe against the Soviet Union. Christian Democrat statesmen rooted in the traditions of political Catholicism – Konrad Adenauer, Alcide De Gasperi, Robert Schumann – were supposedly committed to the concept of a "Christian West," distinct from both the crass materialism of the United States and Soviet dialectical materialism.[75] However, distinguished by their attempts to integrate and reconcile a plurality of societal groups, often with opposing interests, Christian Democrats became catch-all parties of the center-right, moving away from Catholic doctrines that were cautious about capitalism and sympathetic towards workers.

For all their protestations of autonomy, the parties benefited considerably from church instructions to the faithful to vote Christian Democrat. Washington's interest in the Vatican derived in part from the perception that it had delivered electoral success to the Christian Democrats in an Italy on the "front line" during the Cold War. However, John Pollard contends that without the onset of the Cold War, Catholicism would not have achieved such hegemony in postwar Italy, which he identifies as an era of Catholic "triumphalism."[76] Observing that the atmosphere of cosmic crisis massively increased the value of the Vatican's intervention in Italian politics, Pollard notes that Catholic hegemony in Italian civil society was from the beginning unnatural, artificial, and very fragile. He suggests that the church replaced fascism as the authoritarian system sought by the Italian middle classes. While Vatican pressure on the neutralist and pacifist wings of the Christian Democratic Party secured Italy's entry to NATO in 1949, full decision-making autonomy for the Italian laity in the political and trade union fields was not to be effectively granted until after the death of Pius XII in 1958. Pollard has shown, moreover, how Christian Democratic attempts in the mid-1950s to escape Vatican control began a practice of clientelism and corruption on a massive scale that would eventually lead to the collapse of the Christian Democratic regime itself.[77] The Cold War therefore ensured the survival of a corrupt regime in Italy. It also meant that with anti-communism as the major issue on the church's political agenda, other serious moral issues, including the fight against the Mafia in Sicily, were badly neglected.

Throughout western Europe, Christian Democrat parties wanting to be seen as viable, independent political entities rather than political arms of the church, sought to construct a distinct political identity. In doing so, they reinterpreted the meaning of religion for politics and society. Confessional parties never discarded religion, as it defined their identity and guaranteed their unity. However, the construction of a Christian Democratic identity was achieved through a radical reinterpretation of Catholicism that challenged the church's monopoly in defining the relationship between religion and politics. "In a process of symbolic appropriation, confessional party leaders reinterpreted Catholicism as an increasingly abstract and moral concept, controlled and mediated by them rather than the church." Concepts such as Christian, moral, religious inspiration, values of Christian civilization, even

humanism, replaced Catholic doctrine and the interests of the church as the foundation of the parties' ideology and program. These concepts were as vague as the doctrine of the Catholic Church was detailed and specific. For some, the success of
Christian Democracy, ironically, represented the negation of aspirations for either a
Christian west or a new Christendom. By 1960, America's leading Christian intellectual, Reinhold Niebuhr, celebrated the successful inoculation of the west against
communism "by the historical dynamism of the Judaeo-Christian tradition."[78] In
contrast, the French Catholic thinker Jacques Maritain identified the "so-called
Christian parties" as the reason behind the total destruction of any hope for
truly Christian policies.[79]

Eastern Europe

In western Europe the appropriation of Christian traditions for Cold War purposes
reflected a process of assimilation and translation of a religious system of values
into secular ethics that did not require the approbation or even active involvement
of the major churches.[80] While this can be interpreted as positive for Christianity,
it can also be seen as compromising the position of the churches. Nonetheless, it
was the churches in eastern Europe that confronted the most profound and
precarious challenges. The initial period of toleration accorded most churches in
the Eastern bloc began to change as East–West relations deteriorated in the course
of 1947 and the Americans openly moved closer towards the Vatican. That the
activities of their Western counterparts contributed to the harsher treatment and
attitudes accorded the churches in the new regimes was indicated by the archbishop
of York, Cyril Garbett. In June 1948, the archbishop spoke out about the potential
dangers for eastern Europe's churches should their regimes suspect anti-Soviet
church–state collusion by their sister institutions in the West. Garbett warned that
in addition to "making a breach with millions of Orthodox and other Christians,
we might easily also prejudice their position with their communist rulers; and
we should certainly be giving the militant atheist an excuse for demanding
the resumption of persecution on the ground that Christianity is a danger to the
State."[81]

Churches were accorded a degree of protection by the importance attached to
religious freedom, albeit interpreted very differently by the two sides. In the global
Cold War battle for hearts and minds, communist regimes had no wish to
provide fuel for Western propaganda eager to portray religious persecution as a key
trait of the new regimes. Although outright persecution was too often a reality, legislation was directed towards the control and domestication of the churches, often
through state support for religion. The question of religious persecution was further
complicated by the determination of the communist authorities to pursue war criminals and collaborators, regardless of clerical status, and often involving trials seen as
suspect in the West. The existence of the underground churches, plus the implication
of some leading churchmen in dubious wartime behavior and then anti-regime
activities linked to support from Western elements, meant communist regimes
felt able to repudiate Western charges of religious persecution by citing national
security concerns.[82]

Religion confronted Soviet leaders with a range of policy problems, including domestic and foreign affairs, state security, issues related to ethnicity and nationalism, not to mention ideological differences. In each case the fate of churches and religious institutions in the Soviet bloc was dictated by a complex play of factors. These included historical attributes, political cultures, the caliber and attitudes of religious leaders and their interaction with their political counterparts. The evolving policies of the different communist regimes were additional factors. Levels of persecution varied tremendously between different countries, time periods, and denominations. Certainly all religious groups in the Soviet bloc confronted difficulties that included imprisonment, surveillance, censorship, and other means of oppression and control. However, as "modernizing" regimes, east European countries were inherently inclined towards some degree of experiment, change, and adaptation, a process that to some churchmen seemed to allow no more than a means of survival, for others a chance for the church to realize a far more meaningful place in communist societies.

In both East and West, significant numbers of Christians, including members of the clergy, accepted the social analysis developed by Karl Marx. William Temple, perhaps Europe's most outstanding twentieth-century ecclesiastic, archbishop of Canterbury during World War II and a committed ecumenist, defined socialism as "the economic realisation of the Christian Gospel."[83] For Christians in western Europe, socialism represented a political option; for their eastern counterparts, however, it increasingly represented state dictatorship and hence elicited very different responses from most churchmen, including those with some empathy for socialist economics. Nonetheless, the ethical dimensions of socialism and Christianity created a space in which church and state could justify working together. For example, the concept of the "Church in Socialism" that evolved in the GDR suggested a workable compromise between the church and a communist state.

The GDR was the only communist country with a Protestant majority. Although Germany was divided after the war, the Evangelical church retained an all-German institutional structure until 1969 that provided additional resources and income and constrained communist harassment. From the late 1950s the churches and both governments engaged in financial deals:

> The wealthy West German churches financed the greater part of the eastern churches and in addition some 10 per cent of the GDR's health services, traditionally run by Catholic and Protestant religious communities, and never closed down. Not only church money flowed east, but large hidden subsidies from the Bonn government.[84]

Soviet readiness to negotiate Germany's political future meant that it was not until mid-1952 that the SED (Socialist Unity Party) introduced a Stalinist program that included the Soviet model on religious policy. Before then, the churches, Roman Catholic included, were among the potential allies with which the Red Army was instructed to cooperate. Stalin clung to the idea of one Germany, neutral if not communist, for longer than the West. The Federal Republic was established by 1949. The foundation of the GDR inevitably followed, but Stalin remained ready to negotiate it away. With the SED and GDR in crisis by 1953, a reform program was planned.

It included a new religious policy that entailed the state working with the church. Still, membership of the two was deemed incompatible and the route to success remained the party. The years 1953–1957 were a period of consolidation, at the end of which a state-supported Clergy Federation was formed, as were similar organizations elsewhere in the Soviet bloc. A notable failure, it was subsequently dissolved.

The departure of hundreds of thousands of GDR citizens and the building of the Berlin Wall revealed the significant distance between socialist promises and the reality of GDR life. However, without the possibility of escape or unity, East German churchmen had little option but to work within and with the existing system. By 1969 the state achieved its goal of breaking the church's formal links with the West. The church, however, still managed to establish a strong national structure that, albeit legally separate from the Federal Republic, wrote into its constitution links with its West German counterpart based on a common history and theology.

Church–state détente was represented in the 1970s by the concept of "the church within socialism," which reached its climax in the 1980s when the SED decided to celebrate the 500th anniversary of the Protestant Reformation as a major national event. It appeared a means of enhancing the GDR's international reputation and of attracting foreign currency. Money, of course, is a key factor in explaining how the Protestant and Catholic churches in the GDR were able to maintain their elaborate structures. By 1980 the SED had almost completely abandoned its earlier atheistic propaganda and had adopted a posture of relative openness towards religion, alluding to it as a necessary part of socialist society having "objective roots" in the first phase of the construction of communism.[85] Although the evangelical church did not have the same linkage with nationalism as other churches elsewhere, such as in Poland, it won a broad credibility that made it a threat to the ideological and political monopoly that the SED sought to maintain.

Communist regimes hoped that the accommodation between themselves and the churches would increase their legitimacy and popularity, but the space accorded religion also facilitated a process by which diverse constituent elements in society used the church to bring into question their legitimacy. During the turbulent 1980s the church provided essential space for the reform movement that aimed to effect change within, rather than end, the GDR. The movement contained many radical groups with little or no Christian commitment. Interestingly, "practising non-believers" opposed to communism were joining official non-believers in communist governments, many of whom subsequently turned out to be actual believers, in using the churches for political ends.

Glasnost and *perestroika* meant further opportunities for the churches. Regarded as distinct from the Soviet-imposed system, religious values were perceived as part of pre-Soviet European civilization.

In addition, many churches were viewed as linked to nationalist sentiments and movements, and "in some ways, yielding to the demands of local religious believers rather than those of the nationalists was an easy option for the communists."[86] The religious revivals that followed the demise of the communist regimes were, however, often closely connected with national independence movements. Notably, they proved notoriously short-lived as churchmen and nationalists looked for an idealized world that supposedly existed before communism.

It was, of course, in Poland, that the importance of Catholicism in defining national identity, strengthened by the church's monopoly in representing civil society against the totalitarian state, proved crucially important. It meant Christianity was able to play a key role in challenging the communist regime. In August 1980, the church won an unprecedented victory in the communist world in securing the legalization of Solidarność, an independent trade union with ten million members. Solidarność quickly sought to maximize its political profile. This included demoting the church to a "spiritual force" and replacing it as chief spokesman for civil society. The church was only able to regain its previous status with the declaration of martial law in 1981.[87]

The Catholic Church was most subjected to systematic communist persecution in Czechoslovakia. Here, as elsewhere in the communist bloc, there were a variety of Christian strategies, from collaboration and compromise to dissidence and opposition. This remained the case even during the period of *Ostpolitik* when, to preserve the "visible Church" and reconstitute ecclesiastical hierarchy, Rome implicitly tolerated the government-sponsored association of priests, *Pacem in Terris*, set up in 1970. However, apolitical proselytizing Christians who did not work against the state "did not really encounter repression." Still persecution was inflicted on Catholics who joined Christian and secular dissidents in Charter 77, which called for the application of the UN Convention on the observance of civic, political, and cultural rights, as well as the Final Act of the Helsinki conference, both ratified by Czechoslovakia in 1976. Subsequently, the democratic aspirations of these Catholics prevailed against Vatican preferences for a "Christian democratic alliance" that would increase the church's political power following the collapse of the communist regime in November 1989. In the June 1990 elections, the unwillingness of accommodationist Catholics to work with dissident Catholics contributed to the humiliating defeat of the "Christian Party." It received only 10% of the vote, placing third behind the "reconstructed" Communist Party.[88] The electorate proved reluctant to replace one overarching truth with another.

Conclusion

The role of the churches in the Cold War and the impact on Christianity is extremely complex and will remain subject to scholarly exegesis and debates for some years to come, as will the era itself, particularly with the emergence of new archival material. In the morality play presentation of the Cold War as a Manichaean struggle for the soul of Europe, the churches played an inimitable role. To the extent that the demise of communism represented a victory over modernity for the church, it was at best partial. The real victor throughout Europe was the liberal capitalist model, not a new Christian order. Paradoxically, the failure of Soviet-type systems, long regarded as serious threats to Christianity, weakened the churches. The disappearance of the "godless Soviet bogey" and the advance of deregulated market relations as a renewed feature of market capitalism reduced the churches in Europe, to a certain extent, to becoming one of many competing institutions in a secular world of alternative values and spiritualities. However, the adaptation of the churches to the post-Cold War world has been considerably eased by state power. It is worth noting the degree to which the churches remain in a privileged position. Significantly, most European states have continued to support religious discourses, practices, institutions, mores, and belief in varying ways, even during the process of forging secular political institutions and practices.

Notes

1 Susanne Hoeber Rudolph has argued that religion is not a "master variable" in international relations, but one that acquires or loses salience in particular historical moments. Hill, "Religion as a Category of Diplomatic Analysis."
2 For a survey of the debates surrounding religion in the international arena, see Haynes, *Introduction to International Relations and Religion.*
3 Nye, *Soft Power: The Means to Success in World Politics.*
4 Newman, *An Essay on the Development of Christian Doctrine*, 131–150.
5 Kirby, "Divinely Sanctioned: The Anglo-American Cold War Alliance and the Defence of Western Civilisation and Christianity, 1945–48," 385–412.
6 Kirby, *Religion and the Cold War.*
7 See also Chadwick, *The Christian Church in the Cold War.*
8 McDougall, *Promised Land, Crusader State*, 158.
9 Clayton, "Gatt, the Marshall Plan and OECD."
10 Public Record Office (henceforth PRO), FO371/47881, April 2, 1945.
11 Kirby, "The Church of England and 'Religion's Division' during the Second World War: Church–State Relations and the Anglo-Soviet Alliance"; "Anglican–Orthodox Relations and the Religious Rehabilitation of the Soviet Regime during the Second World War."
12 Harbutt, "British Influence: Winston Churchill and the Iron Curtain Speech."
13 PRO, FO 371/56885, May 14, 1946.
14 Kirby, "Truman's Holy Alliance: The President, the Pope and the Origins of the Cold War."
15 For a detailed account of the experiences of individual churches in the Soviet bloc in the early Cold War, see Kent, *The Lonely Cold War of Pope Pius XI.*
16 PRO, FO 371/56885, May 14, 1946.
17 Davies, *MI6 and the Machinery of Spying*, 205–206.
18 Kirby, "Truman's Holy Alliance."
19 Tsakonas, *A Man Sent by God: The Life of Patriarch Athenagoras of Constantinople.*
20 Dunn, *Religion and Nationalism in Eastern Europe and the Soviet Union.*
21 Ramet, *Eastern Christians and Politics in the Twentieth Century.*
22 Kirby, *Church, State and Propaganda*, 150.
23 See Miliband, Saville, and Liebman, *Socialist Register 1984: The Uses of Anti-Communism.*
24 Pospielovsky, "The 'Best Years' of Stalin's Church Policy (1942–1948) in the Light of Archival Documents."
25 *Tablet*, September 18, 1943, 138.
26 Deutscher, *Stalin*, 506–507.
27 Hitler's mobilization of religion as part of his "crusade" against the Soviet Union was disregarded. See Miner, *Stalin's Holy War: Religion.*

28 Steeves, *Keeping the Faiths*, 85–86.

29 Dickinson, "Domestic and Foreign Policy Considerations and the Origins of Post-war Soviet Church–State Relations, 1941–46."

30 van den Bercken, "Holy Russia and the Soviet Fatherland."

31 Sittser, *A Cautious Patriotism*.

32 Recommendations Concerning Study of Religious Factors in International Strategy, April 13, 1955, Box 2, OCB Central File Series, White House National Security Staff Papers, 1948–61: Eisenhower Library.

33 Beales, *The Catholic Church and International Order*, 131, 139.

34 Toynbee, "Notes on 'The Responsibility of the Churches for a New International Order,'" IMC26.11.46/8; Archives of the World Council of Churches, WCC Library, Geneva.

35 Director of studies at Chatham House, funded by a Foreign Office grant to operate the Foreign Research and Press Service and involved with the Peace Aims Group, Toynbee embodied the intimate political connections between the realms of church and state.

36 Chadwick, *Britain and the Vatican during the Second World War*; Graham, *Vatican Diplomacy: A Study of Church and State on the International Plane*; Gaines, *The World Council of Churches*; Kirby, *Church, State and Propaganda*.

37 John Foster Dulles, "Acceptance of Appointment as General Adviser to the US Delegation, San Francisco Conference," April 5, 1945; Box 292, Dulles Papers, Princeton.

38 Pollard, "The Vatican, Italy and the Cold War," 106.

39 "Meeting with Protestant clergymen," October 20, 1947, Myron C. Taylor Papers, Harry Truman Library.

40 Pius IX, *Qui pluribus*, November 9, 1846; *Acta Pii IX*, vol. 1, 13.

41 Pius XI, *Quadregesimo anno*, May 15, 1931.

42 Coppa, "Pope Pius XII and the Cold War: The Post-war Confrontation between Catholicism and Communism."

43 Kent, op. cit.

44 Phayer, *Pius XII, the Holocaust, and the Cold War*.

45 David Caute, the distinguished historian of America's postwar "Red Scare," remarked how in the carefully constructed Truman Doctrine, the president "inflamed the natural missionary piety of Americans." Bernard Baruch, Dulles's old State Department colleague, described it as "tantamount to a declaration of an ideological or religious war." Caute, *The Great Fear: The Anti-Communist Purge under Truman and Eisenhower*, 30.

46 Truman to Pius XII, August 6, 1947; Pius XII to Truman, August 26, 1947, *New York Times*, August 29, 1947, I and II.

47 Kingsley Martin, *New Statesman and Nation*, April 24, 1948.

48 Gallagher, "The US and the Vatican in Yugoslavia, 1945–50."

49 *New York Times*, August 30, 1947, reported criticism of the pope's descent into the political arena, while *Unita*, official newspaper of the Italian communist party, began to refer to "Truman's new order" as a caustic reminder of Hitler's "new order" and the pope's failure to condemn it.

50 Chandler, "The Church of England and the Obliteration Bombing of Germany in the Second World War," 923–924.

51 't Hooft, *The Ten Formative Years: The First Assembly of the World Council of Churches*; Hudson, *The World Council of Churches in International Affairs*; Hudson, *The Ecumenical Movement in World Affairs*.

52   This was the formula used by William Temple in an explanatory memorandum of 1938.
     't Hooft, *The Genesis and Formation of the World Council of Churches*, 93.
53   't Hooft, *Memoirs*, 219.
54   't Hooft, *Memoirs*, 206.
55   Coleman, *The Liberal Conspiracy: The Congress for Cultural Freedom and the Struggle for
     the Mind of Post-War Europe*; Kotek, *Students and the Cold War*.
56   't Hooft, *Memoirs*, 213.
57   Kirby, "Harry S. Truman's International Religious Anti-Communist Front, the
     Archbishop of Canterbury and the 1948 Inaugural Assembly of the World Council
     of Churches."
58   Coppa, op. cit.
59   McLeod, *The Cambridge History of Christianity c. 1914-c.2000*, vol. 9.
60   See't Hooft, *Memoirs*.
61   See Hebly, *The Russians and the World Council of Churches: Documentary Survey of the
     Accession of the Russian Orthodox Church to the World Council of Churches*.
62   Lehtonen, *Story of a Storm: The Ecumenical Student Movement in the Turmoil of Revolution*,
     331–335.
63   Lehtonen, op. cit., 331–335.
64   Stehle, *Eastern Politics of the Vatican*, 299.
65   Hebblethwaite, *John XXIII: Pope of the Council*.
66   Luxmoore and Babiuch, *The Vatican and the Red Flag: The Struggle for the Soul of Eastern
     Europe*, 110–128.
67   *New York Times*, editorial, March 29, 1967.
68   Klugman, *Dialogue of Christianity and Marxism*.
69   Mulazza-Giammanco, *The Catholic–Communist Dialogue in Italy*, 70–71.
70   Marples, *Collapse of the Soviet Union*.
71   *Sollicitudo rei socialis*, December 30, 1987, no. 14.
72   Kselman and Buttigieg, *European Christian Democracy: Historical Legacies and
     Comparative Perspectives*; Gehler and Kaiser, *Christian Democracy in Europe since 1945*,
     vol. 2.
73   Van Kersbergen, "The Distinctiveness of Christian Democracy," 33.
74   Irving, *The Christian Democratic Parties of Western Europe*, 242.
75   Papini, *The Christian Democrat Internationa*.
76   Pollard, "The Vatican, Italy and the Cold War," 103–117. See also Pollard, *Money and
     the Rise of the Modern Papacy*.
77   Pollard, "The Vatican, Italy and the Cold War."
78   Ellwood, *The Fifties Spiritual Marketplace: American Religion in a Decade of Conflict*,
     107.
79   Kalyvas, *The Rise of Christian Democracy in Europe*, 244–245.
80   Kalyvas, op. cit., 261.
81   *The Guardian*, Church of England weekly newspaper, June 4, 1948. Garbett himself
     worked closely with the British Foreign Office.
82   For a discussion of religious persecution in the Cold War context, see Kirby, "The Cold
     War, the Hegemony of the United States and the Golden Age of Christian
     Democracy."
83   Presto, *Explorations in Theology*.
84   Oestreicher, "Christian Pluralism in a Monolithic State," 263–271.
85   Ramet, "Church and Peace in the GDR," 44–57.
86   Sapiets, "The Baltic Churches and the National Revival," 155–168.
87   Kepel, *The Revenge of God*, 84–86.
88   Kepel, op. cit., 91–96.

Bibliography

Alexander, Stella, *Church and State in Yugoslavia since 1945* (Cambridge: Cambridge University Press, 1979).

Beales, A.C.F., *The Catholic Church and International Order* (Harmondsworth: Penguin Books, 1941).

Bernstein, Carl and Politi, Marco, *His Holiness: John Paul II and the Hidden History of Our Time* (New York: Doubleday, 1996).

Buchanan, Tom, and Martin Conway (eds.), *Political Catholicism in Europe 1918–1965* (Oxford: Clarendon Press, 1996).

Caute, David, *The Great Fear: The Anti-communist Purge under Truman and Eisenhower* (New York: Simon and Schuster, 1978).

Chadwick, Owen, *The Christian Church in the Cold War* (London: Penguin, 1993).

Chadwick, W.O., *Britain and the Vatican during the Second World War* (Cambridge: Cambridge University Press, 1986).

Chandler, Andrew, "The Church of England and the Obliteration Bombing of Germany in the Second World War," *English Historical Review*, October 1993, 920–946.

Clayton, W., "Gatt, the Marshall Plan and OECD," *Political Science Quarterly*, December 1963, 493–503.

Coleman, Peter, *The Liberal Conspiracy: The Congress for Cultural Freedom and the Struggle for the Mind of Post-War Europe* (New York: Free Press, 1991).

Coppa, Frank J., "Pope Pius XII and the Cold War: The Post-war Confrontation between Catholicism and Communism," in Dianne Kirby (ed.), *Religion and the Cold War* (Basingstoke: Palgrave Macmillan, 2003).

Coupland, Philip M., *Britannia, Europa and Christendom: British Christians and European Integration* (Basingstoke: Palgrave Macmillan, 2006).

Davies, Philip H.J., *MI6 and the Machinery of Spying* (London: Frank Cass, 2004).

Deutscher, Isaac, *Stalin* (Harmondsworth: Penguin, 1972).

Dickinson, Anna, "Domestic and Foreign Policy Considerations and the Origins of Post-war Soviet Church–State Relations, 1941–46," in Dianne Kirby (ed.), *Religion and the Cold War* (Basingstoke: Palgrave Macmillan, 2003).

Dunn, Dennis J. *The Catholic Church and the Soviet Government, 1939–1949* (New York: Columbia University Press, 1977).

Dunn, Dennis J. (ed.), *Religion and Nationalism in Eastern Europe and the Soviet Union* (Boulder, CO: Lynne Reinner, 1987).

Ellwood, R.S., *The Fifties Spiritual Marketplace: American Religion in a Decade of Conflict* (New Brunswick, NJ: Rutgers University Press, 1997).

Fogarty, M., *Christian Democracy in Western Europe, 1820–1953* (London: Routledge, 1957).

Gaines, D.P., *The World Council of Churches* (Peterborough, NH: Richard R. Smith Co., 1966).

Gallagher, Charles R., "The US and the Vatican in Yugoslavia, 1945–50," in Dianne Kirby (ed.), *Religion and the Cold War* (Basingstoke: Palgrave Macmillan, 2003).

Gallagher, Charles R., *Vatican Secret Diplomacy: Joseph P. Hurley and Pope Pius XII* (New Haven, CT: Yale University Press, 2008).

Gehler, Michael and Wolfram Kaiser, *Christian Democracy in Europe since 1945*, vol. 2 (London: Routledge, 2004).

Graham, R.A., *Vatican Diplomacy: A Study of Church and State on the International Plane* (Princeton, NJ: Princeton University Press, 1959).

Hanley, D. (ed.), *Christian Democracy in Europe: A Comparative Perspective* (London: Pinter, 1994).

Harbutt, Fraser F., "British Influence: Winston Churchill and the Iron Curtain Speech," in T.G. Paterson and R.J. McMahon (eds.), *The Origins of the Cold War* (Lexington, MA: D.C. Heath, 1991).

Hastings, A., *A History of English Christianity 1920–2000* (London: SCM, 2001).

Haynes, Jeffrey, *Introduction to International Relations and Religion* (London: Pearson Education Ltd, 2007).

Hebblethwaite, P., *John XXIII: Pope of the Council* (London: Geoffrey Chapman, 1984).

Hebly, J.A., *The Russians and the World Council of Churches: Documentary Survey of the Accession of the Russian Orthodox Church to the World Council of Churches* (Belfast: Christian Journals, 1978).

Hill, Patricia R., Commentary, "Religion as a Category of Diplomatic Analysis," *Diplomatic History*, vol. 24, no. 4, Fall 2000, 633–640.

Hudson, Darril, *The Ecumenical Movement in World Affairs* (London: WCC Publications, 1969).

Hudson, Darril, *The World Council of Churches in International Affairs* (New York: WCC Publications, 1977).

Irving, R.E.M., *The Christian Democratic Parties of Western Europe* (London: Allen & Unwin, 1979).

Kalyvas, S., *The Rise of Christian Democracy in Europe* (Ithaca, NY: Cornell University Press, 1996).

Kent, Peter, *The Lonely Cold War of Pope Pius XII* (Montreal: McGill-Queen's University Press, 2002).

Keogh, Dermot, *Ireland and the Vatican: The Politics and Diplomacy of Church–State Relations, 1922–1960* (Cork: Cork University Press, 1995).

Kepel, Gilles, *The Revenge of God* (Oxford: Polity Press, 1994).

Kirby, Dianne, "The Church of England and the Cold War, 1945–56," PhD (University of Hull, 1991).

Kirby, Dianne, "Truman's Holy Alliance: The President, the Pope and the Origins of the Cold War," *Borderlines: Studies in American Culture* 4, no. 1, 1997, 1–17.

Kirby, Dianne, *Church, State and Propaganda* (Hull: Hull University Press, 1999).

Kirby, Dianne, "The Church of England and 'Religions Division' during the Second World War: Church–State Relations and the Anglo-Soviet Alliance," *Journal of International Relations* 1, no. 1, May 2000.

Kirby, Dianne, "Divinely Sanctioned: The Anglo-American Cold War Alliance and the Defence of Western Civilisation and Christianity, 1945–48," *Journal of Contemporary History* 35, July 2000, 385–412.

Kirby, Dianne, "Anglican–Orthodox Relations and the Religious Rehabilitation of the Soviet Regime during the Second World War," *Revue d'histoire ecclésiastique* 96, nos. 1–2, 2001, 101–123.

Kirby, Dianne, "Harry S. Truman's International Religious Anti-communist Front, the Archbishop of Canterbury and the 1948 Inaugural Assembly of the World Council of Churches," *Contemporary British History* 15, no. 4, Winter 2001, 35–70.

Kirby, Dianne (ed.), *Religion and the Cold War* (Basingstoke: Palgrave Macmillan, 2003).

Kirby, Dianne, "The Cold War, the Hegemony of the United States and the Golden Age of Christian Democracy," in Hugh McLeod (ed.), *Cambridge History of Christianity*, vol. 9 (Cambridge: Cambridge University Press, 2006).

Klugman, James (ed.), *Dialogue of Christianity and Marxism* (London: Lawrence and Wishart, 1968).

Kotek, Joel, *Students and the Cold War* (New York: Macmillan, 1996).

Kselman, Thomas and Joseph A. Buttigieg (eds.), *European Christian Democracy: Historical Legacies and Comparative Perspectives* (Notre Dame, ID: University of Notre Dame Press, 2003).

Lehtonen, Risto, *Story of a Storm: The Ecumenical Student Movement in the Turmoil of Revolution* (Cambridge: William B. Eerdmans Publishing Company, 1998).

Lernoux, P., *People of God: The Struggle for World Catholicism* (New York: Penguin Books, 1989).

Longley, C., *Chosen People: The Big Idea that Shapes England and America* (London: Hodder & Stoughton, 2002).

Luxmoore, Jonathan and Jolanta Babiuch, *The Vatican and the Red Flag: The Struggle for the Soul of Eastern Europe* (London: Geoffrey Chapman, 1999).

McDougall, W.A., *Promised Land, Crusader State* (Boston: Houghton Mifflin, 1997).

McLeod, Hugh (ed.), *The Cambridge History of Christianity c.1914–c.2000*, vol. 9 (Cambridge: Cambridge University Press, 2006).

Marples, David, *The Collapse of the Soviet Union, 1985–1991* (Harlow: Pearson Education, 2004).

Michel, P., *Politics and Religion in Eastern Europe* (Cambridge: Polity Press, 1991).

Miliband, Ralph, John Saville, and Marcel Liebman (eds.), *Socialist Register 1984: The Uses of Anti-communism* (London: Merlin Press, 1984).

Miner, Stephen M., *Stalin's Holy War: Religion, Nationalism, and Alliance Politics, 1941–1945* (Chapel Hill: University of North Carolina Press, 2003).

Monticone, Ronald C., *The Catholic Church in Communist Poland, 1945–1985: Forty Years of Church-State Relations* (Boulder, CO: East European Monographs, 1986).

Moyser, G., (ed.), *Church and Politics Today: Essays on the Role of the Church of England in Contemporary Politics* (Edinburgh: T. & T. Clark, 1985).

Mulazza-Giammanco, Roseanne, *The Catholic–Communist Dialogue in Italy* (New York: Praeger, 1989).

Newman, J.H., *An Essay on the Development of Christian Doctrine* (London: Penguin Books, 1974).

Norman, E., *Christianity and the World Order* (Oxford: Oxford University Press, 1979).

Nurser, John, *For All Peoples and All Nations: Christian Churches and Human Rights* (Geneva: WCC Publications, 2005).

Nye, Joseph S., *Soft Power: The Means to Success in World Politics* (New York: Public Affairs, 2004).

Oestreicher, Paul, "Christian Pluralism in a Monolithic State: The Churches of East Germany 1945–1990," *Religion, State and Society* 21, nos. 3 and 4, 1993, 263–271.

Papini, Roberto, *The Christian Democrat International*, trans. by Robert Royal (Lanham, MD: Rowan & Littlefield, 1997).

Petito, F. and Hatzopoulos, P., "Special Issue: Religion and International Relations," *Millennium: Journal of International Studies* 29 (2000).

Phayer, Michael, *Pius XII, the Holocaust, and the Cold War* (Indianapolis: Indiana University Press, 2008).

Pollard, John, "The Vatican, Italy and the Cold War," in Dianne Kirby (ed.), *Religion and the Cold War* (Basingstoke: Palgrave Macmillan, 2003).

Pollard, John, *Money and the Rise of the Modern Papacy* (Cambridge, Cambridge University Press, 2005).

Pollard, John, *Catholicism in Modern Italy: Religion, Society and Politics since 1861* (London: Routledge, 2008).

Pospielovsky, Dimitry, "The 'Best Years' of Stalin's Church Policy (1942–1948) in the Light of Archival Documents," *Religion, State and Society* 23, no. 2, 1997, 139–162.

Presto, R., *Explorations in Theology* (SCM Publications, 1981).

Ramet, Pedro (ed.), *Eastern Christians and Politics in the Twentieth Century* (Durham, NC: Duke University Press, 1988).

Ramet, Pedro (ed.), *Catholicism and Politics in Communist Societies* (Durham, NC: Duke University Press, 1990).

Ramet, Pedro, "Church and Peace in the GDR," *Problems of Communism* 32, no. 4, 1984, 44–57.

Ramet, Sabrina Petra, *Balkan Babel: Politics, Culture, and Religion in Yugoslavia* (Boulder, CO: Westview, 1992).

Rhodes, Anthony, *The Vatican in the Age of the Cold War, 1945–1980* (Norwich: Michael Russell, 1992).

Sapiets, Marite, "The Baltic Churches and the National Revival," *Religion in Communist Lands* 18, 1990, 155–168.

Siegel, Paul N., *The Meek and Militant: Religion and Power Across the World* (London: Zed Books Ltd, 1986).

Sittser, Gerald L., *A Cautious Patriotism* (Chapel Hill: University of North Carolina Press, 1997).

Steeves, P., *Keeping the Faiths: Religion and Ideology in the Soviet Union* (New York: Holmes & Meier, 1989).

Stehle, Hanjakob, *Eastern Politics of the Vatican* (Athens, OH: Ohio University Press, 1981).

Temple, William, *Christianity and Social Order* (London: SCM, 1942).Nye, Joseph S., *Soft Power: The Means to Success in World Politics* (New York: PublicAffairs, 2004).

't Hooft, Visser (ed.), *The Ten Formative Years: The First Assembly of the World Council of Churches* (New York: WCC Publications, 1949).

't Hooft, Visser, *Memoirs* (London: SCM Press, 1973).

't Hooft, Visser, *The Genesis and Formation of the World Council of Churches* (Geneva: WCC Publications, 1982).

Tsanokas, Demetrios, *A Man Sent by God: The Life of Patriarch Athenagoras of Constantinople* (Brookline, MA: Holy Cross Press, 1977).

van den Bercken, William, "Holy Russia and the Soviet Fatherland," *Religion in Communist Lands*, vol. 15, no. 3, 1987, 264–277.

van Kerbergen, K., "The Distinctiveness of Christian Democracy," in D. Hanley (ed.) *Christian Democracy in Europe: A Comparative Perspective*, London: Pinter, 1994, 33.

Vardys, Stanley V., *The Catholic Church, Dissent and Nationality in Soviet Lithuania* (Boulder, CO: East European Monographs, 1978).

West, Charles C., "Foreword", in R. Lehtonen, *Story of a Storm: The Ecumenical Student Movement in the Turmoil of Revolution* (Cambridge: W.B. Eerdmans Publishing Co., 1998).

Further Reading

For standard works dealing with the church and Christianity in the international arena, see Owen Chadwick, *The Christian Church in the Cold War* (London: Allen Lane, 1992); Philip M. Coupland, *Britannia, Europa and Christendom: British Christians and European Integration* (Basingstoke: Palgrave Macmillan, 2006); E. Norman, *Christianity and the World Order* (Oxford: Oxford University Press, 1979); F. Petito and P. Hatzopoulos, "Special Issue: Religion and International Relations," *Millennium: Journal of International Studies* 29 (2000); John Nurser, *For All Peoples and All Nations: Christian Churches and Human Rights* (Geneva: WCC Publications, 2005); Paul N. Siegel, *The Meek and Militant: Religion and Power Across the World* (London: Zed Books Ltd, 1986), and William Temple, *Christianity and Social Order* (London: SCM, 1942).

Among many useful works on Roman Catholicism, diplomacy, and politics, see: Dennis J. Dunn, *The Catholic Church and the Soviet Government, 1939–1949* (New York: Columbia University Press, 1977); Charles R. Gallagher, *Vatican Secret Diplomacy: Joseph P. Hurley and Pope Pius XII* (New Haven, CT: Yale University Press, 2008); John Pollard, *Catholicism in Modern Italy: Religion, Society and Politics since 1861* (London: Routledge, 2008); Carl Bernstein and Marco Politi, *His Holiness: John Paul II and the Hidden History of Our Time* (New York: Doubleday, 1996); Dermot Keogh, *Ireland and the Vatican: The Politics and Diplomacy of Church–State Relations, 1922–1960* (Cork: Cork University Press, 1995); P. Lernoux, *People of God: The Struggle for World Catholicism* (New York: Penguin Books, 1989); Pedro Ramet (ed.), *Catholicism and Politics in Communist Societies* (Durham, NC: Duke University Press, 1990); Anthony Rhodes, *The Vatican in the Age of the Cold War, 1945–1980* (Norwich: Michael Russell, 1992); and Stanley V. Vardys, *The Catholic Church, Dissent and Nationality in Soviet Lithuania* (Boulder, CO: East European Monographs, 1978).

Among the many useful studies on the churches under communism, see Stella Alexander, *Church and State in Yugoslavia since 1945* (Cambridge: Cambridge University Press, 1979); Dennis J. Dunn (ed.) *Religion and Nationalism in Eastern Europe and the Soviet Union* (Boulder, CO: Lynne Rienner Publishers, 1987); P. Michel, *Politics and Religion in Eastern Europe* (Cambridge: Polity Press, 1991); Ronald C. Monticone, *The Catholic Church in Communist Poland, 1945–1985: Forty Years of Church–State Relations* (Boulder, CO: East European Monographs, 1986); and Sabrina Petra Ramet, *Balkan Babel: Politics, Culture, and Religion in Yugoslavia* (Boulder, CO: Westview, 1992).

For informative studies of Christian Democracy, see S. Kalyvas, *The Rise of Christian Democracy in Europe* (Ithaca, NY: Cornell University Press, 1996); Tom Buchanan and Martin Conway (eds.), *Political Catholicism in Europe 1918–1965* (Oxford: Clarendon Press, 1996); M. Fogarty, *Christian Democracy in Western Europe, 1820–1953* (London: Routledge, 1957); D. Hanley (ed.), *Christian Democracy in Europe: A Comparative Perspective* (London: Pinter, 1994), and R.E.M. Irving, *The Christian Democratic Parties of Western Europe* (London: Allen & Unwin, 1979).

For additional works on the Ecumenical Movement, see Charles C. West in the foreword to R. Lehtonen, *Story of a Storm: The Ecumenical Student Movement in the Turmoil of Revolution* (Cambridge: W.B. Eerdmans Publishing Co., 1998); and Visser 't Hooft, *Has the Ecumenical Movement a Future?* (Belfast: Christian Journals Limited, 1974).

For the dilemmas with which the poltical arena confronted a national church in the West, see Dianne Kirby, "The Church of England and the Cold War, 1945–56," PhD (University of Hull, 1991); A. Hastings, *A History of English Christianity 1920–2000* (London: SCM, 2001); C. Longley, *Chosen People: The Big Idea that Shapes England and America* (London: Hodder & Stoughton, 2002); and G. Moyser (ed.) *Church and Politics Today: Essays on the Role of the Church of England in Contemporary Politics* (Edinburgh: T. & T. Clark, 1985).

CHAPTER TEN

The End of the Cold War and the Unification of the European Continent

CARINE GERMOND[1]

When the Berlin Wall fell on November 9, 1989, the Cold War order that had ruled international relations for over fifty year and, to an important extent, had determined the birth and subsequent evolution of the European project came to a sudden end. The international repercussions of the collapse of the bipolar system were far-reaching and diverse, but the end of the Cold War was first and foremost a European event, a truly transnational moment that affected the Old Continent as a whole. It made possible and rendered unavoidable a profound reshaping of Europe.

The end of the "fifty-year war"[2] and the radical change of external circumstances thus presented both a chance and a challenge for Europeans. Bringing together the two parts of Europe was seen as an historic mission intended "to heal the rift in Europe opened up by World War II, the East–West confrontation and the Cold War."[3] It however posed a series of technical and political challenges and implied a transformation of the institutional frameworks originally designed for the Six and more or less successfully adapted for a twelve-member European Community. Europe's response to the end of the Cold War consisted in ever more ambitious integration plans. A deepening European Community reached out to incorporate the newly liberated countries of central and eastern Europe. The deepening and widening European Community then evolved into a pan-European Union.

Whereas historians and political scientists have extensively documented and thoroughly analyzed the processes leading to the end of the Cold War and the demise of the Soviet empire, the study of its impact on and implications for post-Cold War European unification processes remains a work in progress given the still unfolding chain of events. This chapter will first discuss how the successive post-Cold War enlargements shaped a wider and more diverse Europe and the manifold challenges it involved. In a second step, it will analyze the emergence of a new European institutional architecture that ensued from post-Cold War integrationist efforts to build a more decisive, unified, and efficient EU.

A Companion to Europe since 1945, First Edition. Edited by Klaus Larres.
© 2014 John Wiley & Sons, Ltd. Published 2014 by John Wiley & Sons, Ltd.

Reuniting Europe: the Challenge of Enlargement

Within hardly a 15-year time span, the European Union (EU) underwent its most spectacular enlargement and more than doubled its size. It grew from 12 to 27 members, and other, more controversial and problematic candidates, such as Turkey and the Balkan countries, are already knocking insistently at the EU's door. Though the two successive enlargement rounds that occurred between 1990 and 2004 concerned different categories of countries, they all resulted from the end of the Cold War. Neutral states such Austria, Finland, and Sweden were no longer constrained by the Cold War; the newly independent central and eastern European countries, liberated from the Soviet yoke, strove to (rejoin the Western community of nations. Finally, others countries like Norway, Turkey, or smaller southern European states, took advantage of the changing international circumstances to reactivate or initiate membership applications.[4]

The first post-Cold War enlargement: the Austrian and Scandinavian adhesion

Since its inception in 1960, the European Free Trade Association (EFTA) had failed to become a credible counterpart of the successful European Community. Of the original seven founding countries, the United Kingdom and Denmark, followed by Portugal, had already joined the EC during the first and second enlargement round in the 1970s and 1980s. The end of the Cold War prompted most remaining EFTA members, notably Sweden, Norway, Finland, Austria, and Switzerland, to apply for membership in the EU. The motives of the applicants were manifold. The Norwegian, Swedish, and Swiss governments had mainly economic interests. The Austrian and Finnish bid for membership was driven by security considerations, although their neutrality could impede their participation in the common foreign and security policy as foreseen in the Maastricht Treaty.[5] Finland also hoped to escape economic dependence on Russia.

However, not enlargement but internal developments, such as German unification, implementation of the European Monetary Union, completion of the single market and ratification of the Maastricht Treaty, were at the heart of the EC's preoccupations. The EC thus tried to delay the accession of the Scandinavian countries and Austria by proposing the creation of the European Economic Area (EEA), which would allow would-be members to enjoy the benefits of the single market without formal adhesion and, in the process, satisfy some of their economic motives to join the EC. The offer did not fulfill the expectations of the candidates, who, even before the conclusion of the negotiations on the EEA, formally applied to the EU by the end of 1992. In a referendum held in December 1992, Swiss voters rejected the EEA agreement and the Swiss government subsequently withdrew its application. Confronted with the insistence of the four remaining candidates for early membership, the EU emarked on accession negotiations in 1993, a development made possible by the eventual resolution of the Maastricht ratification crisis and agreement on a post-Maastricht budgetary package.

Compared to earlier rounds, the negotiations were relatively easy and progressed at a fairly quick pace. The fact that all four applicants were similar to the current EU member states, both in political and economic terms, smoothed away many of the difficulties which would come to light during accession negotiations with the central and eastern European candidates. Moreover, the EEA agreement of 1992 that entered into force in 1994 already contained many of the "chapters" which would form the substance of the adhesion agreements, although matters specific to each of the applicants, such social and energy policy, environment, and agriculture and fisheries, were hard fought. Negotiations, with a few transitional arrangements and concessions, were brought to a successful conclusion at the Corfu summit on June 28, 1994.

With the accession treaties signed, ratification got underway. The four newcomers held referenda. The outcome was positive in Austria with a majority of 66% and in Finland with a majority of 57%. Sweden followed with only a thin majority of 52%. In Norway, however, EU membership was rejected, by a thin majority of 52%, in an almost exact repetition of the 1972 referendum outcome. Nevertheless, Norway remained in the EEA, which allowed it to participate in the internal market without assuming the responsibilities of a full EU member state. On the EU's side, ratification proceeded smoothly although the European Parliament (EP) attempted to push forward institutional change. The EP opposed a Council of Ministers' decision of March 1994, the so-called Ioannina compromise, to allow member states failing to reach the blocking minority voting threshold to postpone decision-making until consensus has been reached. Enlargement was nonetheless approved by the EP and took place in January 1995. By raising the institutional issue, it had nevertheless underscored the need to simultaneously follow the two tracks of enlargement and institutional reforms so the enlarging EU could continue to work efficiently. This particular problem would come more and more to the fore as disputes over the institutional implications of enlargement for central and eastern Europe multiplied towards the end of the decade.

The greatest challenge: enlargement to central and eastern Europe

Not only did the geopolitical context highlight the specificity of enlargement to central and eastern Europe, its also nature differed profoundly from previous rounds. Indeed, rather than a regrouping of similar countries, it came down to the geographic extension of the political and economic model developed by western Europeans since the early 1950s.

Despite the apparent consensus about the eastern enlargement, the EC/EU member states were divided. France, for instance, feared being driven to the periphery of an enlarged Union and a seeing its traditional influence marginalized. Moreover, German unification – in actuality, the very first post-Cold War enlargement since the six new *Länder* of the defunct German Democratic Republic were incorporated into the Federal Republic and thus joined the EU – as well as the adhesion of Austria and the Scandinavian countries in 1995 seemed to guarantee Germany a pivotal political role in the EU, which the accession of the eastern European countries would make even more salient. In fact, Germany was a staunch supporter of enlargement, which it hoped would both have a stabilizing effect on its eastern and southern neighbors and lead to the opening up of new markets. Despite their initial, albeit different, reservations, the EU member states and institutions soon had to acknowledge that for historical and strategic reasons, European integration could not limit itself to western Europe. Moreover, the openness and pan-European finality of the EU was written into its founding treaties. Security reasons also spoke in favor of enlargement, which seemed the best instrument to support democratization in the former communist countries and to strengthen Europe's future security and stability.

The road to accession proved strenuous, however. The new applicants were new democracies with weak administrative structures, unstable democratic institutions, and, for some, pervasive ethnic nationalism. They were underdeveloped and poorer than the average EU members and any previous applicants. The situation was hardly made easier by the fact that they had to adopt an even bigger set of European regulations, the *acquis communautaire*, i.e. about 80,000 pages of EU law.[6] The EU's cautious approach during negotiations met with the applicants' impatience, causing many misunderstandings and disappointments on both sides along the way. The EU's reluctance to concede much in key sectors such as agriculture, steel, free movement of labor, etc., also incurred resentment. The applicants felt that they had to undergo "shock therapy" involving politically and economically costly adjustments with little in exchange.

Although the member states were the main negotiating entities during enlargement negotiations, the European Commission was nonetheless responsible for coordinating of Western help to central and eastern Europe via its main assistance program, which was primarily intended for Poland and Hungary (Poland and Hungary Assistance for the Reconstruction of the Economy, known under the acronym PHARE). PHARE provided both financial and technical assistance to support the transition towards a market economy and liberal democracy. The European Bank for Reconstruction and Development (EBRD) created in 1991 also supported the economic and democratic transition in the former communist countries. Mere assistance soon proved too little for the more "enlargement-enthusiastic" EU member states, especially Germany, which encouraged the Commission's initiative to propose association agreements to the three most economically advanced and strategically important central and eastern European countries, i.e. Poland, Hungary, and Czechoslovakia. Signed throughout the 1990s with most central and eastern countries – successively with the Czech and Slovak Republics (after the break-up of Czechoslovakia), the Baltic countries, Slovenia, Bulgaria, and Romania – the agreements provided a framework for trade relations between the EU and the signatories, and prepared the eastern participants to trade liberalization of services and capital.

The relative tardiness of the actual accession negotiations was not only motivated by the need to prepare the candidates but primarily by the still ongoing negotiations on the Maastricht Treaty and the subsequent ratification crisis. Once ratification of Maastricht was secured in 1992, albeit by a very thin majority in France (51%) and after a Danish rejection (given a few "opt-outs," for instance on the euro, Denmark eventually voted "yes" in 1993), the new European Union could focus on enlargement.

At Copenhagen in June 1993, EU members explicitly acknowledged the right of the associated central and eastern European countries to become members of the EU. They also agreed upon accession criteria, the so-called Copenhagen criteria, which the candidates would need to fulfill to be eligible to join.[7] Also significant was the mention in the conclusions of the Copenhagen summit of the EU's "capacity to absorb new members, while maintaining the momentum of European integration". This reflected the concerns of EU members that enlargement might delay the scheduled deepening of European integration or dilute already completed realizations. Some of the would-be members were also reluctant to relinquish their newly recovered sovereignty to Brussels.

Nonetheless, by the mid-1990s the EU and the central and eastern European candidates embarked upon the process of accession. In a white paper adopted in June 1995 by the European Council, the Commission left no doubt about the enormous and complex difficulties that lay ahead of both the applicants and the EU. The aspirants needed to revamp their entire administrative, legal, and economic structures to bring them up to EU standards, while the EU had to second their efforts by way of the PHARE program or detailed pre-accession plans, and closely monitor the progresses. A first Commission report, published as part of the "Agenda 2000" package,[8] concluded that the applicants, although at different stages of development, had progressed well as far as democratic and legal structures and practices were concerned, but it underscored the lengthy efforts still required to achieve a functioning market economy and absorb the EU's regulations. Of the ten original candidates, the Commission thus recommended the opening of negotiations with only five: Poland, Hungary, and the Czech Republic – all of which were scheduled to join NATO by 1999 – as well as Estonia and Slovenia. The Commission's conclusions were approved by the European Council in December 1997 at Luxembourg. The latter also mandated the Commission to draw up annual reports on the remaining candidates to assuage their fears about the emergence of a new post-Cold War divide between them and the EU.

Accession negotiations with the first five candidates began in spring 1998 and the "chapters" were progressively ticked off. In fall 1999, the Commission recommended the opening of adhesion negotiations with the remaining five countries (Latvia, Lithuania, Slovakia, Bulgaria, and Romania), which was an acknowledgment of their important efforts and responded to the strategic preoccupations of the old EU member states given the volatility of the Balkans where war continued to rage. In February 2000, negotiations were formally opened.

Although accession negotiations were launched with all candidates, no precise date for actual accession was set. This was an important leverage for the EU. Only in June 2001 did it fix early 2004 as the accession date, provided negotiations were successfully concluded by the end of 2002. In its 2002 report, the Commission considered eight of the ten candidates eligible to join the EU. Bulgaria and Romania, which failed to fulfill the criteria, could join only in 2007. The EU removed the last obstacle to enlargement by reaching an agreement on the common agricultural policy for the next EU budget. In December 2002 new summit at Copenhagen, where the strenuous road to adhesion had begun in 1993, confirmed EU enlargement to central and eastern Europe. Although this marked the reuniting of Europe, "enlargement-euphoria" as it existed in the early 1990s had long since vanished both in western and eastern Europe by the time the central and eastern European countries became full EU members on January 1, 2004. Among both older and newer members, it even fostered Euroskepticism, right-wing, xenophobic movements and nationalist reflexes. "Enlargement fatigue" also accounted for the 2005 rejection by the French and the Dutch voters of the EU Constitutional Treaty.[9]

Two new Mediterranean members: Malta and Cyprus

The two Mediterranean islands of Malta and Cyprus presented similarities, both being non-aligned and having historic ties to Europe; but the Republic of Malta was undeniably the easier case.

Malta had formally submitted an official EU membership application in 1990, but the Labour government that took office in 1996 suspended it. In September 1998, the newly elected Nationalist Party decided to reactivate Malta's application. Although the EU was not particularly enthusiastic about having another smallish member, hardly six months after Malta had officially applied the Commission considered it could join the accession negotiations already taking place with the five central and eastern European applicants. The Republic of Malta easily completed the negotiations by 2002 and accession was approved by a majority in a referendum held in March 2003, thus setting a positive example for other referenda to be held in other candidate countries.

Cyprus was a more complex problem, mainly because of the island's division into a Turkish-occupied north and a Greek Cypriot south. The EU had postponed dealing with the Greece-supported membership application of Cyprus as long as possible, hoping for a political settlement of the division prior to enlargement. In 1998, accession talks eventually began with the Cypriot government along with the five central and eastern European applicants (the 5+1 negotiations), although Turkey contested the latter's right to negotiate on behalf of the entire island. Turkey's own application to the EU and its poor relations with Greece made the situation more intricate. At the Helsinki European Council, the EU confirmed that settlement of the Cypriot division was not a precondition for accession. But the EU also reaffirmed its support of the United Nations (UN) talks process and reiterated this position in the following summits. In December 2002, Cyprus was invited to join the EU in 2004, a move concomitant with the presentation of a plan by UN Secretary-General Kofi Annan for the resolution of the island's division. UN efforts intensified in the run-up to the signature of Cyprus's accession treaty in spring 2003 but failed to bear fruit. In April 2004, a mere six days before Cyprus's formal accession to the EU, a revised Annan plan was put to a referendum in both parts of the islands. A majority of Turkish Cypriots (65%) voted in favor but an even greater majority of Greek Cypriots (75%) voted against. Thus, only the Republic of Cyprus joined the EU on May 1, 2004. By allowing only the Greek Cypriots to become members, the EU lost any future negotiation leverage on Cyprus's reunification.

Uncertain future enlargements

The unprecedented scope of EU enlargement to the south and the east has reactivated the question of and how much further expansion could bear the EU go and how fast.[10] The delayed accession of Romania and Bulgaria finally took effect in 2007. Three groups of applicants, namely Turkey, the western Balkan countries and the immediate Slavic neighbors of the EU, present greater challenges for the future.

Turkey's membership application is an ancient issue. The 1963 association agreement signed between Turkey and the EC explicitly referred to the ulterior accession of Turkey to the Community. In 1970, an additional protocol was concluded which stipulated that the two signatories would establish a customs union within a 22-year span and, in 1987, Turkey formally applied to join the EC. However, the Turkish candidacy was never considered seriously given, in particular, Turkey's poverty and disrespect of human rights. The customs union that came into effect in 1995 was seen by many in Brussels as a substitute for actual membership, and not until the 1999 Helsinki European Council did the EU grant Turkey the status of a candidate country and even develop a pre-accession road map. Although the Commission reaffirmed in the "Agenda 2000" Turkey's eligibility for membership, it also underscored the many difficulties (economic, political, human rights, etc.) the Turkish government would need to overcome. Spurred by the incentive, the latter successfully conducted a series of reforms to align its norms with the EU's. In recognition of the substantial progress achieved, Turkey was invited in October 2005 to begin accession negotiations and the usual screening process each applicant has to undergo.

The issue of Turkey's EU membership has, however, taken on a political edge in some of the EU countries, mainly France and Austria, where public opinion is largely opposed to it. Various arguments have been brought up to justify this opposition. Some evoke the Christian identity of Europe that would be challenged by such a large, predominantly Muslim country. Others appeal to geography and question whether Turkey is really part of Europe, or whether the EU is ready to have outside borders with states such as Iraq or Iran. Rather than full membership, leading politicians are thus defending a "privileged partnership" that would minimize the destabilizing effect Turkish membership could possibly have on the EU, in economic, societal, political, and foreign policy terms. Should Turkey succeed in meeting the Copenhagen criteria, it would rob the EU of most of the credible arguments against its membership. Nevertheless, actual Turkish membership remains a long-term prospect.

The western Balkans – Albania and the former constituent parts of the Yugoslav federation (Bosnia-Herzegovina, Croatia, Macedonia, Serbia, and Montenegro) – are likely to become EU members at some later date as they are surrounded by present and future EU member states. The EU has been actively involved in the region since the late 1990s, with the Regional Stability Pact for south-eastern Europe. In 2001, Macedonia and Croatia signed agreements similar to the Europe agreements. At the European Council summit at Thessalonica, the EU reaffirmed the membership perspective for the western Balkans and outlined a road map to help them move from their current pre-candidate status to the formal start of preparations for membership.[11] Early 2003, Croatia formally submitted an application. It was invited to begin accession negotiations in October 2005, although actual membership is unlikely to be activated before 2010. Croatia's lack of cooperation with the International Criminal Tribunal for the former Yugoslavia (ICTY) has until recently constituted a major obstacle to its adhesion. For the remaining Balkan countries, membership outlooks are less promising. They all are extremely poor, socially and politically unstable, oftentimes still corrupt states that have a long way to go before their candidacy is likely to be seriously considered. In the longer term, however, their membership appears to be the only way to eradicate what has been a source of instability and war at the very heart of Europe for almost a century. Macedonia is a somewhat different case. It is already a candidate country but negotiations have not been opened yet.

Further to the east, a number of former Soviet satellites (e.g. Ukraine, Moldova) have expressed their interest in EU membership. The EU has remained very cautious about the prospect of their candidacies, tending to discourage them. Beyond the political, social, and economic problems that plague these countries and make them unlikely candidates even in the medium term, there remains the question of Russia's reaction to its "near outside" going over to the West. The Russian government's attitude towards the 2004 Ukrainian "Orange Revolution" seemed to confirm its reluctance to lose the last remains of its buffer zone.

In an effort to thwart a premature application by these countries, the EU has launched a "new neighborhood policy" whose aim is to stabilize the EU's immediate periphery by creating a middle ground between full membership and exclusion. These goals were reaffirmed by the Commission in March 2003.[12] It proposed the creation of a zone of prosperity and friendly neighborhood and the development of close, peaceful, and cooperative relations with a "ring of friends."[13] How successful the EU's new neighborhood policy will be remains open, however. The EU has many other, higher priorities that are likely to absorb most of the EU's financial resources and attention in the near future. Yet, in the longer term, it is doubtful that those countries will accept being relegated to the periphery of the EU, and they are therefore likely to seek full membership at some point.

The new European Architecture: from Maastricht to the Constitutional Treaty

The tension between "widening," i.e. enlargement, and "deepening," i.e. the strengthening of EU institutions and their policy competencies has a long tradition in European integration, but it acquired a new stringency with the unprecedented scale of the latest enlargement wave.[14] Since the early 1970s, all the successive enlargements of the EU had challenged European identity and the European political project, but never before had the EU undergone such a dramatic expansion that not only redefined it geographically but also considerably altered its political, institutional, and economic shape. The new European architecture that emerged during the 1990s was the result of the European efforts to build a more cohesive and assertive EU within a new post-Cold War economic and political pan-European order.

From Maastricht to Nice

The project of a European Monetary Union (EMU) had been launched before the collapse of communism. In fact, in spring 1989 the Commission's president Jacques

Delors had presentedthe "Delors Report," which outlined a three-stage process towards EMU. Yet the changing international situation gave it and the old project for political union a new momentum. Indeed, reforms that had long been on the Community's agenda and new progress were made necessary by the end of the Cold War and German unification. The former had deprived the Community of its political and ideological cement; the latter had altered the power equilibrium between France and Germany. Deepening thus appeared as the logical response, and integrationist efforts accelerated in the 1990s.

The two intergovernmental conferences on EMU and political union opened in December 1990 and were brought to a successful conclusion at the Maastricht summit a year later. The signature of the Treaty on European Union (TEU) in February 1992 was a decisive qualitative leap forward for European integration. The treaty contained a comprehensive blueprint for the implementation of EMU; it formally established a political union and included a series of innovations such as a Social Charter, EU citizenship, a strengthening of the European Parliament's powers, and the "subsidiarity" principle which attempted to define what would fall within the competency of the European institutions and of the member states and responded to the growing "supranationalization" of European integration. A final provision required that the member states convene another intergovernmental conference (ICG) in 1996 in order to review the treaty and remedy some of its tacitly acknowledged shortcomings.

European Union

Common provisions

The new entity, the European Union (EU), resembled a temple with three pillars, each of which dealt with different, partially overlapping policy areas (see Figure 10.1). The first pillar encompassed the three existing Communities – the Economic European Community (EEC), the European Coal and Steel Community (ECSC),

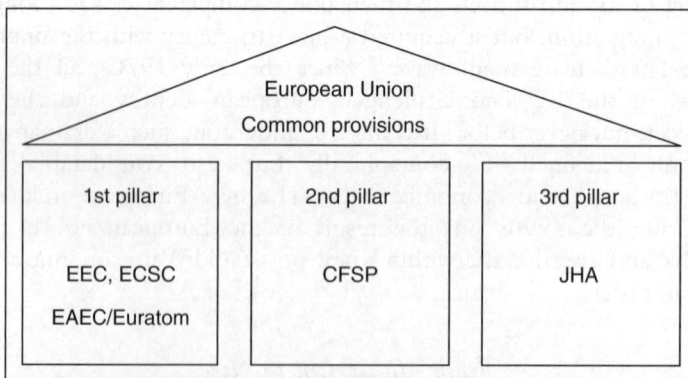

Figure 10.1   The three pillars of the European union, Treaty on European Union, Maastricht, 1992

and the European Atomic Energy Community (EAEC, also known as EURATOM) – and was characterized by the pooling of member states' sovereignty and the transfer of decision-making competencies to the European institutions. The second pillar covered the Common Foreign and Security Policy (CFSP). The third pillar dealt with justice and home affairs (JHA) including immigration issues. The second and third pillars remained largely intergovernmental, with only a limited role for EU institutions.

The ratification of the TEU proved unexpectedly difficult. The ratification crisis accrued from the economic recession precipitated by the unanticipated costs of German unification. Growing unemployment rates in most member states, and fear of uncontrolled immigration from the central and eastern candidates dampened down the integrationist enthusiasm of the late 1980s. The outbreak of the first Gulf War along with the EU's incapacity to manage the collapse of Yugoslavia and the subsequent outburst of civil war in the unstable Balkans added to the uncertainty of voters.

The accelerated pace of enlargement underscored the need for institutional reforms since the existing EU institutions had been built to function both with fewer members and within the context of the Cold War. The 1996 IGC seemed for many member states a welcome opportunity to adjust the institutions so they could cope with the new challenges. Concluded in Amsterdam in June 1997, the IGC delivered a new treaty, which modestly modified the Maastricht Treaty. Neither the Union's institutional structures nor its decision-making procedures were as radically overhauled as the forthcoming enlargement would have required.

The Amsterdam Treaty left the pillar structure established by the TEU largely intact with only a few amendments. It reinforced cooperation in the third pillar, renamed "Police and Judicial Cooperation in Criminal Matters (PJCC)," while immigration-related issues were transferred from the third to the first pillar. Cooperation in the second pillar (CFSP) was also strengthened by the creation of a High Representative. The main institutional innovation of the Amsterdam Treaty consisted in allowing flexibility for "enhanced cooperation" between member states within the Union in specific policy areas, though, in practice, it remained difficult to use. EU leaders also agreed at Amsterdam to extend qualified majority voting (QMV) to a handful of new policy areas but failed to reallocate votes in the Council and redesign the composition and size of the Commission. Instead, they postponed this politically sensitive question to a later date. However, the treaty simplified and extended the legislative cooperation procedure between the Council and the European Parliament, thus granting the latter an increased co-decision right. Despite its deficiencies, the Amsterdam Treaty paved the way for the start of negotiations with the southern, central, and eastern European applicants. Its ratification proceeded without any problems in the 15 EU member states.

In order to tackle the institutional "leftovers" of Amsterdam – i.e. size and composition of the Commission, weighting of votes in the Council of Ministers and the extension of QMV – another IGC convened in 2000 under the French presidency. The central issue was that of the future of the enlarged Union and the functioning of its institutions. The IGC had been prepared by a group of "wise men" appointed by European Commission president Romano Prodi and headed by former Belgian prime minister Jean-Luc Dehaene. The report proposed a new approach to treaty reform, and suggested splitting the main treaty texts into two parts. One would contain constitutional elements (aims, principles, general policy orientations, citizens' rights, and institutional framework); another would contain all provisions relating to specific policy matters.[15] Most member states, however, were reluctant to tackle other issues than those directly relating to the institutional implications of enlargement and preferred to stick to a more limited negotiation agenda.

The 2000 IGC was characterized by tough bargaining, in particular between big and small member states over voting weights, the Commission's and Parliament's size. France was determined to oppose a reweighting of voting in the Council based on demographic criteria only, since it would lose parity of votes with a demographically bigger Germany. The result of hard-fought negotiations between France and Germany, on the one hand, and big and small member states, on the other, was all but a simplification of the Council's decision-making process. The compromise required a double majority to pass legislative decisions: a qualified majority of 72% of votes and an absolute majority of member states. An optional qualified majority of the EU's population of 62% was provided only in case a member state would contest the threshold. The debates over the Commission's and Parliament's future composition also highlighted a growing cleavage between big and small member states. In the end, they all agreed to limit their representation to one commissioner until the EU reached 27 members, after which appointments would rotate between member states according to a system to be determined later but based on strict equality of all member states. EU member states also grudgingly agreed to reduce the size of their national representation in the European Parliament to make room for the delegations of the new member states.

The Nice Treaty which was eventually concluded in December 2000 cleared the way for enlargement but largely failed to prepare the EU to cope with it institutionally. Its main innovation was the adoption of an EU Charter of Fundamental Rights, although its legal status remained unclear. The treaty's complicated, partly abstruse provisions were difficult for the average citizen to understand. It strenghthened people's growing alienation from an EU that was said to lack transparency and legitimacy and laid the ground for the so often disparaged "democratic deficit." This was dramatically confirmed by the rejection of the treaty by the traditionally pro-European Irish electorate in June 2001 by a majority of 64%. Irish voters eventually endorsed the treaty in a second referendum in October 2002, after the European Council confirmed that Ireland's military neutrality would be left untouched by the treaty.

Arguably, the most striking achievement of EU post-Cold War integrationist efforts was the euro, which completed the transition to EMU. By January 2001, twelve member states had qualified to adopt the common currency according to the strict Stability and Growth Pact (SGP), which had been adopted in 1993 to discipline future members of the "Eurozone" thanks to a set of "convergence criteria."[16] In January 2002, the first euro coins and bills were circulated in the participating countries. The euro presented the most tangible proof of the

EU's cohesion and ability to accomplish ambitious, long-term objectives. Several new members are bound to join the "12-nation euro club" once they meet the requirements. Since their accession, six new EU members (the three Baltic countries, Slovenia, Malta, and Cyprus) have joined the European Exchange Rate Mechanism (ERM II) and, meanwhile, the euro has been introduced in Slovenia in January 2007. Poland, the Czech Republic, and Hungary are expected to follow soon. Bulgaria plans to apply in 2007 while Romania intends to join early in the next decade.

CFSP, on the other hand, proved disappointing. The 1998 Franco-British Declaration of Saint-Malo[17] had strengthened the EU's military credibility, and the creation of the post of High Representative for Foreign and Security Policy in 1999 had enhanced its political and diplomatic visibility, although the latter was somewhat diminished by the apparent concurrence between the High Representative and the Commissioner for external relations. Yet, the Union has since made little progress in defining a European Security and Defence Policy (ESDP). The September 11 terrorist attacks showed the necessity for a deepening of cooperation in security and defense matters and, in fact, resulted in a major boost for police and judicial cooperation in the third pillar. In December 2003, the EU adopted a European Security Strategy defining its basic mission and priority areas that, however, did not prevent EU member states from splitting over the American military intervention in Iraq. An "old" versus "new" Europe, as US Defense Secretary Ronald Rumsfeld put it, almost replaced the Cold War East–West fault line.

The future of the union: a European constitution, a constitutional treaty, or a simplified Lisbon Reform Treaty?

The inadequacies and complexity of the Nice Treaty led reform-minded (and other) political leaders to set in motion a wider debate on the future of the European Union that would not limit itself to the usual political circles but, on the contrary, involve the citizens of the Union.

The so-called "post-Nice debate" actually started well before the conclusion of the Nice IGC and gained momentum throughout 2001. German foreign minister Joschka Fischer set the tone in May 2000 at the Humboldt University in Berlin. In a vibrant and ambitious speech, he proposed the conclusion of a Constituent treaty that would establish a European federation.[18] In the next few months, his example was followed by British prime minister Tony Blair, French president Jacques Chirac, and French prime minister Lionel Jospin, who all called for a more imaginative debate about the envisioned finality of the European project and urged more radical institutional reforms.[19] Under the pressure of these calls, the European Commission formally launched the debate along with an EU website, which allowed EU citizens, associations, and organizations to follow and partake in the discussions but failed to attract much attention.[20] It was nonetheless a step forward, albeit a limited one, in the democratization of the EU. The European Convention was to mirror this move towards greater transparency and democratic accountability: plenary sessions were held in public; documentation and work papers were available via the website and the structured consultation with civil-society.

Concerned about growing public alienation from the EU, an increasing sense of frustration over the Nice Treaty and the obvious shortcomings of the IGC method, the European Council agreed at the December 2001 summit at Laeken, to convene a European Convention. This decision rested on a resolution adopted at Nice to convene yet another IGC by 2004. Not only would its agenda be broadened but it would work in a completely novel way. It would include representatives of the member states, members of national parliaments, including those of the candidate states – though they had no decision-making powers – members of the European parliament and Commissions representatives. It was chaired by former French president Valéry Giscard d'Estaing and charged with drawing up the draft of a European constitution. The Convention started its work in February 2002. After intense deliberations, the Convention submitted a draft Constitutional Treaty to the European Council in July 2003.

The Constitutional Treaty contained sweeping innovations. The pillar structure was abolished. The three pillars were merged into a single European Union that would have a legal personality and the ability to conclude binding agreements with other countries and international organizations. The Union's institutions were simplified and rationalized. The rotating presidency was abolished and replaced by a president of the European Council, elected for a two-and-a-half-year duration (renewable once), who would also preside over the Union. This was intended to improve both the European Council's efficiency and the EU's international visibility and standing. The posts of high representative for common and security policy and commissioner for external relations were merged into the position of foreign minister. The latter would chair the Foreign Affairs Council for five years and be the Commission's vice-president. However, the Constitutional Treaty failed to tidy up the still controversial issue of the size and composition of the Commission as well as the complex calculation of QMV. The inclusion of the Charter of Fundamental Rights into the treaty was nonetheless an essential constitutional element. The treaty also reaffirmed the Union's values (democracy, rule of law, respect for human rights and fundamental freedoms) and organizing principles (subsidiarity, proportionality, loyal cooperation).

Signed on October 29, 2004 in Rome, where the founding treaties of the European Community had been signed almost fifty years before, the Constitutional Treaty had to be ratified according to the procedures laid down by the constitutions of the member states to enter into force. By 2007, 18 countries (Germany, Austria, Belgium, Cyprus, Slovakia, Slovenia, Slovakia Spain, Greece, Hungary, Italy, Latvia, Lithuania, Estonia, Luxembourg, Malta, Romania, and Bulgaria) had ratified the Constitutional Treaty, either by parliamentary approval or referendum. France and the Netherlands rejected it in referendums held respectively on May 29, and June 1, 2005. As a result, ratification was put on ice in the United Kingdom, Poland, and Ireland. The reasons for the French and Dutch rejection certainly have many domestic origins, but they also mirrored the growing disconnection between public perceptions of the integration project and the views of pro-integration elites. The anti-treaty campaign in France made abundant use of the "Polish plumber," an imaginary immigrant from the new member states who would compete with local workers and depress wages. The "Polish plumber," as the embodiment of uncontrolled globalization, and the purposefully instrumentalized "Bolkenstein directive" on the liberalization of services served to link enlargement with both economic and social insecurity and motivated many otherwise pro-European French voters to reject the Constitutional Treaty. In the Netherlands, the murder of movie-maker Theo van Gogh by a radical Islamist sent a shock wave through Dutch society and sparked a vivid debate about immigration-related topics. The Dutch rejection of the treaty was also a vote against enlargement, globalization, and open borders.

Following the negative outcome of the referenda in France and the Netherlands, EU leaders called for a "period of reflection." Several ideas were advanced to end the crisis opened by the French and Dutch "No," including new referenda, revisions of the Nice Treaty with inclusion of the less controversial part of the Constitutional Treaty or non-treaty reforms.[21] The 18 member states which have already ratified the constitutional Treaty, were opposed to a Constitutional Treaty "light" or a new text that would require a separate ratification. France and the Netherlands, on the other hand, signalled their opposition to the existing treaty. Other countries such as the United Kingdom, Denmark, and the Czech Republic indicated that they would be satisfied with a shorter, simpler text that could be approved without a referendum. By the December 2006 European Council summit in Brussels, little progress had been made towards a solution.

During the German presidency in the first half of 2007, German chancellor Angela Merkel's diplomatic skills and European commitment contributed to breaking the deadlock over the Constitutional Treaty by building a consensus on a precise mandate for an immediate and short IGC. German efforts were seconded by newly elected French president Nicolas Sarkozy. As early as September 2006, before his election, Sarkozy had suggested a "mini-treaty" that would retain most of the institutional reforms of the Constitutional Treaty but would not require ratification by referendum because of its limited character. Sarkozy was certainly eager to achieve European successes for domestic purposes, but he also intended that the "simplified treaty" be ratified during the 2008 French EU presidency as evidence that "France was back in Europe."

As often in the EU's history, the 27 reached an agreement on a road map for detailed negotiation of a simplified treaty – called the "EU reforming treaty" – in the early morning of June 24, 2007. The new treaty would replace the defunct constitution but not the existing treaties, which it would simply amend. It would be emptied of any reference to symbols (flag, hymn, slogan, etc.). The term "constitution" would disappear. The dispositions of the third part of the Constitutional Treaty, which dealt with the policies and the functioning of the Union, would regain their original place in the existing treaties. The main institutional innovations of the Constitutional Treaty would be maintained, however. The Union would have a stable presidency for a two-and-a-half-year duration; the size of the Commission would also be reduced. QMV would be extended to new policy areas, e.g. judicial and police cooperation, thereby further increasing the powers of the European Parliament. The role of national parliaments would be strengthened too. The double majority (55% of member states and 65% of the population) was left untouched for the most part. The subsidiarity principle would remain firmly anchored in the new treaty which would further delineate the member states' and the Union's competencies. The juridical personality of the Union was preserved along with the merging of the three pillars into a single entity. The content of the Charter of Fundamental Rights would be taken up, but Poland and the United Kingdom obtained assurances that it would not alter their national legislation. The compromise reached by the 27 respected most of the "red lines" drawn by a handful of member states, primarily Poland and Great Britain, and should help overcome the two-year deadlock generated by the French and Dutch rejection of the European constitution.

Portugal, which held the rotating presidency in the second half of 2007, was responsible for conducting negotiations on the EU's simplified Lisbon Treaty, which was adopted at the European Council at Lisbon in October 2007 and signed in December 2007 in the Portuguese capital. It needed to be ratified by the 27 (by parliamentary ratification with the exception of Ireland) and was meant to enter into force in January 2009, shortly before the new European Commission and the newly elected European Parliament were to take office. Even though not perfect, the treaty was designed to facilitate the decision-making process in the enlarged Union. Only time will tell whether yet another reform treaty will be enough to improve the Union's efficiency and decisiveness as well as restore the confidence and faith of its citizens in the European project. The rejection of the ratification of the treaty in a referendum by a majority of Irish voters in mid-June 2008 has thrown the future of the Lisbon Reform Treaty, and with it the future of the EU, wide open. Will the EU find another way (or perhaps ask the Irish to vote again) to become a more efficient and streamlined and much better-structured institution and thus able to project its influence and power globally, or will it merely perform the role of an integrated economic and financial community with a single market, a common currency, and not much else?

Conclusion

Far from meaning the "end of history" for the European continent,[22] the end of the Cold War propelled a radically transformed EU into a new era. Enlargement of the Union completed a process that had begun with the fall of the Berlin Wall. It finally erased the Cold War's long-standing borders and restored the geographic and cultural unity of Europe.[23]

Since the 2004 "big bang" enlargement, the European Union has definitely become a more complex entity. The greater diversity of the enlarged EU in terms of histories, politics, languages, wealth, and geography is likely to increase the multiplicity of interests among its members. But such diversity can also be a source of innovation and power if it is skillfully exploited. Enlargement also brought about essential changes in the EU's external relations. The adhesion of central and eastern European countries has moved the EU's center of gravity farther eastward, thus affecting the way the EU conducts its external relations with potent neighbors, such as Russia, and with the United States. Enlargement has also altered the substance of the EU and changed the way the Union is run, though not as completely and radically as expected or feared. For instance, new coalition-building patterns between old and new members are emerging that are redefining power distribution in the enlarged Union.

In less than 20 years, European integration has made impressive progress despite problems and setbacks. The European Parliament has obtained real legislative powers, even though democratic accountability of the Union remains a problem. QMV has become the rule rather than the exception, even if key policy areas, such as external relations, remain ruled by unanimity. Justice- and immigration-related questions have been incorporated into the Union's policies. And, last but not least, the Union has been endowed with credible representatives. The European constitution would have represented an integrationist leap forward but it proved premature.

Certainly, there remain preoccupying deficiencies in the "EU 27." These are first and foremost of a political nature. With its many "opt-outs" – from the euro to the Charter of Fundamental Rights – the UK is largely offside in the European game. The European Commission, especially under the leadership of its current president José Manuel Barroso, has lost a good part of its role as the engine of European integration. France and Germany need to redefine their privileged partnership if they want to reclaim some of their lost leadership in the enlarged EU and act again as Europe's motor. Furthermore, the Union also needs to take concrete action in policy areas that are of particular concerns for its citizens. Only then will it be able to reconnect its citizens with the European project, an indispensable prerequisite for the future.

All told, the Union needs to process its enlargement, to clarify the issue of its finality and to redefine a European project in the context of globalization. What it is Europeans want to do together is more than ever a relevant question at the dawn of the twenty-first century.

Notes

1 The author wishes to thank Piers Ludlow, Frédéric Bozo, Marie-Pierre Rey, and Leopoldo Nuti who let me see a selection of unpublished chapters of their co-edited book on Europe and the end of the Cold War, and owes many thanks to Stefaan de Rynck of the European Commission for his insightful comments and suggestions on earlier drafts of this paper.

2 Soutou, *La Guerre de Cinquante Ans*.

3 In the words of the European Commission. See *More Unity and More Diversity*, 3.

4 Dinan, *Europe Recast: A History of European Union*, 266–267.

5 Dinan, op. cit., 269.

6 This is at least the number officially claimed by the EU, although it is being constantly revised and increased.

7 The Copenhagen criteria were (1) the stability of democratic institutions, the rule of law, human rights, and respect for and protection of minorities; (2) the existence of a functioning market economy as well as the capacity to cope with competition within the Union; and (3) the ability to take on the obligations of membership, including adherence to the aims of political, economic, and monetary union. See Conclusion of the European Council in Copenhagen, June 21–22, 1993, accessible at http://ue.eu.int/ueDocs/cms_Data/docs/pressdata/en/ec/72921.pdf.

8 On the Agenda 2000, see Avery and Cameron, *The Enlargement of the European Union*, 101–119.

9 For further details, see Graham Bowley, "The New Central and Eastern European Member States in 2004," in Tiersky and Jones, *Europe Today*, 369–399.

10 Van Oudenaren, "EU Enlargement," in Tiersky and Jones, *Europe Today*, 360.
11 Van Oudenaren, "EU Enlargement," 363.
12 See Communication from the Commission to the Council and the European Parliament, March 11, 2003, "Wider Europe-Neighbourhood: A New Framework for Relations with Our Eastern andSouthern Neighbours," accessible at ttp://ec.europa. eu/world/enp/pdf/com03_104_en.pdf.
13 European Commission, *More Unity and More Diversity*, 21.
14 See Neil Nugent, "Distinctive and Recurring Features of Enlargement Rounds," in Nugent, *European Union Enlargement*, 56.
15 Van Oudenaren, *Uniting Europe*, 64.
16 The three main convergence criteria (out of five) include: (1) an annual deficit not higher than 3% of the GDP, (2) a national debt lower than 60%, (3) an inflation rate no more than 1.5 percentage points higher than the three best-performing EU member states.
17 The text of the declaration is available at http://atlanticcommunity.org/Saint-Malo%20 Declaration%20Text.html.
18 Fischer's speech can be consulted in English at http://www.ena.lu/europe/european-union/objective-european-integration-berlin-2000.htm.
19 Tony Blair's and Jacques Chirac's speech are respectively available at http://www. ena.lu/europe/european-union/given-tony-blair-polish-stock-exchange-warsaw-2000. htm and http://www.ena.lu/europe/european-union/given-jacques-chirac-bundestag-europe-berlin-2000.htm.
20 Church and Phinnemore, *Understanding the European Constitution*, 20.
21 See for instance Duff, "Plan B: How to Rescue the European Constitution," in *Notre Europe*, Studies and Research, 52 (2006). Accessible at http://home.um.edu.mt/edrc/ duff_notre_europe_planb.pdf.
22 Fukuyama, "The End of History."
23 Winks and Talbot, *Europe 1945 to the Present*, 144.

Bibliography

Avery, Graham and Fraser Cameron, *The Enlargement of the European Union* (Sheffield: Sheffield University Press, 1998).
Baun, Michael, *A Wider Europe: The Process and Politics of European Union Enlargement* (Oxford: Rowman & Littlefeld, 2000).
Calleo, David P., *Rethinking Europe's Future* (Princeton, NJ: Princeton University Press, 2001).
Church, Clive H. and David Phinnemore, *Understanding the European Constitution: An Introduction to the EU Constitutional Treaty* (London: Routledge, 2006).
Cremona, Marise (ed.), *The Enlargement of the European Union* (Oxford: Oxford University Press, 2003).
Dinan, Desmond, *Europe Recast: A History of European Union* (Boulder, CO and London: Lynn Rienner, 2004).
Dinan, Desmond, *Ever Closer Union: An Introduction to European Integration* (Boulder, CO and London: Lynn Rienner, 2005).
Duff, Andrew, John Pinder, and Roy Price (eds.), *Maastricht and Beyond: Building the European Union* (London: Routledge, 1994).

Eriksen, Erik Oddvar, John Erik Fossum, and Agustín Menéndez (eds.), *Developing a Constitution for Europe* (London: Routledge, 2004).

European Commission, *More Unity and More Diversity: The European Union's Biggest Enlargement*, Europe on the Move series (Luxembourg: Office for Official Publications of the European Communities, 2003). Accessible online at http://ec.europa.eu/publications/booklets/move/41/en.pdf

European Navigator, online resource on the history of European integration and institutions (Luxembourg: Centre Virtuel de la Connaissance sur l'Europe), http://www.ena.lu

Fukuyama, Francis, "The End of History," *National Interest*, no. 16, 3–18, 1989.

Gillingham, John, *European Integration 1950–2003: Superstate of New Market Economy?* (Cambridge: Cambridge University Press, 2003).

Gillingham, John, *Design for a New Europe* (Cambridge: Cambridge University Press, 2006).

Guttman, Robert J. (ed.), *Europe in the New Century: Visions of an Emerging Superpower* (Boulder, CO: Lynne Rienner, 2001).

Heywood, Paul, Erik Jones, Martin Rhodes, and Ulrich Sedelmeier (eds.), *Developments in European Politics* (New York: Palgrave, 2006).

Hitchcock, William, *The Struggle for Europe: The Turbulent History of a Divided Continent, 1945–2002* (New York: Anchor Books, 2004).

Hogan, Michael J., *The End of the Cold War: Its Meaning and Implications* (Cambridge: Cambridge University Press, 1992).

Judt, Tony, *Postwar – A History of Europe since 1945* (New York: Penguin Press, 2005).

Kaiser, Wolfram and Jürgen Elvert (eds.), *European Union Enlargement: A Comparative History* (London: Routledge, 2004).

Ludlow, Piers, Frédéric Bozo, Marie-Pierre Rey, and Leopoldo Nuti (eds.), *Europe and the End of the Cold War* (Abingdon: Routledge, 2007).

McCormick, John, *The European Superpower* (Houndmills: Palgrave Macmillan, 2007).

Mayhew, Alan, *Recreating Europe: The European Union's Policy towards Central and Eastern Europe* (Cambridge: Cambridge University Press, 2002).

Moravcsik, Andrew, *The Choice for Europe: Social Purpose and State Power from Messina to Maastricht* (Ithaca, NY: Cornell University Press, 1998).

Neunreither, Karl-Heinz and Antje Wiener (eds.), *European Integration after Amsterdam: Institutional Dynamics and Prospects for Democracy* (Oxford: Oxford University Press, 2000).

Nugent, Neil (ed.), *European Union Enlargement* (New York: Palgrave Macmillan, 2004).

Preston, Christopher, *Enlargement and Integration in the European Union* (London: Routledge, 1997).

Rice, Condoleezza and Philip Zelikow, *Germany Unified and Europe Transformed* (Cambridge, MA: Harvard University Press, 1995).

Serfaty, Simon (ed.), *The European Finality Debate and Its National Dimensions* (Washington, DC: Center for Strategic and International Studies, 2003).

Shaw, Jo, Paul Magnette, Lars Hoffmann, and Anna Bausili Vergès (eds.), *The Convention on the Future of Europe: Working towards an EU Constitution* (London: Kogan Page, 2003).

Soutou, Georges-Henri, *La Guerre de cinquante ans: Les Relations est–ouest 1943–1990* (Paris: Fayard, 2001).

Tiersky, Ronald and Erik Jones (eds.), *Europe Today: A Twenty-First Century Introduction* (Lanham, MD: Rowman & Littlefield, 2007).

van Oudenaren, John, *Uniting Europe: An Introduction to the European Union* (Oxford: Rowman & Littlefield, 2005).

Winks, Robin W. and John E. Talbot, *Europe 1945 to the Present* (Oxford: Oxford University Press, 2005).

Zielonka, Jan, *Europe as Empire: The Nature of the Enlarged European Union* (London: Oxford University Press, 2006).

Further Reading

Two excellent background readings on post-1945 European general history are Tony Judt's erudite chronicle of postwar European history *Postwar – A History of Europe since 1945* (New York: Penguin Press, 2005), and William Hitchcock's comprehensive account *The Struggle for Europe: The Turbulent History of a Divided Continent, 1945–2002* (New York: Anchor Books, 2004). Desmond Dinan, *Ever Closer Union: An Introduction to European Integration* (Boulder, CO and London: Lynn Rienner, 2005) gives a concise overview of (western) European integration since 1945.

For a standard work in English on the implications of German reunification in Europe, see Condoleezza Rice and Philip Zelikow, *Germany Unified and Europe Transformed* (Cambridge, MA: Harvard University Press, 1995). A valuable collection of essays on the end of the Cold War can be found in Michael J. Hogan, *The End of the Cold War: Its Meaning and Implications* (Cambridge: Cambridge University Press, 1992). For a more recent and European-focused reappraisal of the end of the Cold War, consult Piers Ludlow, Frédéric Bozo, Marie-Pierre Rey, and Leopoldi Nuti (eds.), *Europe and the End of the Cold War* (Abingdon: Routledge, 2007).

The historical literature available on the latest enlargement waves is almost non-existent. Wolfram Kaiser and Jürgen Elvert (eds.), *European Union Enlargement: A Comparative History* (London: Routledge, 2004) provides a comparative analysis of European enlargements between 1973 and 1995, but the 2004 enlargement is not covered. See also Michael Baun, *A Wider Europe: The Process and Politics of European Union Enlargement* (Oxford: Rowman & Littlefield, 2000) and Alan Mayhew, *Recreating Europe: The European Union's Policy towards Central and Eastern Europe* (Cambridge: Cambridge University Press, 2002). Marise Cremona (ed.), *The Enlargement of the European Union* (Oxford: Oxford University Press, 2003), examines the various dimensions of enlargement and its impact on both the candidate and the institution's policies. Christopher Preston, *Enlargement and Integration in the European Union* (London: Routledge, 1997), remains valuable for its focus on the Mediterranean, central and eastern Europe and the former Soviet Countries. For a comprehensive assessment of the evolving nature of the EU and the implications of enlargement for the emergence of new European polity, see Jan Zielonka, *Europe as Empire: The Nature of the Enlarged European Union* (London: Oxford University Press, 2006).

For a critical assessment of the European Union brought into being by the Maastricht and Amsterdam treaties, see Andrew Duff, John Pinder, and Roy Price (eds.), *Maastricht and Beyond: Building the European Union* (London: Routledge, 1994), Michael J. Baun, *An Imperfect Union? The Maastricht Treaty and the New Politics of European Integration* (Boulder, CO: Westview, 1996) and Karl-Heinz Neunreither and Antje Wiener (eds.), *European Integration after Amsterdam: Institutional Dynamics and Prospects for Democracy* (Oxford: Oxford University Press, 2000).

For the Constitutional Treaty, see Jo Shaw, Paul Magnette, Lars Hoffmann, and Anna Bausili Vergès (eds.), *The Convention on the Future of Europe: Working towards an EU Constitution* (London: Kogan Page, 2003) and Erik Oddvar Eriksen, John Erik Fossum, and Agustín Menéndez (eds.), *Developing a Constitution for Europe* (London: Routledge, 2004).

On the debate on the future of Europe, see in particular John Gillingham's *Design for a New Europe* (Cambridge: Cambridge University Press, 2006), which provides a convincing portrait of the problems that afflict the EU and makes interesting suggestions on how to fix them. David Calleo, *Rethinking Europe's Future* (Princeton, NJ: Princeton University Press, 2001) also lucidly re-evaluates Europe's historical legacies and future challenges. For a more optimistic view of Europe's future, see Robert J. Guttman (ed.), *Europe in the New Century: Visions of an Emerging Superpower* (Boulder, CO: Lynne Rienner, 2001) and John McCormick, *The European Superpower* (Houndmills: Palgrave Macmillan, 2007). Interesting reflexions on the finality debate and its national dimensions are to be found in Simon Serfaty (ed.), *The European Finality Debate and its National Dimensions* (Washington, DC: Center for Strategic and International Studies, 2003).

Part III

Europe since 1990: Political and Economic Developments

CHAPTER ELEVEN

Transatlantic Relations since the End of the Cold War: Permanent Alliance or Partnership in Peril?

ROBERT HUTCHINGS

In the middle of the nineteenth century, Lord Palmerston famously remarked that Britain had no permanent allies, only permanent interests.[1] At the end of the Cold War, the question was whether the transatlantic alliance, like alliances before it, would disband with the disappearance of the threat it was formed to counter, or whether it would turn Palmerston's dictum on its head. Was the transatlantic alliance, which had already established itself as the most enduring alliance in history, still cemented by common values and interests that transcended the particular circumstances of the Cold War? Or, on the contrary, would the breakdown of transatlantic solidarity over Iraq beginning in 2002 mark the beginning of the alliance's dissolution? Would international terrorism, so dramatically manifest in the 9/11 terrorist attacks against the United States, provide the alliance's new *raison d'être*? Were the United States and Europe poised to renew their relationship for a new and very different set of twenty-first-century challenges, or were Cold War partners inevitably drifting apart? All those questions were still open.

When the Cold War ended, balance-of-power realists and neo-realists foresaw the inevitable collapse of the transatlantic alliance, as well as other Cold War alliances like the US–Japan pact.[2] Absent a unifying threat, these theorists maintained, strategic alignment would give way to strategic divergence, rivalry, and counterbalancing responses. The values and habits of the bygone era might sustain the alliance for some years, but eventually the structural changes in the international system would lead to erosion. The sense of inevitable drift was later captured in Robert Kagan's claim that "Americans are from Mars and Europeans are from Venus: they agree on little and understand each other less."[3]

Other observers, not persuaded by such deterministic assumptions, remarked on how little had changed in US–European relations after the end of the Cold War.[4] Far from withering away, as realists and neo-realists had predicted, NATO seemed to have gotten a new lease on life, as former Warsaw Pact members eagerly lined up to apply for membership. Liberal internationalists saw a world in which laws and values transcended balance-of-power calculations. States and their leaders, in this view, embraced extensive agendas, not ones limited to the pursuit of power or

A Companion to Europe since 1945, First Edition. Edited by Klaus Larres.
© 2014 John Wiley & Sons, Ltd. Published 2014 by John Wiley & Sons, Ltd.

security, and thus were animated by considerations beyond those of external threats. The international agenda after the Cold War seemed to offer new opportunities, and necessities, for transatlantic cooperation on a host of new issues.

Neo-liberal institutionalists pointed to the critical role played by international institutions in setting agendas, promoting linkages among smaller states, and encouraging coalition formation.[5] The international system, in this view, is politically constructed rather than predetermined. Although obviously affected by post-Cold War realities, European and transatlantic institutions, as associations of democracies, have the capacity to adapt themselves to altered circumstances and new challenges. Successful adaptation was not a foregone conclusion, but neither was it foreclosed.

Competing Visions

For political leaders on both sides of the Atlantic, the challenge of fashioning a new transatlantic bargain was complicated by the manner in which the Cold War ended – "not with military victory, demobilization, and celebration but with the unexpected capitulation of the other side without a shot being fired . . . The grand struggle had ended not with a bang but a whimper."[6] With Western institutions intact and those of the Soviet bloc fast collapsing, the impulse on both sides of the Atlantic was to engage in incremental adaptation rather than wholesale change of those institutions. It was in many ways a sensible calculation, but it tended to inhibit the kind of creativity that was needed to fashion a viable new order.

The very speed of the process had served Western interests well during the period of German unification in 1989 and 1990, in that the US and its European partners were able to present Soviet leaders with a series of faits accompli that they found difficult to counter effectively. However, it also meant that the post-unification, post-Cold War security order in Europe had to be built on the fly, as it were, with little time for far-sighted judgment. In the process, American visions of a "New Atlanticism," intended to reconcile the twin goals of European integration and a US-led transatlantic security order, collided with European efforts to build a more cohesive and assertive European Union (EU) within a "post-Yalta" security order that liberated Europe from American tutelage.

Long-standing American support for European unity, going back to the Marshall Plan and even before, was always tinged with ambivalence, and those misgivings came more clearly to the fore at the end of the Cold War, as Europe embarked on a bold new drive for unity.[7] On the one hand, the United States wanted a more cohesive and capable Europe and knew in any case that American policy had to take into account the reality of a more assertive European Union. On the other, American policy-makers did not always like the kind of EU that seemed to be emerging and so adopted policies that seemed to obstruct these efforts at every turn. It was not that American attitudes towards European integration were duplicitous, but that the two strands of thinking were equally strong and frequently in conflict. In post-Cold War Europe, absent a common external threat, the question was posed starkly: was the ambition of European unity compatible with a continued strong transatlantic link?

At the Paris summit of November 1990, marking the decisive end of the Cold War, three competing visions of the European future were evident. First was the

Europeanist vision of a more united, cohesive European Community (EC), moving resolutely to build economic and political union among its 12 member countries even as it widened its scope to bring in new members. NATO, in this vision, still had a place but no longer a central or permanent one. Second was the Atlanticist vision of a permanent American political and military presence in Europe and a seamless trans-atlantic security community, albeit with a new balance of US and European roles to accommodate a more cohesive EC. Third was the "Vancouver-to-Vladivostok" vision of a pan-European security community, advocated with differing motivations by the Russians, Czechs, and others.[8]

Secretary of State James Baker's "New Atlanticism" idea, expressed in his two Berlin speeches of December 1989 and June 1991, tried to bridge the gap by pro-posing a system of interlocking institutions, with NATO, the European Community (soon to become the European Union), the CSCE (the Conference on Security and Cooperation in Europe), and other organizations playing complementary roles. It was an elegant formulation in the abstract but often clumsy in the execution. President George H.W. Bush offered an even more expansive view of a "new world order," with the Western allies at the core of an expanding democratic community and a revitalized UN system operating as its founders had intended.[9] The hope, as expressed in President Bush's speech in Prague in November 1990, was that the end of the Cold War would create the conditions not only for a continued transatlantic relation-ship but for a stronger and more natural one, freed from the unnatural imbalance of roles and responsibilities that the Cold War had imposed.[10]

American policy proceeded from several core beliefs. First, NATO had to survive as the key instrument of European security and the institutional link binding the United States to Europe. Second, NATO's role in post-Cold War Europe called for its radical transformation, towards a broader security agenda and new balance of European and American roles and responsibilities. Third, the CSCE needed the institutional and operational capacity to play a stronger political role and assume new security responsibilities, particularly in the areas of conflict prevention and crisis management. Fourth and perhaps most important, the United States needed to embrace European unity, including the development of a common European foreign and security policy, while also maintaining the vitality of transatlantic security – com-peting challenges that proved hard to reconcile in practice.[11]

Underlying all this was the conviction that the United States had to remain in Europe to balance Russian power and provide stability so that a more united western Europe could extend its zone of democratic stability eastward. No idea was more strongly or deeply held in the upper levels of the administration. The American role, in Washington's view, transcended Europe's achievement of greater economic and political unity; it had to do with semi-permanent factors of power and geography.

Of course, this American presence had an economic as well as a security dimen-sion. As the military dimensions of security receded, trade issues loomed larger – and now would be played out without the galvanizing element of the Soviet threat. It was, as President Bush put it in a speech in the Netherlands just before the Maastricht summit, "the danger that old Cold War allies will become new economic adversaries – Cold Warriors turned to trade warriors."[12] Indeed, Uruguay Round trade negotia-tions loomed at least as large as security matters in US–European relations after 1990.

Conflict over the first-ever US–EC declaration was a portent of the difficulties ahead. Responding to overtures made by President Bush in his Boston University speech of May 1989 and by Secretary Baker in his Berlin speech the following December, German chancellor Helmut Kohl took the lead in proposing that the United States and the European Community issue a joint declaration aimed at giving US–EC relations a more intense and regular character. Accordingly, US and EC negotiators worked out a text to be issued at the Paris summit of November 1990. The four-page document was mostly hortatory but included a few specific commitments to closer dialogue that were inserted at US insistence over strenuous French objections.[13] As luck would have it, however, US–EC Uruguay Round trade negotiations hit an impasse over agricultural subsidies on the eve of the Paris summit. The declaration, which Bush and Baker were reluctant to endorse under the circumstances, was salvaged by 11th-hour negotiations in Paris, but the new US–EC relationship was off to an inauspicious start.

The European Security "Architecture"

Debate after the Paris summit was similarly fraught in the security arena. US-French differences were particularly acute. Animated by the vision of an EC-centered Europe, France aimed to accelerate European integration while it still had political leverage over newly united Germany. "European construction" in turn required that the EC develop a political and security component to complement its economic institutions. Indeed, during the negotiations towards German unification in April 1990, Chancellor Kohl and French president François Mitterrand had issued a joint call for an accelerated timetable for reaching economic and political union by 1993.

These tasks acquired particularly urgency with two summits looming. A NATO summit to be held in Rome in November 1991 was to present the alliance's "new strategic concept" and complete the vision of a "transformed alliance" heralded at the London summit of July 1990. The following month, in December 1991, the EC was to meet in Maastricht to complete the "single European market" and point the way to European economic and eventual political union.

Under these time pressures, French-led efforts to reinvigorate the Western European Union (WEU) or create a "Eurocorps" became locked in "zero-sum" competition with NATO. The French protested that the United States wanted to preserve a NATO-centric European security order even while gradually disengaging from an active role in European security. Hence efforts to transform NATO and develop new approaches towards the East were always viewed with suspicion in Paris, just as Washington was wary of French-led efforts to set up what appeared to be free-standing European security institutions in competition with NATO.

Behind the scenes, there was an effort on both sides to try to find a way of bridging these differences and bring France back closer to NATO. In the French ministry of defense and at the Elysée (the presidential palace) there was a current of thinking that favored drawing closer to NATO lest France be marginalized in post-Cold War Europe.[14] These sentiments were reciprocated on the American side, which wanted France engaged in NATO and indeed wondered whether the alliance could survive absent full French participation. In a series of secret meetings in late 1990 and early 1991, the two sides explored what changes would need to be made for this to be possible. These were serious discussions but also exploratory, not yet involving Mitterrand directly. Not for the first time or the last, discussions broke down. This became evident in a meeting between Bush and Mitterrand in Martinique in March 1991, when the French president slammed the door on the idea, arguing that Europe had to develop the capacity to defend itself because American disengagement was only a matter of time.[15]

Meanwhile, immediately after the Paris summit, European leaders launched a series of ambitious and ill-considered security initiatives. Kohl and Mitterrand called for the EC's absorption of the Western European Union. Italian foreign minister Gianni de Michaelis likewise called for an early "merger" of the two institutions, also without saying how this new entity would relate to the Atlantic alliance. EC Commission president Jacques Delors went further, proposing that the WEU's mutual defense commitment be inserted into the EC's political union treaty and calling for the WEU to become "a melting pot for a European defense embedded in the Community."[16] What that meant was not clear, but it seemed to have no connection to NATO or the United States. Similarly, the Franco-German proposal for a "Eurocorps" offered no explanation of how it would relate to NATO. Would it be inside NATO or outside? Would it complement NATO or compete with it? These unanswered questions prompted an angry US reaction – in the form of a démarche to all allied capitals – warning against the creation of a European "caucus" within NATO or a free-standing European security organization in competition with NATO.[17]

In his address to NATO's summit in Rome in November 1991, President Bush addressed these concerns directly:

> The United States has been, is, and will remain an unhesitating proponent of the aim and the process of European integration. This strong American support extends to the prospect of political union – as well as the goal of a defense identity . . . Even the attainment of European union, however, will not diminish the need for NATO . . . We support the development of the WEU because it can complement the alliance and strengthen the European role in it . . . But we do not see the WEU as a European alternative to the alliance.[18]

Behind closed doors, Bush was adamant: "If Western Europe intends to create a security organization outside the Alliance, tell me now!"

Neither Rome nor Maastricht settled these fundamental differences, which continued over the Common Foreign and Security Policy (CFSP) and the European Security and Defence Identity (ESDI). For the United States, the question was not just about US support for a more united Europe and its development of a security dimension, but whether this new Europe could be reconciled with a continued vital transatlantic security system. The extravagant assertion, in the opening line of the Maastricht Treaty on European Union (TEU),[19] that "a common foreign and security policy is hereby established," fueled Washington's concerns, as did Delors's invocation of the idea of a "United States of Europe," an ambition that Washington tended to take at face value – not as a long-term aspiration but as a near-term challenge.

Even at the time, these debates seemed overwrought. The United States' NATO-centric approach would have been sound and sustainable if the US were prepared to undertake the kind of fundamental restructuring of the alliance that some in Paris were urging on us. But Washington could not have it both ways – preserving a level of American dominance that was anathema to the French (and others) while also insisting that any European effort be made within the alliance framework. The French position was the mirror image of the American.[20] They wanted a European security capacity but resisted practical efforts to adapt NATO in ways that might have facilitated this goal.

A Pragmatic Truce

By the mid-1990s it was clear that neither vision was going to prevail in the near term and that the two sides needed to find some sort of middle ground. Europe's failure to avert or arrest the violent breakup of Yugoslavia, and then its inability to engage fully alongside more technically advanced US units in the Persian Gulf War of 1991, underlined Europe's dependence on US power for the foreseeable future. In the US, similarly motivated by the experiences in the Balkans (where it, too, had failed) and the Persian Gulf War, the Clinton administration aimed at forging a more balanced US–European relationship. Secretary of State Warren Christopher's June 1995 speech envisioning a "broad-ranging transatlantic agenda for the new century," together with similar overtures by Kohl and others, set the stage for negotiation of a New Transatlantic Agenda, including more regular and substantive consultations between the US and EC.[21]

In the security arena, with defense budgets dropping dramatically on both sides of the Atlantic, the need for a pragmatic meeting of minds became apparent. At the 1991 Rome summit, NATO leaders had approved the alliance's "New Strategic Concept," which outlined a more expansive approach to security, a new mission to promote stability among former adversaries in eastern Europe, a reoriented military posture to include enhanced peacekeeping and crisis management capacities, and a stronger role for NATO's European members.[22] This last stipulation was meant to facilitate the creation of a European Common Foreign and Security Policy (CFSP) as one of the three pillars of the European Union in the Treaty of Maastricht of 1992. That same year, the WEU outlined the so-called Petersberg Tasks – non-combat roles including humanitarian assistance, peacekeeping, and peacemaking – as its appropriate domain, leaving major combat missions to NATO.

Building on these initiatives, the Clinton administration acceded to European demands for greater autonomy, proposing within NATO the creation of a Combined Joint Task Force (CJTF) to enable the dual use of NATO forces and command structures for alliance and/or WEU operations, as well as permitting non-NATO members to join in such operations.[23] This device, in turn, facilitated NATO's official endorsement, in the 1996 Berlin communiqué, of a "European Security and Defence Identity within NATO."[24] Through CJTF and ESDI, European forces would be "separable but not separate" – able to draw on NATO assets for European-only operations but not acting as a free-standing security organization.

Newly elected French president Jacques Chirac responded to these initiatives by signaling France's renewed interest in exploring the possibility of coming back into NATO's integrated command. The idea once again foundered, this time on US unwillingness to accede to French demands that NATO's southern command be transferred from the US to a European country. (One can question the seriousness of Chirac's probe, however, for this episode followed a familiar pattern – of escalating French demands leading ultimately to a French *non* – going back to de Gaulle's protracted withdrawal from NATO's military command in the mid-1960s and indeed all the way back to negotiations towards a European Defence Community in the early 1950s.)

The evolution in transatlantic and European security continued to be overtaken by emerging security challenges, particularly in the Balkans. US–European differences over Balkan policy arose early in the Clinton administration over the latter's opposition to the Vance–Owen peace plan and its push, over European objections, for a policy of "lift and strike" (i.e. lifting the UN-imposed arms embargo and striking Bosnian Serb aggressors). Further developments – the helplessness of Dutch peacekeepers to prevent Serbian atrocities in Srebrenica in July 1995, the US-brokered Dayton peace accords, and the assumption by NATO, led by the US, of responsibility for implementing the accords – underscored European military and therefore political subordination to Washington, even for contingencies within Europe itself.[25]

The 1999 Kosovo war, launched under NATO mandate, reinforced these lessons by demonstrating, as had the 1991 Gulf War, the wide and growing gap between US and European military capacities. In Kosovo, the US flew two-thirds of all strike missions, identified the vast majority of targets, and launched nearly every precision-guided missile.[26] For Americans, the cumbersome decision-making processes produced a growing sense that going it alone was preferable to conducting "war by committee" with allies who contributed relatively little to the military mission. For their part, Europeans saw that American military dominance translated into American dominance in political decision-making as well. Thus were European military capabilities bound up with the aspiration to greater autonomy in foreign and security policy.

In December 1998, British prime minister Tony Blair had joined French president Chirac in issuing the St. Malo declaration, asserting the EU's need to develop "the capacity for autonomous action, backed up by credible military forces, the means to decide to use them, and readiness to do so, in order to respond to international crises."[27] The following June, the European Council endorsed the principles of St. Malo but asked "how much capability the EU needs to possess independently from NATO" in order to fulfill these goals. The Council answered the question six months later in Helsinki, where it proclaimed a European Security and Defence Policy (ESDP) as the successor to the NATO-based ESDI, and established the Helsinki Headline Goals – 60,000 troops capable of deploying within 60 days and sustainable for up to a year.[28] Their missions, as foreseen in the EU Treaty of Amsterdam, would include humanitarian and rescue tasks, peacekeeping, and crisis management, including peacemaking. At the 2001 Laeken summit, the EU announced a European Rapid Reaction Force (RRF) as the partial fulfillment of the Headline Goals, at the same time acknowledging that the RRF was not yet capable of taking on peacemaking and crisis management tasks – i.e. missions at the high end of the Petersberg scale.[29]

Growing Divergence

NATO, meanwhile, was embarked on a similar process of adapting to the new security environment. At the 1999 Washington summit held on its 50th anniversary, NATO brought in three new members – Poland, the Czech Republic, and Hungary – and announced a membership action plan to facilitate further eastward enlargement.[30] Allies also agreed in principle on a highly ambitious "defence capabilities initiative" designed to begin closing the wide gap between US and European military capabilities, but without any realistic appraisal of the higher priority Europeans were likely to attach to the EU's more modest Helsinki Headline Goals. Indeed, the much-discussed "capabilities gap" was at base a "missions gap," because European NATO members were not likely to commit the huge resources necessary to develop high-end military capabilities they had no intention of using.

The growing divergence over NATO's future role was manifest in negotiations towards NATO's 1999 Strategic Concept. Indeed, many of the disputes that surfaced were the same as those that had been with NATO at the creation: the geographic scope of NATO operations, how far NATO's mandate should extend to nontraditional security challenges (in this case, terrorism and proliferation of weapons of mass destruction), the automaticity of the commitment to collective defense, and the relationship between NATO and the United Nations. The strategic concept addressed some of these, papering over differences along the way, but it failed to chart a clear course for the future of transatlantic relations.[31] The American warning that NATO must go "out of area or out of business" turned this challenge into an existential one – a self-imposed litmus test for the very survival of the alliance. One had to wonder about the vitality of an alliance that seemed to face an existential crisis with every new decision.

Because of the amount of political capital and negotiating time required to bring seven new members into the alliance in 2004,[32] the process of NATO enlargement served to mask a growing transatlantic divergence, while at the same time diverting attention from other issues on the transatlantic security agenda. It also served to alienate Russia, Ukraine, and other states of the former Soviet Union, which saw their erstwhile client states joining a formerly adversarial security institution that seemed permanently closed to them. As a consequence, NATO enlargement raised as many questions as it answered about the future of European and transatlantic security.[33] Allied leaders repeatedly proclaimed, with apparent sincerity, that they did not want to draw "new dividing lines in Europe," but the process of NATO enlargement seemed, from Russia's perspective, to be doing precisely that.

EU enlargement proceeded somewhat more slowly at the beginning, owing to policy disputes among EU governments as well as the inherent complexity of the accession process, but soon caught up. The false starts at the Amsterdam and Nice summits (of 1997 and 2000) led finally to the December 2002 decision of the European Council in Copenhagen to admit eight new members from central and eastern Europe, along with Cyprus and Malta, effective from May 1, 2004.[34] Moreover, having moved from 12 members at the end of the Cold War to 15 in 1995,[35] to 25 in 2004 (with Bulgaria and Romania joining in 2007, to bring the total to 27), the EU faced new challenges of streamlining the increasingly cumbersome system of collective decision-making and trying to articulate a vision of the European future. These constituted the mandate of the "Convention on the Future of Europe," or European Convention, launched at the Laeken European Council in December 2001.

Europe was similarly riveted on the challenge of completing the Maastricht commitment to Economic and Monetary Union (EMU), a project whose genesis actually preceded the end of the Cold War. Spurred by a series of Franco-German initiatives in the 1990s, negotiations within the EU led – to the surprise of the many Euroskeptics in the United States (and the UK) – to the creation of EMU in 1999, and the simultaneous adoption by nine EU member countries of the euro as a common currency, which entered into circulation at the beginning of 2002. By 2007, a total of 15 countries had joined the eurozone, and the euro had surpassed the US dollar as the currency with the highest combined value of cash in circulation in the world.

These two huge achievements – EU enlargement and EMU – gave lie to the supposed incompatibility of "widening" and "deepening," but they also meant that the EU agenda was confined almost entirely to Europe itself rather than to the new security challenges beyond. The complaint sometimes heard in Washington that European perspectives were "parochial" betrayed a poor understanding of the enormity of what the EU had actually done since the end of the Cold War, but it reflected the extent to which the American agenda had moved away from Europe towards new global challenges and the growing weight of Asia, especially China, in US thinking.

European and American security perspectives were diverging steadily in the mid- to late 1990s, yet because there was no issue or conflict to bring these differences to a head, they tended to be obscured by the sugarcoated rhetoric of NATO and US–EU communiqués. All that changed one bright September morning in 2001.

Transatlantic Relations after 9/11

During the Cold War it was always assumed that if the collective defense commitment in Article 5 of the North Atlantic Treaty were ever invoked, it would entail America's rising to the defense of Europe after an attack on European territory. Yet the first time Article 5 was invoked, the roles were reversed: it was the European allies who rose to offer "all necessary aid" to the United States after the terrorist attacks of September 11, 2001. Despite the decision of the US administration of George W. Bush to bypass NATO's offer in favor of unilateral American action, Europeans were likewise fully supportive of the US-led invasion of Afghanistan to expel the Taliban regime and go after the Al Qaeda terrorists who had enjoyed its protection.

The instinctive and immediate European expressions of solidarity with the United States after 9/11 may have revealed the depth of the ties across the Atlantic, but they did not translate into a shared perspective on the threat posed by international terrorism. Nor did this new challenge replace the Soviet threat as the glue holding the transatlantic community together. To the contrary: while Europeans saw this new challenge as a more virulent form of a threat they had experienced already, the Bush administration proclaimed a "global war on terror." As the Italian novelist Umberto Eco later put it, "If two airplanes had crashed into Notre Dame or Big Ben, the reaction obviously would have been one of fear, pain, indignation, but it would not have [produced] the instinct to take immediate, unavoidable action that gripped the Americans."[36] What Europeans for the most part saw as a dangerous but manageable threat, to be treated as a matter of domestic security and law enforcement, Americans tended to see (one might say were *led* to see) as an existential threat on a scale approaching that of the early Cold War. Thus 9/11 served more to divide than to unite Americans and Europeans.

There were, of course, other divisive issues, notably the conspicuous US withdrawals from the International Criminal Court and the Kyoto Protocol on climate change in the first few months of the Bush presidency. To Europeans, embarked on the most ambitious effort towards multilateral integration in human history, such acts seemed to demonstrate a growing American unilateralism and disregard for global institutions, including those binding the transatlantic alliance. European public as well as elite attitudes towards the United States deteriorated alarmingly, reflecting differences over basic values as well as about specific policies. But it was the transatlantic clash over Iraq in 2002–2003 that brought these differences to a head.

Even before the dust had settled in Afghanistan, and with only an improvised, poorly designed stabilization plan in place, the Bush administration began building a case for war against Iraq, ostensibly on grounds that Iraq's WMD (weapons of mass destruction) programs and alleged ties to terrorists called for immediate action. For their part, the French insisted that "no military action can be conducted without a decision of the Security Council,"[37] subsequently lobbying to prevent adoption of just such an authorizing resolution. German chancellor Gerhard Schroeder went further, declaring that Germany would not provide material support for a war in Iraq even with Security Council endorsement. Within the United States, former US national security adviser Brent Scowcroft warned against ignoring "a virtual consensus in the world against such an attack."[38] The administration pressed ahead despite this opposition, following Vice President Dick Cheney's admonition that "the risks of inaction are far greater than the risk of action."[39] Thus when the United States and a "coalition of the willing" invaded Iraq in March 2003, it did so without the backing of many of its closest European allies.

The unprecedented breakdown of US–European solidarity over such a seminal security issue produced shock waves on both sides of the Atlantic. In the immediate aftermath of the invasion, the philosophers Jürgen Habermas and Jacques Derrida, odd political bedfellows indeed, issued joint editorials in Germany's *Frankfurter Allgemeine Zeitung* and France's *La Libération*, calling for a united European response "to counterbalance the hegemonic unilateralism of the United States."[40] Other commentators proclaimed it the "end of the West."[41] Yet differences over Iraq policy were only the proximate cause of a longer-term erosion of transatlantic solidarity, as has been discussed. Iraq simply brought these underlying differences into full view. If the breakdown had not occurred over Iraq, it would have occurred over something else.[42]

Relations improved in the second Bush term, beginning in 2005, and with the elections of Angela Merkel as German chancellor and Nicolas Sarkozy as French president, as leaders on both sides came to realize the need to put an end to mutual recriminations over Iraq and restore more civil working relations. Additionally, the US presidential elections of 2008 and the end of the Bush presidency promise to usher in a new and more hopeful chapter in transatlantic relations. Whether these changes in tone and leadership will translate into policy convergence was another matter, however.

While US attention was riveted on Iraq and international terrorism, Europeans were increasingly focused on intra-European challenges: enlargement, Economic and Monetary Union, and the constitutional debacle after the failed French and Dutch referenda on the European constitutional treaty in 2005. It was not so much that US and European leaders disagreed as that they diverged, each side focused on its own set of priorities, without the galvanizing element of an external threat to compel them to find common cause.

After the terrorist attacks of 9/11, some commentators contrasted American fixation on that date with the greater importance Europeans attached to 11/9 – i.e. the collapse of the Cold War order symbolized by the fall of the Berlin Wall on November 9, 1989. Yet this was only part of the story, for there were equally profound global changes underway that were only indirectly related to the East–West conflict or the process of European integration. The accelerating process of globalization was rendering obsolete the old categories – east–west, north–south, developed–underdeveloped, aligned–nonaligned – that had helped define the transatlantic relationship.[43] Finally, the rise of China, India, and other new powers was shifting the global balance away from the US–European partnership, no matter how doggedly political leaders on both sides of the Atlantic continued to assert their primacy.

All these changes added up to a period of flux in world affairs more profound that at any time since the creation of the Western alliance system in the late 1940s. The question for American and European statesmen was whether that alliance, which had served both sides so well in the last half of the twentieth century, could be refashioned to be as relevant to the challenges of the twenty-first.

A New Atlanticism?

The advent of new leaders in Germany, Great Britain, France, and, above all, the United States offered opportunities to strike a new transatlantic bargain, but the challenge was not only about changes of personalities and policies. Opinion surveys conducted early in the new century revealed a growing estrangement between European and American publics. In almost every European country, favorable attitudes towards the United States dropped by between 20 and 30 percentage points between 2002 and 2007.[44] These declines tracked also with measures of diminishing European support for the desirability of US global leadership, for committing additional troops to Afghanistan, and for the US-led war on terror (although Europeans were almost equally concerned with the threat of terrorism). The reasons Europeans overwhelmingly gave for the decline in US–European relations were the US-led invasion and occupation of Iraq, US failure to consider the interests of other countries, and President George W. Bush personally.[45]

European attitudes were obviously driven by what Europeans widely perceived as the assertive unilateralism and militarism of the George W. Bush administration; whether they reflected a temporary shift or something more durable and worrying was a matter of debate.[46] On the one hand, European and American differences over the use of force in international relations, although exacerbated by the Iraq debacle, seemed to reflect a deeper and more durable division that was reflected also in declining support for NATO. On the other hand, the evidence that Europeans continued to hold much more positive attitudes towards Americans than towards US policies, and that, excepting France, they continued to favor addressing threats in partnership with the United States, suggested the possibility of improved transatlantic relations after the 2008 US presidential elections.[47]

However one interpreted these findings, they clearly suggested that fashioning a new Atlanticism would demand more than a nostalgic invocation of the past. As David Gompert put it,

> The old Euro-Atlantic order was based on conditions that no longer exist: US–Allied military interdependence, agreement on the use of force, and a presumption that allies would stand together in crises. Analytically, therefore, the pre-Iraq alliance is not the right point of departure for considering a possible new Euro-Atlantic order. Nor is it wise to proceed from some received wisdom that a close US–European relationship is essential. That intellectual shortcut bypasses the crucial question of how US and European interests match up now and looking to the future.[48]

A "compact" signed by prominent policy-makers and academics on both sides of the Atlantic offered a similar argument: "The Partnership between Europe and the United States must endure, not because of what it achieved in the past, but because our common future depends on it . . . Europe needs America . . . America also needs Europe."[49]

In the same vein, Geir Lundestad called for a "true redefinition of the American–European relationship."[50] But what should be the elements of that new relationship?

To begin with, it was an inescapable reality that almost all the new challenges lay outside the traditional NATO area and many were in areas where US and European approaches had long diverged. Thus it would be too much to ask of the "new Atlanticism" that there be US–European convergence on every such issue. On some, such as engagement with China, agreement was neither likely nor necessary, so long as there was a forum for reconciling issues like arms sales. On others, like the Middle East peace process, US–European differences (as well as intra-European differences) were long-standing and unlikely to change appreciably.

But on many issues, US–European strategic convergence seemed both possible and necessary. These included such immediate security challenges as counterterrorism, Iraq, Afghanistan, and Iran, as well as medium-term issues of energy security and regional stability in the European "near abroad." More broadly, they included issues of global governance related to the Doha trade round, post-Kyoto environmental cooperation, and the refashioning of international institutions to reflect the emerging distribution of global power and influence.

Since 9/11, counterterrorist cooperation had been good, but it was chiefly bilateral and sectoral (i.e. intelligence-sharing, financial tracking, etc.). Over the longer term, given the likelihood that this would be a generational challenge, it would be imperative to develop a shared strategic perspective on how to meet this challenge. The beginnings of such a convergence were dimly visible: if Americans (for understandable reasons) may have overreacted to the attacks of 9/11, Europeans may have underreacted. After the Madrid and London bombings, European publics became more aware of the challenge within their own societies, even as Americans had come to see that the Bush administration's overmilitarized approach had made their country less secure than before. Similarly, as US forces in Iraq began draw down and transfer responsibility to Iraqi authorities, there would be new opportunities to fashion a US–European consensus going forward. This would not mean a US–European meeting of the minds – surely unfeasible, given all that had transpired – but a generally shared political and diplomatic effort to avert destabilization of the wider region. On Iraq as well as other regional issues, most critically Iran and Afghanistan, the essential requirement would be to develop an ongoing transatlantic dialogue as intense as that which characterized the Cold War alliance.

Some argued for a transatlantic division of labor between US "hard" power and European "soft" power, while others contended that Europe needs to close the gap between their military capabilities and those of the United States so that allies can operate together in every contingency.[51] Although the latter argument offered a sounder basis for US–European security cooperation, neither of these formulas could substitute for the development of a shared security perspective. In other words, closing the "missions gap" took logical precedence over closing the "capabilities gap."

One major liability in the transatlantic relationship was the lack of an adequate forum for strategic dialogue. It did not happen in NATO, where the scope of discussion was constrained by the unwillingness of many European countries to submit to NATO's strategic primacy, and the unwillingness of the United States to countenance an "EU caucus" in NATO. Nor did it occur in the US–EU framework, where meetings were too infrequent and formalized to permit the ongoing strategic dialogue that was needed. Of course, the EU itself had trouble enough with an *intra*-EU dialogue, with the result that there was really no place where all of Europe plus the United States could meet to discuss big strategic issues. The consequences were profound, because even issues closer to home – dealing with Russia, managing energy security, bringing Turkey into the EU – never were accorded the sustained transatlantic engagement that was once routine on major security issues.

To fill this need, Weidenfeld proposed creation of "Euro-Atlantic Political Cooperation" as a forum for dialogue;[52] other formulas, such as enhanced NATO–EU cooperation, were also advanced. The precise form was less important than the shared commitment to dialogue, unencumbered by institutional turf warfare.

The same dangers and opportunities presented themselves on the global stage. International institutions were in crisis, owing to the challenges of globalization, the intractability of transnational threats, and the imperative of integrating rising powers into an effective global order. Whether the UN system, the international financial institutions, the World Trade Organization, and the G7/G8 could be transformed successfully was an open question, but it seemed clear that this could happen only if the United States and Europe exercised leadership and mustered the imagination to open these institutions to new actors while preserving the essential values undergirding the global system.

Since the end of the Cold War, it had been a popular rallying cry of political leaders and pundits on both sides of the Atlantic to assert that on almost every issue of the day Americans and Europeans would be better off working together than working separately. It was an inspiring thought, and may even have been true, but the years since the collapse of the old order had shown that just because Americans and Europeans *should* act together in this new era did not necessarily mean that they *would* do so.

Notes

1 "We have no eternal allies and we have no perpetual enemies. Our interests are eternal and perpetual, and those interests it is our duty to follow." (House of Commons, March 1, 1848.)

2 See, e.g., Mearsheimer, "Back to the Future"; Waltz, "The Emerging Structure of International Politics"; Hassner, "Europe beyond Partition and Unity"; Walt, "The Ties that Fray." For a review of realist and other theoretical constructs as they apply to US–European relations after the Cold War, see Matthias Dembinski, "Still Hanging Together?" in Evangelista and Parsi, *Partners or Rivals?* 61–83.

3 Kagan, "Power and Weakness," 5.

4 Lundestad, *The United States and Western Europe*, 249 ff.; Ikenberry, *After Victory*, 249–255.

5 Wendt, "Anarchy is What States Make of It"; Kupchan, "Reviving the West"; Keohane, Nye, and Hoffmann, *After the Cold War*, 34 ff.

6 Hutchings, *American Diplomacy*, 343.

7 For background, see Brimmer, "Seeing Blue."

8 See e.g. Gorbachev's proposal for an "All-European Security Council" in his address to the Paris summit of the CSCE, November 19–21, 1990, and various suggestions in a similar vein by Czechoslovak president Vaclav Havel, Polish prime minister Tadeusz Mazowiecki, and Czechoslovak foreign minister Jiři Dienstbier, as summarized in Hutchings, *American Diplomacy*, 283–287.

9 "Toward a New World Order," Address by President Bush before a Joint Session of the Congress, September 11, 1990, Current Policy no. 1298, Bureau of Public Affairs, US Department of State.

10 "Remarks by the President to the Czechoslovak Federal Assembly," November 17, 1990, White House press release of that day.

11 See e.g. President Bush's intervention at the NATO summit in London, July 5, 1990; declassified May 25, 1999; case no. 98–0142-F.

12 "Remarks by the President at Luncheon Hosted by Prime Minister [Ruud] Lubbers," Binnenhof, The Hague, the Netherlands, November 9, 1991, Office of the Press Secretary, The White House.

13 "Declaration on US–EC Relations," November 23, 1990.

14 This rethinking on the French side was driven in part by lessons taken away from the experience of the Gulf War of 1990–1991. See e.g. "French–US Relations Blossom amid Desert Storm," *Washington Post*, February 26, 1991.

15 The idea of France's rejoining the military command resurfaced in December 1995, when Mitterrand's successor, Jacques Chirac, announced France's rapprochement with NATO's military institutions. See Tiersky, "A Likely Story." This initiative, too, failed to materialize, for essentially the same reasons as in 1991.

16 Jacques Delors, "European Integration and Security," Alastair Buchan Memorial Lecture, International Institute for Strategic Studies, London, March 7, 1991.

17 This was the "Bartholomew message," so dubbed because it happened to be signed out by Under Secretary of State Reginald Bartholomew in the absence of both Secretary Baker and Deputy Secretary Lawrence Eagleburger.

18 "A Time of Decision for the NATO Alliance," Intervention at the NATO summit, Rome, Italy, November 7, 1991, US State Department *Dispatch*, November 11, 1991.

19 Treaty on European Union, Maastricht, 1992.

20 On the French side Frederic Bozo reaches essentially the same conclusion in his *Mitterrand, la fin de la guerre froide et l'unification allemande*, 255–258.

21 For a Clinton administration perspective, see Gardner, *A New Era in US–EU Relations?*

22 Sloan, *NATO, the European Union, and the Atlantic Community*, 91–94.

23 North Atlantic Council declaration, January 11, 1994.

24 North Atlantic Council communiqué, June 3, 1996; Sloan, op. cit., 100–102.

25 Sloan, op. cit., 95–103; Lundestad, op. cit., 250–257.

26 Jean-Yves Haine, "An Historical Perspective," in Gnesotto, *EU Security and Defence Policy*, 39–40.

27 UK Foreign and Commonwealth Office, "Joint Declaration Issued at the British–French Summit."

28 Sloan, op. cit., 185; Keane, "European Security and Defence Policy," 91.

29 Salmon and Shepherd, *Toward a European Army*, 79.

30 The enlargement process was launched at NATO's January 1994 Brussels summit and formalized at the Madrid summit in June 1997.

31 Sloan, op. cit., 107–112.

32 They were: Bulgaria, Estonia, Latvia, Lithuania, Romania, Slovakia, and Slovenia.

33 Kay, *NATO and the Future of European Security*, 89.

34 In addition to Cyprus and Malta, the new members were: the Czech Republic, Estonia, Hungary, Latvia, Lithuania, Poland, Slovakia, and Slovenia. Copenhagen European Council, presidency conclusions, December 12–13, 2002; EU Document SN 400/02.

35 Austria, Finland, and Sweden were admitted in January 1995.

36 *La Repubblica*, May 31, 2003.

37 *New York Times*, August 29, 2002.

38 *Wall Street Journal*, August 15, 2002.

39 *New York Times*, August 27, 2002.

40 May 31, 2003. This article, along with Eco's and others, are translated in Levy et al., *Old Europe, New Europe, Core Europe*.

41 For example, Francis Fukuyama, "Das Ende des Westens," *Die Welt*, September 3, 2002; Charles Kupchan, "The End of the West," *The Atlantic Online*, November 2002.

42 Hutchings, "The World after Iraq."

43 National Intelligence Council, *Mapping the Global Future*.

44 Pew Global Attitudes, *Global Unease*, 13. (In France, favorable attitudes dropped from 62% to 39%; in Germany, from 60% to 30%; in the UK, from 75% to 51%.) See also Kohut and Stokes, *America against the World*.

45 Pew Global Attitudes, op. cit., 22; German Marshall Fund, *Transatlantic Trends 2007*, esp. 5–6 and 17.

46 *Transatlantic Trends* tended to be more sanguine than Pew about the reversibility of European public attitudes.

47 *Transatlantic Trends*, 7. Interestingly, Americans were more optimistic than Europeans on this point.

48 "What Does America Want of Europe?" in Lindstrom, *Shift or Rift*, 57.

49 Centre for European Reform and the Brookings Institution, "A Compact between the United States and Europe."

50 Lundestad, op. cit., 288.

51 Moravcsik, "New Transatlantic Bargain"; Gompert et al., *Mind the Gap*.

52 Partners at Odds, 137.

Bibliography

Bozo, Frederic, *Mitterrand, la fin de la guerre froide et l'unification allemande: De Yalta à Maastricht* (Paris: Odile Jacob, 2005).

Brimmer, Esther, "Seeing Blue: American Visions of the European Union,", *Chaillot Papers* 105 (2007).

Centre for European Reform and the Brookings Institution, "A Compact between the United States and Europe" (2005).

Cooper, Robert, *The Breaking of Nations: Order and Chaos in the Twenty-First Century* (Toronto: McClelland and Steward, 2005).

Delors, Jacques, "European Integration and Security," Alastair Buchan Memorial Lecture, International Institute for Strategic Studies, London, March 7, 1991.

Evangelista, Matthew and Vittorio Emanuele Parsi (eds.), *Partners or Rivals? European–American Relations after Iraq* (Milan: Vita e Pensiero, 2005).

Everts, Steven, et al., *A European Way of War* (London: Centre for European Reform, 2004).

Gardner, Anthony L., *A New Era in US–EU Relations? The Clinton Administration and the New Transatlantic Agenda* (Avebury, 1997).

German Marshall Fund of the United States, Washington, D.C., *Transatlantic Trends 2007*.

Gnesotto, Nicole (ed.), *EU Security and Defence Policy: The First Five Years* (Paris: EU Institute for Security Studies, 2004).

Goldgeier, James M., *Not Whether but When: The US Decision to Enlarge NATO* (Washington: Brookings Institution, 1999).

Gompert, David C., Richard L. Kugler, and Martin C. Libicki, *Mind the Gap: Promoting a Transatlantic Revolution in Military Affairs* (Washington: National Defense University Press, 1999).

Haftendorn, Helga, Georges-Henri Soutou, Stephen F. Szabo, and Samuel F. Wells Jr., *The Strategic Triangle: France, Germany, and the United States in the Shaping of the New Europe* (Washington: Woodrow Wilson Center Press, 2007).

Hassner, Pierre, "Europe beyond Partition and Unity: Disintegration or Reconstitution?" *International Affairs* 66, no. 3, July 1990, 461–475.

Hunter, Robert E., The European Security and Defense Policy: NATO's Companion – or Competitor? (Santa Rouica, CA: Rand Corporation, 2002).

Hutchings, Robert L., *American Diplomacy and the End of the Cold War: An Insider's Account of US Policy in Europe, 1989–92* (Baltimore: Johns Hopkins University Press, 1997).

Hutchings, Robert L., *Permanent Alliance? NATO's Prague Summit and Beyond* (Washington: Atlantic Council of the United States, 2001).

Hutchings, Robert L., "The World after Iraq," Calvin M. Logue, Lynn M. Messina and Jean De Hart (eds), *Representative American Speeches, 2003–2004* (New York: H.W. Wilson, 2005).

Ikenberry, G. John, *After Victory: Institutions, Strategic Restraint, and the Rebuilding of Order after Major Wars* (Princeton and Oxford: Princeton University Press, 2001).

James, Harold, *The Roman Predicament: How the Rules of International Order Create the Politics of Empire* (Princeton and Oxford: Princeton University Press, 2006).

Kagan, Robert, "Power and Weakness: Why the US and Europe See the World Differently," *Policy Review*, no. 113, June–July 2002, 5–23.

Kay, Sean, *NATO and the Future of European Security* (New York and London: Rowman & Littlefield, 1998).

Keane, Rory, "European Security and Defence Policy," *Global Society* 19, no. 1, 2005, 128–143.

Kennedy, Paul, *The Rise and Fall of the Great Powers: Economic Change and Military Conflict from 1500–2000* (New York: Random House, 1987).

Keohane, Robert, Joseph Nye, and Stanley Hoffmann (eds.), *After the Cold War: International Institutions and State Strategies in Europe, 1989–91* (Cambridge, MA: Harvard University Press, 1993).

Kohut, Andrew and Bruce Stokes, *America against the World: How We Are Different and Why We Are Disliked* (New York: Time Books, 2006).

Kupchan, Charles, "Reviving the West: For an Atlantic Union," *Foreign Affairs* 75, no. 3, May/June 1996, 92–103.

Kupchan, Charles (ed.), *Atlantic Security: Competing Visions* (New York: Council on Foreign Relations, 1998).

Larres, Klaus (ed.), *Germany since Unification: The Development of the Berlin Republic*, 2nd edition (London and New York: Palgrave, 2001).

Levy, Daniel, Max Pensky, and John Torpey, *Old Europe, New Europe, Core Europe: Transatlantic Relations after the Iraq War* (London and New York: Verso, 2005).

Lind, Michael, *The American Way of Strategy: US Foreign Policy and the American Way of Life* (Oxford and New York: Oxford University Press, 2006).

Lindstrom, Gustav (ed.), *Shift or Rift: Assessing US–EU relations after Iraq* (Paris: EU Institute for Security Studies, 2003).

Lundestad, Geir, *The United States and Western Europe since 1945* (Oxford: Oxford University Press, 2003).

Mead, Walter Russell, *Special Providence: American Foreign Policy and How It Changed the World* (New York and London: Routledge, 2002).

Mearsheimer, John, "Back to the Future: Instability of Europe after the Cold War," *International Security* 15, Summer 1990, 5–57.

Mearsheimer, John, *The Tragedy of Great Power Politics* (New York: Norton, 2001).

Moravcsik, Andrew, *The Choice for Europe: Social Purpose and State Power from Messina to Maastricht* (Ithaca, NY: Cornell University Press, 1998).

Moravcsik, Andrew, "Striking a New Transatlantic Bargain," *Foreign Affairs*, 82, no. 4, July–August 2003, 74–89.

Mottola, Kari (ed.), *Transatlantic Relations and Global Governance* (Washington: Center for Transatlantic Relations, 2006).

National Intelligence Council, *Mapping the Global Future* (Washington, DC: US Government Printing Office, 2004).

Pew Global Attitudes Project, *Global Unease with Major World Powers* (Washington: Pew Research Center, 2007).

Posen, Barry, "European Union Security and Defense Policy: Response to Unipolarity?" *Security Studies* 15, no. 2, April–June 2006, 149–186.

Rifkin, Jeremy, *The European Dream: How Europe's Vision of the Future is Quietly Eclipsing the American Dream* (Cambridge: Polity Press, 2004).

Salmon, Trevor C. and Alistair J.K. Shepherd, *Toward a European Army: A Military Power in the Making?* (London: Lynne Reiner Publishers, 2003).

Sloan, Stanley, *NATO, the European Union, and the Atlantic Community: The Transatlantic Bargain Challenged* (Lanham, MD: Rowman & Littlefield, 2005).

Tiersky, Ronald, "A Likely Story: Chirac, France-NATO, European Security, and American Hegemony," *French Politics and Society* 14, no. 2, Spring 1996, 1–8.

Walt, Stephen, "The Ties that Fray: Why Europe and America are Drifting Apart," *National Interest*, no. 54, Winter 1998/1999, 3–11.

Waltz, Kenneth, "The Emerging Structure of International Politics," *International Security* 18, Fall 1993, 44–79.

Weidenfeld, Werner, *Partners at Odds: The Future of Transatlantic Relations – Options for a New Beginning* (Gütersloh: Verlag Bertelsmann Stiftung, 2006).

Wendt, Alexander, "Anarchy is What States Make of It: The Social Construction of Power Politics," *International Organization* 46, no. 2, 1992, 391–426.

Zaborowski, Marcin (ed.), *Friends Again? EU–US Relations after the Crisis* (Paris: EU Institute for Security Studies 2006).

Further Reading

There is of course an enormous body of material on US–European relations since the end of the Cold War. On the broad sweep of European and transatlantic relations, see Tony Judt's *Postwar* (New York: Penguin Books, 2005), Geir Lundestad's *The United States and Western Europe since 1945* (Oxford: Oxford University Press, 2003), Harold James's *Europe Reborn* (Harlow, UK: Pearson Longman, 2003), David Calleo's *Rethinking Europe's Future* (Princeton, NJ: Princeton University Press, 2003), Timothy Garton Ash's *Free World* (New York: Random House, 2004), and, on NATO specifically, Sean Kay's *NATO and the Future of European Security* and Stanley Sloan's *NATO, the EU, and the Atlantic Community* (Lanham, MD: Rowman & Littlefield, 1998). (The burgeoning literature on the European Union is beyond the scope of this short essay, but Andrew Moravcsik's *The Choice for Europe* (Ithaca, NY: Cornell University Press, 1988) merits singling out.)

The following four books offer contrasting applications of international-relations theory to post-Cold War transatlantic relations: John Ikenberry's *After Victory* (Princeton, NJ: Princeton University Press, 2001), John Mearsheimer's *The Tragedy of Great Power Politics* (New York: W.W. Norton & Co., 2001), Michael Lind's *The American Way of Strategy* (Oxford: Oxford University Press, 2006), and *After the Cold War* (Cambridge, MA: Harvard University Press, 1993), edited by Robert Keohane, Joseph Nye, and Stanley Hoffmann.

On the lively debate between the America-firsters and Euro-enthusiasts, see especially Robert Kagan's *Of Paradise and Power* (New York: Alfred A. Knopf, 2003), Joseph Nye's *Bound to Lead* (New York: Basic Books, 1991), Robert Lieber's *The American Era* (Cambridge: Cambridge University Press, 2007), Robert Cooper's *The Breaking of Nations* (London: Atlantic Books, 2003), Mark Leonard's *Why Europe Will Run the 21st Century* (New York: Public Affairs, 2005), and Jeremy Rifkin's *The European Dream* (New York: Penguin Books, 2004).

Finally, of the volumes dealing with the most recent past (and prospective future) of US–European relations, see in particular Werner Weidenfeld's *Partners at Odds* (Gütersloh: Bertelsmann Stiftung, 2006); David Andrews (ed.), *The Atlantic Alliance under Stress* (Cambridge: Cambridge University Press, 2005); Kari Möttölä (ed.), *Transatlantic Relations and Global Governance* (Washington, DC: Center for Transatlantic Relations, 2006); Marcin Zaborowski (ed.), *Friends Again? EU–US Relations after the crisis* (Paris: European Union Institute for Security Studies, 2006); Gustav Lindstrom (ed.) *Shift or Rift: Assessing US–EU Relations after Iraq* (Paris: European Union Institute for Security Studies, 2003); and Matthew Evangelista and Vittorio Emanuele Parsi (eds.), *Partners or Rivals? European–American Relations after Iraq* (Milan: Vita a Pensiero, 2005).

Chapter Twelve

Europe and Economic Globalization since 1945

Alfred E. Eckes Jr.

During the long Cold War demonstrators frequently took to the streets to protest atomic weapons and the dangers of nuclear war. With the collapse of the Soviet Union that concern faded, but globalization emerged as the next hot-button issue to ignite widespread political protests. Protests began in Europe with attacks on McDonald's restaurants in August 1999. A few months later, the protests spread to Seattle, where thousands of demonstrators marched, smashed storefront windows, and disrupted a ministerial of the World Trade Organization (WTO). Quickly, the antiglobalization protests ricocheted around the planet to intergovernmental summits, meetings of international agencies, and top-level business conferences. Over time new issues, such as the war in Iraq, would occupy the protestors. But public opinion polls indicate continuing widespread unease about globalization in most high-income countries. A BBC poll, released in 2008, showed an average of 56% in six western European countries (France, Germany, Italy, Portugal, Spain, and the United Kingdom) saying that economic globalization is growing too quickly.[1]

So what is globalization and why has it become so controversial to many ordinary people, but an irreversible new reality to most business and government leaders? In a modern setting globalization can be viewed broadly as a dynamic, synergistic process which over time integrates people and nations into larger structures and communities, as it dissolves traditional barriers. At the core of this process are international trade and investments. Corporations, headquartered and managed in one country, invest abroad, producing goods and services in distant locations for both local and world markets. Facing unrelenting competitive pressures, transnational firms increasingly shift factories to countries with low-cost labor and business-friendly environmental and regulatory policies.[2]

Among the critical long-term drivers of this globalization process are innovations in technology transportation, communications, and information-processing which have dramatically cut the costs and obstacles to international business. Also vital are national government policies supporting open markets and freer trade. Because the complex process involves a number of dynamic variables, some of them relatively

A Companion to Europe since 1945, First Edition. Edited by Klaus Larres.
© 2014 John Wiley & Sons, Ltd. Published 2014 by John Wiley & Sons, Ltd.

new, such as the Internet, there are few reliable statistical measures which capture the expansion of cross-border activities over an extended period of time. Some of the better indicators involve trade and foreign direct investments (FDI), and this essay will make extensive use of that data for the period since 1950, as it focuses on economic aspects of European globalization.[3]

The word globalization is new. Futurist John Naisbitt may have been the first to use it his 1982 book *Megatrends*, but Harvard Business School professor Theodore Levitt offered the first academic analysis, emphasizing business aspects.[4] By the end of the decade, a term first employed to describe business strategies had expanded to cover many other types of linkage, including culture, communications, and politics. Scholars in dozens of disciplines debated the origins, nature, or consequences of this phenomenon.

Europe and Globalization before 1945

In public discussions and demonstrations, many who criticize globalization associate it with rapacious capitalism, powerful transnational corporations, and American corporate and government power (cowboy capitalism and hegemony). French parliamentarian and author Jean-Jacques Servan-Schreiber did the same in 1967, when he published a book, *The American Challenge*. He warned that better-organized American companies were rolling from Naples to Amsterdam with the ease of Israeli tanks in Sinai during the 1967 war. Europe might lose its economic identity, Servan-Schreiber feared, and become a US subsidiary.

Critics of globalization sometimes forget that for centuries Europeans drove the globalization process. Before America achieved independence and emerged as a major power, European innovations and ideas integrated people and regions, overcoming barriers of time, distance, and lack of information. European ideas (individual rights, the rule of law, the efficacy of markets), institutions (democratically elected parliaments, independent judiciaries, professional civil services), capital (portfolio and direct), goods (including services), and people flowed to other regions of the world, integrating people and transforming relationships. From the Middle Ages European traders and explorers roamed the Mediterranean world, looking for precious metals and tradable goods. In the late fifteenth and early sixteenth centuries improvements in navigation enabled them to explore Africa, the Americas, and even the vast Pacific region. The explorations of Christopher Columbus to the Americas and Ferdinand Magellan in the Pacific were among the most significant of these early globalization initiatives.[5]

Thanks to the Industrial Revolution, and spread of laissez-faire economic ideas, the pace of European-led globalization accelerated during the nineteenth century. British inventors developed the steam engine, the basis of steam-powered shipping and railroads, and British business and political leaders seized opportunities in cable and wireless to create global communications networks, centered on London. After repeal of the Corn Laws in 1846, and Parliament's decision to remove tariffs on almost all imports, Britain became the center of world commerce and shipping. The City of London dominated global finance, and managed the international gold standard. British investors sent a large portion of their wealth overseas to build railroads and electrify developing countries. On a smaller scale, the thrifty Dutch matched the commercial and financial prowess of the British. And all of the major European powers competed for empire, exporting their systems of government, laws, and business enterprise to far corners of the world, and integrating colonial areas of Africa, Asia, and Latin America into their empires.[6]

"Europe has long . . . been the world's leading global investing and trading region," observed John Dunning, a British economist specializing in foreign direct investment. Until the nineteenth century, "most European trade and investment continued to be intra-regional, and conducted by small or relatively small family enterprises". Then the UK emerged as a major player "with its extra-European trade and investment considerably exceeding . . . its intra-European equivalent". By 1914 there were hundreds of British multinational firms operating factories in western Europe, North America, and other areas of the empire. The British were not alone. The Dutch, French, Germans, Swiss, Swedes, and others had major foreign investments. In 1914 outward FDI of European firms accounted for 76.9% of the world's FDI stock, valued at $14.5 billion. Continental western Europe had 31.4%, while the United Kingdom had 45.5%. The technologically advanced German electronics and chemical industries had significant overseas investments in 1914, and Germany accounted for about 10.5% of the world stock. The US held another 18.5%. On the eve of World War II, Europe was still the world's leader, accounting in 1938 for nearly 64% of the stock of foreign direct investment. This included 24.1% for continental western Europe, 39.8% for the UK. The United States had another 27.7%, its share up significantly from before World War I. Dunning estimates that 90% of European FDI was invested outside Europe, reflecting the appeal of global opportunities rather than the attraction of European regionalism.[7]

The evolving pattern of international trade before World War II demonstrates in another way how European commerce drove globalization. During the seventeenth, eighteenth, and nineteenth centuries Britain, France, Belgium, and the Netherlands established formal overseas commercial empires, some of them based on political control of dependent areas (such as India, Malaya, Hong Kong, and Singapore in the case of the British), large areas of west and north Africa in the case of France, the mineral-rich Congo for Belgium, and the Dutch East Indies (modern-day Indonesia) for the Netherlands, among others. Britain and some of the other European powers used finance and trade to bind other independent areas informally to the industrializing countries of western Europe. As the British case suggests, a substantial share of Europe's trade before 1914 involved exchange of value-added products manufactured in the developed country for precious metals, oil, foodstuffs (such as sugar, coffee, tobacco, wheat, and meat products) or industrial raw materials like cotton and forest products. Before World War I, according to Swiss economic historian Paul Bairoch, 37.2% of Britain's exports went to colonies and self-governing areas. Other continental countries had similar ties to colonial areas. For France the comparable figure was 13%; Portugal, 14.2%; and the Netherlands 5.3%.[8]

Phases of European Economic Globalization after World War II

Despite the devastation and casualties (some 10 million civilian and military casualties in western Europe alone), Europe recovered relatively quickly from World War II, and soon displayed renewed interest in global commercial and financial linkages. Viewed retrospectively, the period since 1945 appears to have three distinct phases. The first one, of European recovery, decolonization, and regional integration, lasted about 25 years from the end of World War II to the early 1970s. During this defensive phase the United States briefly displaced Europe as the leader of the globalization process. But during a second distinct period of approximately twenty years (lasting until approximately 1992) Europe recovered, and on the basis of rising productivity steadily closed the income gap with North America. Soon it was reasserting leadership in commerce and finance. During these years, western Europeans fulfilled plans to create a single market and sought closer economic ties with North America. Finally, with the collapse of communism in eastern Europe and completion of the single-market initiative, a third stage began. It was distinguished by the integration and consolidation of industries along global lines, as transnational corporations came to view the world as a single market for producing and selling goods. As competition intensified, Europe, America, and Japan looked for new ways to cut costs in complex supply chains. They began moving assembly functions, back-office operations, and even research facilities offshore to low labor-cost nations with abundant skilled personnel.

Phase One: World War II to the Mid-1970s

Despite the devastation of World War II, Europe remained a major factor in overseas trade and investments after the war. Initially, old imperial patterns of trade predominated, with raw materials and foodstuffs flowing into Europe, and manufactures leaving for overseas colonies and dependencies. Europe accounted for 33% of world exports in 1950, and 39% of world imports, compared to 21% for North American exports and 20% for imports (see Table 12.1). While Germany, Italy, and the Benelux countries all relied more on European countries for imports and than on developing areas, it is significant that in 1950 Britain and France imported more from developing countries than from the developed nations of western Europe. On the export side the pattern was similar (see Table 12.2).[9]

In finance Europe experienced some erosion in its international investment position during and immediately after World War II. Europe's overall share of world FDI stock declined sharply from prewar levels, reflecting the need for Britain to sell off 25% of its overseas assets to finance the war. Other foreign assets were destroyed during the war (Singapore, Hong Kong), or lost subsequently as the British empire and China disintegrated. Also, there were expropriations in Argentina, Burma, and Iran. Nonetheless, by 1960 Europe still accounted for 42.1% of world foreign direct investment (estimated stock), but this was down sharply from 64% in 1938. Of the 1960 share, the Continent supplied 25.8%, the UK 16.3%.[10]

In the immediate postwar years, European business leaders understandably focused on recovery from World War II and integration of Europe through the common market and the parallel European Free Trade Association (Inner Six and Outer Seven) so as to avoid future wars. This left the United States as the principal exporter of

Table 12.1 Shares of world merchandise trade (imports/exports)

Country	1950	1973	1992	2001
Developed countries	66/61	73/72	71/72	67/64
Belgium/Luxembourg	3/3	4/4	3/3	3/3
Canada	5/5	4/5	3/4	4/4
United States	15/16	12/12	14/12	19/12
Western Europe	39/33	47/45	45/45	37/39
France	5/5	6/6	6/6	5/5
Germany	4/3	9/12	10/11	8/9
Italy	2/2	5/4	5/5	4/4
Japan	2/1	7/6	7/9	6/7
The Netherlands	3/2	5/5	3/4	3/4
Sweden	2/2	2/2	1/1	1/1
Switzerland	2/1	2/2	2/2	1/1
UK	12/10	6/5	6/5	5/4
Developing countries	29/33	18/20	26/26	29/31
Developing Africa	6/5	3/4	2/2	2/2
Developing Asia	10/12	9/10	16/16	21/24

Source: UNCTAD, *Handbook of Statistics*, Report 1.1. Online at http://www.unctad.org/

Table 12.2 Share of imports/exports – 1950

Trade partners

Country 100%	Developed Europe	European Union	US + Canada	Japan	Developing Countries	Developing Africa	Developing E + SE Asia
Belgium/ Luxembourg	50/65	46/60	19/10	0/1	22/19	9/6	3/4
Canada	15/20	15/19	65/62	0/1	12/8	0/0	2/2
France	32/49	28/41	14/5	0/0	39/40	20/29	3/2
Germany	51/68	46/60	17/6	0/0	24/19	7/2	5/4
Italy	35/52	30/45	24/7	0/0	27/27	5/5	3/5
Japan	4/12	4/11	48/25	n/a	37/53	2/4	27/42
The Netherlands	57/71	54/66	12/5	0/0	22/18	3/3	9/8
Sweden	61/66	57/55	9/7	0/0	19/15	1/2	2/2
Switzerland	54/55	54/54	17/15	1/0	20/20	3/2	4/5
UK	27/31	25/27	16/12	0/0	34/31	10/9	8/10
US	15/30	13/28	23/20	2/4	53/39	3/2	12/18

Table 12.2 *Continued*

Share of imports/exports – 1973

Country 100%	Developed Europe	European Union	US + Canada	Japan	Developing Countries	Developing Africa	Developing E + SE Asia
Belgium/ Luxembourg	76/81	74/78	7/6	1/1	12/8	5/3	2/2
Canada	13/14	12/13	69/65	4/7	9/7	1/0	2/3
France	63/68	60/62	9/6	1/1	21/19	8/10	2/2
Germany	64/67	60/60	9/9	2/2	18/14	5/3	3/3
Italy	57/64	54/59	10/10	1/1	25/17	7/6	2/2
Japan	10/17	9/15	29/29	n/a	45/42	3/2	23/27
The Netherlands	68/82	66/79	9/4	1/1	19/9	4/2	3/2
Sweden	75/75	65/62	7/7	2/1	10/10	2/2	2/2
Switzerland	80/62	79/60	7/9	3/4	8/17	2/3	2/5
UK	49/48	43/42	15/15	3/2	22/20	6/5	5/6
US	27/29	25/27	25/21	14/12	30/30	3/2	10/10

Share of imports/exports – 1992

Country 100%	Developed Europe	European Union	US + Canada	Japan	Developing Countries	Developing Africa	Developing E + SE Asia
Belgium	80/81	77/78	5/4	2/1	10/9	3/2	3/4
Canada	12/8	10/7	64/78	7/5	12/8	1/0	7/5
France	66/68	62/64	9/7	40/2	15/18	4/6	6/5
Germany	66/70	60/64	7/7	6/2	15/14	2/2	8/6
Italy	69/67	63/62	6/8	2/2	18/18	6/4	5/5
Japan	16/21	14/20	26/31	n/a	49/45	1/1	32/34
The Netherlands	73/83	70/80	8/4	4/1	13/9	2/2	6/3
Sweden	70/71	60/60	10/10	5/2	11/12	1/1	6/5
Switzerland	79/65	79/65	7/9	4/4	8/17	1/1	4/9
UK	63/63	57/60	12/13	6/2	14/16	1/2	9/7
US	20/25	19/24	18/20	18/11	41/39	2/2	23/16

Share of imports/exports – 2001

Country 100%	Developed Europe	European Union	US + Canada	Japan	Developing Countries	Developing Africa	Developing E + SE Asia
Belgium	72/78	70/76	8/6	3/1	12/10	2/2	7/5
Canada	13/5	11/4	64/88	4/2	16/5	1/0	9/3
France	70/65	65/61	8/10	2/2	15/18	4/5	6/6
Germany	58/60	52/55	9/11	4/2	16/14	1/1	10/7
Italy	61/58	56/54	6/11	2/2	21/20	6/3	7/6
Japan	14/17	13/16	20/32	n/a	58/48	0/1	42/40
The Netherlands	53/81	50/79	10/5	5/1	24/8	2/1	15/4
Sweden	76/60	68/52	6/13	2/3	8/16	0/2	5/8
Switzerland	74/59	74/59	11/12	2/3	9/20	1/1	5/12
UK	52/58	47/54	16/18	4/2	19/14	2/2	13/7
US	21/23	19/22	19/22	11/8	46/42	2/1	25/17

Source: UNCTAD, *Handbook of Statistics*, Report 3.1. Online at http://www.unctad.org/

private capital. Nonetheless, not until the 1970s did private US FDI outflows surpass intergovernmental aid and lending.[11] For about a quarter-century after World War II, the US remained the leading supplier of direct investment to the world. In 1973, for example, the US accounted for 48.1%, Europe 37.5% (24.7% for continental western Europe, 12.8% for the UK).[12] Interestingly, until the 1960s, when the lure of rapid growth and Europeanization attracted American investors, most US direct investment flowed into other western hemisphere countrie's–Latin America or neighboring Canada – where US investors accumulated a large stock, much of it in mining and raw materials.[13]

There had been a distinctive change to that pattern by the mid-1970s. With its high growth, expanding consumer markets, and potential for a large integrated market, western Europe became a target for US investors eager to participate in this prosperity and to establish long-term positions in a big, recovering, high-income markets. They focused on opportunities in manufacturing. By 1973, some 37% of US FDI was in western Europe (10.6% in Great Britain, 18.3% in the common market countries), 24.6% in Canada, and 15.9% in Latin America. This was the period when IBM and other American-based multinationals relentlessly expanded market share in western Europe and bought up local producers. Not surprisingly, this aroused French politicians like Charles de Gaulle and Jean-Jacques Servan-Schreiber. They worried Europe might succumb to American commercial dominance. Servan-Schreiber offered this gloomy forecast: "Fifteen years from now it is quite possible that the world's third greatest industrial power, just after the United States and Russia, will not be Europe, but *American industry in Europe.*"[14] European nationalists interpreted this as a call to arms, and political leaders like de Gaulle attempted to restrict American investments and to establish strong national champions. This occurred in electronics, information-processing, and aviation. Also, de Gaulle and other European leaders discovered another way to slow the American business advance. Recalling that the Bretton Woods international monetary system rested firmly on the American pledge to redeem dollars for gold at a fixed price, they threatened to do exactly that. Because the US Treasury lacked adequate gold to support the conversion pledge, and sustain the dollar exchange rate at existing levels, the Johnson administration reluctantly imposed controls on private capital exports during the Vietnam War.[15]

From another perspective, it is arguable that Europe was its own worst enemy during the late 1960s and early 1970s. Despite the recovery and a series of steps to promote European integration, it remained divided on the final form of integration, and its markets remained small and segmented. Political differences, such as French president de Gaulle's efforts to keep Great Britain out of the common market and French efforts to protect family farms, slowed Europeanization and delayed the re-emergence of Europe's leadership in the globalization process. Lacking the benefits of a large market, European business could not achieve cost reductions and economies of scale.

Before the mid-1970s most European business leaders had national, or regional, horizons. Except for a few dozen large multinationals – such as British Petroleum (BP), Ericsson, Philips, Shell, Siemens, Unilever, and Volkswagen – few had global ambitions, and most were content to serve foreign markets with exports from Europe. In the auto industry, for example, a series of dominant national firms (Volkswagen,

Renault, and Fiat) sought to expand market share via exports to other national markets in the European region.[16] Ericsson, the giant Scandinavian telecommunications firm, offers another example. Long active in international business, this Swedish company used post-World War II opportunities to reinternationalize, and in particular to establish a strong presence in the European common market. The export share of the Swedish parent increased from one-third to two-thirds between 1946 and 1970, and Ericsson's employment quadrupled, much of this growth being in west European manufacturing subsidiaries. In the oil industry, however, Shell and BP pursued global strategies, seeking to compete in all major markets. Until the late 1960s BP was the only major international oil firm without a stake in the highly profitable US market. Then, to develop a lease in Prudhoe Bay (Alaska), it sought an American partner with political connections and an extensive distribution system. In 1969 BP purchased a 25% equity share in Standard Oil Company of Ohio (Sohio), founded by John D. Rockefeller. Over the next quarter-century, it would gradually expand that stake and eventually substitute the BP logo for the Sohio name.[17]

Phase Two: 1973 to 1991

As it turned out, European fears of the American business challenge were exaggerated. By the mid-1970s the shoe was on the other foot. Much-criticized European business had reorganized and taken the offensive both regionally and globally. European capital began to flood the American market. Continental firms such as French tire-maker Michelin and German automaker Volkswagen set up plants in North America. Uncertain about the future of Europe, with its high labor costs and rigid work rules, they wanted to establish a manufacturing presence in the huge North American market close to millions of affluent consumers. In effect, they chose to serve foreign high-income markets through local production rather than to rely on high-cost European assembly and exports, which might become targets for trade barriers. One sign of changing circumstances occurred in 1978 when *Newsweek* focused on the buying of America. Many European firms, it said, used export earnings to build and buy factories, purchase real estate, and invest in US equities. Two years later London's *The Economist* described the challenge in reverse by which European, Japanese, and Canadian investors bought such household names as Saks Fifth Avenue and Baskin-Robbins ice cream, and constructed tire plants in South Carolina and auto assembly facilities in Tennessee and Ohio. Dutch electronics giant Philips acquired television-maker Magnavox. While press accounts may have exaggerated the intensity of the challenge in the 1970s, the net book value of foreign investment in America grew at nearly twice the rate of outward investment from the United States during that decade.[18]

What explained the swift turn around? For one thing, Britain, Ireland, and Denmark, all European Free Trade Association (EFTA) members, joined the European Community in 1973, and the expanded regional market became more outward-looking. The newcomers especially the British had a long tradition of global business activity. For another, the fall of the dollar and the collapse of the Bretton Woods international monetary system (1971) soon enabled currency markets to set exchange rates. Over the next 20 years, the dollar purchasing power of the German mark, Dutch guilder, Japanese yen, and Swiss franc doubled, helping to fuel a surge in overseas investments. With their currencies rising against the dollar, European and Japanese firms could afford to establish a long-term presence in the American market.

Several other structural factors help to explain the sharp rise in flows of FDI in the early 1970s. For one thing, by 1973 the full Kennedy Round multilateral tariff concessions had been implemented, essentially removing tariffs as impediments to trade in manufactured goods among the industrial powers, and allaying lingering fears that an integrated Europe might turn inward. Tariff liberalization made it easier for businesses to ship parts, as well as finished products, across frontiers and to supply foreign assembly facilities with world-class capital equipment and the best components. Finally, technological innovations in satellite communications, containerization, wide-bodied ships, and wide-bodied aircraft, like the Boeing 747, transformed the business environment. Big corporations could now oversee and integrate global operations, establish global supply chains, and move production and assembly to areas where labor costs were low. As a result of these developments, transportation costs fell sharply, and air freight offered immediate delivery for high-value cargoes. Responding to these developments, Dutch electronics giant Philips set up assembly operations in Southeast Asia during the late 1970s to take advantage of lower labor costs.[19]

The last quarter of the twentieth century thus witnessed a surge of European investments in North America, with longtime capital exporters Britain and the Netherlands leading the way. By 1980 Europe had recovered its historic position as the world's leading investor, and its accumulated stock of FDI surpassed that of the United States. Western Europe accounted for 46% of the world's outbound FDI stock (continental Europe 31%, UK 15%) compared to the United States with 41% (see Table 12.3). A parallel liberalization of finance in the mid-1980s would accelerate these trends and enhance the standing of London as a world financial center. Successful negotiations in the next GATT round (the Uruguay Round) to extend trade liberalization to services would also stoke the fires of global business expansion.

Among the Continental countries, these developments produced an important shift in national FDI rankings. Until the late 1970s the Netherlands had been the leading Continental investor, a fact that reflected a long tradition of overseas investments as well as the presence of several large multinationals such as Shell, Unilever, and Philips. Ten large multinationals reportedly accounted for 75% of the Netherland's accumulated stock of FDI in 1980.[20] But German companies began to move abroad during the 1970s, and soon Germany held a larger stock of FDI.

The German case merits special attention. Although German firms such as Siemens first went abroad as early as 1855, Germany twice lost its FDI stock in world wars, and its firms approached the post-World War II period cautiously. During the recovery period they invested domestically, and used export expansion to penetrate foreign markets. As a result, German exports exceeded foreign production, quite the opposite what happened in of the United States, Britain, and the Netherlands. The German

Table 12.3 Percentage of world foreign direct investment (stock) inward/outward

Country	1980	1985	1992	2002
Developed countries	64/97	63/96	72/94	65/87
Canada	9/5	7/4	5/4	3/4
United States	13/41	20/34	20/25	19/22
Western Europe	37/46	31/47	41/50	39/55
Belgium/Luxembourg	1/1	2/1	4/3	7/7 [2001]
France	9/5	7/5	6/8	6/10
Germany	6/8	4/9	6/9	6/8
Italy	1/1	2/2	2/4	2/3
The Netherlands	3/8	3/7	4/6	4/5
Sweden	0/4	0/2	1/2	2/2
Switzerland	1/4	1/4	2/4	2/4
United Kingdom	10/15	7/15	8/11	9/15
Japan	1/4	1/6	1/12	1/5
Developing countries	36/3	37/4	27/6	33/12
Brazil	2/7	3/5	2/2	3/1
China	–/–	1/–	2/–	6/1
Hong Kong	25/–	19/–	10/1	6/5

Source: UNCTAD, Foreign Direct Investment database, online at http://www.unctad.org/

chemical, electrical, and automobile sectors, as well as banking and finance, would gradually advance overseas. Siemens, for example, had some 210 factories outside Germany in 1990. Volkswagen, which established a position in Brazil in the 1950s, used mergers and acquisitions in western European markets to become a market leader by 1990, and it attempted to set up a US assembly plant near Pittsburgh in the late 1970s. But Mercedes Benz and BMW, makers of prestige vehicles, lagged. Given the tradition of quality production in Germany, they were reluctant to manufacture their best models abroad, until rising labor costs and rigid labor practices in the 1990s forced them offshore.[21]

On a per capita basis, however, the smaller European countries remained more outward looking than the French, Germans, and Italians. With small domestic markets Belgium, the Netherlands, Switzerland, and Sweden had long been accustomed to exporting and scouring the world for business opportunities. Data for 1985 reveal how integrated, and globalized, the smaller countries had become. That year the per capita outward stock of FDI for all of western Europe was $869. Falling below the average were Germany ($771), France ($683), and Italy ($293). The United States ($983) and Canada ($1,669) were both above western European levels. But the smaller European countries invested far more abroad on a per capita basis. For the Netherlands the comparable figure was $3,305 and for Switzerland $3,839 (see Table 12.4).

In international trade the second period – from the early 1970s to the early 1990s – saw a surge in intra-European regional trade. This reflected the dissolution of long-

Table 12.4 World foreign direct investment per capita (outward stock)

Country	1980	1985	1992	2001
Developed countries	$644	$815	$2,171	$5,951
Developing countries	11	9	30	168
Canada	970	1,669	3,095	7,883
United States	935	983	1,930	4,832
Western Europe	657	869	2,538	8,643
France	451	683	2,727	8,670
Germany	551	771	2,125	6,266
Italy	130	293	1,247	3,172
Japan	168	364	1,995	2,357
The Netherlands	2,976	3,305	7,987	20,617
Sweden	430	1,290	5,628	13,881
Switzerland	3,401	3,839	10,687	32,976
UK	1,428	1,770	3,823	15,835

Source: UNCTAD, *Handbook of Statistics*, Report 6.2. Online at http://www.unctad.org/

established trading patterns between Britain and its Commonwealth partners following admission to the common market in 1973, and the attractions of an increasingly integrated and prosperous Europe. In 1973 western Europe accounted for 45% of world exports, and 47% of world imports, a significant rise in shares from 33% of world exports and 39% of world imports in 1950. Britain and France now (1973) relied far more on European partners for imports (49% in the case of Britain, 63% France) than on developing areas (22% Britain, 21% France; see Table 12.2). On the export side the same pattern applied. Britain sent 20% of its exports to developing markets, 48% to the advanced countries of western Europe. France exported 19% to developing countries, 68% to the developed countries of western Europe. It was evident that Europeanization, the development of a vast regional market as EFTA and the EEC (European Economic Community) merged, was binding the economies and people of western Europe. It was also supplanting traditional colonial relationships that once tied France and Britain to overseas colonies and informal commercial and financial empires.[22]

During the second phase, lasting until the early 1990s, Europe moved forward haltingly, under pressure from business leaders, to convert the European Community into a single market. In the early 1980s, European business leaders awoke to the region's costs and inadequacies. Borders continued to segment the national markets and to encourage inefficiencies. Product standards varied enormously from country to country. Intra-European commerce moved slowly because of customs formalities. The presence of different currencies, tax, and monetary systems increased the costs of transactions. Concern about lagging growth (Eurosclerosis), rising protectionism, American competition, and even Japanese penetration of European markets all prompted a group of top European business executives to form the European Roundtable of Industrialists, and to press the corporate agenda for a single market.[23]

At a time when some outsiders feared European integration might enhance a "fortress Europe" mentality, more and more European business leaders had begun to understand the potential of the new technologies and to think globally. Claude Noel Martin of France's Général Biscuit said a European flag should fly at his company's headquarters. Asserting that European companies were too provincial, he urged them to collaborate and compete internationally against American and Japanese firms. Wisse Dekker, the chairman of Dutch electronics giant Philips, warned that multinationals might leave Europe if it failed to complete a single market. If Europe did not unite, industrial innovation would pass Europe by. Multinational companies would then be forced to adjust their geographic priorities. The new technologies, they realized, made global competition a fact of life. High costs of product development required that corporations amortize costs over a larger base of consumers.[24]

Having already established positions in European regional markets, the big European firms focused on acquiring properties in North America, and on achieving strong competitive positions in the high-income triad countries (North America, Japan, and the European Union). As a result, according to a study by business analyst Joseph Quinlan, European inflows to the US soared in the 1980s, totaling $216 billion for the decade versus cumulative inflows of just $28 billion in the 1970s. By 1983 Europe's investment position in the US on a historical-cost basis was almost equal to America's investment stake in Europe. By end of the decade Europe's US investment was 26% larger than the figure for US investment in Europe.[25]

The strategies of firms from smaller European economies mirror these trends. Sweden's Ericsson tried, and failed, to establish a competitive position in the US market before World War I, and then during the 1950s, but in the 1980s it made a third and successful attempt. Ericsson succeeded after an antitrust decision against ATT & T opened the American market to foreign telecommunications suppliers. By 1986, the 20 large Swedish multinationals had become increasingly globalized, with foreign sales accounting for over three-quarters of total sales.[26] The Dutch also targeted North America at this time. While investment in the European Community was 52% of Dutch FDI in 1975, over the next decade that declined to 33% as Dutch guilders flowed into North America. In 1985, some 41% of Dutch FDI was in the United States, compared with 33% in the European Community.[27]

Phase Three: 1992 to the Present

The pace of globalization and Europeanization accelerated during the 1990s, as the Cold War ended and the European Union completed its single-market initiative. Information and economics had helped end the long Cold War. They continued to transform the global marketplace, and of course the European Union. With collapse of the Soviet empire and triumph of market-oriented economics came opportunities to privatize state-owned enterprises and to integrate the well-educated people of eastern Europe into the European Union and the global economy. Germany was soon reunited, and business leaders looked eastward for new markets and low-cost production facilities. Ten central and eastern European states, including three Baltic countries, Poland, Hungary, the Czech Republic, Slovakia, and Slovenia, qualified for full membership in the EU by 2004.

Elsewhere, important regional and multilateral initiatives also reshaped the global economy. A series of regional trading agreements – particularly the North American Free Trade Agreement (NAFTA), Mercosur in South America, and a South East Asian regional agreement (ASEAN) – opened markets to trade, services, and investment on terms benefitting parties to the agreements, and raised concerns in Europe about continued access. Meanwhile, completion of the Uruguay Round of multilateral trade negotiations in 1994, conducted under the auspices of GATT, presented new opportunities. The final agreement sought to integrate developing markets into the world trading system, and it extended the reach of the new World Trade Organization (WTO) to agriculture, intellectual property, customs harmonization, government procurement, and services. Negotiators also created a binding dispute resolution mechanism under the auspices of the WTO.

Despite the progress of trade diplomats, big business chaffed at the glacial pace of intergovernmental negotiations. The Uruguay Round had taken nearly nine years, and it had accomplished little in services and telecommunications. In the private sector technological innovations transformed competitive conditions in product markets much more rapidly. Business wanted more specific terms of access for service providers, greater transparency in decision-making, and impartial dispute resolution panels to resolve business conflicts. The influential International Chamber of Commerce, based in Paris, explained its support for a world investment agreement this way:

> Worldwide economic integration requires business to produce and market goods and services on a global scale, by integrating the skills of people and various assets – tangible (e.g. land and resources), intangible (e.g. intellectual property) and monetary (e.g., stocks). In this process, trade and investment have become indistinguishable parts of a single strategy. Indeed, companies trade to invest and they invest to trade.[28]

In this challenging business environment European producers struggled to stay competitive. Grumbling about high labor costs (labor in France and Germany cost $22 per hour, compared to about $20 in the US), lagging productivity, and cultural barriers to risk-taking and innovation, they invested more abroad where costs were lower. Some pursued "green-field" investments in new markets, and constructed plants. Automakers like BMW and Mercedes, and their suppliers, built assembly facilities in North America in southern states like South Carolina and Alabama where state governments offered generous incentives and labor unions lacked influence.[29] Thyssen Krupp, the large German capital-goods manufacturer, also seized opportunities to move beyond its traditional European base. At the beginning of the 1990s, it had 37,000 German workers. By 1997, it had trimmed the German workforce to 27,000, while adding 28,000 non-German workers, many of them in the NAFTA region.[30]

Other European competitors took advantage of strong European currencies and open markets to buy up foreign assets, and even to reinvent themselves. Sweden's Volvo sold its automotive division to Ford in 1999, and then purchased the truck divisions of Mack and Renault to become a global producer of trucks, the second-largest in the US market, and to launch a joint venture in the Chinese truck industry. One of the most flamboyant failures involved Vivendi, a staid 150-year-old French water and sewage company. Under CEO Jean-Marie Messier, it embarked on a global acquisition binge to become a glamorous media giant. Messier succeeded in purchasing Universal Studios, Seagram, and USA Networks, adding a bevy of stars, and planting the French flag in Hollywood. But he succumbed to Americanism, moving to Park Avenue, insisting executives speak English, and declaring the French "cultural exception" dead. In the final act, Vivendi collapsed from excessive debt, and an angry French board dismissed Messier.

By the late 1990s, the world's transnational corporations – based in Europe, North America, and Japan – had awoken to the potential of big emerging markets like China and India. Each had over a billion people, and each had a government anxious to attract investments and to participate in the international trading system. From a business point of view interest in China and India had two attractions. One was to gain a foothold in a large and potentially lucrative market for the future. The other was to cut costs and thus more efficiently serve international markets. The successful strategy involved substituting cheap Asian labor for high-cost workers in developed nations. In China the transnationals discovered a virtually unlimited supply of highly motivated, cheap labor. Given an opportunity to choose between a traditional life, working rice paddies with a water buffalo, or taking factory jobs, several hundred million residents of rural areas opted for the latter, despite paltry wages of 50 cents per hour or less. In India the transnationals found an abundance of English-speaking software engineers and other professionals prepared to work for a fraction of comparable costs in high-income nations. Soon call centers were closing in Britain and their service jobs moving to India.

Similarly, in eastern Europe, European manufacturers discovered a nearby supply of cheap labor, many with German language skills and technical skills. Glimpsing the opportunities of globalization, they constructed new plants in eastern Europe where wages were 15% of German levels, and encouraged their suppliers to join them. By 2002, Volkswagen employed 37,000 workers and another 200,000 at supplier companies. Detlef Wittig, a Volkswagen group director, told the *Financial Times*, "Central Europe gives us a low-cost supply base, which makes a big contribution to our profit statements. Back home in high-cost EU countries, employment stagnated and jobless workers grumbled. Trade union leaders complained about a "race to the bottom".[31]

A new paradigm for the working world had emerged. According to neo-classical international-trade theory, nations exchanged goods in which they had an absolute, or comparative, advantage, based on relative production costs. In this model only goods moved between countries; capital, labor, and technology did not. Moreover, this explanation assumed that trade remained in balance, and that trading countries enjoyed full employment. By the 1990s this model diverged far from conditions in the global economy. Improvements in information technology, communications, and transportation enabled corporations to think globally and run complex business empires. They obtained raw materials and assembled goods where costs were lowest, borrowed capital where it was cheapest, and moved goods quickly from production facilities to the world's consumers. In the contemporary age of globalization, labor, capital, and technology all became highly mobile, and a large share of international trade involved transactions among units of large corporations at non-market prices.

As the twentieth century closed, trade and investments continued to expand. Europe, along with the United States, provided leadership to the globalization process. In the year 2000, western Europe accounted for 73% of the world's outbound flows of FDI ($1.2 trillion), compared to 12% for the United States. It is true, as UNCTAD has observed, that the largest share of EU direct investment went to other EU countries, but the US remained the most attractive location for EU outward FDI. Europe also appealed to foreign investors. In 2000, western Europe received 51% of the world's direct investment (see Table 12.5). From this peak the quantity of FDI fell sharply in the next two years (down 46%), as a global economic recession and terrorist attacks created uncertainties. Nonetheless, in 2002 (the most recent year for available data), Europe still generated 64% of outflows, and hosted 59% of inflows. But, based on flows and accumulated stocks of foreign investments, Europe remained highly integrated with the rest of the world. As a share of gross domestic product, in 2002, the outward stock of the European FDI was 43%, up from 6% in 1980. The stock of inward investment was 32% of GDP, up from 6% in 1980. In contrast, America's external stock of FDI rose from 8% to 14% of GDP in the same time period, and its inward stock climbed from 3% to 13% (see Table 12.5).[32] No other large market – China, India, the United States, Indonesia, Russia, or Brazil – was as interlinked with the world as western Europe.

At the beginning of the twenty-first century, the larger European countries now surpassed Canada and the US in per capita FDI. In 2001, the average was $8,643 for western Europe, $7,883 for Canada, and $4,832 for the US. Among the medium-sized countries, the United Kingdom had the highest per capita stock of outward FDI ($15,835), and Germany, considerably below the European average ($6,266), was now ahead of the United States. France had made enormous strides. Its per capita FDI level ($8,670) exceeded the European average and surpassed both Canada and the US. Not surprisingly, the smaller European countries remained far ahead. In the Netherlands per capita FDI was $20,617 and in Switzerland $32,976. As a share of the world total, in 2002, western Europe had 55% of the outward stock, compared to 22% for the US and 4% for Canada. Europe also attracted large quantities of investments. As a share of inward FDI stock, it accounted for 39%, the US 19%, and Canada 3%.[33] China and Hong Kong accounted for 12% of the inward stock, more than any single country except the United States (see Tables 12.3 and 12.5).

In world trade the major economies were more tightly integrated than ever at the opening of the new millennium. Nowhere was this more evident than in the North Atlantic region. North America's exports to western Europe and western Europe's exports to North America accounted for about half of world trade, if intra-bloc transactions were excluded. But globalization had also accelerated

Table 12.5 FDI inward/outward stock as share (%) of GDP

Country/group	1980	1985	1992	2002
Developed countries	5/6	6/7	8/10	19/24
Canada	20/9	18/12	19/15	30/38
United States	3/8	4/6	7/8	13/14
Western Europe	6/6	9/11	11/12	32/43
Belgium/Luxembourg	6/5	21/11	31/23	–
France	4/4	7/7	10/12	28/46
Germany	4/5	5/8	6/8	23/29
Italy	2/2	4/4	4/6	11/16
The Netherlands	11/24	19/36	22/36	75/85
Sweden	2/3	4/10	6/19	46/61
Switzerland	8/20	10/26	14/31	44/111
United Kingdom	12/15	14/22	16/21	41/66
Japan	0/2	0/3	0/7	1/8
Developing countries	13/4	16/4	12/3	36/14
Brazil	7/17	12/18	10/11	52/22
China	3/–	3/0	10/2	36/3
Hong Kong	624/1	525/7	205/22	266/227

Source: UNCTAD, Foreign Direct Investment database, online at http://www.unctad.org/

Table 12.6 Percentage of world FDI flows (inflows/outflows)

Country/group	2000	2001	2002
World	100/100%	100/100%	100/100%
Developed countries	80/91	72/93	71/93
Western Europe	51/73	49/66	59/64
France	3/15	7/13	8/10
Germany	15/5	4/6	6/4
Italy	1/1	2/3	2/3
The Netherlands	4/6	6/7	4/4
Sweden	2/3	1/1	2/2
United Kingdom	9/21	8/10	4/6
Switzerland	1/4	1/2	1/2
Canada	5/4	3/5	2/4
United States	23/12	17/15	5/18
Japan	1/3	1/5	1/5
Developing countries	18/8	25/7	25/7
Brazil	2/–	3/–	3/–
China	3/–	6/1	8/–
Hong Kong	4/5	3/2	2/3

Source: UNCTAD, Foreign Direct Investment database, online at http://www.unctad.org/

the integration of Asian peoples and nations. Japan's share of the European market had doubled in about 30 years. As late as 1970, only Germany among the major European traders obtained more than 1% of its imports from Japan and Japan's share was only 2%; 15% of US imports came from Japan. Thirty years later Japan's share of European imports had doubled; German and Britain were at 4%, France and Italy at 2%. On the export side the pattern was similar. Developing areas of Asia had also re-established closer commercial ties with western Europe. In 1950, 9% of Dutch imports and 8% of British imports came from developing Asia, as did 5% of German imports and 3% of French and Italian imports. Those import shares would decline by 1970, reflecting the growth of intra-European trade, but they revived in the 1990s as the globalization process spread to Asia's low-cost suppliers. In 2001, developing Asia supplied 25% of imports to the US, 15% to the Netherlands, 13% to Britain, 10% to Germany, and 6–7% of imports to France and Italy.[34]

With rising flows of trade and investments, and jobless recoveries in high-income countries, low-skilled and even white-collar and professional workers in high-income countries wondered what was next. Did globalization mean a race to the bottom, in which globally competitive companies scoured the world for the cheapest labor even for white-collar and professional workers, while unemployment rose and communities disintegrated in their home countries?[35]

That fear motivated many critics of globalization. Except for a few modern-day Luddites and anarchists who gleefully trashed McDonald's and Starbucks, and espoused a return to inefficient "localization," most parties to the great globalization debate recognized that technological innovations were irreversible and inevitable. They would continue to erase barriers of time, distance, and lack of information, and to integrate residents of many nations into a global market. What was uncertain was whether democratic electorates in western Europe and North America would continue to tolerate open borders and free trade in the face of rising unemployment, deflation, environmental destruction, and social disintegration. Growing numbers of anxious and dislocated workers – including skilled and professional workers – complained that politicians were sacrificing their interests as stakeholders to accommodate the priorities of transnational corporations and their shareholders. If trends continued, elected officials might feel public pressure to reassert control over national and regional borders. In the long run, John Gray, a professor of European thought at the London School of Economics, forecast that "like other twentieth-century utopias, global *laissez-faire* . . . will be swallowed into the memory hole of history".[36]

The debate over economic globalization, which began in Europe during the late 1990s, and swept around the world, seemed destined, like the synergistic globalization process itself, to impact twenty-first-century markets and politics, but in ways that defied easy prediction. Whatever path the future took, the peoples of western Europe, along with their North American partners, could be expected to provide leadership, as they had in the past. As the world's foremost investors and traders, European businesses and governments would shape the age of globalization. But other European activists, who gave energy to the counterglobalization movement, could be expected to play prominent roles in efforts to tame and regulate these market- and technology-driven forces, and to make them more responsive to the interests of the world's poor. The dot.com bubble of the 1990s and the subsequent housing bubble in many developed countries (not least in the US, the UK, Ireland, and Spain) spurred on further cross-country trade and economic interconnectedness in the age of globalization. The bursting of the housing bubble in 2008 and the turmoil in the financial markets in the Western world, including the credit crunch, soon had very real consequences for the real economy.[37] These developments would provide serious challenges to the continued forces of globalization. Political nationalism and its economic counterpart, protectionism, were on the rise again.

Notes

1 BBC Poll. See also Pew Global Attitudes Project, October 4, 2007. Online at http://pewglobal.org/reports/display.php?ReportID=258.
2 See generally the annual *World Investment Report* of the United Nations Conference on Trade and Development (UNCTAD). Online at http://www.unctad.org.
3 For some of the definitional issues, see Hopkins, *Globalization in World History*, 18–25. Foreign direct investment (FDI) involves corporate mergers and acquisitions, as well as the construction of new plants and facilities, but does not involve short-term capital flows or purchase and sale of equities and debt.
4 Naisbitt, *Megatrends*, 64–65, 76; Levitt, "Globalization of Markets," 1–11.
5 Marino, "Economic Encounters," 278–295; Kierzkowski, *Europe and Globalization*, 4–7; Braudel, *Wheels of Commerce*, 138–230.
6 Dunning, "Globalizing Europe," 43–61. Jones and Schroter, *Rise of Multinationals*, 3–27; Mathias, *First Industrial Revolution*, 121–123, 267–307; Ferguson, *Empire*, xxii–xxviii; Headrick, *Invisible Weapon*.
7 Dunning, op. cit., 43–61. Jones and Schroter, op. cit., 10–11; Schroter, "German Multinationals," 28–48.
8 Bairoch, "European Trade Policy," 127.
9 World Trade Organization, *International Trade Statistics 2002* (calculated from WTO table II.2).
10 Jeremy, *Business History of Britain*, 246–247.
11 US Bureau of the Census, *Historical Statistics of the United States*, vol. II: 866–867; Hansen, *European Economic History*, 251–433.
12 Jones and Schroter, op. cit., 10. This is estimated accumulated stock.
13 Zettler and Cutler, "United States Direct Investments," 8.
14 Servan-Schreiber, *The American Challenge*, 35. Emphasis in original.
15 Kunz, *Butter and Guns*, 164.
16 Hiraoka, *Global Alliances*, 1–27.
17 Bamberg, *British Petroleum*, 271–275; Olsson, "Swedish Multinationals," 114–117.
18 Kilborn, "Buying of America," 78.
19 Gales and Sluyterman, "Dutch Multinationals2, 84.
20 Gales and Sluyterman, op. cit., 66.
21 Schroter, "German Multinationals," 44–54.
22 NCTAD database, Table 3.1. On-line at http://www.unctad.org.
23 Lintner, "European Community," 140–157; Balanya et al., *Europe Inc.*, 19–25.
24 Housego, "European Business"; "Multinationals May Leave 'if Europe Does Not Unite,'" Section 1, 1.

25 Quinlan, *Drifting Apart*, 8–10.
26 Olsson, op. cit., 117–21.
27 Gales and Sluyterman, op. cit., 80.
28 International Chamber of Commerce, WTO Investment Agreement.
29 Powers, "German Plants Head Abroad"; Parkes, "Driven to 'Think Global and Act Local,'" 3.
30 "No Fear: Thyssen's Strategy," 30.
31 Testault, "Central Europe Poised to Be Automaking Giant"; Wagstyl, "VW Brings Skoda up to World-class Speed," 13; Pris, "Panic among Unions."
32 UNCTAD, *World Investment Report*, 2002, 40; UNCTAD, *Handbook of Statistics*, online.
33 UNCTAD, *Handbook of Statistics*, online, Table 6.2.
34 UNCTAD, *Handbook of Statistics*, online, Table 3.1.
35 See, generally, Tonelson, *Race to the Bottom*.
36 Gray, *False Dawn*, 235.
37 See for example Fleckenstein, *Greenspan's Bubbles*.

Bibliography

Bairoch, Paul, "European Trade Policy, 1815–1914," in Peter Mathias and Sidney Pollard (eds.) *Cambridge Economic History of Europe*, vol. 8 (Cambridge: Cambridge University Press, 1989).

Balanya, Belen, et al., *Europe Inc.: Regional and Global Restructuring and the Rise of Corporate Power* (Sterling, VA: Pluto Press, 2000).

Bamberg, James, *British Petroleum and Global Oil 1950–1975: The Challenge of Nationalism* (Cambridge: Cambridge University Press).

BBC World Service Poll, "Widespread Unease about Economy and Globalization," February 2008, http://www.worldpublicopinion.org/pipa/pdf/feb08/BBCEcon_Feb08_rpt.pdf

Braudel, Fernand, *Civilization and Capitalism 15th–18th Century*, vol. 2: *Wheels of Commerce* (New York: Harper & Row, 1979).

Dunning, John H., "Globalizing Europe: The Overall Picture," in Thomas L. Brewer, Paul A. Brenton, and Gavin Boyd (eds.), *Globalizing Europe: Deepening Integration, Alliance Capitalism and Structural Statecraft* (Cheltenham, UK, and Northampton, MA: Edward Elgar, 2002).

Ferguson, Niall, *Empire* (New York: Basic Books, 2003).

Fleckenstein, William A., with Frederick Sheehan, *Greenspan's Bubbles: The Age of Ignorance at the Federal Reserve* (New York: McGraw Hill, 2008).

"Foreign Direct Investment in the United States," *Survey of Current Business*, September 2002, 39.

Gales, Ben P.A. and Keetie E. Sluyterman, "Outward Bound: The Rise of Dutch Multinationals," in Geoffrey Jones and Harm G. Schroter (eds.), *The Rise of Multinationals in Continental Europe* (Cheltenham, UK, and Northampton, MA: Edward Elgar, 1993).

Gray, John, *False Dawn: The Delusions of Global Capitalism* (New York: The New Press, 1998).

Hansen, E. Damsgaard, *European Economic History: From Mercantilism to Maastricht and Beyond* (Copenhagen: Copenhagen Business School Press, 2001).

Headrick, Daniel, *The Invisible Weapon: Telecommunications and International Politics, 1851–1945* (New York: Oxford University Press, 1991).

Hiraoka, Leslie S., *Global Alliances in the Motor Vehicle Industry* (Westport, CT and London: Quorum Books, 2001).

Hopkins, A.G. (ed.), *Globalization in World History* (New York: Norton, 2002).

Housego, David, "European Business 'Must Link to Face Outside Competition'," *Financial Times*, September 27, 1984, Section 1, 1.

International Chamber of Commerce (Paris), "ICC's Expectations Regarding a WTO Investment Agreement," March 7, 2003, http://www.iccwbo.org/home/statements_rules/statements/2003/

Jeremy, David J., *A Business History of Britain, 1900–1990s* (Oxford: Oxford University Press, 1998).

Jones, Geoffrey and Harm G. Schroter (eds.), *The Rise of Multinationals in Continental Europe* (Cheltenham, UK, and Northampton, MA: Edward Elgar, 1993).

Kierzkowski, Henryk (ed.), *Europe and Globalization* (New York: Palgrave Macmillan, 2002).

Kilborn, Peter T., "The Buying of America," *Newsweek*, November 27, 1978, 78.

Kunz, Diane B., *Butter and Guns: America's Cold War Economic Diplomacy* (New York: Free Press, 1997).

Levitt, Theodore, "The Globalization of Markets," *Harvard Business Review*, May–June 1983, 1–11.

Lintner, Valerio, "The European Community 1958 to the 1990s," in Max-Stephan Schulze (ed.), *Western Europe: Economic and Social Change since 1945* (London: Longman, 1999).

Marino, John A., "Economic Encounters and the First Stages of a World Economy," in Guido Ruggiero (ed.), *A Companion to Worlds of the Renaissance* (Oxford, UK, and Malden, MA: Blackwell Publishers, 2002).

Mathias, Mathias, *The First Industrial Revolution: An Economic History of Britain 1700–1914*, 2nd edition (London: Routledge, 1983).

"Multinationals May Leave If Europe Does Not Unite," *Financial Times*, April 25, 1985, Section 1, 1.

Naisbitt, John, *Megatrends: Ten New Directions Transforming Our Lives* (New York: Warner Books, 1982).

"No Fear: Thyssen's Strategy for the Global Marketplace," *Industry Week*, June 23, 1997, 30.

Olsson, Ulf, "Securing the Markets: Swedish Multinationals in a Historical Perspective," in Geoffrey Jones and Harm G. Schroter (eds.), *The Rise of Multinationals in Continental Europe* (Cheltenham, UK, and Northampton, MA: Edward Elgar, 1993).

Parkes, Christopher, "Driven to 'Think Global and Act Local': A Look at Mercedes-Benz's Commercial Vehicle Strategy," *Financial Times*, January 20, 1994, 3.

Powers, Mary Buckner, "German Plants Head Abroad," *Engineering News-Record*, October 9, 1995, 11.

Pris, Frederique, "Panic among Unions as British Call-Centre Jobs go to Anglophone India," Agence France Presse, July 20, 2003.

Quinlan, Joseph P., *Drifting Apart or Growing Together? The Primacy of the Transatlantic Economy* (Baltimore, MD: Johns Hopkins University Center for Transatlantic Studies, 2003).

Schroter, Harm G., "Continuity and Change: German Multinationals since 1850," in Geoffrey Jones and Harm G. Schroter (eds.), *The Rise of Multinationals in Continental Europe* (Cheltenham, UK, and Northampton, MA, Edward Elgar, 1993).

Schroter, Harm G., "Swiss Multinationals in Historical Perspective," in Geoffrey Jones and Harm G. Schroter (eds.), *The Rise of Multinationals in Continental Europe* (Cheltenham, UK, and Northampton, MA: Edward Elgar, 1993).

Servan-Schreiber, Jean-Jacques, *The American Challenge* (New York: Avon Books, 1968).

Testault, Jean-Luc, "Central Europe Poised to Be Automaking Giant," *Baltic Times*, November 7, 2002.

Tonelson, Alan, *Race to the Bottom* (Boulder, CO: Westview Press, 2000).

UNCTAD, *Handbook of Statistics*, online.

UNCTAD, *World Investment Report 2002* (Geneva: UNCTAD, 2003).

US Bureau of the Census, *Historical Statistics of the United States: Bicentennial Edition* vol. II (Washington: GPO, 1975).

Wagstyl, Stefan, "VW Brings Skoda up to World-Class Speed," *Financial Times*, September 3, 2002, 13.

World Trade Organization, *International Trade Statistics 2002* (Geneva: WTO, 2003).

Zettler, Joseph A. and Frederick Cutler, "United States Direct Investments in Foreign Countries," *Survey of Current Business*, December 1952, 8.

Further Reading

There is an extensive literature on economic globalization. One of the most important recent works by economic historians is Ronald Findlay and Kevin H. O'Rourke, *Power and Plenty: Trade, War, and the World Economy in the Second Millennium* (Princeton, NJ: Princeton University Press, 2007). It contains a excellent bibliography. Another study especially pertinent to this essay is Henryk Kierzkowski (ed.), *Europe and Globalization* (New York: Palgrave Macmillan, 2002).

On big business and globalization see Geoffrey Jones, *Multinationals and Global Capitalism: From the Nineteenth to the Twenty-first Century* (New York: Oxford University Press, 2005). On the European economy more generally see Barry Eichengreen, *The European Economy since 1945: Coordinated Capitalism and Beyond* (Princeton, NJ: Princeton University Press, 2007) and Ivan T. Berend, *An Economic History of Twentieth-Century Europe: Economic Regimes from Laissez Faire to 2006* (Cambridge: Cambridge University Press, 2006). Another valuable history is Derek H. Aldcroft, *The European Economy 1914–2000*, 4th edition (London: Routledge, 2001).

Readers may also be interested in my essay "Globalization" in Gordon Martel (ed.), *A Companion to International History 1900–2001* (Malden, MA: Blackwell Publishing, 2007); and in A.G. Hopkins (ed.), *Globalization in World History* (London: W.W. Norton, 2002). For a more general introduction to issues of public debate, see Frank J. Lechner and John Boli (eds.) *The Globalization Reader*, 2nd edition (Malden, MA: Blackwell, 2004).

CHAPTER THIRTEEN

Economic Integration since Maastricht

CHRISTOPHER FLOCKTON

The Maastricht Treaty was adopted in December 1991 by EC heads of state and government and subsequently put to referendum or parliamentary approval in member states, often hotly contested, not least in the UK. As the formal outcome of the two intergovernmental conferences (IGCs) which had been convened at the end of the 1980s, the clear purpose was to promote the deepening of the EU (European Union) through ever closer integration, buttressed by reforms to the distribution of powers. The key provisions in the treaty were the creation of the so-called three pillars of economic and monetary union, common foreign and security policy, and internal and judicial affairs. Economic and monetary union (EMU) comprised the completion of the single market, also known as the "1992" project, to be accompanied by the creation of a single currency, in the sense of "one market, one money".[1]

Nobody was in any doubt, however, that the underlying political purpose was to anchor a newly unified Germany into an EU deepened by monetary union, and to secure the course of economic integration among the western European nations, before widening took place to embrace the emerging central and eastern European countries (CEEC) which had escaped Soviet domination with the fall of the Iron Curtain. The strategy would lock a unified Germany into the west, free from temptations to recast a "Mitteleuropa" with the emerging neighboring states in the east. A single-currency strategy would also have the inestimable value for countries such as France of replacing the deutschmark and the Bundesbank at the core of European monetary arrangements: a truly European currency and central bank would be created.[2] The fact that deepening, in the direction of EMU, was to precede widening, and that the widening process took the form of separate bilateral trade agreements with individual CEEC countries, displays the imperatives and priorities of the time. Widening was achieved hesitantly and with delay, although the path to monetary union also displayed some surprises and uncertainties.

The early 1990s, the period of the Maastricht Treaty, saw also milestones in other key areas of Community economic integration, notably the programmed terminal

A Companion to Europe since 1945, First Edition. Edited by Klaus Larres.
© 2014 John Wiley & Sons, Ltd. Published 2014 by John Wiley & Sons, Ltd.

date for the completion of the internal market (single European market – SEM) on December 31, 1992, and these were also the years of the first fundamental attempts to reform the common agricultural policy (CAP). Budgetary decisions, so often closely associated with CAP strains and crises, were adopted at the Edinburgh summit, and set the financial framework for the decade. From December 1991 onwards, the so-called Europe Agreements began to be signed with central European countries (as the most advanced on the transition path to a market economy) and these association agreements held out the possibility of future EC (European Community) membership.

These agreements confirmed the close economic ties which were already being forged, helped underpin the transition to the market and set a template for the adoption of a social market economy constitution in these east European countries. Looking further back, the first half of the 1980s had been years of serious recession in western Europe and it was only from 1985 onwards, with brightening economic prospects, that the single-market program and discussions for a single currency gave an enhanced allure to the European project. However, the early 1990s were years of the deepest postwar recession in key western European countries: deepening and widening therefore posed a significant challenge to governing and business elites both to construct a future European political and economic order and, concurrently, to overcome voter resistance fueled by recession.

The Single Market Programme (SMP) was clearly perceived as a key liberalizing, supply-side agenda attacking non-tariff barriers to trade and as such it retained the close support of the British prime minister, Margaret Thatcher. However, the Single European Act of 1986, which provided the necessary legislation and which was signed by Mrs. Thatcher, contained in its preamble the injunction to promote an ever closer monetary union. Neither the British nor the Danes could accept the sovereignty impacts of such a transfer of monetary powers to an independent central bank and so they gained treaty opt-outs.[3] The British, in particular, felt confirmed in their views concerning the restrictiveness of multilateral monetary arrangements when sterling was ejected in September 1992 from the EMS exchange rate mechanism, after intense speculative pressure.[4]

However, for other large countries these critical economic policy choices offered major attractions. As noted, France saw monetary union as a way of locking unified Germany into the west and at the same time replacing the hegemonic Bundesbank at the core of European monetary arrangements. Germany accepted the implied trade-off and was intensely aware of the geopolitical as well as economic significance of an extension of EC integration eastwards to embrace countries on its new eastern German border. Nonetheless, agricultural, budgetary, and competition policy imperatives also continued to exert their influence, as they had through earlier decades. Partial CAP reforms, attempted primarily under budgetary pressure, had been introduced in the 1980s, with a relatively innovatory reform package in 1988, which also set budgetary ceilings for the CAP. However, at the beginning of the 1990s, external pressures in the shape of the renewal of the GATT (General Agreement on Tariffs and Trade) agreement, the so-called Uruguay Round, imposed difficult choices for the design and operation of a CAP which depended on the dumping of subsidized surplus foodstuffs on world markets.

As for the SEM, while this rested primarily on a desire among elites to kick-start EC trade and investment once again and so allow the Community to contest US and Japanese superiority in manufacturing, there were also court decisions over competition policy issues which gave the program further impetus. These covered the mutual-recognition principle, the free supply of insurance services, and the opening of network industries to cross-border trade, from which these latter had been previously exempt due to a particular reading of Treaty of Rome clauses.[5]

This chapter seeks, then, to analyze the construction of the SEM, the paths of CAP reform attempts, enlargement to the east, and the move to EMU. To varying degrees, these issues show interconnections, particularly between agricultural reform and enlargement and between monetary union and enlargement. In the background is the ever-present issue of the EU budget. Enlargement, were it to have included an unreformed CAP, would swamp budgetary provisions and threaten world trade agreements by the dumping of foodstuffs. As will become evident, the intervening years since the commencement of the 1990s have seen further attempts at a partial reform of the CAP under world trade and enlargement pressures. There has been the consolidation of the internal market, accompanied by the ambitious liberalization of network industries, and the successful introduction of the euro, even if its economic governance arrangements and the conditions for its long-term success remain still somewhat uncertain. Eastern enlargement itself was subject to delay, but has been be a signal achievement, establishing a new geopolitical reality in the form of the widened Europe; enlargement does, however, intensify many pressures – budgetary, CAP, flexible adjustment – which have been inherent in the EC/EU as it has grown over the decades.

The Completion of the Single European Market

The Single Market Programme was devised in 1985 in the shape of the Cockfield white paper, "The Completion of the Single Market," and took the form of 182 draft directives. Each proposed to attack specific non-tariff barriers (NTBs) which remained in place in spite of the tariff abolition which had ended with the final establishment of the customs union in 1968. NTBs, in a wide array of guises, continued to fragment the common market and prevented the full economic gains from being reaped from integration. At the time, weaker EU performance, compared with the US and Japanese economies, was of primary concern, as was a desire to kick-start growth again through trade. The Single Market Programme set a deadline of the end of 1992 for the completion of NTB abolition and the Single European Act of 1986 gave the required powers to this end, primarily in the form of qualified majority voting on these economic issues.

NTBs constraining trade in goods and services typically took one of five forms: the customs barriers themselves, fiscal frontiers, norms and standards, public procurement, and services regulation by nation states which prevent the free movement of services.[6] Economically, the gains from NTB abolition are largely comparable to those of tariff abolition, with enhanced competition driving price convergence on lower price levels, the promotion of allocative and technical efficiency, the reaping of scale economies and dynamic gains through higher investment rates, and R & D expenditure in response to market enlargement. This enhanced competitiveness of the European market would also bring foreign, extra-EU, trade gains and there would be public budget gains through higher net revenues, and lowered costs of public procurement. Of course, consumers would have access to a much greater range of products at keener prices, previously monopolized sectors would be opened to competition, and public authorities would pursue more cost-conscious procurement.[7]

The Emerson Report of 1988 (published also in the more popular version, the Cecchini Report of 1988) spelled out the nature of these barriers and the economic gains which would flow from their abolition, and sought also to quantify the scale of these gains. The report has sometimes been criticized as political for its excessive optimism, which served to gain acceptance of this ambitious program of supply-side reforms. The report documented the cost in waiting time and form-filling for exports to cross a customs post (estimated at 2% of cross-border sales, but at 30–45% of the value of a consignment by a small- or medium-sized firm). There was the allied problem of fiscal frontiers, where differential VAT and excise duty rates meant a good had to be detaxed before it crossed the border and retaxed on the other side. Norms and standards, where these were government-imposed technical standards for public health and environmental control could be very beneficial, but product standards, such as those of the BSI (British Standards Institute), often restricted import competition, since they were devised to give a specification for home-produced goods but could thereby exclude foreign production by the details of the specification itself. Since many commercial insurance policies specified a particular standard, the constraining effect of the standards was the greater: there were 100,000 such standards in the EC in the later 1980s. Public procurement also favored home producers and represented a significant part of GDP: large budgetary savings of perhaps one-quarter could be made.[8]

Public purchasing represented 15% of GDP and perhaps one-half of this comprised internationally tradable goods and services, yet the proportion of cross-border supply was minimal. In sectors closely allied to public purchasing – namely output such as power station equipment, rail rolling stock, or telecommunications equipment – the fragmentation of markets and their dominance by local producers meant that sub-scale output and diversity of technologies held back EU producers often in the face of US and Japanese competition – the Cecchini estimate of potential cost reductions in the case of telecoms equipment supply was of 40% in some member states.

Finally, in the matter of services regulation in transport and the utilities, national monopolies often existed with protected, inefficient production and with no competing cross-border supply. To remedy this market fragmentation, the white paper proposed that customs posts be abolished and export documentation be radically simplified in the form of the Single Administrative Document, that indirect sales taxes be harmonized so that goods could be exported tax-inclusive according to the origin principle of taxation (namely tax is levied at the point of production), that mutual recognition of standards should operate (or harmonization of standards in technologically advanced or sensitive products), and that there should be strict notification of public invitations to tender in public purchasing.[9]

The opening of transport, utilities, and financial services markets was treated separately for treaty reasons, but a stream of directives through the 1990s prised open

and abolished protected monopolies. The Cecchini Report of 1988 estimated opti-
mistically the gains at 4.5% of EC GDP as a first-round effect, but potentially at 7%
with the creation of 5 million new jobs, were the first-round effects to lead to less
restrictive macroeconomic policy. The greatest gains would derive from the assumed
large economies of scale in a single market, and from the opening of the financial
sector to competition (including a fall in interest and bank charges on consumer and
investment credits).

A subsequent large-scale study for the EU Commission pointed to more limited
gains than those forecast by Cecchini/Emerson, namely to a growth impact of 1.5%
of GDP and a net job creation of between 300,000 and 900,000 jobs. This study
concluded that although the gains were more modest, they were still significant.
Intra-EU trade growth had been primarily of intra-industry character (trade in similar
goods) and this indicated that consumers preferred product variety rather than simply
standardized products at lower prices.[10] However, intra-industry trade could constrain the potential gains from economies of scale (given greater variety in production
rather than output-volume increases) and the 1997 report pointed to the limited
effect of economies of scale, which in fact were felt largely in advertising, marketing,
and logistics rather than in production itself.

In November 2002, the Commission produced a further assessment of the
SEM impact called the "The Internal Market – Ten Years without Frontiers"[11] and
this pointed to achievements as well as to shortcomings in completion. The achievements can be found in much lower price variation (though this narrowing of price
differentials between markets came to a halt in the late 1990s) and in large price falls
in certain areas such as airline fares and telephone calls. There was also a strong
expansion in intra-EU trade, while imports from non-EU sources also expanded
strongly (pointing to the absence of any "Fortress Europe" trade diversion effect).
Foreign direct investment (FDI) into EU locations also expanded much more strongly
than trade itself. The resulting GDP growth was estimated to be 1.8% higher, though
the report states that this may be an underestimate, with an employment gain
in aggregate from all these market-opening measures (including telecoms and
utilities) of 2.5 million jobs.[12]

Finally, a survey of the first 15 years of the single market concluded that there had
been a total rise in EU GDP of 2.15%, or €518 per citizen, compared with the absence
of an SEM. This study stressed the gains in terms of personal and occupational mobility, the marked falls in telephone and airline prices, falls of between 10% and 30% for
typical products of public purchasing, and falls in the cost of setting up a new
company.[13]

Much remains, though, to be accomplished, as evidenced by the implementation
reports of the Commission, and also its 2003–2006 Internal Market Strategy, its
November 2007 package of initiatives, the Financial Services Action Plan, the Services
Directive, and repeated attempts by the Competition Directorate-General to prise
open energy markets and weaken the strength of incumbents in telecommunications.
Concerning the transposition of directives into national legislation, this has improved
with time such that the Internal Market Scoreboard in February 2006 indicated that
only 1.6% of the relevant legislation required national implementation, a proportion
very close to the official target of 1.5%. The SOLVIT network is a relatively informal

way of resolving problems of cross-border access to markets, which brings the parties together and seeks to ensure a common interpretation and implementation of the single-market rules. Infringement cases of single-market legislation have been a problem, however, and in September 2003 a record 1,500 cases outstanding was reached.[14]

The Ten-Point Plan of the Internal Market Strategy 2003–2006 made clear that there remained considerable work for completion in the four domains of enforcing internal market law, making the free supply of services a practical reality, removing the remaining obstacles to trade, and building a genuinely European public procurement market. The Commission report of July 2002 on the internal market for services[15] showed that integration in this sector had been very limited both in services generally and particularly in financial services. While the directives of the late 1980s and early 1990s – such as the Directive on Investment Services (which created a "passport" for EU-registered financial services companies), the succession of banking and insurance directives, and the more recent prospectus and pensions directives – all sought to make free right of establishment for financial product suppliers and free supply of financial products a concrete reality, there remained largely a fragmentation of markets and the Financial Services Action Programme[16] sought to address key remaining obstacles.

The Commission's November 2007 package of initiatives shows that there is still much to be done in all these service areas. The package focuses on achieving a European market in retail financial services; creating a "start-up" initiative to ease the creation of small- and medium-sized enterprises (SMEs); easing worker mobility; strengthening the intellectual property, copyright, and patenting systems; and exploiting more effectively the potential for cross-border public procurement, including e-procurement.[17]

The Draft Services Directive (COM 2004)2 of January 13, 2004 sought to bring the large swathe of the services sector previously scarcely touched by the SEM under single-market rules. Goods and utilities markets had been the target of the SEM, but although services made up 70% of output and more than 70% of employment in the EU, they make up only 20% of total EU cross-border trade and much of this is in travel and tourism. Of course, much of the services sector is residentiary, providing local services, but diverse branches such as leisure, IT, medicine, legal and fiscal advice, and construction and employment services could be opened up to cross-border competition, with similar types of economic gain to those of goods-market liberalization. Many national restrictions prevented cross-border supply or the establishment of a subsidiary in another country by a services company. Discriminatory requirements such as authorization and licensing procedures, and other bureaucratic red-tape processes, hindered effective cross-border competition, and were especially dissuasive for SMEs. Differing tax, accounting, and professional qualification rules, and residence requirements, and restrictions on the "unbundling" of services, all acted as hindrances.[18]

The directive did not cover financial, postal, transport, and telecommunication services, already covered by other measures, nor did it affect non-pecuniary public-sector services. The key principles to opening markets in support services were mutual recognition, as for goods, and, connected to this, the "home-country" principle, whereby the home-country regulations, including business and employment regulations, would apply in the supply of the service across the border. A "one-stop shop" or single official point of reference and access would be created in each country to ease registration by potential foreign competitor firms, which should be particularly beneficial to SMEs. The draft directive created a storm of protest among trade unions and some national politicians, who saw in these provisions the perfect mechanism for "social dumping," whereby competitive pressures ensure that looser regulations would force relaxation of tighter ones, including employment protection legislation. It was feared that companies in more regulated countries would set up subsidiaries in those less regulated and then supply services from that jurisdiction. However, the storm over the draft directive had a strong ideological element, with caricatures of the "Polish plumber," since it had always been made clear that the Posting of Workers Directive (96/71/EC) would continue to apply: this would ensure that host-country employment legislation, such as minimum wages, would apply to workers temporarily employed there, although of course the team of workers might not be subject to collectively bargained terms, unless these terms applied to the sector as a whole in the host country. Only employees, not the self-employed, are covered by the directive. There are also derogations from the Services Directive for public safety, health, and environment reasons, and of course postal and network services are excluded.[19]

Following much critical debate in the EU Council and the Parliament, a much diluted directive was agreed in late 2006, with a deadline for implementation of practical measures specified for the end of 2009. In essence, the revised directive seeks to ensure that the European Social Model is sustained and that cross-border supply of services must acknowledge host-country rules. There is much here that is weakly specified, but it is clear that this is tighter than the rules governing goods trade, where outside of the importing country's public health, safety, and environmental regulations, the exporting country's rules apply.

Separately, the phased opening of air travel and telecoms markets through the 1990s had brought large savings to the consumer and a large increase in traffic, while member state resistance to the opening of monopolized gas and electricity markets had led to very variable performance, but the price differentials here between states reflected closely the degree to which the market had been liberalized.[20] Over the 1990s and the 2000s, competition policy has become very active in policing the single market and in prising open monopolized markets. Frustration at the slow pace of energy liberalization and in loosening incumbent power over the "local loop" in broadband/telecommunications has led to renewed threats of further forced liberalization by the Competition and Telecommunications Directorates-General.[21] Separately, the fact that the Commission could only find acceptance among member states (particularly Germany) for a very diluted takeover directive continues to hamper the creation of a single market in company ownership rights.

The Common Agricultural Policy: in Perpetual Reform?

While the CAP (Common Agricultural Policy) has long been the EU's most developed and most interventionist common policy, it remains the most criticized, particularly by economic liberals.[22] Reform seems perpetual, always a work in progress. Common criticisms of the CAP – apart from its high consumer prices, its dominance of the EU budget, and its subsidized ("dumped") exports – were that it failed signally to meet many of its objectives. It favored "northern" products rather than upland or Mediterranean produce; it rewarded large producers very handsomely, while transferring little to the small farmer, it induced intensive farming with damaging ecological consequences, and it had negative impacts on Third World farming.[23]

After a partial reform in 1988, the last decade through to the present day has seen fundamental shifts in the CAP mode of support,[24] from high support prices and accompanying intervention to buy up the surplus produce, to direct payments to farmers which are increasingly decoupled from production and so are less economically distorting. Price cuts meanwhile have narrowed the gap with world prices and a period of very high world prices may now characterize the wider context for the policy. Both internal and world trade pressures continue to force change. It was the 1992 MacSharry Reform and the 1993 Blair House (GATT) agreement which first demonstrated an EC/EU willingness to confront fundamental reform. Though the EU farm commissioner, Ray MacSharry, claimed that his reform was independent of the pressures originating from the GATT world trade talks, it is clear that it laid the groundwork for a compromise world trade agreement.

Around 1990, the USA, Canada, and the so-called "Cairns Group" of Australasian and Latin American temperate foodstuff producers threatened non-renewal of the GATT world trade agreements if large-scale cutbacks in subsidized (dumped) farm exports were not agreed in the approaching Uruguay Round. This group sought a "tariffication," namely the conversion of all protection into tariffs, which would then be cut over time, lowering domestic protection and lowering export subsidy.[25]

The MacSharry package of 1992, reached after fierce resistance by France, among others, produced large cuts of up to 35% in the cereals support price, and an obligatory set-aside of 12% of arable land (for all but farmers of less than approximately 20 hectares of land), but coupled these with full compensation for associated revenue losses. Such compensation, it was argued, since it was linked to past output levels, was not a direct incentive to produce more – it was, to a degree, uncoupled from production. In the jargon of the GATT negotiations, this meant they were no longer in the "amber box," the most trade-distorting. (The "green box" covered permissible non-distorting instruments, while the "blue box" measures had some distortionary effect).[26] Small price cuts affected beef, butter, and oilseeds. In spite of violent resistance and street protests by farmers, the 1993 Blair House accord sealed a compromise between the USA and the EU over farm export subsidies, which therefore allowed the Uruguay Round to be concluded. Here, the focus was clearly on subsidized exports by volume and value. A cut in the value of subsidized exports by 29% and in volume by 24% was agreed for wheat, and binding constraints over time were set. (These latter concerned the volume of subsidized exports and the associated protective levy permitted on wheat imports – the so-called "bound tariff," which was a specific but decreasing level of tariff, so lowering protection over time.)

For the EU, these changes affected largely only the cereals sector, with little reform in other products and a partial switch in support from consumers to taxpayers.[27] In aggregate, the Uruguay Round Agreement on Agriculture (URAA) cut the average measure of support for cereals by 20%. In the first half of the 1990s, then, the reforms appeared to be highly successful such that production surpluses and food mountains temporarily melted away. The compulsory land set-asides temporarily lost their force.

To an important extent, it was shortages on world markets, and the associated high prices, which eased external pressures on the CAP. This market situation proved only temporary in the 1990s.

From the mid-1990s, discussion again came to focus on further reform, partly because the constraints of the URAA were expected finally to begin to bite, and because enlargement to include large agricultural producers in central Europe would make it impossible to hold to the EU's international commitments on export subsidy volumes and levels. A further trade round in the form of the WTO Millennium Round was scheduled for the end of the decade. Under an unreformed CAP, applied to the accession countries, excess production would swamp the storage facilities and world markets with potentially millions of tonnes of surpluses.[28] Even without enlargement, the declining bound tariff (i.e. falling specific level of tariff) on cereals imports would force further cuts in the EU wheat support price towards the end of the decade. The limit on the volume of subsidized cereals exports might also become a serious constraint. Precious little reform had occurred in the beef and dairy sectors, with none in the sugar sector.[29] Furthermore, under the URAA, no new production subsidies could be introduced and this would act as a serious constraint on CEECs should they wish to raise support prices closer to EU levels; equally, only some CEECs possessed negotiated GATT/WTO quotas for subsidized farm exports and their bound tariff levels were lower than the EU's. A straightforward extension of an unreformed CAP to the east would therefore be impossible.[30] The prospect was also that other, largely unreformed, sectors such as dairying, beef, and sugar would come under strong attack at the WTO 2000 Millennium Round from non-EU temperate foodstuffs producers.

A preparatory EC Commission study in 1996 assumed that the CAP, as reformed in 1992, would when applied to ten CEECs cost an extra ECU 9 billion by 2000 (where the ECU, or European Currency Unit, as a composite currency, preceded the single currency). Building on these results, the "Agenda 2000 for a Stronger and Wider Europe" proposals therefore sought to introduce fundamental reforms to the CAP and structural funds, while concurrently establishing a financial perspective for 2000–2006, which would encompass enlargement.[31] These Agenda 2000 farm reform proposals clearly sought a shift to non-production-related aid, namely decoupled aid, and extended the thrust of the 1992 MacSharry reforms further, to encompass large price cuts in beef, dairy product, and cereals prices. Full compensation payments would be made, but these would henceforth require fulfilment of environmental objectives such as a less intensive mode of farming (the so-called "cross-compliance").[32]

Following strong debate between reformers and CAP defenders, the agricultural ministers agreed a less radical package of measures in March 1999, further watered down by the heads of government at the Berlin summit of July 1999, under French intransigence and a German desire to restrict the budgetary consequences. The cost, including enlargement, it was envisaged, would be contained within the overall EU budget ceiling of 1.27% of GDP. Of course, these costs covered essentially the taxpayer costs of transfers via the budget and not the continuing consumer costs in the form of high prices. In essence, the Agenda 2000 settlement put off the difficult issues of CEEC enlargement and the WTO Round. By far the greater part of farm support remained market-distorting and key farm product sectors remained un-reformed.[33] The difficult issue of whether compensation payments would be extended to the east also remained unresolved, although the assumption was they would not be made.

The most recent completed EU farm reform covered the Medium-Term Review of 2002–2003,[34] proposed by farm commissioner Fischler and again strongly disputed by France. Mr. Fischler, however, was addressing the issues that enlargement in 2004 posed, together with those of the Doha Round (the extended WTO Millennium Round) negotiations of September 2003. It was clear that the Agenda 2000 agreement of 1999 had failed signally to address either issue, with the CAP instruments still not WTO-compatible and with the fundamental problems of incorporating the CEECs into the CAP. As noted, CEECs each had various WTO-permitted subsidized export volumes and different bound tariff levels, which made harmonization and integration into the existing CAP highly complex.

After considerable opposition by France and after a Franco-German bilateral deal which set the level of farm funding to 2013, a diluted agreement was finally reached in June 2003, so enabling the EU to present a united front at WTO negotiations and, it was hoped, to absorb CEECs in a coherent manner. The final EU agreement of June 2003 diluted the proposals but the thrust and principles remained. Mr. Fischler sought to convert all support into direct payments and to "decouple" these fully from production by linking the grant of aid to good farm practice and environmental objectives – the so-called "cross-compliance." Such payments would be made as the Single Farm Payment (SFP) from 2005, and at the latest by 2007.

In this way, previous "blue box" payments would become "green," and so WTO-compatible, since farmers would respond in future to market pricing to orient their production decisions. However, for livestock farmers (to prevent many giving up farming altogether), up to 30% of the current support could continue as output-related for several years, rather than support comprising very largely only the SFP. Set-aside requirements would remain in place. The total volume of expenditure would stay at the planned level of €43 billion, but would of course be converted from price support and compensation payments to the SFP direct payments. External protection in the form of a (declining) levy would remain in place and so the domestic price level would be protected externally, albeit in a declining manner.

Meanwhile, Mr. Fischler sought for aid per farm to be capped at €300,000 (to ensure it flowed to medium and small farms rather than to the largest) and for direct payments based on historic levels to be converted over time to payments made in fulfillment of environmental, animal welfare or organic farming objectives (the so-called Pillar II). With some price cuts and a scaling-back of excess production, export subsidies would fall. There would also be reductions in payments to larger farmers (payments exceeding €5,000 pa) on a sliding scale of 3% in 2005, 4% in 2006, and 5% in 2007, a mechanism known as "modulation." These withheld funds would be devoted to project finance under national rural development plans. Finally, price cuts would be introduced over the four years to 2007 of 10% for butter and 15% for skimmed milk powder, additional to the Agenda 2000 phased cuts, but the dairy regime would not be reformed before 2008.[35] The cereals intervention price was maintained, but adjustments were made in some lesser product market support organizations. The highly distortionary sugar regime at that stage continued unreformed.

In aggregate, the Commission then maintained that 80% of farm spending would be switched to non-trade-distorting support (i.e. decoupled), while leaving the overall level of payments to farmers untouched. The CEECs (as well as Cyprus and Malta) would be progressively integrated into this system, as in their transitional periods they moved to the common price level and the common product market organizations, adopting also the external protection system. For the EU10 (the ten accession states of the 2004 enlargement), the SFP would be paid at the rate of 25% initially (Poland: 40% via a diversion of farm structural aid to direct payments), rising to 100% by 2013.[36] Impact studies foresaw that this 2003 reform should lead to more extensive modes of production and also to income gains for EU farmers, though compared with the policy programmed by the Agenda 2000 decisions, the impact would be broadly neutral for EU15 (the fifteen EU states prior to the 2004 enlargement) farmers. For enlargement-country farmers, however, there would be significant staged income rises of perhaps 45% in real terms in aggregate by 2009.[37]

Reminiscent of the changed world agricultural markets situation of the mid-1990s, the 2007/2008 world markets are ones of rapidly rising foodstuffs prices and a rapid rundown of food stocks. Poor harvests, but particularly high demand for cereals, milk products, and meat emanating from Russia, China, and India and the conversion of corn into ethanol, have led to heavy excess demand pressures. Between mid-2006 and mid-2007, world wheat prices rose by 80% and those of maize by 50%, while the EU's wheat stocks fell from 14 million tonnes to 1 million tonnes over the same period. The EU farm commissioner responded with a temporary derogation from all set-aside for a twelve-month period, and the suspension of wheat import duties and dairy export subsidies.[38] The proposal now is that this temporary ending of set aside, of intervention buying (except for milling wheat), and export subsidies should be made permanent. The commissioner, Mrs. Fischer Boel, seeks also to introduce degressive farm payments to larger farmers, such that the SFPs are cut by increasing amounts at over €100,000, over €200,000, and €300,000, thereby seeking (as Mr. Fischler had sought) to limit the payments to farm barons. As occurs in some other distributional settings, the largest 20% of farms receive 80% of the support. Finally, Mrs. Fischer Boel is seeking to stimulate milk production by increasing milk quotas well before they come to an end in 2015.[39] In the intervening period, sugar reforms and wine-lake reforms have been instituted or negotiated. For 2013, the end of the present EU budgetary period, all expectations are that the current forms of subsidy under the CAP will fall and that more radical change will ensue.

The Challenges of Enlargement to the East

In May 2004, the EU was enlarged once more, this time adding ten new members, comprising eight central and eastern European countries (CEECs) and the two Mediterranean islands of Cyprus and Malta, and subsequently, in January 2007, Romania and Bulgaria joined. The earlier enlargement of 1995 to include the ex-EFTA (European Free Trade Area) countries of Austria, Finland, and Sweden had proven largely unproblematical, given their status as advanced, wealthy economies, which would be net contributors to the EU budget. Enlargement to include CEECs has presented, conversely, a large-scale challenge in spite of the fundamental transformation which has occurred there with their transition from central planning. The fall of the Berlin Wall in 1989 offered the historic opportunity, but also the huge challenge, of uniting Europe once more. The EU's response has proven to be somewhat slow and half-hearted, ever sensitive to the adjustments which would be required. While the initial EU response was to offer free-trade agreements, more ambitious integration measures were delayed (partly due to Germany's early focus on its own unification), and the prospect of full membership was only broached in 1993, with formal procedures put in place from 1997. While countries in the vanguard of reform, such as Hungary, had hoped to gain membership by 2000, the delay in the process was evident and disappointment at the less than generous terms of membership widespread.[40]

The successive steps in EU opening to the east concerned the early bilateral free-trade agreements for industrial goods in 1990, the transformation of these into association agreements (the so-called "Europe Agreements") signed from 1991 to 1996 and the decision to set criteria and procedures at the Copenhagen EU Council in 1993. The process (building on decisions taken at the Essen summit in 1994) was clarified in the Luxembourg Council meeting of December 1997 when procedures for vetting and approving progress for membership were put in place, to cover an envisaged first wave of seven applicant countries. This approach was speeded up at the Helsinki Council of December 1999, when it was agreed to treat the eight CEECs and two island states as a group (while acknowledging that Romania and Bulgaria would then be considered for subsequent entry). Such had been the incentive of EU membership for the so-called "second wave" that most applicants introduced the rapid reforms needed for them to become eligible for assessment for full membership.[41] Meanwhile, a separate process known as the Stabilization and Association Process for five Balkan states was instituted in May 1999. The CIS (Commonwealth of Independent States), including the Russian Federation, has Partnership and Cooperation Agreements, which lie outside the association process, reflecting in part the fact that only four of these CIS countries have joined the WTO.

The 1993 European Council in Copenhagen decided on three main criteria candidates had to fulfill for EU membership:

1 achievement of stability of institutions guaranteeing democracy, the rule of law, human rights, and respect for and protection of minorities;
2 the existence of a functioning market economy as well as the capacity to cope with competitive pressure and market forces within the union; and
3 the ability to take on the obligations of membership, including adherence to the aims of political, economic, and monetary union.[42]

Candidate countries must also demonstrate that they have incorporated the *acquis communautaire* into their legislation and have the capacity to implement this effectively through their administrative and judicial structures. The economic criteria in practice involve meeting sub-criteria such as economic growth rates, monetary stability, fiscal consolidation, market functioning, and productivity prospects.

The accession strategy came to comprise six stages, as follows:

1 Association agreements are first negotiated bilaterally between EU and candidate.
2 A White Paper on the preparation of candidates for the single market specifies the essential elements for adoption and the priorities for legal harmonization.
3 The PHARE Programme acts as the key financial support instrument.
4 Bilateral accession partnership programs specify short- and medium-term objectives, together with the EU financial aid which would underpin them. Each candidate country prepares a program for the adoption of EU law, specifying a timetable for this commitment and the national resources involved.
5 Progress made in each member state is assessed for the 31 chapters of the *acquis* and published annually in the form of progress reports.
6 Accession negotiations began in November 1998 for the first wave and in April 2000 for the second wave.[43]

The challenge for candidate states in assuming and meeting EU legislation cannot be over-emphasized. The 31 chapters of EU legislation covered the full range of EU activity, including the free movement of labor, capital, services, and products. Chapters varied significantly in terms of their complexity and the most controversial areas – such as justice and home affairs (migration, visas, etc.), tax, competition, transport, and the budget, and agricultural and regional assistance – were left until later. Indeed in some of these much-debated policy areas, EU reforms among existing member states were required first. A compromise was reached on free movement of labor in that countries such as Germany and Austria could rely on a seven-year transition period, while the UK opened its borders to CEEC migrants from their accession onwards. As for the applicant countries themselves, there were many requests for longer transition periods, delaying complete fulfillment of EU legislative requirements.

The adoption of the *acquis* involved very significant resource costs indeed for applicants and the EU made available pre-accession funding in areas such as institution-building, technical assistance, training, economic and social cohesion (under the PHARE Programme), infrastructural and environmental improvement (ISPA – Instrument for Structural Policies for Pre-Accession) and agricultural modernization (SAPARD – Special Accession Programme for Agricultural and Rural Development). In total, financial support under these programs was of the order of €10 billion in the years 1990–2003, and in 2005 approximately €1.8 billion was transferred, equalling 0.3% of EU10 GDP.[44] In general, these programs functioned well, although SAPARD experienced set-up problems at the outset.[45] The continuing costs involved in raising standards in CEECs to EU requirements are huge. The adoption of the *acquis* requires more than 14,000 legal changes in accession countries, posing huge technical, administrative, and financing challenges. For example, the infrastructure investments in transport and the environment alone needed to achieve EU standards would amount over a 20-year period to between 8% and 10.5% of CEECs' GDP (in 1998 prices).[46] The EU budget assists, particularly through its structural aid, but this assumes a 50% contribution by the recipient country – a heavy burden.

The Nice summit of December 2000 closed the EU's IGC (inter-governmental conference) on enlargement's impact on EU institutions and the reforms required. Concurrently, the heads of state and government approved final plans to complete enlargement negotiations. The ensuing Treaty of Nice provided for a revision in the size and composition of the Commission upon enlargement, revision of voting rules in the Council, the extension of qualified majority voting, the associated expansion of co-decision powers of the European Parliament (EP), a redistribution of EP seats to favor the reunited Germany, and an enhanced cooperation procedure, permitting certain countries willing to advance integration further to do so. Of course, the Lisbon Reform Treaty of late 2007 adjusts and extends many of these changes, although it is not discussed in any detail here, since it has very little economic content.

Trade and FDI links expanded rapidly from 1990 onwards, enmeshing CEECs into close economic integration with western Europe. There was a fundamental reorientation of CEEC trade flows towards the west in the early 1990s and the EU had completely supplanted the former Soviet Union as the CEECs' prime trading partner as early as 1993. Trade links in goods are now very close: in 2003, for example, the EU15 took 67% of the EU10's total goods exports and supplied 58% of their goods imports. The relevant proportions in 1993 were 57% and 55%.[47]

There is no strong evidence that this trade creation between western and eastern Europe has harmed non-European exports to the area in the form of trade diversion. Trade development has helped the acceding countries develop new product specializations, such as vehicles and components and refined food, petroleum, chemical, rubber, and plastics products. In all, such goods exchanges show a certain complementarity in the structures of goods production between the EU15 and the EU10, where the latter show specializations in labor-intensive and low- and medium-to-low technology products, while in the west medium-to high-technology and capital intensive products characterize the structure of goods output. To a considerable extent, this restructuring and reorientation of output specialization is linked to FDI generally and to FDI by European multinationals. The stock of FDI from EU15 into EU10 countries amounted to 47% of their GDP in 2004 and over three-quarters of the total FDI stock in EU10 derives from the EU15.[48] The FDI flows also show a heavy concentration upon the central European states as the chief host countries, with 80% of the stock located in Poland, the Czech Republic, and Hungary. Much of the FDI flowed from Germany and Austria, their close neighbors, although the USA has also been a key investor.[49]

Concerning the provisions for trade preferences, EU Trade and Cooperation Agreements were first signed with Poland, Hungary, and Czechoslovakia in 1990 and trade preference was then extended to other CEECs. These initially provided for the application of the GSP (Generalized System of Preferences) regime traditionally offered to less-developed countries and, additionally, specific and nonspecific quantitative restrictions on imports were lifted for one year, with the exception of import restrictions on "sensitive" products, such as steel, textiles, coal, and CAP products. These provisions were then extended to remaining CEECs (though not to the former Soviet Union): Article 238 discussions were opened with central European countries on association agreements, which offered the potentiality of eventual full EU membership.

These "Europe Agreements" came into force from March 1992 onwards and were bilateral, asymmetric free-trade agreements, whereby the EU would engage in tariff abolition on industrial goods imports from the associated state over a six-year period, and the partner state would commence market-opening later, from 1995 for a ten-year period. In practice, Poland, the Czech Republic, and Hungary permitted tariff-free entry for approximately three-quarters of their manufactured goods imports by the end of 1994, while the EU for its part was engaging in "managed trade" with "contingent protection" (the threat of trade barrier imposition if imports caused market disruption) rather than free trade.[50] Managed trade refers to the restrictions on imports of sensitive products: these products made up 50% of central Europe's manufactured exports to the EU, though they represented only a tiny fraction of EU imports. Even were CEEC sensitive product exports to be admitted to the EU market duty-free, this would have produced a fall in the EU's output of such products by only 2–4%. Examples of such managed trade were the crisis cartel pricing rules on iron and steel products, managed EU domestic coal production limits, the strict quota limits on imports of CAP products, the application of the GATT/WTO multi-fiber agreement on textile and apparel imports, and, finally, the use of severe antidumping rules on chemicals imports.[51] EU rules of origin are also restrictive.

There was much discussion of where the costs of adjustment to cheaper imports from CEECs would be felt in the west. Would CEEC exports challenge the labor- and raw material-intensive output more characteristic of "southern" Europe, or would they compete directly with "northern" output, which is typified by skill- and capital-intensive, medium- and high-technology manufactures?[52] We now know from the structure of product specialization that there is a broad complementarity between the type of goods produced in EU10 and those in EU15. However, there can be little doubt that the pressure of low wage competition has been felt in the west not solely in labor-intensive and material-intensive goods output, but also in transport equipment, other metal goods, electrical products, and some capital equipment. There has been much discussion of the outsourcing of production to the east and of the "delocalization" of production to sites there. Evidence appears to show that these fears are much exaggerated, although lower value-added and low-skilled production in the west has been under competitive threat, and for many years now. Likewise, the flows of eastern migrants to the west have displaced some lesser-skilled labor and have lowered wage pressure at the low end of the wages hierarchy.[53] Studies of the potential growth gains from enlargement to CEEC have pointed to small adjustment costs in the present EU15, but to quite large gains in accession countries, which would be amplified if membership brought a much lower cost of capital through a reduced risk premium.[54]

Budgetary Implications of Enlargement

Key economic concerns in enlargement focused on the CAP impact and on budgetary matters, which were and are clearly linked. The budgetary issues (accompanied by parallel debates on farm reform) were addressed in the Agenda 200 proposals, settled at the Berlin summit in 1998 and, secondly, at the Copenhagen summit in December 2002, which finalized the accession terms, though the budgetary frame for the new 2007–2013 period was only settled in mid-2006.

Under the Agenda 2000 proposals, the CAP reform component assumed that compensation payments would not be applied to applicants, since they had never benefited from high farm support prices. The Berlin Agreement of 1999 gave a financial perspective for the period 2000–2006 and capped total EU expenditure, including that for new members, within the allowable ceiling of 1.27% of the EU15 GDP. Of this, €42.6 billion was dedicated to new members. Gross annual expenditure for new members would rise from initially €11 billion to €16 billion in 2006 and, in terms of functional areas, agricultural support would initially make up 18–26% of payments and 60–70% of structural reform, the remainder would support internal policies and administration. A key change occurred, though, in early 2002 when it was finally confirmed that the compensation payments to EU15 farmers would have to be extended to accession countries.[55] In negotiations between Brussels and the accession countries in 2002, accession countries stressed that the total net benefit (primarily from the agricultural and regional funds) would be far lower, at approximately €25 billion, taking account of their contributions, and that in the first year they would hit budgetary crises, since contributions are paid early, while receipts can arrive after long delays. A special cash facility was therefore established of €1.3 billion to avoid such cash-flow problems.

After intense haggling in December 2002, the final settlement allowed gross EU15 transfers to accession states of €40.2 billion (in 1999 prices) in 2004–2006 (plus a further €0.9 billion for training associated with the Schengen Agreement border controls and €0.6 billion for the closure of nuclear power stations in Lithuania and Slovakia). Sweeteners for Poland's farmers were also negotiated.[56] However, in terms of development aid per head under the agricultural and regional funds, accession countries would receive only €137 per head annually or 60% of that pertaining in the EU15's poorest member states. The outcome allowed the 1999 Berlin Agreement's limits on budgetary spending for enlargement to be observed. However, it must be borne in mind that net transfers (net of their budgetary contributions) to the newcomers represented only 3.5% of the EU budget and less than 2% of the newcomers' GDP, and 0.1% of the EU15 GDP.[57]

There remained, though, the question of the consequences for the new 2007–2013 budgetary period. Here, the prime issue remained that of the extension of the CAP in its entirety to the EU27, as well as of future changes to EU regional policy. In a study which utilizes five different scenarios, ranging from the status quo to the progressive phasing-out of direct farm payments, Brücker and Weise concluded that there would be just sufficient in the rising EU budget to 2013 to accommodate an EU25 (Bulgaria and Romania were not included in the assessment) under unchanged CAP and structural funds.[58] This derives largely from the 1% inflation uprating annually permitted for the farm spending ceiling. The full rise in the EU budget to 2013 would still, however, only represent 0.9% of EU27 GDP, scarcely an impossible burden for present members. Under the new Financial Framework 2007–2013, net financial transfers are expected to rise through time to up to three times the 2006 net level of transfers, with poorer countries among accession states expected to benefit more. Net transfers will vary over time and by accession country from 1.6% to 3.3% of national GDP in the period to the end of 2013.[59] This framework was agreed after the inevitable public rows among EU leaders in mid-2006 and the UK had to agree a reimbursement mechanism for the parts of its rebate which would otherwise have to have been met by accession states themselves.

The European Monetary System in Crisis and the Path to EMU

By the early 1990s the first stage in the move to monetary union had commenced, but the EMS (European Monetary System), the then prevailing exchange rate regime, was in full crisis. Following the commitment to "closer monetary integration" contained in the 1986 Single European Act and the 1989 Delors Report, an intergovernmental conference led to agreement in December 1991 on the Maastricht Treaty, which itself set out clearly the steps and requirements for transition to a single currency. The first phase of the euro project had commenced on July 1, 1990, when barriers to capital movements were lifted and states intending to participate joined the ESCB (European System of Central Banks). Concurrently, the EMS, with its Exchange Rate Mechanism (ERM) system of fixed but adjustable exchange rates, had erroneously come to be viewed as the "glide path" to monetary union. As a result, it had in 1987 entered the phase known as the "hard ERM." During the 1987–1992 period, there were almost no currency realignments and investors had come to consider the ERM exchange rates prevailing as essentially "hardened," as forerunners of the final exchange rates which would pertain when national currencies were replaced by the single currency. However, the underlying economic reality did not permit such rigid currency relations and economic performance among the participating member states diverged markedly. Not only did the real exchange rates of a range of currencies rise against the Deutschmark (DM) (implying a loss of competitiveness for those states), but a key background condition for the 1992–1993 ERM crises was the contrast between the deep recessionary conditions in the UK, France, and Belgium and the boom in a newly reunified Germany.

The EMS was suffering the so-called "asymmetric shock" of German unification, which called for a revaluation of the DM, but this was ruled out on political grounds, as the Community had entered stage one of monetary union. To counter the overheating of the unification boom, the Bundesbank raised interest rates to historic high levels and these, through Germany's dominance of the Exchange Rate Mechanism, led to very high real interest rates in the countries in recession, rates which ruled out any prospect of recovery. The way was free for speculators to engage in a one-way bet on deep devaluations of currencies such as sterling, particularly since controls on capital movements among EMS currencies had been abolished by mid-1990.

When the referendum in France on the Maastricht Treaty only passed with the narrowest of majorities, investors came to believe that the single-currency project was no longer such a certainty and a tidal wave of speculation was unleashed. This forced the pound sterling and the lira out of the system and a deep devaluation of the peseta, and the French franc was saved at its prevailing DM exchange rate only by punitively high interest rates. A second speculation against the franc in August 1993 led to the widening of the ERM's permitted bands of fluctuation (around the central ECU rate) from +/− 2.25% to the very broad and scarcely constraining bands of +/− 15%. This came to be known as the ERM II and member currencies largely regrouped quickly within it around the previous narrow bands as a "hard core," with the lira rejoining only in 1996 and with sterling floating freely.[60]

This episode merely strengthened the views of both protagonists and antagonists in the debate over the wisdom of a single currency, pointing as it did to the problem of a single interest rate level in a grouping of divergent economies. Opponents of the single currency pointed to the rigidities of the exchange rates and to the inappropriateness of a single interest rate level, while proponents claimed that currencies should therefore either float freely or fix rigidly, with, it is claimed, a rigid fixing of currencies forcing convergence.[61]

The gains of a single currency can be elaborated fairly simply: they are the allocative gains of higher price transparency and so price competition and of greater trade, FDI, and free capital movements, the potential dynamic gains of higher investment rates owing to the abolition of currency risk premia within the zone; and the secondary gains of lower transactions and currency hedging costs, lower foreign exchange reserves holdings, and a wider and deeper eurozone capital market.[62] The Maastricht Treaty spelled out the stages and the criteria to be fulfilled before a country could participate in the single currency. Two countries, the UK and Denmark, had negotiated opt-outs, with the UK in particular fearing the loss of sovereignty involved in a single exchange rate and interest rate system for diverse economies. Many in the UK were very conscious of the regional problems which pertain in a single currency area and feared that the UK would become a depressed region if it lost external competitiveness and could not devalue to compensate. Of course, the ERM debacle had merely served to reinforce this view in the eyes of many. With the pound sterling floating freely after September 1992, and as a consequence of the deep in-fighting in the Conservative Party, the Major government announced in April 1996 that a referendum would have to be held in the UK before the adoption of the single currency. This confirmed Britain's long-standing approach of "unripe time,"[63] which was in evidence again in June 2003 when Chancellor of the Exchequer Gordon Brown announced the results of a set of exhaustive studies of the five tests.[64]

The Maastricht Treaty set out the path for the three-stage transition to the single currency, it specified the convergence criteria which had to be met by participating states (which were then extended in the form of budgetary guidelines for the single currency regime itself), and it set out the conditions for an independent European Central Bank (ECB), dedicated to price stability. The first stage, as noted, commenced on July 1, 1990 and lasted until the end of 1993. During this stage, all controls on capital movement had to be abolished, coordination enhanced, and cooperation intensified between central banks, in the frame of the ESCB. Stage two, as the forerunner to the single-currency stage, was clearly essential and this could last until either 1997, should a majority of states qualify, or end of 1998, when at least two qualifying states could then create the single currency.

During stage two, the European Monetary Institute, as forerunner to the ECB, was established, so as to strengthen monetary cooperation and surveillance, to specify closely the organizational and regulatory frame of the ESCB, and to observe the degree of economic convergence in progress. During this phase, all central banks had to become independent and participating states had to narrow the fluctuation of their currencies well within the narrow bands of the ERM. 1997 was the test year for assessment of whether the Maastricht convergence criteria had been met, and the ECB announced in March 1998 that all 11 states wishing to participate in the first round would constitute the eurozone on January 1, 1999: it was therefore to be a wide union. Greece joined in January 2001. The exchange rates prevailing in the second half of 1998 were then the rates to be irrevocably fixed with the replacement of the national currencies by the euro, the ECU, which had been the composite currency of the EMS, would be "hardened" into the euro. In practice, the "legacy" national currencies remained in being until 2002, with prices quoted in both domestic currency and euros. After a brief transition period effectively in the first two months of 2002, euro notes and coin replaced the legacy currencies.

The Maastricht convergence criteria were designed as rules to ensure that monetary and budgetary laxity was supplanted by the practice of sound finance, during the stages leading to the single currency. In this way countries with a history of weak currencies could prepare for life in a system designed principally on the German "sound-money" pattern. The criteria covered inflation and interest rate convergence and currencies had to have participated in the "normal" fluctuation bands of the ERM without severe tensions for at least two years before examination for fitness to join the single currency. Most attention was, however, paid to the general government deficit and debt criteria maxima of 3% and 60% of GDP respectively.

These criteria were criticized at the time for having no basis in economic principles,[65] and the coordinated move to budgetary discipline among continental states from 1994/1995 onwards exerted a marked deflationary effect on interlinked economies. (It was indeed only from 1998 onwards, after the criteria had been met, that a more sustained loosening of interest rates began and exerted a stimulus on these economies.) The assessments in March 1998, by the EU Commission, the European Monetary Institute and the Deutsche Bundesbank that these criteria had been met by 11 states[66] were widely regarded at the time as "political," since creative accounting had been used to achieve the 3% threshold and several countries had debt positions far in excess of 60%. As will be discussed below, these budgetary rules continue in strengthened form in the Stability and Growth Pact, which was agreed under German government pressure in December 1996 and took the form of a regulation in 1997. It was designed as an amplification of the excessive deficit procedure references of the Maastricht Treaty itself, strengthening both the "preventive" and "dissuasive" aspects of the EMU architecture, as discussed further below.

ECB Monetary Policy and the Performance of the Euro

Before the commencement of the single currency on January 1, 1999, the ECB announced the essentials of its monetary policy. The then 18-member ECB Governing Council, comprising 12 central-bank governors and the six management board members of the ECB itself, announced that the definition of price stability, and therefore the ECB's target, was to be "less than 2%" measured according to the harmonized index of consumer prices (HICP). In pursuance of price stability, the ECB would follow a two-pillar strategy and would use intervention instruments similar to those of other central banks, the prime one being the intervention rate. The two-pillar strategy rested, on the one hand, on monetary targeting as previously practiced by the Bundesbank and, on the other, on a range of forward-looking indicators of inflation. The practice of monetary targeting therefore involved an annual target growth of €3 million, "broad money," comprising money and credit.[67] The target annual growth rate of 4.5% for €3 million comprised the three elements of the inflation target, the velocity of circulation of money, and an assumed rate for the underlying growth in productive potential of the eurozone.[68]

As will be seen, the ECB faced criticism from a variety of quarters. In more technical terms, there is criticism that the demand for money function is highly uncertain in the eurozone and the short-term interest rate sensitivity of the demand for money is much lower than in Anglo-Saxon countries,[69] that the two-pillar strategy and particularly the monetary targeting pillar is misleading and confusing, that the inflation target is asymmetrical and too low, and that the operations of the ECB lack transparency and therefore do not guide expectations sufficiently.[70] More political criticisms assert that the ECB is fixed upon very low inflation, at the expense of growth and that generally it acts too little, too late. These points I expand below.

A brief sketch of the performance of the ECB would indicate a quite laudable success in that although inflation has consistently overshot its target, it has remained largely under control, with low and stable inflation expectations secured among the wider public.[71] The annual growth rate of euro M3 (the broad money aggregate of the euro money stock) millionfar exceeded its target both in the early years and in mid-decade, though without apparently inducing inflation after a time lag. Estimations of stability in the historic trend of the demand for money in eurozone countries were flawed, since the eurozone is not a mere aggregation of participating countries[72] and money holdings continue to be higher than estimates. The path of interest rates showed an early, sustained rise to 4.75% to counter inflation; they were kept on hold and then lowered to a low of 2% in summer 2003 in the light of recessionary tendencies, and held at a low level for a long subsequent period, which suggests an accommodative official stance. In fact, both nominal and real (taking account of inflation) interest rates have been as low as those practiced in the early 1970s and real interest rates have been significantly lower than those the Bundesbank practiced in the 1990s.[73] The external value of the euro has, of course fluctuated and was weak for much of the period, recovering its January 1999 value only in mid-2003. From mid-decade, however, it has strengthened markedly against the US dollar, sterling, and emerging market currencies linked to the dollar, presenting major challenges for eurozone export industries, and its rise does represent of course a monetary tightening. (It must be stressed, though, that a given exchange rate is not among the objectives of the ECB.)

There are signs that the single currency is gaining reserve-currency status and is playing an ever larger role in capital market issuance. The euro has gained ground on the US dollar as a share of known official foreign exchange reserves, reaching 26.4% in the third quarter of 2007, compared with 63.8% for the dollar. The euro's share at the beginning of the 2000s was no greater than that enjoyed in 1998 by its constituent currencies, namely, 15%. The weakening of the dollar in the mid- to late 2000s and a desire by central banks of OPEC and emerging market countries to broaden the portfolios of their foreign exchange reserves generally are linked explanations. The pace of financial market development within eurozone countries will also exert influence on the international role of the single currency. In general, there are greater shares of the euro in reserve holdings in countries geographically closer to the zone and in countries with close trade links with it. There are, though, forces of inertia and incumbency which will continue to favor the dollar, in addition to the fact that the US economy can be expected to show greater dynamic performance over the medium and longer terms. While there are very significant gains to the issuing country of a major reserve currency, reserve status also poses considerable constraints, as the UK could attest in the interwar and postwar decades. In 2006, the value of euro currency notes in circulation overtook that of the US dollar, and the euro also plays a larger role than the US currency as a denomination for international debt issues.[74]

Finally, there is the issue of whether, in bringing improved macroeconomic stability and in offering the allocative and dynamic gains of a single currency, the euro has helped raise the trend rate of output growth in the zone. Over the years since January 1999, real growth in the eurozone has been disappointing, with generally slow growth in Germany and France, in spite of better performance from mid-decade. Improved macroeconomic stability has not translated into raised growth potential for the area as a whole, in spite of evidence of greater integration through trade and FDI.[75] The ECB and EU Commission claim regularly, however, that slow growth is not due at all to monetary tightness, but to structural rigidities and overregulation in eurozone countries.[76]

Stepping back, one might conclude that the ECB has successfully introduced the euro payments system and notes and coin; that it has embedded quite impressively an operating monetary policy framework for the eurozone as a whole; that its conduct of monetary policy has been relatively assured, even with some early weaknesses of communication; and that the euro is becoming a significant international reserve currency, playing also a very significant role in capital market issuance. The discussion below focusing on the Stability and Growth Pact shows that there is both academic debate and more damaging critical political debate over the institutions and economic governance of the zone. Also, the adjustment strains among participating countries in a single currency system, which may be a pointer to the longer-term viability of the eurozone, are discussed briefly below.

First, there is the issue of whether the ECB has an excessive price stability bias (at the expense of growth) and of whether its response is "too little, too late." Assessing interest rate decisions in "Taylor rule" terms, whereby a central bank is assumed to respond equally to the deviation of actual inflation from target and to the output gap, the EU Commission study finds that the ECB has been largely accommodative.[77] Artus finds that the ECB, without acknowledging it, has acted anti-cyclically to support demand (namely by interest rate reductions in excess of those "justified" by a Taylor rule), and that its reaction times are similar to those of other central banks, and faster than the Bundesbank had been.[78] Goodhart also argues that the ECB has been as lenient as possible in its monetary decisions, as would be consistent with its primary aim of maintaining price stability.[79] The central bank cannot therefore be seriously branded as slow and too focused on price stability, as many eurozone politicians claim is the case. Secondly, more specific criticism issues relate, however, to the misleading nature of M3 growth (and therefore of the first pillar of policy) and of the asymmetry of the inflation target. This latter is of considerable concern in Germany, where inflation over the 2000s has often been below 1%, near to a falling price level, and so real interest rates remain high, depressing demand growth in stagnant or recessionary economic times.[80] Other countries such as Ireland or Spain experienced boom conditions, and this clear divergence in performance points to the fundamental difficulties of operating a "one size fits all" monetary policy.

Partly in response to the mounting criticisms, the ECB announced in late 2002 that it would review all aspects of its monetary policy. The outcome of the review in June 2003 offered some concessions to critics.[81] The inflation target was clarified as being below, but close to, 2% on the HICP over the medium term and that, while the monetary targeting pillar would be retained, this had primarily a medium- and longer-term significance, such that growth targets for €M3 would no longer be announced, except for a minimum two-year time frame.

Reference has been made to divergence in performance since the introduction of the euro between a slower-growth, low-inflation, high-exporting Germany at the core of the eurozone and smaller, "peripheral" countries (particularly Ireland and Spain) which have boomed and overheated, with higher inflation rates and external payments imbalances. Italy represents something of a special case, since it has lost external competitiveness to a very serious degree since 1999. The "one size fits all" monetary policy, with its single interest rate level for a diverse set of countries, means that monetary loosening (or tightening) cannot be adopted for stagnating (or booming) economies; meanwhile states are very constrained in their budgetary policy, since in actual practice the SGP does not leave them with large room for maneuver for stabilization purposes. Underlying these considerations is the old debate of whether the eurozone constitutes an OCA (optimum currency area), in other words of whether states have alternative means of adjustment to the loss of external competitiveness which threatens depression or, alternatively, to the problem of excessive overheating. An asymmetric shock, such as a particular sensitivity to energy prices, dependence on a particular branch for exports, or a poorly developed IT sector, could all trigger difficulties affecting individual states but not the generality.

Of course, a lack of synchronization of business cycles can also lead to temporary difficulties under a single interest rate regime. If countries cannot readily adjust, the sustainability of the currency union is called into question in the longer term. Principally, adjustment mechanisms would include price and wage flexibility, labor and capital mobility, and official financial flows such as social transfers or public investment: all these represent significant tools for adjustment when the exchange rate and interest rate setting are lost to a nation – which has now become a region in a monetary union. The so-called "Walters critique" (first enunciated by Professor Alan Walters, a special adviser to Margaret Thatcher in the early 1980s) addressed the supposed fundamental flaws in the ERM, but its essence is equally pertinent when in the context of a common set of interest rates applied to divergent economies in a monetary union. Monetary policy could here have a pro-cyclical effect, exacerbating divergence and rendering convergence all the more problematic. Countries experiencing inflationary growth would face low or negative real interest rates (where the high inflation rate may equal or exceed the single interest rate), and in contrast countries in recession and having very low inflation would face very high real interest rates (where real interest rates indicate the real cost of borrowing). Both nominal and real convergence would hereby be far more difficult to achieve, particularly as fiscal policy is also constrained.

In the debates over EMU, some analysts favor the arguments that forces for convergence would prevail: here, increased competition and increased trade, FDI, and labor migration in EMU should all promote greater convergence. Opponents feared the pro-cyclical impact of a single interest rate and the loss of national exchange rates, and adverse movements in the common currency exchange rate could also have very negative impacts on individual states.[82] Studies by the European Commission stress that there has been greater synchronicity of business cycles in the eurozone, although disappointing aggregate rates of growth,[83] while Langedijk and Roeger find that there has been some divergence in performance in the first half of the 2000s, although the main influences may have run their course.[84] Previously higher-inflation, less developed members such as Spain, Portugal, and Ireland gained very significantly in terms of the much lower nominal and real interest rates in EMU, because of the eradication of the earlier exchange rate risk premium in their previous national interest rates.

This gain signified enhanced growth, capital inflows, and, particularly, real-estate investment, with an overheating of property markets. Demand shifted from external to domestic demand and so capital inflows were matched by deteriorating current account balances. In contrast, Germany was particularly influenced by its post-unification heritage, but the loss of the negative risk premium associated with DM interest rates meant higher nominal and real interest rate burdens than were justified for a country with stagnant growth, very low inflation, and large current account surpluses. Overall, since 1999, many countries have markedly lost external competitiveness as measured by relative unit labor costs compared with the Federal Republic.[85] A continuing policy challenge concerns how states can re-achieve such external competitiveness, other than by deep structural reform and years of unit cost control.

The Stability and Growth Pact: Observed in the Breach and Now Much Diluted?

As part of its "preventive" surveillance arm to secure budgetary soundness, the pact stipulates that each year all member states, including non-eurozone members, must submit a "stability program" to the Commission setting out how their public finances will meet the objective of being in balance or near balance over the medium term. In the early years, this meant achieving a balanced general government budget by 2004, but in this period of declining growth (in which governments faced increasing budgetary difficulties) the end date was extended to 2006. The Commission issues an assessment of each program, which is subsequently discussed in the Eurogroup of eurozone ministers and subsequently by Ecofin (the Committee of Ministers of Finance and Economy). Where a member state is departing from this agreed path towards balance the Commission may issue a formal warning, and here we come to the "dissuasive" arm of the pact, the excessive deficit procedure. Where the deficit ceiling of 3% of GDP has been breached, the Commission can admonish the state concerned and demand that the state move closer to balance by instituting annual reductions in its deficit by 0.5% of GDP and come within target in a given time frame. Further, the Commission can threaten that persistent excess deficits in the form of a third annual transgression may lead to formal institution of the sanctions procedure. Here, upon the proposal of the Commission, Ecofin may, by majority vote, agree that an excessive deficit was incurred and that the countervailing measures taken were inadequate. Unless clear deficit reduction measures are then agreed, the sanction may be applied of a compulsory, non-interest-bearing loan of 0.2% of GDP. Finally, if there has been no progress after two years, a fine equal to 0.5% of GDP will be imposed (which in Germany's case would have reached €10 billion).

In reality, aspirant member states struggled relatively successfully in the 1990s to reduce their budget deficits and force debt ratios down. By contrast, in the first half of the 2000s, there was a general failure to improve underlying fiscal deficits and such cyclically adjusted, structural deficits have remained close to 3% (although Germany from mid-decade onwards has achieved some deficit reduction). States generally have not improved their underlying budgetary positions in good years of growth, preferring tax reductions rather than expenditure reduction and debt amortization, with the result that budgetary deterioration sets in rapidly upon an economic downturn. This pattern indicates that, once admitted to EMU, little further progress was made on average in budget consolidation. Such a comment obscures the fact, however, that small states have tended to comply, while large states have behaved as if scarcely constrained – the SGP has had little effective disciplining and enforcement power and the preventive arm did not guide good behavior. Persistent failure by bigger states to meet the pact targets and observe the deficit ceiling led to deep controversy and a loss of credibility of the rules. In the first half of the decade, slow or stagnant growth on top of large structural deficits led to a widening of deficits.

Thus, early in 2002, Portugal and Germany failed to meet the deficit target, but were soon accompanied by Italy and France. Germany and France exceeded the ceiling for a fourth year in 2005. Germany, for example, received warning letters in 2002 and 2003, but it was France who openly flouted the constraints and attracted the ire not only of the Commission but also of a range of smaller states, alarmed by this asymmetry of commitment between large and small. The warning of October 2003 made clear that France was expected to reduce its structural (cyclically adjusted) deficit by at least 0.5% in 2004.[86] Overall, since 2002, six of 12 member states have been subject to the excessive-deficit procedure and the early-warning mechanism was invoked in four cases.[87] Opposition to the pact's rigid interpretation was growing, particularly in deficit countries, which sought to stimulate demand and to meet electoral commitments. Also, while most public discussion focuses on the deficit position, it is the case that more countries are breaching the 60% debt/GDP limit. Signs that political pressure for a deep reform was building were evident in 2002, when Ecofin was unwilling to let the early-warning mechanism run its course for Germany and Portugal. The crisis in the enforcement mechanisms of the pact occurred in November 2003, when the excessive-deficit procedures initiated against France and Germany were effectively put in suspension, as the Council refused to act on the Commission's recommendation. The Commission sought and gained an opinion from the European Court of Justice that the Council's action did not comply with the legal provisions, but this was a moral victory only.

One has to ask whether the pact exacerbates recessionary tendencies. Many see the pact as exerting a pro-cyclical effect: observance of the deficit ceilings in a recession deepens the fall in aggregate demand, while countries in a boom phase and in a budget surplus position can face overheating since they are not enjoined to cut public spending and pay down debt rather than reduce taxes. The pact is not cyclically adjusted and therefore does not focus on the underlying structural deficits; the 3% and 6% limits are also not rooted in economic principle.[88] It focuses too little on debt ratios, national net public asset positions, public finance sustainability issues such as longer-term pension commitments and other costs of an aging population, the need for enhanced public investment, or indeed the costs of structural reforms (which are politically unpopular and may require a "sweetener"). These point to the need for a longer time frame and sensitivity to national difference.[89]

Of course, as will be discussed briefly below, by disciplining states individually the pact takes no aggregate, eurozone-wide view and so has no stabilizing or "policy mix" role at that level. It is of no surprise to find that continuing supporters of the pact "mark 1" were the ECB and the EU Commission's Economic and Monetary Affairs Directorate-General. The ECB stressed the key role of the credibility of public finances for private-sector consumers and investors, holding that increased budget deficit financing would induce private agents to save rather than spend (in anticipation of a later tax increase).[90] Both the Commission and the ECB argued consistently that the main reasons for economic stagnation lay not at all in the conduct of eurozone policy, but in a failure by governments to free sufficiently product, labor, and capital markets. Neither EU Economic and Monetary Affairs Commissioner Solbes nor the ECB perceived any need for reform, with both stressing the gains from a rule-based system, where sustainable fiscal positions would automatically allow adequate room for the anti-cyclical working of automatic stabilizers. The ECB itself was clearly concerned that more far-reaching reforms both would loosen fiscal discipline and could tie the ECB into short-term demand management in response to political pressures.[91]

We move to the disputed issue of the required level and institutional form of macroeconomic coordination in the eurozone; after all, there is a single, independent central bank with its prime objective of price stability, while there are as many fiscal policies as there are national budget ministers! Should there be active fiscal policy coordination between members and some coordination with the ECB to achieve an appropriate policy mix? There is broad academic agreement that a certain coordination of the fiscal policy stances of member states is needed, to ensure that there is no coordinated deflation or excess demand for the zone as a whole and, further, to illuminate the interest rate setting decisions of the ECB.[92] Fiscal policy stances should be set in full knowledge of the reaction function of the ECB. The pact as constructed was not intended to achieve this, since it addresses states' budgetary positions individually and takes no zone-wide view. Equally, there is no provision for formal Eurogroup discussions with the ECB Council.

This takes us to the ongoing debate over reform of the institutional architecture of the eurozone, which centers on the notion of "European economic governance," an expression commonly used, particularly by French politicians and commentators. In a report assessing eurozone economic governance, prepared for the Commissariat général du plan in Paris, Coeuré and Pisani-Ferry show a marked preference for intergovernmentalism rather than any strengthened role for the Commission: they stress that the Eurogroup of eurozone finance ministers requires a more formalized status, with clear mandate and clear and transparent decision-making powers.[93] (This the Lisbon Reform Treaty accomplishes, including the creation of a speaker for the Eurogroup of finance ministers as a "Mr. Euro," appointed for up to two years, although no increase in formal powers is granted.) For the authors, the Eurogroup would discuss key issues for the zone, such as financial stability and labor market reform, and would set general economic priorities and guidelines for the grouping. Currently, arguments over the model of economic governance for the zone continue: they reflect long-held differences between the historic German governance-by-rules approach, favoring automatic procedures for disciplining contraventions of the rules, and the alternative French-favored approach of governance by coordination. Existing legal provisions clearly stress the "rules" approach, while they exert only weak force for "coordination." As Pisani-Ferry argues, poor enforcement has weakened governance by rules, while the intellectual arguments in favor of governance by coordination need to be strengthened, and arguments for a "political union" to buttress the single currency remain only very imperfectly formulated.[94] The institutional architecture and operational procedures of the eurozone remain a work in progress.

Enlargement and EMU: Early Euro Accession or Careful Deliberation?

Accession demands that the new entrant countries adopt all the *acquis*, including membership of the ERM II and, finally, of the eurozone. Having had their macroeconomic progress scrutinized under the progress report procedure throughout the accession negotiations period, new EU members will become subject to the Maastricht convergence criteria upon becoming members of the ERM II and later to the constraints of the Stability and Growth Pact upon participation in the eurozone. Certain accession countries were anxious to join the eurozone as soon as possible, with Slovenia adopting the euro in 2007 and Malta and Cyprus in January 2008. The

Czech Republic, though, favors a later entry in 2009–2010 and Hungary by 2012–2014. Country situations vary, but in principle a longer delay and better preparation are advisable for reasons of meeting the convergence criteria, and more fundamentally to accelerate economic catch-up. With the objective of growing more rapidly and enjoying high productivity growth, it may be that an early and irrevocable currency link to the euro may pose too great a constraint. Such countries are presently often running quite large budget and external deficits, with inflation too high.[95]

Equally, they need to discover the underlying fundamental real equilibrium exchange rate at which they would seek to link eventually to the euro. A period of more competitive, lower real exchange rates would foster export growth and very significant structural challenges persist from the period of transition from central planning. An early locking of exchange rates could force painful disinflation on less competitive economies.[96] More specifically, catch-up economies can suffer higher relative inflation due to the so-called Balassa–Samuelson effect (which points to higher inflation in the non-tradables sector), which with a premature fixing of their exchange rates in the narrow bands of the ERM II would lead to a loss of competitiveness associated with a rising real effective exchange rate. There is debate as to whether the ERM II membership should take place within the wide bands, affording greater national freedom over interest rate and exchange rate policy and so permitting nominal convergence and structural change, or, alternatively, whether this membership should be the briefest possible because of the destabilizing impacts of speculative capital movements at such a time when exchange rates are hardening in advance of euro entry.[97] Careful deliberation is required here.

It is clear, then, that with the introduction of the euro and the enlargement to the east, the EU has been responding to the challenges of a new era. Much accommodation and adjustment has already been achieved. However, the debates over the Convention for the Future of Europe and Lisbon Reform Treaty, the issues of economic governance and flexibility in the eurozone, and fundamental thinking over the EU's central tasks and budgetary distributions demonstrate that while the challenges have been recognized, serious issues remain to be addressed, even as world competition and climate-change pressures intensify.

Notes

1 European Economy, "One Market, One Money."
2 Dyson, *The Politics of the Eurozone.*
3 George, *An Awkward Partner.*
4 Cobham, *European Monetary Upheavals.*
5 Tsoukalis, *The New European Economy Revisited.*
6 Pelkmans and Winters, *Europe's Domestic Market.*
7 Emerson et al., *The Economics of 1992.*
8 Cecchini, *The European Challenge 1992.*
9 EU Commission, *The Internal Market – Ten Years without Frontiers*, 24.
10 European Economy 1997, "Economic Evaluation of the Internal Market."
11 EU Commission, *The Internal Market – Ten Years without Frontiers.*
12 EU Commission, *The Internal Market – Ten Years without Frontiers*, 28.
13 EU Commission, press release IP/04/150 and MEMO/07/464. All EU IP, MEMO and SPEECH texts can be found by typing in the reference in search at http://ec.europe.eu.

14 EU Commission, press release: IP/03/1273.
15 EU Commission, "The Internal Market Strategy for Services."
16 EU Commission, press release: IP/02/1649.
17 EU Commission, press releases IP/04/150 and 1095; *Financial Times*, November 22, 2007.
18 OECD, *Economic Survey of the Euro Area*.
19 OECD, *Economic Survey of the Euro Area*.
20 EU Commission, *The Internal Market – Ten Years without Frontiers*, 32; Pelkmans, *European Integration*.
21 EU Commission, Kroes, SPEECH/07/443, June 28, 2007.
22 Institute of Economic Affairs, "The CAP."
23 OECD, "Agricultural Policies in OECS Countries."
24 Ackrill, *The Common Agricultural Policy*; El Agraa, *The European Union*.
25 El Agraa, op. cit.
26 Ackrill, op. cit.
27 Tangermann, "Europe's Agricultural Policies and the Millenium Round"; Grant, "Change and Resistance to Change in the CAP."
28 Ackrill, op. cit., 149.
29 Tangermann, op. cit.
30 Ackrill, op. cit., 147.
31 EU Commission, *Agenda 2000 for a Stronger and Wider Union*.
32 Thurston, *How to Reform the CAP*, 10.
33 Landau, "The Agricultural Negotiations in the WTO: The Same Old Story?"
34 EU Commission, "Communication from the Commission to the Council and to the European Parliament: *Medium-Term Review of the CAP*.
35 *Financial Times*, various.
36 EU Commission, "CAP Reform."
37 EU Commission, "Reform of the CAP: A Long-Term Perspective for Sustained Development."
38 *Financial Times*, various, November 2007.
39 *Financial Times*, November 21, 2007.
40 Grabbe and Hughes, *Enlarging the European Union Eastwards*.
41 European Bank for Reconstruction and Development, *Transition Report*, 2001, 25–26.
42 Grabbe and Hughes, op. cit.
43 Brüggemann, "EU-Osterweiterung," 213.
44 EU Commission, "Enlargement: Two Years After," 29.
45 European Bank for Reconstruction and Development, *Transition Report*, 2001, 27.
46 Brüggemann, op. cit., 213.
47 EU Commission, "Enlargement: Two Years After," 61.
48 EU Commission, "Enlargements Two Years After," 69.
49 Pain and Lansbury, "Regional Economic Integration and FDI "; International Monetary Fund, *World Economic Outlook*; EU Commission, "Enlargement: Two Years After."
50 Faini and Portes, *EU Trade with Central and Eastern Europe*; Winters and Wang, *Eastern Europe's International Trade*.
51 Smith, "The EU and the Challenge of Enlargement."
52 Smith, op. cit.
53 EU Commission, "Enlargement: Two Years After."
54 Baldwin et al., "The Costs and Benefits of Eastern Enlargement."
55 European Economy, "Public Finances in EMU."
56 *Financial Times*, various, December 2002.

57 *Financial Times*, December 12, 2002; EU Commission, "Enlargement: Two Years After," 31.
58 Brücker and Weise, "Die EU vor der Osterweiterung," 832.
59 EU Commission, "Enlargement: Two Years After," 34.
60 Cobham, *European Monetary Upheavals*; De Grauwe, *The Economics of Monetary Union.*
61 De Grauwe, op. cit.
62 De Grauwe, op. cit.; El Agraa, op. cit.
63 Sumner, "European Monetary Integration."
64 *Financial Times*, various.
65 Buiter et al., "Sense and Nonsense in the Treaty of Maastricht."
66 Deutsche Bundesbank, "Stellungnahme."
67 Artis, "The ECB's Monetary Policy."
68 Issing et al., *Monetary Policy on the Euro Area.*
69 Artus, *La BCE.*
70 Artus, op. cit.
71 EU Commission, "EMU after Five Years."
72 Goodhart, "The ECB and the Conduct of Monetary Policy."
73 European Central Bank, "Current Euro Area Interest Rates from A Historical Perspective"; EU Commission, "EMU after Five Years."
74 *Financial Times*, December 31, 2007.
75 EU Commission, "EMU after Five Years."
76 European Central Bank, "Current Euro Area Interest Rates from A Historical Perspective"; EU Commission, "EMU after Five Years."
77 EU Commission, "EMU after Five Years."
78 Artus, op. cit.
79 Goodhart, op. cit.
80 Deutsches Institut für Wirtschaftsforschung, "Die Lage der deutschen Wirtschaft im Frühjahr 2003."
81 European Central Bank, "The Outcome of the ECB's Evaluation of Its Monetary Policy Strategy."
82 Langedijk and Roeger, "Adjustment in EMU. A Model-Based Analysis of Country Experiences."
83 EU Commission, "EMU after Five Years."
84 Langedijk and Roeger, op. cit.
85 Goodhart, op. cit.
86 *Financial Times*, various.
87 Buti, "Will the New Stability and Growth Pact Succeed?"
88 Buiter et al., op. cit., Sumner, op. cit.
89 Buti, op. cit.
90 European Central Bank, "The Outcome of the ECB's Evaluation of Its Monetary Policy Strategy."
91 European Central Bank, "The Relationship Between Monetary Policy and Fiscal Policies in the Euro Area."
92 Sumner, op. cit.; Buiter, "The Sense and Nonsense of Maastricht Revisited."
93 B. Coeuré and J. Pisani-Ferry, 'Eurozone members must take their own decisions', *Financial Times*, May 2, 2003, 17.
94 Pisani-Ferry, "Only One Bed for Two Dreams."
95 European Bank for Reconstruction and Development, *Transition Report*, 2002, 2007.
96 Lahrèche-Révil, "Les PECO et l'adhesion a l'union monetaire"; Beaudu, "Quelle convergence pour les futurs nouveaux membres de l'UE?"

97   Bladen-Hovell, "The Creation of EMU"; EU Commission, "EMU after Five Years"; Schadler, "Charting a Course Toward Successful Euro Adoption."

Bibliography

Ackrill, R.W., "CAP Reform 1999: A Crisis in the Making?" *Journal of Common Market Studies* 38, no. 2, 1999, 343–353.

Ackrill, R.W., *The Common Agricultural Policy* (Sheffield: UACES-Sheffield Academic Press, 2000).

Artis, M., "The ECB's Monetary Policy," in M. Artis and F. Nixson (eds.), *The Economics of the European Union* (Oxford: Oxford University Press, 2007).

Artus, P., *La BCE* (Paris: Conseil d'Analyse Économique, 2002).

Baldwin, R., J. François, and R. Portes, "The Costs and Benefits of Eastern Enlargement: The Impact on the EU and C. Europe," *Economic Policy: A European Forum*, no. 24, 1997, 125–176.

Beaudu, A., "Quelle Convergence pour les futurs nouveaux membres de l'UE?" *Problèmes économiques*, no. 2794, 2003, 1–5.

Bladen-Hovell, R., "The Creation of EMU," in M. Artis and F. Nixson (eds.), *The Economics of the European Union* (Oxford: Oxford University Press, 2007).

Brücker, H. and C. Weise, "Die EU vor der Osterweiterung: Reformchancen im europäischen Konvent nutzen," *DIW-Wochenbericht* 48, 2002, 831–838.

Brüggemann, A., "EU-Osterweiterung: Qualität hat Vorrang vor Geschwindigkeit," *Wirtschaft im Wandel*, 7, 2000, 210–215.

Buiter, W., "The Sense and Nonsense of Maastricht Revisited: What Have We Learnt about Stabilisation in EMU?" *Journal of Common Market Studies* 44, no. 4, 2006, 687–710.

Buiter, W., G. Corsetti, and N. Roubini, "Sense and Nonsense in the Treaty of Maastricht," *Economic Policy: A European Forum*, no. 16, 1993, 57–101.

Buti, M., "Will the New Stability and Growth Pact Succeed? An Economic and Political Perspective," *European Economy Economic Papers* 241 (EU Commission, Brussels, 2006).

Cecchini, P., *The European Challenge 1992: The Benefits of a Single Market* (Aldershot: Wildwood House, 1988).

Cobham, D. (ed.), *European Monetary Upheavals* (Manchester: Manchester University Press, 1994).

De Grauwe, P., *The Economics of Monetary Union* (Oxford: Oxford University Press, 2003).

Deutsche Bundesbank, "Stellungnahme des Zentralbankrates zur Konvergenzlagen der EU im Hinblick auf die dritte Stufe der WWU," *Monatsbericht*, April 1998, 17–40.

Deutsches Institut für Wirtschaftsforschung, "Die Lage der deutschen Wirtschaft im Frühjahr 2003," *Wochenbericht* 16, 2003, 438–461.

Dyson, K., *The Politics of the Eurozone: Stability or Breakdown?* (Oxford: Oxford University Press, 2000).

El Agraa, A., *The European Union: Economics and Policies* (Cambridge: Cambridge University Press, 2007).

Emerson, M., M. Aujean, M. Catinat, P. Goybet, and A. Jacquemin, *The Economics of 1992* (Oxford: Oxford University Press, 1988).

EU Commission, *Agenda 2000 for a Stronger and Wider Union* (Brussels, 1997).

EU Commission, *The Internal Market – Ten Years without Frontiers*, 2002, http://europa. eu.int/comm/internal_market/en/update (accessed November 2003).

EU Commission, "The Internal Market Strategy for Services," July 2002, press statement IP/01/31.

EU Commission, "Communication from the Commission to the Council and to the European Parliament: Medium-Term Review of the CAP," 2002, COM(2002)394 Final, Brussels, July 10.

EU Commission, "Reform of the CAP: A Long-Term Perspective for Sustained Development. Impact Analysis," March 2003, Brussels.

EU Commission, "EMU after Five Years," 2005, Brussels.

EU Commission, "Enlargement, Two Years After: An Economic Evaluation," *Occasional Papers* 24(2006), ECFIN/REP/53347, Brussels.

EU Commission, "CAP Reform," 2007, http://europa.eu/agriculture/Capreform/index_en.htm (accessed December 2007).

European Bank for Reconstruction and Development, *Transition Reports* (London: EBRD, 2001, 2002, 2007).

European Central Bank, "The Relationship between Monetary Policy and Fiscal Policies in the Euro Area," *Monthly Bulletin*, February 2003, 37–49.

European Central Bank, "The Outcome of the ECB's Evaluation of Its Monetary Policy Strategy," *Monthly Bulletin*, June 2003, 79–92.

European Central Bank, "Current Euro Area Interest Rates from a Historical Perspective," *Monthly Bulletin*, September 2003, 25–28.

European Economy, "One Market, One Money," no. 44, 1990 (Luxemburg: EU Commission).

European Economy, "Economic Evaluation of the Internal Market," Reports and Studies, 1997, Luxemburg: EU Commission.

European Economy, "Public Finances in EMU," no. 3, 2002, Luxemburg: EU Commission.

Faini, R. and R. Portes (eds.), *EU Trade with Central and Eastern Europe: Adjustment and Opportunities* (London: CEPR, 1995).

George, S., *An Awkward Partner: Britain in the European Union*, 3rd edition (Oxford: Oxford University Press, 1998).

Goodhart, C., "The ECB and the Conduct of Monetary Policy: Goodhart's Law and Lessons from the Euro Area, *Journal of Common Market Studies* 44, no. 4, 2006, 757–778.

Grabbe, H. and K. Hughes, *Enlarging the European Union Eastwards* (London: Royal Institute of International Affairs, 1998).

Grant, W., "Change and Resistance to Change in the CAP," *Current Problems and Economics of Europe* 8, no. 1, 1998, 103–117.

Institute of Economic Affairs, "The CAP: History and Attempts at Reform," *Economic Affairs* 20, no. 2, 2000, 2–48.

International Monetary Fund, *World Economic Outlook – Focus on Transition Economies* (Washington: International Monetary Fund, 2000).

Issing, O. et al., *Monetary Policy on the Euro Area: Strategy and Decision-Making at the European Central Bank* (Cambridge: Cambridge University Press, 2001).

Lahrèche-Révil, A., "Les PECO et l'adhésion à l'union monétaire," *Les Lettres du CEPII*, no. 217, November 2002, 1–4.

Landau, A., "The Agricultural Negotiations in the WTO: The Same Old Story?" *Journal of Common Market Studies* 39, no. 5, 2001, 913–925.

Langedijk, S. and W. Roeger, "Adjustment in EMU: A Model-Based Analysis of Country Experiences," *European Economy Economic Papers* 274 (2007).

OECD, "Agricultural Policies in OECD Countries: A Positive Reform Agenda," 2001, http://www.oecd.org (accessed November 2003).

OECD, *Economic Survey of the Euro Area* (Paris: OECD, 2005).

Pain, N. and M. Lansbury, "Regional Economic Integration and FDI: German Investment in Europe," *NIESR Economic Review* 2, 1997, 87–99.

Pelkmans, J., "*European Integration: Methods and Economic Analysis* (Harlow: Pearson–Prentice Hall, 2006)

Pelkmans, J. and L.A. Winters, *Europe's Domestic Market* (London: Routledge, 1988).

Pisani-Ferry, "Only One Bed for Two Dreams: A Critical Retrospective on the Debate over the Economic Governance of the Euro Area," *Journal of Common Market Studies* 44, no. 4, 2006, 823–844.

Sapir, A., "An Agenda for a Growing Europe: Making the EU Economic System Deliver," report of an independent high-level study group established on the initiative of the president of the European Commission, 2003, http://europa.eu.int/comm/lisbon_strategy/pdf/sapir_report_en.pdf (accessed November 2003).

Schadler, S., "Charting a Course toward Successful Euro Adoption," *IMF Finance and Development*, IMF, June 2004, 29–33.

Smith, A., "The EU and the Challenge of Enlargement," in D. Dyker (ed.), *The European Economy* (London: Longman, 1999).

Sumner, M., "European Monetary Integration," In D. Dyker (ed.), *The European Economy* (London: Longman, 1999).

Tangermann, S., "Europe's Agricultural Policies and the Millennium Round," *World Economy* 22, no. 12, 1999, 1155–1178.

Thurston, J., *How to Reform the CAP* (London: Foreign Policy Centre, 2002).

Tsoukalis, L., *The New European Economy Revisited* (Oxford: Oxford University Press, 1997).

Winters, L.A. and Z.K. Wang, *Eastern Europe's International Trade* (Manchester: Manchester University Press, 1994).

Readers may wish to pursue topics further with the following websites:
http://europa.eu.int
www.ebrd.org
www.imf.org
www.oecd.org
http://ec.europa.eu

The following journals cover the topic area well:
Journal of Common Market Studies
Economic Policy
Economics of Transition

CHAPTER FOURTEEN

Political Parties in Europe since 1945

ROGER EATWELL

After 1945, there was a widespread belief in western Europe that political parties were vital to building democracy.

> ### Defining political parties
>
> Modern political parties first emerged as countries began to move towards universal suffrage. They are organizations which typically seek to take part in government, or at least influence public policy, by electoral or other means. They normally have a broader range of programmatic concerns than interest groups, though it is not always easy to make a neat distinction between such groups and parties.

The churches and the labor movement especially helped foster moderate parties in countries which had succumbed to dictatorship during the interwar years, or which had seen party activity curtailed by occupation. In the subsequent waves of democratization in Greece, Portugal, and Spain during the mid-1970s, and in eastern Europe after the sudden collapse of communism at the turn of the 1990s, the creation of stable political parties was again seen as vital.

Indeed, until recently it has been widely held that democracy is virtually unthinkable without political parties to perform a broad variety of tasks. A frequently cited summary of these roles was set out by V.O. Key in the 1960s, in which he distinguished between different party functions: i) in the electorate, ii) as organizations, and iii) in government:

A Companion to Europe since 1945, First Edition. Edited by Klaus Larres.
© 2014 John Wiley & Sons, Ltd. Published 2014 by John Wiley & Sons, Ltd.

The roles of democratic parties

i   to simplify choices, and to politically educate and mobilize citizens;
ii to aggregate interests and train future political elites and select leaders; and
iii to organize government majorities, implement policy objectives, and check executives via parliamentary opposition.[1]

However, during recent decades western Europe has been characterized by the growing divorce of parties from civil society. There have also been increasing signs of alienation from party politicians, who are seen as corrupt, incompetent, and unable significantly to change key policies which are now determined at a more global level. A 2003 European Union (EU) poll showed that a remarkable 75% of respondents "tended to mistrust" political parties.[2] These trends have been accompanied by volatile voting patterns, including the rise of new parties such as greens and regionalists. Another overt sign of malaise is a general decline in turnout. Symptomatically, the 60% of electors who voted in the French 2007 legislative elections was the lowest ever.

Nevertheless, it is important not to overstate change. In the same elections, the incumbent government was returned to office for the first time in France since 1978. And the preceding presidential elections saw the highest turnout since 1974, following a contest in which significant personality, policy, and gender differences separated the socialist (Parti-Socialiste – PS) and the neo-Gaullist Party (Union Pour un Mouvement Populaire – UMP) candidates who made the second ballot run-off.[3] In Spain in 2008, both the governing socialists (Partido Socialista Obrero Espãnol – PSOE) and the conservative Popular Party (Partido Popular – PP) increased their share of the votes at the expense of the small parties.

Turning to eastern Europe the scene at first seems more problematic, with fewer than 10% of voters in recent years conforming to the textbook democratic ideal of having a clear party preference and trusting parties.[4] The vast majority of new parties in this region are typically weakly implanted in civil society, and their support can be highly unstable.

However, extremists have in general not performed well electorally, though ultranationalist parties have occasionally been an exception to this rule (for example, the candidate of the Serbian Radical Party (SRS) only narrowly lost the 2008 presidential election). Moreover, the 54% turnout in the hotly-contested 2007 Polish parliamentary elections was the highest since the country's transition from communism. While the government changed hands yet again from a Law and Justice to a Civic Platform led coalition, the share of the vote going to the two main parties was the largest since 1989, leading some commentators to predict that a bipolar left–right system, typical of much of western Europe, was emerging.

The historic left–right party spectrum

The terms "left-wing" and "right-wing" in a political context first emerge at the time of the French Revolution, when defenders of traditional authority sat on the right of the Estates General, whereas those on the left sought greater political freedoms. By the early twentieth century, left-wing parties tended to focus on egalitarian socioeconomic policies, whereas the right had become more associated with laissez-faire, though it could advocate forms of welfarism. The right also became more associated with nationalism in a further attempt to counter the appeal of the left to the working class.[5] However, boundaries between the two can be movable, and there can also be notable divisions within both left and right, not least over the legitimacy of violence.

These introductory comments indicate that complex trends are taking place, developments which have led to notably different analyses concerning the trajectory of European parties and party systems. A first academic school puts great emphasis on change. Particular emphasis is placed on features such as weakening links between parties and civil society, accompanied by a growing emphasis on leader image as a means of appealing to "dealigned" voters.[6] According to this analysis, even the largest parties are potentially vulnerable to sudden decline. For example, the collapse of the once-dominant Italian Christian Democrat Party (Democratia Cristiana – DC) at the turn of the 1990s was followed by the rise of Forza Italia, a new party led by the charismatic business and media tycoon Silvio Berlusconi, who proceeded to form a coalition government in 1994 with a reformed fascist and separatist regionalist party which was highly critical of central government.[7]

A second school argues that, while changes have taken place in both European party organization and support, there is a basic stability at the level of broad left–right blocs and even major parties in many countries.[8] Thus the main electoral contest in Germany remains between the Christian Democrats (Christlich Democratische/ Christlich Soziale Union – CDU/CSU) and Social Democrats (Sozialdemokratische Partei Deutschlands – SPD). Moreover, government is normally party government. In only a small number of western European countries, such as Finland and the Netherlands, do ministers frequently come from outside political parties. This school sees specific examples of rapid change as stemming more from unique factors, such as the exposure of widespread corruption in the Italian DC at precisely the time that the threat from communism at both home and abroad receded, thus removing an important cement which had helped maintain the party edifice.

In order to analyze these radically different visions of parties' futures, this chapter is divided into three main sections:

- The first is an historical overview. What have been the main "party families" which have characterized European politics since 1945?
- The second is more conceptual. What have been the main organizational forms of European party, and how have party systems been classified?

- The third is essentially theoretical. What determines support for parties? Is it cleavages such as class and religion, institutions such as electoral systems; or "agents" such as party leaders and programs?

The Conclusion will argue that while the second school noted above offers the best broad analysis of European party development since 1945, the first raises ominous warnings about the future of not just parties, but of democracy more generally.

Europe's Post-1945 Party Families

Academics frequently classify contemporary parties in terms of "families." A "party family" in this sense should not be confused with groups such as the British Whigs and Tories before the nineteenth century, which were parliamentary factions based on family connection and nepotism. Rather, "party family" is a term used to group parties together, most typically in terms of ideology and program.[9] Within families there can be variations both across country and through time, but members of a specific family should share essential resemblances.

In the period before World War II, a list of the major European families would need to include agrarian and fascist parties. However, since 1945, the five most important party families in electoral and/or governmental terms have been: i) liberal, ii) conservative, iii) social democrat, iv) communist), and v) Christian democrat. More recently, three significant new families have emerged: vi) green, vii) regionalist, and viii) extreme right.

It is important to note that the family names set out above are not always employed by the parties themselves. For example, in countries like France and Italy the term "conservative" has tended to be pejorative. Moreover, some parties do not fit neatly into one category. The Irish parties Fianna Fail and Fine Gael provide good examples of parties cannot neatly be classed as conservative or liberal, as they owe their founding identities more to the traumatic aftermath of the 1920s Irish civil war. These caveats point once again to the need to be sensitive to specific national and time contexts, and to the dangers of excessive comparative political "science" generalization.

Liberal parties

Liberal parties made the early running in the process of democratization, pushing for greater political and social rights, such as the extension of the franchise and freedom of worship. Initially, they tended to attract middle-class professionals, though later many liberal parties acquired a business link through their free-market economic policies, which has given them a more right-wing dimension. In recent years, support for such parties has tended to be relatively small, though they have often been important to coalition formation as a result of their ability to find common ground with both left and right. However, there have been exceptions such as the Danish liberals (the Venstre, literally "left," or "radical," party), which was the largest party in the 2007 elections with 26% of the vote. In the case of the Venstre, support has been boosted in recent years by some notably unliberal policies, especially restrictions on immigration. Conversely, the more "social" liberal policies of the British Liberal

Democrats have also attracted growing support in recent years. In eastern Europe, too, liberals have tended not to be a major force. Notable exceptions include Hungary, Slovenia, and Romania. In the last case, the National Liberals have been the most successful party since the overthrow of communism, though recently they have lost support.

Conservative parties

Conservative parties stress the defense of established institutions and traditional values such as the importance of family and religion. Historically, they had strong links with rural elites, more recently with business ones. Conservatives have tended to be weakly organized, though the British Conservative Party built up a strong base in the late nineteenth century and successfully appealed to an important minority of the working class on grounds such as welfarism and nationalism. During the 1980s, Thatcherism showed that it is possible to appeal on a mix of free-market policies with nationalism (including anti-EU sentiments), although recently the Conservatives have moved back to the center in the quest for votes. Similarly, the Moderate Party in Sweden gathered support and entered government in 2006 by moving away from the right, with little or no emphasis on issues such as tax cuts and labor market reform. Several conservative parties have been established in post-communist eastern Europe, such as the Czech Civic Democrats, who were the largest party in the 2006 elections. A coalition of conservative and nationalist parties also formed a governing coalition in Poland from 2004 to 2007, helped by growing euroskeptic sentiment as well as corruption among the previous left-of-center governing parties.

Social democrat parties

Socialist parties grew rapidly in several European countries around the turn of the twentieth century, often linked to trade unions. There were notable splits within some parties over the extent and speed to which state ownership and redistribution should be pursued. However, parties such as the Swedish Social Democrats (SPD) have supported a "middle" or "third way" (neither capitalist nor communist) since their early years. Increasingly after 1945 this form of social democracy prevailed.[10] Symbolically, the SPD met in Congress at Bad Godesberg in 1959 and dropped the last vestiges of Marxism from their program, although a more radical group remained in the party. The British "New" Labour Party moved even further from classic statist socialism, adopting parts of the Thatcherite economic legacy and finding in Tony Blair a mediagenic leader, who helped bring Labour back from what had appeared to be terminal decline. After the collapse of communism, several important social democratic parties emerged in eastern Europe. In some cases, these parties emerged through the rebirth of communist parties, though others grew more out of former second-rank dissident communists linking with other groups. The Bulgarian Socialist Party, which won a third of the vote in the 2005 elections, is a good example of the first trajectory, while the Social Democratic Party of Romania came out of the second mold.

Communist parties

Communists emerged after the 1917 Russian Revolution. Most such parties remained small compared to the mass membership-oriented social democrats. However, some parties after 1945 attracted a major electoral base, especially the Italian communists (Partito Communista Italiquo – PCI) in northern cities and the central rural "red belt," which at its peak gave the party over 30% of the national vote. The PCI also led the way in developing a more moderate form of "Eurocommunism," which sought to distance the western parties from both domestic violence and the USSR. The French Communist Party (Parti Communiste Français – PCF) too moved in this direction, which helped it participate in the post-1981 socialist government. However, the responsibility of office further undermined its once significant support, and by the 2007 legislative elections this had dwindled to 4%. After the collapse of Soviet communism, the majority of the PCI reformed itself into the relatively moderate Party of the Democratic Left (Partito Democratico della Sinistra – PDS), which has subsequently undergone several mutations, becoming the major Democratic Party (Partito Democratico – PD) in 2007. In spite of benefiting from an existing party organization, communists in the former Soviet republics have only been democratically elected in Moldova. In Russia, the communists (Kommunisticheskaya Partiya Rossiskoy Federatsii – KPRF) have often sought to exploit nationalist sentiments, and appealed to the losers in the transition rather than to radical ideology. In the 2008 presidential elections the latter factor especially helped the party's candidate win almost 18% of the vote.

Christian democrat parties

Although overtly Protestant parties have emerged in areas such as Scandinavia, the main confessional parties have been Catholic. Christian democrats after 1945, like the Italian DC, were strongly anticommunist and essentially defenders of the existing social order.[11] However, they often had important "social Catholic" wings, which helped attract a section of the working class (and helped lead to policies such as the 1970 Italian Workers' Statute). The role of Catholics in the antifascist resistance in some countries also helped to build wider links. In recent decades, with the notable exception of Germany, these parties have declined in importance. Even in Germany, the CDU/CSU's links with the Catholic church are weaker than in the past. In post-communist eastern Europe, too, religion tends to be a declining political force. Notable minor parties include the Christian People's Party in Slovenia and the League of Polish Families, which formed part of the ruling coalition between 2005 and 2007. The latter, which was backed by the traditionalist Catholic Radio Maryja, campaigned on ultranationalist and euroskeptical views, which markedly differentiated it from the classic Christian democrat parties, whose leaders were prominent advocates of the movement towards European "ever-closer union."

Green parties

Greens first began to make electoral headway in countries like France and West Germany during the 1970s and 1980s, though fighting elections was often combined with more direct forms of action.[12] Such parties have shown a notable tendency to split, with major differences emerging between the "red greens" (initially often former members of left-wing parties) and "green greens," and between the purists and those willing to compromise with other parties. In general, the moderates have emerged in the ascendancy. Electorally, greens have carved a niche especially among the more highly educated young. This has allowed green parties to share government in some countries. For instance, they formed a coalition with the German Social Democrats from 1998 to 2005, which led some to see such alliances as forming part of a strengthening of the center-left. However, in Ireland the greens have allied with the centrist Fianna Fail. Moreover, in eastern Europe green parties tend not only to be small but to be more right-wing (less concerned with issues such as participation and women's rights). The three most important parties in this region can be found in the Czech Republic, Estonia, and Latvia. For ten months during 2004, the last of these witnessed the world's first green prime minister at the head of a center-right coalition

Regionalist parties

Regionalist parties have grown significantly in recent decades, though in some cases these might be better termed "ethnic" or "neo-nationalist." For instance, in Spain parties have emerged in historically independent areas like Catalonia and the Basque country. Although regionalist parties typically play on old traditions, they are often strongest in more affluent regions, some of which do not have clear separate identities. Thus the Italian Lega Nord has exploited resentment against southerners and "thieving" central government in Rome in its attempt to invent a "Padanian" tradition. Like many regionalist parties, the Lega seeks to stress that it is modern in the sense that it supports "multi-level governance," seeking to move decision-making on many issues to a lower tier of government nearer the people, and to move others moving up to the EU level.[13] In the former communist areas of Europe several countries, especially the USSR, broke up into new nation states. However, it is possible to find regionalist parties here, such as the Democratic Union of Hungarians in Romania, while the Istrian Democratic Alliance in Croatia shows that regionalism can feature even in the more ethnically pure states.

Extreme-right parties

The French Front National (FN) is one of several extreme-right parties which have defied initial predictions that they would be "flash parties." Some commentators differentiate these from a "populist family." Examples of the latter include the Swiss People's Party (Schweizerische Volkspartei – SVP), which became the largest party in the 2007 elections, albeit with slightly less than 30% of the vote. Certainly parties like the SVP lack the FN's connections with authoritarian traditions. However, populism is best seen as a style which can be found on the left as well as on the right. It centers around appeals such as defense of the "true" people, hostility to a corrupt Establishment, and celebration of charismatic leaders – all of which can be found in both the FN and the SVP. Moreover, there are other notable similarities, including nationalism, hostility to immigration, and social "welfare chauvinism."[14] In eastern Europe, notable examples of such parties include the Serbian Radical Party and Vladimir Zhirinovsky's misnamed Liberal Democratic Party of Russia, though this has lost support since its 1990s peak. The same is true of the FN since its 2002 high point, when Jean-Marie Le Pen made it to the run-off ballot of the French presidency.

Types of Party and Party System

As well as distinguishing between party families, it is important to differentiate parties in terms of their organization and strategy. It is also necessary to distinguish between the different configurations of parties which can emerge within a country. Arguably the greatest single difference has been that some parties have been willing to use violence, and in some cases have sought to set up single-party states.

The Leninist theory of the political party saw communists as a "vanguard" who would seize power through revolution as the old order crumbled. They would then rule as an enlightened "dictatorship of the proletariat" until the masses were converted to the cause of a more egalitarian and fraternal world. In practice, this vision helped to legitimize communist dictatorship in the USSR after 1917, and later across eastern Europe. Nevertheless, by the 1980s there were signs of change in the communist world. For example, the Polish Solidarity trade union movement founded in 1980, and supported by prominent figures in the Catholic church, helped lead to semi-free elections by 1989.

In post-1945 western Europe, forms of authoritarian government have ruled in Greece, Portugal, and Spain. While these regimes have often been termed "fascist," none were based on the classic German and Italian fascist model of the party. Fascists saw para-military organizations as vital to fight with the left for control of the streets, while also seeking to win mass electoral support on a radical program. While General Franco coopted the small fascist Falange Party into his Spanish regime, it was mainly as a means of inducting new elites and disseminating conservative state propaganda.

Notable versus mass parties

Democratic parties, too, can be distinguished on more than just party family grounds. Maurice Duverger classically categorized them on two major axes. The first was the extent to which they were "notable" (or "cadre," though this term is largely applied to parties with high levels of doctrinal commitment, such as communists) rather than mass parties.[15] The Christian Democrats in southern Italy immediately after 1945 were very much a party of local notables, such as wealthy landlords and businessmen. The Greek Socialist Party (Panellinio Sosialistikó Kinima – PASOK) founded in 1974 was initially dominated by Andreas Papandreou and a small number of lesser national leaders. On the other hand, most socialist parties, such as the German Social Democrats, developed a very different form of organization. This was based on mass membership, often linked to existing trade unions. In Germany after 1945, the CDU/CSU also initially developed a mass organization. This was vital for a variety of functions, including raising money and political campaigning.

Office-oriented v. programmatic parties

Duverger's second axis concerned the extent to which parties were office-oriented ("brokerage") rather than programmatic. In the first decades of the twentieth century, social democratic parties campaigned on relatively clear programs aimed at their core constituencies. Some Christian democratic parties like the CDU/CSU also tended to develop relatively clear program after 1945. However, some parties, especially centrist ones, have sought to eschew too-clear policy commitments as this makes coalition formation easier. A classic example is the French Radical Party, which allied with both center-right and center-left during the Third and Fourth Republics. More recently, social democrats have also often tended to play down previous radical policies which are seen as vote-losers, such as extensive state ownership and radical redistribution via taxation.

Catch-all parties

A seminal work on political parties written by Otto Kirchheimer in the 1960s argued that the age of the mass-programmatic party was coming to an end. Instead, he forecast that a new form of catch-all party was emerging.[16] This was influenced both by theoretical developments in political science and more concrete developments within west European politics. After the 1950s, the rational-choice school argued that large modern parties are vote-"maximizers" rather than proselytizers, which requires competing for the crucial center ground in the prosperous postwar democracies. This approach undoubtedly pointed to important changes, such as the SPD's Bad Godesburg strategy. Nevertheless, there are dangers in overstating the quest for the center ground. The British Conservatives fought the 1979 general election on a program which specifically called for a radical break with the postwar consensus, remaining in office until 1997 (helped in the early 1980s by a move to the left by the Labour Party, though Labour was also harmed by major divisions and weak leadership).

The electoral-professional party

Conservative success in the UK can further be linked to what Angelo Panebianco has termed the "electoral-professional party."[17] This analysis has similarities with the pioneering sociological work in the early twentieth century of Robert Michels, who had argued that an "iron law of oligarchy," namely domination by leaders, existed even in apparently internally democratic parties.[18] Panebianco further stressed on the role of political professionals, such as "spin doctors" and image consultants, who helped make Margaret Thatcher into a formidable personality after the late 1970s. The role of television is seen as especially vital to honing the leader's image. Forza Italia is an even better example of this trend – a party founded by a man

(Berlusconi) – who owned several television networks, which were ruthlessly exploited by him for his own political ends. However, it is important not to overstate the ability of the media to tell people what to think, rather than what to think about, as Forza Italia lost general elections in both 1996 and 2006, although it won in April 2008, enabling Berlusconi to become prime minister for the third time and succeed Romani Prodi.

The cartel party

Prior to the collapse of the old Italian party system, the leading positions in the state media had been colonized by the major parties, and used to maintain their own interests. These links provide a good example of what Katz and Mair have termed the "cartel party."[19] This model stresses the ways in which parties can benefit from factors like generous state funding which exist in some countries, or by appointing sympathizers to key nongovernmental offices. In eastern Europe, where parties have never been firmly planted in civil society, such developments have become relatively common. Nevertheless, there are dangers in overstating cartel parties' powers to marginalize challengers and preserve a relatively stable party system. For example, revulsion against extensive patronage was an important factor in the rise of the extreme right Austrian Freedom Party (Freiheitliche Partei Österreichs – FPÖ), which came a narrow second in 1999 and entered national coalition with the Christian Democrat People's Party (Österreichische Volkspartei – ÖVP) in 2000.

Two- and multi-party systems

Duverger also distinguished between two main types of party system. He saw two major parties as typical of the Anglo-Saxon democracies. The multi-party system was common in Continental western Europe (and more recently in eastern Europe). In practice, very few countries have pure two-party systems. In Britain, the high point in terms of voting came in 1951, when 97% of electors cast their vote for the Conservative or Labour parties. However, by the 2005 general election this share was down to 69%, with Labour winning a parliamentary majority on a record low of 36% (reviving debates about the dangers of "elective dictatorship" which had figured prominently during the Thatcher era). More common have been "two- and a half" party systems with significant third parties which share office. For example, the liberal Free Democrat Party (Freie Demokratische Portei – FDP) in Germany has participated in national government for over forty years since 1949. However, since the 1980s Germany has witnessed the growth of further "third" parties, becoming a multi-party system in terms of representation, even if governing coalitions have remained based on two parties.

Moderate and polarized party systems

Giovanni Sartori has argued that distinguishing between systems in terms of party numbers is far too blunt a tool.[20] Instead, he placed great emphasis on the relationships of parties within systems, especially moderate and polarized systems.

This distinction points to a major weakness in the argument of those who see the British two-party system as necessarily more efficient in policy-implementation terms, and in terms of holding governments to account. Countries such as West Germany and Sweden have shown that coalitions can produce stable and successful government (though as post-1990s debates about German decline have highlighted, there are dangers of ossification when systems become too consensual). However, in countries like Italy, which have had significant anti-system communist and neo-fascist parties, the absence of a "loyal opposition" limits both coalition possibilities and wider social cohesion. Another example of a party system in which major parties were excluded from government was the French Fourth Republic, which had to cope with a major Communist Party (PCF) and a classic extreme-right "flash party," the Poujadists, who in 1956 campaigned against existing deputies with the slogan "throw the rascals out!" Russia in the 1990s would be yet another example of strong communist and extreme-right parliamentary parties – though in this case the powerful, directly elected president made parliament less important.

Dominant parties

Italy also highlights the importance of whether a system has a dominant party. The Christian Democrats always provided the prime minister, together with most government ministers, until the 1980s, with party factionalism leading to a regular game of ministerial musical chairs. In terms of longevity in office, Europe's two most successful parties have been Ireland's Fianna Fail and the Swedish Social Democratic Party. Between 1932 and 2006 the latter party was out of office for just nine years. However, the Social Democrats' 2006 result was the worst since the 1920s, partly because of growing accusations of corruption and misuse of state patronage. Although not on the scale of that revealed within the DC, this case highlights a potential danger when one party dominates government for long periods. In former communist countries, party systems tend to have been too volatile to produce dominant parties. However, a dominant party may be emerging in Russia. Vladimir Putin came from a non-party background, but having become president in 2000 a pro-Putin United Russia Party was formed. On the coattail of widespread support for the president, this won almost 65% of the vote in the 2007 parliamentary elections, and his designated successor Dmitry Medvedev won 70% of the vote in the March 2008 presidential elections. In both cases, the winners were helped by privileged access to the media and some election monitoring agencies reported other forms of malpractice.

Sub-national party systems

Party systems also need to be considered in terms of the sub-national level. Since the 1960s, Belgium has effectively developed two different party systems within its French- and Flemish-speaking areas. Politics in what was East Germany exhibit some important differences from what was West Germany, including the rise of the radical Left Party and pockets of significant extreme-right support. Important regionalist parties exist in many countries, such as the Convergence and Union Party (Convergència i Unió – CiU) in Catalonia and the Northern League (Lega Nord – LN) in Italy. Especially in federal systems, parties which are out of office at the national level can hold important office at lower levels, thus providing elite training and other useful system functions. For example, while the German Social Democrats were out of office nationally from 1949 to 1966, they held office in several *Länder*. The same is true for more local elections, although in general these levels of government perform few major tasks, and appear to be a less important route to national political careers than in the past. Last, but by no means least, even in countries like Britain which since 1945 have had a relatively "nationalized" political system, there are growing signs of local and regional variation, resulting from factors such as local issues and differences in party campaigning.[21]

The European Union and party systems

Within the European Parliament, a variety of formal party groupings have emerged. The Party of European Socialists (PES), made up of social democratic parties, is relatively coherent program-wise. While the second major grouping, the European People's Party–European Democrats (EPP–ED) includes Christian democrats and increasingly "Euroskeptical" conservatives, a recent study has argued that there are signs that a broad left–right bipolarism is emerging in the Parliament.[22] However, the relationship of the EU to party systems has also to be understood in the domestic context.[23] One aspect of this relationship concerns Euroskepticism, which has grown in some countries in recent years. There have even been parties formed, such as the hardline United Kingdom Independence Party (UKIP), whose main policy plank is withdrawal from the EU. More commonly, Euroskepticism has led to splits in major parties, such as the French Gaullists and Swedish Social Democrats. There has also been a spate of referenda about EU treaty reform which have implications for the party system – including whether there will be a growing demand for referenda on a wider set of issues.

Theorizing Party Support

There seems little doubt that both parties and party systems are changing; for example, parties in general are less ideological and membership is much lower than it was 50 years ago. Nevertheless, there is no simple pattern of party birth and death, or system regeneration. In order to analyze these questions further, the next section therefore turns to a more theoretical analysis. Three broad, and to some extent competing, schools have emerged which seek to explain party and party system formation in terms of i) cleavages, ii) institutions, and iii) agency.

It is important to note that these terms are not always defined precisely, and there can be notable overlaps. For instance, the "new institutionalism" of the 1980s was a school which sought to bring institutions and the state back to center-stage in political analysis. In some versions, however, the approach was broadened to include economic and social "institutions," such as churches and even class, which many would see as more central to cleavage analysis. Similarly, agency approaches normally focus on leaders and parties themselves, but can encompass the media and other "institutions" which can "set the agenda."

A further theoretical caveat is that parties and systems can be affected by external factors. An example of the former can be seen when the EU Commission stated in 1997 that Slovakia did not fulfill the democratic conditions required to join the Union, which appears to have led some Slovaks to reject more extreme parties. More generally, international norms about democracy have influenced both elites and voters in former communist countries. However, arguably the least democratic of these countries, Belarus, provides a good example of the limits to this influence. Here a powerful president has curtailed democratic competition through acts such as limiting media access to opposition parties, and has used a classic populist, father-of-the-people appeal to delegitimize parties, labeling them divisive.

Cleavages

Arguably the most common way of understanding the basis of parties in western Europe involves analyzing social or value-based conflicts. A seminal example of such an approach was published in the 1960s by Seymour Martin Lipset and Stein Rokkan, who traced the origins of European parties to four major cleavages which emerged during the nineteenth and early twentieth centuries:

i   employer versus worker;
ii   church versus state;
iii   urban versus rural; and
iv   national versus regional.[24]

According to Lipset and Rokkan, there had been a "freezing" of party systems after World War I around these cleavages.

Some parties have changed name, such as the interwar Catholic Centre Party (Zentrumsparti) in Germany, which provided an important basis for the post-1945 CDU/CSU. Other parties have risen and fallen, such as the French Popular Republican Movement (Mouvement Républicain Populaire – MRP), which emerged mainly from Catholic wartime Resistance circles rather than an earlier party. However, according to this analysis the broad party families in western Europe during the 1960s were very similar to those which had emerged after the completion of universal male suffrage, which had been achieved in most western European countries by 1919 (women often acquired the vote much later).

Party development and stability can further be analyzed in terms of sub-cultures. For instance, until recently the Netherlands was characterized by an overarching sense of national identity, below which was a "pillared" society made up of relatively closed Protestant, Catholic, and secular groups, which had their own unions, newspapers, and so on. This meant that there was very limited crossover of votes between these groups. Localized sub-cultures have also affected party systems. For example, from the 1950s to the 1980s, the neo-fascist Italian Social Movement (Movimento Sociale

Italiano – MSI) could win 10–30% of the vote in parts of southern Italy, helped by the "amoral familist" culture, which encouraged the (not entirely unjustified) belief that mainstream politicians were self-seeking fraudsters and that the vote should be used for clientelistic and/or anti-system protest purposes.

However, since the 1960s there has been considerable academic discussion about the breakdown of traditional cleavages. In particular, two major cleavages have been diminishing in political salience in western Europe – religion and class. Evidence to support this thesis includes factors such as declining church attendance and the "*embourgeoisement*" of the western European working class. Even stronger evidence points to a decline in identification with major parties, and especially party membership. For example, an estimated 3.5 million Britons belonged to parties during the 1950s, compared to under 0.5 million in the first decade of the new millennium, with the main fall coming among trade union members (though this is partly explained by changes in the law about political donations).

After the 1970s, many academics highlighted the emergence of a new cleavage based on the rise of a "postmaterial" society.[25] This portrayed social democrat parties as threatened by the rise of green issues, such as ecologism, and women's rights' and by the decline of issues such as union rights. The analysis also envisaged a reduction in the salience of themes which had been important for mainstream right-wing parties, such as reverence for the nation and traditional institutions. A corollary to the postmaterial thesis holds that extreme-right parties are typically based on the support of less-skilled males who feel threatened by new agendas, and who are still attracted by the community of the nation.[26] However, the analysis has notably over-stated the potential for both green and extreme-right parties to become major players in western Europe.

These approaches offer some insights into why such parties have remained weak in eastern Europe, where postmaterial values are rare. More generally, cleavage analysis helps explain the unstable pattern of voting in much of this region and the fact that parties are weakly implanted in civil society. Communist culture sought to stress collective rather than plural identities, and suppressed related groups such as trade unions or regional associations. In some ways, the main value cleavage which had emerged by the closing stages of communism was a populist one, in which the exploited "people" were left suspicious of parties in general. Nevertheless, it is impor-tant not to overstate flux in eastern Europe, as some commentators hold that there is a broad movement towards a stable and moderate pluralism based on growing affluence in many sectors – and wider factors.

Institutions

Duverger is a classic exponent of an institutionalist approach, holding that two-party systems are largely found in countries which have first-past-the-post electoral systems, like Britain. On the other hand, multi-party systems are more a feature of the pro-portional representation (PR) systems used in western Europe – and now common in eastern Europe, though some countries like Hungary and Russia use mixed systems of list and majoritarian constituencies.

Duverger further developed the important point that electoral systems can have "psychological" as well as "mechanical" effects. A majoritarian system encourages people not to waste their vote on small parties, especially in "first-order" national elections, rather than second-order local or European Parliament ones. This has often been a problem for the extreme right and greens, as opinion polls indicate that they often have a significantly greater potential than election results suggest. Conversely, large parties can gain votes because electors seek to express a meaningful choice over which party will enter government, rather than endorse the party whose views are closest to their own.

However, the link between party and electoral systems is more complex than this suggests. In Italy, after the First Republic collapsed at the turn of the 1990s, the move towards a majoritarian system served to encourage the development of a center-left–center-right bipolarism rather than the emergence of two large parties. In both 1996 and 2001, the largest party, Forza Italia, won under 30% of the vote. Even in Britain, the majoritarian system has not prevented parties winning elections with as little as around 30% of the vote in contrast with four or more cornered contests, which have become increasingly common in recent years. On the other hand, two-and-a-half or three-party systems have emerged in proportional systems like West Germany betweeen 1949 and1990.

Lijphart notes that the impact of proportional representation on party systems needs to be related specific aspects of such laws.[27] Various types of PR exist in Europe, including ones with notably different "district magnitudes." The Netherlands uses a national list, whereas Spain uses regional lists, which has helped the rise of regionalist parties there. There are also different "thresholds" which need to be reached before gaining representation. Both the Czech Republic and Germany have used a 5% cutoff, but in the Netherlands the threshold has been under 1%, which has helped proliferating small parties gain representation. Electoral systems can also vary in some countries between tiers of government, allowing different party systems within a single state (election systems for the European Parliament can also differ from those used for national parliaments).

Other constitutional features which can affect party systems include state subsidies and bans on extremist parties. West Germany banned both neo-Nazi and communist parties in the 1950s, while Spain banned the Basque Batasuna Party in 2002 on account of alleged links with separatist terrorism. Many European countries use forms of state subsidy for parties, often based on the number of votes received in the last election. The practice is especially common in eastern Europe, where parties have limited ability to raise funds by other means. While the practice can be defended as a way of minimizing the ability of rich groups to buy influence, it tends to harm new and small parties – although such funds can be useful to smaller parties once they gain an electoral foothold.

A powerful directly elected presidency can have a party system effect too. Under the French Fifth Republic, the main presidential candidates know that they have to appeal to voters from neighboring party families if they are to win over 50% of the vote on the second ballot. This has, therefore, been a further factor encouraging bipolarism, especially since the resignation of founding-father President de Gaulle in 1969. In Russia, the powerful directly elected presidency has even led to the creation of major party, United Russia, though whether it can survive the loss of Putin's patronage and popularity is another matter.

Agents

The appeal of leaders, especially "charismatic" ones like Putin, features prominently in accounts which stress the role of "agents." The concept of political charisma was first developed by Max Weber to apply to leaders who are driven by a great sense of mission, and who at times of crisis arouse an intensely emotional bond among followers. Understood in this way, it is debatable whether any political leader in western Europe since 1945 has been "charismatic," except perhaps briefly de Gaulle. However, if charisma is understood more in terms of dominant leaders who come to personify a party, then it applies to a much wider number of cases, such as Le Pen and Zhirinovsky.[28]

Even among well-established parties there has been a strong personalization of politics, and some party leaders undoubtedly attract a personal following. The ability to use television effectively has been an especially important attribute for party leaders in recent decades. For example, Germany in 2005 saw televized debates between the two main party leaders, Gerhard Schröder (SPD) and Angela Merkel (CDU). After the last debate, opinion polls showed that Schröder had turned a sixth point deficit into a 14-point advantage on the issue of who was the preferred chancellor, with many respondents highlighting his television performances. In the 2007 Swiss elections, voters gave leader personality as the main reason for supporting the SVP, which was led by rich businessman Christoph Blocher, who attracted significant media attention (though part of the reason for this was his radical policies on issues such as immigration).

Perception of leaders is especially important on so-called "valence issues," namely issues on which there is widespread agreement – for example, the need to manage the economy well – but notably different assessments of parties' abilities. Thus Blair in 1997 was judged much more highly than Conservative prime minister John Major, even though the economy had been relatively strong under Major's Conservative government. Leader image and the media are again seen as crucial in making such judgments.[29] Nevertheless, it is important not to overstate the importance of agency in this example. Other poll evidence shows that voters consider factors such as globalization and the EU important to policy, which can limit their willingness to accord leaders or parties great powers to achieve policy goals.

"Agency" refers to more than just the role of leaders, encompassing factors such as the efficiency of party organization and the appeal of its program. Program has been especially central to many recent analyses of party performance, as voters now seem more concerned with specific issues. Although economic issues such as unemployment were most frequently cited in a 2007 EU poll, close behind are a set of issues including crime and immigration, while concern with ecological issues is growing too.[30] One reason why the major parties have limited the breakthroughs by new parties is that they have often adapted parts of the latters' programs to assuage fears. There has been a general "greening" of mainstream parties in western Europe since the 1980s, while center-right parties have tended to pay more attention to issues

such as law and order, often broadening their appeal to a working class which historically voted for the center-left.

Cleavage theorists see parties as emerging from social divisions. However, it is
possible to reverse this approach and see party leaders as political entrepreneurs
who seek to politicize specific cleavages. For example, Yugoslavia existed as a
peaceful multiethnic and multinational state for decades after 1945 until Slobodan
Milošević and others, starting in the late 1980s, inflamed divisions as a way of boosting personal and party support. Moreover, parties, as institutions, can reinforce or
weaken cleavages. Socialist parties in particular historically promoted class consciousness not only through rhetoric, but through a sub-culture of unions and other
workers' organizations. In recent decades, working-class consciousness has undoubtedly declined because of structural changes, such as the decline of "solidaristic"
occupations like coal mining. But the role of social democratic downplaying class
and often concerned with more middle class issues such as taxation should not be
ignored.

The same point about causal direction can be made about institutions. The discussion of Duverger above implied that electoral systems were a major determinant of
what type of party system emerges. But it is possible to reverse "Duverger's law" and
argue that parties choose electoral systems rather than the other way round. Certainly
in France in 1986 the ruling center-left coalition altered the two-ballot majoritarian
system to a regional-list system in the hope that it would help split the right, especially
by helping the Front National to win representation. Italy in the run-in to the 2006
elections offers another example of where the election system was changed to help
the governing parties – although the fact that Berlusconi's coalition narrowly
lost offers another caveat to attributing too much power to both agency and
institutions.[31]

Conclusion

In the opening section, it was noted that there are two very different academic schools
of thought about the future of parties and party systems in Europe.

Two schools on the future of parties

1 The first school puts considerable emphasis on flux, looking at issues such
   as the divorce between parties and civil society even in western Europe,
   growing signs of alienation from mainstream parties, and the potential for
   dramatic governmental change.
2 The second accepts that parties are changing organizationally, and that there
   is some change within party systems, including a gradual loss of support by
   many mainstream parties. However, it does not hold that radical change is
   on the horizon.

The second school offers a better understanding of developments so far since 1945. Even in recent years, change has often been limited. Indeed, in the 2008 Spanish elections the two main parties, the PSOE and PP, increased their combined share of the vote. Moreover, turnout was only slightly down on the record 2004 figure, which followed major Islamic extremist bombings in Madrid, which the governing PP had initially blamed on Basque terrorists.

However, the first school points to dangers for the future. While parties remain central to functions such as running government and seeking to check executives via parliamentary opposition in most European countries, many people have become more cynical about the motives of politicians and/or their ability to enact change. At the same time, far fewer people are active in party politics at the local level, or in institutions such as universities. This raises the Big Question: how can democracy legitimize itself if there is widespread alienation from mainstream party politics?

Some commentators argue that, far from being a source of concern, systems are becoming more democratic in the sense that parties are now more responsive to popular views, and less driven by sweeping ideologies which are mainly the concern of party elites and hardcore activists. It has even been argued that the decline of parties would offer an opportunity for new forms of democracy, especially the use of the Internet to create a new direct democracy which had previously only flourished in small communities, like city-state ancient Athens.[32]

A more dystopian vision would hold that the Web is hardly likely to provide the policy outputs, interest aggregation, leader-training, and other functions parties have classically performed. Moreover, a surfeit of propaganda is likely to confuse most voters, perhaps resulting in a further retreat into private life, or to help extremes, which often have a strong Web presence. Ominously, in March 2005 a YouGov poll indicated that more first-time electors voted in reality television shows like Big Brother than planned to vote in the 2005 British general election.[33] There is clearly much to ponder, not least by the young.

Notes

1 Key, *Politics, Parties and Pressure Groups*.
2 *Eurobarometer*, 59, July 2003, 12.
3 Many parties are commonly referred to by their initials.
4 Rose and Munro, *Elections and Parties in New European Democracies*, 54–55.
5 For an introduction to the terms see Bobbio, *Left and Right*.
6 Dalton and Wattenberg, *Parties without Partisans*. See also Poguntke and Webb, *The Presidentialization of Politics*.
7 Fella and Ruzza, *Reinventing the Italian Right*.
8 Mair, *Party System Change*. See also Webb et al., *Political Parties in Advanced Industrial Democracies*.
9 Mair and Mudde, "The Party Family and Its Study."
10 Ladrech and Marlière, *Social Democratic Parties in the European Union*.
11 Gehler and Kaiser, *Christian Democracy in Europe since 1945*.
12 Burchell, *The Evolution of Green Politics*.
13 For an excellent example of a study of such parties see Bull and Gilbert, *The Lega Nord and the Northern Question in Italian Politics*.

14 Eatwell and Mudde, *Western Democracies and the New Extreme Right Challenge*.
15 Duverger, *Political Parties*.
16 Kirchheimer, "The Transformation of the Western European Party Systems."
17 Panebianco, *Political Parties*.
18 Michels, *Political Parties*.
19 Katz and Mair, "Changing Models of Party Organization and Party Democracy."
20 Sartori, *Parties and Party Systems*.
21 For example, Geddes and Tonge, *Britain Decides*.
22 Hix et al., *Democratic Politics in the European Parliament*.
23 Ladrech, "Europeanization and Political Parties."
24 Lipset and Rokkan, *Party Systems and Voter Alignments*.
25 Inglehart, *Culture Shift in Advanced Industrial Society*.
26 Ignazi, "The Crisis of Parties and the Rise of New Political Parties."
27 Grofman and Lijphart, *Electoral Laws and their Political Consequences*.
28 Eatwell, "The Rebirth of Right-Wing Charisma."
29 Clarke et al., *Political Choice in Britain*.
30 *Eurobarometer*, 68, December 2007.
31 Gallagher and Mitchell, *The Politics of Electoral Systems*.
32 Budge, *The New Challenge of Direct Democracy*.
33 *Sunday Times*, March 13, 2005.

Bibliography

Bobbio, N., *Left and Right: The Significance of a Political Distinction* (Cambridge: Polity, 1996).

Budge, I., *The New Challenge of Direct Democracy* (Cambridge: Polity, 1996).

Bull, A. Cento and M. Gilbert, *The Lega Nord and the Northern Question in Italian Politics* (Basingstoke: Palgrave Macmillan, 2001).

Burchell, J. *The Evolution of Green Politics: Development and Change within European Green Parties* (London: Earthscan, 2002).

Clarke, H.D., D. Sanders, M.C. Stewart, and P. Whiteley, *Political Choice in Britain* (Oxford: Oxford University Press, 2004).

Dalton, R.J. and M.P. Wattenberg (eds.), *Parties without Partisans: Political Change in Advanced Industrial Societies* (Oxford: Oxford University Press, 2000).

Duverger, M., *Political Parties*, English edition (London: Allen and Unwin, 1954; 1st French edition 1951).

Eatwell, R., "The Rebirth of Right-Wing Charisma? The Cases of Jean-Marie Le Pen and Vladimir Zhirinovsky," *Totalitarian Movements and Political Religions* 3, 2002, 1–24.

Eatwell, R. and C. Mudde (eds.), *Western Democracies and the New Extreme Right Challenge* (London: Routledge, 2004).

Fella, S. and C. Ruzza, *Reinventing the Italian Right* (London: Routledge, 2009).

Gallagher, M. and P. Mitchell, *The Politics of Electoral Systems* (Oxford: Oxford University Press, 2005).

Geddes, J.A. and J. Tonge (eds.), *Britain Decides: The UK General Election of 2005* (Basingstoke: Palgrave, 2005).

Gehler, M. and W. Kaiser, *Christian Democracy in Europe since 1945* (London: Routledge 2004).

Grofman, B. and A. Lijphart (eds.), *Electoral Laws and their Political Consequences* (New York: Agathon, 1986).

Hix, S., A.G. Noury, and G. Roland, *Democratic Politics in the European Parliament* (Cambridge: Cambridge University Press, 2007).

Ignazi, P., "The Crisis of Parties and the Rise of New Political Parties," *Party Politics* 2, 1996, 549–566.

Ingle, S., *The British Party System* (London: Routledge, 2008).

Inglehart, R., *Culture Shift in Advanced Industrial Society* (Princeton: Princeton University Press, 1990).

Katz, R.S. and P. Mair, "Changing Models of Party Organization and Party Democracy: The Emergence of the Cartel Party," *Party Politics* 1, 1995, 5–28.

Key, V.O., *Politics, Parties and Pressure Groups* (New York: Crowell, 1964).

Kircheimer, O., "The Transformation of the Western European Party Systems," in J. LaPalombara and M. Weiner (eds.), *Political Parties and Political Development* (Princeton: Princeton University Press, 1966).

Kopecky, P. (ed.), *Political Parties and the State in Post-communist Europe* (London: Routledge, 2007).

Ladrech, R., "Europeanization and Political Parties: Towards a Framework for Analysis," *Party Politics* 8, no. 4, 2002, 389–403.

Ladrech, R. and P. Marlière (eds.), *Social Democratic Parties in the European Union: History, Organization, Policies* (Basingstoke: Palgrave, 1999).

Lipset, S.M. and S. Rokkan, *Party Systems and Voter Alignments* (New York: Free Press, 1967).

Mair, P., *Party System Change: Approaches and Interpretations* (Oxford: Clarendon Press, 1997).

Mair P. and Mudde C., "The Party Family and Its Study," *Annual Review of Political Science* 1, 1998, 211–229.

Michels, R., *Political Parties: A Sociological Study of the Oligarchical Tendencies of Modern Democracy* (New York: Macmillan, 1966; 1st Italian edition 1911.)

Millard, F., *Elections, Parties, and Representation in Post-communist Europe* (Basingstoke: Palgrave, 2004).

Panebianco, A., *Political Parties: Organization and Power* (Cambridge: Cambridge University Press, 1988).

Poguntke, T. and P. Webb (eds.), *The Presidentialization of Politics: A Comparative Study of Modern Democracies* (Oxford: Oxford University Press, 2005).

Rommele, A., D.M. Farrell, and P. Ignazi (eds.), *Political Parties and Political Systems: The Concept of Linkage Revisited* (New York: Praeger, 2005).

Rose, R. and N. Munro, *Elections and Parties in New European Democracies* (Washington: CQ Press, 2003).

Sartori, G., *Parties and Party Systems: A Framework for Analysis* (Cambridge: Cambridge University Press, 1976).

Webb, P., D. Farrell, and I. Holliday (eds.), *Political Parties in Advanced Industrial Democracies* (Oxford: Oxford University Press, 2002).

Further Reading

Often the best source for up-to-date academic analyses of parties and party systems are journals like *Electoral Politics* and *Party Politics*. See also the special issues on "Party Types, Organisation and Function," *West European Politics* 28, no. 1, 2005, and on "The Future of Parties," *Parliamentary Affairs* 58, no. 3, July 2005. Articles on specific parties and elections, as well as books about specific countries, can offer notably more detail. See, for instance, S. Ingle, *The British Party System* (London: Routledge, 2008).

Some works on specific countries are also useful, especially where a country has been a model for developments elsewhere. For example, on the rise of political marketing see J. Lees-Marshment, *Political Marketing and British Political Parties* (Manchester: Manchester University Press, 2001). A. Rommele, D.M. Farrell, and P. Ignazi (eds.), *Political Parties and Political Systems: The Concept of Linkage Revisited* (New York: Praeger, 2005) seeks to correct the excessive focus in much of the literature on parties in elections, stressing more the way parties forge links between citizens and policy-makers.

Much of the literature on European parties focuses on western Europe rather than the communist successor states. F. Millard, *Elections, Parties, and Representation in Post-communist Europe* (Basingstoke: Palgrave, 2004) offers a good survey of the latter region. P. Kopecky (ed.), *Political Parties and the State in Post-communist Europe* (London: Routledge, 2007) is more specialized, looking at issues such as state financing and party patronage within states. Various websites carry details of parties, including the parties' own sites nationally and party groupings within the European Parliament. Wikipedia is a useful starting point especially for election results (though its entries on party histories, especially more controversial ones, must be treated with caution).

CHAPTER FIFTEEN

The Genesis of a European Security and Defence Policy

RALPH DIETL

The year 1989 marked the end of the Cold War. It also marked the end of bipolarity. A deconstruction of the Cold War security architecture followed suit. A new global order was in the making – a devolution from a bi- to a multipolar order.[1] The Europeans, freed from the constraints of the Cold War system, almost instantly started to question the Cold War division of labor between the North Atlantic Treaty Organization (NATO) and the European Community (EC). Some EC member states now reclaimed the lost "European Security and Defence Identity" of 1948. The idea emerged to complete the European construction by creating a fully fledged European Union (EU). This attitude found a clear expression in the Treaty of Maastricht on European Union (TEU). The TEU not only established a Common Foreign and Security Policy (CFSP), but further envisaged "the eventual framing of a common defense policy, which might in time lead to a common defence."

Almost 15 years have passed since the signing of the Maastricht Treaty. The TEU has been revised twice; the WEU (Western European Union) integrated into the EU, and a treaty project establishing a Constitution for Europe signed, aborted, and replaced by the Treaty of Lisbon of 2007. Notwithstanding this development the EU is still unable to act as a unit. This was poignantly revealed during the Balkan crisis and the way in Iraq. This experience seems to vindicate Stanley Hoffmann's argument about the natural limits of integration and the "logic of diversity" in "high politics." The lack of institutionalization in the field of CFSP, however, cannot be exclusively ascribed to the natural resilience of the nation state or to an "irreducible minimum realm of high politics – the vital interests of national diplomacy and strategy."[2] The "limits of integration" differ widely among nation states. It is a nation's vision of "Europe" that defines the limits of integration, and it is the size of the group that defines the common vision.

This chapter challenges the principle of the "natural" resilience of the nation state by shifting the emphasis towards the integrationist/Atlanticist dichotomy so lucidly analyzed by Hoffmann in *Gulliver's Troubles*. In fact, the lack of institutionalization in the field of CFSP is the product of a competition between two basic visions of Europe: Europe as an independent actor and Europe as a subset of the Atlantic

A Companion to Europe since 1945, First Edition. Edited by Klaus Larres.
© 2014 John Wiley & Sons, Ltd. Published 2014 by John Wiley & Sons, Ltd.

alliance. Proponents of the former plead for a deepening of integration in order to ensure Europe a voice in global affairs. They neither shy away from a gradual transfer of sovereignty to EU institutions nor from a duplication of NATO functions. Their counterparts see in EU enlargement an avenue to rescue the nation state from a further encroachment of national sovereignty, but also and in particular a means to save the integrity of NATO. While the former try to overcome the Cold War division of labor between the Atlantic and the European institutions, the latter try to preserve it. In the last resort it is the integrationist/Atlanticist dichotomy, it is the contest between countries who challenge the status quo and those who try to preserve it, that blocks further institutionalization of the CFSP. Correspondingly, the "limits of integration" differ widely, between Atlanticist states, committed to bandwagoning, and integrationist states, committed to balancing.[3]

This chapter on the genesis of a common security and defense policy (CSDP) breaks with the linear progressive interpretation of European integration that dominates academic literature. The linear interpretation is the result of a rather narrow focus of the prevalent European-studies literature on developments within the EC/EU in general, and on aspects of formal integration in particular. The common limitation of the time frame to current developments only contributes to this perception. The integration of the WEU into the EU, however, makes it indispensable to broaden the historical analysis to institutions and developments outside the EEC (the European Economic Community)/EC framework that contributed to European unity. As a result of this wider perspective the dialectical interpretation outlined above emerges – revealing now a dialectic between "emancipation" and "control." This dialectic dominates the relations among the European powers, as well as those between "Europe" and the United States in the transatlantic framework. The result is a cyclical interpretation of European integration – in the sphere of "high politics." The analysis will show that, though the names have changed, the "game" has remained essentially the same. Even the transformation from a Cold War to a post Cold War order did not change the rules of the "game" – since bipolarity was not replaced by a multipolar order but a unipolar order with a European sub-set.[4]

The Lost Heritage

The Brussels Treaty Organization

Knowledge of the genesis of Euro-Atlantic postwar security architecture is the key to an understanding of the architectural debate on European security since the end of the Cold War. Schemes to form a European defense system predate the creation of both the European Communities and the Atlantic alliance. They originated with the British during World War II.[5] Foreseeing a power vacuum on the European continent and a failure of the UN, British planners drafted blueprints for a European alliance system based upon Franco-British postwar cooperation. This European vision heavily influenced the policy for European reconstruction of the Attlee government. It underpinned the signing of the Franco-British Treaty of Dunkirk (1947) and the formation of the Brussels Pact (1948).[6] The Attlee government envisaged the Brussels Pact as the core of the future Europe. Although the historical debate on the Brussels Pact continues, it is safe to maintain that it was formed to serve as a security guarantee against a resurgent Germany. The Brussels Pact was signed to assure the agreement of Germany's Western neighbors to the gradual formation of Western Germany. The fact that a fully fledged military organization, the Western Union (WU), was established, however, gives credence to the still disputed thesis that the members of the Brussels Pact envisaged the organization as forming the core of a reconstructed Europe that would act as a "third force" in international affairs.[7]

The gradual intensification of the tensions between the Western powers and the Soviet Union since the end of the World War II made the UK and France look towards supplementing the existing Brussels Treaty Organization (BTO) with an Atlantic guarantee treaty. The US, however, hesitated. This hesitation was not only due to traditional American fears of entangling alliances, but also to geopolitical considerations. A security guarantee would help Britain to re-create the old European order of the nation states; it would furthermore pave the way for the formation of a European power bloc. The US favored a security architecture that supported a progressive integration of the Continent and therefore a fully fledged Atlantic alliance to act as an umbrella organization. France soon shifted allegiance, which led to the formation of the ultimate framework for Western security and reconstruction: the Atlantic alliance.[8]

The French had realized that a hierarchical, instead of a "dumbbell," structure of the West would allow France to partake in the integration of Europe without sacrificing her national sovereignty. French sponsorship of Continental integration followed almost immediately. With the Schuman Plan France took the lead in integrating the Continent. Fearing the emergence of a Continental competitor, capable of being substituted for the BTO, the United Kingdom pushed for an integration of the WU into NATO to establish the WU as the European pillar of a two-pillared alliance structure. The Korean War shattered Britain's hopes of maintaining the European command structure of the WU. The intensification of the Cold War made the US plead not only for the formation of internationally balanced forces under the command of a US supreme Allied commander Europe (SACEUR), but for a strengthening of the West by arming the recently formed Federal Republic of Germany.[9]

The US plans met French objections. France insisted on a European defense force under European political control. After long negotiations a compromise was achieved. France agreed to the formation of a provisional NATO command structure while the United States assented to the formation of a European Defence Community (EDC) along the lines of the French Pleven Plan. With the formation of the NATO command structure the WU ceased to exist. This ended the short-lived "ESDI" (European Security and Defence Identity) established in 1948. A substitute, however, was in the making. The French envisaged the European Defence Community not only to replace the WU, but – in time – NATO as well.[10]

The European Defence Community project

The Treaty Establishing a European Defence Community signed on May 25, 1952 fell short of expectations.[11] The EDC Treaty neither resembled the European Army model proposed to the Council of Europe by Winston Churchill, nor the "army of a united Europe" under "a single European political and military authority" as outlined by French prime minister René Pleven. The EDC Treaty created only an integrated unit of continental European countries under the strategic and political guidance of NATO. The ambitious European project had degenerated into a system of "triple containment";[12] a system that allowed the US to "cope with difficult European behavior" instead of enabling the Europeans to command their own destiny. The EDC Treaty perfectly matched US geopolitical blueprints for a disengagement from a reconstructed Europe. The integrated and denuclearized Europe of the EDC seemed to form the ideal basis for an all-European settlement of the German question guaranteed by the superpowers. The US, therefore, rejected any treaty revision that questioned the supremacy of the guarantor powers. The US even threatened to undertake an "agonizing re-appraisal" of her defense policy in Europe in the event that the EDC Treaty of 1952 were not to be ratified.[13]

Washington supported attempts by the EDC member states to create a separate source of political guidance for the European Defence Community, insofar as this remained compatible with the US reconstruction of Europe. The de Gasperi proposal for a European Political Community was compatible with the American scheme. His proposal envisaged the creation of federal institutions and thereby helped to drive a wedge between the nuclear power Great Britain and the Continent.[14] Intergovernmental schemes, like the Eden Plan of 1952, were rejected outright, as were French attempts to amend or revise the EDC Treaty in order to liberate France from the EDC arms control regime. The Eisenhower administration rejected anything that could blur or undermine the division of the West into a conventionally armed continent, i.e. "Europe" and a nuclear-armed Anglo-American directorate. The US considered this division indispensable for an all-European settlement of the German question under super-power control.[15]

Left with no chance to revise the EDC Treaty the French National Assembly postponed the discussion of the treaty *sine die*, thus effectively killing the EDC project.[16] The collapse of the EDC project was a serious setback for the US reconstruction of Europe. For the Europeans, however, it offered an opportunity to renegotiate the Western security architecture and to regain control over their national destinies. Winston Churchill, who considered a European alliance an attractive alternative to the EDC project, approved the French decision to reclaim national sovereignty. The French initiative, furthermore, offered the British government the chance to table an alternative framework for German rearmament. A central feature of those plans was the revival and revision of the BTO. Similar plans emerged in France. There a duplication of NATO structures was advocated in order to rebalance the Atlantic alliance. In 1954 the classic concept of an Atlantic Alliance based on two equal pillars regained popularity on both sides of the Channel.[17]

The Western European Union

The attempts of the Europeans to transform the hegemonic alliance were nurtured by the "little détente" in East–West relations following Stalin's death.[18] Europeans started to reclaim the lost ESDI of 1948, causing great alarm in Washington in the process. The US now tried to separate the question of German rearmament from the process of European integration to forestall the emergence of a European "third force" on the basis of a revised and enlarged BTO. Washington, therefore, pushed for rearmament of the Federal Republic within NATO, and sought to limit the functions of a revised BTO to those of an arms-control agency. The Eisenhower administration objected to any duplication of NATO structures and any European vocation for the WEU. The US planned to relaunch the European integration process of the Continental Six (France, Italy, West Germany, Benelux countries).[19]

The Paris Treaties of 1954, brokered by Sir Anthony Eden, allowed the Federal Republic to rearm and to join the Atlantic alliance. Simultaneously the Federal Republic became a member of an enlarged and revised BTO – the Western European Union (WEU). The WEU was not re-established, but Article III/3 of the revised Brussels Treaty made the WEU Council an ideal forum for European political cooperation. The Standing Armaments Committee formed in 1955 to enhance arms cooperation among the WEU member states finally made the WEU a power to be reckoned with. It was a potential substitute for NATO. The US acted accordingly; it successfully worked towards an incorporation of the WEU into NATO.[20]

The US, having reasserted her leadership, insisted on an unambiguous framework for the further reconstruction of Europe: a strict division of labor between European economic integration and Atlantic defense. Security and defense became a "taboo subject" in a purely European context.[21] Notwithstanding the "peculiar constraints of the Cold War" the European nation states rebelled against the new "European" order. The US reconstruction of Europe was twice seriously challenged during the Cold War – namely at Suez in 1956/1957 and during the EPU negotiations in 1962/1963.[22] Both conflicts went far beyond mere transatlantic disputes about burden-sharing (so prevalent in the history of NATO); both conflicts involved the formation of an alternative framework for European security. The common assumption that questions of security and defense were disassociated from the European integration process in the 1950s and 1960s is erroneous – but widespread. A parallel process of policy integration – of intergovernmental cooperation – has always accompanied the formal process of European integration.

The "loss of the cement of fear" that had set in after the death of Stalin, nurtured by the Geneva summit of 1955 and Khrushchev's policy of peaceful coexistence, had made the Europeans question the US reconstruction of Europe, yet again.[23] The year 1956 witnessed, with the Anglo-French military intervention in Suez, an open rebellion against a bipolar global order. The endeavor ended in a fiasco. The super-powers collaborated to consolidate the blocs of the Cold War. The forced retreat of France and Great Britain from Suez triggered an architectural debate within the WEU.[24]

Just weeks after the Suez Crisis, plans emerged to develop the potential for politico-military cooperation of the WEU. The WEU member states agreed that only an institutionalized political cooperation among the European nation states could stop a further erosion of the power of "Europe." Britain toyed with the idea of a thorough rationalization of Euro-Atlantic organizations. The British concept ascribed to the WEU the role of today's European Council as a directing council, overseeing all of the other European organizations. Simultaneously, the WEU was to act as the European pillar in NATO. Britain's foreign secretary, Selwyn Lloyd, even envisaged the formation of a WEU nuclear force. The project, however, collapsed on January 7, 1957. The British Cabinet rejected Selwyn Lloyd's European grand design.[25] It asked for a policy of Anglo-American reconciliation. Harold Macmillan, who took over from Sir Anthony Eden, acted accordingly. The successful re-creation of the

Anglo-American "special relationship" at the summit meetings in Bermuda and Washington ended a direct challenge to the US reconstruction of Europe. It made the creation of a European defense organization capable of detaching itself from NATO virtually impossible. With the re-creation of the special relationship, the importance of the WEU faded, cooperation among the Continental countries blossomed, and esteem for Britain on the Continent plummeted.[26]

The Fouchet Plans

The Anglo-American realignment speeded the integration process on the Continent. Obstacles that so far had hindered an agreement on EURATOM (European Atomic Energy Community) and the European Economic Community (EEC) were quickly overcome. The development was actively supported by the United States, who envisaged complementing Continental integration militarily with the formation of NATO nuclear forces. The US reconstruction of Europe, the formation of an economically integrated Continent under a NATO umbrella had seemed to bear fruit.[27]

Yet again, the US project faltered. De Gaulle rejected French membership in NATO nuclear forces without proper representation in a political control council. He demanded a trilateral politico-military global directorate.[28] As an amendment to this design de Gaulle foresaw the formation of a Continental European Union on whose behalf France would act on the trilateral politico-military directorate.[29] With the advent of the Berlin Crisis the French proposal, and especially its European amendment, gained the support of the Federal Republic.[30] Konrad Adenauer started to fear a *pax atomica*, a settlement of the German question that would freeze Germany's emancipation once and for all.[31] The German chancellor pushed to develop Europe as an independent power factor before an agreement among the superpowers could emerge. A central tenent of his policy was to enhance Franco-German cooperation, in order to forestall a common approach of the Western powers in East–West negotiations. De Gaulle was happy to reciprocate; Franco-German cooperation strengthened de Gaulle's hand in his negotiations with the "Anglo-Saxons." Furthermore, de Gaulle shared Adenauer's geopolitical vision. Both statesmen agreed that the unification of Germany should lead to the unification of Europe and thereby end the bipolar order of the Cold War. To be precise, de Gaulle envisaged a three-step approach to a Europe from the Atlantic to the Urals. Step one was the formation of a European Political Union of the Six. Having achieved this, an enlarged union under Franco-British leadership was foreseen, which would form the foundation for the envisaged all-European structure from the Atlantic to the Ural.[32]

The first-ever EEC summit, convened in February 1961 by the French government, took the first step towards an implementation of the French vision. The EEC member states agreed to the formation of a Study Committee on European Political Union, chaired by the French diplomat Christian Fouchet. The ensuing discussions on the institutionalization of a "CESDP ('Common European Security and Defence Policy')" were further boosted by the Bonn summit of July 18, 1961, where the EEC member states reiterated their support for a harmonization of their foreign and security policy "so as to promote the political union of Europe." Just days later the UK announced her application to join the EEC. The British decision to join the EEC soon overshadowed the EPU negotiations.[33]

The Fouchet proposals aimed at an intergovernmental European Political Union of the Six. The Benelux countries, however, preferred a supranational structure to check the natural weight of France and Germany; as an alternative they discussed an intergovernmental EPU of the Seven. Notwithstanding the differences, a compromise solution for an EPU of the Six seemed to emerge owing to Italo-German brokerage. French hopes to conclude the EPU negotiations successfully were shattered on April 10, 1962. In a statement made to the Council of the WEU, the Lord Privy Seal Sir Edward Heath stressed that following Britain's accession to EEC, a "European point of view on defense will emerge," which will alter "the balance within the Atlantic alliance." He even spoke of the formation of "two great groupings in the West": Europe and North America. Britain's obvious support for a gradual transformation of the Atlantic alliance towards a two-pillared security structure made the Benelux countries now insist on immediate British EPU membership. However, France and Germany, who intended to consolidate the Continent before admitting Great Britain, made participation in the EPU negotiations dependent on EEC membership. The EPU negotiations arrived at an unbridgeable gap and broke down.[34]

France did not reject British EPU membership per se, but feared that a premature and unconditional admission would allow Britain to dominate the future Europe. De Gaulle, wedded to the three-step approach to European Union, now intensified Franco-German cooperation in order to form a power bloc able to dictate Britain's terms of admission. Simultaneously, Franco-British negotiations about the structures of the foreseen "double-headed alliance" set in. In talks with the French ambassador Macmillan proposed the creation of a European pillar within NATO capable of "matching the United States." Assuming that only a Franco-British program of nuclear sharing might ease the entry negotiations he even floated the idea of forming a Franco-British nuclear trusteeship group.[35]

The Anglo-French talks about the future European defense architecture alarmed the United States. The European schemes seriously endangered the bedrock of US hegemony in Europe: NATO supremacy. President John F. Kennedy responded by publicly pronouncing a renewal of the Atlantic partnership. Although interpretations of the grand design vary, Kennedy proposed anything but a blueprint for an equal partnership.[36] It was far more "a cleverly concealed maneuver to keep the Europeans dependent on America" – as Sir Pierson Dixon observed.[37] One of the core features of the grand design was the formation and later Europeanization of multilateral NATO nuclear forces (MLF). The State Department proposed to hand over political control over the MLF as soon as the Europeans had succeeded in establishing a supranational EPU. The grand design appealed to the conventionally armed European powers, but France and Britain rejected the project. They rightfully suspected that the real aim of the grand design was to centralize nuclear decision-making, not to proliferate it.[38]

The Cuban Missile Crisis made matters worse. The quick resolution of the crisis persuaded Konrad Adenauer – as we now know – to rightfully suspect a far-reaching deal between the superpowers.[39] The Chancellor now interpreted the MLF project as a nuclear control mechanism disguised as a nuclear sharing program. The threat of a *pax atomica* now seemed real. To face down the danger which this development represented for European emancipation the Six had to come to terms with Great

Britain. London and Paris, however, were not able to agree on a procedure. Britain made EEC membership a prerequisite for an agreement on the future European defense structures, while de Gaulle envisaged that EEC membership would follow such an agreement. John F. Kennedy, who started to fear being confronted with a fait accompli by the Europeans, now used the SKYBOLT cancellation to force Britain to negotiate the future European defense structures before being admitted to the EEC.[40]

Kennedy offered Britain the Polaris missile as a compensation for the Skybolt. By doing so, he offered a continuation of the special relationship. Kennedy must have been fully aware that "the continental reactions to this discrimination will do great – perhaps decisive – damage to the EEC negotiations."[41] He nevertheless proceeded to forestall the development of a European defense organization. For Macmillan it was a choice between Scylla and Charybdis. A rejection of the offer and nuclear cooperation with the Continent would surely pave Britain's way into the EEC, but would have far-reaching implications for the transatlantic relationship; acceptance of the offer, however, might endanger the application to join the EEC. The implication of the offer for the development of a 'CESDP', the strings attached to the rocket deal, was to decide the future role of Britain in Europe. British participation in MLF would provoke a veto by de Gaulle because it would undermine the formation of an autonomous European defense organization deemed indispensable for an emancipation of Europe.[42]

Clever diplomacy at Nassau saved the situation. Macmillan managed to chart a middle ground, by paying tribute to trilateralism. The Nassau agreement foresaw the creation of two separate nuclear forces: the Inter-Allied Nuclear Forces (IANF) composed of the nuclear forces of France, Britain, and the United States, and a multi-manned element, the MLF. Yet it was only a pyrrhic victory. The official interpretation of the Nassau agreement by the United States, given on January 11, 1963, left no doubt that the IANF were nothing but a temporary measure, while the future NATO Nuclear Forces (NNF) would be the MLF. Three days later General de Gaulle announced in his infamous press conference his rejection of the Nassau agreement, followed by his veto of British EEC membership.[43]

The French *grand dessin*, the formation of a fully fledged European Union topped by a Franco-British nuclear trusteeship group, faltered, as the Fouchet negotiations had done before. Adenauer and de Gaulle now decided to form a nucleus for an EPU by implementing bilaterally the concept underlying the Fouchet proposal of the Six. On January 22, France and the Federal Republic of Germany signed the Elysée Treaty, which led to an institutionalized harmonization of the foreign and security policies of the two countries. The United States were extremely alarmed by the creation of a Franco-German Defence council. London did not fear the duplication of NATO functions, but her exclusion from Europe. Macmillan, therefore, pleaded for the construction of Europe on the basis of the WEU. The initiative failed, because France rejected the use of a sub-organization of NATO, while the United States feared the implied duplication of NATO functions.[44]

The fact that no possibility emerged to reform the alliance towards a two-pillared structure left the Federal Republic with the choice either to merge her destiny with that of France and to work towards the formation of an autonomous Europe, or to place her destiny in the hands of the United States, which repeatedly had stated a willingness to Europeanize the planned MLF forces. The precarious political situation of Germany made the Federal Republic opt for the latter, hoping to be able to initiate a movement which would serve Germany, Europe, and the preservation of the Atlantic alliance.[45]

Although no institutionalization of European political cooperation occurred, although no EPU or 'CESDP' emerged, the defense architecture of Europe and the West had never before been the object of such fierce struggle, and would not be so again. Never during the Cold War was Europe closer to duplicating NATO defense structures; never was it closer to the formation of a transatlantic alliance based on two separate pillars: the European Community and North America. It is this prehistory that will give the following study of the institutionalization of the CFSP form and direction.[46]

From Détente to the End of the Cold War

European political cooperation and ostpolitik

The year 1963 marks a turning point in the history of the Cold War. Since the resolution of the Cuban Missile Crisis the United States had intensified their contacts with the Soviet Union in order to stop the proliferation of nuclear weapons. The danger of nuclear annihilation, but also the growing assertiveness of the allies, the dangers of "splintering alliance systems," led both super powers to discover shared interests. Both Khrushchev and Kennedy envisaged a nuclear test ban as a potential starting point towards the creation of an East–West regime for the management of the Cold War. The superpowers tried to stabilize the bipolar order.[47]

The US preferred a *pax atomica* to the concept of Euro-Atlantic partnership. Great Britain gradually adjusted to the new framework and became a party in the East–West negotiations that led to the signing of the limited test-stop agreement in Moscow on August 5, 1963. France rejected the test-stop agreement, even after being offered membership in a trilateral NATO directorate. Nevertheless, the Cold War had changed its face. With the test-ban treaty the Cold War had entered a new phase, characterized by the formation of an East–West non-proliferation regime that eased East–West tensions and stabilized bipolarity, but left Europe in shambles.[48]

Years of uncertainty and stagnation followed. Political Europe was torn between adjustment to and a challenging of the new framework. The stalemate left a deep imprint on the European integration process. It finally ended with the French retreat from NATO's integrated structures. With this, a reform of NATO emerged that ended the Western architectural debate and safeguarded NATO central command and control. The challenge to bipolarity, however, continued. France openly challenged the United States in East–West relations. De Gaulle's independent foreign policy, his strategy of emphasizing traditional national interests in order to overcome the "artificial" ideological divide between East and West, threatened to erode bloc stability. To forestall détente provoking a split of the alliance, a harmonization of East–West negotiations within NATO became indispensable. The Harmel Report of 1967 revitalized NATO as a policy forum and thus unintentionally paved the way for a European détente that aimed at overcoming the Cold War without challenging NATO.[49]

European détente, or *Ostpolitik*, took account of the Soviet fear of "Europe," which had led to Moscow's decision to co-create an East–West security regime for the preservation of bipolarity. Trust-building measures lay at the very heart of *Ostpolitik*. They were meant to overcome bloc tension and to ease the Soviet fear of Germany and Europe, and thereby of a multipolar world order. *Ostpolitik* replaced traditional power politics with a civil-power approach. The political aim, namely to overcome the division of Germany by overcoming the division of Europe, remained unchanged.[50]

The concept of *Ostpolitik* evolved in the years of stagnation. It was a conscious reaction to the Cold War reality. The breakthrough of the soft-power approach occurred after Willy Brandt had assumed office in 1969. The new German chancellor was dedicated to making *Ostpolitik* work. Aware that *Ostpolitik* begins in the West, the German chancellor first turned to the EC. A European power platform was indispensable before launching negotiations with the East. The Hague summit of 1969 offered the opportunity necessary for a relaunch of the European integration process. The circumstances were extremely favorable. De Gaulle's departure had removed the main obstacle to a fresh approach to the construction of Europe within an Atlantic framework. A package deal comprising completion, deepening, and enlargement allowed the deadlock to be broken in the construction of Europe. At The Hague the Six agreed to tackle again the thorny subject of "political unification." The net outcome was the Davignon Report of 1970, which created European Political Co-operation (EPC). The EC member states agreed to ensure through regular exchanges of information and consultations a better mutual understanding on the great international problems. The EC member states created, with EPC, a thinly institutionalized structure for enhanced cooperation among the national foreign ministries. The discussion of defense issues was avoided.[51]

The EPC promoted European independence in world politics, thereby weakening the superpower "autocracy in world politics" (Wilkens). The EPC provided the Federal Republic with the multilateral support needed for her *Ostpolitik*. EPC, furthermore, provided useful machinery for the preparation of the meetings of the Conference on Security and Cooperation in Europe (CSCE), and thereby markedly improved Europe's negotiating position. Owing to EPC, Europe had a major impact on the Helsinki Final Act, which, by guaranteeing the inviolability of the borders, by regulating East–West trade, and by fostering human rights, formed a decisive step towards lifting the Iron Curtain.[52]

Underlying European assertiveness in foreign policy was a conflict in transatlantic relations, nurtured by the Vietnam War, the abrogation of the Bretton Woods monetary system, the Middle East crisis and US alliance policy.[53] Europeans were rejecting the notion that Europe the regional power had to support US global policies. They were reluctant to concede to the US demand, formulated by Henry Kissinger in 1973, to consult the US before formulating any common European policy.[54] To ease the tensions created by European détente and the Euro–Arab dialogue, the other bone of contention, the EC member states finally decided at Gymnich to ask the presidency to keep the US informed about major developments within the EPC. Frictions, however, remained. This is reflected in the Tindemans Report of 1975.[55] The report proposed integrating foreign, defense, and fiscal policies, in order to allow Europe to "recover some control over its destiny." It furthermore spoke of the need for Europe to "speak with one voice in its relations with the United States."[56]

The Europeans, however, remained reluctant to follow Tindemans's advice to embrace defense cooperation. This attitude changed with the advent of the so-called Second Cold War from 1979 to 1981. The US drift towards renewed confrontation with the Soviet Union, which threatened to replace the East–West dialogue with a new ideological crusade, set two movements in motion: a strengthening of EPC and the revival of the WEU.[57]

The Single European Act and the revival of the WEU

The US drift towards renewed superpower enmity set a movement in motion that overcame the Eurosclerosis that had befallen the European community shortly after the British admission to the EC in 1973. This led not only to the signing of the Single European Act (SEA) of 1986, but to a revival of the WEU as well. It was due to the political foresight of Mitterrand and the dedication of Germany's new Chancellor Helmut Kohl that the deadlock was broken.[58] Kohl – committed to boosting the feeble EPC and saving European détente – was guided by Adenauer's European vision and the Genscher–Colombo Plan of 1981. The latter envisaged an EU with more "effective decision-making structures," and a "common foreign policy" under the political direction and guidance of the European Council – instituted in 1975.[59]

Kohl and Mitterrand first revived Franco-German cooperation. Having achieved this, both statesmen started – as Moravcsik so pointedly stresses – to threaten Britain with a Europe of two speeds, in order to break the stalemate that threatened Europe's marginalization in future East–West talks. The revitalization of Franco-German cooperation instantly bore fruit. The Fontainebleau summit (1984), held during a French presidency, witnessed an interstate bargain that led to the solution of the British budget question, paved the way to a further EC enlargement and lifted British opposition to institutional reform. With the formation of an ad hoc Committee for Institutional Affairs the negotiations leading to the SEA had taken off.[60]

The SEA of 1986 led to a first revision of the treaties of Rome. It finally brought together the EC and EPC under the single umbrella of the European Council, established in 1974. The SEA did not communitarize EPC, but codified common practice. Title III, however, specified that the Commission "shall be fully associated with the proceedings of political co-operation," to guarantee consistency between the external EC policies and the EPC. This stipulation opened the door for a slow and gradual communitarization of EPC. The EPC structures remained almost untouched, the reinforcement of the EPC mechanism limited. The SEA did not lead to an extension of the competences of the EC into the field of defense. Yet the scope of the EPC was extended to "political and economic aspects of security." More important, however, Article 30, Section 6 SEA stipulated that "nothing . . . shall impede closer co-operation in the field of security between certain of the High Contracting Parties within the frameworks of the Western European Union or the Atlantic Alliance." This article, referring to the parallel process that had emerged within the Western European Union, underlined the close correlation of the two processes.[61]

One of the major manifestations of the Second Cold War in Europe was the NATO "dual-track" decision of 1979. It combined an INF deployment in western Europe with an offer to eliminate INF from Europe altogether. The deployment decision threatened European détente. It contained a double threat: first, a revival of East–West confrontation, and second, a renewal of the superpower management of the Cold War. In Germany a strong peace movement emerged that tried to block the first by buying into the second. Mitterrand, fearing a settlement of the Germany question that would leave Germany neutralized and France isolated, spoke out for a deployment and a relaunch of the Franco-German defense dialogue dormant since 1963.[62]

Soon thereafter, the US Strategic Defense Initiative (SDI) prompted Mitterrand to embark on resurrecting the long-dormant WEU. The SDI project threatened to undermine European deterrence. The deployment of missile defense shields by the superpowers would invalidate the deterrent value of the British and French nuclear forces. Faced with a possible renewal of the superpower management of the Cold War, the WEU member states committed themselves in the Rome Declaration of 1984 to reactivate the WEU as a European security forum. It needed, however, the Reykjavik summit of 1986 to transform commitment into action.

It was the "zero option," the possible elimination of all INF in or targeted at Europe, emerging at the Reykjavik summit that shocked the Europeans into action. The WEU "Platform of European Security Interests" adopted at The Hague on October 27, 1987 re-established the WEU as a European security forum.[63] It outlined a distinct "European identity" in defense matters and described the revitalization of the WEU "as an important contribution to the broader process of European unification." According to its charter, the WEU was deemed to preserve and shape the peace dialogue, in order to overcome "the division of Europe" by "making full use of the CSCE process." The platform established the WEU as a forum at the crossroads of European integration, transatlantic relations, and European unification. It failed, however, to address institutional questions necessary to transform the WEU into a European defense organization.[64]

Owing to a policy of compartmentalization, utilized to circumvent British and Dutch opposition to a duplication of NATO structures, progress in defense cooperation was made bilaterally. Chancellor Kohl and President Mitterrand agreed in 1987 to establish a joint Franco-German Brigade, so as to allow a future European Union to draw on existing defense and military structures. The Franco-German Brigade was instituted in 1990.[65]

Winds of change

In the meantime the international climate had changed dramatically. The superpower diplomacy of Mikhail Gorbachev did not lead to US–Soviet collusion – a renewed superpower détente – as feared in Europe, but to a genuine de-escalation of tensions. Gorbachev's policy of glasnost and perestroika, and his advocacy of unilateral force reductions, demilitarization, and deideologization of interstate relations, made the Europeans realize that Gorbachev was committed to the CSCE process. Gorbachev was not interested in stabilizing the Cold War, but in replacing the coexistence of the Cold War by co-creation. The Soviet Union envisaged an all-European security system, a "Common House of Europe"– excluding the United States.[66]

The US, having focused on superpower détente, was taken by surprise. The specter of an all-European settlement on European terms made the US take up the gauntlet. The fear that Gorbachev might play the "German card" as a joker made the US push the German question herself. Soon the superpowers competed to win the favor of the Europeans and especially of Germany. Thereby a spiral of de-escalation set in which developed its own momentum, slipped out of the control of the superpowers and led not only to the unification of Germany, but to the destruction of the bipolar Cold War order and the dissolution of the Soviet Union.

The breaching of the Berlin Wall in November of 1989 and the quick dissolution of the Eastern bloc came as a surprise to all parties involved. The lifting of the Iron Curtain caused jubilation, but also consternation. Concern about the future dominated the political agenda in Moscow and Washington. The European revolution challenged the whole Cold War security architecture. It ended bipolarity and called into question the very existence of NATO and the Warsaw Pact. Would Europe, as some US analysts mourning the demise of bipolarity predicted, return to anarchy, to ethnic and religious conflict, or to a German domination of the Continent?[67] To forestall such a development a new security architecture was urgently needed. The first contours of the future European security architecture emerged in December 1989 when US secretary of state James Baker envisaged a three-track security architecture consisting of the EC, NATO, and the CSCE. The Treaty on the Final Settlement with Respect to Germany, commonly referred to as the Two + Four Treaty, of September 12, 1990 reflects the three-track approach. It remained undecided, however, whether the CSCE/OSCE, the EC/EU or NATO should dominate the future security architecture of Europe.[68] Preferences differed widely. France, faithful to her European vision, preferred a European framework for German unification. A deepening of European integration, and a merger of the EC and the WEU, would not only allow containment of a unified Germany, but also establish the EC as an independent factor in world politics. The US and Great Britain, in contrast, worked towards a transformation of NATO. The "Atlanticists," dedicated to the preservation of NATO supremacy, envisaged an integration of a reinforced WEU into NATO in order to form a "European pillar" of NATO. The Soviet Union remained committed to her vision to create a Common European Home by turning the CSCE into a fully-fledged regional collective security organization. The dissolution of the Soviet Union, however, markedly weakened the vision of a Common House of Europe.[69]

Europe set the tone. Mitterrand and Kohl revived the vision of de Gaulle and Adenauer, to use the unification of Germany to form a "European third force." The 1980s had prepared the terrain. The time of implementation had arrived. After months of anxiety and hesitation both statesmen agreed in April 1990 to accelerate the political construction of Europe, and to transform the existing European structures into a European Union (EU). Their call for an intergovernmental conference (IGC) on political union, to complement the IGC on economic and monetary union (EMU), was favorably received by the EC member states at the Dublin summit of June 1990. A European Political Union (EPU) would offer an institutional framework capable of containing "the potential regional hegemony of a united Germany."[70]

After German reunification, on October 3, 1990, Kohl and Mitterrand developed further their plans for European political union. Both statesmen envisaged "a real common security policy and eventually a common defence," and therefore "a clear organic relation with WEU" or even a fusion of the future EU and the WEU in 1998, the year the WEU charter expired.[71]

Shortly after the IGC on EMU and EPU opened in December 1990, deliberations about the future of the WEU started. France and Germany supported a relationship closely tying the WEU to the EU; Great Britain and the Netherlands preferred linking the WEU with NATO. Either way a reappraisal of NATO structures became indispensable.

The attempt of the EC member states to bring security and defense into the European integration process alarmed the United States. The US opposed any marginalization of NATO. The famous Bartholomew/Dobbins mission bears witness to this, as well as to US pre-emptive diplomacy. The US floated a NATO reform project that competed with the construction of Europe in order to forestall the possibility that NATO might be sidelined by the European community's defense aspirations. The US initiative strengthened the negotiating position of those Europeans who intended to keep the EC as a sub-set of the Atlantic alliance. As a result the European dynamic slowed markedly.[72]

It needed an agreement on a pillar structure for the future EU to refloat the negotiations. The pillar model separated the EEC from EPC and from home and justice affairs, creating three separate pillars, for which the European Council provided "political guidance and impetus". The pillar model envisaged separate decision-making procedures for each pillar. This allowed a Europe of different speeds. It afforded an enhancement of European economic integration, while policy-making in foreign and security policy could remain largely outside the community decision-making procedures. With the pillar model the contours of a compromise emerged that hardly concealed the tensions between the two competing visions of Europe: Europe as an autonomous partner of the US, and Europe as an economic sub-set of NATO. Those tensions are reflected in the ambiguous text of the Treaty Establishing a European Union (TEU) signed on February 7, 1992.[73]

European Security after the Cold War

Nevertheless the Maastricht Treaty improved EPC. The Common Foreign and Security Policy (CFSP) established under Title V, Article J of the TEU led to a rationalization of EPC, without changing its intergovernmental character. It arranged for systematic cooperation between the member states on "any matter of foreign and security policy." The CFSP "shall include all questions related to the security of the Union, including the eventual framing of a common defense policy, which might in time lead to a common defence." The Union, however, does not deal with defense issues as such, but may, according to Article J.4 TEU, request the WEU "to elaborate and implement decisions and actions of the Union with defence implications." The WEU remained an autonomous organization, although the TEU foresaw a very close interplay. The TEU earmarked the WEU to act in the future "as the defense component of the European Union." The Declaration on Western European Union, attached to the Maastricht Treaty, therefore outlined a further harmonization of cooperation between the EU and the WEU, and an enhancement of the operational role of the WEU.[74]

Pending the ratification of the TEU, a dynamic set in to develop the WEU as the defense component of the EU. Inspired by the Declaration on WEU, plans emerged to create a European Reaction Force under the WEU umbrella – to enable the Europeans to act collectively outside the NATO area. France and Germany even acted upon the expressed need to form military units answerable to the WEU. The Franco-German Defence and Security Council, assembled in La Rochelle on May 22, 1992, formed a Franco-German Corps and invited the WEU member states to participate in the formation of further EUROCORPS in order to "provide the EU with the possibility of conducting its own military affairs."[75]

One month later, on June 19, 1992, the WEU adopted the Petersberg Declaration.[76] Herewith the WEU member states declared their willingness to improve and to use their operational capabilities for the "effective implementation of conflict prevention and crisis management measures," including peacekeeping activities under the auspices of the CSCE and the UN. The formation of multinational and multiservice military units, as well as a Planning Cell, would enable the WEU to engage in humanitarian and rescue missions, peacekeeping, and peace making. On October 1, 1992 the WEU Planning Cell was established in Brussels, to work out contingency plans and the command and control structures of a future European headquarters. Notwithstanding differences in approach, a breakthrough in the formation of a European pillar within NATO seemed imminent in 1992.[77]

The implied duplication of NATO structures threatened to sidetrack NATO and allowed the formation of a European security architecture based on the EU/WEU, the OSCE and the UN. The vision of de Gaulle to form a Europe from the Atlantic to the Urals seemed to become reality. The European dynamic, however, collapsed with the advent of the Yugoslav crisis.

Yugoslavia and NATO enlargement

The emerging new security architecture of Europe based on the UN, the OSCE, and the EU/WEU was not able to meet the challenge posed by the crisis in Yugoslavia. The hostilities commenced in 1991, at a time when the EC still operated according to the old EPC rules. Without adequate crisis-management procedures, and hindered by infighting among the Europeans and conflicts with Russia about the future order of the Balkan region, the Europeans were incapable of formulating an adequate response to the instability in Yugoslavia. This was aggravated by the fact that the US showed no interest in breathing life into the European security architecture. At the very moment when the EC sought, with the Vance–Owen plan of 1992, to put forward a "European solution" to the regional crisis in the Balkans, the US laid the groundwork for NATO enlargement, and thereby for a security architecture that maintained US influence in European affairs.

Under the Vance-Owen plan UNPROFOR (the UN Protection Force), created by the UN Security Council in 1992, would supervise the formation of a Federation of Bosnia-Herzegovina with large-scale autonomy of the provinces. This decision was in line with the new composite European security architecture, but it completely sidestepped NATO. This fateful decision ensured the Vance–Owen plan's failure. The US objected to the peace plan. This prolonged the conflict and led to an escalation of violence, peaking in the Serb attack on the "safe haven" of Sarajevo. The threat of ethnic cleansing forced the EU member states to end the architectural debate, which so far had inhibited a settlement, and to embrace NATO involvement. The US decision to block the Vance-Owen plan had hindered the emergence of an all-European security system including Russia, marginalizing the EU as well as the CSCE. The ensuing Bosnian crisis led to NATO's first out-of-area deployment, which offered the United States the opportunity for a revival of the ailing NATO. The United States used the situation for a far-reaching reform of the Atlantic alliance, re-establishing a hegemonic security architecture in Europe.[78]

Committed to the principle of "enlargement and engagement" by National Security Advisor W. Anthony Lake,[79] the United States based the reform program on two pillars: NATO enlargement and the development of combined joint task forces (CJTFs). The linchpin of the new security concept was the extension of the Western security architecture of the Cold War towards the East. The enlargement of NATO and of the EU would lead to a reconstruction of the entire continent. Enlargement offered an alternative to deepening as a strategy to balance German power. In addition, enlargement excluded Russia from the European security architecture and thereby guaranteed US preponderance. The extension of the security architecture of the Cold War to the East abetted the formation of a unipolar instead of a multipolar world order. This program was complemented by the project to develop CJTFs, which would allow "coalitions of the willing" to draw on "separable but not separate" NATO assets to conduct military operations globally. Such a flexibilization of NATO structures would allow the EU to plan and the WEU to conduct military operations without duplicating NATO structures. This would make an ESDI within the Atlantic alliance possible without detriment to the central command and control structure of NATO.[80]

The US initiative paid off. The reform package was adopted at the NATO summit in Brussels (1994). The member states herewith agreed to the most radical reform in NATO's history. It was a historic decision with wide implications for eastern and western Europe alike. To a degree, however, it was a reform that changed everything in order to change nothing; it changed structures to maintain power structures. In short, NATO expansion, in membership and mandate, was an important tool to sustain US primacy in Europe and to "ensure that no peer competitors arise that might challenge American power in the region".[81] CJTFs did not serve the emancipation of Europe, as long as the use of NATO assets by the WEU required the consensus of the NATO Council, and thereby the *placet* of the United States. The CJTF proposal resembled the MLF project of the 1960s. To make it serve European instead of US interests "Europeanization" was required. It took two years of hard bargaining, until the process of alliance adaptation and reform led to a further definition of the CJTF concept at the Berlin NATO Council meeting of 1996. The Berlin agreement finally addressed the question of European political control; it allowed the temporary formation of European command arrangements for WEU-led CJTF operations. With the CJTF concept, the United States had developed a workable alternative to the emerging European security architecture, which slowed down the European dynamic remarkably.[82]

The pendulum was, however, to swing back yet again. The Kosovo crisis of 1998/1999 challenged the CJTF concept and herewith – as Stuart Croft put it – the victory of the Anglo-Saxon idea.[83]

The new European security architecture

With the 1996 IGC, convoked under Article N of the TEU to revise said treaty, the focus shifted back to the EU. But the Treaty of Amsterdam (ToA) of October 2, 1997, resulting from the 1996 IGC, lacked the confidence and vision of the TEU. Notwithstanding the possible denunciation of the Brussels Treaty in 1998, the EU member states took no final decision on the future of the WEU. The treaty retained the separation of the EU and the WEU and the intergovernmental character of the CFSP. No "variable geometry" emerged that allowed "enhanced cooperation" in pillar two, i.e. the formation of core groups. Instead of "enhanced co-operation" the ToA introduced a "creative abstention" clause (Article 23.1 consol TEU) – a rather ambiguous provision for case-by-case opt-outs from CFSP initiatives. The implementation of a decision with defense implications herewith required the unanimous approval of the EU, the WEU, and – in case CJTFs are brought into play – the NATO Council as well. The balance sheet, however, was not entirely negative. The protocol to Article 17 of the ToA explicitly affirmed the necessity to provide the EU "access to an operational capability" in order to develop an ESDI in accordance with the decisions taken by the NATO Council in Berlin. The protocol asked the EU and the WEU to work out an "arrangement for enhanced co-operation" within a year from the entry into force of the Treaty of Amsterdam. This included the possibility of a merger of the WEU and the EU.[84]

The Kosovo conflict of 1998 revived the architectural debate. To the surprise of many it was the British prime minister Tony Blair who proposed the development of a EU defense capacity at the EU summit meeting at Pörtschach (Austria). Blair, however, ruled out the formation of a European army. Two months later, at the Franco–British summit of St. Malo, Blair and Chirac agreed to implement the ToA and to increase the military capability of the EU in order to achieve a "capacity for autonomous action." The reforms focused on European capabilities, so as to enable the EU to act without having recourse to NATO assets. None of these measures threatened the integrity of the NATO command and control structure. There is no indication that Blair supported the formation of a European pillar. It is therefore questionable whether the Franco-British summit at St. Malo marks a departure from past practice. St. Malo was without doubt a watershed, but no Rubicon was crossed. It marked the adoption of "a European tactic to keep a NATO strategy alive."[85] The Blair government hoped to end the "sterile institutional debate" about a second pillar, by making the Berlin "grand bargain" work – nothing more and nothing less.[86] The British now envisaged a merger of the WEU and the EU that would leave NATO as the only organization with a mutual defense clause (Article V). This would forestall the emergence of a two-pillar structure, but allow the EU to develop the politico-military expertise of the WEU for out-of-area tasks. The latter would give the EU more clout in global affairs. Given such a framework any augmentation of European defense capabilities would not be to the detriment of NATO. This pragmatic approach seemed to cut the Gordian knot; it enabled Britain, France, and Germany to agree on a EU defense component. The latter opened the avenue to an institutional reform that supplied the EU with the "appropriate structures and capacity."

St. Malo set two dynamics in motion: a rush by the Europeans to create the capacity for "autonomous action" foreseen in the Declaration of St. Malo and an attempt by the US to channel this movement. The NATO summit in Washington (1999) advanced both dynamics. NATO's acknowledgment of the EU's resolve "to have the capacity for autonomous action" boosted the European ambition. The elaboration of the CJTF formula for its part bolstered the formation of an ESDI within NATO. The EU was granted ready access to collective assets and NATO planning capabilities. Further command options for EU/WEU-led CJTF missions were developed. The so-called Berlin+ arrangement, however, left Europe's autonomy critically limited. It entailed NATO's right of first refusal, i.e. the EU could only act in case NATO chose not to do so. Furthermore, NATO retained a veto right concerning the use of its assets.[87]

The limitations of the so-called Berlin+ arrangement made France and Germany look for an enhancement of Europe's defense capacity. At the Franco-German Defence and Security Council meeting in Toulouse, both countries pledged to use all their weight to build up EU assets to make the EU a genuinely autonomous actor in world politics. Days later, at the Cologne European Council summit, the EU formally adopted the St. Malo Declaration, and sketched the capability requirements and institutional structures necessary for the EU to contribute to international peace and security in accordance with the principles of the UN or the OSCE. The WEU "Audit of Assets and Capabilities for European Crisis Management," focusing on C3 (command, control, and communication) capabilities, complemented a development that peaked at the Helsinki European Council summit with the launch of the institutional framework for an ESDP/CESDP.[88]

The enhancement of Europe's autonomy in crisis management owes much to Franco-British cooperation. Weeks before the Helsinki summit, both countries called upon the EU to form a self-sufficient corps for EU crisis management. Even more important, however, was the decision by both governments to make the UK permanent Joint HQs and France's Centre opéerationnel interarmées available to act as command centers for EU-led operations. France and Britain furthermore pledged their support for the formation of a European strategic airlift capacity and for restructuring Europe's defense industry. This paved the way for the Helsinki European Council of December 10–11, 1999, which decided to put the whole range of political, economic, and military instruments at the disposal of the EU Council when responding to crisis situations. At Helsinki the EU member states agreed to build up a force of 60,000 men deployable within 30 days and capable of fulfilling the whole range of Petersberg tasks. With the formation of a Political and Security Committee, Military Committee and Military Staff, and the creation of the position of a secretary general, the necessary structures were set in place.

Although the EU member states assured that the process will avoid "unnecessary" duplication and would not involve the "creation of a European Army," the US started to be alarmed. The United States had enthusiastically supported enhanced European capabilities, but had warned of "decoupling," "duplication" and "discrimination."[89] The institutionalization of the ESDP prompted Strobe Talbott to remind the EU that Washington would not like to see an "ESDI that comes into being first within NATO but then grows out of NATO and finally grows away from NATO, since that would lead to an ESDI that initially duplicates but that could eventually compete with NATO."[90] The US was determined to preserve the existing NATO structures which guaranteed the US the status of a European power and therefore the possibility to partake in the shaping of the future European order. Any reform of NATO structures, which would question the centrality of NATO for territorial defense, would deprive the US of its prime regulatory instrument for the US reconstruction of Europe.[91]

US fears were valid. France objected to the preservation of the existing NATO command structures. Independence in foreign policy demanded genuine autonomy, and herewith the capacity for territorial defense. President Chirac's "action plan" called for a European command structure, autonomous intelligence, and a European armaments base – i.e. a further duplication of NATO structures.[92]

The vision of a multipolar world order underlying French policy set France apart from Britain, for whom no contradiction existed between "being a good European and being a good Atlanticist."[93] Great Britain tried to increase Europe's importance by increasing Europe's utility for the US. Britain did not intend to challenge NATO supremacy but looked for a more subtle mix of instruments to meet the diverse threats of the post-Cold War world. The latter had been achieved, thus London focused on stabilizing the new European security architecture.

But not every European nation agreed to the Anglo-American model for transatlantic "burden-sharing," which envisaged EU peacekeeping and NATO peacemaking. According to that model the EU, commanding over the full range of external policies, should focus on reconstruction policies in areas pacified by NATO. This strategy necessitated nothing but an implementation of the Berlin+ agreement as interpreted by Washington. Paris, however, was quick to point out that the aspired increase of military capabilities, without a simultaneous build-up of an institutionalized CESDP, would allow the United States to pursue a policy of *divide et impera* and to resort to "coalitions of the willing" in pursuance of US policy aims. A continuing lack of a European decision-making mechanism would not only prevent a rebalancing of the power structure within the alliance, but also guarantee a latent usability of Europe as a source of support for US foreign policy.

Fearing a further balancing of US power at the Nice European summit la *gouvernante américaine* – to use a phrase by Stanley Hoffmann[94] – threatened the EU member states with an "agonizing reappraisal" of US foreign policy, in case the EU decided to create a "separate operational planning capability".[95] The EU member states brought the work carried out since Cologne and Helsinki to a successful conclusion. The Treaty of Nice made the EU a fully fledged political actor able to respond effectively to requests by the UN and the OSCE. But Nice did not go beyond Helsinki; it consolidated past practice. Nice deferred the task – as President Chirac put it in a speech at Paris, on June 8, 2001 – to work out a balanced relationship between the EU and the alliance. The Treaty of Nice, however, distinguished between missions which do comprise the use of NATO assets and those which do not. The former will be organized and guided by NATO planning cells, the latter by national European HQs.[96]

ESDP after 9/11

The Clinton administration, although having used the Yugoslav crisis to revive NATO, had grudgingly acquiesced to a gradual emancipation of Europe. George W. Bush was less forthcoming. Bush insisted on a CESDP "properly integrated with NATO." The Bush administration openly objected to the formation of a European *über*-state capable of challenging the US in global affairs. Washington preferred – as Bush revealed in his famous Warsaw speech of June 2001 – an enlarged and more diverse Europe, i.e. a weak "Europe," thoroughly embedded into a transatlantic community.[97]

The tragic act of terrorism on September 11, 2001 brought a change of focus. Some analysts argue that 9/11 led to a paradigm shift equal in importance to 1989.[98] A Euro-Atlantic architectural debate on ESDI/CSDP seems to be anachronistic in a time of global terrorist threat. According to exponents of this "school" – prevalent in the UK – the time had come for the Europeans to shift priorities, to "bandwagon rather than balance," to offer military support in order "to remain relevant to a determined US" and to safeguard an effective response to the new threat. Others contradict this analysis, and warn of a possible instrumentalization of 9/11 by the US. The attack on the World Trade Center on September 11, 2001 offered the Bush administration the unique opportunity to demand from its European allies allegiance to America's "war on terror." The Bush administration acted accordingly. It grasped the opportunity not only to fight terrorism, but also to prevent the emergence of a multipolar order.

The "global threat" did not lead the Europeans to close ranks with the United States. The Europeans "reacted as much to American reactions to terrorism as they have to the terrorist threat itself."[99] The "war on terror" exposed the tensions in transatlantic relations, sharpened the existing contradictions in European foreign policy-making and split Europe in to two camps. The "old Europe" – to use a phrase coined by US secretary of defense Rumsfeld – opposed the militarization of the fight against terrorism. The member states of the "old Europe" assumed that a military campaign would increase the danger of terrorism instead of containing it – and possibly even drag the world into the "clash of civilizations" predicted by Samuel Huntington. Notwithstanding the doubts of some of its traditional NATO allies, the United States invaded Iraq. The endeavor was supported by the so-called "New Europe" – "bandwagoning" states from eastern and western Europe. Unable to achieve consensus within NATO, the US sidelined international organizations and replaced them with "coalitions of the willing." US acts were guided by the principle articulated by Deputy Secretary of Defense Wolfowitz, that the mission defines the coalition and not the coalition the mission. This policy demoted NATO to a valuable reservoir from which ad hoc coalitions could be formed.[100] The US – as Stanley Hoffmann put it – picked and chose its clients, just as it picked "in the mass of international norms and agreements, those which it deemed necessary to maintain international order."[101]

US disregard for consensus-building and the resulting utter inability of the EU to influence American foreign policy made some EU member states increasingly question the utility of an alignment with the United States.[102] France and Germany in particular pushed for a further institutionalization of the CFSP to forestall the US pitting the "New Europe" against the "Old Europe" ever again. Both countries were well aware that the decision of the EU summit at Copenhagen on December 12–13, 2002 to enlarge the EU from 15 to 25 by May 1, 2004 would change the dynamics of the EU, unless met by a successful conclusion of the negotiations on a European constitution. The EU member states had decided at the Laeken summit in December 2001 to convene a constitutional convention in order to "organize politics" in an enlarged Europe and "to develop the union as a stabilizing factor and a model in the new multi-polar world." Despite a supranational/intergovernmental dichotomy separating the European visions of Germany and France, both countries harmonized their policies to ensure the adoption of a constitution which would, among other provisions, contain a mutual-assistance clause, strengthen the principle of mutual solidarity in foreign policy, introduce "enhanced co-operation" in pillar two, and lead to the formation of a European arms agency.[103] Both countries were determined to master the double challenge to EU coherence posed by US unilateralism and EU enlargement, and to foreclose a possible disintegration of the EU.

The plan to establish an EU operational planning staff projected by the prime ministers of France, Germany, Belgium, and Luxembourg at the Tervuren summit, as well as the discussion initiated by French foreign minister Dominique de Villepin about a Franco-German Union of States, were foreshadowing the development of a core Europe as envisaged by Article III, 211–214 of the draft constitution. The stipulations on structured cooperation allowed any number of EU member states, "whose military capabilities fulfil higher criteria" to form a core group, in order to advance defense cooperation independently from the EU at large. The specter of Franco-German bilateralism within or outside the EU framework made it virtually impossible for the United Kingdom to reject the draft constitution. The UK could not afford to be sidelined from structured cooperation. A rejection of the constitution meant a loss of influence in Europe and by extension in the United States.[104]

At the EU foreign ministers' meeting at Naples in November 2003, Foreign Secretary Jack Straw thus confirmed Britain's willingness to partake in the formation of a core group to be formed around a Franco-German-British directorate. Britain's acceptance of structured cooperation led France and Germany to abandon the Tervuren project. The "Big Three" now agreed that the EU should develop the planning capability of the military staff at EU HQs in Brussels, and to create a planning cell at SHAPE (Supreme Headquarters Allied Powers Europe), in order to increase the EU's capacity to stage Berlin+ missions autonomously. Franco-German compliance with British planning was eased by Britain's acceptance of Article 40.7, a mutual defense clause. The latter assures participants in the core group who fall victim to armed aggression on their territory the unlimited support of their fellow core group members. This limited mutual-defense clause will be generalized the moment the EU Council unanimously decides – in accordance with Article 40.2 of the draft constitution – on a common defense. The constitution, herewith, refrains from duplicating NATO functions, but enabled the Europeans to form an autonomous European Defence Organization at their earliest convenience. This architecture was meant to restrain US unilateralism as well as the Franco-German drive towards European autonomy.[105]

Britain's cooperation on ESDP went hand in hand with attempts to achieve a balance between those powers who support the maintenance of the European and Euro-Atlantic structures grown during the Cold War, and those powers who have

used the European institutions since 1954 for a peaceful revision of the power structures in Europe, i.e. for the emancipation of their nation states and of Europe as a
whole. Spain's reaction to the Madrid bombing of March 2004, the replacement of
prime minister Aznar by Jose Luis Zapatero, an avowed opponent of the war in Iraq
and supporter of European integration, underlined the fact that Britain's efforts to
sustain the current power structures in Europe were of no avail, should as the United
States continue to prefer unilateralism and pre-emptive strikes to consensus-building,
alliance politics, and international law. Under those circumstances, more and more
EU member states will be compelled to back the Franco-German vision of Europe,
enhance the "toolbox" of the EU, duplicate NATO structures, and develop a model
of global governance that sidetracks the Atlantic alliance by strengthening the EU's
capabilities to enforce UN decisions autonomously.

The adoption of the European Security Strategy in 2003 and of the Headline Goal
for 2010 points in this direction. The European Defence Agency, the development
of a European Airlift Command and the creation of rapid deployable EU battle
groups are a further case in point – the EU enhances its operational capabilities. Thus
the impasse created by the failure of the Constitutional Treaty in the French and
Dutch parliaments did not affect the European dynamic in the field of foreign and
security cooperation; in fact the contrary was the case. The Treaty of Lisbon (ToL),
which emerged out of the IGC of 2007, will strengthen the EU's structures for collective action further. A "mutual solidarity clause" governing the fight against terrorism and a "mutual assistance article" (ToL 28.A7) will change the character of
the EU forever. The Brussels Treaty's mutual-defense clause was now incorporated
into the EU. This turn the EU into a mutual defense organization – without permanent command structure. These far-reaching decisions are complemented by the
formation of flexible defense structures to ensure the European ability to act in international relations. The EU "enhanced cooperation" provision is now extended to
the field of CSDP. The ToL furthermore foresees "permanent structured co-operation" in military affairs.[106] The latter project aims at a "Defence G6" comprising
France, the UK, Germany, Italy, Spain, and Poland, who – according to French
plans – will act as a vantguard in defense procurement and peacekeeping or peace-
enforcement missions.[107] The ToL thus finally incorporates peace enforcement into
the Petersberg tasks. The EU will thus command over a full-fledged "toolkit" for its
streamlined CFSP. The EU, as an independent actor, will try to replace unipolarity
with global governance, if possible, and multipolarity, if necessary.[108]

The question discussed in British historiography with reference to the BTO –
whether Europe has been an intermediary state on the way to a transatlantic community, or the transatlantic alliance a necessary transitional stage on the way to
European unity – remains unanswered. The existing NATO structure is transitory.
The question of whether there will be a place for an Atlantic alliance in the future
European security architecture will be decided by the external environment, and – in
the absence of an external threat – by the ability of the transatlantic structures to
adjust to changed power structures. This in turn presupposes the transformation of
a still hegemonic transatlantic alliance into a Euro–Atlantic partnership. This inturn
presupposes a transatlantic bargain that would allow a united and "autonomous" EU
to decide freely to join with the United States in the formation of a new Atlantic
Covenant, whose integration will be as binding for the United States as for the United

Europe. Looking at past practice, such a bargain seems improbable. Europeans and Americans alike should nevertheless aspire to a reform that would dissolve the dialectic between Atlanticism and Europeanism, by internalizing it into a new structure which would guarantee the EU equality of status and US partnership, and offer the US the improved cooperation of a more capable European partner.

In the last resort, it remains in the hands of the United States to decide whether the emergence of the EU as a power factor will lead to confrontation or to enhance cooperation.As Charles Kupchan put it:

> Those Americans who are reluctant to endorse fully Europe's defense moves are afraid of upsetting the status quo and thereby threatening the still important transatlantic bargain. They are making a critical mistake, however, in failing to recognize that the traditional Atlantic bargain is already unravelling, that the status quo is unsustainable, and that the Atlantic link can be preserved only if Europe and America strike a new and more equitable bargain.[109]

Notes

1 Layne, *The Peace of Illusions*, 94ff., 134ff.; Sloan, "The United States and European Defence," 13ff.

2 Hoffmann, *Gulliver's Troubles*; Hoffmann, *The European Sisyphus*.

3 Walt, *The Origins of Alliances*, 17ff.

4 Layne, *The Peace of Illusions*, 134ff.

5 Melissen and Zeeman, "Britain and Western Europe, 1945–1951"; Wiebes and Zeeman, "Baylis on Post-War Planning"; Baylis, "British Wartime Thinking about a Post-war European Security Group."

6 Baylis, "Britain, the Brussels Pact and the Continental Commitment"; Greenwood, "Return to Dunkirk."

7 Baylis, "Britain, the Brussels Pact and the Continental Commitment"; Young and Dockrill, *British Foreign Policy, 1945–1956*; Kent, *British Imperial Strategy*.

8 Foerster and Wiggershaus, *The Western Security Community*; Baylis, *The Diplomacy of Pragmatism*; Ireland, *Creating the Entangling Alliance*; Schmidt, *A History of NATO*; DiNolfo, *The Atlantic Pact*.

9 Heller and Gillingham, *NATO*; Hitchcock, *France, the Western Alliance*; Schmidt, op. cit.

10 Dietl, *Emanzipation und Kontrolle. Der Ordnungsfaktor Europa 1948–1958*, 90ff.

11 Köllner, *Die EVG-Phase*.

12 Pruessen, "Cold War Threats."

13 Duchin, "The Agonizing Reappraisal"; Ruane, *The Rise and Fall of the European Defence Community*.

14 Griffiths, *Europe's First Constitution*.

15 Trachtenberg, *A Constructed Peace*; Dietl, "Une Déception Amoureuse?"

16 Clesse, *Le Project de C.E.D.*

17 Guillen, "Die französische Generalität, die Aufrüstung der Bundeswehr und die EVG"; Dietl, "Une Déception Amoureuse?"

18 Larres and Osgood, *The Cold War after Stalin's Death*.

19 Küsters, "Souveränität und ABC-Waffen Verzicht"; Dietl, "Une Déception Amoureuse?"; Dietl, *Emanzipation und Kontrolle. Der Ordnungsfaktor Europa 1948–1958*.

20 Abelshauser and Schwengler, *Wirtschaft und Rüstung. Souveränität und Sicherheit*; Dietl, *Emanzipation und Kontrolle. Europa in der westlichen Sicherheitspolitik 1948–1963. Der Ordnungsfaktor Europa 1948–1958*.

21 Howorth, "European Integration and Defence."

22 Neustadt, *Alliance Politics*; Risse-Kappen, *Cooperation among Democracies*.

23 Bischof and Dockrill, *Cold War Respite*.

24 Heinemann and Wiggershaus, *Das Internationale Krisenjahr 1956*; Tal, *The 1956 War*; Troen and Shemesh, *The Suez–Sinai Crisis 1956*; Beaufre, *The Suez Expedition*.

25 Dietl, "Une Déception Amoureuse?"

26 O'Driscoll, "Les Anglo-Saxon, F-I-G and the Rival Conceptions of Advanced Armaments Research & Development Co-operation in Western Europe, 1956–1958"; Baylis, "Exchanging Nuclear Secrets"; Dietl, "Une Déception Amoureuse?"; Jones, "Anglo-American Relations after Suez."

27 Pitman, "Un Général qui s'appelle Eisenhower"; Dietl, "Une Déception Amoureuse?"

28 Vaisse, "Aux origins du memorandum de septembre 1958."

29 Soutou, "Le Général de Gaulle et le Plan Flouchet."

30 Bariéty, "Les Entretiens de Gaulle–Adenauer de juillet 1960 à Rambouillet."

31 Kosthorst, *Brentano und die deutsche Einheit*, 247ff.

32 Lucas, *Europa vom Atlantik bis zum Ural*; Soutou, "Le Général de Gaulle et le Plan Flouchet"; Lappenküper, *Die deutsch-französischen Beziehungen 1949–1963*; Dietl, "Sole Master of Western Nuclear Strength?"

33 Kaiser, *Using Europe, Abusing the Europeans*; Soutou, Plan Fouchet, 1999; Koopmann, *Das schwierige Bündnis*; Dietl, *Emanzipation und Kontrolle*, vol. II.

34 Deighton and Milward, *Widening, Deepening and Acceleration*; Koopmann, op. cit.; Dietl "Sole Master of Western Nuclear Strength?"; special issue *Revue d'Allemagne et des pays de langue allemande* (1997).

35 Kaiser, "The Bomb and Europe"; Pagedas, *Anglo-American Strategic Relations and the French Problem*; Dietl, *Emanzipation und Kontrolle*, vol. II.

36 Costigliola, "Kennedy, the European Allies and the Failure to Consult"; Giauque, *Grand Designs and Visions of Unity*; Conze, *Die gaullistische Herausforderung*.

37 National Archives, UK/PRO: FO 371/167024 – September 13, 1962.

38 Pagedas, *Anglo-American Strategic Relations and the French Problem*; Dietl, "Sole Master of Western Nuclear Strength?"

39 Nash, *The Other Missiles of October: Eisenhower, Kennedy and the Jupiters 1957–1963*.

40 Neustadt, *Report to JFK*; Dietl, "Sole Master of Western Nuclear Strength?"

41 Henry Owen to Acting Secretary, 6 December 1962, cit in Dietl, *Emanzipation und Kontrolle*, vol. II, 256f.

42 Pagedas, op. cit.; Dietl, "Sole Master of Western Nuclear Strength".

43 Middeke, "Anglo-American Nuclear Weapons Co-operation"; Dietl, *Emanzipation und Kontrolle*, vol. II.

44 Davis, "The Problem of de Gaulle"; Steininger, "Groß britannien und de Gaulle. Das Scheitern des britischen EWG Beitritts im Januar 1963"; Dietl, "Sole Master of Western Nuclear Strength?"

45 Heuser, *NATO, Britain, France and the FRG*; Marcowitz, *Option für Paris?*; Dietl, *Emanzipation und Kontrolle*, vol. II.

46 Kissinger, "Strains on the Alliance"; Kissinger, "Coalition Diplomacy in a Nuclear Age"; Bowie, "Tensions within the Alliance."

47 Trachtenberg, op. cit.; Wenger, "Crisis and Opportunity."

48 Schrafstetter and Twigge, "Trick or Truth?"; Dockrill, "Britain's Power and Influence"; Dietl "Sole Master of Western Nuclear Strength?"

49 Bozo, *Deux stratégies pour l'Europe*; Bozo, "Détente vs Alliance"; Ludlow, "Challenging French Leadership in Europe"; Loth, *Europe, Cold War and Co-existence*; Heuser, *NATO, Britain, France and the FRG*.

50 Davy, *European Détente: A Reappraisal*; Garthoff, *Détente and Confrontation*; Loth, op. cit.

51 Smith, *Europe's Foreign and Security Policy*; Regelsberger et al., *Foreign Policy of the European Union*; Hiepel, "In Search of the Greatest Common Denominator"; see also the special issue of the *Journal of European Integration History*, edited by Van der Harst.

52 Wilkens, "Westpolitik, Ostpolitik and the Project of the Economic and Monetary Union"; Smith, op. cit.

53 Simonet, "Energy and the Future of Europe."

54 Hamilton, "Britain, France and America's Year of Europe, 1973."

55 *Bulletin of the European Communities*, Suppl. 1/76.

56 Smith, op. cit.; Forster and Wallace, "Common Foreign and Security Policy"; Forster and Wallace, "What Is NATO For?"

57 Crockatt, *The Fifty Years War*.

58 Moravcsik, *Negotiating the Single European Act*.

59 Smith. op. cit.; Lappenküper, op. cit.; Regelsberger, op. cit.

60 Moravcsik, op. cit.

61 Smith, op. cit.

62 Myers, *The Western European Union*; Cahen, "The Western European Union and NATO"; Calleo and Saal, *Europe's Franco-German Engine*.

63 See http//www.weu.int – key documents.

64 Myers, op. cit.; Gambles, *European Security Integration in the 1990s*; Taylor, *Western European Security and Defence Co-operation*.

65 Schmid, Franco-German.

66 Crockatt, op. cit.; Brands, *The Devil We Knew*; Garthoff, *The Great Transition*; Larson and Sherchenko, "Shortcut to Greatness. The New Thinking and the Revolution in Soviet Affairs."

67 Mearsheimer, "Back to the Future"; Mearsheimer, "Why We Will Soon Miss the Cold War."

68 Lansford, "The Triumph of Transatlanticism"; Sloan, "The United States and European Defence."

69 Van Ham, "Europe's Precarious Centre"; McCarthy, *France–Germany, 1983–1993*.

70 Foster and Wallace, "Common Foreign and Security Policy."

71 McCarthy, op. cit.

72 Hunter, *The European Security and Defence Policy*; Regelsberger et al., op. cit.; David, *The Future of NATO*.

73 Regelsberger et al., op. cit.; Smith, op. cit.; Aybet, *The Dynamics of European Security Co-operation*.

74 Missiroli, "CFSP, Defence and Flexibility"; Taylor, op. cit.

75 McCarthy, op. cit.

76 See www.weu.int – key documents.

77 Gordon, "Does the WEU have a Role?"; Hunter, op. cit.

78 Crawford, "The Bosnian Road to NATO Enlargement"; Sperling, *Europe in Change*; Rauchhaus, *Explaining NATO Enlargement*.

79 Kay, *NATO and the Future of European Security*; David, *The Future of NATO*.

80 Hunter, op. cit.; Bensahel, "Separable but Not Separate Forces."

81 Kay, op. cit.

82 Ruggie, "Consolidating the European Pillar"; Flockhart, "The Dynamics of Expansion"; Cornish, *Partnership in Crisis*; Sloan, *NATO, the European Union, and the Atlantic Community*, 181ff.

83 Croft, "The EU, NATO and Europeanisation."

84   Whitman, "Amsterdam's Unfinished Business"; Philippart and Edwards, "The Provisions on Closer Co-operation in the Treaty of Amsterdam."
85   Howorth, "European Defence and the Changing Politics of the European Union", p. 769.
86   Howorth, "European Integration and Defence"; Howorth, "Britain, France and the European Defence Initiative"; Hoffmann, "US–European Relations"; Hoffmann, "Towards a Common European Foreign and Security Policy," 193; Cornish, "Britain, the WEU and NATO."
87   Hunter, op. cit.; Rutten, *From St. Malo to Nice*; Cornish and Edwards, "Beyond the EU/NATO Dichotomy."
88   Howorth, "Britain, France and the European Defence Initiative."
89   Cornish and Edwards, op. cit.; Howorth, *Defending Europe*.
90   Sloan, "The United States and European Defence," 24.
91   Howorth, "European Integration and Defence"; Howorth, "Britain, France and the European Defence Initiative"; Roper, "Two Cheers for Blair?"; Kupchan, "In Defence of European Defence."
92   Howorth, "Britain, France and the European Defence Initiative."
93   Roper, op. cit.
94   Hoffmann, op. cit., 192.
95   Hunter, op. cit.
96   Rutten, op. cit.
97   Daalder, "The End of Atlanticism."
98   Gordon, "NATO after September 11."
99   Gnesotto, "Reacting to America.", p. 99.
100   Daalder, op. cit.; Gnesotto, op. cit.
101   Hoffmann, "US–European Relations," 1033.
102   Daalder, op. cit.
103   Menon, "Britain and the Convention on the Future of Europe." Lahen Declaration, http://european-convention.eu.int/pdf/LKNEN.pdf
104   Smith, "The Future of the European Union and the Transatlantic Relationship"; Everts and Keohane, "The European Convention and EU Foreign Policy"; Howorth, "The European Draft Constitution Treaty and the Future of the European Defence Initiative."
105   Howorth, "The European Draft Constitution Treaty and the Future of the European Defence Initiative."
106   Quille, "The Lisbon Treaty and Its Implications for CFSP/ESDP."
107   Dagand, "The Impact of the Lisbon Treaty on CFSP and ESDP," 1–7.
108   Deighton, "The European Security and Defence Policy."
109   Kupchan, "In Defence of European Defence," 21.

Bibliography

Abelshauser, W. and W. Schwengler, *Anfänge der westdeutschen Sicherheitspolitik*, Bd. 4: *Wirtschaft und Rüstung. Souveränität und Sicherheit* (Munich: Oldenbourg, 1997).

Aybet, G., *The Dynamics of European Security Co-operation, 1945–91* (London: Palgrave, 2001).

Bariéty, J., "Les Entretiens de Gaulle-Adenauer de juillet 1960 à Rambouillet," *Revue d'Allemagne et des pays de langue allemande* 29, no. 2, 1997, 167–175.

Baylis, J., "British Wartime Thinking about a Post-war European Security Group," *RIS* 9, 1983, 265–281.

Baylis, J., "Britain, the Brussels Pact and the Continental Commitment," *International Affairs* 60, 4, 1984, 615–629.

Baylis, J., *The Diplomacy of Pragmatism: Britain and the Foundation of NATO 1942–1949* (Basingstoke: Macmillan, 1993).

Baylis J., "Exchanging Nuclear Secrets: Laying the Foundations of the Anglo-American Nuclear Relationship," *Diplomatic History* 25, no. 1, 2001, 33–51.

Beaufre, Andre, *The Suez Expedition* (New York: Praeger, 1969).

Bensahel, N., "Separable but Note Separate Forces: NATO's Development of the Combined Joint Task Force," *European Security* 8, no. 2, 1999, 52–68.

Bischof, G. and S. Dockrill, *Cold War Respite: The Geneva Summit of 1955* (Baton Rouge: Louisiana University Press, 2000).

Bowie, R., "Tensions within the Alliance," *Foreign Affairs* 42, 1963–1964, 49–69.

Bozo, F., *Deux Stratégies pour l'Europe. De Gaulle, les Etats-Unis et l'Alliance atlantique, 1958–1969* (Paris: Plon, 1996).

Bozo, F., "Détente vs. Alliance: France, the US and the Politics of the Harmel Report (1964–1968)," *Contemporary European History* 7, no. 3, 1998, 343–360.

Brands, H.W., *The Devil We Knew: Americans and the Cold War* (Oxford: Oxford University Press, 1993).

Cahen A., "The Western European Union and NATO," *Brassey's Atlantic Commentaries* 2 (1989).

Calleo, D. and E. Saal, *Europe's Franco-German Engine* (Washington, DC. Brookings Press, 1998).

Cioc, M., *Pax Atomica: The Nuclear Defense Debate in West Germany during the Adenauer Era* (New York: Columbia University Press, 1988).

Clesse, A., *Le Projet de C.E.D. du Plan Pleven au "crime" du 30 août* (Baden-Baden: NOMOS, 1989).

Conze, E., *Die gaullistische Herausforderung: Die deutsch-französischen Beziehungen in der amerikanischen Europapolitik 1958–1963* (Munich: Oldenbourg, 1995).

Cornish, P., *Partnership in Crisis: The US, Europe and the Fall and Rise of NATO* (London: Chatham House, 1997).

Cornish, P., "Britain, the WEU and NATO," in Carl Lankowski and Simon Serfaty (eds.), "Europeanizing Security: NATO and an Integrated Europe," AICGS (American Institute for Contemporary German Studies) Report 9 (1999).

Cornish, P. and J. Edwards, "Beyond the EU/NATO Dichotomy: The Beginnings of a European Strategic Culture," *International Affairs* 77, no. 3, 2001, 587–603.

Costigliola, F., "Kennedy, the European Allies and the Failure to Consult," *Political Science Quarterly* 110, no. 1, 1995, 105–123.

Crawford, B., "The Bosnian Road to NATO Enlargement," *Contemporary Security Policy* 21, no. 2, 2000, 39–59.

Crockatt, R., *The Fifty Years War: The United States and the Soviet Union in World Politics, 1941–1991* (London: Routledge, 1995).

Croft, S., "The EU, NATO and Europeanisation: The Return of Architectural Debate," *European Security* 9, no. 3, 2000, 1–20.

Daalder, I., "The End of Atlanticism," *Survival* 45, no. 2, 2003, 147–166.

Dagand, Sophie, "The Impact of the Lisbon Treaty on CFSP and ESDP," *European Security Review* 37, March 2008, 1–7.

David, C.P. (ed.), *The Future of NATO: Enlargement, Russia, and European Security* (Montreal: McGill University Press, 1999).

Davis, R., "The 'Problem of de Gaulle': British Reactions to General de Gaulle's Veto of the UK Application to Join the Common Market," *Journal of Contemporary History* 32, 1997, 4.

Davy, R. (ed.), *European Détente: A Reappraisal* (London: Sage, 1992).

Deighton, A., "The European Security and Defence Policy," *Journal of Common Market Studies* 40, no. 4, 2002, 719–741.

Deighton, A. and S. Milward (eds.), *Widening, Deepening and Acceleration: The European Economic Community 1957–1963* (Baden-Baden: NOMOS, 1999).

Dietl, R., " 'Une Déception Amoureuse'? Great Britain, the Continent and European Nuclear Co-operation, 1953–1957," *Cold War History* 3, no. 1, 2002, 29–66.

Dietl, R., " 'Sole Master of Western Nuclear Strength'? The United States, Western Europe and the Elusiveness of a European Defence Identity, 1959–1964," in W. Loth (ed.), *Europe, Cold War and Co-existence 1953–1965* (London: Cass, 2004).

Dietl, R., *Emanzipation und Kontrolle. Europa in der westlichen Sicherheitspolitik 1948–1963. Der Ordnungsfaktor Europa 1948–1958* (Stuttgart: Steiner, 2006).

Dietl, R., *Emanzipation und Kontrolle. Europa in der westlichen Sicherheitspolitik 1948–1963. Europa 1958–1963. Vom Ordnungsfaktor zum Akteur?* (Stuttgart: Steiner, 2007).

DiNolfo, E., *The Atlantic Pact. Forty Years Later: A Historic Re-appraisal* (Berlin: de Gruyter, 1991).

DiNolfo, E., *Power in Europe II. Great Britain, France, Germany and Italy and the Origins of the EEC 1952–1957* (Berlin: de Gruyter, 1992).

Dockrill, S., "Britain's Power and Influence: Dealing with Three Roles and the Wilson Government's Defence Debate at Chequers in November 1964," *Diplomacy and Statecraft* 11, no. 1, 2000, 211–240.

Duchin, B., "The Agonizing Reappraisal: Eisenhower, Dulles, and the European Defence Community," *Diplomatic History* 16, 1992, 201–221.

European Union, Report by Leo Tindemans, *Bulletin of the European Communities, Supplement* 1/76.

Everts, S. and D. Keohane, "The European Convention and EU Foreign Policy: Learning from Failure," *Survival* 45, no. 3, 2003, 167–186.

Flockhart, T., "The Dynamics of Expansion: NATO, WEU, and EU," *European Security* 5, no. 2, 1996, 196–218.

Foerster R. and N. Wiggershaus (eds.), *The Western Security Community 1948–1950: Common Problems and Conflicting National Interests during the Foundation Phase of the Atlantic Alliance* (Oxford: Berg, 1994).

Forster, A. and W. Wallace, "Common Foreign and Security Policy: A New Policy or Just a New Name?" in H. Wallace and W. Wallace, *Policy-Making in the European Union* (Oxford: Oxford University Press, 1996).

Forster, A. and W. Wallace, "What is NATO for?" *Survival* 43, no. 4, 2001–2002, 107–122.

Gambles, J., "European Security Integration in the 1990s," *Chaillot Papers* 3 (1991).

Garthoff, R.L., *Détente and Confrontation: American–Soviet Relations from Nixon to Reagan* (Washington: Brookings, 1999).

Garthoff, R.L., *The Great Transition: American–Soviet Relations and the End of the Cold War* (Washington: Brookings, 1994).

Giauque, J., *Grand Designs and Visions of Unity: The Atlantic Power and the Reorganization of Western Europe 1955–1963* (Chapel Hill: University of North Carolina Press, 2002).

Gnesotto, N., "Reacting to America," *Survival* 44, no. 4, 2002–2003, 99–106.

Gordon, P., "Does the WEU Have a Role?" *Washington Quarterly* 20, 1997, 125–140.

Gordon, P., "NATO after September 11," *Survival* 43, no. 4, 2001–2002, 89–106.

Greenwood, S., "Return to Dunkirk: The Origins of the Anglo-French Treaty of March 1947," *Journal of Strategic Studies* 6, 1989, 49–65.

Griffiths, R., *Europe's First Constitution: The European Political Community, 1952–1954* (London: Kogan, 2001).

Guillen, P., "Die französische Generalität, die Aufrüstung der Bundesrepublik und die EVG (1950–1954)," in Hans-Erich Volkmann and Walter Schwengler (eds.), *Die Europäische Verteidigungsgemeinschaft. Stand und Problem der Forschung* (Munich: Oldenbourg, 1985).

Hamilton, K., "Britain, France and America's Year of Europe, 1973," *Diplomacy and Statecraft* 17, no. 4, 2006, 871–895.

Heinemann, W. and N. Wiggershaus, *Das Internationale Krisenjahr 1956. Polen, Ungarn, Suez* (Munich: Oldenbourg, 1999).

Heller, F. and J. Gillingham (eds.), *NATO: The Founding of the Atlantic Alliance and the Integration of Europe* (New York: St. Martin's Press, 1992).

Heuser, B., *NATO, Britain, France and the FRG: Nuclear Strategies and Forces for Europe, 1949–2000* (Basingstoke: Macmillan, 1997).

Hiepel, C., "In Search of the Greatest Common Denominator: Germany and the Hague Conference 1969," *Journal of European Integration History* 9, no. 2, 2003, 63–81.

Hitchcock, W., "France, the Western Alliance and the Origins of the Schuman Plan 1948–1950," *Diplomatic History* 21, 1997, 603–630.

Hoffmann, S., *Gulliver's Troubles, Or the Setting of American Foreign Policy* (New York: McGraw-Hill, 1968).

Hoffmann, S., *The European Sisyphus: Essays on Europe 1964–1994* (Boulder, CO: Westview Press, 1995).

Hoffmann, S., "Towards a Common European Foreign and Security Policy," *Journal of Common Market Studies* 38, no. 2, 2000, 1989–1998.

Hoffmann, S., "US–European Relations: Past and Present," *International Affairs* 79, no. 5, 2003, 1029–1036.

Howorth, J., "Britain, France and the European Defence Initiative," *Survival* 42, no. 2, 2000, 33–55.

Howorth, J., "European Integration and Defence: The Ultimate Challenge?" *Chaillot Papers* 43 (2000).

Howorth, J., "European Defence and the Changing Politics of the European Union: Hanging Together or Hanging Separately?" *Journal of Common Market Studies* 39, no. 4, 2001, 765–789.

Howorth, J., "The European Draft Constitution Treaty and the Future of the European Defence Initiative: A Question of Flexibility," *European Foreign Affairs Review* 9, 2004, 483–508.

Howorth, J. and J. Keeler, *Defending Europe: The EU, NATO and the Quest for European Autonomy* (London: Palgrave, 2003).

Hunter, R., *The European Security and Defense Policy: NATO's Companion – or Competitor?* (Santa Monica: RAND, 2002).

Ireland, T., *Creating the Entangling Alliance: The Origins of the North Atlantic Treaty Organization* (Westport: Greenwood, 1981).

Jones, M., "Anglo-American Relations after Suez, the Rise and Decline of the Working Group Experiment, and the French Challenge to NATO, 1957–59," *Diplomacy and Statecraft* 14, no. 1, 2003, 49–79.

Kaiser, W., "The Bomb and Europe: Britain, France and the EEC Entry Negotiations, 1961–1963," *Journal of European Integration History* 1, 1995, 65–85.

Kaiser, W., *Using Europe, Abusing the Europeans: Britain and European Integration, 1945–1963* (London: Macmillan, 1996).

Kay, S., *NATO and the Future of European Security* (Lanham, MD: Rowman & Littlefield, 1998).

Kent, J., *British Imperial Strategy and the Origins of the Cold War, 1944–49* (Leicester: Leicester University Press, 1993).

Kissinger, H., "Coalition Diplomacy in a Nuclear Age," *Foreign Affairs* 42, 1963–1964, 525–545.

Kissinger, H., "Strains on the Alliance," *Foreign Affairs* 41, 1962–1963, 261–285.

Köllner, L., *Anfänge westdeutscher Sicherheitspolitik 1945–1956 II. Die EVG-Phase* (Munich: Oldenbourg, 1990).

Koopmann, M., *Das schwierige Bündnis. Die deutsch-französischen Beziehungen und die Außenpolitik der Bundesrepublik Deutschland 1958–1965* (Baden-Baden: NOMOS, 2000).

Kosthorst, D., *Brentano und die deutsche Einheit. Die Deutschland- und Ostpolitik des Aussenministers im Kabinett Adenauer 1955–1961* (Düsseldorf: Droste, 1993).

Kupchan, C., "In Defence of European Defence: An American Perspective," *Survival* 42, no. 2, 2000, 16–32.

Küsters, H.-J., "Souveränität und ABC-Waffen Verzicht. Deutsche Diplomatie auf der Londoner Neunmächtekonferenz 1954," *Vierteljahrshefte für Zeitgeschichte* 42, 1994, 499–536.

Lansford, T., "The Triumph of Transatlanticism: NATO and the Evolution of European Security after the Cold War," *Journal of Strategic Studies* 22, no. 1, 1999, 1–28.

Lappenküper, U. (2001), *Die deutsch-französischen Beziehungen 1949–1963. Von der Erbfeindschaft zur Entente elementaire,* 2 Bde. (Munich: Oldenbourg 2001).

Lappenküper, U., "Die Deutsche Europapolitik zwischen der Genscher-Colombo-Initiative und der Verabschiedung der Einheitlichen Europaeischen Akte 1981–1986, *Historisch-politische Mitteilungen* 10, 2003, 275–294.

Larres, R. and K. Osgood (eds), *The Cold War after Stalin's Death. Missed Opportunity for Peace* (Lanham, MD: Rowman & Littlefield, 2006).

Larson, D.W. and A. Shevchenko, "Shortcut to Greatness: The New Thinking and the Revolution in Soviet Affairs," *International Organization* 57, no. 1, 2003.

Layne, C., *The Peace of Illusions: American Grand Strategy from 1940 to the Present* (Ithaca, NY: Cornell University Press, 2006).

Loth, W. (ed.), *Europe, Cold War and Co-existence 1953–1965* (London: Frank Cass, 2004).

Lucas, H.-D., *Europa vom Atlantik bis zum Ural. Europapolitik und Europadenken im Frankreich der Ära de Gaulle (1958–1969)* (Bonn: Bouvier, 1992).

Ludlow, N.P., "Challenging French Leadership in Europe: Germany, Italy, the Netherlands and the Outbreak of the Empty Chair Crisis of 1965–66," *Contenpotory European History* 8, no. 2, 231–248.

Lundstrom, G., "Enter the EU Battlegroup," *Chaillot Papers* 97 (2007).

McCarthy, P. (ed.), *France–Germany, 1983–1993: The Struggle to Co-operate* (Basingstoke: Macmillan, 1993).

Marcowitz, R., *Option für Paris? Unionsparteien, SPD and Charles de Gaulle 1958 bis 1969* (Munich: Oldenbourg, 1996).

Mearsheimer, J., "Back to the Future: Instability in Europe after the Cold War," *International Security* 15, no. 4, 1990, 5–56.

Mearsheimer, J., "Why We Will soon Miss the Cold War," *The Atlantic*, August 1990, 35–90.

Melissen, J. and B. Zeeman, "Britain and Western Europe 1945–1951," *International Affairs* 63, no. 1, 1986–1987, 81–95.

Menon, A., "Britain and the Convention on the Future of Europe," *International Affairs* 79, no. 5, 2003, 963–978.

Middeke, M., "Anglo-American Nuclear Weapons Co-operation after the Nassau Conference: The British Policy of Interdependence," *Journal of Cold War Studies* 2, no. 2, 2000, 69–96.

Missiroli, A., "CFSP, Defence and Flexibility," *Chaillot Papers* 38 (2000).

Moravcsik, A., "Negotiating the Single European Act: National Interests and Conventional Statecraft in the European Community," *International Organization* 45, no. 1, 1991, 19–56.

Myers, J., "The Western European Union: Pillar of NATO or Defence Arm of the EC?" *London Defence Studies* 16 (1992).

Nash, P., *The Other Missiles of October: Eisenhower, Kennedy and the Jupiters 1957–1963* (Chapel Hill: University of North Carolina Press, 1997).

Neustadt, R., *Alliance Politics* (New York: Cambridge University Press, 1970).

Neustadt, R., *Report to JFK: The SKYBOLT Crisis in Perspective* (Ithaca, NY: Cornell, 1999).

O'Driscoll, M., "Les Anglo-Saxon, F-I-G and the Rival Conceptions of Advanced Armaments Research & Development Co-operation in Western Europe, 1956–1958," *Journal of European Integration History* 7, no. 1, 1997, 105–130.

Pagedas, C., *Anglo-American Strategic Relations and the French Problem, 1960–1963: A Troubled Partnership* (London: Cass, 2000).

Philippart, E. and G. Edwards, "The Provisions on Closer Co-operation in the Treaty of Amsterdam: The Politics of Flexibility in the European Union," *Journal of Common Market Studies* 37, no. 1, 1999, 87–108.

Pitman, P., "'Un Général qui s'appelle Eisenhower': Atlantic Crisis and the Origins of the European Economic Community," *Journal of European Integration History* 6, no. 2, 2000, 37–59.

Pruessen, R., "Cold War Threats and America's Commitment to the European Defence Community: One Corner of a Triangle," *Journal of European Integration History* 2, no. 1, 1996, 51–69.

Quille, Gerrard, "The Lisbon Treaty and Its Implications for CFSP/ESDP," *European Parliament, Policy Department External Policies, Briefing Paper* (Brussels: EP 2008).

Rauchhaus, R., *Explaining NATO Enlargement* (London: Frank Cass, 2001).

Regelsberger, E. et al. (eds.), *Foreign Policy of the European Union. From EPC to CFSP and Beyond* (Boulder, CO: Lynne Rienner, 1997).

Risse-Kappen, T., *Cooperation among Democracies: The European Influence on US Foreign Policy* (Princeton: Princeton University Press, 1995).

Roper, J., "Two Cheers for Blair? The Political Realities of European Defence Co-operation," *Journal of Common Market Studies* 38, 2000, 7–23.

Ruane, K., *The Rise and Fall of the European Defence Community: Anglo-American Relations and the Crisis of European Defence, 1950–1955* (Basingstoke: Macmillan, 2000).

Ruggie, J., "Consolidating the European Pillar: The Future Key to NATO's Future," *Washington Quarterly* 20, no. 1, 1997, 109–123.

Rutten, M., "From St. Malo to Nice: European Defence: Core Documents," *Chaillot Papers* 47 (2001).

Rutten, M., "From Nice to Laaken: European Defence: Core Documents," *Chaillot Papers* 51 (2002).

Schmidt, G. (ed.), *A History of NATO: The First Fifty Years* (New York: Palgrave, 2001).

Schmidt, Peter, "The Special Franco-Germany Security Relationship in the 1990s", *Chaillot Papers* 8 (1993).

Schrafstetter, S. and S. Twigge, "Trick or Truth? The British ANF Proposal, West Germany and US Non-proliferation Policy, 1964–1968," *Diplomacy and Statecraft* 11, no. 2, 2000, 161–184.

See, J., "An Uneasy Truce: John F. Kennedy and Soviet–American Détente, 1963," *Cold War History* 2, no. 2, 2002, 161–194.

Simonet, H., "Energy and the Future of Europe," *Foreign Affairs* 53, 1974–1975, 450–463.

Sloan, S., "NATO's Future in a New Europe: An American Perspective," *International Affairs* 66, no. 3, 1990, 495–511.

Sloan, S., "The United States and European Defence," *Chaillot Papers* 39 (2000).

Sloan, S., *NATO, the European Union, and the Atlantic Community: The Transatlantic Bargain Challenged* (Lanham, MD: Rowman & Littlefield, 2005).

Smith, J., "The Future of the European Union and the Transatlantic Relationship," *International Affairs* 79, no. 5, 2003, 943–949.

Smith, M., *Europe's Foreign and Security Policy: The Institutionalisation of Cooperation* (Cambridge: Cambridge University Press, 2004).

Soutou, G.-H., *L'Alliance incertaine: Les Rapports politico-stratégiques franco-allemands 1954–1996* (Paris: Plon, 1996).

Soutou, G.-H., "Le Général de Gaulle et le plan Fouchet d'union européeane: on project strategique," in Anne Deighton and Alan Milward (eds), *Widening, Deepening & Acceleration: the EEC, 1957–1963* Brussels: Nomos, 1999).

Sperling, J. (ed.), *Europe in Change: Two Tiers or Two Speeds* (Manchester: Manchester University Press, 1999).

Steininger, R., "Gro ß britannien und de Gaulle. Das Scheitern des britischen EWG Beitritts im Januar 1963," *Viertelijahrshefte für Zeitgeschichte* 44, 1996, 87–118.

Tal, D., *The 1956 War: Collusion and Rivalry in the Middle East* (London: Frank Cass, 2001).

Taylor, T., "Western European Security and Defence Co-operation: Maastricht and Beyond," *International Affairs* 70, no. 1, 1994, 1–16.

Trachtenberg, M., *A Constructed Peace: The Making of the European Settlement 1945–1963* (Princeton: Princeton University Press, 1999).

Troen, S. and M. Shemesh, *The Suez–Sinai Crisis 1956: Retrospective and Re-appraisal* (New York: Columbia, 1990).

Vaisse, M., *La Grandeur: Politique étrangère du Général de Gaulle 1958–1969* (Paris: Fayard, 1998).

Vaisse, M., "Aux Origins du memorandum de septembre 1958", *Belations Internationales* 58 (1989), 253–268.

Van Ham, P., "Europe's Precarious Centre: Franco-German Co-operation and the CFSP," *European Security* 8, no. 4, 1999, 1–26.

Walt, S., *The Origins of Alliances* (Ithaca, NY: Cornell University Press, 1987).

Welch, D. and A. Sherchenko, "Shortcut to Greatness: The New Thinking and the Revolution in Soviet Foreign Policy," *International Affairs* 57, 2003, 77–109.

Wenger, A., "Crisis and Opportunity: NATO's Transformation and the Multilateralization of Détente, 1966–1968," *Journal of Cold War Studies* 6, no. 1, 2004, 22–74.

Whitman, R., "Amsterdam's Unfinished Business? The Blair Government's Initiative and the Future of the Western European Union," *Occasional Papers* 7 (1999).

Wiebes, C. and B. Zeeman, "Baylis on Post-war Planning," *Review of International Studies* 10, 1984, 247–250.

Wilkens, A., "Westpolitik, *Ostpolitik* and the Project of the Economic and Monetary Union: Germany's European Policy in the Brandt Era (1969–1974)," *Journal of European Integration History* 5, no. 1, 1999, 73–102.

Young, J. and M. Dockrill (eds.), *British Foreign Policy 1945–1956* (New York: St. Martin's Press, 1989).

Zeeman, B. (1986), Britain and the Cold War, An Alternative Approach. The Treaty of Dunkirk Example, *European History Quarterly*, 16, 3 (1986), 343–367. 16.

Further Reading

The literature on European security co-operation is part of a wider literature on the multilayered security architecture of the West – it is thus intimately connected with the literature on the Cold War, NATO, and the European institutions. Useful information on the Cold War setting is offered by the publications of the Militärgeschichtliche Forschungsamt (MGFA) and the Cold War Study Centers in Princeton, Harvard, London, and Rome. Marc Trachtenberg's seminal study *A Constructed Peace The Making of the European Settlement* (Princeton, NJ.: Princeton University Press, 1999) deserves special attention due to its impact on current Cold War historiography.

The NATO context is well captured in the editions of Gustav Schmidt and Ennio DiNolfo, and the excellent studies of Beatrice Heuser, Richard Hunter, Simon Serfaty, Stanley Sloan, David Yost, and Lawrence Kaplan. The publications of Trevor Taylor and Jolyon Howorth analyze the complex dynamics of European security co-operation. A good insight into the institutionalization of the European Foreign and Security policy is offered by, inter alia, David Allen and Michael Smith. The Western European Union development has received little attention in the literature – notable exceptions are the classics by Alfred Cahen and Armand Imbert and the edition of Anne Deighton.

An indispensable source for the study of any aspect of European Security and Defence issues are the *Chaillot Papers* of the Institute for Security Studies of the European Union in Paris and the *Adelphi Papers* published by the International Institute for Strategic Studies in London.

Chapter Sixteen

Europe's Experience of Terrorism since 1945: A Brief Overview

Paul Wilkinson

The key attractions of terrorism as a weapon of asymmetrical conflict are that it is a low-cost yet potentially high-yield method of struggle and that terrorist attacks can have a major psychological impact, can bring short-term gains, and in some cases can influence strategic change. There is also the fact that since the end of the colonial independence struggles, national borders have become firmly established. It is now very difficult for any minority movement to achieve a renegotiation of frontiers in its favor through some general diplomatic conference. Moreover, even though strategic objectives are very hard to achieve through terrorism, tactical gains such as publicity, ransom payments, and release of prisoners have frequently been obtained. Another factor is relative-deprivation psychology – the feelings of political injustice felt by particular groups. Research has shown that feelings of political injustice – deprivation of political rights or exclusion from power or influence within a community – are especially likely to lead to violent rebellion.

Weaknesses in general within the international community and in particular nation states in responding to terrorism also contributed to the rise in terrorism. This was particularly true up until 1972. Since then, certain western European states began to take a firmer line; and there has been a widespread growth of elite units of special forces designed for hostage rescue, a development inspired by the success of the Entebbe and Mogadishu rescues. However, following the TWA hijack to Beirut in 1985 and the disastrous loss of life in a hijack to Malta in the same year, it has become clear that such rescue forces are not a panacea and do not necessarily restrain potential hijackers of the more fanatical type. The shift of revolutionary theory from the guerrilla concept towards the idea of urban struggle is an important feature of contemporary terrorism. European revolutionaries in the nineteenth century and the early twentieth went through a similar process. The hunger for publicity tends to drive the revolutionary to the cities. Other factors precipitating the move to cities were technological opportunity and the vulnerability of industrial societies and cities to terrorist techniques. One should also stress the contagion. The information flow effects of

A Companion to Europe since 1945, First Edition. Edited by Klaus Larres.
© 2014 John Wiley & Sons, Ltd. Published 2014 by John Wiley & Sons, Ltd.

terrorism over a long span of time can cause a kind of bandwagon reaction. There is also the growth of pro-terrorist ideologies and sub-cultures in Western cities right in the hearts of the countries that had the highest numbers of terrorist attacks in the last decade. Maverick states have also been active in funding and giving sanctuary to terrorists.

But of course all the factors mentioned so far are of a general nature. They characterize the international system of the late 1960s. How does one explain the significance of 1968 as the starting point for the upsurge in modern international terrorism? All specialists in the study of terrorism would agree that there were two international developments which had a key role in triggering this outbreak.

First and foremost there was the overwhelming defeat of the military forces of the Arab states in their June 1967 war with Israel. Terrorism was by no means new to the Middle East, but there was no doubt that as a result of this setback and of the Israeli occupation of the West Bank, Gaza, and the Sinai peninsula, and the Israeli takeover of the whole of Jerusalem, Palestinian militants concluded that the routes of defeating Israel by conventional military force, or regaining their homeland by diplomatic negotiation, were blocked to them. The Arab states were too divided and Israel was too militarily powerful. They concluded that they would gain more by a campaign of ruthless political violence striking at Israel and its supporters internationally in a war of terrorist attrition. Hence from 1968 to 1972 there follows a tremendous upsurge of hijack attempts, bombings, shootings, and other terrorist attacks against Israeli targets both in Israel and abroad and against airline facilities and personnel of the United States and other Western powers seen in Palestinian eyes to be guilty of supporting and collaborating with Israel. This shift to terrorism was intensified after the further disastrous defeat of the Fedayeen at the hands of KingHussein's forces in Jordan in autumn 1970. Between 1967 and 1974, about 15% of all international terrorist incidents were carried out by Palestinian groups, many of them spilling over into western Europe.

The impact of Palestinian terrorism should not be assessed purely in quantitative terms. Reports of their actions and the huge international publicity they achieved undoubtedly had the effect of interesting other militant groups in other parts of the world in exploiting the techniques of international terror. And we should not neglect the direct influence of the PFLP (Popular Front for the Liberation of Palestine) and Fatah and the other Palestinian organizations through their work of training foreign terrorists in various camps in the Middle East and in the constant Palestinian contacts with other terrorists groups around the world.

The second historical development was the resurgence of the extreme neo-Marxist and Trotskyist left among the student population of all the industrial countries. Their common rallying points were bitter opposition to US policy in the Vietnam War, and to American policy in the Third World generally, which they designated neo-imperialism. Although the majority of the student left abandoned political violence following the street demonstrations and battles with the police in 1968–1969, there was in each case a small hardcore of ideological extremists who decided that what was really needed was a more professional and long-term campaign of urban violence against the "system." These groups decided to form an "underground" which engaged in a sustained campaign of terrorism. The main groups that sprang from this movement included the Baader-Meinhof Gang in the Federal Republic of Germany, the Red

Brigades in Italy, and the Japanese Red Army. With their shared neo-Marxist ideology and self-perceptions as part of a broader international revolutionary movement, they maintained international links with movements abroad, including the Palestinians. There is considerable evidence that they learned from each other.[1]

Terrorism against European Targets in Europe and Overseas after 1945

European nation states had experienced a variety of campaigns of terrorist violence by non-state groups within their borders in the nineteenth century and early twentieth. For example, the tsarist regime in Russia faced frequent attacks by Narodnaya Volya (People's Will), the group responsible for assassinating Tsar Alexander II in March, 1881, and later by the Social Revolutionary Battle Organization. And in the early twentieth century the Internal Macedonian Revolutionary Organizations (IMRO) waged a campaign of terrorism in an attempt to obtain an independent state of Macedonia. The Fenian movement seeking liberation from British rule in Ireland conducted spasmodic attacks in the nineteenth century. There was an upsurge of anarchist terrorism in the 1890s, the so-called "dynamite decade," in which France was a major target.

In the mid-twentieth century it was the mass terror committed by the totalitarian regimes of Hitler and Stalin which dominated the terror scene, totally eclipsing the terrorist efforts of small non-state groups.

However, in the immediate aftermath of World War II non-state terror once again presented challenges to those European countries which faced violent liberation struggles in their overseas colonies. The French faced a war of independence fought by the National Liberation Front (Front de libération nationale – FLN) (FLN) in Algeria[2] in which terror became a major weapon. The atrocities committed in Sétif in May 1945 were a horrific precursor to what Alistair Horne has called a "Savage War of Peace."[3] Over a hundred Europeans were killed by an Arab crowd. Women were raped and mutilated and men's genitals were severed and sewn into their mouths. In response French security forces killed thousands of Muslims. *Colons* (French settlers) killed many Muslims in revenge. The FLN intensified its attacks in the mid-1950s but found they were unable to defeat the French army in the rural areas. They decided to mount a terrorist campaign in Algiers in 1956 which in the eyes of the nationalists brought great success, virtually drying up the flow of information from informers collaborating with the French. General Massu's Parachute Division was deployed to defeat the general strike called by the nationalists in Algiers in 1957.

Although Massu's troops crushed the strike and virtually suppressed terrorism in Algiers, this was only achieved by the use of torture and other draconian measures. The savagery of the conflict led to increasing international pressure on the French government and a huge exodus of French settlers. Ultimately President Charles de Gaulle recognized that the aim of maintaining "Algérie française" was unsustainable and negotiated independence for Algeria at Evian.

The Secret Army Organization (Organisation de l'Armée Secrète – OAS,) made up of former soldiers, students, and *colons*, thirsting for revenge, were outraged by what they saw at de Gaulle's surrender. There was an attempted coup in Algiers, and the OAS attempted a bombing campaign in both Algeria and France. Both failed. In the eyes of the FLN and many foreign observers what the Algerian case showed was that terrorism could achieve a strategic victory over a militarily far more powerful adversary.

Britain also confronted serious challenges from liberation groups using terrorism as a weapon in Cyprus (1954–1958), Malaya (1948–1951), and Kenya (1952–1956).[4] In Malaya and Kenya the security forces succeeded in defeating the terrorists, but in Cyprus the EOKA (National Organization of Cypriot Fighters) terrorists eventually succeeded in forcing the British to hand over government to a divided island, one section ruled by Greek Cypriots and the other section ruled by Turkish Cypriots. EOKA did not achieve Enosis (union with Greece).

The most serious and long-term impact of the period of anticolonial struggle arose from another colonial situation. Britain was awarded a mandate for governing Palestine after World War I. In the 1930s and 1940s there was a big influx of Jewish refugees into Palestine, precipitated by the Nazi persecution of the Jews in Germany and in Occupied Europe as a whole, and by the Holocaust. The British authorities attempted to limit the flow of refugees because it was recognized that a major influx would be likely to lead to an escalation of the conflict that had already broken out between Palestinian Arabs and Jews, but more and more refugees managed to reach Palestine. The British military and the police were unable to prevent the militants on both sides from preparing for full-scale war. To the surprise of many observers the newly established state of Israel, founded in 1948, managed to beat off successive attempts by the Arab states that surrounded it to suppress the Jewish state. It is hard to understate the anger and resentment this created among Palestinians. They felt that their rightful home had been stolen from them and they demanded the right of return to their homes now occupied in Israel. The British government had swiftly washed its hands of responsibility for the situation, and the newly established United Nations was too weak and divided to find a viable solution to the Israeli–Palestinian problem.

Radical Palestinian groups turned to the weapon of international terrorism following the massive defeat of Arab forces in the June 1967 war with Israel.[5] Militant Palestinians concluded that they could no longer rely on the armies of Arab states to liberate their homeland; they saw international terrorism in the form of hijackings, bombings, and hostage-taking as the only weapon left to them, a weapon that was low-cost, relatively low-risk, and potentially high-yield. The PLO (Palestinian Liberation Organization), founded in 1964, was an eclectic umbrella group of many groups, dominated by Yasser Arafat's Fatah. The Palestinian National Covenant, issued in May 1964, committed the PLO to the destruction of Israel. The most radical of the Palestinian groups, dominated by the Popular Front for the Liberation of Palestine (PFLP) led by George Habash,[6] favored the tactics of international terrorism and soon embarked on their campaign.

The PFLP believed in international revolution and that by hastening its coming the militants, in collaboration with other revolutionaries, could bring a major change in the international system which, in turn, would lead to the founding of an independent Palestinian state.

From the start of the PFLP's campaign it was clear that Europe was going to be one of their most favored venues for international terrorist attacks. For example, in December 1968 PFLP gunmen attacked an El Al airliner in Athens, in February 1969

PFLP gunmen attacked an El Al airliner in Zurich, in July the PFLP firebombed Jewish-owned stores in London, and in September a PFLP group threw grenades at Israeli embassies in the Netherlands and West Germany, and at the El Al office in Belgium.

However, it was the massacre by Black September of Israeli athles and West German security personnel in Munich during the 1972 Olympics which brought home not only to European governments, but also to the US, that international terrorism presented a major challenge to governments and security forces. Although Yasser Arafat was careful to deny responsibility for the attack at the Olympics, it is known that Black September was a unit of the PLO and that his brother-in-law, Hasan Salamah, was one of the unit's members.

By the late 1980s Yasser Arafat and his associates in the PLO had decided to shift to a more political and diplomatic strategy in their efforts to establish a Palestinian state, but more militant extremist groups, such as the Abu Nidal Organization (ANO), which fiercely rejected the PLO's leadership and policies, continued to wage terrorism, including attacks in Europe. For example, the ANO carried out airport massacres at El Al's airline desks at Rome and Vienna airports.

Ideological Terrorism

Europe had extensive experience of ideological terrorism of the extreme left in the 1970s and the early 1980s, and from the extreme right in the 1980s. The best-known of the extreme-left terrorist groups were the Baader-Meinhof Gang, also known as the Red Army Faction (RAF), in Germany and the Red Brigades (BR) in Italy, and there were some lesser-known groups such as Action directe in France and GRAPO (Grupo de Resistencia Antifascista, Primero de Octubre) in Spain. One such group, November 17, in Greece, continued with terrorism into the 1990s[7] until the capture and trial of its leader effectively ended its campaign.

The Red Army Faction was generally known as the Baader-Meinhof Gang after its joint leaders, Andreas Baader and Ulrike Meinhof. The group developed out of student revolt in the late 1960s and hostility to US capitalism and foreign policy, particularly US support for Israel and the Vietnam War. Its first act of terrorism was a bomb attack on a department store in Frankfurt. The bombing was claimed by the perpetrators to be a protest against the Vietnam War. The group was very small, consisting of no more than a few dozen hardcore militants who went "underground" to carry out terrorist operations and the bank robberies which they mounted to finance their activities, though they had many sympathizers and supporters among the alienated and pro-violence wing of the student movement. The group attacked American and Israeli-linked targets in West Germany as well as key members of the political and business elite.[8] For example, in 1977 they murdered Siegfried Buback, the state prosecutor-general, and Jürgen Ponto, head of one of Germany's major banks. In September 1977 the RAF kidnapped Hanns-Martin Schleyer, president of the West German employers' association, having murdered his four bodyguards. The terrorists demanded the release of Andreas Baader, Gudrun Ensslin, and other jailed members of the gang as the price for the release of Hanns-Martin Schleyer. Chancellor Helmut Schmidt's government refused to give in to the terrorists. The RAF, with the help of Palestinian terrorists, reacted by hijacking a Lufthansa airliner on October

13, 1977. Their aim was to put additional pressure on the government. They threatened to kill passengers at regular intervals. The airliner eventually landed at Mogadishu, the capital of Somalia. The West German government adopted a clever dual strategy to deal with this major challenge by the terrorists. An envoy was sent to Mogadishu, apparently to negotiate for the hostages' release. Meanwhile, West Germany's specialist antiterrorist unit, GSG-9, and members of Britain's SAS were flown to Somalia.

The surprise rescue assault by the GSG-9 succeeded in rescuing all the passengers on board and killing or capturing all the hijackers. Hanns-Martin Schleyer was murdered by the terrorists and his body was found in a car in Alsace on the French side of the Franco-German border. This marked the beginning of the end for the Baader-Meinhof group. Meinhof, Baader, and Ensslin committed suicide in prison, and the group gradually withered away, finally issuing a communiqué announcing an end to its terrorist campaign in 1992.

The Red Brigades, founded in Italy in 1970, had a similar ideology to the Baader-Meinhof Gang.[9] It was bitterly opposed to capitalism, and believed that the Italian Communist Party had betrayed the working class and the cause of revolution by working within the Italian parliamentary and party system. Its founders were Renato Curcio and Margherita Cagol. The group was organized into small cells of terrorist militants and larger structures or "columns" throughout the major cities of Italy. In addition it had many hundreds of supporters and sympathizers during its most active period from 1973 to 1987. Like the RAF, it raised funding from bank robberies. Initially it tried to spread its propaganda among the factory workers, but found most workers were more interested in practical matters such as wages and conditions. In the mid 70s it became increasingly violent: it did not generally seek mass fatalities, it wanted propaganda of the deed. It kidnapped and murdered former prime minister Aldo Moro in 1978. This outraged the vast majority of Italians and concentrated the minds of the Italian authorities, including the judiciary, on finding more effective measures to suppress the movement. In the 1980s the Italian judiciary was given the scope to offer real incentives to convicted terrorists to turn state's evidence. The so-called *pentiti* law gave courts the discretion to substantially reduce sentences where convicted terrorists provided tangible information leading to the arrest and conviction of fellow terrorists. By 1982, 389 *pentiti* had come forward, of whom 78 had actively cooperated with the police and judiciary. This measure was highly effective: it helped the police to crack open the Red Brigade cells and columns. By the late 1980s the group was on its last legs. All this had been achieved without undermining the independence of the judiciary and the viability of the country's democratic institutions.

Nationalist Terrorism in Europe since 1945

There is a long history of armed rebellion against British rule in Ireland. The antecedents of the modern conflict go back to the Catholic revolt in Ireland in the 1640s, eventually suppressed by Oliver Cromwell's army, and the efforts of groups such as the Society of United Irishmen (1798) and the Fenians, a movement formed in the 1850s and dedicated to winning Irish independence. The Fenians launched raids from the United States into British Canada, and in the 1880s mounted a bombing campaign in England, including an attack on the Houses of Parliament.

The major underlying causes of Irish rebellion in earlier centuries were resentment against English efforts to implant or impose Protestantism in Catholic Ireland and hostility to the policy of settling Protestant immigrants from Scotland and England in the northern provinces of Ireland. By the early twentieth century it was clear that successive Liberal prime ministers from Gladstone to Asquith had become committed to granting Home Rule for Ireland. Sadly, peaceful progress towards this objective was delayed by the outbreak of World War I. Militant supporters of total Irish independence mounted an uprising in Dublin at the Easter of 1916.

Although the Easter rebellion was suppressed, Irish support for total independence from Britain grew and in the 1918 general elections Sinn Fein, the pro-independence party, won a majority of the Irish vote. In 1919 a group of militant supporters of full independence, led by Michael Collins, formed the IRA (Irish Republican Army) and started a guerrilla war against British rule. This war for Irish independence ended in 1921 when the British government offered the nationalists a treaty (the Anglo-Irish Treaty) which would establish an Irish Free State in the Catholic-dominated south, but would leave six counties in the north of Ireland, where there was a Protestant majority, firmly under British control. A parliament of Northern Ireland was established at Stormont and was accorded a considerable amount of autonomy over Ulster's internal affairs. Michael Collins and moderate nationalists were willing to accept the treaty, but the hard-line faction of the IRA, led by Eamon de Valéra, opposed the treaty, and this split triggered a civil war. The Irish Free State was ruthless in its suppression of the rebels. Seventy-seven IRA members from the dissident section were executed and over 12,000 were jailed. By the end of the 1920s the IRA again split. Eamon de Valéra led the more pragmatic majority within the IRA into mainstream Irish politics as a peaceful democratic political party (Fianna Fail).

However, the hard-line faction of the IRA, led by Sean Russell, continued with its campaign of violence and mounted a bombing campaign in mainland Britain in World War II. In the 1950s and early 1960s IRA militants launched a series of attacks in Northern Ireland (the so-called "Border War"), but the Republic's government reintroduced internment of IRA members and the campaign was a complete failure.

It was in the late 1960s that the Northern Ireland Civil Rights Association emerged, campaigning peacefully against discrimination in housing and employment and against what they saw as gerrymandering and other abuses which they claimed were used by the Protestants to dominate councils and other public bodies. In July 1969 the B-Specials of the Royal Ulster Constabulary used disproportionate violence to break up an entirely peaceful civil rights demonstration in Derry. It became obvious to the British government that the police were no longer able to maintain law and order and were seen as a sectarian force by the Catholic community. The then home secretary in Harold Wilson's Labour government had no alternative but to deploy the British Army to restore order and maintain peace.

In 1970 there was another major split in the IRA, and a militant wing emerged known as the "Provisionals," putting itself forward as the true defenders of the Catholic minority community against the British Army and promising to expel the British from Northern Ireland.[10] The Provisionals soon eclipsed the old IRA leadership (the "Officials") and acquired the recruits, explosives, guns, funds, and expertise to become the most formidable and deadly indigenous terrorist movement in Europe.

The situation was further complicated by the activities of Protestant Loyalist terrorists, the Ulster Defence Association (UDA), and the Ulster Freedom Fighters (UFF) – the latter a breakaway faction from the UDA. As in the case of the Republican terrorists, there were bitter rivalries among the groups involved and their most frequent tactics were bombings and assassinations. The main difference was that the Loyalist terrorists, unlike the IRA and the other Republican terrorist groups, did not attack the British security force.

The British government and army and the RUC made some major errors of judgment in the early years of the "Troubles." The decision to accede to the Stormont government's request to intern terrorist suspects proved to be a major disaster. The intelligence available to the security forces that rounded up suspects was grossly inaccurate, and this acted as a recruiting sergeant for the IRA. As for those who were interned, their confinement gave the IRA hard-liners, some of whom were interned, the chance to use their imprisonment as a kind of terrorist staff college. "Bloody Sunday," when British soldiers fired on Catholics rioting in Derry, proved to be another tragic disaster. Thirteen civilians were killed. This also acted as a recruiting sergeant for the IRA.

The year 1972 proved to be the worst for deaths caused by terrorism; 475 died. In one attack on "Bloody Friday" the Provisional IRA set off 22 bombs in Belfast, killing nine civilians. In 1972 alone the IRA was responsible for killing 255 people. The problem of countering terrorism was also complicated by the fact that the IRA mounted major bombing attacks in London and other cities in the British mainland. The most deadly was the bombing of pubs in Birmingham in 1974 which killed 21 and injured 164.

It is a tragic irony that while the Provisional IRA was escalating its atrocities the British government, led by prime minister Edward Heath, was working imaginatively and urgently to address the underlying grievances of the minority population in Northern Ireland, legislating against discrimination in employment and housing and ending the gerrymandering in the electoral system. Though it is now often forgotten, the Heath government also attempted to reform the entire political system in Northern Ireland through the Sunningdale Agreement and established, if only briefly, a genuinely power-sharing government and assembly which included Catholics such as John Hume of the Social Democrat Labour Party as well as leading members of the Ulster Unionist Party.

Sadly, this brave effort at a long-term solution was sabotaged by the actions of Loyalist extremists who masterminded the so-called Ulster Workers' Council strike, paralysing all the key public services in Northern Ireland. If one examines the Good Friday Agreement of 1998, the basis of the present power-sharing government in Northern Ireland, there are many uncanny similarities. Far from being a "creative force" in Northern Ireland, terrorist extremism became the major obstacle to a peaceful settlement and reconciliation in Northern Ireland.

Moreover the severity of attacks carried out by the IRA on the British mainland, such as their attempt to blow up prime minister Margaret Thatcher and half her cabinet at the Grand Hotel, Brighton, in 1984, and the City of London bombings, only tended to polarize the situation still further and made it more difficult to get the IRA to declare and sustain a ceasefire.

Ultimately the Northern Ireland peace process, which started in the mid-1990s, and was pushed forward by prime minister John Major and his Northern Ireland secretary, Patrick Mayhew, in close alliance with the Irish prime minister, brought a remarkable power-sharing devolved government in Northern Ireland with the Rev. Ian Paisley as first minister and Martin McGuiness, formerly of Sinn Fein/IRA, as his deputy. Prior to this the IRA, contrary to earlier predictions, agreed to the decommissioning of its weapons under the supervision of the international disarmament commission established for this task.

The huge problems involved in initiating and sustaining this peace process should not be underestimated. Nor should one overlook the contribution of the British Army and the RUC. By the 1990s their intelligence and technical skills in thwarting major terrorist attacks had become so well developed that it became clear to the leaders of Sinn Fein/IRA that they stood a greater chance of influencing politics in Northern Ireland by adopting the political pathway than by blattering on with bombs and guns.

It has proved extremely difficult to replicate the success of the peace process in Northern Ireland elsewhere in Europe or anywhere in the world.

ETA[11]

The Basques live at the western end of the Pyrenees, with over 2 million on the Spanish side of the border and over 200,000 in France. ETA (Euskadi Ta Askatasuna – Basque Fatherland and Liberty) has its origins in the early 1960s. Its aims were to try to protect Basque language and culture from the Franco regime's attempts to suppress them, and ultimately to establish an independent Basque state incorporating the Basque provinces on both the Spanish and French sides of the border. It was not until the 1970s that ETA began a serious terrorist campaign. Their most spectacular achievement was the 1973 assassination of Admiral Luis Carrero Blanco, the Spanish prime minister and designated successor to General Franco.

There were several major factions in the Basque nationalist movement in the 1970s. Some were straightforward supporters of national independence for the Basques, and many of these accepted the Spanish government's offer of "social reinsertion" in the 1970s, meaning that they agreed to use exclusively nonviolent means to further their cause in return for their freedom from jail or the dropping of charges against them. However, others, especially those in the Marxist–Leninist wing of the movement, planned terrorist attacks on what they claim are "the most important instruments of state repression" – the police, the military, and the Civil Guard. They believed that this would sting the authorities into taking brutal and indiscriminate counterterrorist actions, that this would trigger a wider civil war, and that this in turn would force the Spanish government to relinquish control of the Basque region.

It is again a tragic irony that ETA militants started to develop this campaign at just the time when the Spanish parliament was adopting an imaginative and radical Statute of Autonomy for the Basques which gave them the greatest degree of autonomy of any region in Spain.

Despite their complete failure to realize their objectives, a hardcore of ETA terrorists have continued their campaign of bombings and assassination attempts right up to the time of writing (2008).

ETA terrorists have, since the mid-1980s, experienced a crackdown against ETA terrorists living on the French side of the border or moving across it. Greatly improved Franco-Spanish cooperation has repeatedly resulted in the capture of key ETA leaders and members.

Those who hope for a Northern Ireland-style peace process and resolution of the Basque terrorism problem seem likely to be disappointed. The hard-liner ETA leadership seems determined to pursue its maximalist demands, without any hint of compromise. Meanwhile the Spanish government is determined to resist any dismemberment of Spain, and in this they have the backing of the other major political parties and of overwhelming majority of Spaniards. By the beginning of 2008 ETA had succeeded in killing over 800 people since the beginning of its violent campaign in the 1970s.

FLNC

The Corsican National Liberation Front (Front de Libéracion Nationale de la Corse – FLNC) was a much smaller and far less deadly group than the IRA and ETA. In 1990 it announced that it was going to abandon the violence, but a breakaway faction is still committed to its use.

The FLNC was set up by a group of Corsicans bitterly opposed to immigration from France and the impact of the tourist industry, which they claim damages their local culture. They also express concern about the survival of their own island language, a dialect of Italian. The FLNC's main targets have been the tourist industry, settlers' homes and symbols of the French administration. They have also mounted occasional attacks in mainland France, for example a bombing of the Ministry of Finance in Paris.

By the 1980s it had become clear that a very high proportion of violent incidents were acts of organized crime rather than political violence.

The FLNC and other small violent groups in Corsica have at no stage posed a significant threat to the civilian population in Corsica or to French security.

Al Qaeda-linked terrorism in Europe[12]

Al Qaeda ("the base") is an extremist network, founded by Osama bin Laden and Abdallah Azzam in 1988, which declared a jihad against the US and its allies and Muslim states which they claim are "apostates" because they cooperate and trade with Western countries. European countries – especially the UK, seen as a key ally of the US, and France, with its history of suppressing Algerian terrorists, are clearly seen as appropriate targets and convenient venues for attacks.

Al Qaeda has a network in Europe which clearly poses a more significant threat to international security than any of the small nationalist and ideological groups discussed above. It is far more dangerous than the other types of non-state terrorist phenomena discussed earlier because it:

- is explicitly committed to mass-lethality attacks;
- has taken a particular interest in acquiring chemical, biological, radiological and nuclear weapons (CBRN) knowledge and materials and its track record

(e.g. the 9/11 attacks which killed nearly 3,000 people) shows that it would have no compunction about using a CBRN weapon;

- has "global reach" (i.e. a presence in at least 60 countries); and
- is incorrigible (i.e. it shows no signs of following a more pragmatic path and abandoning terrorism in favor of peaceful politics).

There is tragic evidence of Al Qaeda-linked groups' commitment to attacking targets in Europe.

In March 2004 a Moroccan cell based in Spain and linked to Al Qaeda carried out a massive multiple bombing of trains at Madrid railway stations killing 191 and injuring 2,051. And in July 2005 another group linked to Al Qaeda carried out suicide bombings on London Underground trains and a double-decker bus, killing 52 and injuring 700.

Conclusion

Al Qaeda is undoubtedly the most serious terrorist threat to European countries. It is true that there are signs of divisions spreading within the networks. Some leading radicals such as Dr. Fadl, based in Egypt, have scathingly attacked Al Qaeda for its indiscriminate killing of fellow Muslims. And in May 2008 at a Deobandi conference attended by 70,000 Muslims, a group of leading Deobandi scholars issued a fatwa condemning terrorism as "an inhuman crime."

Nevertheless, Al Qaeda is still in business, still recruiting new suicide bombers, including young Muslims in the UK and other European countries, and actually consolidating its position in Pakistan. It is also spreading its influence in both East and West Africa.

Terrorism and counterterrorism are likely to remain on the agenda of European ministers for some time ahead. In Academia, Europe needs to encourage scientific research into terrorism, drawing on all relevant disciplines. Europe is well behind the United States in this key field.

Notes

1 See Alexander and Pluchinsky, *Europe's Red Terrorists*.
2 Horne, *A Savage War of Peace*.
3 Horne, op. cit.
4 See Townshend, *Britain's Civil Wars*.
5 See Cubert, *The PFLP's Changing Role* and Cobban, *The Palestinian Liberation Organisation*.
6 See Cubert, op. cit.
7 See Kassimeris, *Europe's Last Red Terrorist*.
8 See Becker, *Hitler's Children*.
9 For a perceptive account of the Red Brigade's mind-set see Jamieson, *The Heart Attacked*.
10 On the Provisional IRA see Bell, *The Secret Army* and English, *Armed Struggle*.

11   On ETA's history see Clark, *The Basque Insurgents.*
12   On Al Qaeda see Gerges, *The Far Enemy* and Gunaratna, *Inside Al Qaeda.*

Bibliography

Alexander, Yonah and Dennis Pluchinsky, *Europe's Red Terrorists: The Fighting Communist Organizations* (London: Frank Cass, 1992).

Becker, Jillian, *Hitler's Children: The Story of the Baader Meinhof Gang* (St. Albans: Granada, 1978).

Bell, J. Bowyer, *The Secret Army: The IRA 1916–1979* (Dublin: The Academy Press, 1979).

Clark, Robert P., *The Basque Insurgents: ETA, 1952–80* (Madison: University of Wisconsin Press, 1984).

Cobban, Helen, *The Palestinian Liberation Organisation* (Cambridge: Cambridge University Press, 1984).

Cubert, Harold, *The PFLP's Changing Role in the Middle East* (London: Frank Cass, 1997).

English, Richard, *Armed Struggle: The History of the IRA* (London: Pan-Macmillan, 2003).

Gerges, Fawaz A., *The Far Enemy: Why Jihad Went Global* (New York: Cambridge University Press, 2005).

Gunaratna, Rohan, *Inside Al Qaeda* (Columbia: Columbia University Press, 2002).

Horne, Alistair, *A Savage War of Peace, Algeria 1954–62* (Harmondsworth: Penguin, 1977).

Jamieson, Alison, *The Heart Attacked: Terrorism and Conflict in the Italian State* (London: Marion Boyars, 1989).

Kassimeris, George, *Europe's Last Red Terrorist: The Revolutionary Organisation 17 November* (London: C. Hurst & Co. 2001).

Townshend, Charles, *Britain's Civil Wars* (London: Faber, 1986).

PART IV

Europe Since 1990: Social and Cultural Developments

Part IV

CHAPTER SEVENTEEN

The Quest for a European Identity: A Europe without Europeans?

RUTH WITTLINGER

Much has happened in the 50 years since the signing of the Treaties of Rome on March 25, 1957 which established the European Economic Community (EEC) and the European Atomic Energy Community (EURATOM). The Europe of 2007 is very different from that of 1957. Not even optimists among the heads of state or government who signed the treaties in 1957 could have expected so much progress in just 50 years. The European Economic Community of six has developed into the world's largest internal market made up of 27 members with several more waiting to be admitted. Not much has been left untouched and a single market and – at least in the eurozone countries – a common currency as well as considerable migration among its member states are normal features of life in the EU 50 years after the formal launch of the European project. The Europeanization of national polities, economies, and societies is far advanced, in most areas and where it is still lagging behind, for instance in foreign and security policy, there are serious efforts under way which are aimed at adopting a common approach here also. In spite of the diversity which the large number of member states brings to the Union, the convergence achieved in key areas is remarkable.

Economic and, to some extent, political integration has had an overall positive effect on the continent as a whole. The evolution of the European project has been accompanied by a relatively long period of peace among its member states, and through various rounds of enlargement it has succeeded in overcoming some of the continent's divisions and ensuring stability and security. Particularly remarkable has been the way the Cold War division of the continent has been overcome by the European Union's eastern enlargement, which has been described as the "most cost-effective Western instrument for advancing global democracy and security."[1]

The "Identity Deficit"

The popularity of the EU to aspiring members and the "deepening" and "widening" that has taken place in the wake of the collapse of communism – with the initiatives of the 1990s making it the EU's most successful decade – has resulted in the paradox

A Companion to Europe since 1945, First Edition. Edited by Klaus Larres.
© 2014 John Wiley & Sons, Ltd. Published 2014 by John Wiley & Sons, Ltd.

of increasing convergence in many areas accompanied by more and more diversity caused by the various waves of enlargement that have happened since the end of the Cold War. Furthermore, the success story of the larger and more integrated Union has not been accompanied by steady progress towards a European identity and the emergence of a "European citizen." In fact, perhaps even the opposite has happened. The more integrated Europe has become, the more Eurosceptic sections of national societies have become, even in traditionally very integration-friendly member states such as France and the Netherlands.

In view of the planned Europeanization of more and more policy areas, however, notions of a "European consciousness" or a "European identity" are considered to become increasingly important. There is also the question of how the European Union is perceived from an outside perspective. The lack of a common identity combined with the EU's unique system of multi level governance can have serious implications for its credibility as a global actor. Especially from an American perspective, this has been expressed on numerous occasions, for example when John F. Kennedy asked the rhetorical question "I'm the President of the United States, but who's the President of Europe?"[2] or when Henry Kissinger jokingly asked what telephone number to ring for Europe.[3]

Hence the emergence of a European political culture based on a shared sense of identity is considered to be pivotal for the legitimacy and future success of the European Union, internally as well as for its position as a credible global actor. This was made explicit in the Copenhagen Declaration on European Identity of 1973 which located the "originality and dynamism" of European identity in "the diversity of cultures within the framework of a common European civilization, the attachment to common values and principles, the increasing convergence of attitudes to life, the awareness of having specific interests in common and the determination to take part in the construction of a United Europe." Experience so far has shown, however, that identification at national level is more deeply entrenched and resilient than first assumed. This is why the relationship between the envisaged European identity and other regional and national identities is nowadays seen as complementary rather than as providing an alternative. Accordingly, "hybrid collective identities" would correspond to the EU's hybrid form of multilevel governance.[4]

Although there is clearly some attachment to Europe and, to a lesser extent, to the European Union, it by no means matches the degree of Europeanization that has taken place in EU member states over the last 50 years. Eurobarometer data suggest that nearly two out of three Europeans (63%) "feel attached to Europe" but only 50% of European Union citizens "feel attached to the European Union," suggesting that a sense of cultural belonging to Europe is more widespread than perceptions of "civic" belonging to the economically and politically integrated European Union. And although these figures show at least some degree of identification with Europe and less with the European Union, identification is still much stronger at and below the national level, with 90% of respondents to their own country, 87% to their region and 86% feeling attached to their city, town, or village.[5]

Of late, a greater realization has set in that there appears to be no general trend discernible which indicates an increasing identification with Europe.[6] Not even Germany – which for a long time probably came closest to the goal of its population identifying with Europe rather than the nation because of its National Socialist past

– has managed to progress towards more and more identification with Europe. Especially since German unification in 1990, identification with the German nation and its symbols have played a strong role in what has been referred to as the "normalization process," with the result that especially since the end of the Kohl chancellorship German political leaders have fewer qualms about articulating Germany's national interests and representing them on the European stage. The World Cup celebrations in 2006 in particular seem to have given huge impetus to a new German "feel-good patriotism" which appears much more successful than the "constitutional patriotism" that German intellectuals had prescribed for the Bonn Republic and which was supposed to provide a kind of "ersatz identity" by suggesting an identification with German democratic institutions rather than with the nation.

Partly responsible for the fairly low degree of identification with Europe and especially with the EU is no doubt the fact that there is a multitude of different definitions as well as visions of Europe and of its economically and to some extent also politically integrated part, the European Union. In addition to widespread semantic imprecision in everyday speech, as well as in political rhetoric, which equates Europe with the EU, it is not even clear what kind of entity it is, famously leading Jacques Delors to describe it as a UPO, an "unidentified political object." With its steadily increasing influence on member states and the growing weight it carries internationally, it is clearly more than an international organization but still less than the "superstate" so feared by Euroskeptics. Several recent studies have therefore resorted to describing the European Union as an "empire"[7] which states outside the EU seek to join rather than aim to counterbalance.[8]

The "Consensus Deficit": Perceptions of Europe

Identification requires – at least in terms of perceptions – a certain degree of commonality. In order for its citizens to be able to identify with the EU and feel some commitment towards it as well as solidarity with the other member states, a shared sense of what defines Europe and what it means to be a citizen of the EU would be helpful. Apart from the values of liberal democracy and the free market, however, it is not easy to find commonalities in the EU and construct what Anderson in the case of the nation state has called an "imagined community." Efforts to construct a common past are seriously hampered by the fact that the continent was divided for most of the postwar period and that member states joined at different points in time, making the logo adopted for the 50th anniversary celebrations of the signing of the Treaties of Rome "Together since 1957" appear highly inapt. Especially since the end of the Cold War, it has also become very apparent how deep-seated and divisive collective memory of World War II and its immediate aftermath still is, for example in Polish–German relations.

There is also no agreement on what Europe *is* or what it *ought to be*. Is it a geographical entity – if yes, where are its borders – or does it consist only of the countries that are members of the European Union? Or is Europe composed of the collection of member states that make up the Council of Europe, the oldest European organization, which has 46 member states and concentrates its efforts on human rights, education, youth, and culture and which chose and adopted the European flag and anthem long before they also became symbols of the European Union?

Linked to this is also the question of what Europe is based on. Is it historical, ethnic, or cultural commonalities which provide at least a degree of cohesion and common interest or is it a set of common values which provide the vital ties between countries?

Crucially, there is also the question of where the European project is going, whether there is some finality about it, or whether integration can continue indefinitely. Is Europe now indeed, as American scholar Andrew Moravcsik has suggested, a "mature" political system which has passed "the point of no return" and therefore "does not need continually to move forward on a neo-functionalist bicycle in order to be stable"?[9]

Whereas the beginning of European integration was clearly grounded in the destructive experience of World War II, 50 years later it is much more difficult to articulate the *raison d'être* of the European Union. In his speech to the British think tank Chatham House in October 2006, José Manuel Barroso, the president of the European Commission, pointed out that "60 years of peace has meant that the image of Europe as a bastion against war is losing its resonance." Hence, he argued, "the European Union needs new foundations. A new core purpose. One which looks forward, recognizes new realities, that draws inspiration from but does not depend upon the achievements of the past." Barroso considers this "new core purpose" to consist of the European Union meeting the challenges facing Europe today, i.e. climate change, growing competition from China and India, global pandemics, mass migration, international terrorism, demographic change, and energy security.[10] Along similar lines, Jürgen Habermas has pointed out that at the beginning "Europe" was a response to problems within Europe, whereas it is now directed at meeting the challenges brought to Europe from the outside.[11]

Different understandings of "Europe" have also led to different perceptions of what the "European project" is or should be about. The United Kingdom, for instance, has traditionally approached the issue in a very pragmatic way and largely considered it to be an economic project with the key achievement provided by the single market. From this perspective, the cultural diversity created by various waves of enlargement does not constitute a problem since the single market is something to which all member states subscribe. The implications for a European identity are also clear: it is redundant. Margaret Thatcher's position made this very apparent with her pro-European stance in economic matters – the single market as "Thatcherism on a European scale"[12] – and her utter dislike of any other initiatives which suggested integration and ultimately an erosion of national sovereignty.

In his speech to the European Parliament on the eve of the UK's EU presidency in 2005, British prime minister Tony Blair tried very hard to challenge the widespread perception that Britain appreciated the EU only for its market value. He declared himself to be "a passionate pro-European" and denied that the current debate about the future of Europe was about the choice between a 'free market' Europe and a social Europe, between those who want to retreat to a common market and those who believe in Europe as a political project." Accordingly, he described the European Union as "a union of values, of solidarity between nations and people, of not just a common market in which we trade but a common political space in which we live as citizens." Claiming to "demolish" the caricature that "Britain is in the grip of some extreme Anglo-Saxon market philosophy," he nevertheless spoke out in favor of a modernization of the European social model the purpose of which, in his view, should be "to enhance our ability to compete." Furthermore, he promoted further enlargement without appearing to dedicate much reflection to questions of cohesion in terms of values.[13]

Similarly, Gordon Brown, still chancellor of the exchequer at the time, spoke of the need for a Europe which "can move from the older inward-looking model to a flexible, reforming, open and globally-oriented Europe." Asserting that a European identity had failed to develop, Brown pleaded for the adoption of a "pro-European realism" which accepts intergovernmental cooperation as the way forward since "the old assumptions about federalism do not match the realities of our time."[14]

This is in stark contrast to the rhetoric of German leaders, for whom European integration has traditionally meant much more than just an economic project. Helmut Kohl, named Honorary Citizen of Europe by the heads of state or government in 1998 for his achievements in European integration, declared European integration a matter of "war and peace" and suggested that German and European unification were "two sides of the same coin". Taking into account the concerns of Germany's neighbors, Kohl made European integration a central tenet of his Ten-Point Programme for Policy on Germany in the immediate aftermath of the fall of the Berlin Wall. It subsequently also found entry into the preamble of the Treaty on German Unity of August 1990. Together with the French president, Helmut Kohl worked hard to tie united Germany into a European framework which would make European integration irreversible for future generations of German political leaders whose attitudes towards Europe were not influenced any more by the experience of World War II and who therefore might be more critical regarding the benefits of European integration for Germany.

At the beginning of his chancellorship in 1998, Gerhard Schröder's rhetoric did in fact suggest that he represented a new pragmatism which was based on a cost–benefit analysis in European matters. He, too, however, saw the purpose of the European project going far beyond economics and envisaged the cultural identity of the people of Europe in future to be enriched by a European dimension.[15] And it was Joschka Fischer, Germany's foreign secretary from 1998 to 2005, who – with his Humboldt speech of May 2000 – contributed considerably to the creation of the Convention on the Future of Europe which later presented the draft treaty establishing a constitution for Europe.

In her first speech to the European Parliament during Germany's EU presidency in 2007, Chancellor Angela Merkel – borrowing an image from the former president of the European Commission Jacques Delors – at least rhetorically went in search of "the European soul" and claimed to have found it: "Europe's soul is tolerance."[16] Even though it was clearly yet another attempt to make a virtue of diversity, it also showed that Merkel's conception of Europe goes well beyond the economic project and sees common values as providing the basis for identification. In her view, "there is no doubt that the single market and the Euro and a lot more besides are very important for the European Union." At the same time she stressed, however, that "we should be clear that it is the common understanding of basic values that holds Europe together internally." In particular, Merkel mentions freedom, justice, democracy, the rule of law, and a respect for human rights.[17] During Germany's presidency of the EU in 2007, Merkel also voiced her opinion that European unity continues to be a question of "war and peace" since peace and democracy "should never be taken for granted," even though the EU has made peace in Europe a "familiar normality."[18]

The lack of agreement on what Europe *is* or what it *ought to be* became particularly apparent during the run-up to the 50th-anniversary celebrations of the signing of the Treaties of Rome on March 25, 2007 and in the aftermath of the "Berlin Declaration" which the German government issued on this occasion. It was a difficult balancing act to produce a declaration for this event which was acceptable to all member states since certain issues – such as the constitutional treaty, the "European social model," references to religion and traditions and whether the euro should be listed as an achievement or not – were and are likely to remain highly divisive. In the end, the "Berlin Declaration" made no reference to the constitutional treaty but promised to place the European Union on a "renewed common basis before the European Parliament elections in 2009," it spoke of a "European model" which "combines economic success and social responsibility," and it declared that the EU was striving for "peace and freedom, for democracy and the rule of law, for mutual respect and shared responsibility, for prosperity and security, for tolerance and participation, for justice and solidarity." In spite of some member states not being part of the eurozone and considerable skepticism at grassroots level in those countries that are, it asserted that the euro made "us strong."[19]

The celebrations were hardly over when Poland and the Czech Republic started to voice their opposition to the core aim stated explicitly in the "Berlin Declaration": to place the European Union on a "renewed common basis" before the elections to the European Parliament in 2009. Whereas Polish president Lech Kaczynski called the aim possibly desirable but the timetable "unrealistic," Czech president Vaclav Klaus went further and pointed out the nonbinding character of the "Berlin Declaration" and indicated that he did not consider a new treaty to be a priority.[20]

Just as there is no consensus regarding the nature of the European project and what direction it should take after 50 years, there is also no agreement on what constitutes Europe's "other." Whereas the bipolar Cold War division allowed democratic western Europe to define itself in opposition to its communist and undemocratic eastern "other," the end of the Cold War and the transitions to liberal democracy in eastern Europe put an end to this convenient construction of alterity.

Illustrating the centrality of "the other" for identity construction, there is no shortage of attempts which try to identify what distinguishes Europe and the EU from other parts of the world. In spite of the European Union's commitment not to discriminate against its citizens on grounds of religion,[21] a distinction based on religion has turned out to be quite popular. Jacques Delors, for example, suggested that Europeans should "unite behind the label of 'Christian European Civilization.'"[22] Similarly, Angela Merkel has professed her "allegiance to Europe's Christian principles"[23] and argued in favor of acknowledging the centrality of Christianity for Europe in the constitutional Treaty. Referring to the centrality of the individual and the inviolability of his dignity, in her speech as president of the Council at the official ceremony to celebrate the 50th anniversary of the signing of Treaties of Rome, she added what she called a "personal comment": "that this view of the individual is for me also part and parcel of Europe's Jewish–Christian heritage."[24]

Especially since 9/11 and the ensuing unilateralization of American foreign policy under President George W. Bush, there have been constructions of alterity which define Europe in opposition to the US. This became particularly obvious in the run-up to the war in Iraq when a number of European states refused to support the United States in a military campaign. What US defense secretary Donald Rumsfeld referred to as "old Europe" was a group of countries led by France and Germany which formed the major European opposition to the American plans to invade Iraq.[25]

In an article which instigated a major intellectual debate on the relationship between Europe and the US,[26] philosophers Jürgen Habermas and Jacques Derrida suggested that the simultaneous demonstrations against the war in major European cities on February 15, 2003 would "go down in history as a sign of the birth of a European public sphere."[27] However partial, since not all governments of EU member states opposed the war against Iraq, this "European public" was clearly defined in opposition to the United States. Survey results also show that anti-Americanism is on the rise in Europe. *Transatlantic Trends*, a survey conducted by the German Marshall Fund, for example, has found a persistent decline in views of the United States in Europe since 2002. It found that the proportions of Europeans who consider American leadership in world affairs desirable has reversed since 2002, from 64% positive in 2002 to only 37% in 2006 and from only 31% negative in 2002 to 57% in 2006. The only exceptions to this downward trend are provided by the Netherlands, Romania, and the United Kingdom.[28]

"Bringing Europe Closer to Its People"?

Even if there were indications that a European public is emerging, as Habermas and Derrida suggested, the European project clearly lacks emotive elements which could add up to something even faintly resembling a kind of "European patriotism." In spite of the existence of appropriate symbols such as a European flag, an anthem, and even a "Europe Day," the relationship between the European Union and its people is dominated by a cognitive rather than an affective dimension. As Ernest Renan pointed out in his famous lecture on what constitutes a nation "a customs union is not a fatherland". Similarly, but more recently, Jacques Delors stated that "you cannot fall in love with a Single Market."[29] Accordingly, support for European integration is very often based on an evaluation of its outputs and an assessment is made of how it affects the individual in economic terms and what the advantages and disadvantages of being a member state are. Whereas for the founders of Europe and the war generation the main motivation for an integrated Europe was to ensure peace, more recent, debates about European integration are increasingly dominated by cost–benefit analyses. Whereas approval of membership and an appreciation of its advantages continually rose throughout the 1980s, this trend was reversed at the beginning of the 1990s. What was referred to as the "permissive consensus" or "benevolent indifference," the unquestioning supportive position based on either tacit approval or lack of interest, started to give way to more critical attitudes regarding European integration, in particular regarding its costs.[30]

Judgments regarding the advantages and disadvantages of EU membership are not always well informed and are often based on the performance of national economies

in terms of growth, inflation rates, unemployment figures, and a cost–benefit analysis
as to whether one's country is benefiting from European funds or is largely subsidiz-
ing them.[31] Very often, these discussions are based on myths rather than on the
complex facts, and negative issues are more likely to make the headlines. The evaluation of the common currency is a case in point. Although all statistical data suggest
the opposite, many people in the eurozone countries are convinced that the euro has
made life more expensive.[32]

More widespread Euroskepticism and the problems the European Union has
encountered in the process of ratifying the proposed constitutional Treaty – leading
some to diagnose the EU's deepest crisis yet – indicate the discrepancy between the
degree of Europeanization that has been achieved and the difficulty of developing
and sustaining an underlying supportive European political culture based on general
approval of the EU and its institutions as well as on political participation at European
level. The failed referenda on the constitutional Treaty in France and the Netherlands
in 2005 – even though their outcome, especially in the case of France, had much to
do with national issues – served as a reminder that the European project not only
requires political elites entertaining and pursuing their visions of Europe but also
grassroots support to sustain it. Even among political elites, however, skeptical attitudes are much more prevalent now than during the years of the "permissive consensus." What used to stand out as the "British approach" has become quite common.
Tony Blair referred to this phenomenon in his speech on "The Future of Europe"
in February 2006 when he suggested that "the very cultural/political reservation
that was particularly British, is now widely shared by millions of our fellow
Europeans."[33]

In view of increasing criticism and the difficulty of creating an emotive attachment to Europe in the quest for a European identity, much effort has gone into
"bringing Europe closer to its citizens." The European Union, it has been claimed,
is so undemocratic, that it would not even be accepted as one of its own member
states! Attempts to bridge the gap between political elites and European institutions on the one hand, and the citizens of Europe on the other, are designed
to alter the perception of the EU as an "elite project" which lacks grassroots
support. More citizen participation as well as transparency of EU decision-making
processes, it is assumed, would lead to a "European demos," thereby alleviating the "democratic deficit" and ensuring the legitimacy of the EU in the long
term.

There have been several attempts and initiatives aimed at rectifying the "democratic deficit" by allowing citizens of EU member states to become more engaged in
the European process and to develop a European identity. A milestone in the attempt
to make Europe a Europe of its citizens was the introduction of direct elections to
the European Parliament in 1979, even though turnout at European Parliament
elections has been very low since then, with the election result very often being
determined by national issues. Furthermore, the Maastricht Treaty introduced
European citizenship for every person holding nationality of one of its member
states.[34] It complements national citizenship rather than replacing it and confers a
number of rights on EU citizens, such as freedom of movement within the EU, the
right to vote and to stand as a candidate for election to the European Parliament and
at local elections in the member state of residence. The notion of rights for European
citizens was taken a big step further by the European Union Charter of Fundamental

Rights, which was signed at the European Council meeting in Nice in December 2000 and which, for the first time, set out in one single text the whole range of civil, political, economic, and social rights of European citizens and others resident in EU member states.

One year after the Treaty of Nice, on December 15, 2001, the European Council adopted the so-called "Laeken Declaration," a "Declaration on the Future of the European Union" which committed the Union to becoming more democratic, transparent, and effective. To this purpose, a Convention was set up which was to discuss four key issues regarding the future of Europe: the division of powers, the simplification of treaties, the role of national parliaments, and the status of the Charter of Fundamental Rights. In July 2003 the Convention presented its draft treaty establishing a constitution for Europe which – having been further discussed by the Intergovernmental Conference starting in October 2003 – was signed on October 29, 2004 in Rome by the heads of state or government of the EU25, the twenty-five members of the EU.

In spite of all this, however, there is currently a consensus that efforts to create a "European citizen" have failed. Ironically, the proposed constitutional Treaty, the venture which was envisaged as a remedy for the EU's "democratic deficit" and perceived "crisis of legitimacy," was thrown into complete disarray by the negative referenda outcomes in 2005. It was supposed to be "an exercise in *public relations*" which was "to increase trust and support among European public" in order to "legitimate the EU not, as had been the case since its origin, by facilitating mutually beneficial trade, regulation, and economic growth, but instead by politicizing and democraticizing it in a way that encouraged a shared sense of citizen engagement in a common project."[35] In view of the outcomes of the referenda and the subsequent stalling of the process, this exercise has clearly failed. Even if the constitutional Treaty will eventually come into effect in some form, it has certainly failed as a public relations exercise aimed at increasing trust and support among EU citizens. If anything, it has highlighted once again the paradox of a "Europe without Europeans."

Whereas the politicization of the European Union has been happening incrementally since the introduction of the Single European Act, this has not been accompanied by a parallel development of democratization. Attempts to politicize the European Union have been driven forward in the same top-down fashion which has traditionally characterized Europe as an economic project. When the same method was attempted regarding its democratization, however, somewhat predictably this model failed. As the traditionally low turnout to European Parliament elections illustrates, the citizens of the EU member states do not appear to be interested in participating and engaging even if appropriate opportunities exist.

Political leaders in Europe are very aware of this even though recognition of the problem does not mean that they have an appropriate remedy at hand. Commission President Barroso, for example, had no trouble identifying the problem but his "solution" remained vague. In a speech in 2006, he pointed out that the "distance is growing between Europe and its citizens." Asserting that this must change, he suggested injecting "greater accountability and transparency into Europe's institutions" in order to close the gap. According to Barroso, this means "letting fresh air into smoke-filled rooms, and developing a more political way of building Europe, rather than a diplomatic or technocratic one."[36] In a debate in the European Parliament shortly after the Berlin summit in 2007, Angela Merkel became more concrete and suggested that the European Parliament should conduct a "hearing of civil society" in order to ensure that the expectations of the "European public" regarding the process of "placing the European Union on a renewed common basis," as announced in the Berlin Declaration, will find their way into the debates of European leaders.[37]

The need for an identification of its citizens with Europe is usually explained by suggesting that the legitimacy of the EU will remain fragile as long as it is based only on its output and its performance.[38] As long as the populations of the EU member states do not become involved in its input structures, and participate, a European identity will remain a distant aim. The persistent "democratic deficit" would thus ensure the continued persistence of a "Europe without Europeans" which in turn would become increasingly untenable with further integration.

For Habermas, for instance, the nature of European integration is in the process of fundamental change that goes well beyond economics. Whereas the construction of a common market and the eurozone have driven reforms until now, he argued, these "driving forces" are now "exhausted" and a "*transformative* politics which would demand that member states not just overcome obstacles for competitiveness but form a common will, must take recourse to the motives and the attitudes of *the citizens themselves*."[39] Whereas the "Monnet method" had ensured the spillover effect of economic integration into other areas, with the single market bringing clear advantages to its members, a constitutional framework for common policies requires more. According to Habermas, it requires a common political will which moves beyond the issue of economic advantage for individual nation states.[40]

Although these calls for a "European demos" and a common political will that support further integration sound plausible, the question is, of course, to what extent participation is actually necessary. Andrew Moravcsik has pointed out that there is no empirical evidence to suggest that "salient political rhetoric and increased opportunities to participate" necessarily produce "more intensive and informed public deliberation or greater public trust, identity and legitimacy."[41] Hence the most reasonable explanation for European citizens' reluctance to participate at EU level is that the issues predominantly dealt with by the EU such as trade, industrial regulation, technical standardization, etc. are far less salient to them than issues dealt with by national governments: "The most salient issues, notably those involving fiscal outlays, remain firmly national."[42]

There is no doubt that the European project has so far managed quite well without a strong underlying European identity to support it. The lack of a widespread emotive dimension in the relationship between the EU and its citizens has certainly not hindered integration in the first 50 years since its inception. Similarly, supporters of a European "constitutional patriotism" might identify a lack of commitment by its citizens towards the EU's institutions, but again this certainly has not manifested itself as an obstacle to a considerable degree of integration so far.

Nevertheless, the recent failure of the constitutional Treaty has led some to ask why "this beneficial European dynamics has waned,"[43] and whether this means that we are now witnessing a "renationalization" in Europe.[44]

Former German chancellor and staunch pro-integrationist Helmut Kohl has commented on the emerging Euroskepticism that Europe is currently facing. This negative mood towards the European idea, Kohl argued, has arisen from insufficient acknowledgment of national and regional independencies and identities of the peoples of Europe.[45] Accordingly, at least on the level of rhetoric, European leaders go to great lengths to pay tribute to Europe's diversity and acknowledge the importance of national identities. The Berlin Declaration, for example, proclaimed the European Union to be committed to the preservation of the identities and diverse traditions of its member states with the system of multilevel governance ensuring that tasks are shared between the Union, the member states, and their regions and local authorities.

Similarly, pro-integrationist European leaders tend to dismiss the concern voiced by member states like the UK, for example, that the European Union is eroding the national sovereignty of its member states. Commission President Barroso explicitly dismissed this traditional concern of UK governments. In a speech in the UK in 2006, Barroso dismisses it as belonging to the "old debates." Quoting former British prime minister Harold Macmillan, Barroso points out that it is not a one-sided surrender of sovereignty but a pooling of sovereignty by all concerned which in turn means receiving a share of the sovereignty renounced by other members. In view of the degree of European integration already achieved, for the UK this means, according to Barroso, a choice: be in a position "to shape a positive agenda, or be dragged along as a reluctant partner."[46]

In view of the way that the European project has managed to flourish without the parallel emergence of a European identity, it can probably continue to do so. It does, however, depend on the future direction of the EU. If it continues to enlarge, it is likely to remain an economic project with further deepening and the development of a transnational identity being improbable. In case of further deepening, however, especially in home affairs and foreign policy, a common identity based on more widespread participation as well as a degree of emotional attachment might become increasingly important.

In view of the already existing heterogeneity and lack of cohesion which is likely to increase with further future waves of enlargement, the notion of a "core Europe" has been brought forward as a possible way ahead. Already the Schäuble–Lamers paper which was published in 1994 brought a two-tier Europe into the discussion. Wolfgang Schäuble und Karl Lamers, two German Conservative politicians, suggested that the European integration process had reached a critical point and that the whole project ran the risk of turning into a "free trade area" rather than the "ever closer union" envisaged by the Maastricht Treaty unless a solution was found to the institutional overstretch, the increasing diversification in terms of interests, and the rise of a "regressive nationalism" which – in their view – the EU at this point faced. Schäuble and Lamers envisaged that a core of five or six of the more pro-integrationist member states would continue on the path to further integration but that the core would remain open for others to join.[47]

Nearly ten years later, with the membership of the European Union in the meantime having risen to 27, the idea of a "core Europe" has recently started to enjoy a renaissance. Jürgen Habermas, for example, has argued in favor of a European core which acts as an avant-garde for further integration. It is important, in his view, that the leading role of the core countries does not mean exclusion. The more closely operating core would welcome new members to its inner circle. The more effective it becomes externally and the more it can demonstrate its "soft power of negotiating agendas, relations and economic advantages," Habermas argues, the better are the chances that other countries want to join the core.[48]

Suggesting that the overwhelming success of the European Union was now threatening to overwhelm the Union itself, Karl Lamers has also returned to the idea of a "core Europe."[49] In his view, national identities are threatened and the emergence and development of a European identity in doubt since Europe does not seem to have any boundaries or borders. This lack, he argued, has resulted in a loss of identity because the new member states are perceived – by the core – as too alien to be trusted with influence over their own fate.[50] Accordingly, Lamers argued, "the political union will be limited or it will not happen at all,"[51] and the core will have to demonstrate what its member states consider to be a "political Europe."[52] Or, as Ulrich Beck has put it, a core of states could show the others "that it works."[53]

Arguably, this has already happened to some extent when, on January 1, 1999, the euro was launched, and when it became legal tender on January 1, 2002. Out of the 15 member states at the time, only 12 took part in the venture to create an Economic and Monetary Union and to have their monetary policy directed by the European Central Bank. Britain, Denmark, and Sweden did not join the "currency core." As it did in this instance, the concept of a "core Europe" has the potential to overcome the inherent friction caused by the parallel widening and deepening processes of the European Union, even though it does carry the risk of institutionalizing renewed divisions.

Regardless of whether EU member states will advance at different speeds or together, the European Union is not and probably never will be on a par with the nation state when it comes to offering opportunities for identification, especially in terms of emotive attachment. Through its citizenship law the European Union might succeed in turning many a German into a French person and vice versa, as one commentator has pointed out, but it does not turn the French and the Germans into Europeans.[54] It is equally difficult to achieve a kind of European "constitutional patriotism" that would at least offer some degree of "civic" underpinning for a European political culture. There is a common lack of knowledge of European institutions at grassroots level due to the complexity as well as the lack of transparency of decision-making processes. Furthermore, it is difficult for people to get involved in genuinely European politics since many political institutions which normally allow political participation are still largely grounded in the national level. Apart from some examples of cross-border cooperation, the media landscapes of the different EU member states operate within a largely national framework. And even though a "European public" might have been momentarily apparent in the run-up to the war in Iraq, there is a distinct lack of European media which would foster such a "European public" and sustain it. Three years after suggesting that the antiwar demonstrations which took place in European capitals in February 2003 may go down in history as a sign of "the birth of a European public," Habermas himself resignedly has come to the conclusion that "there is no European public."[55] Just as Moravcsik has interpreted the collapse of the constitutional project as a demonstration of "the EU's stability and success" since it "rests on a pragmatically effective, normatively attractive, and politically stable 'European constitutional settlement'" as set out in the various treaties since 1957,[56] the lack of a European identity does not necessarily have to be seen as a severe flaw. Even though there is no indication of a widespread emotive attachment to and identification with the EU and its institutions, there is certainly a European consciousness which is based on a consensus regarding basic values as well as the best political order to sustain them. Liberal democracy might not distinguish Europe from other parts of the world but together with the member states" geographical proximity and economic interdependencies, it will continue to provide a very good basis for intensive cooperation, peace, and more widely shared prosperity.

German academic Gerd Strohmeier has recently argued that it would be a grave mistake to attempt to shape the representative democracy of Europe according to the representative democracy of the nation state.[57] The same applies to identity. Over the last 50 years, the European Union has turned into something unique. It is inappropriate to use the criteria of the nation state to evaluate the EU with regard to its identificatory potential. At the same time, however, it was rivalries between the nation states of Europe, nationalism at its worst, and the ideological battle of a bipolar world which led Hobsbawm to describe the twentieth century as the "Age of Extremes." In view of this, a European Union that does *not* bind its citizens emotionally, *is* evaluated in terms of costs and benefits, and does *not* manage to mobilize its citizens can be considered a welcome and appropriate response to the twentieth century.

Nevertheless, a number of very mundane things are likely to make Europe grow together. A sense of belonging based on symbols such as the common currency and everyday experiences such as traveling (made easier and more accessible through cheap air travel), popular European study exchange programs like Erasmus/Socrates, and working or buying holiday homes abroad will result in increasing familiarity and, as a consequence, the transnational extension of civic solidarity often considered to be crucial for further European integration to happen successfully. Rather than emulating the structures and processes of the nation state, it might be different forms of civic engagement which will help to support the European Union's democratic legitimacy. It has been suggested, for instance, that rather than strengthening representative democracy by giving more power to the European Parliament, deliberation in the sense of consultation would be a more fruitful way forward. Similarly, an enhanced role for contestation could provide useful opportunities for EU citizens to express their opposition to decisions reached by EU institutions.[58]

A poll conducted on the eve of the European Union's 50th birthday in its five largest member states suggested that 44% of its citizens thought that life had got worse since their country joined. At the same time, however, only a minority thought that their country would do better if it pulled out.[59] This brings to mind parallels with Churchill's thoughts on democracy. The European Union might be the worst form of governing Europe except for all those others that have been tried.

Notes

1   Moravcsik, "What Can We Learn from the Collapse of the European Constitutional Project?" 235.
2   Quoted in Lundestad, *"Empire" by Integration*, 16.
3   Pond, *The Rebirth of Europe*, 17.
4   Schild, "Europäisierung nationaler Identitäten in Deutschland und Frankreich," 32.
5   Standard Eurobarometer 65, Full Report.

6   Nissen, "Europäische Identität und die Zukunft Europas," 24–25.
7   See for example, Beck and Grande, "Empire Europa,," 397–420 and Zielonka, *Europe as Empire*.
8   Zielonka, "Europa als Empire," 301.
9   Moravcsik, op. cit., 237.
10   Barroso, "Seeing Through the Hallucinations: Britain and Europe in the 21st Century."
11   Habermas, "Europa: Vision und Votum," 517.
12   Young, *This Blessed Plot*, 333.
13   Speech by prime minister Tony Blair to the European Parliament on June 23, 2005.
14   Speech by the chancellor of the exchequer Gordon Brown at the Mansion House, London, on June 22, 2005.
15   Speech by chancellor Gerhard Schröder at a conference entitled "A Soul for Europe."
16   Speech by Angela Merkel, chancellor of the Federal Republic of Germany, to the European Parliament during Germany's EU presidency, January 17, 2007.
17   German chancellor Angela Merkel in a speech to the Deutsche Gesellschaft für Auswärtige Politik, November 8, 2006.
18   Bild-Interview with German chancellor Angela Merkel, March 23, 2007.
19   Berlin Declaration.
20   Parker, Benoit, and Williamson, "Merkel Lays out Tight EU Treaty Timetable"; Bacia, "Neinsager sollen austreten."
21   This is laid out in Chapter II, Article 9 of the Charter of Human Rights of the European Union, which assures everyone of "the right to freedom of thought, conscience and *religion*" (my emphasis).
22   Billig, *Banal Nationalism*, 141.
23   Speech by Angela Merkel, chancellor of the Federal Republic of Germany, to the European Parliament during Germany's EU presidency, January 17, 2007.
24   Speech by Angela Merkel as President of the European Council at the official ceremony to celebrate the 50th anniversary of the signing of the Treaties of Rome.
25   US Defense Secretary Donald Rumsfeld, press conference on January 22, 2003.
26   For an edited collection in English which documents the intellectual debate that followed the Habermas/Derrida initiative, see Levy, Pensky, and Torpey, *Old Europe, New Europe*.
27   Habermas and Derrida, "February 15, or What Bind Europeans Together," 291.
28   German Marshall Fund, *Transatlantic Trends 2006*.
29   Delors quoted by German chancellor Angela Merkel in her speech at the Vision for Europe Award ceremony in Luxembourg, November 15, 2006. For the Delors quote, see Ernest Renan, 'Qu'est-ce qu'une nation?' lecture delivered at the sorbonne 11 March 1882, http://archives.vigile.net/04-01/renan.pdf.
30   Nissen, op. cit., 23.
31   Nissen, op. cit., 25.
32   Flash Eurobarometer Report 193.
33   British prime minister Tony Blair, speech on The Future of Europe, February 2, 2006.
34   Details of EU membership are set out in Part Two (Articles 17–22) of the EC Treaty.
35   Moravcsik, op. cit., 220. Emphasis in the original.
36   Barroso, op. cit.
37   European Parliament debate, March 28, 2007.
38   Schild, op. cit., 32.
39   Habermas and Derrida, "February 15," Emphasis in the original., 293.
40   Habermas, "Europa: Vision und Votum," 518.
41   Moravcsik, op. cit., 219.

42 Moravcsik, op. cit., 225.
43 Habermas, "Die Bewährung Europas," 1453.
44 Zürn, "Zur Politisierung der Europäischen Union," 242.
45 Bild-Interview with Germany's former Chancellor Helmut Kohl, March 22, 2007.
46 Barroso, op. cit.
47 Schäuble and Lamers, "Überlegungen zur europäischen Politik."
48 Habermas and Derrida, "February 15," 293.
49 Lamers, "Die Fundamente tragen noch," 31.
50 Lamers, op. cit., 31.
51 Lamers, op. cit., 32.
52 Lamers, op. cit., 31.
53 Quoted in Hofmann, "Der Kosmopolitist," 12.
54 Christoph Schöneberger quoted in Kemmerer, "Was Europa zusammenhält," 36.
55 Habermas, "Die Bewährung Europas," 1454.
56 Moravcsik, op. cit., 221.
57 Strohmeier, "Die EU zwischen Legitimität und Effektivität," 30.
58 See Zielonka, "Europa als Empire," 296–297.
59 Anon, "Jubiläums Umfrage: Die EU ist schlecht, ohne EU wäre alles noch viel schlechter."

Bibliography

Anon., "European Parliament Elections 2004," http://www.euractiv.com/en/elections/european-parliament-elections-2004-results/article-117482

Anon., "Jubiläums Umfrage: Die EU ist schlecht, ohne EU wäre alles noch viel schlechter," *Der Spiegel Online*, March 19, 2007, http://www.spiegel.de/wirtschaft/0,1518,472462,00.html

Bacia, Horst, "Neinsager sollen austreten," *FAZ.NET*, March 26, 2007, http://www.faz.net/s/Rub99C3EECA60D84C08AD6B3E60C4EA807F/Doc~ED8F0838CCBF748A6BE939FD8F4BCDA74~ATpl~Ecommon~Scontent.html

Barroso, José Manuel, "Seeing through the Hallucinations: Britain and Europe in the 21st Century," Hugo Young Lecture, October 16, 2006, http://ldeg.org/pages/barrosospeech.html

Beck, Ulrich and Edgar Grande, "Empire Europa: Politische Herrschaft jenseits von Bundesstaat und Staatenbund," *Zeitschrift für Politik* 52, no. 4, 2004, 397–420.

Berlin Declaration, http://www.eu2007.de/de/About_the_EU/Constitutional_Treaty/BerlinerErklaerung.html

Billig, Michael, *Banal Nationalism* (London: Sage, 1995).

Blair, Tony, speech to the European Parliament on June 23, 2005, http://www.number10.gov.uk/output/Page7714.asp

Blair, Tony, speech on The Future of Europe, February 2, 2006, http://www.pm.gov.uk/output/Page9003.asp

Brown, Gordon, speech at the Mansion House, London, on June 22, 2005, "Global Britain, Global Europe: A Presidency Founded on Pro-European Realism," http://www.hm-treasury.gov.uk/newsroom_and_speeches/press/2005/press_57_05.cfm

European Parliament Debate, March 28, 2007, http://www.europarl.europa.eu/sides/getDoc.do?type=CRE&reference=20070328&secondRef=ITEM-012&language=EN

"European Parliament Elections 2004" http://www.euractiv.com/en/elections/european-parliament-elections-2004-results/article-117482

Flash Eurobarometer Report 193, "The euro, 5 Years after the Introduction of the Banknotes and Coins," http://ec.europa.eu/public_opinion/archives/flash_arch_en.htm

German Marshall Fund, *Transatlantic Trends 2006*, http://www.transatlantictrends.org/trends

Habermas, Jürgen, "Die Bewährung Europas," *Blätter für deutsche und internationale Politik* 51, no. 12, December 2006, 1453–1456.

Habermas, Jürgen, "Europa: Vision und Votum," *Blätter für deutsche und internationale Politik* 52, no. 5, May 2007, 517–520.

Habermas, Jürgen and Jacques Derrida, "February 15, or What Binds Europeans together: A Plea for a Common Foreign Policy, Beginning in the Core of Europe," *Constellations* 10, no. 3, 2003, 291–297.

Hofmann, Gunter, "Der Kosmopolitist," *Die Zeit*, March 1, 2007, p. 12.

Kemmerer, Alexandra, "Was Europa zusammenhält," *Internationale Politik* 62, no. 1, January 2007, 34–38.

Kohl, Helmut, Bild-Interview, March 22, 2007, http://www.bild.t-online.de/BTO/news/2007/03/23/kohl-interview-europa/deutsche-einigung-teil-1.html

Lamers, Karl, "Die Fundamente tragen noch," *Internationale Politik* 60, no. 7, July 2005, 29–34.

Levy, Daniel, Max Pensky, and John Torpey (eds.), *Old Europe, New Europe, Core Europe: Transatlantic Relations after the Iraq War* (London, 2005).

Lundestad, Geir, *"Empire" by Integration: The United States and European Integration, 1945–1997.* (Oxford, Oxford University Press 1998).

Merkel, Angela, speech to the Deutsche Gesellschaft für Auswärtige Politik, November 8, 2006, http://www.bundesregierung.de/nn_23272/Content/DE/Rede/2006/11/2006-11-08-rede-bkin-deutsche-gesellschaft-fuer-auswaertige-politik.html

Merkel, Angela, speech at the Vision for Europe Award Ceremony in Luxembourg, November 15, 2006, http://www.bundesregierung.de/nn_6566/Content/EN/Reden/2006/11/2006-11-14-bkin-visions-for-europe-award.html

Merkel, Angela, speech to the European Parliament, January 17, 2007, http://www.bundes-regierung.de/nn_1514/Content/DE/Bulletin/2007/01/04-2-bk-ep.html

Merkel, Angela, Bild-Interview, March 23, 2007, http://www.bundesregierung.de/nn_1500/Content/DE/Interview/2007/03/2007-03-23-interview-merkel-bild.html

Merkel, Angela, speech at the Official Ceremony to Celebrate the 50th Anniversary of the Signing of the Treaties of Rome, March 25, 2007, http://www.eu2007.de/de/About_the_EU/Constitutional_Treaty/RedeBundeskanzlerin.html

Moravcsik, Andrew, "What Can We Learn from the Collapse of the European Constitutional Project?" *Politische Vierteljahresschrift* 47, no. 2, June 2006, 219–241.

Nissen, Sylke, "Europäische Identität und die Zukunft Europas," *Aus Politik und Zeitgeschichte. Beilage zur Wochenzeitung Das Parlament*, B38, 13 September 2004, 21–29.

Parker, George, Bertrand Benoit, and Hugh Williamson, "Merkel Lays out Tight EU Treaty Timetable," *Financial Times Europe*, March 25, 2007, http://www.ft.com/cms/s/a1e08896-dac9-11db-ba4d-000b5df10621.html

Pond, Elizabeth, *The Rebirth of Europe* (Washington: Brookings Institution Press, 1999).

Rumsfeld, Donald, press conference on January 22, 2003, http://www.defenselink.mil/transcripts/transcript.aspx?transcriptid=1330

Schäuble, Wolfgang and Karl Lamers, "Überlegungen zur europäischen Politik," September 1, 1994, http://www.cducsu.de/upload/schaeublelamers94.pdf.

Schild, Joachim, "Europäisierung nationaler Identitäten in Deutschland und Frankreich," *Aus Politik und Zeitgeschichte. Beilage zur Wochenzeitung Das Parlament*, B3–4, 20 January 2003, 31–39.

Schröder, Gerhard, speech at a conference entitled A Soul for Europe, November 26, 2004, http://archiv.bundesregierung.de/bpaexport/rede/12/751512/multi.htm

Standard Eurobarometer 65, Full Report, January 2007, http://ec.europa.eu/public_opinion/archives/eb/eb65/eb65_en.htm 71

Strohmeier, Gerd, "Die EU zwischen Legitimität und Effektivität," *Aus Politik und Zeitgeschichte. Beilage zur Wochenzeitung Das Parlament*, no. 10, 5 March 2007, 24–30.

Young, Hugo, *This Blessed Plot: Britain and Europe from Churchill to Blair* (Basingstoke: Macmillan, 1999).

Zielonka, Jan, *Europe as Empire: The Nature of the Enlarged European Union* (Oxford: Oxford University Press, 2006).

Zielonka, Jan, "Europa als Empire," *Blätter für deutsche und internationale Politik* 52, no. 3, March 2007, 294–301.

Zürn, Michael, "Zur Politisierung der Europäischen Union," *Politische Vierteljahresschrift* 47, no. 2, June 2006, 242–251.

Further Reading

After several decades during which socioeconomic issues and the history of European integration dominated the academic field, there is a steadily growing body of literature in English which examines and, occasionally questions, the emergence of a supranational European identity and its relationship with national identities. A standard work on European identity, past and present, is, however, still missing.

For an interesting recent account which examines the emergence of a new European identity based on civic as well as cultural components since the 1970s, see Michael Bruter's *Citizens of Europe? The Emergence of a Mass European Identity* (Basingstoke: Palgrave Macmillan, 2005). Questioning one of the most basic assumptions in this context, i.e. that a convergence towards a common political identity is actually under way, in her book *Europolis: Constitutional Patriotism beyond the Nation State* (Manchester: Manchester University Press, 2006), Patrizia Nanz suggests that Europe needs what she describes as a "situated constitutional patriotism."

A wide range of contributions discussing various aspects of European identity, in particular vis-à-vis the United States, followed the publication of the article in which Jürgen Habermas and Jacques Derrida suggested that the mass antiwar demonstrations which took place simultaneously in European capitals against the war in Iraq constituted "the birth of a European public sphere." These contributions have been published in one volume edited by Daniel Levy, Max Pensky, and John Torpey entitled *Old Europe, New Europe, Core Europe* (London: Verso, 2005).

There are a number of works which examine the role of "the East" in European identity formation past and present, e.g. Iver B. Neumann's book *Uses of the Other: "The East" in European Identity Formation* (Minneapolis: University of Minnesota Press, 1998); David D. Laitin, "Culture and National Identity: 'The East' and European Integration," *West European Politics* 25, no. 2, 2002, 55–80); and Dieter Fuchs and Hans Dieter Klingemann, "Eastward Enlargement of the European Union and the Identity of Europe," *West European Politics* 25, no. 2, 2002, 19–54).

Questions of the European Union's identity in the context of enlargement are also discussed in Helene Sjursen (ed.): *Questioning EU Enlargement: Europe in Search of Identity* (London: Routledge, 2006) and the relationship between national and supranational identities is examined in Richard Robyn (ed.), *The Changing Face of European Identity* (London: Routledge, 2005).

A number of studies examine legal aspects of EU citizenship and migration, e.g. Elspeth Guild, *The Legal Elements of European Identity: EU Citizenship and Migration Law* (The Hague: Kluwer Law International, 2004); and Rémy Leveau, Khadija Mohsen-Finan, and Catherine Wihtol de Wenden, *New European Identity and Citizenship* (Aldershot: Ashgate, 2002).

Specific cultural aspects of European identity are discussed in the following books: Wendy Everett (ed.), *European Identity in Cinema* (Oxford: Intellect, 2005); Thomas M. Wilson (ed.), *Food, Drink and Identity in Europe* (Amsterdam: Rodopi, 2006); Liz Crolley and David Hand, *Football and European Identity: Historical Narratives through the Press* (London: Routledge, 2006).

CHAPTER EIGHTEEN

Europe and Post-Cold War Nationalism

CLAIRE SUTHERLAND

To understand nationalism, we have to understand the practical uses of the category "nation," the ways it can come to structure perception, to inform thought and experience, to organize discourse and political action.[1]

Nationalist ideology has shaped the way in which the world is organized. Political maps are divided into differently colored states – often called "nation states" – suggesting that the nation is intimately linked to the state as a territorial entity and a reservoir of power. As the primary focus of nationalist ideology, the nation is both a way of justifying where borders are drawn and a means of contesting those borders, because it serves to underpin not only the legitimacy of modern states but also the conflicting claims of sub-state nationalists. In an era of globalization and integration into the European Union (EU), nationalists also strike alliances which may at first seem surprising. How can some nationalists be pro-European, for instance, if the core of their demands is greater independence? How does globalization impact on the sovereignty and legitimacy of the nation state and the demands of minority nationalists? How do we account for the many varieties of nationalist movements, and how have they evolved since the end of the Cold War? How can some nationalists espouse left-wing views, when nationalism is also associated with fascism?

This chapter offers ways of thinking about these questions in today's European context. Space limitations mean that other important aspects of post-Cold War nationalism receive scant attention, however, such as the impact of postcolonialism on Europe and the implications of multiculturalism.[2] The discussion focuses on a few illustrative cases – Scotland, the Basque country, Catalonia, Yugoslavia, Czechoslovakia, France, and Germany – rather than offering broad generalizations. This specificity entails selectivity, and swathes of Europe – namely Scandinavia, the Baltic and Alpine republics, much of eastern Europe, and parts of the Mediterranean – are not covered as a result. Nevertheless, the types discussed are applicable to a wide range of cases.

The first section of the chapter offers some preliminary definitions to guide the discussion. The following section then puts contemporary nationalism in the context

A Companion to Europe since 1945, First Edition. Edited by Klaus Larres.
© 2014 John Wiley & Sons, Ltd. Published 2014 by John Wiley & Sons, Ltd.

of its twentieth-century antecedents, before elaborating on the characteristics of state and sub-state nationalism. With particular reference to the process of European integration, it asks whether this distinction is still relevant to a globalizing world, in which the locus of power and authority is likely to become more fluid and diffuse. The third section goes on to discuss the usefulness of nationalism theory for explaining post-Cold War nationalism, including primordialist and modernist approaches. Does theory help to illuminate the systemic change which took place in central and eastern Europe at the end of the Cold War? Accompanied by a reconfiguration of state nationalism which drew on real or invented tradition, its results ranged from "velvet revolution" to "ethnic cleansing."[3] The final section draws on the examples of Czechoslovakia, Yugoslavia, and the Basque country in considering what distinguishes "hot" from "banal" nationalism. The chapter concludes that contemporary European nationalism is a multifacetted and evolving ideology, which underpins both continuing state legitimacy and demands for sub-state autonomy. It is a powerful and flexible political instrument which resonates with every individual – the vast majority – who identifies with a particular nation. The relevance of nationalism is thus undiminished in the post-Cold War world.

The chapter sets up three dichotomies as a means of navigating the complexity of post-Cold War nationalism: state and sub-state, primordial and modern, "hot" and "banal." Running through the discussion is a fourth distinction between civic and ethnic nations, which can be defined respectively as "the bearer of universal political values [and] an organic, cultural, linguistic or racial community."[4] None of these binaries should be understood as fixed categories, but rather as end points on a sliding scale which can be used to analyze specific nationalisms. At the same time, they make comparisons possible; some manifestations of post-Cold War European nationalism will be "hotter" than others, and might be influenced to a greater or lesser extent by civic or ethnic principles. Nationalism continues to provide states with a sense of community and to fuel independence movements in the face of globalization and the process of EU integration. It is also linked to the salient current issues of immigration and citizenship. Whether "hot" or "banal," primordial or modern, nationalist ideology is here to stay, underlining the need for a differentiated understanding of its contemporary manifestations.

Defining the Nation

The category "nation," referred to in the epigraph which opened this chapter, is a notoriously nebulous term. It has been described as "one of the most puzzling and tendentious items in the political lexicon."[5] One definition which has proved extremely popular is the nation as an "imagined political community – and imagined as both inherently limited and sovereign."[6] The nation is imagined in the sense that it is too large for all of its members ever to meet in person, and yet they still believe they belong together. This sense of community may be grounded in perceptions of shared ancestry, traditions, history, language, or religion, but there are no necessary, objective criteria defining the nation. Whether commonalities actually exist is ultimately less important than the "psychological bond"[7] uniting members of the community, a bond which may well be articulated negatively in terms of common opposition to an "Other."

Some national communities emphasize ethnic or cultural markers over civic ones, the latter being usually understood as the rights, obligations, and democratic values shared by state citizens. This, in turn, influences the relative ease with which one can become a member of a given nation – through naturalization as a citizen, for example – or more restrictively, through birth into a national community following laws of descent (*jus sanguinis*). Definitions of the nation and markers of belonging are articulated and contested by nationalist movements, states, and political parties alike. All of these actors play a role in trying to mobilize national identity for a variety of political ends.

Within the United Kingdom, for instance, promoting the linguistic and cultural identity of the Welsh nation is an important feature of the self-styled "Plaid Cymru" – the "Party of Wales." Similarly, the Scottish National Party (SNP) appeals to voters as "Scotland's Party" in its pursuit of political independence for Scotland within the European Union. At the same time, the UK Labour Party and the Conservatives, both unionist parties, are nationalist insofar as they consider the United Kingdom to be a legitimate "nation state" and seek to promote a sense of British national identity. It remains to be seen how the SNP and Plaid Cymru, in government in Scotland and Wales for the first time in 2007, will influence this constitutional debate from a position of power.

Definitions of nationalism are necessarily linked to theoretical approaches. These can be divided into "three conceptual languages, which see nationalism as, respectively, an instinct (primordialism), an interest (situationalism) and an ideology (constructivism)."[8] The first focuses on a belief in common origins, the second sees the nation as a means of pursuing group interests, whereas the third considers it a tool of elites used to legitimate political projects, notably states. In practice, most manifestations of nationalism draw on all three aspects. They profess to speak for a community, however defined, as part of a political ideology, which aims to achieve greater national autonomy or lend authority to state power as a "limited and sovereign" territorial entity. This last element, included in Anderson's definition above, is what distinguishes a nation from ethnic groups. These also claim to have "distinctive attributes,"[9] but they do not necessarily link these to a political ideology or demands for self-determination within a given territory.

Finally, the term "nationality" is sometimes used to designate ethnic groups associated with a particular sub-state region or nation, such as in Spain. Confusingly, nationality is also often used as a synonym of state citizenship, indicating how closely state-building is bound up with the presumption of a common national identity. We will return to this question in the following discussion, which will sketch some aspects of contemporary nationalism as an instinct, an interest, and an ideology.

State and Sub-state Nationalisms

The years 1918, 1945, and 1990 were key dates in the twentieth-century history of European nationalism, which help to put its post-Cold War variants into context. The first marked the end of World War I and the breakup of the Austro-Hungarian and Ottoman empires, to be replaced by a series of new states premised on the idea of national self-determination as articulated by then US president Woodrow Wilson, among others. These included the re-established state of Poland, and the newly formed state of Yugoslavia, which would be held together by Josip Tito's force of character and the circumstances of the Cold War until its own breakup in the 1990s. The Turkish secular republic, based on Mustafa Kemal Atatürk's vision of the Turkish nation, emerged from the ruins of the Ottoman Empire. The Treaty of Versailles, signed in 1919, also imposed crippling reparations and responsibility for the war on Germany. This sowed the seeds for hardship and resentment among the German population, which would be skilfully exploited by Adolf Hitler and his National Socialist German Workers' (Nazi) Party. Unspeakable crimes against humanity would be perpetrated in the name of Nazi ideology, a murderous mix of chauvinistic nationalism, fascism, and populism, leading to a second global conflict only 25 years after the beginning of the first.

In the aftermath of World War II, the map of Europe was reconfigured once again. The fledgling "nation-states" of Latvia, Lithuania, and Estonia, briefly independent between the wars, were incorporated into the Soviet Union. Germany was divided along the ideological cleavage of communism versus capitalism, which defined the Cold War and dominated international relations for the next four decades. At the same time, the architects of European integration stressed the need to overcome the nationalism held responsible for World War II, in order to prevent any future conflict. Plans to create a form of supranational federalism have since met with varying degrees of resistance from member states, often justified in the name of national sovereignty. In November 1989, the fall of Berlin Wall symbolized the beginning of the end of the Cold War era. With the collapse of the Soviet Union in 1990, the Baltic republics recovered their independence and other Soviet republics, including Belarus, Ukraine, and Moldova, also joined the ranks of European "nation-states." States once cut off by the Iron Curtain became eligible to join the EU after a period of transition to democracy and a free market economy. By January 2007, a total of ten central and eastern European countries had become members of the organization.

To indicate one's nationality as Polish, Italian, French, German, or Estonian today is to evoke a national construct. Every nationalist variant, from terrorist nationalists, through democratic independence movements, to established "nation-states," aims to represent the nation through control of territory and institutions. This is what existing "nation-states" and those nationalists aspiring to greater autonomy, or self-determination, have in common. What differs is how the nation is defined and the nature of appeals to it, but it remains the focal point of mobilization. European "nation-states" can endure, and have endured, a "crisis of the hyphen" between the two concepts of nation and state.[10] Instances include the breakup of Yugoslavia and Czechoslovakia. Some commentators also see Scottish devolution as heralding de facto, if not *de jure* independence.[11] This case highlights "the tension between the claims of an established nation state and the claims of an emergent peripheral nationalism."[12]

How does the process of European integration impact on the claims and aims of nation-builders and autonomy-seekers alike? Comparison of Catalonia and Spain, Scotland and the United Kingdom exemplifies different understandings of national sovereignty within the European Union. Neither Scotland nor Catalonia fit any neat correspondence between nation and state. The nationalist movements there incorporate a broad social base and are progressive in their discourse; that is, they accept both the concept of limited sovereignty and the existence of multiple identities.

Contemporary sub-state nationalism is often characterized by a mix of civic and ethnic markers, mobilized differently according to the changing constellations of power at state and international levels. For such sub-state movements to be successful, competence in economic matters is also important.

Nationalism plays a role in articulating a new political arena and thereby providing a focus for collective action. Given declining loyalty to the "nation-state" construct, sub-state territories are reinvented as centers of social, economic, and political activity, as well as an alternative locus of identity. A similar phenomenon accompanied the breakup of the Soviet Union, where nationalities were already associated with well-established sub-state republics.[13] The way in which conflicts between the sub-state group and its encompassing "Other" are managed will also affect the internal dynamics of sub-state movements. However, the nationalist ideology of individual parties must be carefully distinguished from a more diffuse sense of national identity, which is not party-political. This will be illustrated with reference to Scotland, which has recent experience of both political devolution and nationalist electoral success.

The SNP claims to speak for the Scottish nation as a whole. By styling itself as "Scotland's party," it aims to politicize an inchoate sense of loyalty to Scotland and make the link between party, people, and nation appear self-evident. The 1970s saw the SNP's evolution from a single-issue movement to a party with a wide range of policies. This went hand in hand with the discovery of North Sea oil and the economic boost this gave to the independence cause, as well as the party's first real taste of power in local government and at Westminster. Part of the SNP's initial success was due to protest votes against the incumbent United Kingdom government, which the party then successfully exploited by offering an alternative political identity to the traditional left/right and class cleavages.[14] The decline and stagnation in SNP support during the 1980s can be attributed to a lack of voter loyalty and internal rivalries, as well as party inexperience in handling the devolution debate and exploiting "emotional–economic" issues such as North Sea oil.[15] The SNP's nationalist ideology, however, must not be confused with a more widespread sense of Scotland as an "imagined community."[16]

An independent state until its political union with England and Wales in 1707, Scotland retained its separate church, legal system, and education system even then. Today, its status as a nation is accepted in UK political discourse, even if the nationalist project derived from this status is not.[17] Postwar investment in the British welfare state was an important political project which united Scottish civil society but emphasized the continued worth of UK membership.[18] At the same time, Scotland was allowed considerable administrative leeway in adapting policy to the country's needs.[19]

By the late 1960s and early 1970s, however, Scottish voters had become increasingly discontented with a political and – by extension – constitutional system which was not delivering prosperity. Although the Labour-led referendum of 1979 on devolution of power to a Scottish Assembly resulted in a narrow "yes" vote, it did not meet the stipulated threshold of 40% of the electorate, and the project was abandoned. Soon, Scottish voting patterns diverged so markedly from those in England that between 1987 and 1997 the Conservatives governed Scotland with only about one-seventh of Scottish seats. The loss of all these at the 1997 general election marked the end of what was widely perceived in Scotland as an unfairly imposed government.

The incoming Labour government's renewed promise of a devolved parliament proposed a remedy backed by three of Scotland's four main parties, demonstrating that support for a degree of political autonomy is not purely the preserve of nationalist politicians.

A 74.3% "yes" vote in the referendum of September 1997 paved the way for a parliament with far more powers than its abortive predecessor of 1979. Economic, defense, and foreign policy (including European affairs), and social security, consumer protection, and immigration, were some of the areas reserved to the Westminster parliament, with everything else being devolved to Edinburgh. The advent of the Scottish parliament means that "all parties are thus forced to play on the nationalist field,"[20] since a great swathe of policy preferences are now articulated at the Scottish, not the British, level. Not all parties are comfortable with this; the Conservative Party is still more strongly associated with its British than its Scottish identity in the minds of Scottish voters, for instance. The same can be said for the Partido Popular in Catalonia.[21]

In May 2007, the Scottish National Party pipped the Labour Party to gain the largest number of seats in the third Scottish parliamentary election, and went on to form a minority government. It plans to hold a referendum on independence near the end of its term, a policy which alienated all potential coalition partners (but for the Green Party). For the first time, this will directly confront two competing constructions of the "nation-state" – as Scotland or the UK – since elections are fought on a wider range of issues and by no means all SNP voters support independence for Scotland.

Catalonia, like Scotland, is part of a unitary state which has engaged in substantial, asymmetric devolution of power, to the point of "semi-federalism" in the Spanish case.[22] Article 1 of the Spanish constitution tortuously seeks to guarantee the "indissoluble unity of the Spanish nation" while recognizing the right to autonomy of both nationalities and regions. No precise definitions are offered to distinguish nation, nationality, and region, however. This illustrates the view that "nationalism as a state-building force is ambiguous if ethnic heterogeneity is present."[23]

Following the end of General Franco's centralizing dictatorship in 1975, Catalonia enjoyed a privileged transition to autonomy together with other "historic nationalities," including the Basques (discussed below). Catalan was restored as an official language after years of repression, which had only served to unite an otherwise ideologically divided civil society.[24] A coalition of Christian democrat and Liberal parties, Convergència i Unió (CiU), won the first Catalan elections in 1980. During their long incumbency up to 2003, they promoted the Catalan language as a passport to the integration of migrants in an otherwise civic and voluntaristic definition of national identity; "Everyone who lives and works in Catalonia and has the wish to be so and feels tied to this land, is Catalan."[25] Although CiU do not demand complete independence from the Spanish state (in contrast to a rival party, the Esquerra Republicana de Catalunya), and their policy agenda might otherwise contrast with that of the left-leaning SNP, both parties profess support for European integration.

Sub-state nationalist parties characteristically respond to contemporary social and political developments, including opposition-party tactics, by attempting to make a national identity politically relevant. In order to create a rhetorical link between the nationalist principle of self-determination and a vote for the party, appeals are made to an alternative national loyalty to that of the existing "nation state." The party's construction of national identity is often translated into "emotional–economic" rhetoric, a mix of emotive and rational appeals. If nationalism is viewed as a "thin" ideology capable of being supplemented by a variety of policies and strategies,[26] then it is not incompatible with support for European integration.

The SNP pursues its core goal of promoting Scottish independence within a larger European framework. Its flagship policy of "independence in Europe" plays an important symbolic role in the party's ideology, providing a backdrop to a full policy agenda. The party thus uses the European Union to support, rather than undermine, its core aim. Whether the European periphery can be reconciled with the national core depends in every case on the nature of each ideological construct.

In the SNP's case, it is designed to counter accusations of isolationism from its opponents and display a pragmatic understanding of self-determination within the post-Cold War context of shared sovereignty. Likewise, CiU embraces European networks, although it also places Catalonia within the Spanish context and is vague about its ultimate ambitions for the nation in a potentially post-sovereign world.[27] The SNP and CiU have adapted to contemporary circumstances and espouse different ideal power configurations. Single-issue parties have limited electoral viability, and so they have supplemented the nationalist core with elements of socialist, liberal, or conservative ideology to offer voters an agenda for government.

European integration has also had a different impact in Spain and the United Kingdom as a whole. Generally welcomed in Spain as a boost to national democracy and development in 1986, it was a source of national pride in marking a definitive end to the era of dictatorship.[28] In the United Kingdom, on the other hand, European integration is considered a threat to national sovereignty by a significant, "Euroskeptic" strand of public opinion.[29] Far from "rescuing" the nation state,[30] this portrays the European Union as sapping British autonomy through an inexorable transfer of power to Brussels, and endangering national symbols such as the British pound. Britain's belated entry into the then European Economic Community in 1973 was associated with the country's decline as a world power, and the negative aura surrounding membership of the EU has failed to dissipate with time. Contrasting Spanish and British attitudes to the EU are exemplified in the prolonged debates surrounding the European constitutional treaty. Spain resoundingly ratified the original treaty in a referendum, a procedure which the British government was keen to avoid, in the expectation that it would be defeated. Sub-state nationalists are thus no more isolationist in European matters than member states, and can actually be more open to the prospect of multilevel governance. It remains to be seen how nationalism interacts with globalization.

There is no generally accepted definition of globalization. It has variously been interpreted as an intensification of all forms of cultural and economic transfer and an increase in worldwide communication characterized by the compression of distances and time delays. The implications for nationalism clearly depend on how globalization is understood. Theoretical approaches to the phenomenon can be divided into three very broad and much simplified trends.[31] The so-called hyperglobalist thesis holds that globalization heralds the end of the nation state, which is increasingly being bypassed as a source of authority and legitimacy by ever-accelerating flows of goods, capital, people, and information.[32] More skeptical scholars, on the other hand, question whether globalization is such a new phenomenon at all,[33] highlighting its uneven impact across the world and its manipulation by both left and right for ideological ends.[34]

This suggests that some nation states will be affected more than others and will have differing abilities to control the flows crisscrossing their borders. Still other theorists stress that globalization is an unprecedented product of technological advances and imbue it with the potential to reconfigure global relations of power, regional organizations such as the European Union being one example.[35] This requires moves away from nineteenth-century theories of the state towards some form of post-sovereign construct.[36]

The preceding examples have shown that sub-state nationalists may be quite relaxed about flexibly apportioned power. Similarly, small states may be accustomed to deep integration, such as the long-standing agreements between Belgium, the Netherlands, and Luxembourg. Indeed, nation-builders may use the economic potential of globalization to bolster their legitimacy through rising living standards, in return for national and labor solidarity.[37] Other effects of globalization include the greater economic and political visibility of minorities through international labor movements and the mass media, which will affect the nation-building process.[38]

For instance, international organizations such as the United Nations manage human rights regimes which vie with states' rights to regulate migrants and asylum-seekers.[39] Domestic and external terrorist threats also influence nation-building and perceptions of the "Other." A decoupling of the concepts nation and state remains unlikely in post-Cold War Europe, however, where citizenship legislation still builds on nation-based criteria and sub-state demands are still made in nationalist terms. Despite the changing international context and tensions at, above, and below the state level, the political map of Europe continues to be established, challenged, and reconfigured in predominantly nationalist terms.

Primordial and Modern Nationalisms

A long-standing academic debate between so-called primordialist and modernist scholars has sought to pinpoint the origins of nations and nationalism.[40] Primordialists trace the roots of nations far back in time to an actual or symbolic ethnic community,[41] whereas modernists argue that European nationalism was a product of nineteenth-century industrialization and urbanization. Few adopt positions at the extremes of this spectrum, and most share common ground. The debate continues to be relevant today in that many nationalists themselves claim to represent an ancient nation, and demand recognition on that basis.

What are the implications for the people who live within the territorial boundaries of that nation? Who is deemed to belong to a nation, and who is thereby excluded? Is it possible to become a member, or is belonging based purely on descent? Does one have to possess certain skills, such as mastery of a particular language, or profess a specific religion? In the case of nation-states, these questions have important implications for citizenship and immigration. A closer look at France and Germany, which have been traditionally regarded as pursuing very different policies in these areas, will help to illustrate this point.

Contemporary nationalisms differ from older variants, which have been the subject of much theorizing. Nineteenth-century European nationalism emerged in the context of the Industrial Revolution and the breakdown of agrarian society. Scholars have variously sought to explain this as an elite-driven method of promoting solidarity among uprooted citizens,[42] as a consequence of modernization and urbanization,[43] or as a result of the development of print capitalism.[44] Ernest Gellner's highly influential theory argues that from the eighteenth century on, states pursued internal legitimacy through the fiction of the nation. The new hierarchies and mass dislocation characteristic of the time gave rise both to middle-ranking clerks and to a working class, ready to mobilize and be mobilized behind a new conception of society promising them greater opportunities. Nevertheless, this was a slow process of national identity creation where once there was none. The EU's relative failure in fostering a sense of European identity is often contrasted to well-established national identities within its member states. However, fledgling European states had to overcome feudal regimes, establish their right to exist, and build legitimacy.[45] Although military might continued to be central to state authority, nineteenth-century states began to seek to legitimate their rule by popular consent rather than coercion.[46]

Well-established national identities may be taken for granted today, but they are neither primordial nor perennial. In turn, mass loyalty to the nation must be contrasted to the beliefs of a small elite. Eugen Weber has argued that only mass education, a growing infrastructure, and military conscription turned "peasants into Frenchmen" in the early twentieth century.[47] Where before there had been only Bretons, Basques, Gascons, and Provençals, or even more localized identities, common experiences and the inculcation of a shared history were crucial in fostering popular patriotism. Similarly, Alon Confino has shown how the German term *Heimat* was gradually widened to mean not only the locality, but also the nation, between the creation of a modern German state in 1870 and the onset of World War I.[48] It functioned as a mediating concept between local life and the abstract nation, until the idea of *deutsche Heimat* became corrupted by Nazi ideology.

Celia Applegate takes up the story by arguing that *Heimat* was "pulled out of the rubble of the Nazi *Reich* as a victim, not a perpetrator,"[49] and came to embody once more the local patriotism which had been discouraged by Nazism. Following World War II, France and Germany would espouse different official understandings of the national community; Germany was not a country of immigration (*kein Einwanderungsland*)[50] and France was depicted as a "color-blind" community open to all who were ready to adopt her civic, republican values.[51] This nation-building rhetoric perpetuated by successive state governments shows that "it is not the existence of language and culture policies which determine whether a nationalism is ethnic or civic, but the uses made of language and culture, whether to build a civic nation or to practise ethnic exclusion."[52]

Circumstances have changed and other approaches have been used to explain contemporary nationalism, but familiar themes emerge. One Marxian analysis, for instance, reads nationalism as a product of relative deprivation in an already modern, industrialized environment.[53] It emphasizes the relevance of "material circumstances" to political mobilization, while acknowledging the importance of symbols in cementing national solidarity. Social negotiation is also important in shaping the strategies and interests of today's collectivities. In another reading, the nation can be seen as a conceptual tool manipulated by contemporary nationalist movements in order to legitimate their political project.[54] Such "neo-nationalisms" must be ready to adapt the way in which they articulate the link between the individual and the collective; "different ideological elements are mixed and mobilized: right/left; ethnic/civic; past/future; local/global; corporatist/neo-liberal; separatist/autonomist."[55] A further possible typology distinguishes civic, ethnocultural, and multicultural nationalisms, the last having recently emerged from the "unraveling" of the first two.[56]

Germany and France are often held up as archetypes of an ethnic nation based on bloodlines and a rights-based, civic nation respectively. Their respective citizenship laws are cited as evidence: Germany's legislation is founded on the principle of descent, or *jus sanguinis*, in determining state citizenship;[57] in France, citizenship was largely decoupled from markers of ethnic belonging, however, birth on French territory being enough to satisfy the requirements of *jus soli*.[58] Subsequent work has further refined this analysis.[59] France, as an imperial state, grappled with the inconsistencies of egalitarian republicanism and imperialism, with the hierarchies of belonging this entailed.[60]

Germany, although committed to a state built around the concept of the German *Volk*, always permitted naturalization based on more or less restrictive criteria.[61] With the fall of the Berlin Wall, West Germany in particular was confronted with the consequences of a policy which had upheld the principle of a single German nation despite the existence of two German states. East Germans who managed to make their way to the West German Federal Republic automatically enjoyed its citizenship. On German unification in October 1990, this provision supposedly made state and nation congruent once more.

The prevailing principle of German citizenship also included all people of German descent living east of the Iron Curtain, who came to Germany in great numbers as it crumbled and travel restrictions eased. These so-called *Aussiedler* had a right to residence and citizenship quite distinct from Germany's generous asylum provisions, as they were deemed German by virtue of their lineage. In 1996, however, German language tests were introduced.[62] As many spoke only the language of the Eastern bloc country in which they had been raised, this proved a significant hurdle. At the same time, second- or third-generation descendants of immigrant "guest workers" (*Gastarbeiter*), who came from Turkey, Yugoslavia, and several other Mediterranean states to fuel Germany's postwar "economic miracle," had only the option of taking the costly and discretionary road to citizenship through naturalization, despite having lived in Germany all their lives. The irony was not lost on governments keen to promote integration and social cohesion; a significant, though watered-down, reform of citizenship law eventually took place in 2000.[63] Thus the construction of the German nation was placed under scrutiny in the post-Cold War era, leading to some change in national self-understanding, at least in legal terms.

The hyphenated term "nation-state" indicates how closely the two concepts are linked, with the former providing legitimacy for the latter. By extension, citizenship, as the mark of official belonging to a state, is a legal expression of how the nation is defined and thus closely bound to it. A purely civic nation, then, would require no demonstrations of linguistic or cultural competence more redolent of ethnic belonging, such as the citizenship tests administered in the United Kingdom and Germany today. The most it could demand would be an oath to respect the rights and duties bestowed with citizenship, perhaps linked to a set period of residence and an absence of criminal convictions.[64] In practice, however, contemporary nation-states also tend to advocate some cultural homogeneity in the population through integration measures. Once avowedly multicultural states such as the Netherlands and the United Kingdom are now using citizenship and language tests to encourage immigrants to integrate (if not assimilate), as a response to fears of social fragmentation.[65] The effects of the Islamic fundamentalist terrorist threat are also making themselves felt in German citizenship tests.[66]

The French presidential election of 2007 featured nationalist rhetoric from both main candidates, not only to woo right-wing voters, but also to make national identity the subject of debate once more.[67] The socialist candidate Ségolène Royal encouraged voters to fly the French flag and sing the national anthem at her rallies, while the eventual winner, Nicolas Sarkozy, took a hard-line approach to issues of immigration and integration both as interior minister and presidential candidate.[68] This illustrates that nationalist rhetoric is alive and well in post-Cold War Europe. It continues to underpin government legitimacy at the state level, and permeates current debates surrounding immigration and citizenship.

The discourse of French and German nation-building and citizenship speaks for a view of the nation as percolating from the level of the elite to the masses through the medium of ideology. It is more than merely a top-down process, however. A.D. Smith has put forward the "ethno-symbolist" argument that nationalist movements draw on the pre-existing myths and symbols of an established ethnic group to facilitate the creation of a national consciousness, thereby grounding their political appeals on familiar identifiers.[69] This is not to suggest that post-Cold War nationalism, be it at state or sub-state level, necessarily rests on age-old foundations or "natural origins." Contemporary nationalism is not only flexible enough to adapt evidence of long-standing community links to the current political environment but also capable of manipulating and inventing traditions along the way. The Lega Nord's construction of Padanian nationalism in northern Italy is one extreme example of the latter.[70]

National divisions are not immutable but constructed. One need look no further than Europe's changing frontiers since 1990 to see that these are flexible; Germany, Estonia, Latvia, Czechoslovakia, and Yugoslavia, among others, have all been affected by conflicting interpretations of national identity and ideology. One need only recall the highly charged symbolism of historic Serb battlefields and churches in today's Kosovo to grasp the continuing significance of the primordialist versus modernist debate for post-Cold War nationalism, to the extent that nationalist ideologues continue to mobilize followers using appeals to primordial symbols. During the Bosnian conflict, the foreign media often colluded in presenting ethnic rivalries as "ancient" and "atavistic," suggesting that hatred was ingrained and ineluctable when in fact different ethnic groups had long lived together in peace.

"Hot" and "Banal" Nationalisms

"Hot" nationalism, which tends to be virulent, chauvinistic, and sometimes violent, can be contrasted with "banal" nationalism, understood as taken-for-granted markers of national loyalty which have been so oft-repeated as to become mundane.[71] Every citizen of a "nation state" construct is subject at the very least to the banal nationalism expressed in the symbolic markers of belonging to a "nation state": the limp flag (one being waved would be making an explicit statement), the emphasis of the media on "home" news, singing the national anthem at football matches, and the repeated use of the adjective "national" to describe affairs of state.[72] Examples from the Basque country and the Balkans demonstrate a range of manifestations of "hot" European nationalism in contrast to the more "banal" state-led nation-building discussed in the previous sections. Just as nationalism can be chauvinistic and exclusionary, so it can be defined more openly by offering a share in a common project. The former Czechoslovakia is interesting in that it combines a transition to democracy with a peaceful breakup into two new "nation-states."

It is a mistake automatically to associate "hot," or violent nationalism with atavistic ethnic loyalties and long-standing tensions. Such animosities can also be instigated for political ends where previously there was peaceful cohabitation. Yugoslavia was created after World War I from the ruins of the Ottoman and Austro-Hungarian empires. Following World War II, its communist incarnation under Tito moved towards a federal framework in order to ensure territorially based representation of ethnic diversity. By frequently rotating representatives and encouraging collective decision-making in the interests of Yugoslav unity, Tito actually sowed the seeds of its demise.[73] After his death in 1980, nobody had the authority to address rising frustration at the continuing economic disparities between the different republics. Political rhetoric began to shift from Yugoslav to ethnically based appeals.

Slobodan Milošević won a platform based on an articulation of Serb nationalism which, on the one hand, advocated a "greater Serbia" to include the ethnic Serb minority living in the incipient Croatian "nation-state" and, on the other, evoked historic events in order to assert rights to the territory of Kosovo as a Serb "homeland."[74] Ironically, his ethnic demands were linked to clearly demarcated administrative units established under the communist system. According to the 1981 census, one in seven marriages was interethnic and a small but rising minority identified themselves as Yugoslav rather than by an ethnic category.[75] By the early 1990s, however, as battle lines were being drawn, people were fleeing their erstwhile neighbors to become refugees and former classmates found themselves on opposing sides of what would become a series of bloody wars. In contrast to Czechoslovakia, Milošević would not countenance a breakup which would leave ethnic Serbs in Croat territory, pointing to the persecution of Serbs during World War II as justification. Neither would he accept a lack of control over Kosovo, replete with Serb nationalist symbolism.

In an ambitious typology of "ethnic cleansing," Michael Mann places its murderous and genocidal manifestations at the end of a spectrum of discrimination, which he calls "the dark side of democracy."[76] He argues that the prevalence of "ethnic cleansing" in the twentieth century is bound up with nationalism (or what he calls the politicization of ethnicity) as "an essential part of modern state-building. Only when people and state are mutually related within the sphere of a legitimate political order does the question arise as to which "people" is the legitimate owner of the state."[77] The reasons for an extreme response must be sought in the degree of economic, political, social, and cultural conflict in each case. Communism trumped nationalism within the USSR and its satellite states during the Cold War, although the two ideologies are not incompatible.[78] However, the Yugoslav case has shown that Soviet-era territorial units could provide the basis for demands formulated in ethnic nationalist terms, which would degenerate into an extreme policy of "purification." Yet the fate of the former Czechoslovakia demonstrates that national divorce can also be amicable in certain circumstances.

Although Czechoslovakia's constituent parts of Bohemia, Moravia, and Slovakia had all been under Austro-Hungarian imperial rule, the first two had been subject to strong German influence in the nineteenth century, whereas Slovakia had been faced with policies of Magyarization emanating from Budapest. A sense of cultural nationalism, including the development of a standardized orthography, had thus evolved along different lines in each.[79] With the creation of Czechoslovakia following World War I, Slovaks found themselves rubbing shoulders with the Czech "dominant *ethnie*" in politics and administration,[80] but their first president considered a united front against the threat of the "Other" to be a source of solidarity.[81] A common Czechoslovak identity proved difficult to foster, however, despite attempts at economic redistribution. The short-lived Slovak state under Nazi domination proved less divisive than in the Croat case and, despite the subsequent communist regime's lack of political legitimacy, Slovakia had largely caught up economically with the Czech lands by 1989.[82]

Slovak politicians wanted to protect this state of affairs as Cold War systems collapsed, and disagreements with their Czech counterparts over economic policy hardened into distrust. To everyone's surprise, talk of separation quickly became reality. The lack of territorial disputes or of fears for the safety of Czechs and Slovaks living in each other's territory ensured a remarkably smooth transition, without any kind of "cleansing"; "Today . . . with the breakup of the Soviet Union, Yugoslavia, and Czechoslovakia, the last of the region's avowedly multinational states have disappeared. Everywhere, political authority has been reconfigured along putatively national lines."[83]

The Basques, living on both sides of the Pyrenees in Spain's northwest and France's southwest, seem to offer strong evidence of ethnic particularities. The Basque language does not belong to the Indo-European family and their relatively isolated position long discouraged inter-ethnic marriage and miscegenation.[84] This alone, however, cannot account for Basque nationalism, especially as adherence to the Basque Nationalist Party (Partido Nacionalista Vasco – PNV) rose in the twentieth century as the number of Basque-speakers declined.[85] Important socioeconomic factors included the early industrialization of the Basque country in the late nineteenth century and the influx of migrant workers from other parts of Spain. Despite close economic links with the rest of the country, the PNV enjoyed the support of many keen to preserve their economic interests against what they deemed to be the Spanish "Other."

A second economic upswing in the 1960s took place within Franco's politically and culturally repressive regime, another important factor in mobilizing support behind the PNV and the newly formed Euskadi ta Azkatasuna (ETA) Party, whose name means freedom for the Basque country. An offshoot of the PNV, it offered a competing version of Basque nationalism with linguistic and socialist dimensions, but grew increasingly factionalized over how inclusive its definition of the Basque nation should be, particularly with reference to Spanish migrants. Despite important civic elements, it espoused a radical terrorist strategy for achieving its aims, waging a campaign which has dogged Basque and Spanish politics for decades.

Today, different strands of Basque nationalism still disagree over whether to work with the autonomy guaranteed by the Spanish constitution or to pursue complete independence (within the constraints on sovereignty represented by European integration and globalization). Their strategies have also diverged considerably. As the PNV, the SNP, and the Catalan CiU have shown, democracy and nationalism are not incompatible. Indeed, the people, or *demos*, can be equated with the civic nation in an ideal-type nation state based on the principle of popular sovereignty. However, some nationalist movements, and not only the narrowly ethnocultural variety, spurn electoral politics. Although progress towards peace is being made in the Basque country (and most spectacularly in Northern Ireland), ongoing ethnopolitical conflict in the Caucasus reminds us that "hot" nationalism continues to play a role on the European scene.

People's sense of national identity can be politicized in many different ways, or not at all. Nonetheless, individuals are likely to be exposed to forms of "banal" nationalism all the time. Voter choices are based on a host of reasons, including class loyalties, policy preferences, and protest. Any combination of economic, ethnic, and ideological reasons may underlie individual decisions to support nationalist parties, recalling the earlier definition of contemporary nationalism as an instinct, an interest, and an ideology.[86] Nationalist movements, in turn, often use "emotional-economic" rhetoric in an attempt to channel these potentially conflicting sentiments, with varying success. Nationalism may be more or less exclusionary, defining national belonging along more ethnic or civic lines. Its strategies may also be more or less extreme, espousing democratic or terrorist methods to further the nationalist cause.

This is exemplified in the case of the Basque country, where the PNV and ETA use very different means to pursue core nationalist goals. The PNV seeks to advance Basque autonomy through democratic elections. ETA, on the other hand, continued to advocate terrorist violence as a response to the policies of successive Spanish central governments after the end of the Cold War. Meanwhile, the brand of Serb nationalism propagated by Milošević played on images of ancestral battlefields to lay claim to the territory of Kosovo, translating an ideology of national purity into a murderous policy of "ethnic cleansing." What emerges from the discussion is that nationalism is an infinitely flexible, protean ideology which continues to play a central role in the politics of post-Cold War Europe. Nationalism can tap into a wealth of evocative myths, symbols, and community ties to add resonance to its appeals, and continues to do so in manifold ways across Europe today.

Conclusion

In post-Cold War Europe, many nationalist variants, whether state or sub-state, contain some element of "the ethnocultural nationalist concern with cultural regeneration and the civic nationalist concern with territorial autonomy."[87] Like their nineteenth-century predecessors, they have evolved in an environment where statehood and sovereignty continue to play a central role. Unlike them, however, they have to contend with the discourse of globalization and supranational integration. Some nationalist parties are open to shared sovereignty and the implications of globalization. Whether of the left or right, several support further European integration. The end of the Cold War removed one territorial and ideological dividing line from the European map. The pervasive influence of nationalist ideology, however, continues unabated across the continent. Nation-building remains the main source of legitimacy for established nation-states. Nationalism has also provided the ideological underpinnings for both peaceful and violent struggles to create new ones. Tellingly, the language of national belonging is shared by people across Europe as constitutive of identity and imagined community.

The cases discussed offer a glimpse of how differently the nation and nationalism can be articulated in distinct contexts. The binaries suggested in each section provide a basic framework within which to compare and contrast further nationalist movements. Beyond core ideological principles of prioritizing national autonomy and culture, the strategies and success of nationalist movements will depend on many factors, including economics, leadership, emotion, (perceived) injustice, oppression, conflict, and the nature of the "Other" with which they are confronted. The ideological cleavage of the Cold War may have melted away, but post-communist countries continue to grapple with the experience. National unification in Germany cannot erase 40 years of divergent development, for example, and the policies of the nationalist right in contemporary Poland include a reappraisal of citizens' activities during the communist era. All forms of nationalist politics in today's Europe draw on a recent or more distant past in their reading of the current climate, be it the injustices of the Soviet system or premodern myths. Yet nationalism's enduring mix of instinct, interest, and ideology help explain why it remains, in the post-Cold War era, resolutely up to date.

Notes

1   Brubaker, *Nationalism Reframed*, 7.
2   Kumar, "English and French National Identity: Comparisons and Contrasts," 424; Parekh, *Rethinking Multiculturalism*, 230; Modood, *Multiculturalism*.
3   On invented tradition, see Hobsbawm and Ranger, *The Invention of Tradition*.
4   Brubaker, *Citizenship and Nationhood in France and Germany*, 1.
5   Tilly, "Reflections on the History of European State-Making," 6.
6   Anderson, *Imagined Communities*, 6.
7   Connor, "A Nation Is a Nation, Is a State, Is an Ethnic Group, Is a . . . ," 36.
8   Brown, *Contemporary Nationalism*, 5.
9   Brown, op. cit., 6.
10 Anderson, cited in McCrone, *The Sociology of Nationalism*, 173.
11 Nairn, *Faces of Nationalism*, 222.
12 Brown, op. cit., 70.
13 Brubaker, *Nationalism Reframed*, 41.
14 Webb, *The Growth of Nationalism in Scotland*.
15 Levy, *Scottish Nationalism at the Crossroads*.
16 Anderson, *Imagined Communities*.
17 Brown, et al., *Politics and Society in Scotland*, 39.
18 Brown, et al., op. cit., 14.

19   Paterson, *The Autonomy of Modern Scotland*.
20   Keating, *Nations Against the State*, 93.
21   Keating, *Nations against the State*, 149.
22   Share, "Politics in Spain," 263.
23   Armstrong, "Postcommunism and Nationalism," 186.
24   Keating, *Nations against the State*, 147.
25   Mercadé, cited in Keating, *Nations against the State*, 155.
26   Freeden, "Is Nationalism a Distinct Ideology?" 748–765.
27   Keating, *Nations against the State*, 189; Keating, *Plurinational Democracy*.
28   Jáuregui, "National pride and the meaning of 'Europe'."
29   Geddes, *The European Union and British Politics*, 194.
30   Milward, *The European Rescue of the Nation State*.
31   Guibernau, "Globalization and the Nation-State," 244.
32   Ohmae, *The End of the Nation-State*.
33   Hirst and Thompson, *Globalisation in Question*.
34   Hay and Rosamond, "Globalization, European integration and the discursive construction of economic imperatives," 147–167.
35   Held, *Democracy and the Global Order*.
36   McCormick, "Liberalism, Nationalism and the Post-Sovereign State," 553–567; Keating, *Plurinational Democracy*.
37   Brown, *Contemporary Nationalism*, 105.
38   Guibernau, op. cit., 259.
39   Soysal, *Limits of Citizenship*.
40   Smith, *The Ethnic Origins of Nations*; Gellner, *Nations and Nationalism*; Gellner, *Nationalism*.
41   Van den Berghe, "A Socio-biological Perspective."
42   Hroch, *Social Preconditions of National Revival in Europe*; Smith, *The Ethnic Revival*, 90.
43   Gellner, *Thought and Change*; Gellner, *Encounters with Nationalism*.
44   Anderson, *Imagined Communities*.
45   Tilly, "Reflections on the History of European State-Making."
46   Breuilly, *Nationalism and the State*; Mann, *The Sources of Social Power*.
47   Weber, *Peasants into Frenchmen*.
48   Confino, *Nation as a Local Metaphor*.
49   Applegate, *Heimat*, 228.
50   Green, *The Politics of Exclusion*.
51   Wilder, *The French Imperial Nation-State*.
52   Keating, *Nations against the State*, 12.
53   Nairn, *The Break-up of Britain*.
54   Jenkins and Sofos, *Nation and Identity in Contemporary Europe*.
55   McCrone, *The Sociology of Nationalism*, 129.
56   Brown, op. cit.
57   Green, op. cit.
58   Brubaker, *Citizenship and Nationhood in France and Germany*.
59   Nathans, *The Politics of Citizenship in Germany*; Wilder, *The French Imperial Nation-State*.
60   Wilder, op. cit., 13.
61   Nathans, op. cit., 67.
62   McNamara, "21st Century Shibboleth," 360.
63   Green, op. cit., 121.
64   Kostakopoulou, "Why Naturalisation?" 85; Brubaker, *Nationalism Reframed*, 105.

65 Joppke, "Beyond National Models," 8.
66 Joppke,op. cit., 15.
67 "It's Sarko v Ségo."
68 Joppke, op. cit., 11; "Seconds Away, Round Two."
69 Smith, "The Origins of Nations," 151.
70 Giordano, "Italian Regionalism or 'Padanian' Nationalism," 445–471.
71 Billig, *Banal Nationalism*.
72 Billig, op. cit., 93.
73 Ferdinand, "Nationalism, Community and Democratic Transition in Czechoslovakia and Yugoslavia," 481.
74 Brubaker, *Nationalism Reframed*, 79.
75 Ferdinand, op. cit., 481.
76 Mann, "Explaining Murderous Ethnic Cleansing: The Macro-Level," 217.
77 Mann, op. cit.
78 Sutherland, "Conceptual Combat: Twentieth-century Vietnamese Nationalism," 334.
79 Maxwell, "Unintended Consequences."
80 Smith, *Nations and Nationalism in a Global Era*, 106.
81 Ferdinand, op. cit., 471.
82 Ferdinand, op. cit., 477.
83 Brubaker, *Nationalism Reframed*, 3.
84 Brown, op. cit., 71.
85 Brown, op. cit., 72.
86 Brown, op. cit., 5.
87 Brown, op. cit., 83.

Bibliography

Anderson, B., *Imagined Communities*, 2nd edition (London: Verso, 1991).

Applegate, C., *Heimat: A Nation of Provincials* (Berkeley, Los Angeles, and Oxford: University of California Press, 1990).

Armstrong, J., "Postcommunism and Nationalism," in M. Guibernau and J. Hutchinson (eds.), *Understanding Nationalism* (Cambridge: Blackwell, 2001).

Billig, M., *Banal Nationalism* (London: Sage, 1995).

Breuilly, J., *Nationalism and the State* (Manchester: Manchester University Press, 1993).

Brown, A., D. McCrone, and L. Paterson, *Politics and Society in Scotland* (Basingstoke: Macmillan, 1996).

Brown, D., *Contemporary Nationalism* (London and New York: Routledge, 2000).

Brubaker, R., *Citizenship and Nationhood in France and Germany* (Cambridge, MA: Harvard University Press, 1992).

Brubaker, R., *Nationalism Reframed* (Cambridge: Cambridge University Press, 1996).

Confino, A., *Nation as a Local Metaphor* (Chapel Hill and London: University of California Press, 1997).

Connor, W., "A Nation Is a Nation, Is a State, Is an Ethnic Group, is a . . . ," in J. Hutchinson and A.D. Smith (eds.), *Nationalism* (Oxford and New York: Oxford University Press, 1994).

Eley, G. and R. Suny, *Becoming National* (Oxford: Oxford University Press, 1996).

Ferdinand, P., "Nationalism, Community and Democratic Transition in Czechoslovakia and Yugoslavia," in D. Potter, G. Goldblatt, M. Kiloh, and P. Lewis (eds.), *Democratization* (Cambridge: Polity and Open University Press, 1996).

Freeden, M., "Is Nationalism a Distinct Ideology?" *Political Studies* 46, no. 4, 1998, 748–765.

Geddes, A., *The European Union and British Politics* (Basingstoke and New York: Palgrave, 2004).

Gellner, E., *Thought and Change* (London: Weidenfeld & Nicolson, 1964).

Gellner, E., *Nations and Nationalism* (Oxford: Blackwell, 1983).

Gellner, E., *Encounters with Nationalism* (Oxford: Blackwell, 1994).

Gellner, E., *Nationalism* (London: Weidenfeld & Nicolson, 1997).

Giordano, B., "Italian Regionalism or 'Padanian' Nationalism: The Political Project of the Lega Nord in Italian politics," *Political Geography* 19, no. 4, 2000, 445–471.

Green, S., *The Politics of Exclusion: Institutions and Immigration Policy in Contemporary Germany* (Manchester: Manchester University Press, 2004).

Guibernau, M., *Nations without State* (Cambridge: Polity, 1999).

Guibernau, M., "Globalization and the Nation-State," in M. Guibernau and J. Hutchinson (eds.), *Understanding Nationalism* (Oxford: Blackwell, 2001).

Hay, C. and B. Rosamond, "Globalization, European Integration and the Discursive Construction of Economic Imperatives," *Journal of European Public Policy* 9, no. 2, 2002, 147–167.

Held, D., *Democracy and the Global Order: From the Modern State to Cosmopolitan Governance* (Cambridge: Polity, 1995).

Hirst, P. and G. Thompson, *Globalisation in Question: The International Economy and the Possibilities of Governance*, 2nd edition (Cambridge: Polity, 1999).

Hobsbawm, E. and T. Ranger (eds.), *The Invention of Tradition* (Cambridge: Cambridge University Press, 1983).

Hroch, M., *Social Preconditions of National Revival in Europe* (Cambridge: Cambridge University Press, 1985).

"It's Sarko v. Ségo," *The Economist*, April 26, 2007, http://www.economist.com/opinion/displaystory.cfm?story_id=9079843 (accessed July 16, 2007).

Jáuregui, P., "National Pride and the Meaning of 'Europe': A Comparative Study of Britain and Spain," in D. Wright and S. Smith (eds.), *Whose Europe? The Turn towards Democracy* (Oxford: Blackwell, 1999).

Jenkins, B. and S. Sofos, *Nation and Identity in Contemporary Europe* (London and New York: Routledge, 1996).

Joppke, C., "Beyond National Models: Civic Integration Policies for Immigrants in Western Europe," *West European Politics* 30, no. 1, 2007, 1–22.

Keating, M., *Nations against the State: The New Politics of Nationalism in Quebec, Catalonia, and Scotland*, 2nd edition (London: Palgrave, 2001).

Keating, M., *Plurinational Democracy: Stateless Nations in a Post-sovereignty Era* (Oxford: Oxford University Press, 2001).

Kostakopoulou, D., "Why Naturalisation? Perspectives on European Politics and Society," *Regulation and Identity in the New Europe* 4, no. 1, 2003, 85–115.

Kumar, K., "English and French National Identity: Comparisons and Contrasts," *Nations and Nationalism* 12, no. 3, 2006, 413–433.

Levy, R., *Scottish Nationalism at the Crossroads* (Edinburgh: Scottish Academic Press, 1990).

McCormick, N., "Liberalism, Nationalism and the Post-sovereign State," *Political Studies* 44, 1996, 553–567.

McCrone, D., *The Sociology of Nationalism* (London: Routledge, 1998).

McNamara, T., "21st Century Shibboleth: Language Tests, Identity and Intergroup Conflict," *Language Policy* 4, no. 4, 2005, 351–370.

Mann, M., *The Sources of Social Power: The Rise of Classes and Nation States, 1760–1914* (Cambridge: Cambridge University Press, 1993).

Mann, M., "Explaining Murderous Ethnic Cleansing: The Macro-level," in M. Guibernau and J. Hutchinson (eds.), *Understanding Nationalism* (Oxford: Blackwell, 2001).

Maxwell, A., "Unintended Consequences: Language Politics and Slovak Nationalism," in W. Burszta, T. Kamusella, and S. Wojciechowski (eds.), *Nationalisms across the Globe*, vol. 1 (Poznan: School of Humanities and Journalism, 2005).

Milward, A., *The European Rescue of the Nation State* (London: Routledge, 1994).

Modood, T., *Multiculturalism* (Cambridge and Malden, MA: Polity Press, 2007).

Nairn, T., *The Break-up of Britain* (London: Verso, 1981).

Nairn, T., *Faces of Nationalism: Janus Revisited* (London: Verso, 1997).

Nathans, E., *The Politics of Citizenship in Germany: Ethnicity, Utility and Nationalism* (Oxford: Berg, 2004).

Ohmae, K., *The End of the Nation-State* (New York: Free Press, 1996).

Ozkirimli, U., *Theories of Nationalism* (London: Macmillan, 2000).

Parekh, B., *Rethinking Multiculturalism* (Basingstoke and London: Macmillan, 2000).

Paterson, L., *The Autonomy of Modern Scotland* (Edinburgh: Edinburgh University Press, 1994).

Schopflin, G., *Nations, Identity, Power* (New York: New York University Press, 2000).

"Seconds Away, Round Two," *The Economist*, April 26, 2007b, http://www.economist. com/opinion/displaystory.cfm?story_id=9079957 (accessed July 16, 2007).

Share, D., "Politics in Spain," in G. Almond, R. Dalton, G. Bingham Powell, and K. Strøm (eds.), *European Politics Today*, 3rd edition (New York: Pearson Longman, 2006).

Smith, A.D., *The Ethnic Revival* (Cambridge: Cambridge University Press, 1981).

Smith, A.D., *The Ethnic Origins of Nations* (Oxford: Blackwell, 1986).

Smith, A.D., "The Origins of Nations," in J. Hutchinson and A.D. Smith (eds.), *Nationalism* (Oxford and New York: Oxford University Press, 1994).

Smith, A.D., *Nations and Nationalism in a Global Era* (Cambridge: Polity and Blackwell, 1995).

Soysal, Y., *Limits of Citizenship: Migrants and Postnational Membership in Europe* (Chicago and London: University of Chicago Press, 1994).

Sutherland, C., "Conceptual Combat: Twentieth-Century Vietnamese Nationalism," in W. Burszta, T. Kamusella, and S. Wojciechowski (eds.), *Nationalisms across the Globe*, vol. 2 (Poznan: School of Humanities and Journalism, 2006).

Tilly, C., "Reflections on the History of European State-Making," in C. Tilly and G. Ardant (eds.), *The Formation of National States in Western Europe* (Princeton, NJ: Princeton University Press, 1975).

Van den Berghe, P., "A Socio-biological Perspective," in J. Hutchinson and A.D. Smith (eds.), *Nationalism* (Oxford and New York: Oxford University Press, 1994).

Webb, K., *The Growth of Nationalism in Scotland* (Glasgow: Molendinar, 1977).

Weber, E., *Peasants into Frenchmen: The Modernization of Rural France, 1870–1914* (London: Chatto & Windus, 1977).

Wilder, G., *The French Imperial Nation-State* (Chicago: University of Chicago Press, 2005).

Further Reading

A good overview of theories of nationalism can be found in U. Ozkirimli, *Theories of Nationalism* (London: Macmillan, 2000). However, it is also worth going back to some of the key texts which originally shaped the primordialism-versus-modernism debate, such as Ernest Gellner, *Thought and Change* (London: Weidenfeld & Nicolson, 1964); Ernest Gellner, *Nations and Nationalism* (Oxford: Blackwell, 1983); and A. D. Smith *The Ethnic Origins of Nations* (Oxford: Blackwell, 1986). Another hugely influential work is Anderson, *Imagined Communities*, 2nd edition (London: Verso, 1991). Although his empirical focus is Southeast Asia, his ideas can be applied to European cases.

Theoretical analyses of contemporary nationalism include M. Keating, *Plurinational Democracy: Stateless Nations in a Post-Sovereignty Era* (Oxford: Oxford University Press, 2001); and T. Nairn, *The Break-up of Britain* (London: Verso, 1981); with more wide-ranging essays to be found in T. Nairn, *Faces of Nationalism* (London: Verso, 1997). Another thought-provoking collection of essays is G. Eley and R. Suny *Becoming National* (Oxford: Oxford University Press, 1996).

A good means of getting to grips with the particularities of "neo-nationalism" is D. McCrone, *The Sociology of Nationalism* (London: Routledge, 1998), while case studies of specific European nationalisms can be found in Brown, *Contemporary Nationalism* (London: Routledge, 2000); M. Guibernau, *Nations without States* (Cambridge: Polity, 1999); and M. Keating *Nations against the State* (London: Palgrave, 2001). Insights into how nationalism is used on a daily basis to boost state legitimacy can be found in M. Billig, *Banal Nationalism* (London: Sage, 1995), while G. Schopflin, *Nations, Identity, Power* (New York: New York University Press, 2000; and R. Brubaker, *Nationalism Reframed* (Cambridge: Cambridge University Press, 1996) discuss this and other issues with specific reference to central and eastern Europe.

CHAPTER NINETEEN

The Participatory Revolution: New Social Movements and Civil Society

INGOLFUR BLÜHDORN

In the age of globalization the experiences and hopes of European citizens regarding the scope for democratic participation and the role of civil society are highly diverse. Across Europe, liberal democracy is recognized and valued as a norm for political systems. Yet the promises implicit in the ideal of democracy often remain unfulfilled. While in the formerly communist countries of eastern Europe a stable democratic culture is only gradually evolving, the ever-increasing extent to which the life of European citizens is determined by actors and developments at the transnational or even global level draws attention to the fact that, beyond the nation state, satisfactory structures of democratic governance have not yet been established. Perceived democratic deficits, i.e. the discrepancy between normative ideals of democratic self-determination and the factually experienced lack of control over key conditions shaping everyday life, are a continuous source of political mobilization at the grass roots of European societies.

Since the 1960s, in particular, social movements have been struggling for access to the centers of power and for direct political influence. Distrust in established elites, dissatisfaction with existing political institutions, and growing confidence in the capabilities of the increasingly educated citizenry have given rise to ever newer waves of mobilization and fueled a general shift of preference from representative democracy to more direct forms of participation. The transformation of democratic systems and political cultures across western Europe may legitimately be described as a participatory revolution in which traditional forms of political involvement have been supplemented by a host of new forms of political articulation. Since the 1990s, the term may, *mutatis mutandis*, also be applied to eastern Europe. The normalization of often informal and unconventional political participation at the grass roots of society has prompted sociologists to describe contemporary European democracies as *social movement societies*.[1] Curiously, however, there is, at the same time, also talk of increasing political apathy, democratic sclerosis, and even of the *end of politics*.[2]

Across Europe electoral turnout at democratic elections, party membership, and other traditional forms of political participation have gradually declined over the past

A Companion to Europe since 1945, First Edition. Edited by Klaus Larres.
© 2014 John Wiley & Sons, Ltd. Published 2014 by John Wiley & Sons, Ltd.

few decades. Given the rise of alternative ways of political expression, it would be simplistic to interpret these developments as evidence that democratic systems are experiencing a severe crisis. But beyond the anticipated deepening of democracy, the participatory revolution has, indeed, also given rise to unexpected negative side effects; for example, the widening range of political actors and articulated interests has much increased the complexity of the political process. This not only triggers politically exploitable desires for new simplicity and simplification, but as ever more diverse sectional interests are pushing for direct influence and representation, democratic compromise and agreement on a genuinely common good are becoming increasingly difficult to achieve.

Furthermore, the resources required to make practical use of new participatory opportunities are unevenly distributed across the different sections of society, which gives rise to new forms of political inequality, disempowerment, and feelings of exclusion. Indeed, higher demands for political inclusiveness, transparency, and accountability render the political process more costly while reducing the pace and flexibility of decision-making – which in turn breeds suspicions that politicians are unresponsive, incompetent, and inefficient. This list of unforeseen problems could easily be extended.

Thus the participatory revolution has indeed expanded political opportunities in European democracies, but it has also given rise to new problems. It has inflated public expectations and augmented the potential for political disappointment and disaffection. In recent years, political elites and academic observers have become increasingly concerned about widespread disengagement and cynicism. Democratic reform, civic re-engagement, and the enhancement of civil society have become a priority issue. Hence citizens in many European countries have experienced a curious reversal of the direction of the democratic struggle: while historically the participatory revolution has been a bottom-up process, carried forth, in particular, by underprivileged social groups striving to wrench some power from established elites, European governments have more recently been trying to activate their somewhat ambivalent citizenry in a top-down fashion. Understandably, this new agenda of civic self-responsibility, empowerment, and inclusion raises suspicions about the true underlying motives.

The emancipatory social movements which since the 1960s have challenged established hierarchies and demanded democratic self-determination for the increasingly self-confident and critical citizenry are the focus of this chapter. While the democratic revolutions in eastern Europe are briefly touched upon, the main emphasis is on the new social movements in western Europe and on their attempts to turn into *genuinely* democratic societies what they perceived as only *formally* democratic systems. It ought to be noted that over the past 60 years some European countries have also experienced social movements which did not pursue democratic and participatory agendas oriented towards the establishment of an inclusionary civil society: nationalist, separatist, religious, and other sectarian movements are not covered in this chapter. The first section offers some general observations about the nature and action repertoire of social movements as political actors. This is followed by an attempt to describe the participatory revolution since the 1960s as successive waves of social movement mobilization. The third section focuses more closely on specific social movement issues and their varied significance in different European countries. A brief overview of major analytical approaches that have been developed by social movement researchers is provided in the fourth section. The chapter concludes by trying to assess the success and failure of the participatory revolution. This entails, *inter alia*, further discussion of the thesis that in recent years the original optimistic confidence in the democratic capacities of civil society has been dampened by something that might be described as postdemocratic disillusionment about participatory politics.

Social Movements and Repertoires of Collective Action

In many respects, the participatory revolution since the 1960s continued the agenda of earlier democratic movements. Its primary agents, the new social movements, are commonly defined as mobilized networks of individuals, groups, and organizations which are integrated by a common concern or shared political vision and engage in sustained collective action relying on unconventional political means. While some social movement have focused on very narrowly defined strategic goals, others were more strongly oriented towards the expression of marginalized social identities. These different types of social movements are united in their attempt to improve the representativeness and responsiveness of governments by providing citizens with more direct access to and control over processes of political decision-making. Their project of democratization entails increasing the thematic scope, expanding the franchise, and deepening the authenticity of political participation. Improving the transparency of political processes and making political elites more accountable to the electorate are key strategies for reducing the distance between those who exercise political power and those who are affected by their decisions. Social movements are distinct from other political actors in that they are fluid entities with no formal membership, but decentralized structures, weak internal hierarchies, and limited functional differentiation. They foster political communication and cooperation across traditional social cleavages and established ideological or geographical division lines. They redefine the political space by redrawing the boundaries between the public and the private spheres.[3]

The most common form of action taken by social movements across Europe has been collective protest. The term describes a variety of nonconventional forms of political disruption, persuasion, or coercion. Once the social movements became institutionalized and had established social movement organizations (SMOs), other forms of activity gained in significance. But in the early phases of a movement's development, in particular, protest is the main form of action, not least because in contrast to political parties and lobbying groups, social movements have no other form of influencing political decision-makers. The logic of originality and provocation, the logic of mass mobilization, and the logic of inflicting material damage or disadvantage are their main weapons.[4]

Protest action, which is often highly symbolic, aims to disrupt the established order of things. In some instances it is on the margins of legality or is straightforwardly illegal. At the more moderate end, the social movements' repertoire of collective action includes, for example, information campaigns, the signing of petitions,

demonstration rallies, public meetings, sit-ins, concerts, theater or dance performances, vigils, torchlight processions, human chains, etc. More radical ways in which
social movements have tried to exert political influence are strikes, litigation, picket-
ing, blockades, product boycotts, hunger strikes, and a wide range of forms of civil
disobedience. Openly confrontational strategies include actions such as occupations
of embassies; smokestacks or bridges; withholding rent or tax; acts of sabotage; blocking access to military bases; obstructing construction work at road projects, airports,
nuclear power stations, or similar projects; and physical attacks on property and
people.

In their search for innovative and creative forms of political articulation, social
movements across Europe have increasingly learnt to use the media and modern
communication technologies. Dramatic protest events have been staged specifically
for the media, thus enabling relatively small groups of activists to reach mass
audiences for their often highly symbolic protests. Computer technology, the
Internet, and cellular phones have revolutionized strategies of mobilization and
campaigning, accelerating the distribution of information and facilitating the
constitution of virtual as well as physical activist networks from the local to the
global level.[5]

The social movements' unorthodox forms of political participation have often
presented a challenge to the authorities, catching them unprepared. Although social
movements in Europe have overwhelmingly condemned physical violence, radical
currents as well as inadequate responses by politicians and police forces have sometimes led to an escalation of confrontations, culminating in violent clashes between
demonstrators and the security forces. Violent protest action, in particular, has
brought some social movements into disrepute. It challenges the state's monopoly
on the legitimate use of force and has raised concerns about social movements representing a threat to the democratic system and the rule of law. In the sense that
social movements lack confidence in the established institutions and insist on direct
participation and action, they have indeed always implied a challenge to established
forms of representative democracy. Yet, contrary to concerns that their activism may
spell political chaos and anarchy, social movements in European countries have almost
always perceived themselves as a constructive challenge: with the exception of some
right-wing as well as left-wing extremist movements, they have been inspired by the
ethos of pursuing the further democratization of democracy and the full realization
of the democratic promise.

Waves of Mobilization

The participatory revolution since the 1960s has evolved in waves of social movement
mobilization. In a strongly simplifying way, and neglecting protests that remained
restricted to individual countries, five major waves of mobilization may be distinguished. The specific issues raised in each phase, and the way in which different
movements blended into one another, will receive closer attention at a later stage.
For the moment the emphasis is primarily on identifying the main periods of movement activism which, in each case, were separated by quieter periods of restabilization
and reform.

1   In the 1960s a youth movement, carried primarily by university students, initiated a cultural revolution that targeted the political and social arrangements which had been established in the immediate postwar era. Protests against inappropriate conditions at the rapidly expanding universities widened into emancipative protests against restrictive social norms and authoritarian structures of government. Traditional state-centered politics had emphasized law and order, economic growth, and the social distribution of material wealth. It had tended to regard citizens as immature, incompetent, and unwilling to play an active role in politics. Against this background, the student movement of the 1960s demanded a new politics that would abandon the reductionist emphasis on economic and political stability, involve new political actors, and adopt decentralized policy approaches. Contrary to its American counterpart, the European student movement was intellectually largely based on Marxist analysis and conceived of itself as the revolutionary subject of the class struggle. Cuba's Fidel Castro, the Argentinean revolutionary Che Guevara, Mao Zedong's Cultural Revolution in China, Ho Chi Minh's resistance in North Vietnam, and the Czechoslovakian reform communist Alexander Dubček were major sources of inspiration. The student protests peaked in 1968–1969 and then rapidly declined.

2   The mid-1970s saw the adoption of the students' repertoire of collective action and emancipative goals by much wider sections of European societies. A clearly post-Marxist wave of citizens' initiative groups shifted the emphasis to environmental issues, gender issues, social justice, and Third World poverty. Growing sections of an increasingly politicized public regarded the Western model of consumer capitalism as exploitative and unsustainable, not least because it relied on new mega-technologies (such as nuclear technology) bearing unmanageable and unacceptable risks. The demand for more participation and better representation blended into the desire for a radically different form of society. Mobilized citizens pioneered alternative lifestyles. The earlier preference for provocative transgressions of established social norms was superseded by constructive attempts to make political processes more accessible and reshape socioeconomic conditions. Self-transformation (rather than revolution) now appeared as the key to comprehensive societal change. The political vision was a post-ideological civil society that could provide comprehensive quality of life instead of a numbing mass consumption. A new sense of civic responsibility and self-restriction counterbalanced the older emphasis on emancipation and liberation. It reflected a new awareness of moral, social, and ecological limits to quantitative growth and technological feasibility.

3   In the early 1980s the nuclear arms race between the Cold War superpowers and increasing concerns about accelerating environmental degradation brought a sense of unprecedented urgency to the European protest movements. The uncontrollable dynamics of a depersonalized techno-economic system seemed to be pushing European risk societies[6] unremittingly into environmental catastrophes and nuclear apocalypse which would threaten the survival of the entire human species. Radical democratization appeared as the only way of breaking the irrational and eventually lethal logic of this system. Civil society was idealized as the public political sphere for the rational and democratic negotiation of the conditions of

human survival, of the kind of society that is worth living in, and of the path of modernization that ought to be pursued. The new social movements' diverse range of concerns merged into something resembling a new political ideology which found its expression in the foundation of national green parties across western Europe.

4   In the second half of the 1980s the epicenter of the participatory revolution and the struggle for civil society shifted to central and eastern Europe. While protest activity in Western countries somewhat declined, the civil rights movements in eastern Europe rapidly gained momentum. Especially after Soviet president Michael Gorbachev had started his politics of perestroika and glasnost, dissident intellectuals intensified their efforts to develop networks of oppositional forces.[7] In Poland the Catholic church had provided a framework for the limited development of civil society structures, and from 1980 the workers' union Solidarity became the center of opposition to the regime. In the German Democratic Republic, environmental groups and a small peace movement evolving under the auspices of the church were the germ cells of collective action. In Hungary opposition against the proposed construction of a dam on the river Danube in the mid-1980s acted as a catalyst for the formation of protest networks. In Czechoslovakia a small civil and human rights movement had existed since the second half of the 1970s, but the strongly repressive Communist Party had not allowed the movement to expand. In 1989 and 1990 the gradual rise of oppositional movements culminated in the mass demonstrations in Leipzig, Prague, Bucharest, and elsewhere which contributed significantly to the collapse of the communist regimes. Yet following the "velvet revolutions" in the central eastern European countries their civil rights movements quickly disintegrated.

5   After the victory of liberal democracy and consumer capitalism across Europe, the social movement sector went through a process of deideologization, differentiation, and institutionalization. Comprehensive alternatives to the established socioeconomic order became ever more difficult to imagine, yet the struggle for the further democratization of European democracies continued. In the diverse and fragmented protest landscape of European social movement societies, three major strands of protest-movement activity deserve particular attention: neo-nationalist and xenophobic right-wing movements; new direct-action movements focusing primarily on environment-related issues; and antiglobalization movements fighting the neo-colonialist agenda of international corporations, neo-liberal governments, and institutions such as the International Monetary Fund and the World Trade Organization.

The right-wing movements, in many cases materializing primarily as electoral move-ments, have tended to mobilize social groups feeling disadvantaged by processes of modernization in the new climate of global economic competitiveness. Accelerated innovation and hypercomplexity generate feelings of uncertainty and anxiety, which in turn increase the responsiveness to populist simplifications and promises of security offered by right-wing movements. While their demands sometimes seem to echo the leftist critique of established political elites, they do not subscribe to the liberal values and democratic agenda that have powered the participatory revolution.[8] Radical direct-action groups have sprung up not least in response to the mainstreaming and cooptation of green parties and the large social movement organizations. They have lost confidence that the structures of representative democracy will ever give due consideration to social movement concerns and regard the incalculable ecological and social consequences of certain technological and infrastructural innovations as threats sufficiently serious to warrant direct intervention.[9] Antiglobalization movements, finally, which are also referred to as global justice movements or by the French term *autre-mondialisme* ("other-worldism" – another world is possible), are concerned that the increasing power of global corporations might spell the end of democratic politics and of cultural and ecological diversity. They regard ever increasing social inequality, polarization, and conflict as the inevitable consequence of the neo-liberal agenda. Opposition to the wrong kind of globalization is integrating a broad spectrum of social movement actors and networks into an emergent global movement.[10]

Thus dissatisfaction with established political elites and with the performance of the institutions of representative government has been the mobilizing force behind consecutive waves of social movement activity. Spreading in concentric circles, the struggle for more direct participation and more authentic representation engaged ever larger sections of European societies. In certain periods and for some movement strands, the participatory revolution seemed to imply no less than radical system change. Yet emancipation from self-serving authorities and the achievement of genuine democratic self-determination have been the common denominator of most European social movements throughout the second half of the twentieth century. Table 19.1 (pp. 414–415) aims to provide a schematic overview of the waves of mobilization in Europe since the 1960s. In certain respects the table anticipates aspects which will be discussed in the next section. Inevitably, any such periodization and the criteria used to distinguish different phases are reductionist attempts to capture the complexity and diversity of the social movement sector. It is useful to keep in mind that they are simplifications which neglect considerable differences in national constellations and developments. They suggest the existence of clearly distinguishable waves where it is equally plausible to emphasize significant overlaps, incremental shifts, and lines of continuity.

Movement Strands and Protest Issues

The vast array of issues that European social movements have politicized in the course of their participatory revolution is commonly organized into major thematic strands such as anti-authoritarian movements, the peace movement, the environmental movement, the international solidarity movement, the women's and gender movement, and so forth. In different European countries, these thematic strands have had varied significance, emphases, and ideological orientations. When talking about such major strands of social movement activity it needs to be kept in mind, firstly, that not all protest issues can easily be assigned to one of them. Secondly, each of these broad strands of mobilization comprises a diversity of different

Table 19.1 Waves of social movement mobilization in the participatory revolution since the 1960s

	1960s	1970s	1980s		Since 1990s		
	Student movement	Citizens' initiatives	New social movements (western Europe)	Civil rights movements (eastern Europe)	Right-wing movements	Direct-action movements	Anti-globalization movements
Dominant understanding of *participation*	Emancipation from established authorities and rigid social norms	Reshaping local communities and societal infrastructure	Negotiation of common good, deliberation on objectives and path of societal progress	Emancipation from authoritarian state, civil liberties, freedom of expression	Direct intervention because state fails to act	Direct intervention because representative democracy is structurally incapable	Civil society against corporate power, transparency and accountability of corporations and politics
General concerns	Authentic life, self-development, cultural identity, social equality	Quality of life, social justice, environmental integrity	Human survival, global peace, environmental integrity	Lack of civil rights and liberties	*Überfremdung*, competition for jobs, benefits, and social opportunities	Social and ecological blindness of techno-economic system	Neo-imperialism, neo-colonialism, end of democracy, end of politics
Specific issues	Universities, repressive social morality, exclusive political structures, sexual liberation, fascist past, Vietnam War	Gender, environment, finite resources, nuclear energy, social opportunities	Environment, nuclear armament, peace, gender, social justice, Third World poverty	Civil rights, environment, freedom of mobility	Asylum-seekers, economic migrants, multiculturalism	Roads and transport, environmental and bio-technology, nuclear installations, animal rights	Cultural and ecological diversity, fair trade, global social justice, global democracy

Main enemy	Capitalist class, authoritarian state, established moral authorities	Bureaucratic institutions, cartel of productivism and economic growth	Depersonalized systemic forces, the machine, high-tech and large-scale technologies	Communist Party, authoritarian state and its agents	Foreigners, ethnic and cultural minorities	Research laboratories, scientific elites, big firms, big government	Global corporations, neo-liberal governments WTO, IMF, World Bank
Main objective	Cultural–political revolution, post-capitalism	More participation, democratization, social equality	Radical system change for rehumanization, revaluation of life world vis-à-vis system	Overthrow of communist system	Prioritize nationals, reduce number of foreigners and asylum-seekers	System change, self-expression	Reregulation, relocalization, grass roots democracy
Ideological orientation	Marxist, socialist, anti-authoritarian	Social democratic, left–libertarian	Left–libertarian, anticapitalist, feminist, ecologist	Anti-communist, liberal	Nationalist, xenophobic, neo-fascist, populist	Leftist radical	Leftist radical, neo-Marxist
Main strategy	Provocative, disruptive	Constructive	Demonstrative, confrontational	Underground capacity building, demonstrative	Provocative, direct action	Direct action	Demonstrative, confrontational

and often even competing currents. Thirdly, these different thematic strands have always been closely connected to each other in discursive, strategic, and ideological coalitions. Just as the distinction of consecutive waves of mobilization will always remain artificial, the variety of thematic strands cannot really be seen as separate entities.

Already the student movement of the 1960s combined a number of very diverse concerns. In Italy, France, and Germany, which were the countries where the student protests turned most violent, inappropriate conditions at the expanding but underresourced universities were the immediate trigger, yet much more wide-ranging issues were implicit. The hierarchical structures of the universities, and the aging professors who presided over a curriculum that students perceived as irrelevant, symbolized the authoritarian and repressive structures that dominated the respective societies at large. In many European countries institutional reform had not kept pace with socioeconomic progress. The achieved levels of economic prosperity implied promises of self-fulfillment which were in stark contrast with the social reality of ongoing poverty, inequality, and political exclusion. Italy and Germany, in particular, had not appropriately come to terms with their fascist past, and although formally democratic structures were in place a genuinely democratic culture had not yet taken root. In France, opposition to the Algerian war and General de Gaulle's conservative and restrictive domestic policy agenda were a major motor of mobilization. In all three countries the Catholic church had a firm grip on social values and private morality. The heavy-handed approach the respective police forces took to incidents of social unrest only aggravated the experience of repression.

In accordance with the psychoanalytical-cum-sociological analyses of Sigmund Freud, Wilhelm Reich, and Herbert Marcuse, the revolting students interpreted social and political repression as the immediate consequence of sexual repression. For this reason, sexual liberation and gender equality were regarded as necessary preconditions for societal liberation from authoritarian structures and for the establishment of a genuinely democratic culture. The writings of Antonio Gramsci in Italy, of the Frankfurt school in Germany, and of Jean-Paul Sartre in France led to a strong resurgence of neo-Marxist thinking. In Britain, in contrast, the influence of Marxist thinking and the impact of intellectually driven radical protest was much more limited. Prior to 1968–1969 Britain experienced very few student protests. But in Britain, too, the 1960s were a decade of increasing student politicization, primarily through the Campaign for Nuclear Disarmament (CND), which had been established in the late 1950s. In the mid-1960s the Vietnam Solidarity Campaign became the center of student politics in the UK. Indeed protest against the Vietnam War was a theme that was shared by student movements across Europe and in the US.[11]

Environmental issues came to the fore towards the end of the 1960s, not least in response to rapid industrial development and the chemical revolution. The European Economic Community declared 1970 European Year of the Environment, thereby officially acknowledging the state of the natural environment as an important political concern. Yet the established economic and political institutions were slow to address the new environmental imperatives. Hence the struggle for environmental quality and integrity became a core dimension in the social movements' bottom-up politics.

Friends of the Earth, founded in the US in 1969 and in Britain the following year, became the first of a new type of radical social movement organization which soon emerged in many European countries.[12] In 1972, the UN Conference on Development and Environment in Stockholm put further emphasis on the relationship between economy and ecology. The Club of Rome's report on the *Limits to Growth* demonstrated that the further expansion of living standards and welfare systems, rather than continuing ad infinitum, would be limited by finite natural resources.[13] When in 1973 the oil-producing countries of the Middle East reduced their crude oil exports to the Western industrialized world, the dependence of European countries on natural resources became painfully visible: severe economic slowdown, power cuts, driving bans, and in some countries a shortening of the working week seemed to provide evidence that the social movements were right in pushing for major socioeconomic change. Hoping to break the institutionalized logic of unlimited growth and expansion before irreparable damage to the environment occurred, the environmental activists and social movement organizations gathered expertise and sought to expand their opportunities to directly influence environment-related policy decisions as well as their implementation. For the internationalization and eventually globalization of environmental movements, the UN Brundtland Report (1987) on sustainable development and the 1992 UN Earth Summit in Rio de Janeiro were further milestones.[14]

A specific issue that, since the 1970s, has had an unrivaled effect on social movement mobilization is that of nuclear energy. Following the oil crisis of 1973–1974, European governments made concerted efforts to expand their capacities for nuclear energy. This necessitated the construction of dozens of new power plants as well as appropriate reprocessing and final storage facilities for large quantities of nuclear waste. In France, Germany, the Netherlands, Sweden, Austria, Italy, Switzerland, and elsewhere opposition to this policy became a focal point of social movement politics, firstly because the nuclear energy program reconfirmed the dubious logic of unlimited economic growth and material consumption, and secondly because it underpinned this logic with a kind of technology that implied incalculable risks to society and the natural environment.[15]

Anticipating today's concerns about terrorist attacks on nuclear facilities, German antinuclear activists, in particular, warned that the safe operation of nuclear technology would necessitate comprehensive, centralized security measures which would lead directly into the semi-fascist surveillance state. While this particular argument had less purchase elsewhere, antinuclear activists across Europe were deeply concerned that nuclear technology rendered the public dependent on scientific experts, that it undermined citizens' rights and capabilities of democratic control, and that it exposed them to the secrecy of governments and the nuclear industry. These concerns were confirmed after the explosion of the nuclear reactor in Chernobyl (Ukraine) in 1986. But already, at the turn to the 1980s, the phasing-out of nuclear energy became one of the key demands of the emerging green parties which, across Europe, represented a new stage in the struggle for grassroots participation and the comprehensive democratization of European risk societies.[16]

As the reprocessing of nuclear waste provides access to plutonium that can be used for the production of nuclear weapons, the issue of nuclear energy was also important for the peace movement. In the early 1980s, mass protests and direct obstruction of weapon deployment policies were essential tools for stopping what peace activists saw as the nonsensical dynamics of the Cold War and bringing irresponsible world leaders back under democratic control. The main trigger for large-scale peace protests across Europe was NATO's decision in December 1979 to modernize its medium-range nuclear weapons by deploying 572 Cruise and Pershing II missiles in Germany, Italy, Belgium, the Netherlands, and the UK. In response to this decision, the tradition of Easter marches was resumed, which dated back to the late 1950s and early 1960s, when peace marches to Trafalgar Square in London had drawn significant support. In Germany, too, Easter marches to military sites had, throughout the 1960s, mobilized increasing numbers of peace activists. In the early 1980s, peace rallies in Brussels, London, Bonn, Rome, and other major cities mobilized hundreds of thousands of peace protesters. In Britain, a group of women set up the first peace camp at the Greenham Common Air Base near Newbury, Berkshire, in 1981. Following their example, a host of similar camps were set up across Europe. Their residents attempted to disrupt and obstruct construction work for the stationing of nuclear missiles, cutting down fences or blockading the gates of military bases.

The peace movement peaked in October 1983 when more than 3 million people demonstrated in European cities. For the German Green Party, which at the time was the first social movement party in Europe to enter a national parliament, the peace movement had been a crucial source of mobilization. In Italy, which in the late 1970s had been characterized by violent escalation, extremist tactics, and hard-line policing,[17] the peace movement of the 1980s marked a break with the tradition of violent strategies. In France, which was itself in possession of nuclear weapons, and in Switzerland, which had adopted a strategy of neutrality, the NATO missiles raised much less concern. When it had failed to prevent the stationing of the Cruise and Pershing missiles, the European peace movement largely collapsed. Yet the belief that the application of common sense and strict democratic control of political, economic, or military elites by the grass roots of society would help to prevent military conflict and violence remained unshaken. The Gulf War of 1991, Jacques Chirac's 1995 announcement that France would launch a new series of nuclear tests in the Pacific, and the war in Iraq in 2003 provided powerful evidence that the European peace movement has a lasting ability to mobilize mass protests.

Even this brief and very selective account of social movement issues and their varying significance in different European countries demonstrates how the seemingly separate thematic strands of grassroots politics have always been closely connected to each other, and how throughout decades of movement activity more direct political participation and better democratic representation have been regarded as key to the solution of ever new categories of societal problems. In 1969, at rather early stage of the participatory revolution, the then German federal chancellor Willy Brandt promised to "dare more democracy," implicitly reminding citizens that there are significant risks and responsibilities inherent in transferring political power from societal elites to the wider citizenry. Across Europe, the social movements have consistently insisted that civil society has acquired the maturity and capability to bear these responsibilities. In no other European country was the social movement sector as diverse and well developed as in Germany. Up to the present the German social movement organizations are stronger than many of their European counterparts, and the German greens have so far remained the most successful green party in Europe. In Britain, in contrast, social movements have, until very recently,[18] remained relatively weak, not least because the British political system has been more open to consultation with, and accommodation of, interest and lobbying groups.

Social Movement Research and Social Movement Theories

As social movements and direct interventions by mobilized citizens in the political process became a standard feature in European societies, academic research into new forms of political participation quickly developed into a specific field of sociological enquiry and political science.[19] The conservative–elitist as well as the Marxist tradition had regarded the masses in industrial society as passive, immature, politically uninterested, and lacking the intellectual and organizatory skills for effective political action. Mass mobilization under fascism, for example, had been investigated primarily as a phenomenon of mass psychology. By the 1960s, however, the increasingly self-confident democratic grass roots of society had clearly begun to emancipate themselves from their dependence on political elites. The political do-it-yourself culture[20] of the emerging social movement society necessitated an analysis in terms of collective action rather than collective behavior.[21] Marxist, post-structuralist, and functionalist social theory have generated very different interpretations of the social movement phenomenon. More empirically oriented social science has developed approaches such as *resource mobilization* theory, the analysis of *political opportunity structures*, *framing* theory, and the *new social movements* approach. Together, social theorists, political sociologists, and political scientists have tried to reach beyond the simple observation that social movements across Europe are struggling for more direct political participation and better democratic representation. They have dealt with questions such as: why did the new social movements emerge at that particular juncture in European history? Why did they develop differently in different countries? How do they recruit and maintain public support, and who are their supporters? What political impact do they have? What is the relationship between new social movements and the established political institutions?

Throughout the 1970s and into the 1980s, much attention was devoted to distinguishing new social movements from the older labor movements. European social theorists in the Marxist tradition believed that the new social movements had to be interpreted, in the Marxist sense, as the historical subject of societal progress. They accepted that with the transition from industrial to postindustrial society,[22] with the relative pacification of the social question through the welfare state, and with the structural transformation of the working class, orthodox Marxist analysis had become outdated. Nevertheless, from a post-Marxist perspective, the social movements since the 1960s represented a new subject for the old struggle for freedom, equality, and solidarity. Empirical research established that the new social movements recruited their support primarily from young, well-educated, middle-class cohorts who were either still in (higher) education or working as public-sector employees, teachers, journalists, social workers, doctors, or artists, or in similar occupations. In the sense that this new postindustrial service intelligentsia could be regarded as a new social class, it seemed possible to conceptualize social movement politics as the postindustrial extension of the Marxist class struggle.[23]

Major arguments against the conceptualization of new social movement politics in socioeconomic terms have been, firstly, that the social movements since the 1960s were not primarily concerned with economic issues, and, secondly, that the the so-called new middle class has been increasingly diverse. The specific emphasis of the social movements on noneconomic issues, their politicization of formerly unpolitical questions, their provocative transgression of established cultural norms, and their deliberate transition from the "old politics" of material production and distribution towards a "new politics" of multidimensional identity clearly pointed beyond Marxist approaches. Furthermore, the rapid differentiation of the service sector implied that patterns of work, economic conditions, social opportunities, and personal lifestyles became too diverse to warrant talk of a cohesive new middle class with a broadly common horizon of experience and interests. Shifting the emphasis to socio-cultural aspects, Ronald Inglehart therefore developed his theory of post-materialism which suggests that for the postwar generations, who had grown up in conditions of unprecedented material wealth and security, cultural autonomy and political self-determination had become the new priority. Under conditions of material saturation, Inglehart argued, the marginal utility of further economic growth triggered a shift of emphasis towards postmaterial issues such as environmental quality, democratic participation, and cultural self-expression. Inglehart's sociocultural explanation of the post-1960s protest movements provided the basis for post-structuralist analyses which put the emphasis on the contestation of cultural norms, the social construction of individual and collective identities, and practical experiments pioneering alternative life styles.[24]

In contrast to (post-)Marxist and post-structuralist approaches, functionalist social theorists have interpreted the new social movements as something like the "immune system" of advanced modern societies triggered into action by problems emerging from the ever increasing complexity of modern societies. According to their analysis, social movements emerge in response to processes of functional differentiation.[25] As functionally differentiated societies are polycentric and lose the capability of strategically coordinating their overall development, their ongoing evolution generates negative side effects which the economy, politics, the legal system, or any of the other function systems cannot easily address. Social movements highlight and politicize these side effects, and by trying to adopt an integrating overall perspective, they enhance the reflexivity of advanced modern society. In processes of reflexive modernization these problems can then be addressed and remedied.[26]

While social theorists (Marxist, post-structuralist, and functionalist) were interested in the new social movements primarily in so far as these can be analyzed as indicators for the overall condition and development of advanced modern societies, empirically oriented social scientists have devoted closer attention to the mobilizing structures, organizational dynamics, and political narratives of these new social actors, as well as to their relationship with the established political system. In the 1970s, the Americans John McCarthy and Mayer Zald established the resource mobilization approach to social movement research, which is based on the tradition of liberal individualism and the notion of rational actors developing their strategies on the basis of cost–benefit analyses. Accordingly, resource mobilization theory focuses on the entrepreneurial side of the social movement industry. The formal and informal organizational structures which mobilize and coordinate collective action are analyzed as key factors in social movement development. The success or failure of social movement politics is explained as depending on the extent to which campaigning resources such as money, activists, time, specialist knowledge, and access to officials are available and can be mobilized.[27] Network research is a relatively recent strand within this approach.[28]

Resource mobilization theory has tended to overemphasize the extent to which social movements are rational actors. It is reductionist in regarding them as primarily instrumental, and it is insensitive to the processes of collective construction in which social movement concerns are shaped and packaged into comprehensive narratives. Furthermore, the development and success of social movements are not just determined by the resources that can be mobilized, but depend to a significant extent on the way in which established political structures facilitate or repress social movement activity. This latter point, in particular, is the focus of research into the political opportunity structures for new social movements. Comparative studies by Herbert Kitschelt, Hanspeter Kriesi, and many others (McAdam et al.) have revealed that factors such as the responsiveness of the established political parties to social movement concerns, the availability of public funding, the use of legislation to control or suppress social movements, or the policing of protest activity have major impact on the emergence and endurance of social movements.[29]

In addition to efficient resource mobilization and favorable political opportunity structures the availability of an integrating and motivating narrative is an equally important condition for sustained social movement activity. In social movement research the "framing approach" has focused on these cognitive and ideational foundations of collective action. David Snow, Robert Benford, Bert Klandermans, and others have used the concept of framing to capture the process in which movement participants fashion a shared interpretation of themselves, the world around them, and their political action.[30] The framing approach focuses on the social construction of collective concerns, causes, enemies, legitimacy, and solutions. The integrating narrative that is generated in a three-dimensional process of diagnostic, prognostic, and motivational framing constructs meaning and identity and may, in the post-ideological era, be regarded as the functional equivalent of a political ideology.

With their specific focus on the conditions for social movement success, resource mobilization theory, the analysis of political opportunity structures, and the framing approach all tend to neglect the radical, subversive, and countercultural dimension of the new social movements. If Marxist social theory overemphasized this system-changing dimension, empirically oriented social science approaches often leave it underexplored. New social movement theory, which was established by scholars such as Alain Touraine and Alberto Melucci, may be regarded as a middle way between the progressive Marxist perspective and the inherently conservative perspective of the positivist social sciences.[31]

New social movement theory explains the emergence of the post-1960s social movements as the result of structural strains which are not, as Marxists had suggested, of an economic, but of a cultural nature. Processes of rapid modernization are assumed to have disrupted the normal functioning of society, giving rise to feelings of uprootedness, uncertainty, and disorientation. The new social movements are interpreted as a reaction of defense against the increasing colonization and commodification of human individuals and communities by the economic and administrative system.[32] New social movement theory regards the social movements not simply as a new collective actor on a par with more established political actors, but as the subject of a completely new politics. It suggests that the post-1960s social movements were not about participation in a political game whose rules remain predetermined and fixed, but about a form of democratization that makes the rules of the political game themselves accessible to democratic scrutiny. Rather than being instrumental to the achievement of particular political goals, social movements are seen as networks or spaces within which alternative cultures and lifestyles are being rehearsed and new social identities forged.[33] Table 19.2 (opposite) provides a simplified overview of the approaches and theories which have now been discussed. Once again, this schematization is no more than a heuristic device: in contemporary social movement research, the different approaches have merged and are cross-fertilizing each other.

Success and Failure of the Participatory Revolution

The success or failure of the participatory revolution is notoriously difficult to assess, not least because social movements pursue their goals, often at the same time, at very different levels. Some of them focus on very specific grievances, others aim to raise fundamental debates. In the longer term, they contribute to the selection of new social elites, effect the modernization of social and political institutions, and reconfigure public discourses in which societal goals and priorities are negotiated. To the extent that the European social movements wanted to achieve a radical turn away from the growth-dependent and exploitative capitalist consumer society, they have clearly failed. But measured by the degree to which they have reconfigured political institutions and political culture in individual countries and at EU level, their impact has been immense.

In contemporary European societies issues such as environmental integrity, cultural diversity, gender equality, human rights, and (international) social justice have been adopted as noncontroversial collective concerns – even though these ideals are, obviously, far from being realized. Social movements have achieved the extension of women's and minority rights, the establishment of new nature reserves, and the setting up of comprehensive monitoring systems for environmental quality and social standards. Throughout Europe, they have contributed to the deepening of democratic cultures and of the commitment to democratic principles. Since the 1960s, elements of direct democracy have been introduced in many European countries, and power has been devolved from central governments to regional and local authorities. European citizens have secured far-reaching rights to information. Both public and private sectors are required to fulfill tightened standards of transparency and accountability. Overall, there is clear evidence that citizens

Table 19.2 Approaches and theories in social movement research

	Collective behavior	Resource mobilization theory	Political opportunity structures	Framing theory	New social movement theory
Key scholars	Smelser, Turner, Killian	McCarthy, Zald	Kitschelt, Tarrow, Kriesi	Snow, Benford	Touraine, Melucci
Explanatory emphasis	Emergence	Emergence, stabilization, regeneration	Emergence stabilization	Stabilization, regeneration	Emergence, stabilization
Main focus	Mobilizing anxieties	Mobilization and campaigning resources	Institutionalized structures of political system	Integrating and motivating narrative	Radical objectives
Informed by	Mass psychology	Liberal individualism, rational choice theory	Organization theory, political science	Social constructivism, discourse analysis	Critical social theory
Relevant for	Affective movements	Instrumental movements	Instrumental and subcultural movements	Subcultural and countercultural movements	Countercultural movements
Short-comings	Regards social movements as irrational	Overemphasizes rational-actor model, neglects political framework and cultural dimension	Neglects mobilizing structures and cultural dimension	Neglects resource issues and significance of systemic structures	Overestimates desire for radical system change

have gained more access to, and influence on, political decision-making. Their range of opportunities for political articulation and democratic participation has widened substantially.[34]

Beyond this, the social movement sector has given rise to a diversity of alternative scientific and social institutions, self-help groups, and information networks. Social movement organizations command considerable resources and gradually they achieved formal representation in business advisory boards, government commissions, and bodies of public administration. Green parties have been established in most European countries and have pursued an agenda that integrates the full range of social movement concerns. In a number of countries they have not only won parliamentary seats, but entered government coalitions, thus taking direct (co-)responsibility for domestic and foreign policy.[35] Furthermore, social movements have directly and indirectly contributed to the emergence of international policy regimes regulating the exploitation of natural, human, and social resources, and protecting global commons such as biodiversity, climate stability, and cultural plurality. In their ongoing battle to remove democratic deficits they have developed multilevel strategies corresponding to the ascendance of multilevel governance.

The period from 1992 to 2002, in particular, was a decade of international NGO (nongovernmental organization) and social movement euphoria. At the UN summits in Rio (1992, environment), Cairo (1994, population), Bejing (1995, women), Kyoto (1997, climate), Durban (2001, racism), Rome (2002, food) and Johannesburg (2002, Rio + 10), to name but some of the most important ones, social movements and their organizations had an unprecedented level of input, which triggered a wave of considerable optimism. Since 2001, the World Social Forum held first in Porto Alegre (2001–2003) and then in Bombay (2004) has become the global countersummit to the annual World Economic Forum in Davos. Major protest events first in Seattle (December 1999), and then at international summit meetings in Prague (September 2000), Nice (December 2000), Gothenborg (June 2001), Genoa (July 2001), and elsewhere provided further evidence that resistance to the politics of market liberalism has for the first time forged a genuinely global social movement pursuing an agenda of democratic participation, decentralization, and autonomy in opposition to the globalist project of neo-liberal market capitalism. Therefore social movements can legitimately claim to have contributed not only to the downfall of authoritarian regimes in eastern Europe and to the further democratization of western European democracies, but also to the promotion of social movement concerns at EU level, and to the defense of European beliefs and values at the level of global politics. But despite all this, there are also reasons to be more skeptical as to how much they have really achieved. At the beginning of the twenty-first century we are confronted with the irritating coincidence of the victory of the participatory revolution and its failure.

Two developments, in particular, ought to be considered in some detail: first, the transformation of the social movements themselves, and second, the emergence of exaggerated expectations and unmanageable levels of complexity in the democratic process. These developments are important because both of them contribute to the dramatic erosion of public trust in politics and the rise of cynicism and post-democratic disillusionment with participatory governance. The transformation of the movements themselves is often captured in terms of their professionalization, institutionalization, and cooptation. In many policy areas social movement networks and organizations soon proved much more effective and efficient than the official institutions of the state. On a range of matters they had local knowledge and expertise that government authorities were lacking. They were able to relate to local people and obtain their trust and cooperation. The movements were therefore encouraged to work as partners rather than opponents of the authorities. Similarly, private businesses discovered that social movement organizations could help them improve their social and environmental credentials. For the social movements this brought desirable opportunities to enhance their capacities and political influence. Yet state facilitation and private cooptation also implied that they had to accept the rules of the political game and speak the language of the established system.

The social movements had to formalize their organizational structures and often became dependent on public- as well as business-sector funding. As they competed for subsidies and were integrated into policy-making processes, political realism and strategic pragmatism compromised their more radical demands and idealistic visions. In the interest of efficiency, cherished social movement practices needed to be reviewed. As extensive democratic deliberation and participation consume large quantities of resources but do not necessarily lead to qualitatively better and politically more legitimate policies, participatory beliefs which had been precious to the pioneers of social movement politics had to be reassessed. In the process of professionalization, the principles of DIY-politics partially turned back into those of delegation and representation. In an equally efficien, and for both sides convenient, division of labor, many social movement supporters confined themselves to cheque-book activism, while their organizations provided a professional campaigning service. Thus these institutionalized and professionalized movements metamorphosed from pioneers of a radically different socioeconomic as well as political order into reformist service providers for the established system. More and more, they operated in accordance with the logic they had once opposed. Their cooptation undermined the hope and belief that democratic politics really can be categorically different. The German Green Party, which has above been described as the most successful social movement party in Europe, may also be regarded as one of the most prominent examples illustrating this transformation. New radical direct action groups have sprung up not least in response to the mainstreaming and – from their perspective – failure of the participatory revolution.

As regards the overload and fragmentation of the democratic process, two equally important dimensions may be distinguished: the pluralization of articulated interests and the erosion of public trust in political institutions and personnel.[36] The participatory revolution has generated thoroughly unrealistic expectations of direct influence and representation. Mobilization entrepreneurs and the networks of the social movement industry have continuously emphasized government failure and expanded political demands. What they have failed to acknowledge is that in the protest society, the main problem is no longer the lack of opportunities for political articulation, but the lack of ability to integrate the increasingly fragmented interests into a common good. The new social movements have contributed significantly to the erosion of public trust in established institutions and elites, but they have been much less successful in providing new institutions and processes which can synthesize the diverging demands into manageable policy agendas. Inadvertently, they have contributed to the reinterpretation of democratic participation in terms of vociferously articulating specific interests rather than cooperatively integrating diverse perspectives into an inclusive societal agenda. Nowhere in Europe is there evidence that democratic values per se are in decline, but confidence that institutional reform can pave the way towards a new overarching societal consensus is indeed diminishing. Yet, if the pluralization and fragmentation of competing rationalities and sectional interests cannot be cured by institutional reform, the participatory revolution has chipped away at its own foundations and given rise to post-democratic tendencies.

At the beginning of the twenty-first century, European governments are confronted with the impossible task of having to regenerate public trust in political institutions and confidence in democratic processes. They have to address a triple crisis of mounting public deficit, sluggish economic growth, and declining political legitimacy. They are responding to this challenge, firstly, by employing strategies of depoliticization: for the sake of improving the efficiency and quality of public administration, they rely on expert commissions, think tanks, regulating authorities, and other non-majoritarian bodies. Given the complexity of contemporary problem constellations, the level of specialist knowledge that is required, and the nature of media-driven political discourse, this strategy of delegating responsibility to bodies which are insulated from political competition seems fully rational. However, while such strategies may increase the output legitimacy of political institutions, the postdemocratic delegation of power also gives rise to new feelings of political disempowerment, alienation, and exclusion.

Secondly, European governments have discovered civil society as an antidote to the three ills they have to address: decentralized and community-based welfare systems are believed to be more responsive and cost-effective than centralized provision; the social capital of local communities is seen as a resource for new economic growth; and the devolution of decision-making capacities to regional and local bodies seems a promising strategy for reducing political apathy while at the same time deflecting electoral discontent from central government. Across Europe, lean administration, the shrinking of the "nanny state," and the promotion of self-responsibility have, therefore, emerged as key objectives. Political elites from diverse party backgrounds are calling in unison for more freedom from state regulation, more subsidiarity, and more flexibility, diversity, and choice. Yet what might appear like the full mainstreaming of social movement demands and a resounding success for the participatory revolution in fact reflects a comprehensive reframing of the whole civil society debate.

From the social movement perspective, civil society had been conceptualized as the counterpart to the realm of economic efficiency and strategic and instrumental thinking. It was supposed to be the sphere in which cultural diversity and vitality would freely thrive. In the era of globalization, however, civil society has been redefined as a resource for the enhancement of economic efficiency and profitability. This colonization of the social movements' ideal by the discourse of competitiveness and efficiency severely reduces the movements' ability even to imagine any alternative to the status quo. It nurtures disillusionment, cynicism, refusal to participate, and – where frustration turns into mobilization – a readiness to resort to radical action. Given the overwhelming power of the neo-realist dogma that European societies have no choice but to adapt to the imperatives of the global market, it is difficult to argue that the participatory revolution has really provided European citizens with the power and means to democratically determine the conditions that shape their everyday lives. However, the new social movements have indeed succeeded in establishing a wealth of institutions and codified procedures which stand as symbols of democratic participation, self-determination, transparency, and accountability.

Notes

1 Etzioni, *Demonstration Democrary*.
2 Bauman, *In Search of Politics*; Gamble, *Politics and Fate*.
3 Dalton and Kuechler, *Challenging the Political Order*; Kriesi et al., *New Social Movements in Western Europe*; Crossley, *Making Sense of Social Movements*.
4 Della Porta and Diani, *Social Movements*.
5 Grossman, *The Electronic Republic*; Norris, *Digital Divide?*; Della Porta and Tarrow, *Transnational Protest and Global Activism*.
6 Beck, *The Risk Society*.
7 Beyme, *Transition to Democracy in Eastern Europe*; Nagle and Mahr, *Democracy and Democratization*; Kaldor and Vejvoda, *Democratization in Central and Eastern Europe*; Glenn, "Contentious Politics and Democratization."
8 Merkl and Weinberg, *Right-Wing Extremism in the Twenty-first Century*; Eatwell and Mudde, *Western Democracies and the Extreme Right Challenge*; Kopecky and Mudde, *Uncivil Society? Contentious Politics in Post-communist Europe*.
9 Wall, *Earth First! And the Anti-Roads Movement*; Seel et al., *Direct Action in British Environmentalism*.
10 Bennholdt-Thomsen et al., *There is an Alternative*; Waterman, *Globalization, Social Movements and the New Internationalism*; Klein, *No Logo*; Della Porta and Tarrow, op. cit.; George, *Another World is Possible if. . . .*
11 Marwick, *The Sixties*.
12 Dalton, *The Green Rainbow*.
13 Meadows et al., *The Limits to Growth*.
14 Rootes, *Environmental Movements*; Rootes, *Environmental Protests in Western Europe*.
15 Flam, *States and Anti-nuclear Movements*; Welsh, *Mobilising Modernity*.
16 Richardson and Rootes, *The Green Challenge*; O'Neill, *Green Parties and Political Change in Contemporary Europe*; Bomberg, *Green Parties and Politics in the European Union*; Burchell, *The Evolution of Green Politics*; Müller-Rommel and Poguntke, *Green Parties in National Governments*.
17 Tarrow, *Democracy and Disorder*.
18 Wall, op. cit.; Seel et al., op. cit.
19 Dalton and Kuechler, op. cit.; Jenkins and Klandermans, *The Politics of Social Protest*; McAdam et al., *Comparative Perspectives on Social Movements*; Klandermans and Staggenborg, *Methods in Social Movement Research*.
20 McKay, *DiY Culture*.
21 Turner and Killian, *Collective Behavior*; Smelser, *Theory of Collective Behavior*.

22 Touraine, *The Post-industrial Society.*
23 Offe, "New Social Movements."
24 Inglehart, *The Silent Revolution*; Inglehart, *Modernization and Postmodernization.*
25 Luhmann, *Ecological Communication*; Luhmann, *Social Systems.*
26 Beck, *The Reinvention of Politics.*
27 McCarthy and Zald, *The Trend of Social Movements in America*; McCarthy and Zald, "Resource Mobilization and Social Movements."
28 Castells, *The Rise of the Network Society*; Diani and McAdam, *Social Movements and Networks.*
29 Kitschelt, "Political Opportunity Structure and Political Protest"; Kitschelt, "Left-Libertarian Parties"; Kriesi, "The Political Opportunity Structure of New Social Movements"; McAdam et al., *Comparative Perspectives on Social Movements.*
30 Snow et al., "Frame Alignment Processes, Micromobilization and Movement Participation"; Snow and Benford, "Ideology, Frame Resonance, and Participant Mobilization"; Klandermans, *International Social Movement Research.*
31 Touraine, *The Voice and the Eye*; Touraine, *Can We Live Together?*; Melucci, *Nomads of the Present.*
32 Habermas, "New Social Movements."
33 Nash, *Contemporary Political Sociology.*
34 Cain et al., *Democracy Transformed?*
35 Müller-Rommel and Poguntke, *Green Parties in National Governments.*
36 Cain et al., op. cit.; Dalton, *Democratic Challenges – Democratic Choices.*

Bibliography

Bauman, Zygmunt, *In Search of Politics* (Cambridge: Polity, 1999).

Beck, Ulrich, *The Risk Society: Towards a New Modernity* (Cambridge: Polity, 1992).

Beck, Ulrich, *The Reinvention of Politics: Rethinking Modernity in the Global Social Order* (Cambridge: Polity, 1997).

Bennholdt-Thomsen, Veronika, Nicholas Faraclas, and Claudia von Werlhof (eds.), *There Is an Alternative: Subsistence and Worldwide Resistance to Corporate Globalization* (London and New York: Zed Books, 2001).

Beyme, Klaus von, *Transition to Democracy in Eastern Europe* (London: Macmillan, 1996).

Bomberg, Elizabeth, *Green Parties and Politics in the European Union* (London: Routledge, 1998).

Brundtland Report, *Our Common Future* (London: Earthscan, 1987).

Burchell, Jon, *The Evolution of Green Politics: Development and Change within European Green Parties* (London: Earthscan, 2002).

Cain, Bruce, Russell Dalton, and Susan Scarrow, *Democracy Transformed? Expanding Political Opportunities in Advanced Industrial Democracies* (Oxford: Oxford University Press, 2003).

Castells, Manuel, *The Rise of the Network Society* (Oxford: Blackwell, 1996).

Crossley, Nick, *Making Sense of Social Movements* (Buckingham and Philadelphia: Open University Press, 2002).

Dalton, Russel, *The Green Rainbow: Environmental Groups in Western Europe* (New Haven, CT and London: Yale University Press, 1994).

Dalton, Russel, *Democratic Challenges – Democratic Choices: The Erosion of Political Support in Advanced Industrial Democracies* (Oxford: Oxford University Press, 2004).

Dalton, Russel and Manfred Kuechler, *Challenging the Political Order: New Social and Political Movements in Western Democracies* (Cambridge: Polity, 1990).

Della Porta, Donatella and Mario Diani, *Social Movements: An Introduction* (London: Blackwell, 1999).

Della Porta, Donatella and Sidney Tarrow (eds.), *Transnational Protest and Global Activism* (Boulder, CO: Rowman & Littlefield, 2004).

Diani, Mario and Doug McAdam (eds.), *Social Movements and Networks: Relational Approaches to Collective Action* (Oxford: Oxford University Press, 2003).

Eatwell, Roger and Cas Mudde (eds.), *Western Democracies and the Extreme Right Challenge* (London: Routledge, 2003).

Etzioni, Amitai, *Demonstration Democracy* (New York: Gordon and Breach, 1970).

Flam, H. (ed.), *States and Anti-nuclear Movements* (Edinburgh: Edinburgh University Press, 1994).

Gamble, Andrew, *Politics and Fate* (Cambridge: Polity, 2000).

George, Susan, *Another World Is Possible If...* (London and New York: Verso, 2004).

Glenn, John, "Contentious Politics and Democratization: Comparing the Impact of Social Movements on the Fall of Communism in Eastern Europe," *Political Studies* 51, 2003, 103–120.

Grossman, Lawrence, *The Electronic Republic: Reshaping Democracy in the Information Age* (New York: Penguin, 1995).

Habermas, Jürgen, "New Social Movements," *Telos* 49, 1981, 33–37.

Inglehart, Ronald, *The Silent Revolution: Changing Values and Political Styles among Western Publics* (Princeton, NJ: Princeton University Press, 1977).

Inglehart, Ronald, *Modernization and Postmodernization: Cultural, Economic, and Political Change in 43 Societies* (Princeton, NJ: Princeton University Press, 1997).

Jenkins, Craig J. and Bert Klandermans (eds.), *The Politics of Social Protest: Comparative Perspectives on States and Social Movements* (Minneapolis: University of Minnesota Press, 1995).

Kaldor, Mary and Ivan Vejvoda (eds.), *Democratization in Central and Eastern Europe* (London: Continuum, 1999).

Kitschelt, Herbert, "Political Opportunity Structure and Political Protest: Anti-nuclear Movements in Four Democracies," *British Journal of Political Science* 16, no. 1, 1986, 58–95.

Kitschelt, Herbert, "Left-Libertarian Parties: Explaining Innovation in Competitive Party Systems," *World Politics* 40, no. 2, 1988, 194–234.

Klandermans, Bert (ed.), *International Social Movement Research*, vol. 1 (Greenwich, CT: JAI Press, 1988).

Klandermans, Bert and Suzanne Staggenborg (eds.), *Methods in Social Movement Research* (Minneapolis: University of Minnesota Press, 2002).

Klein, Naomi, *No Logo* (London: Flamingo, 2001).

Kopecky, Petr and Cas Mudde, *Uncivil Society? Contentious Politics in Post-communist Europe* (London: Routledge, 2003).

Kriesi, Hanspeter, "The Political Opportunity Structure of New Social Movements: Its Impact on Their Mobilization," in Craig J. Jenkins and Bert Klandermans (eds.), *The Politics of Social Protest: Comparative Perspectives on States and Social Movements* (Minneapolis: University of Minnesota Press, 1995).

Kriesi, Hanspeter, Ruud Koopmans, Jan Willem Duyvendak, and Marco Giugni, *New Social Movements in Western Europe: A Comparative Analysis* (London: UCL Press, 1995).

Luhmann, Niklas, *Ecological Communication* (Cambridge: Polity, 1989).

Luhmann, Niklas, *Social Systems* (Stanford, CA: Stanford University Press, 1995).

McAdam, Doug, John D. McCarthy, and Mayer N. Zald (eds.), *Comparative Perspectives on Social Movements: Political Opportunities, Mobilising Structures, and Cultural Framings* (Cambridge: Cambridge University Press, 1996).

McCarthy, John D. and Mayer N. Zald, *The Trend of Social Movements in America: Professionalization and Resource Mobilization* (Morristown, NJ: General Learning Press, 1973).

McCarthy, John D. and Mayer N. Zald, "Resource Mobilization and Social Movements: A Partial Theory," *American Journal of Sociology* 82, no. 6, 1977, 1212–1241.

McKay, George (ed.), *DiY Culture: Party and Protest in Nineties Britain* (London: Verso, 1998).

Marwick, Arthur, *The Sixties: Cultural Revolution in Britain, France, Italy and the United States* (Oxford: Oxford University Press, 1998).

Meadows, Donella, Dennis Meadows, Jürgen Randers, and William Behrens, *The Limits to Growth: A Report from the Club of Rome's Project on the Predicament of Mankind* (London: Pan, 1972).

Melucci, Alberto, *Nomads of the Present: Social Movements and Individual Needs in Contemporary Society* (London: Hutchinson Radius, 1989).

Merkl, Peter H. and Leonard Weinberg (eds.), *Right-Wing Extremism in the Twenty-First Century* (London: Frank Cass, 2003).

Meyer, David S. and Sidney Tarrow, *The Social Movement Society: Contentious Politics for a New Century* (Lanham, MD, Boulder, CO, New York, and Oxford: Rowman & Littlefield, 1998).

Müller-Rommel, Ferdinand and Thomas Poguntke, *Green Parties in National Governments* (London: Frank Cass, 2002).

Nagle, John and Alison Mahr, *Democracy and Democratization: Post-communist Europe in Comparative Perspective* (London: Sage, 1999).

Nash, Kate, *Contemporary Political Sociology: Globalization, Politics, and Power* (Oxford: Blackwell, 2000).

Norris, Pippa, *Digital Divide? Civic Engagement, Information Poverty and the Internet in Democratic Societies* (New York: Cambridge University Press, 2001).

Norris, Pippa, *Democratic Phoenix: Reinventing Political Activism* (New York: Cambridge University Press, 2002).

Offe, Claus, "New Social Movements: Challenging the Boundaries of Institutional Politics," *Social Research* 52, no. 4, 1985, 817–869.

O'Neill, Michael, *Green Parties and Political Change in Contemporary Europe: New Politics, Old Predicaments* (Aldershot: Ashgate, 1997).

Richardson, Dick and Chris Rootes, *The Green Challenge: The Development of Green Parties in Europe* (London: Routledge, 1995).

Rootes, Christopher (ed.), *Environmental Movements: Local, National and Global* (London: Frank Cass, 1999).

Rootes, Christopher (ed.), *Environmental Protest in Western Europe* (Oxford: Oxford University Press, 2003).

Seel, Benjamin, Matthew Paterson, and Brian Doherty (eds.), *Direct Action in British Environmentalism* (London and New York: Routledge, 2000).

Smelser, Neil, *Theory of Collective Behavior* (New York: Free Press, 1962).

Snow, David and Robert Benford, "Ideology, Frame Resonance, and Participant Mobilization," in Bert Klandermans (ed.), *International Social Movement Research*, vol. 1 (Greenwich, CT: JAI Press, 1988).

Snow, David, Burke Rochford, Steven Worden, and Robert Benford, "Frame Alignment Processes, Micromobilization, and Movement Participation," *American Sociological Review* 51, 1986, 464–481.

Snow, David, S. Soule, and Hanspeter Kriesi (eds.), *Blackwell Companion to Social Movements* (Oxford and Malden, MA: Blackwell, 2003).

Tarrow, Sidney, *Democracy and Disorder: Protest and Politics in Italy 1965–1975* (Oxford: Clarendon Press, 1989).

Touraine, Alain, *The Post-industrial Society. Tomorrow's Social History. Classes, Conflicts and Culture in the Programmed Society* (London: Wildwood House, 1971).

Touraine, Alain, *The Voice and the Eye: An Analysis of Social Movements* (Cambridge: Cambridge University Press, 1981).

Touraine, Alain, *Can We Live Together? Equality and Difference* (Cambridge: Polity, 2000).

Turner, Ralph H. and Lewis M. Killian, *Collective Behavior* (Englewood Cliffs, NJ: Prentice-Hall, 1957).

Wall, Derek, *Earth First! and the Anti-Roads Movement: Radical Environmentalism and Comparative Social Movements* (London and New York: Routledge, 1999).

Waterman, Peter, *Globalization, Social Movements and the New Internationalism* (London and New York: Continuum, 2001).

Welsh, Ian, *Mobilising Modernity: The Nuclear Movement* (London and New York: Routledge, 2000).

Further Reading

Donatella della Porta and Mario Diani's *Social Movements: An Introduction* (London: Blackwell, 1999) and Nick Crossley's *Making Sense of Social Movements* (Buckingham and Philadelphia: Open University Press, 2002) provide excellent overviews of the significance of new social movements as political actors. The *Blackwell Companion to Social Movements*, edited by David Snow (Oxford and Malden, MA: Blackwell, 2003), offers, among other things, reliable and comprehensive accounts of the wide range of different types of social movement. Christopher Rootes's *Environmental Protest in Western Europe* (London: Frank Cass, 2003) provides a comparative analysis of what is probably the most lasting type of social movement, addressing, in particular, the questions whether the new social movements are in decline. The contributions to Bruce Cain et al.'s edited volume *Democracy Transformed?* (Oxford: Oxford University Press, 2003) demonstrate how elements of direct democracy, improvements in representative democracy and the ascendance of advocacy democracy (through judicial courts) have provided citizens with new avenues of democratic participation. Russell Dalton's *Democratic Challenges – Democratic Choices* (New Haven and London: Yale University Press, 2004) analyzes how advanced democratic systems have come under pressure from the fragmentation of political interests and argues that public trust in the institutions and processes of democracy can be regenerated if the right democratic choices are made.

CHAPTER TWENTY

Postwar Europe: A Continent Built on Migration

PANIKOS PANAYI

In 1945 "Europe choked with refugees"[1] as the Nazi empire unraveled itself. Tens of millions of people made their way home in every direction out of central Europe. Forced laborers left the German cities where they had found themselves working for the Nazi war regime.[2] From further east over ten million people tramped towards a devastated rump Germany traversed with shells of buildings searching for accommodation among the ruins. Local long-standing border conflicts resolved themselves through an exchange of populations.[3]

Following the end of the refugee crisis in the late 1940s, labor recruitment began to develop. While Britain and France could call on their colonial populations, other industrialized western European states turned to workers available in the south of the continent, a process which would last into the middle of the 1970s. In the eastern half of the continent migration remained much more limited as the command economies of the industrializing Soviet bloc used their own internal surplus labor supplies.[4]

Although western European states had all stopped direct recruiting by the mid-1970s, migration has, nevertheless, continued to develop due to a range of processes. These have included family reunification, whereby mainly male migrants brought over their wives and children. The end of the Cold War led to a refugee crisis reminiscent (but not on the same scale as) the one which had characterized Europe in the second half of the 1940s, as the death of communism made way for new mainly nationalist ideologies, which made "ethnic cleansing" one of their goals. While Yugoslavia created most refugees, other parts of eastern Europe would experience new movements. The end of the Cold War also brought the old eastern European economies into the global migration system, as movement from east to west replaced passage from the Mediterranean to northern Europe.[5] The southern European states had gradually changed from labor exporters to labor importers as their demographic structure and changing economies created a need for workers not met by their domestic populations.[6] All these movements across Europe increasingly found their grounding in the expanding European Union (EU), allowing free movement of labor. However, people from beyond the borders of the EU have also tried to make

A Companion to Europe since 1945, First Edition. Edited by Klaus Larres.
© 2014 John Wiley & Sons, Ltd. Published 2014 by John Wiley & Sons, Ltd.

their way to Europe to experience the riches of the west, whether they have moved from areas beyond the southern periphery of "Fortress Europe," in the form of Africa, or from areas of eastern Europe which had not or still have not joined the EU.[7]

The migratory movements which have occurred into Europe since 1945 have had a deep impact upon the nature of the continent: they have affected both the already existing populations and the newcomers themselves. In general, migrants have tended to find themselves towards the bottom end of the social scale, often carrying the tasks shunned by natives, although in some nation states, particularly Great Britain, significant social mobility has taken place.[8]

Migrants have interacted (or failed to interact) with natives in a variety of ways. At one extreme it may seem tempting to view migrant communities as blots on the traditional demography of Europe, unable to assimilate into wider society. This picture works on the assumption of self-created, isolated ghettoes, with their own economies, which fail to interact with wider society. However, this image remains simplistic and deeply flawed. In the first place the "ghettoes" largely emerge both as a result of hostility from wider society and, more particularly, as a result of the relative poverty of many of the newcomers, forced to live in the poorest areas of cities.[9] These newcomers have entered nation states which have allowed them in to carry out generally low-paid economic tasks. Most migrants and their offsprings have experienced racism, whether it consists of a full-frontal physical attack or the more subtle example of hostility in the labor market, especially as children attempt to move away from carrying out the menial tasks of their parents.[10] But despite the racism of European states and societies, migrant populations have also interacted with dominant populations in a variety of positive ways. Most obviously, intermarriage has become the norm in many parts of Europe, although this pattern varies from one ethnic group to another. Migration has also had a transformative impact upon European societies, culture, and economy, so that the continent which emerged from the ruins of 1945 has developed under the impact of migration.[11]

Migratory Movements and Phases

Migration into postwar Europe fits into three phases. Within these three phases a series of movements has taken place simultaneously. These differing streams may have a variety of reasons behind them, which deserve analysis on an individual basis, but a range of underlying factors determine much of the migration which has taken place since 1945. These underlying factors include the wealth and economic strength of the continent, which has allowed the most developed economies to import labor from poorer areas from either within Europe or beyond. This connects with the demography of most of the continent since the 1960s, which has seen declining birth rates and, therefore, falling domestic labor supplies, resulting in the movement of people from parts of Europe or the world beyond with high birth rates and underemployment. At the same time the most politically stable parts of Europe have also proved the most attractive for refugees.[12]

In the first phase of postwar migration a massive refugee crisis developed following the collapse of Nazism. During this phase, which lasted from about 1944 to the early 1950s, a series of migratory streams fled across Europe in different directions, counting as many as 25 million people between 1945 and 1947,[13] with Germany as the focus.

As many as 13 million Germans may have fled westwards towards rump Germany between 1944 and 1947 as a result of the collapse of the Nazi empire. These included people who simply escaped the advancing Soviet armies. However, much of the migration occurred as a result of the movement westward of the Soviet border, which took over much of Poland. In turn the Polish border also moved further to the west, leading to an ethnic cleansing of German parts. At the same time, those nation states invaded by, but now liberated from, the Nazis, including Czechoslovakia, Hungary, and Romania, also expelled their ethnic German populations, which had lived in these nation states before they had emerged as such entities in the fall-out from the collapse of the Austro-Hungarian Empire in 1918. These westward movements received sanction in the Potsdam Treaty. As a result the rump Germany found itself housing millions of refugees. By 1950, out of a total population of 50.8 million living in the newly created Federal Republic, 7.9 million consisted of refugees and expellees. In addition, another 1.6 million people had fled from the German Democratic Republic (GDR), a stream that would continue into the 1950s, so that by 1960 German refugees accounted for 23.8% of the population of the Federal Republic. The GDR itself counted 3.5 million expellees in 1966, while the figure in Austria totalled around half a million.[14]

At the same time as this westward movement occurred, millions of foreign workers and prisoners of war, who had found themselves working in the Nazi Reich during the war, made their way home in all directions, especially towards eastern Europe and the Soviet Union where most of them had originated. Some of the 5 million who eventually reached the USSR were transported there by force.[15] Those who refused to return found themselves "displaced persons," living in camps set up for them, especially in Germany, although several European states, above all Britain, imported thousands of such individuals as part of the drive to fill the gap in their domestic labor shortages. Both France and Britain also retained some of the German prisoners of war they had held on their soil for the same reason.[16] Jews liberated from concentration camps located in Poland also, paradoxically, made their way to Germany partly escaping from a resurgence of postwar murderous anti-Semitism in the former and reaching a total figure of around 200,000 by 1947. Most would subsequently make their way to Palestine/Israel.[17]

While Germany may have formed the epicenter of European refugee movements in the immediate postwar years, displacement took place in locations throughout the continent as a result of border and regime change. For instance, 145,000 Poles (consisting of troops and their dependents) who had fought with the British armed forces decided to remain in Britain rather than return to the new Soviet-controlled Polish state.[18] Elsewhere, a change in the Italian–Yugoslav border gave the latter an extra 900,000 Italians, 300,000 of whom decided to cross the boundary. Italy also took in Italian nationals from Tunisia, Egypt, Libya, and other parts Africa. Together with Austria, Italy also attracted about 100,000 anticommunist Yugoslavs.[19]

During the late 1940s and early 1950s three further small refugee movements, not directly connected with World War II, also occurred. Firstly, about 100,000 people fled the Greek Civil War and headed towards eastern bloc states. Second, at the same time the Bulgarian government, pursuing a policy of "re-educating" its

Turkish minority, forced around 180,000 members of this group to leave between 1949 and 1951. Thirdly, and just as significantly, the Soviet crushing of the Hungarian revolution of 1956 led to the flight of over 200,000 people, largely to Austria and Yugoslavia, most of whom would subsequently move to other European destinations including Britain, France, Switzerland, and Germany.[20]

The Hungarian revolution represents the end of the postwar refugee crisis. The ensuing Cold War freeze meant relatively little movement of a purely political nature in Europe took place until the 1980s and, more especially, the 1990s. In the meantime, mass migration motivated by economic factors, connected with the longest sustained phase of growth in the history of capitalism, predominated. This period of labor migration would eventually pull in millions of people from beyond Europe, especially Africa but also South Asia and the West Indies.

The underlying pull factors which brought people to Europe fall into two groups. Firstly, there was sustained growth of the economy initiated by the need to rebuild the cities destroyed by Nazi and allied policies. Between 1950 and 1970 gross domestic product increased by about 5.5% per annum. Increasing investment, productivity, and mechanization, and more direct state intervention in the economy, fueled the boom.[21] Most of the migrants who made their way towards western Europe would find manual employment, above all building and manufacturing, which had the greatest need for labor. Secondly, the demography of postwar Europe witnessed a slowing of the growth rate to about 0.6% per annum by 1970, which created a need for labor to sustain economic expansion.[22] The areas of the world from which migrants would eventually originate had economic and demographic characteristics almost the direct opposite of Europe – not least they had high birth rates; for example, Turkey's population increased from 36.5 million in 1972 to 55 million by the end of the 1980s. As economic growth did not keep pace with the population explosion, high levels of unemployment resulted, creating a classic migratory push factor.[23]

The labor migration from the late 1940s until the 1970s moved towards the most industrialized economies of western Europe, above all Britain, France, and Germany, as well as smaller states such as Sweden, Switzerland, and the Netherlands. These years did not simply witness an importation of people from beyond Europe but also a move from the Mediterranean periphery, still undergoing rapid population growth, towards the industrialized north and west. For instance, millions of Italians moved towards Britain, France, Germany, and Switzerland. Much migration took place on a fairly local scale from predominantly agricultural economies to industrialized ones. A classic example consists of the movement of over half a million Irish to Britain by 1971, continuing a historical pattern.[24] Similarly, France counted a Portuguese population of 649,714 by 1990.[25]

The Federal Republic of Germany provides an example of a state which pursued a policy of organized labor recruitment from the European periphery. Despite the fact that millions of ethnic Germans from further east had moved towards the country from the 1940s until the end of the 1950s, continuing economic growth led to the signing of labor importation agreements between the federal government and several states on the European periphery during the late 1950s and 1960s, including Spain,

Greece, Turkey, Morocco, Yugoslavia, Portugal, and Tunisia, which meant that 2.6 million foreigners lived in Germany by 1973, making up 11.9% of the labor force.[26]

While Britain and France certainly used people from the Mediterranean rim, they also had more readily available supplies of labor from their colonies, which they utilized from the 1950s. Multicultural Britain evolved because governments in the immediate postwar decades somewhat halfheartedly allowed the entry of people from the empire and the Commonwealth as a result of the introduction of the British Nationality Act of 1948.[27] By the 1960s further legislation curtailed this movement, but by this time a series of visible groups had emerged, especially Indians, Pakistanis, and West Indians.[28] In contrast the French Office national d'immigration signed treaties with a series of former African colonies during the 1960s, including Morocco, Tunisia, and Algeria. By 1990 a total of 614,207 Algerians lived in France, a figure which excludes the 850,000 white Algerians who migrated after independence in 1962.[29] The Netherlands also imported people from its colonies, especially in the West Indies.[30]

Migration occurred on a far more limited scale in the Eastern bloc, although movement certainly took place within the Soviet Union as a result of industrialization. Some labor recruitment occurred in the GDR on a far smaller scale than had taken place in western Europe. Nevertheless, by 1990 about 250,000 workers from Soviet bloc states, including Poland, Czechoslovakia, Hungary, Vietnam, and Cuba lived in East Germany.[31]

A third phase in the history of European migration has occurred since the mid-1970s. Unlike the first two, which have the two major characteristics of mass refugee movements and labor recruitment respectively, the latest period has seen a series of apparently contradictory developments, which, nevertheless, have meant an increase in the number of migrants and refugees in Europe. In the first place, the organized and large-scale labor recruitment practiced especially by France, Germany, and Switzerland had ceased by the mid-1970s. In fact, many people who had entered Europe as part of this process returned home as they only held short-term resident permits. The change of policy came as a result of a hostile public opinion, manifesting itself in the evolution of anti-immigrant parties, and the slow-down in the European economy of the 1970s, which meant that the need for foreign workers had lessened.[32]

The official stop in labor recruitment on the continent, mirrored by the introduction of increasingly tight legislation in Britain, has not, however, lessened the scale of migration in Europe, as people have moved into and across the continent for a variety of reasons. For much of the 1970s and 1980s the most important reason consisted of family reunification, as many of those who had moved from the 1950s consisted of young men and, to a lesser extent, women. Often single, many had spouses and families in the homeland and rather than return, the migrants chose to bring over their dependents. The South Asian population of Britain and the Turkish population of Germany provide good examples of this process. In 1964, 90% of Pakistanis and Bangladeshis and 69% of Indians in Britain consisted of males. As the 1960s and 1970s progressed changes took place in the ratio of men to women, which in the case of Indians had reached 56:44 by 1974 and for Pakistanis 65:35.[33] Meanwhile, the number of Turks in the Federal Republic of Germany increased from 599,000 in 1973, the year of the stop on labor recruitment, to 1.6 million by 1989.[34]

While the migrants of the years of labor recruitment tended to move to the industrialized north and west of the continent, often from the Mediterranean periphery, the states of southern Europe have increasingly attracted foreign workers themselves since the mid-1970s as their economies, based largely on tourism and agriculture, have strengthened and their demographic growth has slowed. Their proximity to a much poorer African continent also acted as a factor increasing the movement to the states of southern Europe. In fact, much of the migration to Greece, Spain, and Italy has consisted of the movement of illegal immigrants from Africa.[35]

Nevertheless, illegal immigration does not remain confined to southern Europe. As a result of global inequality and the restrictive policies of the European Union towards those wishing to enter from beyond its borders, illegal residents characterize many of the major European cities so that a total of several million such individuals probably live in Paris, Berlin, and London, in particular, as well as in other locations in France, Germany, and Britain.[36]

The Cold War thaw resulted in a second postwar refugee crisis. Some people moved towards Europe from conflicts outside the continent, especially from the Middle East and Africa. However, most refugee movements occurred within Europe. Above all, the disintegration of Yugoslavia, accompanied by policies of ethnic cleansing, meant that 20% of Yugoslavs had found themselves refugees by 1995. The Cold War thaw also meant the movement of millions of ethnic Germans from eastern Europe to their "homeland" in the late 1980s and early 1990s. But by the end of the latter decade European Union states had made it increasingly difficult for refugees to cross their borders.[37]

Instead, movement within the European Union has increasingly become the norm in recent decades, especially with the incorporation of states from eastern Europe. The migration of as many as 600,000 Poles to Britain provides a good example. Such individuals often leave skilled or professional jobs for the higher pay available in Britain, with the aim of returning home.[38] Nevertheless, much of the movement within the EU represents a skilled migration; for instance there exists a community of 266,136 middle-class Germans who now live in Britain.[39]

European Union states with powerful economies and state structures have reached a stage where they can pick and choose the populations to which they allow entry. While, backed up by a hostile press, they attempt to exclude unskilled migrants from beyond the continent, they all operate a work permit system which allows those holding the right qualifications and abilities, especially in the technology sector, to settle within their borders.[40]

The Impact of Immigration

The migration of tens of millions of people into and across Europe since World War II has had a profound impact upon the society, economy, and culture of Europe, although national and regional variations clearly exist. Those states which have experienced the most significant migratory movements, especially France, Britain, Germany, Switzerland, and the Netherlands, have noticed some of the most significant changes.

Most obviously, migrants have changed the ethnic makeup of the populations of the countries of settlement. For instance, by 1990 foreigners made up 6.35% of the population of France, including over 500,000 Portuguese, Algerians, and Italians and more than 400,000 Moroccans and Spaniards.[41] Similarly, by 1989 Germany counted nearly 5 million foreigners.[42] According to the 2001 British census, about 8% of the population regard themselves as ethnic minorities, although these largely consist of people with origins outside Europe, rather than those with origins within Europe such as Greek Cypriots, the Irish, and Italians, who would increase the proportion further.[43]

Migrants of the first generation in particular, especially those from outside Europe, tend to have more children than natives, mirroring their homelands. For instance, during the 1980s, while French fertility remained the same for both southern European and French women, at 1.8 children each, it stood at 4.2 for Algerian women in 1982, having fallen from 8.5 during the 1960s. Foreigners accounted for 11% of all births in 1982. Similarly, in 1981, while 17.9% of Germans were under 15, the figure for foreigners stood at 26.3%. Various explanations present themselves for these differences, including the fact that the migrants arrive from parts of the world with higher fertility rates than those in Europe. At the same time a large percentage in the earlier stages of the migration process tended to fall into younger age groups, as the nation states which imported them simply needed their labor power. Family reunification facilitated the fertility of migrants.[44] Nevertheless, over time, these reproductive patterns tend to mirror those of the majority population, as the example of South Asian communities in Britain suggests.[45]

Migrants have had a profound impact upon the urban geography of Europe as they have concentrated upon cities, where they have tended to develop their own neighborhoods. Three explanations exist for this development: the desire of newcomers to live next to people similar to themselves; fear of racism in wider society; and the fact that many of the newcomers, constituting the poorest in society, simply move to areas with the cheapest accommodation.[46] However, not all migrations have moved purely towards cities. The refugees who made their way to rump Germany after World War II found themselves directed away from devastated German urban landscapes and towards smaller locations, including villages, which had experienced little or no allied bombing.[47] But this remains unusual. In Britain the inner city tended to become the domicile of the West Indian newcomers. This was already recognized by some of the early sociological studies of this community examining London during the 1960s.[48] Forty years later South Asian communities, divided according to religion and area of origin, remain highly concentrated, whether within London, in the Midlands, or in the north of England.[49] In France, meanwhile, over 90% of migrants lived in cities in 1990, with 35.6% resident in Paris.[50] Similar patterns reveal themselves in Germany, where migrant neighborhoods often developed near to the factories where the newcomers found themselves working. Thus, in Duisburg the streets nearest to the steelworks, which imported immigrants during the 1960s, tended to count the highest proportion of foreigners. In West Berlin, meanwhile, the Turkish quarter has developed in Kreuzberg, one of the poorest areas of the city.[51] Turks in the Netherlands have tended to focus upon areas of low-quality nineteenth-century housing, while the Surinamese community moved out of inner city areas in Amsterdam during the 1970s towards newly constructed state housing in the suburbs. Swiss cities have counted some of the highest percentages of migrants among their populations. In 1980 the figure for Geneva stood at 35.7%, with 23.2% in Lausanne, 18.2% in Basle and 17.7% in Zurich.[52]

Concentration in major European cities meant that migrants often lived in the poorest accommodation available, reflecting their economic and social status. Some of the worst conditions emerged in France during the 1960s where shanty towns (*bidonvilles*) developed in the suburbs of some of the major cities, housing as many as 75,000 people by the mid-1960s. After their disappearance many migrant families found themselves living in unsatisfactory high-rise suburban accommodation in areas experiencing high rates of unemployment.[53] In Germany some of the initial housing for foreign workers during the 1960s included labor camps. While the newcomers gradually left such accommodation, they tended to move into lower-quality accommodation than that used by Germans. In North Rhine–Westphalia, for instance, the living quarters of foreigners were 36% smaller than those of the population as a whole during the 1970s.[54] Meanwhile, more recent migration to southern European states has seen a repetition of the residence patterns experienced in France and Germany during the 1960s.[55]

While political factors have played a large role in migratory movements since 1945, the overwhelming attraction of Europe has consisted of its wealth, which has increasingly spread from the west and north to most of the continent. Any assessment of the impact of immigrants in postwar Europe therefore needs to examine their economic role. It seems questionable whether Europe could have experienced the level of prosperity of the years since 1945 without the labor commodity called immigrants.

Much of the postwar boom which occurred in the Federal Republic of Germany depended upon the millions of people who made their way to the country in a series of waves, from the refugees of the 1940s and 1950s to the foreign workers of the 1960s and 1970s. Richard Overy has identified the availability of refugee labor in the German economic recovery in the immediate postwar years.[56] The labor migration of the 1960s selected migrants at the peak of their economic productivity. The recruitment in Germany, for instance, was organized by a combination of industry and government.

Most migrants who have moved to Europe since 1945 have the aim of economic betterment. The wages which they have received, while often lower than those obtained by their indigenous neighbors, usually exceeded what they earned in their homelands. Turkish migrants to Europe, for instance, often saved some of their small salaries, which would subsequently allow them to build homes when they returned to Turkey.[57]

However, the process of labor recruitment did not take place for the benefit of the migrants, but for the benefit of European economy and society. Western governments, with the support of big business, turned to labor recruitment in order to plug the gap resulting from the demographic stabilization of native populations. Young foreigners could satisfy this demand and help to sustain the long period of economic growth from the 1940s to the 1970s. With the economic slow-down of the 1970s and 1980s labor migration ceased. The recent eastward expansion of the EU has provided new workers for big business in western Europe.

Initially, refugees filled the gap needed for the economic reconstruction of Europe at the end of the World War II, indicated especially by the German case. Like the foreigners who followed them, these German refugees often carried out work below their skill and qualification levels. In the long run these refugees became integrated into West German society, although they still tended to have a lower social status than their neighbors born in the west.[58]

The foreign workers who arrived in western European society have tended to experience less social mobility. The positions which they took at the bottom end of the social scale have entailed working the longest hours under the worst conditions for the worst rates of pay, often rewarded at piece rates, and sometimes employed by their own nationals, especially as ethnic economies took on a life of their own. Initially, the newcomers found themselves heavily employed in building and factory work. In the French case 37.5% of all foreign workers were involved in construction between 1956 and 1967, with 16.5% working in manufacturing, especially textile, motor car and steel production.[59] Clemens Amelunxen, referring to West Germany during the 1970s, wrote that "guest workers perform the most menial and dirtiest tasks. They drag the tar spreaders, carry pig iron, clean toilets, and cart away the garbage of affluence."[60]

In the longer term, migrant workers and their descendants have experienced some social mobility, especially in the British case, where, for instance, a South Asian middle class has developed. A closer analysis of this group, however, reveals that most of its members come from higher-caste Indian backgrounds who never worked in manual employment. On the other hand, Pakistani migrants, who did predominantly carry out manual labor, have less presence in the South Asian bourgeoisie. Some of them have lost their jobs as this group, along with Bangladeshis, has experienced high unemployment rates. This applies to both the first and subsequent generations[61] and repeats itself among other communities throughout Europe, including Turks in Germany and North Africans in France.[62] But migrants all over the continent have experienced some social mobility as smallscale shopkeepers. Newcomers usually establish retail outlets for members of their own communities in areas where ethnic economies have developed.[63]

More recent migration, especially from eastern to western Europe, as well as towards the Mediterranean, reveals similar patterns. For instance, Poles arriving in Britain since 2004 have tended to work in manual employment, shunned by natives, for which they are often too highly qualified. Just as the predominantly industrial economies of the 1960s needed foreign labor to sustain growth, so did the tourist and agricultural economies of southern Europe since the 1970s and the service economy of Britain over the last ten years.[64]

Migrant communities have also had an impact upon other aspects of life in Europe. For instance, they have played a large role in the development of sport, particularly football. This is indicated by the presence of players from all over the world in the major European football leagues, but also by the impact of the children of migrants upon national football teams, epitomized by the French World Cup-winning team of 1998, which counted players from French, African, and European backgrounds.[65] Migrants have also had a significant impact upon food in Europe. This seems most obvious in the evolution of the Indian (essentially Bangladeshi) restaurant, in Britain, which has brought home the food of the British in India.[66] However, the doner kebab has spread just as widely in Germany, so that by the mid-1990s some 200 tonnes were being sold every day, making 720 million such meals per year.[67] Meanwhile Chinese restaurants have become ubiquitous.[68]

Interethnic Relations

The migrant communities which have evolved in Europe since the 1940s have interacted with the majority community in a variety of ways. In the first place, some have followed the path of full integration.[69] Second, most have, to some degree, created their own ethnic communities evolving in local geographic concentrations. This partly results from the desire to continue the traditions of the homeland. However, hostility from the majority community often forces the new groups back into their own shell. This hostility has a variety of manifestations, most seriously racist violence.

Relatively few migratory movements have undergone a process of mass and complete assimilation into the majority group. One of the main exceptions to this rule consists of the German refugees who moved west immediately after the end of World War II. Nevertheless, even this did not take place smoothly. While the refugees may have, in theory at least, spoken the same language, natives and newcomers did not have the same outlook. More specifically, the main desire of the refugees consisted of getting their homes back in eastern Europe. For this purpose they established a series of organizations (*Landmannschaften*) based upon their areas of origin. Relatively little conflict occurred between natives and refugees on the ground largely because the federal government, in contrast to its attitudes to foreigners, did everything possible to ease the path of the refugees into West German society, epitomized by the establishment of a Ministry for Expellees, Refugees, and War Victims. By the fall of the Berlin Wall refugees had become fully integrated into West German society.[70] However, as a result of the changes brought on by the collapse of communism, millions more ethnic Germans stranded in eastern Europe during the Cold War moved west under a clause in the federal constitution, which allowed them to do so. This new group, whose members often spoke little German, received much hostility which led to legal changes to prevent further migration.[71]

While the early postwar German refugees may have assimilated en masse, most other groups have done so at least on an individual level. As social scientists have increasingly demonstrated, identity choices work upon an individual basis.[72] One of the major roads to assimilation consists of intermarriage. In Britain members of all groups have followed this path to some extent, particularly black males, but also, to a lesser extent, South Asian females, especially Sikhs and Hindus.[73] Meanwhile, in Germany 9.6% of marriages by 1990 involved a German and a non-German partner.[74]

This offers one example of the complexity of migrant identities in postwar Europe. But most communities have developed a strong ethnicity, to which individuals adhere according to personal choice. The artificially constructed migrant communities have either formed a completely new identity or rebuilt a version of their lives from the homeland. Black identity in Britain during the 1970s even encompassed South Asians, while, succeeding this, the idea of Asians in Britain unifies vastly diverse groups from Pakistan to Sri Lanka. On the other hand, the concept of a Turkish community in Germany or the Netherlands may have more validity, in the sense that

Turks originate from one nation state, although this ignores the artificiality of national groupings. The most developed ethnic communities, in terms of the evolution of communal structures, exist in northern and western Europe, partly because of the longevity of settlement in these states and partly because they more usually constitute legal migrants.[75]

Turks in Germany provide a good example of the evolution of an organized ethnic community in Europe. They initially arrived in the Federal Republic as predominantly male migrants during the 1950s and 1960s. Following family reunification during the 1970s and 1980s they developed into one of the most visible and organized ethnic groups in the EU. By the 1990s, 11 Turkish newspapers circulated in Germany. From 1964 the German regional radio station, WDR (Westdeutscher Rundfunk), based in Cologne, broadcast radio programs in Turkish, which in 1990 were listened to by 52% of Turks in the city on a daily basis. Many Turks have subscribed to satellite TRT-International broadcasting from Turkey. A high culture has also developed in Germany which has incorporated serious literature. The Turkish community in Germany helped to develop Islam in the country. By the middle of the 1990s about 1.7 million Muslims lived in Germany, 75% of them Turks. Approximately 1,200 Muslim parishes existed by this time, 1,100 of them Turkish. However, perhaps reflecting the secular nature of the Atatürk state, only about 30% of the total Muslim population regularly practiced its religion, while 22% regularly attended mosques. Despite the evolution of communal organizations, such figures point to the importance of personal identities. Turks in Germany have also developed political groupings, mirroring organizations in the homeland. The largest include the Turkish Social Democrats and the conservative Freiheitlicher deutsch-türkischer Freundschaftsverein. The best-known political grouping in Europe with origins in Turkey has consisted of the Kurdistan Communist Party (Partiya Karharen Kurdistan – PKK), which has resorted to violence and which may have counted 50,000 members in Germany during the 1990s.[76]

This examination of the Turkish community in Germany points to the development of ethnic minorities wishing to reinvent their homeland organizations and culture, with perhaps a limited desire to interact with the majority community. An extreme example of such a situation would consist of violent anti-Western groups in contemporary Britain with a particular take on Islam, which they view as justifying war against the west. While members of such groups may often emerge from ghettoized communities, they have usually passed through the British education system and find employment in wider British society.[77]

Nevertheless, the ethnic majority play a role in the rise of tension. State policies, as well as the media, plays a large part in the way in which individuals interact on the ground. While intermarriage may have become increasingly normal in postwar Europe, most members of most groups in Europe marry partners with the same ethnicity.[78] Hostility, and indifference, also characterize interethnic relations.

Government plays a central role and it seems tempting to divide European nation states into a number of categories: first, those which actively pursue multiculturalism, such as Britain, the Netherlands, and Sweden; second, the more assimilationinst French model, which, in theory, rejects the evolution of separate communities; third, states which reject even the idea of themselves as immigration countries, such as Germany until the end of the 1990s, Switzerland, and some of the southern European democracies, which have not fully addressed the presence of large migrant communities in their midst. But this represents a simplification of reality. Alternative ways also present themselves for distinguishing the attitudes of European states towards minorities. France, Britain, and the Netherlands have large minority populations, who, because of imperial connections and the history of nationality legislation, count a large number of people who possess French, British, and Dutch citizenship, which at least gives them the same legal rights as the majority. This contrasts with the mass of disenfranchised migrants in much of the rest of Europe who not only possessed foreign nationality but also, in cases such as Switzerland or Italy – where *jus sanguinis* determines nationality law – have discovered that their descendants have remained foreigners and, therefore, in theory, remain excluded from civil rights in perpetuity.[79]

Racism has affected all nation states in postwar Europe and has also impacted upon most migrant groups within them at some stage. The media play a large role in this, negatively focusing upon particular groups at specific times and therefore bringing to the attention of a wider society the presence of particular minorities. In Britain, for example, the press devoted much attention to West Indians during the late 1950s, which helped to fuel the Nottingham and Notting Hill riots of 1958.[80] The German media also played a similar role in attacks upon foreigners during the early 1990s.[81]

Most European nation states which have experienced immigration have also seen the evolution of extremist political parties which have demanded either the ceasing of further movement or even deportation.[82] The most successful and sustained group consists of the Front National, which has become a fixture in French politics since the early 1980s and which has clearly had a negative impact on interethnic relations in France, as well as making it virtually impossible for migrant communities to disappear, assuming that they wish to do so.[83]

Members of most migrant groups in postwar Europe have experienced racial violence at some stage. In Britain, for instance, full-scale riots occurred throughout the 1950s and early 1960s, which by the early 1970s had turned into murderous attacks upon individuals, especially in the East End of London.[84] Perhaps the most serious incidents of all, looking at the continent as a whole, occurred in 1973 following the murder of a French bus driver by a mentally disturbed Arab. There followed nationwide attacks against North Africans, including bombings and the use of machine guns, which resulted in death or serious injury to 52 individuals.[85] Serious disorder also broke out in Germany in the early 1990s affecting both the old western half of the Federal Republic as well as the new states in the eastern half of the country. Violence took place against the background of mass migration, economic collapse, and nationalistic euphoria consequent upon reunification.[86]

Immigrants and Majorities

Any account of the history of Europe since the end of World War II has to stress the importance of immigration in its development. The western half of the continent, above all the large democracies of Germany, France, and Britain, together with smaller states such as the Netherlands, Switzerland, and Sweden, have experienced the most significant and profound migratory movements throughout the postwar period. By the 1970s, partly because many of these states had stopped labor recruitment, but also because of rising living standards in the Mediterranean, immigration increasingly became a feature of southern European societies. While the Soviet bloc remained largely immune from international migration, the end of the Cold War has increasingly brought this part of the world into global patterns, particularly as a supply labor for western Europe as increasing numbers of eastern European states have joined the EU.[87]

Migration has profoundly impacted upon European economy, society, and culture since 1945. It seems unlikely that the sustained level of growth which has character-ized the majority of postwar European economic history, especially in the capitalist west, would have occurred without the ready supply of cheap labor from other parts of Europe and the world. While some of these newcomers, especially those with ethnic credentials closest to those of the majority population, may have experienced social mobility, many have almost formed an underclass, especially where citizenship remains closed to their descendants.[88] Migrants have also transformed the demogra-phy of European societies, as well as the urban geography, so that it proves almost impossible, at the beginning of the twenty-first century, to find any city without an immigrant quarter. "Culturally," the most profound and visible impact of migrants and their descendants has probably occurred in the areas of sport and food.

Relations between majorities and minorities remain complex. It seems tempting to succumb to the image of ghettoized unassimmilable groups, especially those of Muslim origin, portrayed by the European media. Certainly, some research backs up the idea of "parallel lives."[89] While the desire of ethnic groups themselves to remain separate partly explains such situations, the role of racism also adds to this sense of difference and isolation. Yet this only offers partial reality. Integration takes place at the same time as isolation. This has happened en masse for some groups, especially those with similar ethnic characteristics to the majority.[90] Ultimately, as much identity led research increasingly emphasizes, ethnicity and interaction between different groups functions upon an individual basis.

Notes

1 Marrus, *The Unwanted: European Refugees in the Twentieth Century*, 297.
2 Jacobmeyer, *Vom Zwangsarbeiter zum heimatlosen Ausländer*.
3 Panayi, *Outsiders*, 122–129.
4 Panayi, *Outsiders* 129–46.
5 Ardittis, *The Politics of East–West Migration*.
6 King and Black, *Southern Europe and the New Immigration*.
7 Panayi, *Outsiders*, 146–160.
8 Panayi, *An Ethnic History*.
9 Panayi, *An Ethnic History*.
10 Wrench and Solomos, *Racism and Migration in Western Europe*.
11 Panayi, *An Ethnic History*.
12 Panayi, *Outsiders*, 117–22.
13 Kulischer, *Europe on the Move*, 305.
14 Panayi, *Outsiders*, 123–125.
15 Panayi, *Ethnic Minorities in Nineteenth and Twentieth Century Germany*, 201–203.
16 Panayi, *Outsiders*, 125–126.
17 Gay, *Safe among the Germans*.
18 Lane, *Victims of Stalin and Hitler*.

19 Panayi, *Outsiders*, 127.

20 Panayi, *Outsiders*, 127–128.

21 Aldcroft, *The European Economy, 1914–2000*, 128–62.

22 Salt, "International Labour Migration: The Geographical Pattern of Demand."

23 Panayi, *Outsiders*, 132–133.

24 Delaney, *The Irish in Post-war Britain*.

25 Hargreaves, *Immigration, "Race" and Ethnicity in Contemporary France*, 16.

26 Panayi, *Ethnic Minorities*, 216–17.

27 Paul, *Whitewashing Britain: Race and Citizenship in the Postwar Era*.

28 Panayi, *The Impact of Immigration*, 12–15.

29 Hargreaves, op. cit., McDonald, "Labour Immigration into France, 1946–1965."

30 Panayi, *Outsiders*, 141.

31 Panayi, *Ethnic Minorities*, 228–30.

32 Panayi, *Outsiders*, 143–145.

33 Panayi, *The Impact of Immigration*, 17–18.

34 Panayi, *Ethnic Minorities*, 218–19.

35 King and Black, *Southern Europe*.

36 Jordan and Düvell, *Irregular Migration: The Dilemmas of Transnational Mobility*.

37 Panayi, *Outsiders*, 152–157.

38 Burrell, "War, Cold War and the New World Order: Political Borders and Polish Migration to Britain."

39 Kettenacker, "The Germans after 1945."

40 Cornelius et al., *The International Migration of the Highly Skilled*.

41 Hargreaves, op. cit., 8–14.

42 Panayi, *Ethnic Minorities*, 230.

43 See http://www.statistics.gov.uk/cci/nugget.asp?id=455, 2001 UK Census, Focus on Ethnicity and Identity.

44 Panayi, *An Ethnic History*, 36–37.

45 Singh, "Multiculturalism in Contemporary Britain: Reflections on the 'Leicester Model.'"

46 Panayi, *An Ethnic History*, 44.

47 Müller and Simon, "Aufnahme und Unterbringung."

48 Banton, *The Coloured Quarter: Negro Immigrants in an English City*; Glass, *Newcomers: The West Indians in London*.

49 Cantle, *Community Cohesion: A New Framework for Race and Diversity*.

50 Panayi, *An Ethnic History*, 47.

51 Panayi, *Ethnic Minorities*, 220–221.

52 Panayi, *An Ethnic History*, 49–50.

53 Panayi, *An Ethnic History*, 55–56.

54 Panayi, *Ethnic Minorities*, 220–221.

55 Però, "Immigration and Politics in Left-Wing Bologna," 162–163.

56 Overy, "The Economy of the Federal Republic since 1949," 4–10.

57 Martin, *The Unfinished Story: Turkish Labour Migration to Western Europe*, 40.

58 Rock and Wolff, *Going Home to Germany?*

59 Hollifield, *Immigrants, Markets and States*, 144–59.

60 Amelunxen, "Foreign Workers in West Germany," 119.

61 Ali et al., *A Postcolonial People: South Asians in Britain*.

62 Panayi, *An Ethnic History*, 95–96.

63 Kloosterman and Rath, *Immigrant Entrepreneurs*.

64 Burrell, "War, Cold War and the New World Order"; King and Black, *Southern Europe*.

65 Lanfranchi and Taylor, *Moving with the Ball*.
66 Panayi, "The Spicing Up of English Provincial Life: The History of Curry in Leicester."
67 Seidel-Pielen, *Aufgespießt: Wie die Döner über Deutschland kamen*.
68 Roberts, *China to Chinatown: Chinese Food in the West*.
69 Lucassen, *The Immigrant Threat*.
70 Rock and Wolff, op. cit.
71 Panayi, *Ethnic Minorities*, 251–252.
72 Kershen, *A Question of Identity*.
73 http://www.statistic.gov.uk/cci/nugget.asp?id=1090, "Inter-Ethnic Marriage."
74 Schumacher, *Einwanderungland BRD*, 144.
75 Panayi, *An Ethnic History*, 101–105.
76 Panayi, *Ethnic Minorities*, 225–226.
77 Ansari, *"The Infidel Within": Muslims in Britain since 1800*, 298–406.
78 http://www.statistic.gov.uk/cci/nugget.asp?id=1090, "Inter-Ethnic Marriage."
79 Rex and Singh, *Governance in Multicultural Societies*; Panayi, "The Evolution of Multiculturalism in Britain and Germany: An Historical Survey."
80 Miles, "The Riots of 1958: Notes on the Ideological Construction of 'Race Relations' as a Political Issue in Britain."
81 Panayi, "Racial Violence in the New Germany (1990–3)."
82 Cheles et al., *The Far Right in Western and Eastern Europe*.
83 Marcus, *The National Front and French Politics*.
84 Panayi, "Racial Violence in Britain during the Nineteenth and Twentieth Centuries," 15–21.
85 Lloyd, "Racist Violence and Anti-racist Reactions: A View of France."
86 Panayi, "Racial Violence in the New Germany."
87 Wallace and Stola, *Patterns of Migration in Central Europe*; Górny and Ruspini, *Migration in the New Europe: East–West Revisited*.
88 Castles and Cossack, *Immigrant Workers and Class Struggle in Western Europe*.
89 Cantle, *Community Cohesion*.
90 Lucassen, op. cit.

Bibliography

Aldcroft, Derek, *The European Economy, 1914–2000*, 4th edition (London: Routledge, 2001).

Ali, N., V.S. Kalra, and S. Sayyid (eds.), *A Postcolonial People: South Asians in Britain* (London: Hurst, 2006).

Amelunxen, Clemens, "Foreign Workers in West Germany," in William A. Veenhoven (ed.), *Case Studies in Human Rights and Fundamental Freedoms*, vol. 1 (The Hague: Martinus Nijhoff, 1975).

Ansari, Humayun, *"The Infidel Within": Muslims in Britain since 1800* (London: Hurst, 2004).

Ardittis, Solon (ed.), *The Politics of East–West Migration* (London: Macmillan, 1994).

Banton, Michael, *The Coloured Quarter: Negro Immigrants in an English City* (London: Cape, 1955).

Burrell, Kathy, "War, Cold War and the New World Order: Political Borders and Polish Migration to Britain," *History in Focus*, 11, http://www.history/ac.uk/ihr/Focus/Migration/articles/burrell.html

Cantle, Ted, *Community Cohesion: A New Framework for Race and Diversity* (Basingstoke: Palgrave, 2005).

Castles, Stephen and Godula Cossack, *Immigrant Workers and Class Struggle in Western Europe* (London: Oxford University Press, 1973).

Cheles, Luciano, Ronnie Ferguson, and Michalina Vaughan (eds.), *The Far Right in Western and Eastern Europe* (London: Longman, 1993).

Cornelius, Wayne A., Thomas J. Espenshade, and Idean Salehyan, *The International Migration of the Highly Skilled: Demand, Supply, and Development Consequences in Sending and Receiving Countries* (San Diego: Center for Comparative Immigration Studies, University of Califoria, 2001).

Delaney, Enda, *The Irish in Post-war Britain* (Oxford: Oxford University Press, 2007).

Gay, Ruth, *Safe among the Germans: Liberated Jews after World War Two* (New Haven, CT, and London: Yale University Press, 2002).

Glass, Ruth, *Newcomers: The West Indians in London* (London: Allen Odd Unwin 1960).

Górny, Agat and Paolo Ruspini (eds.), *Migration in the New Europe: East–West Revisited* (Basingstoke: Palgrave, 2004).

Hargreaves, Alec G., *Immigration, "Race" and Ethnicity in Contemporary France* (London: Routledge, 1995).

Hollifield, James F., *Immigrants, Markets and States: The Political Economy of Post-War Europe* (Cambridge, MA: Harvard University Press, 1992).

Jacobmeyer, Wolfgang, *Vom Zwangsarbeiter zum heimatlosen Ausländer* (Göttingen: Vandenhoech & Ruprecht, 1985).

Jordan, Bill and Franck Düvell, *Irregular Migration: The Dilemmas of Transnational Mobility* (Cheltenham: Edward Elgar, 2002).

Kershen, Anne J. (ed.), *A Question of Identity* (Aldershot: Ashgate, 1998).

Kettenacker, Lothar, "The Germans after 1945," in Panikos Panayi (ed.), *Germans in Britain since 1500* (London: Hambledon, 1996).

King, Russell and Richard Black (eds.), *Southern Europe and the New Immigration* (Brighton: Sussex Academic, 1997).

Kloosterman, Robert and Jan Rath, *Immigrant Entrepreneurs: Venturing Abroad in the Age of Globalization* (Oxford: Berg, 2003).

Kulischer, Eugene, *Europe on the Move: War and Population Changes, 1917–1947* (New York: Columbia University Press, 1948).

Lane, Thomas, *Victims of Stalin and Hitler: The Exodus of Poles and Balts to Britain* (Basingstoke: Palgrave, 2004).

Lanfranchi, Pierre and Matthew Taylor, *Moving with the Ball: The Migration of Professional Footballers* (Oxford: Palgrave, 2001).

Lloyd, Cathie, "Racist Violence and Anti-racist Reactions: A View of France," in Tøre Björgo and Rob Witte (eds.), *Racist Violence in Europe* (London, 1993).

Lucassen, Leo, *The Immigrant Threat: The Integration of Old and New Migrants in Western Europe since 1850* (Chicago: University of Illinois Press, 2006).

McDonald, James R., "Labour Immigration into France, 1946–1965," *Annals of the Association of American Geographers* 59, 1969, 116–134.

Marcus, Jonathan, *The National Front and French Politics: The Irresistible Rise of Jean-Marie Le Pen* (Basingstoke: Macmillan, 1995).

Marrus, Michael, *The Unwanted: European Refugees in the Twentieth Century* (Oxford: Oxford University Press, 1985).

Martin, Philip L., *The Unfinished Story: Turkish Labour Migration to Western Europe* (Geneva: International Labor Office, 1991).

Miles, Robert, "The Riots of 1958: Notes on the Ideological Construction of 'Race Relations' as a Political Issue in Britain," *Immigrants and Minorities* 3, 1984, 252–275.

Müller, Georg and Heinz Simon, "Aufnahme und Unterbringung," in Eugen Lemberg and Friedrich Edding (eds.), *Die Vertriebenen in Westdeutschland: Ihre Eingliederung und ihr*

Einfluss auf Gesellschaft, Wirtschaft, Politik und Geistleben, vol. 1 (Kiel: Ferdinand Kirt, 1959).

Overy, Richard, "The Economy of the Federal Republic since 1949," in Klaus Larres and Panikos Panayi (eds.), *The Federal Republic of Germany since 1949: Politics, Society and Economy before and after Unification* (London: Longman, 1996).

Panayi, Panikos, "Racial Violence in Britain during the Nineteenth and Twentieth Centuries," in Panayi (ed.), *Racial Violence in Britain, 1840–1950* (Leicester: Leicester University Press, 1993).

Panayi, Panikos, "Racial Violence in the New Germany (1990–1993)," *Contemporary European History* 3, 1994, 265–287.

Panayi, Panikos, *The Impact of Immigration: A Documentary History of the Effects and Experiences of Immigrants and Refugees in Britain since 1945* (Manchester: Manchester University Press, 1999).

Panayi, Panikos, *Outsiders: A History of European Minorities* (London: Hambledon, 1999).

Panayi, Panikos, *An Ethnic History of Europe since 1945: Nations, States and Minorities* (London: Longman, 2000).

Panayi, Panikos, *Ethnic Minorities in Nineteenth and Twentieth Century Germany: Jews, Gypsies, Poles, Turks and Others* (London: Longman, 2000).

Panayi, Panikos, "The Spicing up of English Provincial Life: The History of Curry in Leicester," in Anne J. Kershen (ed.), *Food in the Migrant Experience* (Aldershot: Ashgate, 2002).

Panayi, Panikos, "The Evolution of Multiculturalism in Britain and Germany: An Historical Survey," *Journal of Multilingual and Multicultural Development* 25, 2004, 466–480.

Paul, Kathleen, *Whitewashing Britain: Race and Citizenship in the Postwar Era* (Ithaca, NY: Cornell University Press, 1997).

Però, Davide, "Immigration and Politics in Left-Wing Bologna: Results from Participatory Action Research," in Russell King and Richard Black (eds.), *Southern Europe and the New Immigration* (Brighton: Sussex Academic, 1997).

Rex, John and Gurharpal Singh, *Governance in Multicultural Societies* (Aldershot: Ashgate, 2004).

Roberts, J.A.G., *China to Chinatown: Chinese Food in the West* (London: Reaktion, 2002).

Rock, David and Stefan Wolff (eds.), *Going Home to Germany? The Integration of Ethnic Germans from Central and Eastern Europe in the Federal Republic* (Oxford: Berghan, 2002).

Salt, John, "International Labour Migration: The Geographical Pattern of Demand," in John Salt and Hugh Clough (eds.), *Migration in Post-war Europe* (London: Oxford University Press, 1976).

Schumacher, Harald, *Einwanderungland BRD: Warum die deutsche Wirtschaft weiter Ausländer braucht* (Düsseldorf: Zebulon, 1992).

Seidel-Pielen, Eberhard, *Aufgespießt: Wie die Döner über Deutschland kamen* (Hamburg: Rotbuch Verlag, 1996).

Singh, Gurharpal, "Multiculturalism in Contemporary Britain: Reflections on the 'Leicester Model,'" *International Journal on Multicultural Societies* 5, 2003, 40–54.

Wallace, Claire and Dariusz Stola (eds.), *Patterns of Migration in Central Europe* (Basingstoke: Palgrave, 2001).

Wrench, John and John Solomos (eds.), *Racism and Migration in Western Europe* (Oxford: Berg, 1993).

Further Reading

Two general texts by Panikos Panayi on migrants in postwar Europe are *An Ethnic History of Europe since 1945: Nations, States and Minorities* (London, 2000); and *Outsiders: A History of*

European Minorities (London, 1999). A good, if rather Marxist and slightly dated, starting point on the migration process and its consequences is Stephen Castles and Godula Cossack, *Immigrant Workers and Class Struggle in Western Europe* (London, 1973). Refugee movements can be traced in Michael Marrus, *The Unwanted: European Refugees in the Twentieth Century* (Oxford, 1985).

Important texts which deal with more recent migration include Solon Ardittis (ed.), *The Politics of East–West Migration* (London, 1994); Agat Górny and Paolo Ruspini (eds.), *Migration in the New Europe: East–West Revisited* (Basingstoke, 2004); and Russell King and Richard Black (eds.), *Southern Europe and the New Immigration* (Brighton, 1997). A good volume on the importance and role of immigration is Panikos Panayi, *The Impact of Immigration: A Documentary History of the Effects and Experiences of Immigrants and Refugees in Britain since 1945* (Manchester, 1999).

Books which trace a variety of aspects of interethnic relations include Ted Cantle, *Community Cohesion: A New Framework for Race and Diversity* (Basingstoke, 2005); Luciano Cheles, Ronnie Ferguson, and Michalina Vaughan (eds.), *The Far Right in Western and Eastern Europe* (London, 1993); Tøre Björgo and Rob Witte (eds.), *Racist Violence in Europe* (London, 1993); John Wrench and John Solomos (eds.), *Racism and Migration in Western Europe* (Oxford, 1993); Anne J. Kershen (ed.), *A Question of Identity* (Aldershot, 1998); and John Rex and Gurharpal Singh (eds.), *Governance in Multicultural Societies* (Aldershot, 2004).

CHAPTER TWENTY-ONE

Changing Norms of Masculinity and Femininity: Development in Gender Relations and Family Structures in Europe

LAURA DEN DULK

All over Europe we have witnessed an increase in female labor market participation as well as major demographic changes, such as declining fertility rates and rising divorce rates. Both trends are related to changing gender relations in Europe. The rise of female employment has challenged the traditional male breadwinner–female homemaker model as the dominant family model, which was prevalent in Europe during the 1950s and 1960s. All European countries have been characterized by an increase of dual-earner families in particular among couples with children. Moreover, it is nowadays more reasonable to talk about "families" rather than "family" as the variation in family patterns has become so immense, with cohabiting couples, married couples, stepfamilies, single-parent families, and same-sex couples.[1] Generally, families have become smaller as a result of fewer children per family and the tendency of women to postpone the births of their first child.[2] Although countries differ with regard to the nature and degree of these demographic and labor market develop-ments, modern working and family life in all welfare states has increased the need to respond to work–family issues and to reconsider the question of which family model(s) welfare states wish to facilitate.[3]

The development of welfare states has been strongly influenced by the traditional breadwinner family model. Founders of current European welfare states in western Europe, like Beveridge and Keynes, based their theories on the implicit assumption of a traditional division of tasks between women and men. The unpaid care work of the wife was paid for indirectly by the paid work of the husband.[4] As a result social insurance schemes and social policies were based on the household rather than the individual. Since the 1970s reforms to promote gender equality between men and women have been on the political agenda.[5] Although all European countries have witnessed an increase in female employment, a rise of dual-earner families. and declin-ing fertility rates, countries do differ in their policy responses. In some countries, like Sweden and Norway, the rise of female employment has been accompanied by a broad range of public policies that support working parents in the combination of

A Companion to Europe since 1945, First Edition. Edited by Klaus Larres.
© 2014 John Wiley & Sons, Ltd. Published 2014 by John Wiley & Sons, Ltd.

paid work and caring responsibilities. In countries like the UK, in contrast, government support for working parents has been minimal or nearly absent.

This chapter describes changing gender relations in Europe. The focus is on a comparison between countries, although people within countries may respond differently to development in their country. Age, gender, and education are important individual characteristics in this respect. The question will be raised of what kinds of family model are emerging in Europe. More specifically, to what extent a pattern of dual-earner–dual-carer families emerging within Europe. Not only are developments in western Europe discussed, but also trends in eastern European countries. Furthermore, we will focus on the different policy responses in countries; i.e. to what extent public policies support new family models in which both women and men combine paid work and caring tasks.

First, the chapter will give an overview of demographic and labor market changes within Europe. In the subsequent sections the dual-earner family in contemporary Europe is discussed and the way the institutional context in countries affects the nature and extent of changing gender relations. Differences between countries are based on historical and cultural differences. An important source for explaining national differences has been the welfare state. A country's timing, pace, and pattern of change from the traditional male breadwinner to the dual-earner family model is affected by its type of welfare state regime.[6] Based on the typology of Esping-Andersen[7] and with the addition of the former socialist regime, four welfare state regimes are distinguished: the social democratic welfare state regime, the liberal regime, the conservative regime, and the postcommunist regime.[8] In particular, the development of work–family policies that support dual-earner families in the various regimes is discussed.

Demographic and Labour Market Changes within Europe
The growing labor market participation of women

One of the major labor market developments in Europe after World War II has been the increase in women's labor market participation. At the beginning of the twenty-first century, it is more likely for a woman to have a paid job than to be a full-time housewife. Although the increase of female labor market participation is true for all European countries, large differences exist between countries. This is especially true for western European countries. Among eastern European countries differences are smaller than in the west. Under the influence of the communist ideology, female labor force participation was stimulated in all eastern European countries and they were the first to show high levels of female labor market participation rates. Hence, in the 1960s, participation rates of eastern European women were high compared to western Europe. Female employment remained high and stable in eastern Europe until the political turnover in 1989, after which female employment rates decreased somewhat.[9]

Table 21.1 presents activity rates for men and women between 1975 and 2005.[10] All European countries are characterized by growing female activity rates and a decline in male activity rates. The decline of male activity rates is mainly due to longer periods of education and lowering of retirement age. In 1975,

Table 21.1 Activity rates (% of population aged 15–64), by sex, 1975, 1985, 1995, 2005

	Men				Women			
	1975	1985	1995	2005	1975	1985	1995	2005
Northern Europe								
Sweden	89	86	80	81	68	79	75	76
Finland	79	83	76	77	69	77	69	73
Denmark	88	91	85	84	63	76	74	76
Western Europe								
Belgium	83	74	72	74	39	45	52	60
Germany	85	83	80	81	50	53	61	67
France	90	80	75	75	54	58	61	64
The Netherlands	93	81	80	84	35	44	59	70
Austria	85	86	81	79	51	54	62	66
Ireland	90	84	76	81	36	40	47	61
UK	92	88	84	82	55	62	67	69
Southern Europe								
Portugal	88	86	77	79	51	55	60	68
Greece	86	83	78	79	34	42	45	55
Italy	83	78	74	75	34	39	42	50
Spain	90	80	75	81	33	34	43	58
Eastern Europe								
Poland	82	82[1]	73[3]	71	67	66[1]	59[3]	58
Hungary	75[4]	84[1]	66[3]	68	48[4]	62[1]	49[3]	55
Bulgaria	83	n/a	n/a	67	67	n/a	n/a	57

1   1983
2   including the new German Länder
3   1997
4   % of population ages 15–60+
n/a   data not available
Sources: *Employment in Europe*, 1999, 2006; for eastern Europe *ILO Yearbook of Labour Statistics*, 1975, 1983.

female activity rates varied between 33% in Spain and 69% in Finland and 67% in Poland. Already in 1975, the Nordic and eastern European countries were characterized by high activity rates of women. Thirty years later, women in Nordic countries are still the most active on the labor market within Europe. In eastern Europe a decline is visible since the political turnover in 1989 and female activity rates have become more similar to those in the west. In 2005, the highest female activity rate was found in Sweden and Denmark (76%) and the lowest in Italy (50%). Male activity rates in 2005 varied between 84% in Denmark and the Netherlands and 67% in Bulgaria. In 2005 the lowest female employment rates were found in eastern and southern Europe, with the exception of Portugal. Overall, the gender employment gap is narrowing in Europe. Nevertheless, activity rates of women are still lower than those of men in all European countries. This is also true for the Nordic countries, although differences are minimal.

Not only is the gender employment gap narrowing, also the gender gap in educational attainment. Moreover, in some countries, women are doing better in higher education than men. All over Europe, highly educated women are more likely to be in employment than less-educated women. "Higher education is likely to give women access to more interesting and better paid occupations, also increasing the opportunity cost of choosing not to work in order to take care of children."[11] Although gender differences in educational attainment are disappearing, important differences remain. Women tend to choose different fields of study than men do. Women are concentrated in fields of study such as health and welfare, the humanities, art, and education. In traditional male fields, such as engineering and applied sciences, physical sciences, and mathematics and computer science, women are still underrepresented. The choice of field of study might be related to differences in attitudes of women and men towards work and work/family issues and to the fact that occupations and professions are seen as "male" or "female."[12]

Occupational segregation by sex is in fact still an actual phenomenon in Europe. Women tend to work in the service sector while men are overrepresented in the industrial sector. In eastern Europe, before the transition, more women used to work in the industrial and agricultural sectors than in western European countries. However, after the collapse of the socialist regime, more women tend to work in the growing service sector and occupational segregation by gender has become more similar to that of the west.[13] In western Europe higher levels of occupational gender segregation are found in Nordic countries, where female labor market participation is high. In southern Europe where lower levels of female employment are found, segregation is less marked. In addition, all over Europe women are underrepresented in managerial job positions.[14]

The fact that men have more senior or higher-level occupations than women is also reflected in a gender gap in earnings. In 1995, the average earnings of women employed full-time in industry and services in the EU were around 75% of men's. Only in Belgium, Denmark, Luxembourg, and Sweden were women's average earnings more than 85% of men's. In Portugal the largest gender pay gap is found: Portuguese women earn only 67% of what men do; in the Netherlands and Greece 70%. Eastern European countries show similar differences in average earnings between men and women: in Estonia and Lithuania women earn on average 75% of men's earnings and in Hungary, Poland, and Romania just over 80%; the highest female earnings compared to male are found in Slovenia (women earn 90% of men's earnings).[15] Over time, the sex wage gap appears to be declining. In the Netherlands, for instance, women earned approximately 60% of men's wages in 1950 and 71% in 1999.[16]

Part-time employment

The increase in female employment has been accompanied by the shift of employment from agriculture and manufacturing towards services and the rise of part-time employment.[17] A first phase of rapid growth in part-time work among women occurred between the 1950s and the 1970s. The second phase contained a more modest growth (with the exception of the Netherlands) and began in the late 1970s.[18] Women in particular use part-time work as a strategy to combine paid work with the care of young children. Men, on the other hand, work more once they have children. In particular, when women have two or more children their employment rates decline. Notable exceptions are Belgium and Sweden, as well as Denmark and Norway. In these countries little impact of motherhood on employment is found. The largest effects of having two or more children on the labor market participation of women are found in the Czech Republic, Germany, and Ireland.[19]

Already in 1985 the Netherlands was characterized by the highest percentage of part-timers: 14% of Dutch men and 58% of Dutch women had a part-time job; in 2005 this was 23% and 75% respectively (see Table 21.2). Other western

Table 21.2   Part-time employed (% of total employment), by sex, 1985, 1995, 2005

	Men			Women		
	1985	1995	2005	1985	1995	2005
Northern Europe						
Sweden	7	7	12	46	36	40
Finland	6	8	9	17	15	19
Denmark	8	11	13	44	35	33
Western Europe						
Belgium	2	3	8	21	31	41
Germany	2	4	8	30	34	44
France	3	5	6	22	29	31
The Netherlands	14	17	23	58	67	75
Austria	3	4	6	23	27	39
Ireland	2	5	63	16	22	323
UK	4	8	10	45	44	43
Southern Europe						
Portugal	3	4	7	10	13	16
Greece	3	3	2	10	8	9
Italy	3	3	5	10	13	26
Spain	2	3	5	14	16	24
Central and eastern Europe						
Poland	n/a	8[1]	8	n/a	14[1]	14
Hungary	n/a	2[1]	3	n/a	6[1]	6
Bulgaria	n/a	n/a	2	n/a	n/a	3
Czech Republic	n/a	3[2]	2	n/a	10[2]	9
Romania	n/a	13[1]	10	n/a	18[1]	11
Slovenia	n/a	8[1]	7	n/a	10[1]	11
Slovakia	n/a	1[2]	1	n/a	4[2]	4

1   1997
2   1998
3   2004

Source: Employment in Europe, 1999, 2006.

European countries also show high percentages of part-time working women: in 2005, 43% of British working women, 41% of working women in Belgium, and 44% of working women in Germany were working part-time. But also one-third of working women Denmark and 40% in Sweden had a part-time job. Finland is an exception to the northern European employment patterns, there only 19% of women are in part-time employment. In southern and eastern European countries part-time work is also less common, although Italy and Spain witnessed a sharp increase of women in part-time employment between 1995 and 2005. Currently, among southern European countries the percentage of women with a part-time job varies between 9% and 26%, while in eastern Europe part-time employment is even less prevalent; only 3–14% of eastern European women have a part-time job. Recently, some countries (Sweden, Denmark, and Norway) have experienced a decline in part-time employment. In other countries, the growth of part-time jobs has remained the same or has even increased.[20] Overall, part-time work is mainly a women's affair; with the exception of the Netherlands, the percentage of men in part-time employment was 13% or less in 2005.

In Italy, Spain, and Greece employment rates for women are relatively low, but women who do work often do so on a full-time basis. Therefore, differences in women's labor market activity are less pronounced when measured in terms of hours worked than employment rates indicate. Moreover, the contribution of women to paid work is less substantial than employment rates suggest. Furthermore, behind the distinction of part-time and full-time, large variations in working hours exist among women within and across countries. In the Netherlands and the United Kingdom, for example, women often work "short" part-time hours (ten hours or less). By contrast, in the Nordic countries women more often work "long" part-time hours – 25 hours or more per week.[21]

The proportion of part-time employment in countries relates, among other things, to working-time regulations, fiscal incentives, and available childcare facilities, but also to existing gender relations and societal values.[22] Italy, being a low part-time country, has, for instance, one of the most rigid labor markets in Europe. Relatively strong unions in the 1970s have led to a comprehensive job security system with many regulations on recruitment, dismissal, and working times.[23] Trade unions in Italy hesitate to encourage part-time work; it is seen as a threat to the position of the regular, full-time worker.[24] In the Netherlands, on the other hand, the government has encouraged the development of part-time work. Part-time work is seen as a way to combine paid work and care for children.[25] Important in this respect is the strong cultural belief in the Netherlands that parents (mothers) should do most of the actual care and upbringing of their children rather than make the state responsible for this. The Dutch government has improved the position of part-timers in several ways and part-time work does not necessarily mean a half-time, lower-status job. In the Netherlands there are discussions about how managerial and higher staff positions can fit into a four-day working week. This pattern is developing slowly, primarily in the public sector and primarily among women.[26] Nevertheless, in general part-time work often means that there are fewer career opportunities as compared to full-time employment. In Europe, part-time jobs are more likely lower-paid jobs and part-timers are more likely to have a temporary work contract than full-timers.[27]

Diefenbach analyzed gender role orientation in various OECD (Organisation for Economic Co-Operation and Development) countries (using International Social Survey Programme – ISSP, 1994 data) based on agreement or disagreement with the statement "a man's job is to earn money; a woman's job is to look after the home and family." An egalitarian gender role orientation (i.e. strong disagreement with the statement) was found in countries like Sweden, Norway, East Germany and the Netherlands. Eastern European countries, in contrast, responded most traditionally. Countries like Ireland, Spain, Italy, and West Germany scored in the middle. Diefenbach also showed that people are not always able to realize their preferences. For example, the economic situation in a country may simply not allow a traditional male breadwinner model because two (full-time) incomes are needed to sustain a family.[28]

However, modern gender role orientation, as well as the rise in female employment, does not guarantee equal division of household tasks. In all European countries, women spend more hours on average on household work than their husbands do, regardless of the number of hours they work outside the home. The most traditional division of paid and unpaid work between men and women in western Europe is found in Italy; Italian women do 74% of the household work and take care of the children. In Sweden the contribution of men to household work and caring tasks is more substantial: 60% of the number of hours that women spend on them. Studies in the UK and the Netherlands indicate that men do about half the amount of unpaid work that women do – 48% and 47% respectively.[29] Generally speaking, the more women are employed, as in Denmark and Finland, the less time they spend on domestic work. On the other hand, the presence of young children increases women's time spend on household work and caring tasks. Over the last decades men's contribution to domestic work have increased somewhat but not enough to compensate for women's increase in hours spent on paid work. Men's contributions to domestic work lies on average at around 10 to 12 hours per week across western European countries, while women's unpaid hours vary between 25 and 45 hours a week. Only Swedish men have a more substantial contribution; they spent on average 21 hours per week on unpaid work.[30] Hence, despite the increase in female labor market participation, women still carry the major burden of household work and care for children in addition to doing their paid job.

Diversification of family forms and declining fertility rates

The growing labor market participation of women in Europe has been accompanied by declining fertility rates and a diversification in family forms. In the last few decades, there has been a general decrease in marriage rates and a tendency to marry at a later age. Cohabitation has become popular, especially for couples without children. Cohabitation is common in particular in Scandinavia and countries like the Netherlands, France, and the UK. Since 1960, we have also seen a rise in divorce rates that have resulted in a growth of one-parent families and patterns of remarriage and stepfamilies.[31] Besides diversification of family forms, there is an overall decline in average household size, primarily because fewer children are born per household and the number of childless families in many countries is increasing. In addition, women are increasingly postponing the birth of their first child. Together these developments result in an overall decline in fertility rates within Europe. These demographic developments occur in all European countries, although the pace and timing of developments differ from country to country.

The United Nations provides an overview of fertility rates over time in northern, western, southern, and eastern Europe (see Table 21.3).[32] All over Europe, fertility was at a lower level in 2000 than in the 1950s, and the majority of countries now have below-replacement fertility. Jensen states that patterns of divergence in family forms and declining fertility rates first emerged in the Scandinavian countries in the 1960s and 1970s. In the 1990s, however, fertility rates in southern European countries (Spain and Italy) have been declining faster than in northern Europe, although divorce rates and extramarital births remain low in these countries. In eastern European countries, on the other hand, fertility rates remained at a relatively high and stable level until the mid-1980s, after which strong declines set in.[33] The most pronounced decline is found in the former East Germany, where the total fertility rate fell from 1.57 per woman in 1989 to 0.80 in 1993.[34] But Italy, Spain, Bulgaria, Romania, and the Czech Republic are also characterized by relatively low fertility rates, i.e. below 1.25.[35] Jensen also notes that the rates of birth outside marriage are highest in the countries where fertility levels are highest; i.e. in the northern countries. In southern Europe, in contrast, the link between fertility and marriage is still strong, and is combined with low fertility. Central Europe can be placed between these two extremes.[36]

The sharp decline in fertility rates is related to the increase in average age of mothers at the birth of their first child. Women are tending to postpone motherhood. Between 1980 and 1990, the mean age of women at first birth rose about 2 to 3 years in western Europe.[37] Eastern European countries have experienced an increase in the mean age of the mother at first birth only since 1989/1990. In 1998 the

Table 21.3 Total fertility rates 1950–1955, 1975–1980, and 2000–2005

	1950–1955	1975–1980	2000–2005
Northern Europe	2,32	1,81	1,61
Western Europe	2,39	1,65	1,58
Southern Europe	2,65	2,25	1,32
Eastern Europe	2,91	2,08	1,18
Europe	2,66	1,97	1,38

Northern Europe: Denmark, Estonia, Faeroe, Finland, Ireland, the Channel Islands, Latvia, Lithuania, the Isle of Man, Norway, UK, Iceland, Sweden.
Western Europe: Belgium, Germany, France, Liechtenstein, Luxembourg, Monaco, the Netherlands, Austria, Switzerland.
Southern Europe: Albania, Andorra, Bosnia and Herzegovina, Gibraltar, Greece, Italy, Yugoslavia, Croatia, Macedonia, Malta, Portugal, San Marino, Slovenia, Spain, Vatican City.
Eastern Europe: Bulgaria, Hungary, Republic of Moldova, Ukraine, Poland, Romania, Russian Federation, Slovakia, Czech Republic, Belarus.
Source: UN, 2003

average age of childbearing women in Bulgaria was 22.9, thwe Czech Republic 24.3; Hungary 24.5 and Poland 23.3. Although the average age of new mothers has increased in these countries since 1990, the mean age is still lower than in western European countries.[38] Presently, the highest average age of women at childbearing in Europe is found in the Netherlands: the mean age of Dutch women at the birth of their first child is 30.2 years, one year older than the average mean age in Europe.[39]

Reasons for women to start a family later in life can be found in the lengthening of the period of education and the increased labor market participation of women.[40] Young people organize and plan their entry into parenthood carefully: education and establishing a position on the labor market usually precede the formation of a family. In addition, research findings suggest that the delay in having children is further lengthened by the lack of work–family policies that facilitate the combination of paid work and caring responsibilities for young children.[41] In addition, it is argued that postponement of starting a family is linked to individualization and consumerism. It is assumed that young couples want to enjoy their freedom and maintain their consumption power as dual-income-no-kids couples. Research shows that having children is costly; children often mean reduced money, time, and career options. Finally, labor market conditions are mentioned as important determinants: unemployment, precarious employment conditions, and job insecurity are also reasons to postpone having children. This may in particularly be true for the current eastern European countries. Postponement may lead to childlessness and the proportion of childless women is increasing in Europe, in particular among more highly educated women.[42] Nevertheless, the two-child family is presently the most common family type in Europe.

The rise of the dual-earner family

The increase in women's labor market participation has resulted in a growth of dual-earner families. Within Europe, there has been a change from the traditional male-breadwinner/female-homecarer to the dual-earner family model. However, European countries do differ in the pace and timing of developments. In the Nordic and Eastern countries (with the exception of Hungary) and Portugal, around two-third of couples are dual-earners, while in southern European countries, like Spain, Italy, and Greece, the proportion of dual earners is around 50% of couples (Aliaga, 2005). The growth of dual-earner families was in particular substantial among couples with children. Nevertheless, among dual earner families with children there are large differences in the way paid work is divided among partners: both partners may work full-time, one partner may have a full-time job whereas the other works part-time; or both partners may work part-time. The latter is fairly uncommon in the investigated countries. There are also very few dual-earner households with children in which the mother works full-time and the father works part-time.[43]

Table 21.4 shows the working-time patterns of couples with a child under 12 in various western European countries. Compared to couples without children, the proportion of households in which both partners work full-time is less substantial.

Table 21.4 Working time patterns of couples aged 20–49 in households with a child under 12 in 2003, percentage of couples with at least one partner in work

	Male FT/female not employed	Male FT/female FT	Male FT/female PT
Northern Europe			
Finland	25	60	8
Western Europe			
Austria	27	36	33
Belgium	26	41	27
France	30	47	17
Germany	37	22	35
Luxembourg	42	30	25
The Netherlands	26	12	55
UK	29	27	39
Southern Europe			
Greece	47	44	6
Italy	50	32	14
Portugal	22	67	7
Spain	48	40	9
Eastern Europe			
Czech Republic	44	50	4
Estonia	37	52	4
Latvia	31	53	7
Lithuania	17	60	11
Hungary	47	44	3
Poland	35	46	9
Slovenia	13	80	(1)
Slovakia	36	57	2

FT   working full-time, that is, 30 or more hours a week
PT   working part-time, that is, less than 30 hours a week
()   reliability uncertain
Source: Eurostat: European Labour Force Survey, 2003

In the Netherlands and the UK couples with children more often have a division of paid work in which the father works full-time and the mother part-time (55% and 39% of couples respectively). In countries were part-time employment is less common, couples with children are less often dual-earners and if both partners work, they both have a full-time job. In Italy, Spain, Hungary, and Greece about half of the couples with children are single earners. It is striking that in Slovenia 80% and in Portugal 67% of couples with children are both working full-time. Table 21.5 shows the actual and preferred employment patterns of couples with a child under 6 in various European countries.

The work patterns of working parents in different European countries show that the one-and-a-half-earner model (men full-time, women part-time) is dominant in

Table 21.5 The actual and preferred employment patterns of couples with a child under 6 in various European countries, 1998

	Male FT/ female FT	Male FT/ female PT	Male FT/female not employed	Other
Northern Europe				
Finland				
Actual	49.3	6.4	32.8	11.5
Preferred	80.3	8.6	10.2	0.8
Sweden				
Actual	51.1	13.3	24.9	10.7
Preferred	66.8	22.2	6.6	4.4
Central and western Europe				
Ireland				
Actual	30.8	18.7	37.0	13.5
Preferred	31.1	42.3	8.1	18.5
UK				
Actual	24.9	31.9	32.8	10.4
Preferred	21.3	41.8	13.3	23.6
Austria				
Actual	19.1	28.2	48.1	4.5
Preferred	35.6	39.9	3.9	20.7
Germany				
Actual	15.7	23.1	52.3	8.9
Preferred	32.0	42.9	5.7	19.4
The Netherlands				
Actual	4.8	54.8	33.7	6.7
Preferred	5.6	69.9	10.7	13.8
Belgium				
Actual	46.0	19.4	27.3	7.3
Preferred	54.8	28.8	13.4	3.0
France				
Actual	38.8	14.4	38.3	8.4
Preferred	52.4	21.9	14.1	11.7
Luxembourg				
Actual	23.5	27.0	49.1	0.4
Preferred	27.5	29.9	12.4	30.2
Southern Europe				
Greece				
Actual	42.2	7.9	36.1	13.8
Preferred	65.6	10.6	9.4	14.4
Italy				
Actual	34.9	11.8	43.3	10.0
Preferred	50.4	27.7	10.7	11.2
Portugal				
Actual	74.5	4.7	18.7	2.2
Preferred	84.4	8.0	4.0	3.6
Spain				
Actual	25.6	6.3	56.9	11.2
Preferred	59.7	11.6	19.7	9.0

Source: OECD, *Employment Outlook*, 2001, based on Options of the Future Survey employment, 1998.

particular in the Netherlands, but also in the UK and Germany. Swedish and Finnish parents prefer a pattern in which both have a full-time job. In southern European countries (with exception of Portugal), the one-earner model is still most prevalent. However, preferences in these countries show that parents would like to realize a dual-earner arrangement in which both partners have a full-time job. British couples with children show much variation: besides a large group of one-and-a-half earners, there is also a group of dual earners in which both parents have a full-time job and a group of one-earner families.

Different factors contribute to the variation found in working patterns of couples with children across Europe. Economic and labor market conditions, the dominant family ideology, and supports offered to working parents within the welfare state and workplaces are all highly relevant and intertwined. People – or couples – need an income and in many countries two incomes are needed to sustain a family, explaining why many couples combine two full-time jobs even though they might prefer another division of paid work. In addition, the availability of part-time employment determines whether people can opt for the one-and-a-half-earner model as is widely common in the Netherlands. Attitudes towards gender roles have been changing and it is increasingly accepted that women should be in paid employment; nevertheless, women still carry the main responsibility for care tasks and domestic work at home.[44] Norms and values concerning what is good motherhood and fatherhood vary within countries and between countries. For instance, more highly educated people often have more liberal or egalitarian views while among the lower educated "traditional" views are more prevalent. National variations are visible in the degree to which it is considered normal practice for parents with young children to have a full-time job or the degree to which care for children at home is the dominant norm. Cultural ideas around motherhood and fatherhood are also incorporated in existing policy responses across countries to the rise of female employment and the increasing wish and need to combine work and family life. The introduction of work–family policies that support dual-earner families are more common in some countries than in others. In the next section I will discuss the development of work–family policies in various welfare state regimes.

The Perspective of Welfare State Regimes

The degree and nature of work–family policies in a country is linked to its welfare state regime. Welfare states are, at least implicitly, based on assumptions about the social roles of men and women, on ideas about families, and on what has to be seen as appropriate behavior for women and men. The availability of work–family policies reflects these cultural ideas and assumptions.

In cross-national research, Esping-Andersen's typology of welfare state regimes is often used as a framework or starting point for interpretating differences and similarities between countries.[45] Central to his typology is the assumption that the relation between the state, the market, and the family varies in different welfare state regimes, using the notions of decommodification and social stratification. Many scholars have criticized the Esping-Andersen typology.[46] A crucial objection was that

Esping-Andersen did not take into account the specific position of women in welfare states and that his analysis is mainly based on (male) paid workers. It is argued that it is not just the degree to which people live independently of market forces that is relevant, but also the degree to which it is possible for people (women) to live independently from families. Based on the work of Esping-Andersen, but with more emphasis on the relations between the market, the state, and the family, and the addition of a fourth regime, four types of welfare state regime can be distinguished: liberal, conservative corporatistic, social democratic, and postcommunist. The different types of welfare state regimes are used to describe the variation in policy responses towards changing gender relations.

In the social democratic regime women's employment is supported by an elaborate system of public work–family policies which makes the combination of work and family life less difficult to manage. Universal services, such as a substantial public day-care system, support the employment of women. Also the tax system is individualized. The state is the main provider of welfare; private welfare provision is almost nonexistent. In this welfare state regime, the state also plays an important role as an employer, especially within the service sector. To a large extent women in particular work in the public services. Sweden, Denmark, and Finland come nearest to this particular welfare state regime within Europe.

In Sweden, for instance, working parents' children aged from one to 12 years are entitled to a place in publicly funded childcare services. During the first year of the child's life, parents are able to use paid parental leave in order to stay at home and care for their child themselves. In fact, Sweden was the first country in Europe to introduce parental leave for both mothers and fathers. As early as 1974, working parents had the right to take paid parental leave and the right to return to the same job or a similar position in the workplace. Nowadays, parents can share 480 days of parental leave between them. The first 390 days are paid at 80% of earnings and after that they are entitled to a flat-rate payment. Of the parental leave, 60 days are reserved for each parent, the so-called daddy and mommy quota. The special daddy months aim to encourage fathers to take leave and thereby stimulate the equal division of caring responsibilities between men and women.[47]

Norway has also introduced a fathers' quota regarding parental leave. In Denmark and Finland, in contrast, no specific fathers' quota for parental leave has been present and special leave for fathers is restricted to paternity leave. Another notable difference between the social democratic countries is that Norway and Finland both introduced "cash-for-care" systems, allowing working parents to choose between public day care and parental care at home when children are young.[48] Denmark and Sweden, on the other hand, do not support parental choice between care at home and the use of public day care. Instead, Danish and Swedish parents are expected to return to full-time employment after their parental leave.[49] However, despite these differences, the attention given to the equal sharing between men and women of caring responsibilities is a striking characteristic of the social democratic welfare state regime.

A typical characteristic of the conservative regime is compulsory social insurance schemes, which uphold status differences.[50] For people without work only a modest social security system is offered. In addition, this type of regime for a long time strongly supported the traditional family unit and motherhood ideals. Day care and other family services are moderate in comparison with the social democratic regime. Aside from this, a principle of subsidiarity is enhanced, which means that the state only interferes when the possibilities of families are exhausted.[51] Within the conservative welfare state regime childcare and parental leave facilities are less common and the participation of women in the labor market is relatively low compared to countries of the social democratic regime. In many conservative countries tax provisions still favor the traditional single-earner/breadwinner family and parental care is emphasized. Within Europe, Germany and Italy most closely resemble this type of welfare state. Some studies distinguish a separate Mediterranean regime.[52]

Much depends on which factors or indicators are taken into account. Anttonen and Sipilä, for instance, look at the availability of caring services, while Esping-Andersen's analysis focuses on the role of families in the provisions of welfare.[53] Southern European countries have extremely low public provisions, but on the other hand they do not support the breadwinner-family model by incorporating disincentives in the tax system regarding paid employment of women. In Austria, Germany, and the Netherlands (in the Netherlands until 2001), tax provisions favor the traditional single-earner/breadwinner family. In Scandinavia and southern Europe, no discouragement of a wife's employment through tax treatment is found.[54] France and Belgium, usually placed in the conservative cluster, can be viewed as ambiguous cases since both countries have extensive day-care and preschool facilities. Like Norway and Finland, a "parental choice orientated model" characterizes France; next to daycare provisions, French parents can also opt for a long paid parental leave.[55] In other conservative countries, such as Germany and the Netherlands, parental care is emphasized much more either by promoting part-time work as a strategy for combining work and care or by offering long leave.[56] Nowadays, the Netherlands is characterized by 16 weeks' paid maternity leave, 13 weeks' unpaid parental leave per parent, and two days' paternity leave. Germany recently introduced the possibility of taking up to three years' parental leave (including maternity leave)[57]

The liberal regime stands out owing to its focus on market forces, the market's self-regulation capacity, and market solutions. Employer-sponsored benefits and private insurance are common. Therefore, universal transfers, benefits, and social insurance plans are mainly modest. The state is seen as a last resort. The individual is seen as responsible for childcare and parental leave and not the government. As a result, support at the national level is not so distinctive. People must acquire care services on the market, but these are expensive and generally less accessible to low-income families. A strong role for employers is envisioned in this welfare state regime and the business side of work–family policies is emphasized; that is, employers introduce work–family support when it gives them a competitive advantage. Because liberal welfare state regimes only have a limited system of breadwinner facilities, the labor market participation of women is still rather high. The US most closely represents this regime type. Within Europe, the United Kingdom comes nearest to this model, even though the British welfare state also has universalistic elements, such as a universal health care system.[58] However, under the Labour government elected in 1997, the UK has introduced more work–family policies and the level of provisions has become more similar to that of countries like the Netherlands.

Esping-Andersen argues that markets only rarely substitute for public services or family self-servicing. Only when market services are cheap (because of cheap labor, as in the US) does it become worthwhile for a majority of families to outsource caring tasks. In Europe, however, the cost of market services is high because of high tax on labor and a relatively egalitarian wage structure (a notable exception is Portugal.[59] Therefore market services, such as private day care, are expensive and inaccessible to a majority of families.

Blossfeld and Drobnič (2001) have suggested a further welfare state type for the former socialist countries, or eastern Europe. Under state socialism, women's participation on the labor market was high and the common family model was the model of two full-time earners. "Work arrangements in these countries could tentatively be described as standard forms of employment, with life-long, secure, permanent, full-time jobs for both men and women."[60] Nevertheless, the equal division of household work and care tasks between men and women was not discussed or debated.[61] The idea of gender equality considered only access to paid work for women. To make a combination of work and care possible for women, childcare services were developed in the late 1950s and early 1960s. Most of the children aged between three and six years at this time attended public day care. Subsequently leave arrangements were introduced. In 1969, Hungary was the first central eastern European country to introduce a parental leave scheme (for mothers only) with a relatively high allowance. Instead of using childcare facilities for children under 3 years of age, mothers stayed at home to care for their children. Job security and pension entitlements were guaranteed. After the transition to a market economy, public provisions declined in most former socialist countries. Nevertheless, eastern European countries are still characterized by relatively long periods of leave, mostly until a child is 3 years old. Until the 1990s, parental leave was mainly targeted at mothers; however, nowadays also fathers are entitled to take leave. But unlike in the social democratic regimes, former socialist countries have not (yet) introduced either paternity leave for fathers or special schemes, like a daddy quota, to encourage take-up by fathers.[62]

After the transition to a market economy in 1989/1990, labor market conditions changed and living standards dropped. In the 1990s childcare services declined as well as wage compensation during the period of leave. A notable exception is Slovenia, which recently increased its facilities with the introduction of a very generous paternity leave scheme for fathers.[63] In eastern Europe the transition to the market economy was expected to give parents the opportunity to opt for the one-earner model. Nevertheless, two incomes were still needed to sustain a family. The proportion of children cared for in public childcare services is still large among the 3- to 6-year-old age group (50% in Poland and 87% in Hungary). This is explained by the fact that a decline in available places in childcare has coincided with the dramatic decline in fertility rates in eastern Europe.[64]

Although the degree and nature of work–family policies that enable people to combine paid work and caring responsibilities seems to affect the employment of women in any given country, the relationship is not straightforward. Low levels of work–family policies do not in all countries go together with low levels of female employment. The case of Portugal shows, for instance, that high female employment levels can be reached without extensive publicly funded childcare. In Portugal coverage rates for public childcare have increased substantially since the 1990s and the level is now similar to rates found in France and Finland.[65] Liberal welfare states, like the United Kingdom but also the United States and Canada, combine low levels of public day care and minimal parental leave provisions with relatively high levels of female employment. Van Dijk concludes in her study on the relationship between childcare provisions and female employment that the main political ideology in a country is an important determinant of childcare provisions. Sweden and Denmark, for example, combine a strong gender equality ideology with substantial public day care, while a country like France combines high levels of public childcare with a largely conservative ideology.[66] Moreover, it is important to note that in most European countries women took up formal employment well ahead of the development of supportive work–family policies, such as childcare and leave arrangements.[67]

Van der Lippe analyzed the number of hours of paid work by women in western and eastern Europe. In doing so, she included both individual characteristics and institutional characteristics of the countries in which women live. Results show that women living in former socialist countries work more hours per week than women in other welfare state regimes; women in eastern Europe are also more often employed full-time. As for Western European countries, women in social democratic regimes work more hours per week than women in liberal or conservative regimes. Moreover, housewives are most often found in conservative regimes.[68] Van der Lippe also notes the importance of the availability of public childcare as well as the average level of income in a country. Where the level of income is low, the more hours women tend to work, emphasizing the need for two incomes. Generally, individual characteristics, such as education and the age of children, are less important in explaining the number of hours worked for pay in the Nordic, social democratic countries and in the eastern European countries.[69]

Conclusion

To summarize, the rise of female employment and declining fertility rates are universal trends within Europe. However, the pace and timing of these trends differ across countries, as do the degree to which new family models are emerging. Despite the fact that women are more active on the labor market, gender inequality on the labor market is a persistent phenomenon and within households the division of unpaid work between men and women remains fairly unchanged. This is true for all European countries. In some countries, the rise of the dual-earner family has been, in fact, a rise of one-and-a-half-earner families in which the man is working full-time and the woman part-time. This is in particular true in countries in which there has been a growth of part-time work and where the development of substantial childcare provisions and leave arrangements remains underdeveloped. While, on the whole, western Europe is showing more differences than eastern Europe, it must be noted that since 1990 eastern Europe has become more similar to western Europe. Nevertheless, in eastern Europe the dual-earner family is still the most common family model, mainly because two incomes are needed to sustain a family.

Scandinavian countries are the only countries that combine a broad range of work–family policies that support dual-earner families with a strong gender equality ideology. In eastern Europe a traditional gender ideology is still prevalent, despite the availability of support for female employment. With the decline of the breadwinner model, more diversity in family models has occurred. Work and family are no longer considered as separate worlds and questions are being raised about how families adjust to these changing circumstances and whether and how institutions accommodate to these new realities.[70] Policy reforms responding to these developments differ across countries. In some countries gender equality is a reason to develop policies that support the dual-earner family, in others worries regarding declining fertility rates have become important determinants. Although differences and similarities across European countries have been analyzed using a typology of welfare state regimes, it is important to note that countries within the same regime may also vary in their approach to changing gender relations and family structures.

Notes

1   Drew, "Re-conceptualizing Families."
2   For example Eurostat, *Demographic Statistics*; Drew, op. cit.; SCP (Netherlands Institute for Social Research), *Sociaal en Cultureel Rapport 2000.*
3   Leira, "Family Change: Policies, Practices and Values."
4   Van Doorne-Huiskes et al., "Work–Family Arrangements in the Context of Welfare States."
5   Sainsbury, *Gender, Equality and Welfare States.*
6   For example Blossfeld and Drobnič, *Careers of Couples in Contemporary Societies.*
7   Esping-Andersen, *The Three Worlds of Welfare Capitalism*; Esping-Andersen, *Social Foundations of Postindustrial Economics.*
8   For example Blossfeld and Drobnič, op. cit.; Van Dijk, "Macro Changes in Public Childcare Provision"; Van der Lippe and Van Dijk, *Women's Employment in a Comparative Perspective.*
9   Van der Lippe and Van Dijk, op. cit.
10 Activity rates are calculated as the percentage of people who either have a job or are unemployed – and looking for a job – in a population aged 15 to 64 years.
11 OECD, *Employment Outlook 2002*, 71.
12 OECD, *Employment Outlook 2002*, 71.
13 Van der Lippe and Van Dijk, op. cit.
14 OECD, *Employment Outlook 2002.*
15 Clarke, "Earnings of Men and Women in the EU."
16 De Ruijter, "Occupational Wage Differences: A Gender Approach."
17 OECD, *Employment Outlook 2002.*
18 MOCHO project, Universite Libre de Bruxelles (Daniele Meulders) 2002 ("The Rationale of Motherhood Choices: Influence on Employment Conditions and on Public Policies").
19 OECD, *Employment Outlook 2002.*
20 MOCHO project 2002.
21 Den Dulk, *Work–Family Arrangements in Organisations.*

22 OECD, *Employment Outlook 2002.*
23 Del Boca, *Structural Change and Economic Dynamics*
24 Den Dulk, op. cit.
25 Plantenga et al., "Towards an Equal Division of Paid and Unpaid Work."
26 Van Doorne-Huiskes et al., op. cit.
27 For example OECD, *Employment Outlook 2002.*
28 Diefenbach, "Gender Ideologies, Relative Resources and the Division of Housework in Intimate Relationships."
29 SCP, op. cit.
30 Esping-Andersen, *Social Foundations of Postindustrial Economics.*
31 Drew, op. cit.
32 United Nations, *World Population Prospects.*
33 Jensen, "Partners and Parents in Europe."
34 Jensen, op. cit.
35 Nimwegen and Esveldt, "Bevolkingsvraagstukken in Nederland anno 2003."
36 Jensen, "Partners and Parents in Europe."
37 Neyer, "Family Policies and Low Fertility in Western Europe."
38 MOCHO Project, 2003.
39 Eurostat, *Demographic Statistics.*
40 For example, Nimwegen and Esveldt, op. cit.
41 For example Esping-Andersen, *Social Foundations of Postindustrial Economics;* Künzler, "Paths Towards a Modernization of Gender Relations."
42 MOCHO Project, 2003.
43 Franco and Winqvist, "Women and Men Reconciling Work and Family Life."
44 Crompton et al., *Women, Men, Work, and Family in Europe.*
45 Esping-Andersen, *Social Foundations of Postindustrial Economics;* Künzler, op. cit.
46 For example, Langan and Ostner, "Gender and Welfare: Towards a Comparative Framework"; Plantenga and van Doorne-Huiskes, "Verschillen in arbeitsparticipatie van vrouwen in Europa"; Lewis, *Women and Social Policies in Europe;* Sainsbury, op. cit.; Leira, op. cit.
47 Plantenga and Remery, "Reconciliation of Work and Private Life."
48 OECD, *Family Database 2006.*
49 Wall, "Leave Policy Models and the Articulation of Work and Family in Europe."
50 Esping-Andersen, *The Three Worlds of Welfare Capitalism;* Sainsbury, op. cit.
51 Esping-Andersen, *The Three Worlds of Welfare Capitalism.*
52 For example Blossfeld and Drobnič, op. cit.
53 Anttonen et al., *The Young, The Old and the State;* Esping-Andersen, *Social Foundations of Postindustrial Economics;* Künzler, op. cit.
54 Esping-Andersen, *Social Foundations of Postindustrial Economics,* 65.
55 Wall, op. cit.
56 Anttonen et al., op. cit.
57 OECD *Family Database 2006.*
58 Sainsbury, op. cit.
59 Crompton et al., op. cit.
60 Blossfeld and Drobnič, op. cit., 44.
61 For example Kocourková, "Leave Arrangements and Childcare Services in Central Europe."
62 Deven and Moss, "Leave Arrangements for Parents."
63 Fagnani, "Context Mapping for the EU Framework 5 Funded Study."
64 Kocourková, op. cit.
65 Wall, op. cit.

66 Van Dijk, "Macro Changes in Public Childcare Provision."
67 For example Leira, "Family Change: Policies, Practices, and Values."
68 Van der Lippe and van Dijk, op. cit.
69 Van der Lippe and van Dijk, op. cit.
70 Crompton et al., op. cit.

Bibliography

Anttonen, Anneli, John Baldock, and Jorma Sipila (eds.), *The Young, the Old and the State: Social Care Systems in Five Industrial Nations* (Cheltenham: Edward Elgar, 2003).

Blossfeld, H.P. and S. Drobnič (eds.), *Careers of Couples in Contemporary Societies: From Male Breadwinner to Dual Earner Families* (Oxford: Oxford University Press, 2001).

Boca, D. Del, *Structural Change and Economic Dynamics* 9, 1998, special issue on Economics of the Family.

Brannen, J., "Mothers and Fathers in the Workplace: The United Kingdom," in L.L. Haas, P. Hwang, and G. Russel (eds.), *Organizational Change and Gender Equity* (London: Sage Publications, 2000).

Clarke, S., "Earnings of Men and Women in the EU: The Gap Is Narrowing but Only Slowly," *Statistics in Focus*, Population and Social Conditions, Theme 3–5 (2001).

Crompton, R., S. Lewis, and C. Lyonette (eds.), *Women, Men, Work and Family in Europe* (New York: Palgrave Macmillan, 2007).

Deven, F. and P. Moss, "Leave Arrangements for Parents: Overview and Future Outlook," *Community, Work and Family* 5, no. 3, 2002, 237–255.

Diefenbach, H., "Gender Ideologies, Relative Resources, and the Division of Housework in Intimate Relationships: A Test of Hyman Rodman's Theory of Resources in Cultural Context," *International Journal of Sociology*, 43, no. 1, 2003, 45–64.

Dijk, L. van, "Macro Changes in Public Childcare Provision, Parental Leave, and Women's Employment: An International Comparison," in T. van der Lippe and L. van Dijk (eds.), *Women's Employment in a Comparative Perspective* (New York: Aldine de Gruyter, 2001).

Doorne-Huiskes, A., L. den Dulk, and J. Schippers, "Work–Family Arrangements in the Context of Welfare States," in L. den Dulk, A. van Doorne-Huiskes, and J. Schippers (eds.), *Work–Family Arrangements in Europe* (Amsterdam: Thela Thesis, 1999).

Drew, E., "Re-conceptualizing Families," in E. Drew, R. Emerek, and E. Mahon (eds.), *Women, Work and the Family in Europe* (London: Routledge, 1998).

Dulk, L. den, *Work–Family Arrangements in Organisations: A Cross-National Study in the Netherlands, Italy, the United Kingdom and Sweden* (Amsterdam: Rozenberg Publishers, 2001).

Dulk, L. den, A. van Doorne-Huiskes, and B. Peper, "Arbeid en Zorg in Europees Perspectief," *Tijdschrift voor Arbeidsvraagstukken* 19, no. 1, 2003, 69–82.

Employment in Europe, *Employment in Europe 1999* (Luxembourg: European Commission, Employment and Social Affairs, 1999).

Employment in Europe, *Employment in Europe 2003* (Luxembourg: European Commission, Employment and Social Affairs, 2006).

Esping-Andersen, G., *The Three Worlds of Welfare Capitalism* (Cambridge: Polity Press, 1990).

Esping-Andersen, G., *Social Foundations of Postindustrial Economics* (New York: Oxford University Press, 1999).

Eurostat, *Demographic Statistics, Data 1960–99* (Luxembourg: European Commission, 1999).

Fagnani, J., "Context Mapping for the EU Framework 5 Funded Study: Gender, Parenthood and the Changing European Workplace," report for the European Commission, Manchester Metropolitan University (2004).

Franco, A. and K. Winqvist, "Women and Men Reconciling Work and Family Life," *Statistics in Focus*, theme 3–9 (2002), Eurostat: European Communities.

Jensen, A.M., "Partners and Parents in Europe: A Gender Divide," in A. Leira (ed.), *Comparative Social Research*, vol. 18: *Family Change: Practices, Policies and Values* (Stamford, CT: JAI Press, 1999).

International Labour Organisation (ILO), *Yearbook of Labour Statistics* (Geneva: ILO, 1975, 1983).

Kaufmann, F.X., A. Kuijsten, H.J. Schulze, and K.P. Strohmeier (eds.), *Family Life and Family Policies in Europe*, vol. 2: *Problems and Issues in Comparative Perspective* (Oxford: Oxford University Press, 2002).

Kocourková, J., "Leave Arrangements and Childcare Services in Central Europe: Policies and Practices before and after the Transition," *Community, Work and Family* 5, 3, 2002, 301–318.

Künzler, J., "Paths towards a Modernization of Gender Relations, Policies, and Family Building," in F.X. Kaufmann, A. Kuijsten, H.J. Schulze, and K.P. Strohmeier (eds.), *Family Life and Family Policies in Europe*, vol. 2: *Problems and Issues in Comparative Perspective* (Oxford: Oxford University Press, 2002).

Langan, M. and I. Ostner, "Gender and Welfare: Towards a Comparative Framework," paper presented at the Social Policy Association conference, Bath, UK, July 12–15, 1990.

Leira, A., "Family Change: Policies, Practices, and Values. Introduction," in Leira (ed.), *Comparative Social Research: Family Change: Policies, Practices and Values*, vol. 18 (Stamford: JAI Press, 1999).

Lewis, J., *Women and Social Policies in Europe: Work, Family and the State* (Aldershot: Edward Elgar, 1993).

Lippe, T. van der and L. van Dijk (eds.), *Women's Employment in a Comparative Perspective* (New York: Aldine de Gruyter, 2001).

MOCHO project, Université Libre de Bruxelles (Daniele Meulders), 2002, 2003 ("The Rationale of Motherhood Choices: Influence on Employment Conditions and on Public Policies").

Neyer, G., "Family Policies and Low Fertility in Western Europe," *MPIDR Working Paper* WP 2003–021 (Rostock: Max Planck Institute for Demographic Research, 2003).

Nimwegen, N. van and I. Esveldt, "Bevolkingsvraagstukken in Nederland anno 2003," *Werkverband periodieke rapportage bevolkingsvraagstukken*, Rapport no. 65 (The Hague: NIDI, 2003).

OECD, *Employment Outlook 2001* (Paris: Organisation for Economic Co-operation and Development, 2001).

OECD, *Employment Outlook 2002* (Paris: Organisation for Economic Co-operation and Development, 2002).

OECD, *Family Database 2006*, www.oecd.org/els/social/family/database

Plantenga, J. and C. Remery, with P. Helming, "Reconciliation of Work and Private Life: A Comparative Review of Thirty European Countries," 2005, http://europa.eu.int/comm/employment_social/gender_equality/docs/2005/reconciliation_report_en.pdf

Plantenga, J. and A. van Doorne-Huiskes, "Verschillen in arbeidsparticipatie van vrouwen in Europa, de rol van verzorgingsstaten," *Tijdschrift voor Arbeidsvraagstukken* 9, no. 1, 1993, 51–65.

Plantenga, J., J. Schippers and J. Siegers, "Towards an Equal Division of Paid and Unpaid Work: The Case of the Netherlands," *Journal of European Social Policy* 9, no. 2, 1999, 99–110.

Rostgaard, T., "Setting Time aside for the Father: Father's Leave in Scandinavia," *Community, Work and Family* 5, no. 3, 2002, 343–364.

Ruijter, Judith de, "Occupational Wage Differences: A Gender Approach" (Thesis, Erasmus University of Amsterdam, 2002).

Sainsbury, D., *Gender, Equality and Welfare States* (Cambridge: Cambridge University Press, 1996).

SCP, *Sociaal en Cultureel Rapport 2000. Nederland in Europa* (The Hague: Sociaal en Cultureel Planbureau, 2000).

United Nations, *World Population Prospects*, the 2002 revision, 2003 (United Nations: New York), http://www.un.org/esa/population/unpop.htm

Wall, K., "Leave Policy Models and the Articulation of Work and Family in Europe: A Comparative Perspective," in P. Moss and K. Wall (eds.), *International Review of Leave Policies and Related Research 2007* (London: Department of Trade and Industry, 2007).

Further Reading

There are some excellent comparative volumes and books on changing gender relations and work and family issues, for instance R. Crompton, S. Lewis, and C. Lyonette (eds.), *Women, Men, Work and Family in Europe* (New York: Palgrave Macmillan, 2007); R. Crompton, *Employment and the Family: The Reconfiguration of Work and Family Life in Contemporary Societies* (Cambridge: Cambridge University Press, 2006); A. Leira, *Welfare States and Working Mothers* (Cambridge: Cambridge University Press, 1992); T. van der Lippe and L. van Dijk (eds.), *Women's Employment in a Comparative Perspective* (New York: Aldine de Gruyter, 2001); J.C. Gornick and M.K. Meyers, *Families that Work: Policies for Reconciling Parenthood and Employment* (New York: Russell Sage Foundation, 2003).

Interesting publications for further reading on gender and welfare states are M. Daly and K. Rake, *Gender and the Welfare State* (Cambridge: Polity Press, 2003); D. Sainsbury, *Gender, Equality and Welfare States* (London: Sage, 1996); A. Orloff, "Gender and the Social Rights of Citizenship: State Policies and Gender Relations in a Comparative Perspective," *American Sociological Review* 58, no. 3, 1993, 303–328; J. Lewis, "Gender and Welfare State Change," *European Societies* 4, 4, 1992, 331–357.

Suggestions for further reading on fatherhood are, for instance, B. Hobson (ed.), *Making Men into Fathers* (Cambridge: Cambridge University Press, 2002); J.W. Duyvendak and M.M.J. Stavenuiter (eds.), *Working Fathers, Caring Men: Reconciliation of Working Life and Family Life* (The Hague and Utrecht: Verwey Jonker Institute, 2004).

An interesting volume on how young people in various European countries experience work and family is edited by J. Brannen, S. Lewis, A. Nilsen, and J. Smithson, *Young Europeans, work and family: Futures in transition* (Routledge: London/New York, 2002).

For those interested in the current state of affairs regarding public work–family policies in different countries the Babies and Bosses series of the OECD is a valuable source. The series covers the following countries: Australia, Denmark, the Netherlands, Austria, Ireland, Japan, New Zealand, Portugal, Switzerland, Canada, Finland, Sweden, and the UK. The latest publication in this series is a synthesis of the preceding reviews and presents data on all OECD countries for 2005 (*Babies and Bosses, Reconciling Work and Family Life. A Synthesis of Findings for OECD Countries*, OECD, 2007). In addition, the OECD Family database is a good source for information on public work–family policies in different countries (www.oecd.org/els/social/family/database). The report of J. Plantenga, C. Remery, and P. Helming (2005) titled *Reconciliation of Work and Private Life: A Comparative Review of Thirty European Countries* not only contains information on public policies present in different countries but also data on the role of employers (downloadable at: http://europa.eu. int/comm/employment_social/gender_equality/docs/2005/reconciliation_report_en.pdf). A discussion of leave policy models across Europe and the type of family model they tend to facilitate by Karin Wall is included in "Leave Policy Models and the Articulation of Work and Family in Europe: A Comparative Perspective," in P. Moss and K. Wall (eds.), *International Review of Leave Policies and Related Research 2007* (Department of Trade and Industry: London).

CHAPTER TWENTY-TWO

Europe and the Welfare State since 1945

STEEN P. MANGEN

An investigation of the evolution of postwar welfare states in the six largest countries of western Europe in so short a space is a daunting task and one which, of necessity, demands compromise. Two coping strategies have been seized. One is to rely on the depiction by Esping-Andersen[1] of "three worlds" of welfare capitalism to survey policy developments in the "liberal" UK; in "conservative corporatist" Germany and France, subsuming Italy and Spain as the Mediterranean "via media"; and in social democratic Sweden. The other is to adopt a broad chronological approach by decade, mindful of the significant variations in the pace – and context – of social policy innovation. The review is set against an introductory discussion of the main theories that have informed cross-national understanding of contemporary European welfare and which, in turn, have assisted scholars to specify parsimonious systemic categorizations of countries with such diverse histories. Theories arguing the primacy of "modernizing" imperatives leading to spontaneous cross-national convergence in welfare provision, on the one hand, and those privileging the role of culturally embedded, path-dependent institutions and the space they afford (or deny) to actors mobilized to advance reform, on the other, stand at the heart of the debate. The review will conclude by questioning whether the EU (European Union) is now directing an institutionally structured and consensually derived Europeanization which, at various levels, evidences a stronger measure of convergence than previously existed.

Theorizing the Welfare State

The structural-functionalist "logic of industrialism" lays emphasis on economic growth arising from industrialization as having been the principal trigger of a converging modernization of states and their welfare systems. For Wilensky this modernization was not driven by class politics, but by the necessities of meeting the demands of an expanding modern urban economy.[2] Context-dependent institutional arrangements, leftist politics, and demographic pressures are secondary in understanding why countries have been welfare "leaders" or "laggards".[3] Wilensky[4] concedes that among contemporary advanced welfare states there are considerable institutional

A Companion to Europe since 1945, First Edition. Edited by Klaus Larres.
© 2014 John Wiley & Sons, Ltd. Published 2014 by John Wiley & Sons, Ltd.

and ideological variations, but this is due to the nature of corporatism rather than the direct impact of the left. Indeed, it is left–right competition and in some countries the hold of Catholic parties that has mattered more.[5]

Nation-state formation and consolidation have been the key catalytic welfare determinants in other modernization theories associated with Rokkan.[6] The approach to modernization theory integrates class and industrialism in a politicized "logic of industrialism" framework: the pace of industrialization is a function of wider, pre-existing sociopolitical contexts that act in combination with workers' mobilization to produce "opportunity structures" favorable to new political and institutional resolutions.[7]

By comparison, what may be termed the "logic of capitalism" invests principal effort in theorizing about social conflict, class struggle, and mobilization as essential agents of change. Informed by a social democrat version of this "logic," Korpi identifies the motor of social transformation as being class alliances that enable parliaments to be democratically "captured" so that allied power may translate into implemented policy. The state, by conceding welfare demands, secures the compliance of the working class; the ultimate beneficiary is a well-functioning capitalism.[8] In social democratic theory, government of the left is the strongest factor. Hence "politics matter," for the strength of workers' mobilization determines not only the range of welfare policy output, but also critically, its redistributive impact and the quality of what Marshall has defined as "social citizenship."[9]

Institutional theories have elaborated on state-centered or state-responsiveness analyses and, additionally, actor-centered analyses. While "politics matters," theorizing prioritizes the mediating effects of institutional frameworks broadly defined. To be sure, while they are influenced by state-formation (as well as social citizenship) interpretations, this stable of theories interprets power as extending beyond the narrow "state" to other key actors who both influence and are influenced by formal institutions. Primacy is afforded to context, since political structures and the wider culture of a nation state mould its approach to welfare: institutional configurations are central to understanding how process mediates the relationship between policy inputs and policy outputs. Case studies, sensitive to socioeconomic and cultural context, and historical uniqueness are privileged, largely empirical a priori cross-national typologies suspect.[10]

In more actor-centered approaches institutions, by setting the rules of the game, crucially influence the motivations and actions of key players across regulatory, normative, and cognitive dimensions. Each welfare state is a unique product of complex and diverse compromises, negotiated over many years by reformist activists (including politicians) and key civil servants who, according to "public choice" theory, maneuver for welfare expansions that extend their power bases.[11]

A recent variant of institutional approaches insisting on the distinct "varieties of capitalism" focuses on contemporary attributes of domestic political institutions and the activities of their constituent key players in an economic environment of globalization. Swank,[12] for example, has examined the evolving "opportunity" and "veto" points facing coalitions of actors seeking to promote – or obstruct – policy innovation. The conclusion is that institutional contexts that support social corporatism or high electoral turnout and depend on proportional representation are more likely than others to resist neo-liberal reforms that threaten the welfare state, since interest groups can exploit their ability to impose vetoes. Thus the balance of vetoes and opportunities helps explain the extent to which states have engaged in retrenchment policies in the face of the perceived threat posed by globalization.[13]

O'Connor and Brym convincingly argue that inconsistent theoretical findings on the evolution of the welfare state obtain from different conceptualizations: there cannot be *one* explanation.[14] This said, "actors-within-institutions" interactive frameworks offers the most premium. However, this assertion needs to be judged within the current context of a post-modern imperative of converging Europeanization that is substantially evolving within the parameters of supranational institutional arrangements.

Harnessing Theory for Cross-National Models

Whatever the perspective taken on the strength of mobilization, most welfare scholars endorse a cross-national framework that privileges the interaction both of key actors and of structural and economic–political institutional factors. This is the approach adopted by Esping-Andersen in his classification of welfare "regimes" that is firmly embedded in theory.[15] Central to this concept is the context-specific nature of regulation; that is, the institutional rules of the game derived from the operation of the state, markets, and civic society. In order to develop his regime model, Esping-Andersen introduced three key concepts: the nature of *corporatism* (employers and employees in partnership), the degree of *decommodification* (compensatory value of welfare benefits in relation to lost earnings), and *social stratification* (differential rights of social citizenship). Despite extensive criticism of elements of his approach, his regime model has remained the principal orientation in cross-national welfare state research.[16] Esping-Andersen employs archetypes to elaborate three welfare regimes: liberal, conservative corporatist, and social democratic.[17] States and markets are brought into the same interactive model of social relations. Regimes emphasize multidimensionality as opposed to the more linear view of power found in working-class mobilization theories; in particular, his approach draws attention to the catalytic role of class coalitions in driving forward welfare developments.[18]

Esping-Andersen's archetype of the *liberal welfare regime* is the USA but, in reviewing developments in the Thatcher era, he insists that the UK increasingly bears attributes of this regime. State encouragement of the market results in minimal statutory welfare provision and what is offered is largely targeted at the poor. There is heavy reliance on discretionary benefits and means-testing. Typically, the social budget takes a low proportion of GDP (gross domestic produce); thus the UK after the 1960s has invested less of its GDP In social expenditure than France, Germany, or Sweden.[19]

Germany is the archetype of the *conservative corporatist regime*, although Esping-Andersen includes France and most continental countries in this category. For much of the postwar era, social and labor market policy-making progressed in corporatist engagement of the state and social partners within a consensus-generating "middleway" social market economy. Apart from federalism, the operation of the "subsidiary principle" confers on lower tiers of government and on nongovernmental agencies much of the responsibility for service provision: a plural "mixed economy" of welfare. Many social security rights are derived from employment through contributions to occupational social insurance schemes managed by the social partners under state supervision. For much of the postwar period adherence to the "equivalence principal" has ensured a large measure of transparency by offering earnings-related entitlement determined by insurance record.[20] In terms of outlays on the social budget Germany has tended to be a mid-field investor, although there was a decline in total expenditure in the 1980s before unification.[21]

By comparison, "conservative corporatism" in France has evolved in what, until the 1980s, was a highly centralized state and an adversarial polity. Freeman *characterizes the French* welfare system has having been "*étatist* in style, *corporatist* in form and *pluralist* in practice."[22] The plural complex that is the policy-making arena has accorded many points for sectional interest groups to exercise much power to shape policy outputs. By contrast with Germany the interaction of contributory insurance and discretionary assistance (discretionary, means-tested principle) has been treated fluidly within the benefits system, although despite creeping partial fiscalization (subsidization of insurance by general taxation) social security in France at the beginning of the 1990s was still largely derived from insurance levies. France, in terms of social expenditure as a proportion of GDP, has been in the above-average range.[23]

The Mediterranean states did not feature prominently in Esping-Andersen's original formulation, although he has subsequent defended his assertion that, in institutional terms, they conform to the conservative corporatist regime, albeit with a strong assumption of familiarism (high propensities of the family to provide).[24] There are criticisms of the failure of this regime typology to explain the evolution of key social policies here, particularly from the late 1970s onwards, such as attempts to establish socialized health care. Thus, for Ferrera,[25] the Mediterranean countries represent a "via media" straDDling Bismarckian and Beveridgean models. These states have been more active in providing in-cash transfers which have privileged groups closest to the core of the labor market focus, thereby creating marked insider–outsider differentials. In-kind welfare provision has been fragmented and effective involvement of the state in the "welfare mix" has been wanting. A shared attribute has been the opportunities the system has offered for the perpetuation of clientelistic practices in access to welfare in environments where, too often, administrative capacities have been inadequate.[26] Table 22.1 (p. 476) provides details indicating that while Italy has tended to be in the middle range of social expenditure outlays, Spain has been a low investor.

Social democratic corporatism is exemplified for Esping-Andersen by Sweden, although to varying degrees other Nordic countries share its attributes. The social democratic model developed in a distinct historical path due to two principal factors: initially a strong coalition between labor movements and agrarian interests (red–green coalitions) and, in the postwar era, a strong working-class and white-collar alliance.[27] The driving role of the social democrats in developing the Swedish model in close alliance with the trade union organization, (Landsorganisationen LO), was critical party in the post war decades. Policy formulation in partnership with the employers has, over the long pull, delivered an anticipatory managerial approach. Within this corporatist model centralized wage bargaining, active labor market policies, and general and consciously maintained consensus over economic and social measures have been central principles. Welfare rights and service provision are based on universalism, although many benefits are graduated according to earnings. The welfare state has been firmly anchored in the public sector and has functioned with a bias towards

Table 22.1 Total gross social protection expenditure (% GDP): a crude analysis over time

	1960	1980	1990	2004
(D) Germany	20.5	28.8	25.4	29.5
(E) Spain	8.2	18.2	19.9	20.0
(F) France	13.4	25.4	27.7	31.2
(I) Italy	16.8	19.4	24.1	26.1
(SE) Sweden	15.4	(33.4)	32.9	32.9
(UK) United Kingdom	13.9	20.5	23.0	26.3
EU	n/a	24.1	25.4	27.6

Sources:
1 1960 – except Spain, OECD, *Social Expenditure 1960–1990: Problems of Growth and Control* (Paris: OECD, 1985). Data refers to social expenditure and includes education, except in the case of France. Spanish data derive from a calculation by Rodriguez for social expenditure including education (1993 – see my book)
2 1980 – except Sweden, European Commission, *Social Protection in Europe, 1995* (DG Employment, Luxembourg: Office for Official Publications of the European Communities). EU is EU12. Swedish figure is for 1981 and is from OECD, *Social Expenditure 1960–1990*, and refers to social expenditure including education.
3 1990 – Eurostat, *Statistics in Focus: Population and Social Conditions.* no. 14 (19998). Figure for Germany exclude the new Länder and EU is EU15.
4 2004 – Eurostat, *Statistics in Focus: Population and Social Conditions.* no. 99 (2007). EU is EU15. Data are provisional except for EU15 where they are estimates.

strong institutional redistribution, universal solidarity, and extensive social citizenship, guaranteeing what have been cross-nationally generous entitlements. Significantly, social insurance levies have largely been borne by employers – those of employees have played a minor role (except in unemployment benefit); the state has also made a large contribution to the total budget.[28] In terms of aggregate expenditure, at least, Sweden has been a welfare "leader," although this did not pertain until the early 1970s.[29]

From Postwar Fordist Welfare to Post-Fordist Restructuration

This review presents a comparative-chronology welfare evolution. Admittedly, focusing on the decade as the unit of investigation may risk overstressing convergent trends because, in reality, the timing, context, and change of policy direction vary among the sampled countries. This said, it may offer possible purchase by throwing into sharper relief the reforms of established policy lines and policy reversals implemented either within THE space of one government or over successive governments, even of the same party formation.[30]

Immediate postwar accommodations

No country negotiated the postwar welfare settlement from the position of a *tabula rasa*. The legacy of the interwar years was significant because this was the period where, at least in the democratic states, many of the obstacles to an expansion of statutory welfare were gradually dismantled, with the result that comprehensive reforms could be speedily negotiated at the end of hostilities.[31] To be sure, postwar institutional renewal offered opportunities for innovation, but set against this were constraints arising from past policy lines and the constellations of interests they represented.

The impact of war on social policy is well documented in the literature: massive infrastructural investments needed to remedy war damage and foster economic recovery, morale-boosting stemming from the exigencies of rewarding the peoples' war effort, and capitalizing on presumed intensified sentiments of national solidarity all played a part. Besides, the contingencies of war had necessitated unprecedented state mobilization of the economy. In its aftermath, versions of Keynesianism displaced the last vestiges of traditional liberalism in official economic policy. Fordist production required that male blue-collar workers and their interest groups would be indispensable allies in an economic environment where the demand for labor was to grow rapidly. Their compliance was vital. Thus the postwar welfare accommodation was essentially an affair of men; women were to be dispatched back to home and hearth, this despite their vital wartime role.[32]

Policy reformulation in Britain had commenced in earnest during the war years once the threat of German invasion had receded. The 1942 "Social Insurance and Allied Services" Report by the Liberal Beveridge set out a politically moderate blueprint to indemnify the major social risks through state social security flanked by a commitment to full employment (his "Full Employment in a Free Society" being published two years later). In 1944 the school leaving age was raised in the "Butler Act," which also specified a streamlined secondary education system. Churchill's personal animosity to Beveridge meant that his report had to await endorsement in the 1946 National Insurance Act by Atlee's Labour government, keen to preserve the loyalty of the unions. During his premiership all the complementary structures of the Fordist welfare state were put in place: industrial-injuries compensation, reform of public assistance, and – most radical of all – a socialized "national health service" (NHS) from 1948. A fillip to the construction sector, as a driver of economic growth, was offered by legislation in 1946 to create new towns and by the instigation of a major house-building program.

Labour's ambitions did not only extend to the UK. The government, with the support of German social democrats and trade unions, had wished to establish a socialized welfare system in the allied zones. This did not find favor with the Americans, who were to win the day. Accordingly, the opportunity for radical reform was lost and the Bismarckian social protection system was denazified and restored. Under the founding Christian Democratic chancellor, Adenauer, rapid economic growth, national reconstruction, and social reintegration dominated the agenda and in 1949 constitutional reform established west Germany as "social state guaranteed under law."

The operation of veto points is also redolent of the immediate postwar French experience. Influenced by the Beveridge prescription, the ambitious Laroque Report of 1945 embraced three principles: full employment, strong income redistribution to families, and a preventive focus in health services. In the event, Laroque had to compromise at every turn. In particular, his plan for comprehensive reform was foiled by vested corporate interests, especially among self-employed and agricultural workers. The result was that the system ultimately agreed was far from the unitary universal model Laroque had originally envisaged: *national* solidarity was rejected in favor of *corporate* solidarity.[33]

A similar situation pertained in Italy. The period heralded in the long domination of politics by the Christian Democrats, initially under Gasperi. Proposals for major social security reform embracing universalism and a unitary organizational system were rejected in 1948 and, instead, the Demochristian coalition opted to restore the prewar institutional framework along Bismarckian lines.

The Bismarckian system would in large measure also be endorsed in Franco's Spain. The generalissimo was attracted to Bismarckian welfare since work-based and risk-related, tripartite-funded insurance appealed as a device for regulating the working class and rewarding those sections that had been loyal to his cause.[34] Thus his welfare system was a central instrument of the corporate state: early rewards to his constituency came in the form of pensions legislation in 1939. But Franco was pragmatic enough to learn policy lessons from elsewhere: he instituted compulsory sickness insurance in 1942 to fund a new health system that would owe much to ideas adopted from the British NHS.

The postwar welfare momentum in neutral Sweden was, by comparison with the UK, relatively modest. After all, many of the key pillars of social democratic corporatism were already in place. This said, in 1946 a controversial pensions reform was proposed that would be the object of continued debate and revision throughout the 1950s. A year later compulsory comprehensive national sickness insurance was instigated.

Consolidation in the 1950s

The overarching concern of postwar reconstruction extended well into the 1950s but there were also consolidations of welfare commitments and in several countries pensions resolution would prove contentious. The 1950s are also characterized by the marked stability of parties in power, assisting consolidation of social policy lines. In fact the party composition of government at the end of hostilities in this sample of countries was to remain in place throughout the decade, with the exception of Britain where the reforming Labour Party was dispatched in 1951, ushering in the long hegemony of the Conservatives until 1964.

Esping-Andersen identifies the UK as recording the highest "decommodification" score among his sample for 1950.[35] The subsequent decline he traces thereafter he ascribes to the failure of the outgoing Labour government to extend the universalism of the NHS to other welfare sectors. Macmillan, as a patrician Conservative, afforded priority to continuing the house-building program, promoting full employment, and helping achieve it by expanding investment in welfare services. His policies bore fruit in the growing prosperity, particularly after Suez.

Similar to the contemporary situation in Sweden, Adenauer's government of the 1950s was to confront a crisis resulting from proposals for pensions reform that sought to ensure greater equality of entitlement between blue- and white-collar workers. After a bitter and protracted debate, the eventual outcome in 1957 was a compromise between social democratic pragmatists and progressive Christian democrats on the "social policy wing" of the party. The popular appeal of the pensions reforms was demonstrated by the election of 1957, which rewarded the CDU (Christlich Demokratische Union) with an absolute majority. In the aftermath of defeat the social democrats agreed the revisionist Bad Godesberg program in which they abandoned radical social reforms and accepted the workings of the social market economy.

From the late 1950s, after the creation of the Fifth Republic, the role of French lower house of parliament in social policy-making was progressively sidelined, since much legislation was passed through special powers that did not need its approval. This executive domination of the welfare agenda was equally evidenced by the propensities of successive presidents to extend their personal remits in social policy.[36] Under de Gaulle, France witnessed a modernization of welfare provisions, with enhancement of benefits through improved index-linking and extension of entitlements for the first time to new groups such as agricultural laborers. In 1958 national unemployment compensation was introduced for the first time and in 1967 it was extended to all employees in the private sector.

In Italy socioregional development aid, particularly for the south, featured prominently as a key welfare objective. The country had been a prime beneficiary of the 1949 European Recovery Program and housing was made a priority. In 1955 the Vanoni Plan prescribed a rapid increase of infrastructural investment over a ten-year period to assist job creation on a massive scale.

Pensions policy in the 1950s was a vital arena for understanding the corporatist nature of Sweden's social policy-making because, in the decade following the war it was the principal object of contention between the political parties. A national referendum on the subject proved inconclusive. Ultimately, a basic flat-rate pension was agreed in 1957, with the compromise that a second-tier earnings-related occupational pension would be legislated later. Mirroring in reverse contemporary events in Germany, the electoral gains secured shortly afterwards by the ruling social democrats, who passed the reform, convinced the "bourgeois parties" of the center-right that conceding extra welfare rights paid electoral dividends and, thereafter, they were willing parties to further welfare expansion.[37]

The innovating 1960s

Growing prosperity in the 1960s, as the highpoint of the *Trente Glorieuse*, afforded governments ample opportunities to modernize welfare systems that had been operating since the war. In many countries there were to be innovatory departures in sectors such as education and social housing. Above all, in maturing postwar democracies there was evidence of growing faith in the state's capacity to plan and provide. On the other hand, the old political order in Germany, France, and Italy would be dealt a blow by the "events" of 1968 and their sequelae.

Britain was the first of the sample to demonstrate the change in political mood in this decade. In 1964 Labour was returned to power, albeit with a minuscule majority. The new premier, Wilson, was anxious to be portrayed as a modernizer but he faced budgetary constraints inherited from the Conservatives. Aping Gaullist France, extensive economic and regional planning machinery was introduced, accompanied by an overarching (but ill-fated) National Plan. Education was adopted as a central platform of reform. Local education authorities were compelled to plan the abolition of matriculation tests at the age of 11 used to determine access to streamed secondary education. Despite much opposition, comprehensive schools were created, although their national imposition was not secured until the re-election of Wilson in 1974.

Tertiary education expanded enormously with the development of a network of new universities which would include an "open" university designed to cater for new kinds of students hitherto excluded. By the mid-1960s, however, the mounting economic problems diverted political attention away from the welfare arena, as Britain became the first major economy to enter the flight path to irreversible deindustrialization.

Conservative corporatism was, admittedly, faring somewhat better. Nonetheless, after the modest welfare advances under Erhard, the classic German "social market economy" came to an end in the mid-1960s with the formation at the onset of a minor recession of the first Grand Coalition government (involving the social democrats). Across the Rhine, during the 1960s family policy was a key object of French innovation. Increasing emphasis was placed on strong pronatalist objectives through improved benefits while draconian laws prohibiting contraception were also retained. But, the "events" of 1968 were to spell the end of de Gaulle and his successor, Pompidou, instigated a new phase of programmatic welfare reforms with a strong planning focus. During the 1960s the triggers for the acceleration of policy reform in Italy were the so-called "events" of 1968, when the institutional profile of the welfare state began to change rapidly. The key elements of this new transformation were acceleration of the secularization and modernization of social services, plans for further regional devolution and the launching of a debate on the socialization of social security funding (that is, funding through general taxation).

In Italy, too, "1968" provided the catalyst for policy reform and the institutional profile of the welfare state began to change rapidly. Plans were announced for further regional devolution and the more progressive local authorities experimented with secularizing and modernizing social services. However, although by the end of the decade the social insurance system had been consolidated through the extension of coverage and the raising of benefit levels, the manner of its doing would sow the seeds of future fiscal problems. Bending to political pressures among its core constituency, the demochristian-led governments had conceded what by international standards was a generous pension package offering possibilities for early retirement. But this generosity was markedly lacking in equity, since those who had the greatest to gain were the most privileged in the labor marker. Similarly, although reform of unemployment compensation in 1968 made benefits among the most generous in the EEC (European Economic Community), many of the jobless were ineligible.

Economic takeoff in Spain came after the Stabilization Plan of 1959 and led to certain modernizing concessions urged by the elite Catholic lay organization, Opus Dei. Under its influence the deeply plural social insurance system was recodified and unified in 1963, with further modernizing reforms in 1972. However, inequalities of treatment both in social and fiscal welfare persisted. And, although there was a 60% increase in welfare outlays in terms of GDP in the last 15 years of Franco's life, undisguised clientelistic practices were perpetuated.[38]

While social outlays in Sweden in the 1960s were not far above the OECD (Organisation for Economic Co-operation and Development) average, the country was at the vanguard of innovations that would provide international benchmarks. The social democrats shared the concerns of their sister parties elsewhere in Europe to drive forward a greater equality of outcome rather than mere access to welfare. As in Britain, the rapid expansion of comprehensive schooling was a principal object of reform. The health services were the fastest-growing area of social expenditure. But the policy landmark of the 1960s was legislation in 1968 fulfilling the promise of an earnings-related contributory occupational pension which was to supplement the first-tier basic pension introduced a decade earlier.

The 1970s: welfare state in crisis?

Albeit at varying speeds, the post-oil shocks to European economies were unambiguously gathering pace, as the postwar welfare accommodation was increasingly called into question. For neo-Marxist scholars the end of rapid economic growth merely served to reveal the underlying contradictions between welfare for all and the monopolistic exigencies of capitalism. The "fiscal crisis of the welfare state" arising from the conflict between legitimation and accumulation could not be ignored: Fordist capitalism had needed the welfare state as a key investment in human capital, but as welfare claims had expanded, the expense of the postwar welfare state was undermining the capitalist accumulation process.[39]

Critics in some mature democracies, like the Conservative Sir Keith Joseph in Britain, were re-evaluating long-held welfare principles and there were concerns that social protection might be causing as many problems at it solved, by inculcating chronic welfare dependency, creating massified service structures, and imposing high non-wage costs. On the other hand, the democratic transitions in the 1970s among the Mediterranean states stimulated considerable new welfare investment.

In the UK Labour, perceived to have hit its own constituency the hardest, lost the 1970 election. The incoming Conservative government of Health expanded retrenchment measures but this only served to exacerbate the widespread industrial unrest which ultimately led to his downfall. Labour returned to power, initially under Wilson, but the critical economic situation offered the party no opportunities to engage in expensive reforms, especially as the IMF (International Monetary Fund) was demanding further retrenchment. Budgetary cuts in education and housing and rising unemployment under Wilson's successor, Calaghan, ultimately led to the unrest of the "winter of discontent" and the victory of the Mrs. Thatcher's Conservatives, that would keep Labour out of power for the best part of 20 years.

Countries of "conservative corporatist" Europe were varyingly vouchsafed more time before the nettle of irreversible industrial decline had to be grasped. While the UK under Heath was battening down the hatches, the German election of 1969 was won by Brandt on a progressive social democratic ticket. As the first social democratic chancellor of postwar Germany, he was anxious to develop a distinct policy line that would break the long-held CDU hegemony over the state. Although over the broad range of welfare sectors, his was a largely consolidating strategy, there were innovative departures, in equality of opportunity in education, for example. Critically, during his chancellorship social expenditure broke loose from economic trends and rose to one third of GDP, the country becoming one of the highest welfare spenders in the OECD. The subsequent SPD-led (Sozialdemokratische Partei Deutschlands) government under Schmidt more or less coincided with the onset of a deepening recession, although less severe than that facing Wilson in the UK. Schmidt's era is, therefore, characterized by a preoccupation with cost containment and one where the power of social partnership began to recede.[40] His legacy was to initiate a re-education of the electorate to expect less from the social state which was now being cast as the main culprit for the predicament facing *Standort Deutschland.*[41]

Concerns with the impact on the faltering economy of high non-wage costs were also being debated in France. Pompidou approached social policy with a technician' eye by adopting national social and health planning, for example. And he was able to universalize access to social security and introduce cross-subsidization of the different social insurance schemes (something that would prove so problematic in Germany), as well as taxation subsidies, to the system. But in the late 1970s, under his successor, Giscard, a national debate was gathering pace about the failures of French welfare to prevent what was being termed "social exclusion," particularly as rising unemployment meant that half of the jobless were falling through the welfare safety net.

In Italy the *autumno caldo* social unrest of 1969 provided further impetus for reform during the era of the "historic compromise" when the demochristians were able to lead a government coalition courtesy of Communist Party tolerance. During the 1970s social security proved one of the most chronic problems in Italian politics, which recurring fiscal crises since this period have only served to emphasize. Reforms of the health system in 1978 were also to be problematic. Great expectations of the universal, largely socialized service to be implemented by the regions were unleashed but they were soon dissipated, as it became apparent that it could not deliver distributional equity or efficiency, with the result that a large private sector has been maintained, thereby institutionalizing a form of two-tier medicine.

The second half of the 1970s, at least in terms of GDP consumed by the social budget, has been the period of major acceleration of the Spanish welfare state, which was identified as a principal instrument of legitimation by new political elites keen to negotiate a peaceful democratic transition. However, this expansion evolved in a context of a deteriorating economic situation and a sharp rise in unemployment. Political and administrative modernization (with a constitution prescribing a "social state" and owing much to the West German), variegated regional devolution, and economic restructuring were the main policies pursued in this era. The pacific transition was facilitated by a series of social pacts among major political and economic actors, key among them being the 1977 Moncloa Pact concluded by the center-right prime minister Suarez: in exchange for wage restraint unions were offered future welfare gains, although they remained unfulfilled in the short-term.[42]

In Sweden the 1969 election was won by Palme, campaigning on a platform of greater social justice. And he delivered: there were large increases in cash benefits, especially earnings-related pensions and sick pay, and innovations such as a parental leave scheme for child care. But the two oil crises took their toll on the Swedish economy. Interparty consensus about welfare was breaking down with the center-right increasingly complaining of the international competition perpetrated by an overbloated, costly welfare system that, moreover, was fostering welfare dependency. Their election in 1976 (though not impressive) ended the hold of the social democrats on government originating in the 1930s. It was during their period of office that the rhetoric of budgetary stability was routinized. Yet this "new realism" produced only short-run effects. Indeed, during their period in office until 1982, the social budget increased four times as fast as the economy and twice as fast as the OECD average, with heavy reliance deficit financing and monetary devaluation.

Fundamentally, the Swedish center-right parties could not curb social expenditure: there were important maturation effects of benefit entitlements, they were essentially centrist parties, and, moreover, they had obtained no clear electoral mandate for radical change in social policy.

The 1980s: retrenchment gathers pace

At the beginning of the 1980s there was still some reluctance among the left in countries like Sweden, France, and Germany to confront the irreversible trend of deindustrialization and hence confront the exigency of revising the postwar social democratic project. But by the end of the decade welfare reforms were making deeper inroads into prevailing welfare frameworks and objectives, something that Hall[43] identifies as "second-order" changes which were to set in train more fundamental restructuring from the 1990s onwards, veering towards his "third-order" change.[44] Trade unions in many countries were divided on how best to respond to rising joblessness beyond pressing for early retirement packages and complying with government tactics to confer incapacity benefits on those made redundant, so that official unemployment rates could be kept artificially low.

The 1980s were an interesting time in European welfare politics. Firstly, new issues were rapidly emerging, not least the growing problem of social exclusion in inner cities and peripheral estates in the larger countries, which demanded new urban-policy formulation. Secondly, new political inpulses from the right began, at least, to provoke revisionist debate on the left, although the impact of the old left was still a force. The future of the welfare state was at the heart of debate.

By far the most radical break with past policy paths was directed by British premier Thatcher.[45] Unencumbered by constraints imposed by corporatist negotiation, she seized the opportunities provided by her retrenchment strategy to undermine existing institutional arrangements on a broad front. While many of the initial cuts largely continued the pattern of expenditure priorities set by the previous Labour government, Thatcher institutionalized welfare retrenchment as an article of neo-liberal faith. Social housing was worst hit, with a virtual moratorium on new building, sharp rent increases, and privatization through "right to buy." There were also retrenchments in education, social services, pensions, and unemployment compensation, although the health service was relatively well protected. The functions and funding of local government were extensively reformed and a wider welfare mix with the private and voluntary sectors was actively endorsed, including in primary and secondary education. In reality, despite her rhetoric, Thatcher was effectively recentralizing the state's supervisory and budgetary powers. Her welfare legacy was rising unemployment and other attributes of social exclusion, increased means-testing in social security, and weakened employment protection, for which EU social legislation – which she routinely opposed – only partly compensated. Yet despite these comprehensive retrenchments she was unable to stem the proportion of GDP the welfare state consumed. Indeed, it increased during her premiership owing to accumulated entitlements in the pensions system, the cost of incapacity and unemployment compensation, and so forth.[46] For Pierson this was evidence enough that, despite reforms of funding and delivery mechanisms, the welfare state – at least in the 1980s – remained the most resilient element of the postwar democratic settlement.[47]

A professed admirer of Thatcherism, Kohl came to power in Germany in 1982 in a CDU-led government. In his initial period of office he made much of his promise of a change of direction (*Wendepolitik*): cutting back the harmful effects of an over-blown welfare system by promoting self-help. But, unlike Thatcher, he was restrained by corporatist engagement and he was exposed to the influential progressive wing of his party and the continual round of federal state elections which impacted on the political composition of the upper house of parliament. Most of his budgetary curbs in welfare were imposed in the first two years, before state elections took their toll on his party, although prior to unification his chancellorship witnessed a decline in the percentage welfare take of GDP.[48]

By contrast the election in 1981 of Mitterrand as the first socialist president of the Fifth Republic raised expectations of the welfare state, since he had promised extensive institutional modernization, state devolution, and avenues for wider public participation. Yet this was the very time when the French economy was increasingly unable to deliver on such an agenda. Decentralization was the major reform of his first office and after an initial flurry of radical welfare reforms such as increased pensions and a reduction in retirement age his presidency settled down to more modest ambitions. Critically, in the wake of massive protest, in part organized by the church demonstrating strong veto tactics, the promised reform of private education did not amount to much. Mitterrand had naively presumed that sustained economic growth could be relied on to pay for welfare advance but, as Freeman observes,[49] when he assumed office it was already too late to build the radical welfare system the socialists had espoused. Accordingly, Mitterrand's second term from 1988 was a quieter affair, although in an environment of rising racial tensions he launched a major urban program to tackle social exclusion and also introduced an innovative guaranteed social minimum income (Revenu Minimum D'insertion – RMI) paid to those eligible who participated, under contract, in inclusion programs.

The 1982 election of the Gonzalez's socialists a year after the political "shock" of the last attempted parliamentary coup in Spain marked the end of the democratic transition. Although while in exile in France he had been under the influence of Mitterrand, Gonzalez had spent the transition years moderating the stance of his party. Like Mitterrand and Kohl, his was to be a lengthy period of office, extending until 1996, albeit at times in coalition. Pactism provided the premier in his first period in office with opportunities to consolidate a policy line that, above all, observed the dictates of fiscal prudence. In this regard, his premiership seems to anticipate the "third-way" revisionist policies of social democrats elsewhere a decade later. Containment of inflation was prioritized over welfare expansion or job creation, although in "going for growth" Gonzalez did opt for selective welfare targets. There was a modest gender equality program and, despite the opposition the church, abortion legislation was passed, although he (like Mitterrand) could not override its ability to marshal a political "veto" impact on plans for radical education reform. By the mid-1980s the opportunities provided by pacts with the social partners were no longer available. In the judgment of the unions, he had reneged on his promise to deliver an adequate unemployment compensation scheme for the growing number of jobless, with the result that many were left without entitlements. Nor did the 1985 pensions reform or the promised universal and socialized health system, legislated in 1986, live up to their expectations (although universal health access was eventually established in 1990). The breakdown of pactism and the effective mobilization in 1988 of a one-day general strike prompted Gonzalez, now in his second term, to make certain welfare concessions such as improved unemployment benefits, although his government rejected calls to introduce a national benefit along the lines of the French RMI. In conclusion, Rodriguez observes a correlation between social unrest and welfare gains in post-Franco Spain,[50] although it has to be said that the cumulative budgetary impact of Gonzalez's welfare reforms in the 1980s was comparatively modest.[51]

In the early 1980s the Swedish social democrats were again in government under Palme, who promised to restore those welfare losses imposed by the outgoing center-right. The new government adopted measures to stimulate the economy and reduce unemployment, a strategy that incurred further devaluation and heavy international borrowing) – the kind of package that social democrat parties elsewhere were increasingly discarding. Economic pressures soon took their toll and while some further welfare concessions were offered, priority was given to achieving greater financial rationalization of social policy. In the aftermath of the election in 1985, again won by the social democrats, policies aiming to reduce budgetary deficits prompted strike action in the public sector. After his assassination, Palme was succeeded by Carlsson, who instigated extensive tax reforms to reduce the very high marginal rates with the aim of restoring international competitiveness and stemming the flow of "tax flight."

The 1990s and beyond: constructing a post-Fordist welfare state?

Some scholars have stressed that the principal threats and opportunities posed by the welfare state in terms of international competitiveness are fundamentally regime-specific.[52] Yet despite the substantial preservation of distinct welfare institutional frameworks – and the specificities of the political and economic context in which they operate – the period since 1990 has witnessed a remarkable degree of convergence in approaches to policy resolution in these six countries. Responses to the economic challenges posed by globalization and the fear that, in the face of it, EU states were being constrained by resistant "eurosclerosis" in efforts to drive forward reforms have progressively embraced key elements of the neo-liberal agenda, irrespective of the parties in power. Besides, many European states are confronting similar sociodemographic problems and to respond to them have been implementing similar new welfare delivery styles associated with "new public management."[53] Postwar principles of social justice and citizenship are being recast in terms associated with increased conditionality, adaptability, and sustainability. While new objectives such as "work–life" reconciliation and actions to alleviate the predicaments of those facing "new social risks" have been officially espoused, there is no doubt that, overall, welfare has become more contingent. Contribution is being reinforced whereas need entitlement is weakened, exacerbating the plight of those least protected and with little mobilizing power. Benefit levels, in general, are subject to a measure of "recommodification." In short, the welfare system is being redesigned more resolutely to "make work pay."[54]

In the first half of the 1990s Major, the UK premier, continued the euroskepticism of his predecessor and, indeed, negotiated the "opt-out" of social provisions of the

1992 Maastricht Treaty. One of the principal targets of Major's social policy was urban regeneration, contemporary with developments in the second Mitterrand presidency. However, in the evolving UK policy line, more explicitly socioeconomic dimensions were elaborated and implemented through utilization of competitive bidding for funding and the exploitation of wider horizontal and vertical partnerships that dispatched solidaristic notions of need to the political margins.

The newly elected Blair government of 1997 revoked the Maastricht "opt out." As a resolutely "new" Labour premier, he embraced a British version of "third-way" politics that resonated elsewhere in Europe. Essentially a political centrist, his was not a distinct theory but borrowed elements of social democracy, "one-nation" conservatism and the "new right." Influenced by Clinton, he embraced the vision of Giddens,[55] who espoused the idea of the "social investment state" exploiting social capital and social networks within a broader political framework that balanced rights with responsibilities. Blair's "third way" incorporated targeted redistribution, communitarianism, and public–private partnership underpinned by government endorsement and facilitated by the exigencies of "new public management." Stakeholding was at the very heart of his approach to social citizenship.

His resounding first electoral victory, coming after revisionist political reform of his party, consolidated the hold he enjoyed on the party. The wide array of opportunities afforded to him to impose his vision is amply demonstrated by the formidable pace of policy output in his ten years of office. In employment a national minimum wage was legislated in 1998, tax credits were introduced for the working poor, and there was a series of "new deal" packages to lure the targeted sectors of the unemployed back into the labor market. Blair acknowledged that the public sector was the anchor of the health service for attaining targeted outcomes but, while increasing total outlays, he looked to private resources and a more commercial strategy as a necessary infusion into management and delivery. Education was a shibboleth of Blairism: expenditure rose, performance indicators were refined, and elements of marketization were introduced, not least in the form of tuition fees for a rapidly expanding university sector.

Blair also had the combating of social exclusion – particularly its urban dimension – centrally on his agenda. Within this broad policy envelope measures to tackle crime and anti-social behavior, while affirming a commitment to eradicate the environments in which they prospered, provided a second shibboleth. New Labour's urban policy manifested the very core of Blairism – and its contradictions. While it restored a measure of social solidarity and was stronger on community-led solutions, it retained – and in critical ways intensified – reliance on new public management, competitive bidding, and performance targets. Increased outlays were made to the urban budget, which was more closely integrated with "new deal" objectives on unemployment and other manifestations of deprivation.[56] Within this policy arena the stressing of "joined-up" government became Blairism's third shibboleth. Drawing lessons from French experiences, refined area-based targeting and longer integrated funding streams were guaranteed to improve sustainability.[57]

Blair – and, to varying degrees, his fellow "third-way" continental social democratic modernizers – engaged in a strategy of targeted social policy advances to benefit workers in order to ensure their acceptance of growing "flexibilization" measures in the labor market and workfare "flexicurity" in the benefits system. The enormous reform output combined pre-existing retrenchment strategies of outgoing center-right governments with policy innovations represented as "new ways of doing things." Above all, this was packaged in a rhetoric of a declining state imperative to act directly, but rather to "enable," thereby affording individuals greater opportunities to respond as customers rather than clients of the welfare system. In this, the new "third way," at least in the Blairite version, has imposed what now appears an irreversible revision of earlier, Fordist "social citizenship" elaborated by Marshall.[58]

German unification was not exploited as an opportunity to tackle the manifest and growing deficiencies of the West German welfare. Rather, the "new Länder" were to be assimilated over stages into the prevailing Western system. This decision would carry serious economic, social, and political costs. In effect, it created in the "united" Germany a two-tier welfare state, with chronic differential quality of welfare access between east and west.[59] Kohl was at pains to stress that the vital infrastructural investment to resolve welfare problems in the east would be obtained through rapid economic takeoff there. In this he was mistaken: rampant unemployment exacted a heavy toll; in the first four years of unification alone almost four million jobs were lost and serious levels of unemployment particularly in the east has dogged the German economy since.

Solidarity transfers to the east, either through earmarked taxation or preferential treatment in policy programs have remained of fundamental importance, with knock-on effects on investment in welfare in the old states. This said, an attempt to resolve one of the thorny problems confronting many European countries – how to fund the growing demand for long-term care, particularly among the elderly – was provided by legislation in 1994 that added a further pillar to the social insurance system.

In the 1998 election the social democrats were returned to power in alliance with the greens. Influenced by Blairite "welfare-to-work" prescriptions and guided also by the recently negotiated EU Amsterdam Employment Strategy, the new chancellor, Schröder, made job creation a central plank of policy and in 1999 launched the "Alliance for Jobs." Schröder was also able to push through further wide-ranging pensions reforms, including the introduction of a form of Blairite "stakeholder" pension. With high unemployment and new jobs more sluggish in their creation than planned, a reinvigorated "alliance" was announced after his re-election in 2002. Henceforth, policy in this sector has evolved in line with the Hartz recommendations of fundamental labor market reform. In a situation of serious levels of job losses the chancellor made extensive retrenchments involving stricter regulation of unemployment entitlements and an allied reform of social assistance. Schröder's approach to social security and the failure to deliver on the labor market front were contributory factors in his narrow defeat in 2005 to the Christian democrat, Merkel, leading a second "grand coalition" government. One of her targets has been the health system, which since the early 1990s has incrementally been restructured, much of which in line with principles of new public management and elements of "marketization." Another has been pensions and the package of reforms negotiated with the key actors involves reduced entitlements and a progressive raising of the statutory retirement age.

Esping-Andersen raised the question of whether "conservative corporatism" embodied a "frozen landscape" of immobilism.[60] This potential effect is not demonstrated by subsequent events. The "shock" of unification, with its long-term fiscal consequences, has inevitably reshaped the priorities of the social state.[61] Vail is among those dismissing the "path-dependency" paradigm as poorly equipped to explain German departures in the last ten years or so.[62] By way of refinement, Lessenich proposes the notion of "path creation,"[63] where new policy pathways are gradually negotiated through the "windows of opportunity" which are the product of by collusion among major political and economic players arguing the case of an unavoidable, new welfare "realpolitik" in order to impose unpopular welfare reforms.[64] The outcome of these processes, according to Leibfried and Obinger,[65] is an on-going streamlining of German welfare as a leaner "social insurance state," fostering new social structuration effects in that the cuts have hit the least mobilized and most marginalized the hardest but there are counterbalances elsewhere in the form of elder care and improved family benefits.

Until 1990 welfare revenue deficits in France were primarily resolved by ad hoc increases in levies, though in declining proportions falling on the employer, and by user charges in health and in-kind services. But, given the imposed budgetary constraints of the Maastricht convergence criteria, there were growing doubts about the future viability of these tactics. Moreover, the social partners were increasingly suspected of having too laxly managed the insurance system. The government took the decision to increase its directorial role in social security and further partial fiscalization was adopted as the preferred solution, complemented by the introduction in 1990 of a new "social contribution," a tax on all types of income, including benefits, to replace insurance funding of noncontributory allowances. The looming demographic crisis in France, as elsewhere, also concentrated political minds on pensions reform, a process launched in 1993 for the private sector.

Widespread disillusion with the achievements of the 14-year socialist presidency assisted the election of the center-right Chirac in 1995. His governments accelerated moves for long-term modernization of social security and health care. But mass popular opposition to proposals to extend pensions reform to the public sector temporarily held back policy-making momentum. In 1997, Chirac was confronted by the need to "cohabit" with new socialist prime minister, Jospin, who pledged a massive job creation program and a 35-hour working week, and rejected Blairite "MacJob" solutions. The prime minister also attached high priority to advancing reform of social protection financing including the family benefits system. Nonetheless, the negotiation of the European Employment Strategy and a meeting of minds on urban exclusion introduced a measure of convergence between competing visions. Subsequently, the "exception Française" in employment and social policy has been giving way to "welfare-to-work" objectives, an example being stricter regulation of the reformed RMI social minimum income.

The "frozen landscape" must also be discounted in the French case, given the substantial accumulation of reforms in the past 30 years. Some innovations – such as partial fiscalization and the introduction of the RMI – have undoubtedly compromised the transparency of the system and undermined the equivalence principle. This said, a wider range of policy and financial instruments is now available to the state to manage social protection and these, for Palier[66] have introduced new elements to the French logic of welfare.

In Spain, the stringencies of the Maastricht criteria and the retrenchment that ensued had an abrupt negative impact on the social budget, which attained a historical high in GDP terms in 1993. In Gonzalez's last period in office there were further deregulations of the labor market and more curbs on unemployment benefits. In 1995 the interparty Toledo Pact agreed a restructuring program for social security, although it substantially protected the relatively favorable position of old-age pensioners. Yet his final years as premier were marked by accusations of administrative corruption, clientelism, and complaints about enduring "insider–outsider" effects in a welfare system that lacked equity, efficiency, and transparency.

Abandoning its previous radical privatization agenda helped Aznar's center-right party to gain power in 1996, albeit forming a minority government. Ploughing the middle ground, and as part of his role in the Toledo Pact, Aznar pledged to preserve commitments to pensions, health care, and unemployment compensation, but espoused a broader mixed delivery of welfare. On labor market policy he took Blair's line and supported him in negotiations for the European Employment Strategy at the EU level. In 2001 a new pensions pact revised the original formula. Against expectation, the socialists were re-elected in 2004, under Zapatero. His legalization of same-sex marriage met with the predictable opposition of the church, but times had moved on and the Holy Mother's veto powers had waned. Proposals for reversing the education reforms of the prior government by reducing the remit of church schools reopened the controversy unleashed by Gonzalez 20 years earlier.

Since 1993, total welfare outlays have continued to decline in GDP terms, widening the gap between the Spanish and EU average and comparing unfavorably with welfare investment in Portugal and Greece.[67] But it is not only quantitative deficiencies that are a hallmark of the evolution of Spanish social policy. Despite the undeniable advances made since the democratic transition, it is in qualitative aspects that divergence with most of the EU15 (the then 15 EU members) is more apparent, with implementation gaps, clientelism, and other problems of welfare management perpetuating a southern European model.

The collapse of the postwar Italian party system after 1992 provided opportunity points for consensus-building among politicians and the social partners. Thus "concertation" assumed an ever more central role in national policy-making as the 1990s progressed. It was in this environment that a new realism emerged, reflected in the attempt, at least, to advance serious social security reform, the main target being pensions. In the event, prime minister Prodi was forced into important concessions in the face of strong opposition not only from the unions but also from Berlusconi's center-right. Incrementally, while reforms since the 1990s have attempted to reduce very high replacement rates and reinstate a stronger contributory principle in the pensions system, they have stopped well short of securing long-term fiscal stability. Successive Italian governments of the time also attempted to displace passive compensatory measures with more active labor market policies. In 1998 new means-testing procedures were legislated for all noncontributory benefits, including unemployment assistance. A version of the French RMI was piloted by some local authorities, although the Berlusconi government in 2003 decided against mainstreaming its funding nationally.

Ostner and Saraceno have castigated the "double deficit of statecraft" deriving from the weak role of the Italian state in delivering welfare and its powerlessness as neutral arbitrator of a plural welfare arena.[68] Reforms in the past 30 years have tended to overload a heavily indebted and inadequate administrative system. Implementation deficits and cross-service coordination problems have coexisted with serious social and spatial inequities of access to welfare. For Ferrera and Gualmini,[69] Italian elite actors have been attempting to develop a more formal model of neo-corporatism within a weak state in order to modernize the economy and moderate welfare. It has been a vital learning process for all involved.

The early 1990s were a grim time for the Swedish economy; the 1991 election gave the social democrats their worst ever electoral result and Sweden another government of the bourgeois parties. Many assessments of the time predicted the serious erosion of social democratic welfare and the end of Swedish corporatism. The official unemployment rate rose fivefold, with a further large reserve of jobless in assisted labor market schemes. The severest economic recession since the 1930s, together with the imperatives of the Maastricht convergence criteria, at least stimulated a certain cross-party merging of minds on the need for structural welfare reforms, although eschewing root-and-branch transformation. Pensions and other reforms were packaged in an agenda arguing for revised entitlements that were realigned to economic realities. Innovations in welfare delivery were to incorporate more extensively new public management techniques in operation in the health and social services since the 1980s.

After three years in opposition the social democrats under Persson returned to power in 1994, following an election fought largely on the sustainability of Swedish welfare and its reconciliation with the competitiveness of a largely export-led economy. But there were mounting internal divisions between modernizers and the traditionalists to which the prime minister belonged. Within the bounds of stricter budgetary policy, Persson's commitment to maintain the best traditions of Swedish welfare was exemplified by symbolic restorations of several entitlement levels reduced by the former government, although they did not survive long. In the late 1990s, after Denmark, Sweden was the highest spender on active labor market measures in the EU. As a further investment in the "leading-edge" labor market, in 1997 Persson launched a national lifelong learning program aimed at skills-upgrading. As one of the largest such projects in the EU it was eventually to involve about 15% of the workforce, although there were critics of its effectiveness on both right and left.

For all but ten years of the postwar period, Sweden's government has been led by the social democrats. However, in 2006 the party was narrowly defeated by a center-right coalition under Reinfeldt on a platform to reduce employers' insurance levies, the quality of unemployment compensation, and the size of the public sector.

Although there has been an observable decline in the path-dependent *Folkhemmet* policy and an infusion of new delivery styles, in large measure the Swedish welfare state still remains distinct.[70] By international standards Swedes exhibit greater support for progressive social policy, albeit now moderated. Employment rates have remained high and labor market inequalities, whether by gender or by high–low wage gaps, are relatively low.[71] Sweden's high social budgetary outlays have stabilized since 1980 but, in crude GDP terms, it is still (just) the most generous provider.[72] The observation by Lessenich[73] in relation to Germany bears comparison with that of Cox,[74] who examines the evolution of contemporary Scandinavian welfare states and identifies the political parties there as having been colluding in the "conceptual stretching" of social democratic welfare. Within this compass, there is greater scope that reforms can be defended on ground of conformity to one or other principles emblematic of the welfare tradition. The willingness of the electorate to accept these devices – the "stickiness" of the model's reputation – is a path-dependency, at least of an idea.

Path Dependency, Reconfiguration, and Europeanization

The concept of path dependency, which may be defined in terms of the high departure costs incurred by veering from established policy frameworks,[75] must be reconsidered in the light of policy innovations introduced in this sample of countries during the period in which the postindustrial crisis of the welfare state gathered pace. Assessments of path changes depend, of course, on the extent, speed, and direction that policy renewal has taken, and here definitions matter. Rothgang and colleagues counsel against focusing on paradigmatic change,[76] for this will underestimate the cumulative effect of minor and "second-order" changes over time which may have greater transformative impact on redefining the objectives of European welfare states, systems which in reality have changed considerably.[77] This said, institutional frameworks – "regimes" – are largely cognate with those negotiated in the postwar settlement. And current welfare "leaders" and "laggards" are to a large extent the same as at the beginning of the period under review.[78]

Owing to different sourcing and definitions, cross-national data over time are notoriously difficult to interpret with great accuracy and the statistics supporting this review are no exception. Nonetheless, despite these limitations, they do broadly demonstrate a growing convergence. For one, the distance in gross public welfare GDP "takes" between leaders and laggards has in most cases been declining (net expenditures which take into consideration such factors as tax clawbacks and state subsidies to private welfare would reduce the distance still further).[79] For another, the distribution and sourcing of that funding shows some signs of convergence: as Table 22.2 indicates, pensions and health take the lion's share of the total budget. Table 22.3 demonstrates that partial fiscalization has been increasing; and the percentage contribution of the employer has, in general, been declining in the attempt to reduce the negative impact of high nonwage costs on competitiveness.[80]

Table 22.2 Contemporary social protection expenditure by allocation type, 2004 (% share)

	D	E	F	I	SE	UK	EU15
Old age and survivors	44	44	44	61	40	45	46
Sickness, health, and disability	35	38	36	32	40	40	36
Family and children	11	4	9	4	10	7	8
Unemployment	9	13	8	2	6	3	7

Source: Eurostat, *Statistics in Focus: Population and Social Conditions*, no. 99 (2007). Data are provisional except for EU15 where they are estimates.

Table 22.3 Source of social protection receipts

D	E	F	I	SE	UK	EU12/15
% employers						
1980	42	64	56	60	33	6	
2004	36	51	46	41	41	33	39
% protected person						
1980	28	19	24	14	14	22	
2004	28	16	21	15	9	16	21
% general government contributions						
1980	7	16	17	24	43	29	
2004	35	30	30	42	49	50	38

Sources:
1980 – *Social Protection Expenditure and Receipts 1980–1994* (Luxembourg: Office of Official Publications of the European Communities, 1996).
2004 – Eurostat, *Statistics in Focus: Population and Social Conditions.* no. 99 (2007). Data are provisional except for EU15 where they are estimates.

These statistical trends help uncover what many argue is a new political logic of welfare in an era where retrenchment is largely accepted as unproblematically orthodox. At root it is a politics reviewing the appropriate role of the state in a post-Fordist era in which interparty differences have progressively been sidelined. It is a politics directed towards making work pay;[81] in short it is, a politics espousing a *Schumpetarian* postnational state endorsing flexibilization and competitiveness and relegating welfare to a subordinate role, increasingly delivered by non-statutory agents.[82] Yet aggregate statistics tell only part of the story. We must look beyond them for a deeper understanding of the dynamics of European welfare: how redistribution has been negotiated in these reconfigurations. For Pierson,[83] what was evolving, at least until the turn of the millennium, was an emerging overarching European consensus about post-Fordist exigencies of streamlining welfare, but one which has been subject to contextual (regime-specific) mediation. Thus liberal regimes in their retrenchment strategies in social and tax policies were becoming more "liberal" in their recommodification of welfare and, thereby, in widening the gap between rich and poor. By contrast social democratic regimes exploited social and fiscal measures in an attempt to spread the pain in a more egalitarian fashion. Conservative corporatist regimes implemented strategies of "recalibration" which varyingly redraw lines between contributory and noncontributory welfare.

Into this regime-dependent scenario must be interpolated the supranational integration effects of Europeanization fostered by the operation of EU-level interventions, a process that institutionally has gathered pace since the stipulations negotiated in the 1992 Maastricht Treaty and the economic strategy specified in Delors's 1993 competition white paper. This integration is more of a pragmatic convergence and dispatches earlier ambitions of stronger harmonization or coordination to history. What is being prized is the positive asset that European welfare offers: the very maturity of many European social protection systems means that they can better cope with the losers in the process of economic transformation than can inchoate systems, while also investing in human capital to meet the demands of the globalizing economy. The welfare *acquis* is multilevel and multidimensional: as the 2000 Nice Treaty specifies, the "European social model" incorporates provisions derived from EU level through to local level via the nation state; it embraces social and labor market interventions, including industrial dialogue. Accordingly, to advance this *acquis*, what is now favored is a flexible balance between "hard" EU legislative output and a measured deepening of EU institutions regulating broad areas of social policy in a context that offers greater scope for national and sub-national policy learning. The instigation of the "open method of coordination" is a case in point, but other social policy networks also input into various stages of the policy cycle beyond it.

To be sure, as Taylor-Gooby reminds us,[84] the effects of Europeanizing convergence in such a broad field of social policy are sector-specific. One critical area where nation states have retained exclusive competence is fiscal welfare. Threlfall has employed the indicator of a "single social area" to examine the integration process from an outcome perspective.[85] This framework enables her to locate policy outputs on a strong–weak integration continuum. Regulations governing workers' freedom of movement guarantee a barrier-free single space. Parallel policies in the member states derived from EU directives such as those governing health and safety represent the "harmonized field." The third is an "approximated field" where EU-level legislation is softer or has allowed extensive derogations – her example is working time. The "weakest approximations" are those social policy fields where competence is effectively retained by nation states but where there has been a stimulation of Europeanization by member states agreeing broad, largely qualitative convergence objectives and common benchmarks through the "open method of coordination," such as those related to social inclusion.

In fact, the "weakest approximation" arena currently offers Europeanization the most purchase, since it is primarily driven by process (styles of collective decision-making and peer monitoring) rather than earlier *dirigiste* attempts directed at quantitative outcomes. It must be conceded that this qualitative Europeanization is an inchoate concept combining both deepening and widening objectives for the Union. Above all, it encapsulates the shared perceptions – at least among political and economic elites – of common social problems and attitudes to their resolution, something Radaelli[86] terms "cognitive Europeanization" and which is predicted over time to have a crucial impact on the evolving multi-level governance of welfare.

Notes

1 Esping-Andersen, *The Three Worlds of Welfare Capitalism.*
2 Wilensky, *Rich Democracies.*
3 For further reading and critique see Higgins, *States of Welfare;* Lockhart, "Explaining Policy Differences," and Castles, "On Religion and Public Policy." Pampel and Williamson's *Age, Class, Politics and the Welfare State* is a historical examination of the impact of the pensioner electoral constituency as a driver in welfare expenditure, identifies this variable as empirically stronger than party competition for predicting the volume of insurance-based welfare expenditure, although not tax-generated discretionary social assistance.
4 Wilensky, "Leftism, Catholicism and Democratic Corporatism"; Wilensky, *Rich Democracies.*

5 Further discussion is contained in Flora and Heidenheimer, *The Development of Welfare States*, and Hage and Hanneman, "The Growth of the Welfare State in Britain, France, Germany and Italy."

6 Flora et al., *State Formation, Nation-Building and Mass Politics in Europe*.

7 Flora and Alber, "Modernization, Democratization and the Development of Welfare States in Western Europe,"provides valuable further reading. Castles and McKinley, "Public Welfare Provisions " offers a refinement of the social democratic hypothesis by arguing that, although the mobilizing strength of workers was the most important variable for the *generosity* of welfare provision, a prerequisite for welfare state *initiation* was the existence of a small, but effective right-wing party.

8 Korpi, *The Democratic Class Struggle*.

9 Marshall, *Citizenship and Social Class and Other Essays*. Proponents of these theories do not discount the role of independent variables (such as industrialization, urbanization, and democratization) but argue that they are given too much weight. Skocpol, "Bringing the State Back In" has been one of the leading advocates of "bringing the state back in," by criticizing pluralist and Marxist accounts of welfare state developments as being too society-centered. State-centered accounts draw attention to the progressive "learning capacity" of the state (and its constituent institutions): a "politics of learning" rather than, crudely, "power." Additional reading: Heclo, *Modern Social Politics in Britain and Sweden*; and Skocpol, *States and Social Revolutions*.

10 Further insightful reading is provided by Ashford, *The Emergence of the Welfare States*.

11 The data presented by Korpi, op. cit., cast doubt on crude correlations between increases in the size of welfare bureaucracies and subsequent additional social policy expansion. However, while insisting on the dominance of left politics as *the* predictor of policy *input*, he confirms that state capacity, its institutions, and constituent actors are of major relevance in determining the nature of policy *output*.

12 Swank, *Global Capital*.

13 For further discussion of "varieties of capitalism" see Hall and Soskice, *Varieties of Capitalism*. They discard a primary focus on worker mobilization in favor of one examining the motives of employers in enhancing productivity. Cross-national differences in industrial structures which require distinct human capital assets are, they assert, a strong predictor of what kind of welfare is conceded. An earlier study by Katzenstein – *Small States in World Markets* – is also recommended. It argues that welfare systems have tended to advance most in small, open economies where both employer and employee are highly exposed to international markets and have vested interests in engaging in corporatist arrangements. For a critique of "varieties of capitalism" see Andersen, "Welfare Crisis and Beyond"; and Andersen and Guillemard, "Conclusion: Policy Change, Welfare Regimes and Active Citizenship."

14 O'Connor and Brym, "Public Welfare Expenditure in OECD countries."

15 Esping-Andersen, *The Three Worlds of Welfare Capitalism*.

16 Overreliance on the archetype approach, the very wide incorporation of a "conservative corporatist" sample, the neglect of southern Europe, the gender dimension, fiscal systems, and services-in-kind are examples. For further reading see Ferrera, "The Southern Model of Welfare in Social Europe," Lewis, "Gender and the Development of Welfare Regimes," and Kleinman, *A European Welfare State?*

17 In fact his classification of archetypal countries is, in key respects, cognate with that proposed 30 years earlier in Titmuss, *Social Policy*, though the latter's "social division of welfare" approach is, by comparison, less theoretically entrenched.

18 Other authors have argued the case for a dimensional rather than categorical approach to designing cross-national models of European welfare systems, arguing that two-axis

classifications are more parsimonious. See, for example, Jones, *Patterns of Social Policy*, and Bonoli, "The Politics of New Social Policies."

19 See Table 22.1.

20 Mangen, "The German Social State 1949–1989."

21 See Table 22.1.

22 Freeman, "Financial Crisis and Policy Continuity in the Welfare State," 192.

23 See Table 22.1.

24 Esping-Andersen, *Social Foundations of Postindustrial Economies*. My emphasis.

25 Ferrera, "The Southern Model of Welfare in Social Europe."

26 Further discussion of Italy is provided by Ferrera, "Italy."

27 See also Pierson, *Beyond the Welfare State*.

28 See Table 22.3.

29 See Table 22.1.

30 Visser and Hemerijck, in *A Dutch Miracle*, discuss these issues in greater detail.

31 Ashford, op. cit.

32 Titmuss, *Essays on the Welfare State*; Marwick, *War and Social Change in the Twentieth Century*, and Thane, *Foundations of the Welfare State*, Section 1.7, are recommended reading.

33 Hantrais, *Contemporary French Society*.

34 Rimlinger, *Welfare Policy and Industrialization in Europe, America and Russia*.

35 Esping-Andersen, *The Three Worlds of Welfare Capitalism*.

36 Freeman, "Financial Crisis and Policy Continuity in the Welfare State."

37 Wilson, *The Welfare State in Sweden*.

38 Mangen, *Spanish Society after Franco*.

39 See, for example, O'Connor, *The Fiscal Crisis of the State*; and Gough, *The Political Economy of the Welfare State*.

40 Streeck and Hassel, "The Crumbling Pillars of Social Partnership."

41 Leibfried and Obinger, "The State of the Welfare State."

42 Moxon-Browne, *Political Change in Spain*.

43 Hall, "Policy Paradigms, Social Learning and the State."

44 In what he admits is a tentative model, Hall, op. cit., adumbrates a three-tier momentum of change: "first-order," simple changes in existing policies: "second-order" change in policy instruments to meet new goals but within existing institutional frameworks; and third-order radical transformation, changing overarching goals and encompassing both first and second order. For a critique of this model, consult Andersen and Guillemard, op. cit., and Rothgang et al., "The State and Its Welfare State."

45 Pierson, "Interests, Institutions and Policy Feeback."

46 See Table 22.1.

47 Pierson, "Interest, Institutions and Policy Feedback."

48 See Table 22.1.

49 Freeman, op. cit.

50 Rodriguez, "Between Welfare State and Social Assistance State in Spain, 1980–1992."

51 See Table 22.1.

52 See, for example, Scharpf and Schmidt, "Introduction"; Pierson, "Coping with Permanent Austerity"; Yeates, *Globalization and Social Policy*.

53 Esping-Andersen, in *Social Foundations of Postindustrial Economies*, argues that transformation is not primarily due to globalization but to the more general social and economic impacts in postindustrialism, reflected in changing labor markets, technological revolution, and profound demographic changes.

54 For further reading see Bonoli, "The Politics of New Social Policies."

55 Giddens, *The Third Way*.

56 Jacobs and Dutton, "Social and Community Issues."
57 Mangen, *Social Exclusion and Inner City Europe.*
58 Marshall, *Citizenship and Social Class and Other Essays.*
59 Mangen, "Social Policy: One State, Two-Tier Welfare."
60 Esping-Andersen, "Positive Sum Solutions in a World of Trade-Offs?"
61 For further discussion see Seeleib-Kaiser, "The Welfare State," who assesses that, but for unification, welfare expenditure in GDP terms would be lower than in the late 1980s.
62 Vail, "Rethinking Corporatism and Consensus."
63 Lessenich, "Frozen Landscapes Revisited."
64 See also Clasen, "Modern Social Democracy and European Welfare State Reform."
65 Leibfried and Obinger, op. cit.
66 Palier, "Beyond Retrenchment."
67 Mangen, "Contextualising Spanish Welfare Performance."
68 Ostner and Saraceno, "Keine Arbeit, keine Kinder, keine Lösung?"
69 Ferrera and Gualmini, "Reforms Guided by Consensus."
70 See Bergh, "The Universal Welfare State."
71 Svallfors, "Class, Attitudes and the Welfare State."
72 See Table 22.1.
73 Lessenich, op. cit.
74 Cox, "The Path Dependency of an Idea."
75 Pierson and Skocpol, "Historical Institutionalism in Contemporary Political Science."
76 Rothgang et al., op. cit.
77 Further discussion is provided by Andersen, op. cit.
78 See Table 22.1.
79 For further analysis see Adema, "Net Social Expenditure."
80 See Table 22.3.
81 Wilensky, *Rich Democracies,* Leibfried and Obinger, op. cit.
82 Jessop, "The Changing Governance of Welfare."
83 Pierson, op. cit.
84 Taylor-Gooby, "Open Markets versus Welfare Citizenship."
85 Threlfall, "European Social Integration."
86 Radaelli, The Europeanization of Public Policy."

Bibliography

Adema, W., "Net Social Expenditure," *Labour Market and Social Policy Occasional Papers* 52, 2nd edition (Paris: OECD, 2001).

Andersen, J.G., "Welfare Crisis and Beyond," in S. Kuhnle (ed.), *Survival of the European Welfare State* (London: Routledge, 2000).

Andersen, J.G. and A.M. Guillemard, "Conclusion: Policy Change, Welfare Regimes and Active Citizenship," in J.G. Andersen, A.M. Guillemard, P.H. Jensen, and B. Pfau-Effinger (eds.), *The Changing Face of Welfare: Consequences and Outcomes from a Citizenship Perspective* (Bristol: Policy Press, 2005).

Ashford, D., *The Emergence of the Welfare States* (Oxford: Blackwell, 1986).

Bergh, A., "The Universal Welfare State: Theory and the Case of Sweden," *Political Studies* 52, 2004, 745–766.

Bonoli, G., "Classifying Welfare States: A Two Dimensional Approach," *Journal of Social Policy* 26, 1997, 351–372.

Bonoli, G., "The Politics of New Social Policies: Providing Coverage against New Social Risks in Mature Welfare States," *Policy and Politics* 33, 2005, 431–449.

Bonoli, G. and M. Powell, "Third Ways in Europe," *Social Policy and Society* 1, 2002, 59–66.

Castles, F., "On Religion and Public Policy: Does Catholicism Make a Difference?" *European Journal of Political Research* 25, 1994, 19–40.

Castles, F. and R. McKinley, "Public Welfare Provision: Scandinavia and the Sheer Futility of the Sociological Approach to Politics," *British Journal of Political Science* 9, 1979, 157–171.

Clasen, J., "Modern Social Democracy and European Welfare State Reform," *Social Policy and Society* 1, 2002, 67–76.

Cox, R., "The Path Dependency of an Idea: Why Scandinavian Welfare States Remain Distinct," *Social Policy and Administration* 38, 2004, 204–219.

Esping-Andersen, G., *The Three Worlds of Welfare Capitalism* (Cambridge: Polity, 1990).

Esping-Andersen, G., "Positive Sum Solutions in a World of Trade-Offs?" in Esping-Andersen (ed.), *Welfare States in Transition: National Adaptations in Global Economies* (London: Sage, 1996).

Esping-Andersen, G., *Social Foundations of Postindustrial Economies* (Oxford: Oxford University Press, 1999).

Ferrera, M., "Italy," in J. Dixon and R. Scheurell (eds.), *Social Welfare in Developed Market Countries* (London: Routledge, 1989).

Ferrera, M., "The Southern Model of Welfare in Social Europe," *Journal of European Social Policy* 1, 1996, 17–37.

Ferrera, M. and Gualmini, E., "Reforms Guided by Consensus: The Welfare State in the Italian Transition," in M. Ferrera and M. Rhodes (eds.), *Recasting European Welfare States* (London: Cass, 2000).

Flora, P. and J. Alber, "Modernization, Democratization and the Development of Welfare States in Western Europe," in P. Flora and A. Heidenheimer (eds.), *The Development of Welfare States in Europe and America* (New Brunswick: Transaction Books, 1981).

Flora, P. and A. Heidenheimer (eds.), *The Development of Welfare States in Europe and America* (New Brunswick: Transaction Books, 1981).

Flora, P., S. Kuhnle, and D. Urwin (eds.), *State Formation, Nation-Building and Mass Politics in Europe: The Theory of Stein Rokkan* (Oxford: Oxford University Press, 1999).

Freeman, G., "Financial Crisis and Policy Continuity in the Welfare State," in P. Hall, J. Hayward, and H. Machin (eds.), *Developments in French Politics* (London: Macmillan, 1990).

Giddens, A., *The Third Way: The Renewal of Social Democracy* (Cambridge: Polity Press, 1998).

Gough, I., *The Political Economy of the Welfare State* (London: Macmillan, 1979).

Hage, J. and R. Hanneman, "The Growth of the Welfare State in Britain, France, Germany and Italy: A Comparison of Three Paradigms," in R. Tomasson (ed.), *Comparative Social Research*, vol. 3 (Greenwich, CT: JAI Publications, 1980).

Hall, P., "Policy Paradigms, Social Learning and the State: The Case of Economic Policy-Making in Britain," *Comparative Politics* 25, 1993, 275–296.

Hall, P. and D. Soskice, *Varieties of Capitalism: The Institutional Foundations of Comparative Advantage* (Oxford: Oxford University Press, 2001).

Hantrais, L., *Contemporary French Society* (London: Macmillan, 1982).

Heclo, H., *Modern Social Politics in Britain and Sweden: From Relief to Income Maintenance* (New Haven, CT: Yale University Press, 1974).

Higgins, J., *States of Welfare: Comparative Analysis of Social Policy* (Oxford: Blackwell and Robertson, 1981).

Jacobs, B. and C. Dutton, "Social and Community Issues", in P. Roberts and H. Sykes (eds), *Urban Regeneration: A Handbook*. London: Sage, 2000).

Jessop, B., "The Changing Governance of Welfare: Recent Trends in Its Primary Function, Scale and Modes of Coordination," *Social Policy and Administration* 33, 1999, 348–359.

Jones, C., *Patterns of Social Policy: An Introduction to Comparative Analysis* (London: Tavistock Publications, 1985).

Katzenstein, P., *Small States in World Markets* (Ithaca, NY: Cornell University Press, 1985).

Kleinman, M., *A European Welfare State?* (Basingstoke, Palgrave, 2002).

Korpi, W., *The Democratic Class Struggle* (London: Rouledge & Kegan Paul, 1983).

Leibfried, S. and H. Obinger, "The State of the Welfare State: German Social Policy between Macroeconomic Retrenchment and Microeconomic Recalibration," *West European Politics* 26, 2003, 199–218.

Lessenich, S., "'Frozen Landscapes' Revisited: Path Creation in the European Social Model," *Social Policy and Society* 4, 2005, 345–356.

Lewis, J., "Gender and the Development of Welfare Regimes," *Journal of European Social Policy* 2, 1992, 159–173.

Lockhart, C., "Explaining Policy Differences among Advanced Industrial Societies," *Comparative Politics* 16, 1984, 335–360.

Mangen, S., "The German Social State 1949–89: A Selective Critique," in E. Kolinsky (ed.), *The Federal Republic of Germany: The End of an Era* (New York: Berg, 1991).

Mangen, S., "Social Policy: One State, Two-Tier Welfare," in G. Smith, W. Paterson, P. Merkl, and S. Padgett (eds.), *Developments in German Politics*, vol. 2 (Basingstoke: Macmillan, 1992).

Mangen, S., *Spanish Society after Franco* (Basingstoke: Palgrave, 2001).

Mangen, S., "Contextualising Spanish Welfare Performance: Fellow Cohesion Countries Compared," *International Journal of Iberian Studies* 17, 2004, 131–151.

Mangen, S., *Social Exclusion and Inner City Europe: Regulating Urban Regeneration* (Basingstoke: Palgrave, 2004).

Marshall, T., *Citizenship and Social Class and Other Essays* (Cambridge: Cambridge University Press, 1950).

Marwick, A., *War and Social Change in the Twentieth Century* (London: Macmillan, 1974).

Moxon-Browne, E., *Political Change in Spain* (London: Routledge, 1989).

O'Connor, J., *The Fiscal Crisis of the State* (New York: St Martin's Press, 1971).

O'Connor, J. and R. Brym, "Public Welfare Expenditure in OECD Countries: Towards a Reconciliation of Inconsistent Findings," *British Journal of Sociology* 39, 1988, 47–68.

Ostner, I. and C. Saraceno, "Keine Arbeit, keine Kinder, keine Lösung? Italien und Deutschland in vergleichender Perspektive," in B. Cattero (ed.), *Modell Deutschland – Modell Europa. Probleme, Perspektiven* (Opladen: Leske and Budrich, 1998).

Palier, B., "Beyond Retrenchment: Four Problems in Current Welfare State Research and One Suggestion on How to Overcome Them," in C. Pierson and F. Castles (eds.), *The Welfare State Reader*, 2nd edition (Cambridge: Polity, 2006).

Pampel, F. and J. Williamson, *Age, Class, Politics and the Welfare State: A Comparative Study* (Cambridge: Cambridge University Press, 1989).

Pierson, C., *Beyond the Welfare State: The New Political Economy of Welfare* (Cambridge: Polity Press, 1991).

Pierson, P., "Interests, Institutions and Policy Feedback," in Pierson (ed.), *Dismantling the Welfare State? Reagan, Thatcher and the Politics of Retrenchment* (Cambridge: Cambridge University Press, 1994).

Pierson, P., "Coping with Permanent Austerity: Welfare Restructuring in Affluent Democracies," in Pierson (ed.), *The New Politics of the Welfare State* (Oxford: Oxford University Press, 2001).

Pierson, P. and T. Skocpol, "Historical Institutionalism in Contemporary Political Science," in I. Katzneslon and H. Milner (eds.), *Political Science: State of the Discipline* (New York: Norton, 2002).

Radaelli, C., "The Europeanization of Public Policy," in K. Featherstone and C. Radaelli (eds), *The Politics of Europeanization* (Oxford: Oxford University Press, 2003).

Rimlinger, G., *Welfare Policy and Industrialization in Europe, America and Russia* (New York: Wiley, 1971).

Rodriguez, G., "Between Welfare State and Social Assistance State in Spain, 1980–1992," paper presented at Comparative Research on the Welfare State in Transition Conference, University of Oxford, September 9–12, 1993.

Rothgang, H., G. Obinger, and S. Leibfried, "The State and Its Welfare State: How Do Welfare State Changes Affect the Make-up of the Nation State?" *Social Policy and Administration* 40, 2006, 250–266.

Samuelsson, K., *From Great Power to Welfare State: 300 Years of Swedish Social Development* (London: Allen & Unwin, 1968).

Scharpf, F. and V. Schmidt, "Introduction," in Scharpf and Schmidt (eds.), *Welfare and Work in the Open Economy*, vol. 2: *Diverse Responses to Common Challenges in Twelve Countries* (Oxford: Oxford University Press, 2000).

Seeleib-Kaiser, M., "The Welfare State," in S. Padgett, W. Patterson, and G. Smith (eds.), *Developments in German Politics 3* (Basingstoke: Palgrave, 2003).

Skocpol, T., *States and Social Revolutions: A Comparative Analysis of France, Russia and China* (Cambridge: Cambridge University Press, 1979).

Skocpol, T., "Bringing the State back in: Strategies of Analysis in Current Research," in P. Evans, D. Rueschmeyer, and T. Skocpol (eds.), *Bringing the State back in* (Cambridge: Cambridge University Press, 1985).

Streeck, W. and A. Hassel, "The Crumbling Pillars of Social Partnership," *West European Politics* 26, 2004, 103–124.

Svallfors, S., "Class, Attitudes and the Welfare State: Sweden in Comparative Perspective," *Social Policy and Administration* 38, 2004, 119–138.

Swank, D., *Global Capital, Political Institutions and Policy Change in Developed Welfare States* (Cambridge: Cambridge University Press, 2002).

Taylor-Gooby, P., "Open Markets versus Welfare Citizenship: Conflicting Approaches to Policy Convergence in Europe," *Social Policy and Administration* 37, 2003, 539–554.

Thane, P., *Foundations of the Welfare State*, 2nd edition (London: Longman, 1996).

Threlfall, M., "European Social Integration: Harmonization, Convergence and Single Social Areas," *Journal of European Social Policy* 13, 2003, 121–140.

Titmuss, R., *Essays on the Welfare State* (London: Allen & Unwin, 1963).

Titmuss, R., *Social Policy* (London: Allen & Unwin, 1974).

Vail, M., "Rethinking Corporatism and Consensus: The Dilemmas of German Social Protection Reform," *West European Politics* 26, 2003, 41–66.

Visser, J. and A. Hemerijck, *A Dutch Miracle: Job Growth, Welfare Reform and Corporatism in the Netherlands* (Amsterdam: Amsterdam University Press, 1997).

Weir, M. and T. Skocpol, "State Structure and the Possibilities for 'Keynesian' Responses to the Great Depression in Sweden, Britain and the United States," in D. Rueschmeyer, T. Skocpol, and P. Evans (eds.), *Bringing the State back in* (New York: Cambridge University Press, 1985).

Wilensky, H., *The Welfare State and Equality: Structure and Ideological Roots of Public Expenditure* (Berkeley, University of California Press, 1975).

Wilensky, H., "Leftism, Catholicism and Democratic Corporatism: The Role of Political Parties in Recent Welfare State Development," in P. Flora and A. Heidenheimer (eds.), *The Development of Welfare States in Europe and America* (New Brunswick: Transaction Books, 1981).

Wilensky, H., *Rich Democracies, Political Economy, Public Policy and Performance* (Berkeley: University of California Press, 2002).

Wilson, D., *The Welfare State in Sweden* (London: Heinemann, 1979).

Yeates, N., *Globalization and Social Policy* (London: Sage, 2001).

Further Reading

There is a large and growing literature on comparative social policy with a European focus. Much of this concentrates on the era of deindustrialization consequent to the mid-1970s. Work on the earlier post-1945 period has tended to neglect France and the southern European states, although more contemporary work goes some way to remedying this.

Several overarching books are indispensable: *The Development of Welfare States in Europe and America*, edited by P. Flora and A.J. Heidenheimer (New Brunswick: Transaction Books, 1981), provides a largely quantitative and extensive analysis stretching pre- and postwar. G. Esping-Andersen in *The Three Worlds of Welfare Capitalism* (Cambridge: Polity, 1990), integrates his analysis through the specification of welfare regimes, although his liberal regime is largely represented by the United States. It has become the most cited comparative text in the literature. His later works, particularly *Social Foundations of Post-industrial Economies* (Oxford: Oxford University Press, 1999) and *Why We Need a New Welfare State* (Oxford: Oxford University Press, 2002) offer refinements and updating of his original approach.

No such list as this would be complete without citation of P. Baldwin's *The Politics of Social Solidarity* (Cambridge: Cambridge University Press, 1990). In an investigation of five European countries this examines how different social-class actors forged risk alliances to drive welfare advance forward in some contexts with relative ease, in others after entrenched conflict. A detailed five-country analysis of social insurance is provided in *The Evolution of Social Insurance: 1881–1981*, edited by P.A. Kohler and H.F. Zacher (London: Frances Pinter, 1982). Finally, within the framework of a comparative cross-national analysis, *In Care of the State: Health, Education and Welfare in Europe and America* (Cambridge: Polity, 1988), A. De Swaan embraces a very broad historical scope, including the post-1945 era, to investigate the consolidation of welfare as a prime concern within centralizing nation states.

In terms of comparative cross-sector analyses two publications can be recommended: the three editions of *Comparative Public Policy: The Politics of Social Choice in Europe and America* by A.J. Heidenheimer, H. Heclo, and C.T. Adams (New York: St Martin's/Macmillan, 1976, 1983, 1990) present a impressive series of specific welfare policy arenas within the broader context of governance and economic policy; and F.G. Castles, *Comparative Public Policy: Patterns of Post-war Transformation* (Cheltenham: Edward Elgar, 1998) investigates the impact of the economy, social and political institutions, and big government on policy transformations in selected welfare areas. Literature on the more recent era does run the risk of being narrowly episodic. Edited collections of country-by-country analyses which are worthy of recommendation are M. Ferrera and M. Rhodes, *Recasting European Welfare States* (London: Cass, 2000); S. Kuhnle, *Survival of the European Welfare State* (London: Routledge, 2000); and A. Cochrane, J. Clarke, and S. Gewirtz, *Comparing Welfare States*, 2nd edition (London: Sage, 2001).

There is a mushrooming of literature concerning the effects of globalization on European welfare states. Among many which are recommendable are the edited collection by M.R. Sykes, B. Palier, and P.M. Prior, *Globalization and European Welfare States: Challenges and Change* (New York: Palgrave, 2000); P. Hall and D. Soskice, *Varieties of Capitalism: The Institutional Foundations of Comparative Advantage* (Oxford: Oxford University Press, 2001); N. Yeates, *Globalization and Social Policy* (London: Sage, 2001); M. Kleinman, *A European Welfare State?* (Basingstoke: Palgrave, 2002); V. George and P. Wilding, *Globalization and Human Welfare* (Basingstoke: Palgrave, 2002); the edited collection by B. Södersten, *Globalization and the Welfare State* (Basingstoke: Palgrave, 2004); and finally the edited essays by P. Taylor-Gooby, *Ideas and Welfare State Reform in Western Europe* (Basingstoke: Palgrave, 2004), examining ideas, policy change, and paradigm shifts in a sample of advanced welfare states.

Index

A Companion to Europe since 1945, First Edition. Edited by Klaus Larres.
© 2014 John Wiley & Sons, Ltd. Published 2014 by John Wiley & Sons, Ltd.